Harald Pechlaner / Wolf von Holzschuher /
Monika Bachinger (Hrsg.)

Unternehmertum und Public Private Partnership

GABLER RESEARCH

Harald Pechlaner / Wolf von Holzschuher /
Monika Bachinger (Hrsg.)

Unternehmertum und Public Private Partnership

Wissenschaftliche Konzepte und praktische Erfahrungen

GABLER

RESEARCH

Bibliografische Information der Deutschen Nationalbibliothek
Die Deutsche Nationalbibliothek verzeichnet diese Publikation in der Deutschen Nationalbibliografie; detaillierte bibliografische Daten sind im Internet über <http://dnb.d-nb.de> abrufbar.

Gedruckt mit freundlicher Unterstützung der

INITIATIVE REGIONALMANAGEMENT
Region Ingolstadt e.V.

Südtiroler Sparkasse AG
Cassa di Risparmio di Bolzano SpA

VHV Allgemeine Versicherung AG

1. Auflage 2009

Lektorat: Claudia Jeske | Britta Göhrisch-Radmacher

Gabler ist Teil der Fachverlagsgruppe Springer Science+Business Media.
www.gabler.de

Umschlaggestaltung: KünkelLopka Medienentwicklung, Heidelberg
Gedruckt auf säurefreiem und chlorfrei gebleichtem Papier
Printed in Germany

ISBN 978-3-8349-1631-0

Geleitwort des Förderers

Südtiroler Sparkasse und Sparim AG

Dem Thema „Public Private Partnership“ wird in den letzten Jahren auf allen Ebenen eine immer größere Aufmerksamkeit geschenkt. Der Konzern Südtiroler Sparkasse – mit seiner Immobiliengesellschaft Sparim AG – beschäftigt sich schon seit einigen Jahren mit der Thematik. So war die Sparkasse an der letztjährigen Tagung „Private Public Partnership: Potenzial von PPP in Südtirol“ nicht nur als Hauptsponsor beteiligt, sondern sie stellte auch einige Referenten. Weiters war die Sparkasse Gründungsmitglied der „Arbeitsgruppe PPP in Südtirol“, welche gemeinsam mit dem Kollegium der Bauunternehmer Südtirols und der Gesellschaft Euregio Finance aus der Taufe gehoben wurde. Wir bieten nämlich sowohl privaten Unternehmen, als auch der öffentlichen Hand Unterstützung bei der Strukturierung und der Finanzierung von Projekten. Wir wollen ein kompetenter Ansprechpartner sein, wenn es um PPP geht. Zum vorliegenden Buch „Unternehmertum und Public Private Partnership“ kann ich deshalb den Autoren sowie der Katholischen Universität Eichstätt-Ingolstadt als Herausgeber nur gratulieren. Vor allem die Kombination zwischen wissenschaftlichen Konzepten und praktischen Erfahrungen gibt diesem Buch einen nicht zu unterschätzenden Mehrwert.

Norbert Plattner

Präsident

Südtiroler Sparkasse und der Sparim AG

Geleitwort des Förderers

INITIATIVE REGIONALMANAGEMENT Region Ingolstadt e.V.

„Gemeinsam sind wir stärker"

Je schneller die Globalisierung voranschreitet, desto mehr gewinnt die Region als Handlungs- und Identifikationsraum an Bedeutung. Die sich immer rascher vollziehenden Veränderungen auf politischer, sozialer und wirtschaftlicher Ebene bleiben auch für Regionen nicht ohne Wirkung. So wird neben Anpassungs- und Steuerungsprozessen auch die Positionierung im Wettbewerb notwendig.

Um diesen Anforderungen gerecht zu werden, wurde im Jahr 2008 die INITIATIVE REGIONALMANAGEMENT Region Ingolstadt e.V. gegründet. Als Public-Private-Partnership wollen wir bei den Bürger/innen der Region eine breite Mitwirkungsbereitschaft wecken, Prozesse für die Region gestalten und uns im Wettbewerb der Regionen positionieren. Dabei wurde von Beginn an Wert auf eine dauerhafte und intensive wissenschaftliche Kooperation gelegt.

Zur Förderung des allgemeinen Verständnisses für die tiefgreifenden Beziehungen zwischen PPP und Unternehmertum möchten wir insbesondere auf den Beitrag „Regionale Kooperation und Unternehmensentwicklung am Beispiel der AUDI AG" von Dr. Werner Widuckel, Vorstandsvorsitzender der INITIATIVE REGIONALMANAGEMENT Region Ingolstadt e.V. und Personalvorstand der AUDI AG, hinweisen.

Martina Schwytz

Geschäftsführerin

INITIATIVE REGIONALMANAGEMENT Region Ingolstadt e.V.

Geleitwort des Förderers

VHV Allgemeine Versicherung AG

Die VHV ist der führende Spezialversicherer der Bauwirtschaft, ein Versicherer, der von Profis getragen wird und Profis Schutz gibt.

Die VHV hat ihren Ursprung in der 1919 gegründeten Haftpflicht-Versicherungsanstalt der Hannoverschen Baugewerks-Berufsgenossenschaft. Weitsichtige und verantwortungsbewusste Bauunternehmer gründeten damals ihre eigene Solidargemeinschaft. Dies war die Geburtsstunde der VHV Vereinigte Hannoversche Versicherung a.G.

Die VHV ist schon immer Impulsgeber gewesen. So hat sie z. B. die Versicherungsangebote und -bedingungen an die sich verändernden Rechts- und Risikosituationen, an neue Bautechniken und neue Baustoffe angepasst und innovative Versicherungsprodukte entwickelt.

Seit 1999 können interessierte bauausführende Unternehmen auch mit der Baugewährleistungs-Versicherung auf eine alternative, weitergehende Sicherheit zur Absicherung von Mängelansprüchen zurückgreifen.

Auf dieser Grundlage wurde gemeinsam mit der HypoVereinsbank, Unternehmensberatern der Kommunen und Verbandsvertretern für PPP-Maßnahmen das VHV-Mittelstandsmodells Bau entwickelt, das durch Veranstaltungen der Rationalisierungsgemeinschaft Bau bundesweit publiziert wurde.

RA Gerhard Steyer

Leiter Verbands- und Kooperationsmanagement Bau
VHV Allgemeine Versicherung AG

Vorwort der Herausgeber

Im Vergleich zu Staaten wie Großbritannien oder den USA, entfalten Public Private Partnership-Projekte beispielsweise in Deutschland gerade erst allmählich eine Wirkung. Im globalen Wettbewerb der Standorte um Unternehmensansiedlungen, qualifizierte Mitarbeiter und insgesamt hohe Lebensqualität spielen kommunale Investitionen eine entscheidende Rolle. Bedenkt man zudem, dass immer neue Teilnehmer das Wettbewerberfeld betreten und mit großer Dynamik voranschreiten (man denke an Dubai, Singapur aber auch osteuropäische Metropolen), dann gehört den PPP-Projekten die Zukunft. Angesichts der Tatsache, dass keine wesentliche Verbesserung der staatlichen Haushaltssituation zu erwarten ist, brauchen die Gebietskörperschaften neue Finanzierungsalternativen - und dies nicht in unerheblichem Ausmaß, denn das Deutsche Institut für Urbanistik schätzt, dass die deutschen Kommunen in den Jahren 2000 bis 2009 jährlich rund 68 Mrd. Euro für Investitionen benötigen werden, wobei der größte Teil auf den Verkehrsbereich sowie auf soziale Infrastruktureinrichtungen entfällt. PPP-Modelle scheinen eine willkommene Lösung. Dass sie nicht nur Vorteile bieten, sondern gerade durch die Kooperation zweier sehr unterschiedlicher Partner auch Risiken bergen, das zeigt der vorliegende Band. Aus der Lektüre der einzelnen Beiträge lässt sich schließen, dass PPP eine große Chance, aber gleichzeitig kein Allheilmittel ist. Es bedarf eines stringenten Abwägens und einer kritischen Haltung gegenüber der Vergabe öffentlicher Leistungen an Private. Planung, Durchführung und Kontrolle erfordern ein Höchstmaß an Genauigkeit und Professionalität. PPP bedeutet nicht die schnelle Lösung unter Handlungsdruck, sondern eher einen „Marathonlauf mit Hürden“[1].

---

1 Losse, B./Ramthun, C. (2008): Marathonlauf mit Hürden, in: WirtschaftsWoche, Nr. 1 und 2 vom 7. Januar 2008, S. 26-29.

Das vorliegende Buch ist unterteilt in zwei große Abschnitte: im ersten Teil werden dem Leser wissenschaftliche Konzepte nahe gebracht, im zweiten Teil liegt das Augenmerk auf praktischen Erfahrungen im Umgang mit PPP-Projekten. Über den einzelnen Anwendungsfall hinaus liefert jeder Beitrag grundsätzliche Information zur PPP-Problematik und ist damit gut in den übergeordneten Kontext einzuordnen. Zahlreiche Beispiele aus den verschiedenen wirtschaftlich und gesellschaftlich relevanten Bereichen machen den Sammelband ebenso anschaulich wie anwendungsorientiert und verdeutlichen die hohe Praxisrelevanz der Thematik.

Zunächst widmet sich der vorliegende Band in Teil I theoretischen Fragestellungen. Dazu zählt die kritische Würdigung des Public-Private-Konzepts unter dem Gesichtspunkt der Stakeholder-Orientierung. Sachs/Rühli fordern in diesem Kontext vor dem Hintergrund der zunehmenden Bedeutung gesellschaftlicher Verantwortung ein Umdenken im Bereich traditioneller Management-Werte. Die besondere Bedeutung der Risikoallokation für PPP-Projekte im Zusammenhang mit dem Entwicklungsfortschritt bei privatem Risikomanagement wird hingegen im Beitrag von Pfnür diskutiert. Freiling/Calliess wiederum übertragen das PPP-Gedankengut auf Fragestellungen des Public-Private-Ordering, um einen möglichen Lösungsansatz für die Governance(-Lücke) internationaler Transaktionen zu erforschen. Mit den Beiträgen von Rufera über die Chancen und Risiken von PPPs aus Sicht der öffentlichen Hand, von Jacob/Schröter, die deren Bedeutung für ein modernes öffentliches Infrastrukturmanagement diskutieren und von Bachinger/Pechlaner/von Holzschuher, die die Bedeutung von PPPs im Bildungssektor beleuchten, schließen sich Informationen an, die jeweils detaillierte Einblicke in spezielle thematische Problemstellungen von PPP-Projekten geben. In diesen Kontext passt auch der Beitrag von Di Domenico/Meneguzzo, die den Einsatz von PPPs auf dem Arbeitsmarkt analysieren.

Während sich letzterer Beitrag auf einen gesamteuropäischen Kontext bezieht, werden im Anschluss daran drei konkrete Beispiele aus einzelnen europäischen Staaten dargestellt. Promberger setzt sich mit den ökonomischen Grundlagen von PPP-Projekten in Österreich auseinander. Nach einem umfassenden Überblick über die Forschungstraditionen bzgl. PPP sowie des politischen Stellenwertes der Projekte stellt er fest, dass diese dort im Vergleich mit anderen Staaten in Europa noch eine eher untergeordnete Rolle spielen. Eine erste Gegenüberstellung der aktuellen Erfahrungen in Italien und der Schweiz nehmen Gianella/Meneguzzo/Bernhart vor, indem sie die Ergebnisse eines Benchmarks vorstellen. Es geht dabei sowohl um politische Programme als auch Veränderungen in strategischer und organisatorischer Hinsicht, wobei Fragen zum Managementverhalten eingeschlossen werden. Mit dem Stellenwert von PPP im Rahmen der regionalen wirtschaftlichen Entwicklung in Estland schließlich befasst sich Mäeltsemees. Er zeichnet die Kontextbedingungen und bisherigen Erfahrungen sowie die Chancen und Risiken von PPPs als aussichtsreichen Lösungsweg für diverse Mängel in der oftmals noch aus der planwirtschaftlichen Vergangenheit stammenden Infrastruktur vor dem Hintergrund der aktuellen kommunalrechtlichen und wirtschaftspolitischen Entwicklungen nach.

In ähnlicher Weise beschreiben neun weitere Beiträge in Teil II des vorliegenden Sammelbandes jeweils konkrete praktische Erfahrungen aus unterschiedlichen PPP-Projekten. Die ersten drei Artikel liefern Beispiele aus der Baubranche. So stellt Littwin den Zusammenhang einer größeren Wirtschaftlichkeit von PPP-Projekten im Vergleich zur Eigenrealisierung mit klar definierten Aufgabenstellungen der Kommunalaufsicht und den Einsatz geeigneter Finanzierungsmodelle in Zusammenhang. Auf der anderen Seite illustriert Lupp – speziell unter Berücksichtigung von Erkenntnissen im Freistaat Bayern – Herausforderungen und Perspektiven bei öffentlichen Baumaßnahmen; Engel wiederum stellt Pilotprojekte im staatlichen Hochbau dar und erläutert Beratungsleistungen seitens der Bayerischen Staatsbauverwaltung für Kommunen. PPP als Möglichkeit zur Effizienzsteigerung im öffentlichen Immobilienmanagement behandeln Glock/Schultheis, indem sie Hintergründe erörtern und praktische Kenntnisse in Form von Vor- und Nachteilen von PPP zusammenfassen. Am konkreten Fall der Innsbrucker Nordkettenbahnen beschreibt Seeber den Einsatz öffentlich-privater Kooperationen bei Seilbahnprojekten und geht dabei insbesondere auf die Vorgehensweise bei der Implementierung der Partnerschaft sowie die bisherige Erfolgsbilanz ein.

Ein bedeutendes Instrument können PPPs zudem in der Wirtschaftsförderung sein. Brandt diskutiert in diesem Kontext potenzielle Steuerungs- und Legitimationsprobleme. Ein prägnantes Beispiel für unternehmerisches Engagement im Bereich des Regionalmanagements ist außerdem der Automobilkonzern AUDI AG mit Sitz in Ingolstadt. Deren Personalvorstand Widuckel stellt dar, wie vor dem Hintergrund der eigenen Unternehmensentwicklung regionale Kooperation zwischen öffentlichen und privaten Partnern gefördert wird. Ob schließlich eine öffentlich-private Zusammenarbeit auch für Stadtwerke von strategischem Interesse sein kann oder aber andere Typen der Kooperation möglicherweise zu bevorzugen sind, diskutiert Wübbels im Rahmen seines Beitrags über PPP im liberalisierten Energiemarkt und Jäkel erörtert die ökonomische und gesellschaftspolitische Beurteilung von PPPs im Strafvollzug. Kloss/Steyer schließen die Darstellung von praktischen Anwendungsfällen mit einem Beitrag zu PPP im Mittelstand ab.

Sicherlich gäbe es noch weit mehr über Public Private Partnership zu berichten. Die Zusammenstellung in diesem Sammelband soll die wissenschaftliche und praktische Auseinandersetzung mit diesem noch sehr jungen Forschungsgebiet verstärkt anregen und Planungshilfen für eine bewusste Herangehensweise an die tatsächliche Implementierung geben. Die Herausgeber hoffen, einige wesentliche Fragestellungen aufgegriffen und damit einen Beitrag zur wissenschaftlichen Diskussion und praktischen Umsetzung von PPPs geleistet zu haben.

Eichstätt und Ingolstadt, im August 2009

Harald Pechlaner
Wolf von Holzschuher
Monika Bachinger

Inhaltsverzeichnis

Teil II – Praktische Erfahrungen

Teil I

Wissenschaftliche Konzepte

The Stakeholder View of Strategy (SHV) – A Comprehensive Approach to Harmonize Public and Entrepreneurial Interaction

Sybille Sachs & Edwin Rühli

Inhaltsverzeichnis

1 The firm's role in society

The meaning of firm's role as a societal institution has gained increasing relevance as a result of globalization. Corporations have begun to manage the globalization processes, while political systems are still primarily oriented towards the idea of the nation state. The main duty of the nation states is to regulate and coordinate social issues within the framework of national boundaries; as their sphere of influence is limited to national boundaries they only limitedly engage in developing and realizing solutions for global problems. This gap is filled at least partially on the one hand by NGOs and supranational institutions like the UN. On the other hand, also the globally active multinational corporations are being increasingly challenged in their societal function. In the same vein STIGLITZ (2006) claims for a reorientation of firms' role in society in his new book on globalization: "One step in the right direction (note of the author: to improve corporate governance) would be to have companies take into account all stakeholders – employees and the communities in which they operate, not just their shareholders."[1]

In taking over this wider concept of (corporate) social responsibility, corporations could actively contribute to the resolution of larger societal problems or issues. However, this new role has neither been thoroughly defined vis-à-vis the state and civil society, nor has it been legitimized through a democratic process.[2] This is even more important as REICH (2007), for example, stresses in his new book "Supercapitalism" the fact that there is a decreasing effectiveness of the democracy due the benefits of supercapitalism. The benefit of the citizen decreases while the benefit of consumer and investor rises.[3]

These developments of the society ask for a new balance between business captured in capitalism and society grounded in democracy. Firms have to contri-

1 Stiglitz, J. E. (2006), p. 203.
2 See e.g. Matten, D./Crane, A. (2005).
3 See Reich, R. B. (2007).

bute to this. We believe that corporations as a fundamental social institution have to adopt approaches that are embedded in a stakeholder network to commonly create value with and for a broad set of different stakeholders. Stakeholders are thereby representatives of different subgroups of the societal, political and economic system. A firm's interaction with the stakeholders and therefore also with society are to a large extent influenced by its strategic management.

2 Approaches and concepts of strategic management

The traditional concepts of strategic management are based on two dominant approaches and streams of literature primarily in the 1990s: the Industry Structure View (ISV)[4] and the Resource Based View (RBV)[5]. At the center of these concepts, the question is how firms can achieve a sustainable economic success in spite of ongoing severe competition.

The ISV is market-oriented and assumes that a firm reaches a sustainable competitive advantage if it takes a clear position in the market as a cost leader or with a unique differentiation. The RBV focuses on the firm's resources and assumes that a sustainable competitive advantage can be reached based on the unique and inimitable core competencies. In reality both approaches can be useful. The problem is that both consider exclusively economic causalities and leave aside important factors which also determine strategic success in real-life situations. Moreover, both focus on the shareholder as the only important stakeholder and therefore neglect the contributions and expectations of other constituencies of a firm.

---

4 See Porter, M. E. (1985); Porter, M. E. (1991); Porter, M. E. (1996); Porter, M. E. (1998); Porter, M. E. (2008).

5 See Barney, J. B. (1991); Barney, J. B. (1996); Barney, J. B. (2002); Newbert, D. (2008); Prahalad, C. K./Hamel, G. (1990); Teece, D. J. (2007); Teece, D. J./Pisano, G./Shuen, A. (1997); Wang, H./Lim, S. S. (2008).

This has been widely criticized by practitioners as well as by academics in the last years. For example BLAIR and STOUT (1999) claim to focus more on the importance of intellectual capital: "Viewing the firm as a bundle of assets owned by shareholders also seems odd once we recognize that one of the key assets a corporation uses in production is 'intellectual capital' – that is, the knowledge and experience residing in the minds of its employees, rather than the hands of its shareholders."[6] Consequently, ASHER/MAHONEY/MAHONEY (2005) argue that "a stakeholder perspective indicates that it is no longer tenable to regard the shareholders as the only residual claimants, where residual claimants are defined as persons or collections whose relationships to the firm give rise to a significant residual interest in the firm's success and failure".[7]And MICHAEL JENSEN (2000), a well-known finance scholar from Harvard, adds that "a firm cannot maximize value if it ignores the interests of its stakeholders".[8]

In practice, more and more firms use concepts such as the triple bottom line including economic, social and ecological indicators for success[9] or the Balanced Scorecard[10] to include a broad stakeholder thinking in their strategic management. The SHV gains also more and more attention in the consulting community. KPMG, for instance, and also PricewaterhouseCoopers, based on their experiences, have published tools considering stakeholder aspects.

The idea of a more comprehensive and stakeholder-oriented view of strategic management is also supported by the UN Commission on Sustainable Development (CSD) and the Global Compact Initiative launched by the General Secretary of the United Nations at the Management Symposium 1999 in Davos. In the same line of thinking, the EU Commission started a project in 2001 focusing "Best Practices for Corporate Social Responsibility".

---

6 Blair, M. M./Stout, L. A. (1999), p. 261.
7 Asher, C. C. /Mahoney, J. M./Mahoney, J. T.(2005), p. 3.
8 Sachs, S./Maurer, M. (2005a).
9 See Elkington, J. (1998); Mowat, D. (2002); Norman, W./MacDonald, C. (2004); Shell (1999); Willard, B. (2002).
10 See Kaplan, R. S./Norton, D. P. (1996).

Finally, recent incidents such as Enron, WorldCom and others have challenged management practitioners as well as scholars to rethink their values and their way of interaction with the firm's constituencies. More and more since companies realize that a one-sided orientation to shareholder value is in a strategic perspective too narrow, especially because the firms' strategically relevant resources are not only of financial nature but most importantly knowledge oriented.

On this background, POST, PRESTON and SACHS (2002) developed and published the concept of the Stakeholder View of Strategy[11] which represents a new and comprehensive approach to strategic management to cope with the challenges resulting from the interaction between firms and society in the early years of the 21st century. This approach is widely discussed and accepted by the scientific community.[12] "By raising the level of analysis form the firm's "internal" resources and the industry level to the socio-political stakeholder network, the authors' version of the SHV simultaneously integrates the other views into a broader framework that provides a more complete explanation of an organization's action and its outcomes."[13]

3 What does a Stakeholder View of Strategy mean?

The SHV posits the capacity of a firm to generate sustainable wealth over time and hence its long-term value is to a large extent determined by its relationships with key stakeholders. The success and survival of the enterprise ultimately depends upon its mutual interactions with its stakeholders. "Thereby, stakeholders are defined as *'all individuals and constituencies that contribute, either volunta-*

---

11 See Post, J. E./Preston, L. E./Sachs, S. (2002).

12 See e.g. Abe, N./Shimizutani, S. (2005); Agle, B. R. et al. (2008); Bracken, D. W. (2003); Buono, A. F. (2003); Caldwell, C. (2004); Marlin, D./Lamont, B. T./Hoffman, J. J. (1994); Mattingly, J. E. (2004); Porter, M. E./Kramer, M. R. (2002); Post, J. E./Preston, L. E./Sachs, S. (2002); Walsh, J. P. (2005).

13 Mattingly, J. E. (2004), p. 521.

rily or involuntarily, to its wealth-creating capacity and activities, and are therefore its potential beneficiaries and/or risk bearers' (Post et al., 2002: 19). Based on this definition, four categories of stakeholders are distinguished:

- Benefit providers
- Benefit receivers
- Risk providers
- Risk bearers".14

In our empirical research (see part 4 below) focusing on best practices of stakeholder management in firms we found that:

- firms see their stakeholders overwhelmingly as benefit receivers or benefit providers
- firms understand that their stakeholders can be risk bearers and very seldom even risk providers.

Type of Firm-Stakeholder Interaction	*Average (all firms)*
Value Creation - Benefit Provider	33%
Value Creation - Benefit Receiver	45%
Value Creation - Risk Bearer	17%
Value Creation - Risk Provider	5%
Total	100%

Tab. 1: Average of the different types of Firm-Stakeholder Interaction
Source: own graphics.

A fundamental aspect of this framework, therefore, is that stakeholders have a "stake" in the operation of the firm. That is, they have something "at risk" and/or something "to win" – some possibility of gaining benefits or experiencing losses or harms – as a result of corporate operations.

[14] Sachs, S./Maurer, M. (2005a), p. 8.

On the one side we can identify resources bearing stakeholders (such as employees) and shareholders (as strategic stakeholders). These stakeholders have access to tangible resources such as capital, technology, and/or intangible resources such as core values, technological know-how, i.e., resources that help firms build unique and inimitable core competencies. On the other side, we have the relations between the corporation and its constituents within the industry, including competitors, suppliers, and customers. These groups have been traditionally considered to be the strategically relevant stakeholders in a firm's stakeholder network. But apart from these stakeholders, other interest groups such as governments, regulators or NGOs increasingly influence a firm's strategy. These strategic stakeholders are part of the social domain in which the firm conducts its business.

In our empirical investigation we found that among the top ten stakeholders firms mentioned in interviews five are directly linked to its value chain but also five belong to the societal arena.

	All Firms	
	Ranking	**%**
Customers	1	26.25
Employees	2	20.53
Shareholders / Investors	3	10.2
Society	4	7.00
Regulators	5	6.22
Business / Industry Partners	6	4.91
Government	7	3.79
Experts / Academics / Universities	8	3.61
Suppliers	9	2.84
Politicians	10	2.66

Tab. 2: Stakeholders of firms
Source: own graphics.

As we can see, firms are not only embedded in business stakeholders' relations but also in non-market stakeholders' relations. Based on the contact with this non-economic type of stakeholders and in gaining and maintaining the "license to operate"[15], new knowledge can emerge which leads not only to a competitive advantage and therefore to strategic success for the firm but contribute also to the fulfillment of societal expectations.

So far, we have focused on the interactions of the firm with its stakeholders to **create** value. In addition to this, the SHV also considers the value **distribution**.

In this perspective, the question arises how the different stakeholders should participate in this value distribution.

Following the principle of **distributive justice** those stakeholders should participate in the dissemination that make firm-specific investments. Similar to the shareholders that are compensated for their specific capital investments in the firm, all other stakeholders making firm-specific investments should be considered according to their contribution to the firm's value creation.

In the SHV this can be complemented by a **procedural justice** which means that stakeholders affected by a firm's activities should be included in an appropriate manner in a firm's strategic decision processes in its corporate governance.

Based on these reflections and the remarks in the previous paragraphs, the main features of the business model of the Stakeholder View of Strategy can be summarized with the following eight statements:

– In the SHV, the corporation is defined as a socio-economic organization to create sustainable wealth with and for its multiple constituencies representing the economic as well as the societal sphere.

[15] Post, J. E./Preston, L. E./Sachs, S. (2002).

- The SHV holds the capacity of a business enterprise to generate sustainable wealth over time which is determined by its dynamic relationships with key stakeholders within its resource base, industry structure and social-political environment.
- Effective stakeholder management aims to insure that relationships with all types of stakeholders are wealth-enhancing (and not wealth-reducing), so that the greatest possible increase in total wealth – and therefore total capacity to generate stakeholder benefits – will be achieved.
- The SHV places the firm – and its management – at the center of a web of stakeholder relationships, and demonstrates that sustainable organizational wealth can be enhanced by a purposeful management of favorable relations (and reduced by unfavorable relations) between the corporation and its strategic stakeholders.
- Based on the network linkages with the stakeholders resources and knowledge can be combined to unique and firm specific competencies.
- The firm is not only embedded in business stakeholders' networks but also in non-market stakeholders' networks. The SHV enlarges the range of causalities influencing corporate success by taking into account economic and societal factors which in turn also enhances managerial discretion. Managers can purposefully use the non-market relations to complement the sources and causalities of strategic success.
- In considering societal and ecological oriented stakeholders the firm contributes directly to societal needs and expectations.
- The SHV argues for a fair distribution of the values created by the interaction of all constituencies. The stakeholders should participate in the value distribution based on their contribution and the risks they bear in their interaction with the firm. This is the normative core of the SHV.

4 The empirical foundations of SHV

Given this concept of SHV, the questions arise to what extent it is already used in practice and what "good practices" are in reality. To contribute to these questions, we undertook a series of empirical case studies (some of the results of this study we have already mentioned above). The concept of SHV and its implementation in practice is still quite unexplored, both in the stakeholder theory and in the strategic management literature. The lack of theoretical understanding and empirical results might be caused by the fact that these stakeholder relations are a very complex social phenomenon with no clearly evident boundaries to its context. Taking account of this high degree of complexity of the real life situations, a qualitative approach seems to be appropriate. Case studies are such a qualitative approach that also considers a comprehensive perspective.

First of all, the three cases analyzed in the book by POST, PRESTON and SACHS (2002) gave basic insights in how Shell, Motorola and Cummins consider stakeholder aspects in their strategic management. Based on this, a second step followed in which we organized a workshop with some 10 firms to discuss their experiences in the light of the SHV. This led to a research project in which we analyzed in depth six firms which already have proven to develop a stakeholder orientation. In this project focusing on good practices for stakeholder view we emphasized firms learning processes to integrate stakeholder management in their business model. We focused on two industry clusters, the telecommunications and the financial services industry. First insights have already been published or presented at professional meetings.[16]

---

[16] See Kern, I./Sachs, S./Rühli, E. (2007); Maurer, M./Sachs, S. (2005); Post, J. E./Preston, L. E./ Sachs (2002); Sachs, S. et al. (2006); Sachs, S./Rühli, E. (2005b); Sachs, S./Rühli, E. (2005c); Sachs, S./Rühli, E. (2007); Sachs, S./Rühli, E./Kern, I. (2007a); Sachs, S./Rühli, E./Kern, I. (2007b); Sachs, S./Rühli, E./Maurer, M. (2006a), Sachs, S./Rühli, E./Maurer, M. (2006b); Sachs, S./Rühli, E./Mittnacht, V. (2007); Sachs, S./Rühli, E./Post, J. E. (2003).

In building up our database we first analyzed external and internal material of the participating firms about the stakeholder orientation of these corporations. This was the basis to conduct semi-structured interviews with top level managers and representatives of these corporations that already were in charge of stakeholder management task. In these interviews the findings of the analysis had been deepened. Finally we conducted a workshop with these companies to exchange experiences.

Some basic insights are:

- The learning process of the firms towards a stakeholder-oriented strategic management we analyzed covered several years and was the result of important events such as liberalization or economic and social shocks in the environment (particularly wake-up calls).
- There is a lack of professional and systematic stakeholder management. None of the firms have fully developed the SHV in such a comprehensive way that we are claiming for. But all have introduced important parts of it and see advantages in developing it further.[17]
- Our case analysis shows that corporations which already have a certain stakeholder orientation clearly see the importance and the potential of stakeholder relations to enhance benefits or reduce risks. Interactions with these categories of economic, social and ecological stakeholders create additional resources or provide a strong position in the industry which is acknowledged as a chance.
- Our investigation also shows that the strategy, the structure and the culture of a stakeholder-oriented firm are strongly influenced by a SHV. This means that the expectations and needs of the society are internalized and therefore accepted and supported (see next paragraph).

---

[17] See Sachs, S./Schmitt, R./Perrin, I. (2008).

5 SHV and economic theory

In economic theory, the only and exclusive criterion managers should apply in their strategic choices is net present value of the cash flow coming from that decision.[18] Other societal effects are excluded and often modelled as external costs. If two or more strategic directions are possible then managers should choose the one providing the highest net present value. This concept is based on a narrow interpretation of what rational behaviour means, namely maximizing the economic outcome.

But when we analyzed firms' behaviour in reality in the context of our research project, we could see numerous situations in which firms invest resources without a direct effect on their cash flow. Why this contradiction? The reasons are obvious. Economic theory and related rational behaviour are based on abstractions and assumptions which are not given in the real life situation. As soon as we move from economic theory to business practice we can see a whole bunch of reasons why firms engage (invest) in strategies even if this does not maximize the net present value of their cash flow. In the following text we present nine reasons.

1. Broad objective function (utility function) of investors

The objective of investors in reality is not always to maximize the net present value of their investment but to satisfy a broader set of objectives. Managers then have a broader fiduciary duty than to serve financial goals. Investors may be ready to reduce their financial expectations if the firm gains a leading position in the list of the most admired companies, contributes to humanistic values of a family company or to a high level of citizen, customer or employee satisfaction. We have clearly seen such "deviations" in family-owned companies in small towns where the social contacts are tight.

---

[18] See e.g. the criticism on the Grand Design Model by Asher, C. C./Mahoney, J. M./Mahoney, J. T. (2005); Blair, M. M./Stout, L. A. (1999); Freeman, R. E./Harrison, J. S./Wicks, A. C. (2007).

2. Maintain the license to operate

The license to operate is often attributed to a firm by a political or legal institution, by a special regulator or in a more fuzzy way by society's expectations. These stakeholders may expect (for political or social reasons) a "certain amount" of non cash flow oriented activities (sponsoring, ecological or social investments, protections against noise and malodour etc.). If a firm neglects these activities it may sooner or later lose its license to operate or the support of these stakeholders in difficult situations.

Investments to gain and sustain the license to operate lead also to "deviations". Their values and dimensions are not determined by a market or a formal contract but open for managerial discretion.

3. Public mandate

Private corporations sometimes have a public mandate to provide public services. (This may be linked to a license to operate, see 2.) Firms then have to provide services to a specific set of citizens even if this happens not at lowest cost of production or highest possible market prices for their services. And the regulator may not be willing to cover the "deviation". We have analyzed a bank with a public mandate to provide favourable conditions to small firms and private home owners and an insurance company with the mandate to offer favourable conditions to people suffering from accidents.

4. Time preferences

Firms have sometimes the opportunity to voluntarily reduce the cash flow in the short run to invest in stakeholder relations that enhance the chance of future cash flows. The "deviation" then appears in the short run. An insurance company may pay a client generously (more than necessary) for the damage of his car, hoping that he will also remain a client in the future.

5. Imperfect markets

Reality shows that firms which do not maximize the net present value are not eliminated immediately by the financial markets or the markets for firms. There is not a strong and absolute mechanism. In addition to this, product markets may also be imperfect (lack of transparency, monopolistic niches, heterogeneity).
Besides the most profitable firm, we can see less profitable ones in reality that survive over long periods of time. In this context, firms may spend money on activities that reduce their cash flow without a danger of failure. We have seen a telecommunication company that pays much more attention to its stakeholder relations (including sponsoring) than its competitor; nevertheless, this company also survives.

6. Enhancement of firm-specific investments

A firm may spend some money to motivate stakeholders to make firm-specific investments that lead in addition to the capital investment to residual profit which then can be distributed to all stakeholders, not only to shareholders. Such firm-specific investments often are made by employees or lead users and are not covered by the salary/remuneration they get.

7. Rents from externalities

A firm may have more favourable conditions than its competitor (e.g. location advantage). This firm may develop activities which do not lead to cash flow and still have a competitive advantage. This is obvious for firms operating in the highly differentiated global context.

8. Uncertainty and managerial discretion

In reality, the optimal production function or value creation process in the firm as well as the market conditions are never clear and certain. This leads to managerial discretions and to room for not exclusively cash flow oriented activities. It depends on the personal values of the manager how much he is willing to invest into not strictly economic activities given these management discretions.

9. History matters

A firm's present position and possible future alternatives are always to a certain extent determined by its past. A firm which in the past had favourable social contracts with its employees or the public can hardly break them without losing its image, acceptance or the motivation of its employees (contribution of the stakeholders as it was in the social contract). Favourable potential from the past always creates room for not immediately cash flow oriented activities.

Given this whole range of possibilities of not strictly and simple profit maximization, management is challenged to handle the complex economic, societal and ecological situation in reality in a comprehensive way, not only in a narrow economic perspective.

6 Managerial implications

The concept of SHV is not only a descriptive framework but it also leads to recommendations on procedures, tools and implementation processes. The SHV as a frame of strategic thinking offers new insights for managers: Fundamentally, managers have to reflect what kind of learning process would be suitable for their own company to adopt a comprehensive stakeholder management perspective that will lead to changes in the corporation's structure and culture, as well as in its strategy.

In the SHV perspective, stakeholder management is more than ad hoc response to crises and occasionally paying attention to an unsatisfied stakeholder (agents provocateurs). Stakeholder management must pervade the firm and result in consistent policies and sustainable practices based on systematic and professional identification of the key stakeholders and of their claims and potential to contribute to the firm's value creation.

As to the **strategy** of the firm, management has to actively identify and integrate these stakeholder potentials in the process of strategy creation and implementation. Systematic stakeholder mapping is the first step. More specifically, the knowledge of the stakeholders not only in the business world (market stakeholders) but also in the social and political environment (non-market stakeholders) offers strategic chances. This leads to new resources and therefore to the chance for new core competencies.[19] Our research shows that on the one hand, the effects of the SHV follow the value chain and go beyond the corporation's limits (e.g. they affect suppliers, alliance partners etc.). The perspective of core competencies is therefore based on several firms. "Intermediaries" like banks and insurances have a significant influence on the implementation of the Stakeholder View within the whole society. They judge more and more their customers' strengths and weaknesses not only on the basis of their financial and business behavior but also according to their ecological and societal qualifications. The price for credits or for insurance coverage a firm has to pay to the bank or the insurance company depends on its social and ecological chances or risks. In strategizing management has to take action for a favourable positioning of the firm not only in the markets but also in the stakeholder network. This contributes to society's needs.

The more our society and economy are developing, the more important the stakeholder network becomes. The bundling of distributed knowledge becomes critical in gaining and sustaining competitive advantages.

One specific aspect of corporate strategy today is to clarify the behaviour with respect to the strategic stakeholders. Useful stakeholder relations very often presuppose trust. And this demands for proactive and interactive, not only for occasional and reactive interactions with the respective stakeholder. Managing these relationships can itself become a core competence.

---

[19] See Rühli, E./Sachs, S. (2005).

Systematic stakeholder management leads to respective **structures and processes**. Two opposing forms can be distinguished in institutionally tying down stakeholder management: On the one hand, specific institutions (departments) are created (e.g. public affairs department, sustainability group or investor relations department). Quite often, corporations have chosen this solution to a certain extent. Some corporations have even declared selected departments to be "the owner" of a given stakeholder-relation process (process owners). On the other hand, the Stakeholder View can be regarded primarily as an integral part of the activities of all instances. From the cases we analyzed, we could notice that most firms have specific institutions to manage the relationships with the stakeholders they consider of strategic importance which facilitates the harmonization of public and entrepreneurial interactions. One of the crucial questions in institutionalizing the SHV is how to make sure that stakeholder aspects are considered in the corporate governance (participation, voting power or information and consultation).

The SHV claims that it is part of management's responsibility to create the necessary structures and processes (e.g. reporting) to maintain professional stakeholder interactions. Since higher level managers have overall responsibility for corporate performance, they are responsible for the impact of the corporation – both favourable and unfavourable – on all of its stakeholders. And therefore on society.

The corporation's **culture** is a critical factor in stakeholder management. The core values of a firm can support or hinder the behavior in dealing with stakeholder relations. Therefore, in the visions or value statements of firms the stakeholder orientation should be clarified and harmonized with the culture of the society in which it operates. In our research we have seen some good examples of basic orientation of core values affecting the relationships to employees, customers, regulators etc. The SHV becomes an integral part of the corporate culture. The cultural aspect of the SHV becomes particularly important in firms in which the employees originally come from different national cultures and in which the customers and business partners are also part of different regional cultures. This is particularly intensified by the general globalization trend. The cultural aspect of SHV is particularly well developed in POST, PRESTON and SACHS's book (2002). "Indeed. One of the important thrusts of the book is a focus on the nature of change in the corporate culture of the firms under scrutiny. Real change, the authors stress, is impossible without real change in corporate culture. They are surely correct in this view, and they devote considerable effort to making the point clear to supplying detailed evidence as to its validity."[20]

In order to implement the Stakeholder View better in the thinking of management, top managers have to change some of the traditional values. Three options exist to achieve this goal: First, top managers' incentives must be changed; second, the assessment process for top management selection must be changed; third, management development programs must be changed as well. So far, managers' incentives have been mostly oriented towards investors' policies based on financial data such as shareholder values or stock prices. These incentive systems do not consider the expectations of a broader range of strategically relevant constituencies, particularly from the societal and ecological spheres. The more the corporate culture takes the SHV into consideration, the smaller the need for its formal institutionalization.

Regarding how the stakeholder orientation is reflected in firm's strategy, structure and culture, our cases provide an obvious interrelationship between their strategy, structure, culture, and their stakeholder relations. On the one hand, changes in these three elements lead to a refocusing on the awareness and the importance of the strategic stakeholders and to a new perception of the stakeholder network. On the other hand, strategies, structures and cultures are clearly influenced by the contributions of the respective set of economic and societal stakeholders. As already mentioned, the knowledge contribution capacity of stakeholders is of paramount importance.

---

[20] Jones, T. M. (2002), p. 473.

7 Final remarks

The Stakeholder View of Strategy as a concept and the corresponding managerial behaviour create a systematic link between business and society. Society's expectations and potentials are important determinants of the firm's strategic decisions. The newest empirical investigations support also the success of this behavior.[21] With this the firms "automatically" contribute to the fulfillment of society's needs.

Bibliography

Abe, N./Shimizutani, S. (2005): Employment Policy and Corporate Governance: An Empirical Analysis on the Stakeholder Model in Japan. SRI Discussion Paper Series.

Agle, B. R. et al. (2008): Dialogue: Towards Superior Stakeholder Theory. In: Business Ethics Quarterly, 18(2): 153-190.

Asher, C. C./Mahoney, J. M./Mahoney, J. T. (2005): Towards a Property Rights Foundation for a Stakeholder Theory of the Firm. In: Journal of Management and Governance, 9(1): 5-32.

Barney, J. B. (1991): Firm resources and sustained competitive advantage. In: Journal of Management, 17(1): 99-120.

Barney, J. B. (1996): The resource-based theory of the firm. In: Organization Science, 7(5): 469.

Barney, J. B. (2002): Gaining and Sustaining Competitive Advantage (2nd ed.). Upper Saddle River: Prentice Hall.

[21] See Hull, C. E./Rothenberg, S. (2008).

Blair, M. M./Stout, L. A. (1999): A Team Production Theory of Corporate Law. In: Virginia Law Review, 85(2): 247-328.

Bracken, D. W. (2003): Book Review: Redefining the corporation – Stakeholder management and organizational wealth. In: Personnel Psychology, 56(4): 1064-1067.

Buono, A. F. (2003): A review of Redefining the corporation: Stakeholder management and organizational wealth. In: Business & Society Review, 108(2): 279-284.

Caldwell, C. (2004): Book review essay: Effective governance in managing change: common perspective from two lenses. In: Academy of Management Review, 29(2): 299-301.

Elkington, J. (1998): Cannibals With Forks: The Triple Bottom Line of 21st Century Business. Stony Creek, CT: New Society Publishers.

Freeman, R. E./Harrison, J. S./Wicks, A. C. (2007): Managing for Stakeholders: Survival, Reputation, and Success. New Haven: Yale University Press.

Hull, C. E./Rothenberg, S. (2008): Firm Performance: The Interactions of Corporate Social Performance with Innovation and Industry Differentiation. In: Strategic Management Journal, 29(2008): 781-789.

Jensen, M. C. (2000): Value Maximization, Stakeholder Theory and the Corporate Objective Function. In: Beer, M./Nohria N. (Eds.), Breaking the Code of Change. Boston, MA: Harvard Business School Press: 37-58.

Jones, T. M. (2002): Book Review: Redefining the corporation – Stakeholder management and organizational wealth. In: Business & Society, 41(4): 469-474.

Kaplan, R. S./Norton, D. P. (1996): The Balanced Scorecard. Boston MA: Harvard Business School Press.

Kern, I./Sachs, S./Rühli, E. (2007): Stakeholder Relations and Maintaining the License to Operate: A Comparative Case Study of the Swiss Telecommunications Industry. In: Corporate Governance, 7(4): 446-454.

Marlin, D./Lamont, B. T./Hoffman, J. J. (1994): Choice situation, strategy, and performance: A reexamination. In: Strategic Management Journal 15: 229-239.

Matten, D./Crane, A. (2005): What is Stakeholder Democracy? Perspectives and Issues. In: Business Ethics: A European Review, 14(1): 6-13.

Mattingly, J. E. (2004): Book Review: "Redefining the Corporation: Stakeholder Management and Organizational Wealth". In: Academy of Management Review, July: 520-523.

Maurer, M./Sachs, S. (2005): Implementing the Stakeholder View: Learning Processes for a Changed Stakeholder Orientation. In: Journal of Corporate Citizenship, 17 (Spring): 93-107.

Mowat, D. (2002): The VanCity Difference: A Case for the Triple Bottom Line Approach to Business. In: International Journal of Corporate Sustainability, 9 (1): 24-29.

Newbert, S. L. (2008): Value, Rareness, Competitive Advantage, and Performance: A Conceptual-Level Empirical Investigation of the Resource-Based View of the Firm. In: Strategic Management Journal, 29(2008): 745-768.

Norman, W./MacDonald, C. (2004): Getting to the Bottom of "Triple Bottom Line". In: Business Ethics Quarterly, 14(2): 243-262.

Porter, M. E. (1985): Competitive advantage – Creating and sustaining superior performance. New York: Free Press.

Porter, M. E. (1991): Towards a dynamic theory of strategy. In: Strategic Management Journal, 12(Special Issue Winter): 95-117.

Porter, M. E. (1996): What Is Strategy? In: Harvard Business Review, (November-December 1996): 61-78.

Porter, M. E. (1998): Competitive strategy: Techniques for analyzing industries and competitors. New York: The Free Press.

Porter, M. E. (2008): The Five Competitive Forces That Shape Strategy. In: Harvard Business Review, (January): 79-93.

Porter, M. E./Kramer, M. R. (2002): The competitive advantage of corporate philanthropy. In: Harvard Business Review, 80(12): 27-64.

Post, J. E./Preston, L. E./Sachs, S. (2002): Redefining the corporation – Stakeholder management and organizational wealth. Stanford: Stanford University Press.

Prahalad, C. K./Hamel, G. (1990): The core competence of the corporation. In: Harvard Business Review, 68(3): 79-91.

Reich, R. B. (2007): Supercapitalism: The Transformation of Business, Democracy, and Everyday Life. New York, NY: Knopf.

Rühli, E./Sachs, S. (2005): Practical Issues in Implementing the Stakeholder View as a Core Competence. In: Sanchez, R./Heene, A. (Eds.), Competence Perspectives on Resources, Stakeholders, and Renewal. Oxford: Elsevier: 217-233.

Sachs, S./Maurer, M. (2005a): Toward Dynamic Corporate Stakeholder Responsibility. Journal of Business Ethics.

Sachs, S. et al. (2006): Corporate Social Responsibility from a "Stakeholder View" Perspective: CSR Implementation by a Swiss Mobile Telecommunication Provider. In: Corporate Governance, 6(4): 506-515.

Sachs, S./Rühli, E. (2005b): Changing Managers' Values Towards a Broader Stakeholder Orientation. In: Corporate Governance, 5(2): 89-98.

Sachs, S./Rühli, E. (2005c): Practical Issues in Implementing the Stakeholder View as a Core Competence. In: Sanchez, R./Heene, A. (Eds.): Competence Perspectives on Resources, Stakeholders and Renewal, Vol. 9 Advances in Applied Business Strategy.

Sachs, S./Rühli, E. (2007): Global Governance as Challenge for the Strategic Management, 6th Annual Colloquium of the European Academy of Business in Society (EABIS). Barcelona.

Sachs, S./Rühli, E./Kern, I. (2007a): Lizenz zum Managen. Mit Stakeholdern zum Erfolg: Herausforderungen und Good Practices. Bern: Haupt.

Sachs, S./Rühli, E./Kern, I. (2007b): Stakeholder Relations as a Corporate Core to Operate, Compete and Innovate. International Association for Business and Society (IABS), Florence, Italy: 470-475.

Sachs, S./Rühli, E./Maurer, M. (2006a): The effects of liberalization and privatization on former monopolist's stakeholder relations. Politeia, Milan.

Sachs, S./Rühli, E./Maurer, M. (2006b): Strategic Management: A New Challenging Perspective, Academy of management (AoM). Atlanta, USA.

Sachs, S./Rühli, E./Mittnacht, V. (2007): How stakeholder relations impact corporate strategy – An empirical investigation. International Association for Business and Society (IABS), Florence, Italy: 476-481.

Sachs, S./Rühli, E./Post, J. E. (2003): Implementing the Stakeholder View in European Firms – an Empirical Investigation. European Management Journal, in review.

Sachs, S./Schmitt, R./Perrin, I. (2008): Stakeholder Value Management System. Paper presented at the Annual Meeting of the International Association for Business and Society (IABS) in June, Tampere/Finland.

Shell (1999): The Shell Report 1999: People, Planet and Profits.

Stiglitz, J. E. (2006): Making Globalization Work: The Next Steps to Global Justice. New York: Norton.

Teece, D. J. (2007): Explicating dynamic capabilities: the nature and microfoundations of (sustainable) enterprise performance. In: Strategic Management Journal, 28 (13): 1319 - 1350.

Teece, D. J./Pisano, G./Shuen, A. (1997): Dynamic capabilities and strategic management. In: Strategic Management Journal, 18(7): 509-533.

Walsh, J. P. (2005): Book Review Essay: Taking Stock of Stakeholder Management. In: Academy of Management Review, 30(2): 426-438.

Wang, H./Lim, S. S. (2008): Real Options and Real Value: The Role of Employee Incentives to Make Specific Knowledge Investments. In: Strategic Management Journal, 29 (2008): 701-721.

Willard, B. (2002): The Sustainability Advantage: Seven Business Case Benefits of a Triple Bottom Line. Gabriola Island, BC: New Society Publishers.

Möglichkeiten und Grenzen der Risikoallokation zur Effizienzsteigerung von PPP-Projekten

Andreas Pfnür

Inhaltsverzeichnis

1 Problemstellung

Public Private Partnerships (PPP) werden in Theorie und Praxis vor allem als Finanzierungsvariante oder, in der weit geringeren Zahl der Fälle, als Realisierungsvariante angesehen.[1] Dabei wird häufig übersehen, dass ein erhebliches, wenn nicht sogar das größte, systemimmanente Potenzial von PPPs in der richtigen Allokation von Projektrisiken zwischen den Partnern liegt. Vergleicht man die derzeitigen Bemühungen um das Risikomanagement des öffentlichen Sektors mit denen der Privatwirtschaft, so wird schnell klar, dass der öffentliche Sektor den privaten Unternehmen deutlich unterlegen ist. Im folgenden Beitrag wird untersucht, wie mit Hilfe von PPPs der Entwicklungsfortschritt des privaten gegenüber dem öffentlichen Risikomanagement zur Steigerung der Effizienz öffentlicher Investitionen gesteigert werden kann. Die Ausführungen bedienen sich dabei insbesondere eines Beispiels aus dem öffentlichen Immobilienmanagement, sind aber grundsätzlich auf jedes Anwendungsfeld von PPPs übertragbar.

2 Risiken und deren Ursachen

Ökonomische Risiken resultieren aus unsicheren Erwartungen über die zukünftige Entwicklung im Rahmen von Planungs- und Entscheidungsprozessen. Die Determinanten des Risikos sind erstens die Wahrscheinlichkeit, mit der Abweichungen von einem Plan eintreten, sowie zweitens die Höhe des daraus resultierenden Schadens. Vice versa gelten auf der Kehrseite der Medaille diese Zusammenhänge auch für die ökonomischen Chancen. Im Folgenden konzentrieren sich die Ausführungen auf die negative Seite der Risiken.

---

[1] Vgl. exemplarisch z.B. Alfen, H./Fischer, K. (2006); BMVBW (2003); Budäus, D. (2004).

2.1 Ausmaß der Unsicherheit als Risikodeterminante

Da in realen Entscheidungssituationen de facto nie Sicherheit über die zukünftige Entwicklung herrscht, sind Risikosituationen im Wirtschaftsleben allgegenwärtig. Typischerweise wird unterstellt, dass die Unsicherheit und damit auch das Risiko mit zunehmendem Planungshorizont ansteigen.

Wie hoch die Unsicherheit über den Erfolg von selbst so vermeintlich sicheren Investitionen wie Immobilieninvestitionen ist, verdeutlichen beispielhaft die Ergebnisse einer empirischen Unternehmensbefragung zu den Risiken von Immobilieninvestments institutioneller Immobilieninvestoren in Deutschland, welche auch erste Hinweise auf die Unsicherheit der Eingangsdaten von öffentlichen Infrastrukturinvestitionen erlaubt. In der als repräsentativ zu bezeichnenden Studie wurden institutionelle Immobilieninvestoren unter anderem nach der Möglichkeit befragt, die aus einer Investition in Gewerbeimmobilien resultierenden Zahlungsströme zu prognostizieren. Konkret sollten die Befragten einschätzen, wie groß voraussichtlich die Abweichungen der realisierten von den geplanten Beträgen in einer zehnjährigen Finanzplanung sein werden. Abbildung 1 veranschaulicht die durchschnittliche Abweichung der erwarteten von den realisierten Zahlungen:

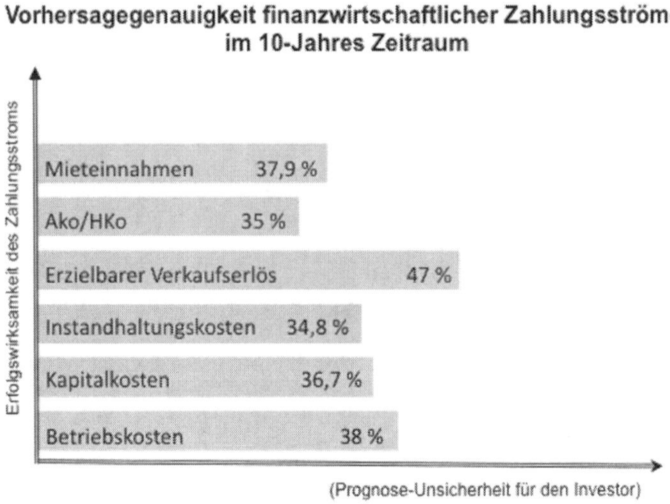

Abb. 1: Unsicherheit in der Finanzplanung von Immobilieninvestments
Quelle: Pfnür, A./Armonat, S. (2001).

Beispielsweise könnten die Anschaffungs- und Herstellungskosten bei einer Unsicherheit von 35% anstatt 10 Mio. Euro mit ebenso hoher Wahrscheinlichkeit 8,25 Mio. Euro oder auch 11,75 Mio. Euro betragen. Angesichts der Prognoseunsicherheiten zwischen über 30 und nahezu 50 Prozent bei den wichtigsten finanzwirtschaftlichen Erfolgsfaktoren wird das Ausmaß des Risikos von Immobilieninvestitionen auch im öffentlichen Sektor deutlich. Genauso wie in der Privatwirtschaft entstehen hier die den Mieteinnahmen gleichzusetzende Nutzenbewertung, Anschaffungs- und Herstellungskosten, die im Verkaufspreis zum Ausdruck kommende Wertentwicklung, die Instandhaltungskosten, Kapitalkosten sowie Betriebskosten.

Verkürzt sich der Prognosehorizont, so nimmt die Unsicherheit im Planungs- und Entscheidungsprozess sukzessive ab, bis sie in der Gegenwart schließlich zur Gewissheit wird. Bei langfristigen Investitionsprojekten begründet sich daraus für die private Immobilienwirtschaft wie auch für die öffentliche

Hand unmittelbar die Notwendigkeit zur laufenden Aktualisierung der Planungen im Rahmen eines prozessbegleitenden Investitionscontrollings.

Weitet man das Betrachtungsspektrum auf ein ganzes Portfolio von Immobilieninvestitionen aus, so nimmt die Unsicherheit mit jedem zusätzlich betrachteten Objekt erfahrungsgemäß ebenfalls ab. Objektspezifische und damit unsystematische Risiken gleichen sich aus. Während in einem Objekt die Instandhaltungskosten deutlich gegenüber dem geplanten Wert liegen, weisen andere Objekte unterplanmäßige Instandhaltungskosten auf. In der Summe gleichen sich Planabweichungen aus.

Auch wenn entsprechende Untersuchungen bislang nicht flächendeckend vorliegen, ist mit sehr hoher Wahrscheinlichkeit davon auszugehen, dass nahezu alle Beschaffungsvorgänge der öffentlichen Hand mit langfristigem Investitionscharakter vergleichbaren, wenn nicht sogar höheren Unsicherheiten, unterliegen. Im Gegensatz zur Privatwirtschaft hat die öffentliche Hand allerdings bislang kaum die Mittel entwickelt, die Informationsunsicherheiten zu verringern. Wie die Kapitel 5 und 6 zeigen, sind sowohl die Datengrundlagen, auf deren Basis die Unsicherheiten strukturiert werden könnten, als auch die zur Reduktion der Unsicherheit notwendigen Prognoseinstrumente im Vergleich zur Privatwirtschaft nur schwach entwickelt. Für die öffentliche Hand besteht bislang weder ein ausreichender Anreiz- noch ein Sanktionsmechanismus.

2.2 Höhe des entstandenen Schadens als Risikodeterminante

Die Unsicherheit ist zwar notwendige Bedingung, begründet aber allein noch kein Risiko. Hierzu bedarf es zusätzlich im Falle des Eintritts einer Planungsabweichung eines daraus resultierenden Schadens. Grundsätzlich geht das ökonomische Risikokonzept davon aus, dass jede Planungsabweichung – egal ob nach oben oder unten – zu einer Verschlechterung der Wirtschaftlichkeit führt. Abweichungen nach unten, zum Beispiel in Form von Kostenüberschreitungen, werden naturgemäß stärker gewichtet. Aber auch Abweichungen zum positiven, zum Beispiel in Form von Kostenunterschreitungen, verursachen in ökonomischen Kalkülen Opportunitätskosten, da man beispielsweise die eingeplanten Ressourcen anderweitig sinnvoller hätte einsetzen können. Schäden können in diesem Zusammenhang nicht nur durch Projekte entstehen, sondern auch durch die Unterlassung von Projekten. So kann gerade durch die Unterlassung einer Instandhaltungsinvestition ein erheblicher Folgeschaden entstehen.

Wichtige Einflussgröße bei der Schadensentstehung ist die Flexibilität von Investitionsalternativen. Flexibilität ermöglicht Reaktionen durch Planänderung zur Abwehr von Schäden oder zumindest zur Verringerung der Schadenshöhe. Die Schaffung von Flexibilität ist nicht umsonst. Im Rahmen eines proaktiven Risikomanagements wird deshalb das Kosten-Nutzen-Verhältnis von flexibilitätsschaffenden Maßnahmen geprüft.

3 Kritische Analyse des Status quo im Risikomanagement der öffentlichen Verwaltung

Ergebnis des vorausgehenden Abschnitts ist der unmittelbare Zusammenhang zwischen unternehmerischen Konzepten und der Fähigkeit, Risiken zu handhaben. Anreize zum Aufbau eines effektiven Risikomanagements werden nur entwickelt, wenn entsprechende unternehmerische Strukturen vorhanden sind. Wendet man diesen Zusammenhang auf die öffentliche Hand an, so stellt sich zunächst die Frage, ob und gegebenenfalls in welchem Umfang die öffentliche Hand eine unternehmerische Verantwortung wahrnehmen kann.

3.1 Unzureichend wahrgenommene „unternehmerische" Verantwortung der öffentlichen Hand

Voraussetzung unternehmerischer Tätigkeit sind starke Verfügungsrechte an den Ressourcen. Liegen die Verfügungsrechte (Nutzungsrecht, Fruchtziehungsrecht, Veränderungsrecht, Veräußerungsrecht) alle bei einer (natürlichen oder juristischen) Person, so kann diese die Verfügungsrechte uneingeschränkt wahrnehmen.

Ein Unternehmer, der die Verfügungsrechte auf sich vereinigt, kann in seinem Unternehmen Wirtschaftlichkeit durchsetzen. Werden dagegen die Verfügungsrechte auf viele Personen verteilt, dann müssen die Rechte der einzelnen Personen aufeinander abgestimmt und gemeinsam wahrgenommen werden. Es sind dann regelmäßig aufwendige Abstimmungsprozesse erforderlich, um zu klaren und konsistenten Handlungsanweisungen zu gelangen. Die Demokratisierung im 20. Jahrhundert hat die Verfügungsrechte im Vergleich zum 19. Jahrhundert in sehr erheblichem Ausmaß verändert. Die Verfügungsrechte von Kaisern, Königen, Fürsten und anderen Potentaten waren vor jener Zeit grundsätzlich sehr stark und sie hatten ein ureigenes, großes Interesse an einer effizienten und effektiven Verwaltung. Unter den demokratischen Bedingungen sind diese Verfügungsrechte auf alle Bürger verteilt worden. Der einzelne Bürger hat dabei aber nur geringe Möglichkeiten, seine Verfügungsrechte angemessen wahrzunehmen. Stellvertretend verfügt in einer demokratisierten Gesellschaft die Verwaltung über starke Verfügungsrechte und kann mit ihnen im Rahmen gesetzlicher Möglichkeiten ihre Partikularinteressen durchsetzen. Ein effizientes und effektives Risikomanagementsystem hat sich in diesen Strukturen aufgrund fehlender beziehungsweise entgegengesetzter Anreize in der Verwaltung naturgemäß nicht entwickeln können.

Das in Abbildung 2 dargestellte Verfügungsrechte-Wettbewerb-Modell[2] geht davon aus, dass neben Verfügungsrechten auch der Wettbewerb eine

---

[2] Vgl. Picot, A. (1984) und Streitferdt, L. (1985).

Determinante der Wirtschaftlichkeit einer Organisation ist. Je stärker der Wettbewerb, desto größer ist die Notwendigkeit, das Fortbestehen der Organisation durch Wirtschaftlichkeit im Handeln zu sichern.

	Starke Verfügungsrechte	Schwache Verfügungsrechte
Starker Wettbewerb	Fall I Wirtschaftlichkeit durch starke Verfügungsrechte und starken Wettbewerb	Fall II Wirtschaftlichkeit durch starken Wettbewerb
Schwacher Wettbewerb	Fall III Wirtschaftlichkeit durch starke Verfügungsrechte	Fall IV Durch schwache Verfügungsrechte bei den Eigentümern und schwachen Wettbewerb gefährdete Wirtschaftlichkeit

Abb. 2: Verfügungsrechte und Wettbewerb als Determinanten der Wirtschaftlichkeit

Quelle: Streitferdt, L.(1985), S. 114.

Für die öffentliche Verwaltung ist generell der Fall IV typisch. Im besonderen Fall der Durchführung öffentlicher Investitionen ist traditionell kein Wettbewerb vorhanden und die Bürger haben nur beschränkte Einwirkungsmöglichkeiten auf den Investitionsprozess.

Die öffentliche Hand ist somit per se nicht wirtschaftlich, wie es etwa die BHO/LHO in ihren Ausformulierungen postuliert. Vielmehr sind der Wirtschaftlichkeit in demokratischen Strukturen mangels entsprechender Anreize enge Grenzen gesetzt. Im Vergleich mit privatwirtschaftlichen Unternehmen wirken sich diese Unterschiede in Bezug auf das Risikomanagement in einer ganzen Reihe, nachfolgend dargestellter wesentlicher Punkte aus.

3.2 Zu kurzer Planungshorizont des öffentlichen Haushalts

Große öffentliche Investitionsprojekte kennzeichnen sich in der Regel durch eine lange Laufzeit, die nicht selten 25 Jahre übersteigt. Eine umfassende Planung setzt voraus, die Investitions- samt ihrer Folgekosten im Rechnungswesen zu veranschlagen. Das kamerale öffentliche Rechnungswesen stellt hierzu das Instrument der Verpflichtungsermächtigungen bereit. Verpflichtungsermächtigungen ermöglichen die Berücksichtigung zukünftiger Belastungen des Haushalts beispielsweise durch zeitlich verteilt anfallende Investitions- oder Betriebsauszahlungen. Allerdings ist der längste Planungshorizont zur Berücksichtigung von zukünftigen finanziellen Verpflichtungen die mittelfristige Finanzplanung, deren Planungshorizont fünf Jahre beträgt. Diese Perspektive ist zu kurz, um die lang laufenden öffentlichen Investitionen in ihren finanziellen Wirkungen über ihren gesamten Lebenszyklus abzubilden. Investitionsfolgekosten bleiben deshalb im Haushalt der öffentlichen Hand weitgehend unberücksichtigt.

3.3 Keine explizite Verpflichtung zur Installation eines Risikomanagements

Zur Sicherung der finanziellen Stabilität der Wirtschaftssysteme sind in den letzten Jahren Unternehmen zur Einrichtung eines Risikomanagementsystems verpflichtet worden. Beispielsweise wurde in Deutschland das Gesetz zur Kontrolle und Nachverfolgung unternehmensbedrohender Risiken (KonTraG) und in den USA der Sarbanes Oaxley Act (SOA) eingeführt. Das privatwirtschaftliche Risikomanagement hat in der Folge enorme Entwicklungssprünge gemacht. Anders als Unternehmen unterliegt die öffentliche Verwaltung in Deutschland nicht dem KonTraG. Folglich sind auch die Fortschritte im Risikomanagement vergleichsweise gering ausgefallen. Während in den letzten zehn Jahren eine große Anzahl an Veröffentlichungen zum Risikomanagement im Unternehmenssektor zu verzeichnen war, fand die Auseinandersetzung mit dem

Thema Risikomanagement in der öffentlichen Verwaltung bislang weder in der Theorie noch in der Praxis in nennenswertem Umfang statt.

3.4 Selbstversicherungsprinzip

Grundsätzlich gilt in der Öffentlichen Hand das Selbstversicherungsprinzip. Es wird davon ausgegangen, dass sie die Risiken aufgrund ihrer Größe und Struktur besser selber tragen kann, als sich zu versichern oder per Risikotransfer auf einem anderen entgeltlichen Weg an Dritte zu übertragen. Die Risikotragung nach dem Selbstversicherungsprinzip ist prinzipiell dann die geeignete Strategie des Risikomanagements, wenn die Institution die Risiken selbst am besten diversifizieren und steuern kann. Wie die Beispiele Kraftfahrzeugversicherung und Altersvorsorge bei Beamten deutlich machen, steigt die Effizienz von Selbstversicherungssystemen mit zunehmender Fallzahl kontinuierlich an. Der öffentliche Sektor zerfällt durch die föderale Struktur und deren weitere kommunale Untergliederung in zahlreiche mehr oder weniger eigenständig agierende und entsprechend Risiko tragende Institutionen. Diese Gliederung erschwert die Prinzipien der Selbstversicherung. Als Problemlösung sind deshalb Pools wie der kommunale Schadensausgleich (KSA) ins Leben gerufen worden, welche nach dem Kostenerstattungsprinzip Versicherungsnehmer und Schadensfälle bündeln.

Das Selbstversicherungsprinzip gilt im Allgemeinen und grundsätzlich auch im Bereich öffentlicher Investitionen. Werden diese allerdings von den Kommunen getätigt, ist fraglich, ob diese nach Größe und Struktur noch die idealen Voraussetzungen der Strategie der Risikotragung aufweisen. Vertiefte Überlegungen zum Schadenausgleich durch Kumulation von Fallzahlen werden in Kapitel 8 noch folgen. Generell bleibt festzuhalten, dass das Selbstversicherungsprinzip der öffentlichen Hand dazu geführt hat, dass Erfahrungen im Umgang mit alternativen Risikomanagementstrategien (z.B. versichern, verkaufen, vermeiden) im öffentlichen Sektor weitgehend fehlen.

3.5 Realisationsprinzip im öffentlichen Rechnungswesen wichtiger als Vorsichtsprinzip

Mit ihrem Rechnungswesen verfolgen Institutionen die konkurrierenden Ziele des Gläubigerschutzes und der Bilanzwahrheit. Je nach institutionellem Hintergrund gewinnt einmal das eine und einmal das andere Ziel die Oberhand. Während in den für Unternehmen geltenden Bewertungsvorschriften des handelsrechtlichen Rechnungswesens der Bundesrepublik Deutschland (§§ 252-256 HGB) der Gläubigerschutz ein wichtiges Ziel ist, welches in das allgemeine Bewertungsprinzip der Vorsicht (§ 252 Abs. 1 Nr. 4 HGB) mündet, ist dieses Ziel im öffentlichen Rechnungswesen aufgrund der rechtlichen Stellung der Gebietskörperschaften nur von untergeordneter Bedeutung. Stattdessen kann das Ziel der Bilanzwahrheit, also einer realitätsnahen Abbildung der wirtschaftlichen Verhältnisse, im öffentlichen Rechnungswesen ohne die Einschränkungen des ausgeprägten Vorsichtsprinzips verfolgt werden. Von herausragender Bedeutung für das öffentliche Rechnungswesen ist nach Ansicht von BUSCHER/LÜDER (1994) deshalb dieses auch als Realisationsprinzip bezeichnete Prinzip, welches eine willkürfreie und intersubjektiv nachprüfbare Bewertung sicher stellt.[3]

Eingegangene Risiken sind per definitionem die Unsicherheit ökonomischer Werte und damit gerade nicht realisierte, sondern rein kalkulatorische Größen. Folglich werden die Risiken im öffentlichen Rechnungswesen nicht ausgewiesen. Dementgegen ist im privaten Rechnungswesen, welches dem Gläubigerschutz und dem Vorsichtsprinzip folgt, der Ausweis von Risiken verpflichtend. Geht man davon aus, dass ökonomische Entscheidungen nach dem im Rechnungswesen ausgewiesenen Erfolg getroffen werden, finden Risiken somit im Management öffentlicher Institutionen per se geringere Beachtung als in der Privatwirtschaft.

---

3 Vgl. Buschor, E./Lüder, K. (1994), S. 168.

3.6 Risikoerfassung im zahlungsorientierten kameralen Rechnungswesen

Das kamerale Rechnungswesen der öffentlichen Hand ist, dem Realisationsprinzip folgend, strikt zahlungsorientiert. Die Möglichkeiten der Zuordnung von Risiken mittels Eventualverbindlichkeiten (Rückstellungen) zu der Periode, in der sie eingegangen worden sind, sind nicht gegeben. Stattdessen werden die Schadenbeseitigungskosten zu den jeweiligen Fälligkeiten bilanziert. Beschafft die öffentliche Hand beispielsweise eine Immobilie, deren Betriebskosten sehr unsicher sind, wird das Kostensteigerungsrisiko weder zum Anschaffungszeitpunkt noch im Zeitraum des Betriebs veranschlagt. Das Risiko zeigt sich im Rechnungswesen erst in späteren Perioden, wenn die Mehrkosten anfallen. Anders als in privaten Unternehmen besteht bei der öffentlichen Hand nicht die Notwendigkeit der Unterlegung eingegangener Risiken mit Risikokapital.

Ein entscheidungsorientiertes internes Rechnungswesen im Sinne einer Kosten- und Leistungsrechnung hat in der öffentlichen Hand keine Tradition. Zwar sind nach § 7 Absatz 3 der Haushaltsordnung des Bundes und der meisten Länder für geeignete Bereiche Kosten- und Leistungsrechnungen einzuführen, eine flächendeckende Bewertung von kalkulatorischen Wagnissen, wie Risiken in der Sprache des Rechnungswesens genannt werden, ist aber noch nicht erfolgt. So werden in vielen Bereichen kalkulatorische Mieten für eigen genutzte Immobilien und kalkulatorische Zinsen für das zur Verfügung gestellte Kapital in Ansatz gebracht, die Berücksichtigung kalkulatorischer Wagnisse wird bislang aber vernachlässigt.

3.7 Wesen des Risikomanagements im öffentlichen Sektor

Zusammenfassend bleibt festzuhalten, dass das Risikomanagement der öffentlichen Hand aufgrund der institutionellen Rahmenbedingungen sehr stark reaktiv im Sinne einer Schadensabwehr ausgestaltet ist. Verantwortlich dafür sind die kurzfristige Orientierung des öffentlichen Rechnungswesens und dessen Realisationsprinzip. Erschwerend hinzu kommen die auf Legislaturperioden ausgerichteten in der Regel kurz- bis mittelfristigen Erfolgszwänge von Politik und Verwaltung, denen gegenüber eine adäquate Risikovorsorge zumeist kontraproduktiv wirkt.

Ein proaktives Risikomanagement beispielsweise im Sinne von Vermeidungs- und Bewältigungsstrategien ist mit Aufwand verbunden, dem aus der Akteursperspektive kein angemessener Nutzen gegenüber steht. Den Entscheidungsträgern in den Verwaltungen fehlen die Entscheidungsgrundlagen aus dem Rechnungswesen sowie die entsprechenden Anreize, das Risikomanagement der öffentlichen Verwaltung zu intensivieren.

Lösungskonzepte zur Verbesserung des Risikomanagements der öffentlichen Hand sind angesichts der tiefgreifenden institutionellen Rahmenbedingungen, die für den derzeitigen geringen Entwicklungsstand ursächlich sind, nicht besonders vielfältig. Eine Übertragung betriebswirtschaftlicher Instrumente aus dem privaten Sektor scheitert in der Regel schnell aufgrund der schlechten Informationsgrundlagen und grundlegend fehlender Anreize der Akteure. Als möglicher Ausweg bleibt die Verlagerung der Aufgabenerfüllung aus staatlichen Strukturen heraus in den privaten Sektor beispielsweise mittels privatwirtschaftlicher Leistungserbringung unter staatlicher Regulierung (Contracting out), die Umstellung öffentlicher Dienstleister auf privatwirtschaftliche Unternehmensverfassungen (Privatisierung) oder mittels Public Private Partnership.

4 Risikomanagement mittels unterschiedlicher Beschaffungsvarianten

Das Ziel dieses Abschnittes ist die Gegenüberstellung der Wirkungsweisen unterschiedlicher Beschaffungsvarianten im Risikomanagement anhand eines stark vereinfachten Beispiels.[4] Dazu werden die idealtypischen Anreizsysteme

[4] Vgl. zu diesem Beispiel auch Pfnür, A./Schetter, C./Schöbener, H. (2008).

und Risikomanagementmechanismen der konventionellen Beschaffung (Eigenleistung der öffentlichen Hand), des Outsourcings (Fremdvergabe per Vertrag) und der Public Private Partnership miteinander verglichen.

4.1 Konventionelle Beschaffungsvariante

In der konventionellen Beschaffungsvariante generiert die öffentliche Hand die notwendigen Planungs-, Bau- und Betreiberleistungen weitestgehend selbst. Dabei wird sicherlich die eine oder andere Aufgabe im Rahmen der einzelgewerkweisen Vergabe von Dritten erbracht.

Ausgangspunkt ist die Errichtung und der Betrieb einer öffentlichen Investition, hier einer Schule mit geplanten Investitionskosten von 25 Mio. Euro. Die weiteren finanzwirtschaftlichen Eckdaten sind in Tabelle 1 dargestellt.

Kostenposition	Geplanter Wert	Realisierter Wert
Investitionskosten	25 Mio.	30 Mio.
Bewirtschaftungskosten p.a.	5 Mio.	5 Mio.; im 7., 9. und 11. Jahr ungeplante Instandsetzungen von je 5 Mio.
Investitionsphase	1 Jahr	1 Jahr
Betriebsphase	12 Jahre	12 Jahre

Tab. 1: Daten für ein Beispiel – Konventionelle Beschaffung
Quelle: Pfnür, A./Schetter, C./Schöbener, H. (2008), S. 30.

Auf die Planung von inflationsbedingten Bewirtschaftungskostensteigerungen wurde der Einfachheit halber verzichtet. Ebenso werden die Planung, Finanzierung, die Kapitalisierungseffekte und die im Rahmen der Verwertung entstehenden Restwerte der Investition hier vernachlässigt. Nachfolgend ist zu klären, wie sich einerseits Investition und Betrieb sowie andererseits die Risiken der Kostensteigerung bei alternativen Beschaffungsvarianten im öffentlichen Haushalt niederschlagen.

Bei der konventionellen Beschaffung werden die Risiken grundsätzlich von der öffentlichen Hand selbst getragen und im Haushalt zum Zeitpunkt ihres Auftretens als Mehrausgaben verbucht.

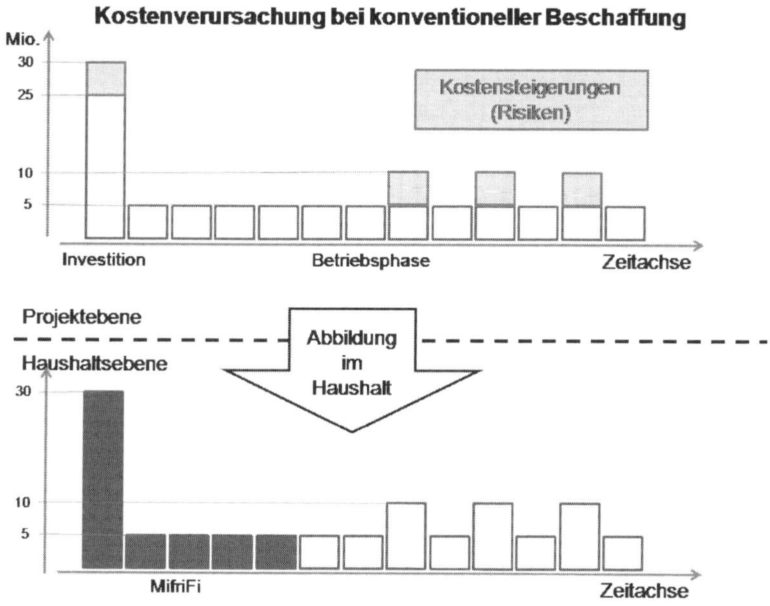

Abb. 3: Prinzip-Schaubild der Finanzströme bei konventioneller Beschaffung
Quelle: Pfnür, A./Schetter, C./Schöbener, H. (2008), S. 31.

Wie im vorausgegangenen Abschnitt bereits erläutert, führen die vermuteten Kostenrisiken in der Bau- und Betriebsphase zu Mehrausgaben in der jeweiligen Haushaltsperiode. Mit Ausnahme der erhöhten Investitionskosten sind die Risiken des Projekts im Haushalt nicht erkennbar, da sie jenseits des Planungshorizonts der mittelfristigen Finanzplanung liegen. Die mit der heute getroffenen

Investitionsentscheidung einhergehenden Risiken führen dem Selbstversicherungsprinzip der öffentlichen Hand folgend zu Haushaltsbelastungen in der Zukunft.

4.2 Fremdvergabe

Im Rahmen des Outsourcings verfolgt die öffentliche Hand die Strategie der Fremdvergabe der notwendigen Leistungen. Die nach Ausschreibung beauftragten Unternehmen werden in unserem idealtypischen Beispiel verpflichtet, ihre Leistungen zu einem Festpreis zu erbringen. Aufgrund günstigerer rechtlicher Rahmenbedingungen bei der Beschaffung von Vorleistungen und der Bereitstellung von Personal, spezifischer Fähigkeiten (Economies of scope) sowie Mengendegressionseffekten (Economies of scale) können die Privaten die Leistungen in der Regel günstiger anbieten als die öffentliche Hand dies selbst könnte. Nach Zuschlag eines Unternehmerlohns ergibt sich in der Regel ein niedrigerer Vergleichspreis. Da die Privaten im Festpreismodell allerdings die Kostenrisiken übernehmen, müssen sie eine entsprechende Risikovorsorge in ihrer Kalkulation treffen. Bedingt durch die kalkulatorischen Risikokosten fallen die Baukosten wie auch die Betriebskosten in diesem Beispiel leicht höher aus als in der Eigenleistungsvariante. Dies muss jedoch nicht immer so sein. Vielfach realisieren Private trotz kalkulatorischer Risikokosten noch Gesamtkostenvorteile.

Kostenposition	Geplanter Wert	Realisierter Wert
Selbstkosten Investition + Unternehmergewinn + Risikovorsorge = Gesamtpreis	22,50 Mio. 1,25 Mio. 2,50 Mio. 26,25 Mio.	30 Mio.
Selbstkosten Betrieb p.a. + Unternehmergewinn + Risikovorsorge = Gesamtpreis p.a.	4,50 Mio. 0,45 Mio. 0,10 Mio. 5,05 Mio.	4,5 Mio.; im 7., 9. und 11. Jahr zusätzlich ungeplante Instandsetzungen von je 4,5 Mio.

Tab. 2: Daten für ein Beispiel – Fremdvergabe
Quelle: Pfnür, A./Schetter, C./Schöbener, H. (2008), S. 32.

Die im Planungsstadium noch unerwartete Kostensteigerung kann der öffentlichen Hand vertragsgemäß nicht in Rechnung gestellt werden. Hier ist es Sache der Privaten, die Risiken mittels eines geeigneten Risikomanagements zu handhaben. Ohne eine entsprechende Abwälzung der Risiken werden sowohl das Bauunternehmen als auch der Betreiber im Projekt einen Verlust erleiden.

Im öffentlichen Haushalt werden, wie in Abbildung 4 dargestellt, die jeweiligen Gesamtpreise in Rechnung gestellt.

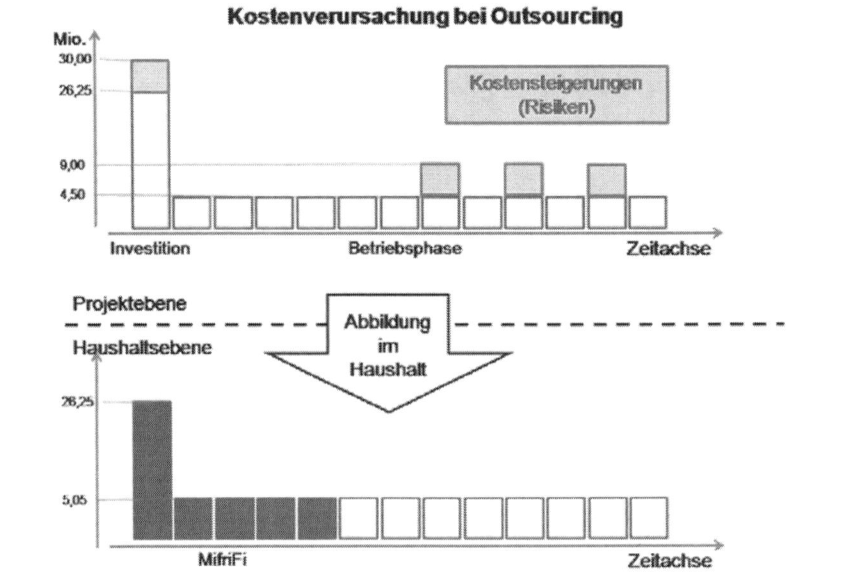

Abb. 4: Prinzip-Schaubild der Risikobehandlung beim Outsourcing
Quelle: Pfnür, A./Schetter, C./Schöbener, H. (2008), S. 33.

Im Vergleich zur konventionellen Beschaffungsvariante fallen die erwarteten Haushaltsbelastungen durch Investition und Betrieb leicht höher aus. Dafür halten die privaten Partner die öffentliche Hand von den unerwartet eingetretenen Kostensteigerungen (Risiken) frei. Aus der Perspektive der mittelfristigen Finanzplanung zum Entscheidungszeitpunkt erscheint die Fremdvergabe auf den ersten Blick teurer als die Selbsterstellungsvariante. Allerdings werden hier Äpfel mit Birnen verglichen, da die Fremdvergabe zusätzlich noch die Absicherung der Risiken im Rahmen der Übernahme beinhaltet. Im Beispiel wird schnell deutlich, dass sich die Absicherung der Kostensteigerungen durch Festpreisregelungen als effizient erweist. Die tatsächlich realisierten Baukosten betragen bei Fremdvergabe 3,75 Mio. Euro weniger als im Falle der Eigenerstellung. Die Betriebskosten fallen in der Summe mit 60,6 Mio. Euro (5,05*12) um 14,4 Mio. Euro günstiger aus als bei der Eigenerstellung in Höhe von 75 Mio. Euro (12*5 + 3*5).

Aus der Perspektive der Privaten ist es eine Frage des Risikomanagements, ob sie den entstandenen Verlust selbst übernehmen müssen. Oft ist durch eine entsprechende Versicherung oder im Zuge einer Unterbeauftragung von Subunternehmern das Risiko an Dritte weitergereicht. Zur Finanzierung dieser oder anderer Maßnahmen des Risikomanagements steht die kalkulierte Risikovorsorge bereit.

4.3 Public Private Partnership

In der PPP-Variante wird die Gesamtleistung von privaten Partnern erbracht. Die öffentliche Hand vergütet die Nutzung der Investition sowie die weiteren Leistungen im Betrieb durch ein vereinbartes Nutzungsentgelt oder gewährt das Recht, ein Entgelt von den Nutzern zu erheben. Auf die in der Praxis üblichen Preisanpassungsklauseln wird in dem Beispiel der Übersichtlichkeit halber verzichtet.

Die Privaten werden in der Regel höhere Investitionskosten haben als die öffentliche Hand im Falle der Eigenrealisierung oder im Falle der Fremdvergabe. Begründet werden die höheren Investitionskosten durch spätere Kostenvorteile im Betrieb, die die Investitionskosten überkompensieren. Im Beispiel sind die im PPP eingesetzten kostengünstig zu reinigenden Bodenbeläge in der Anschaffung teurer als die in den übrigen Varianten verwendeten Ausführungen. Entsprechend sind die Betriebskosten im PPP mit 4 Mio. dagegen die niedrigsten von allen Beschaffungsvarianten.

Die Möglichkeit zur lebenszyklusintegrierten Investitionsoptimierung der PPP schafft nicht nur im Betrieb sondern ebenso im Risikomanagement erheblich erweiterte Handlungsspielräume. Beispielsweise fallen aufgrund einer solideren Bauweise die ungeplanten Instandsetzungen nur in den Jahren 7 sowie

9 an und der entstehende Aufwand ist entsprechend geringer. Zudem ist in der PPP-Variante eine sorgfältige Verteilung der Risiken zwischen beiden Akteuren erfolgt. Das Risikomanagement im PPP-Prozess bezieht dabei die Möglichkeiten der Risikohandhabung beider Parteien unter Federführung der Privaten mit ein. Risiken können durch das Zusammenwirken potenziell früher erkannt und besser bewältigt werden. Entsprechend fällt auch die Risikovorsorge in der PPP-Variante mit 2,0 Mio. Euro deutlich geringer aus als in der Fremdvergabe-Variante, wie nachfolgende Tab. zeigt.

Kostenposition	Geplanter Wert	Realisierter Wert
Selbstkosten Investition	26,25 Mio.	31,25 Mio.
Selbstkosten Betrieb p.a.	4,0 Mio.	4,0 Mio.; im 7. und 9. Jahr zusätzlich ungeplante Instandsetzungen von je 4,0 Mio.
Selbstkosten Betrieb ges.	48,00 Mio.	56,00 Mio.
		87,25 Mio.
+ Unternehmergewinn	7,50 Mio.	
+ Risikovorsorge	2,00 Mio.	
= Gesamtpreis	83,75 Mio.	
Jährliches Nutzungsentgelt	6,98 Mio.	

Tab. 3: Daten für ein Beispiel – PPP
Quelle: Pfnür, A./Schetter, C./Schöbener, H. (2008), S. 35.

Insgesamt schaffen die Möglichkeiten einer lebenszyklusintegrierten Optimierung der Leistungserstellung sowie die erweiterten Handlungsspielräume im Risikomanagement Kostenvorteile zugunsten der PPP-Variante, die sich auch im Haushalt niederschlagen, wie Abbildung 5 zeigt.

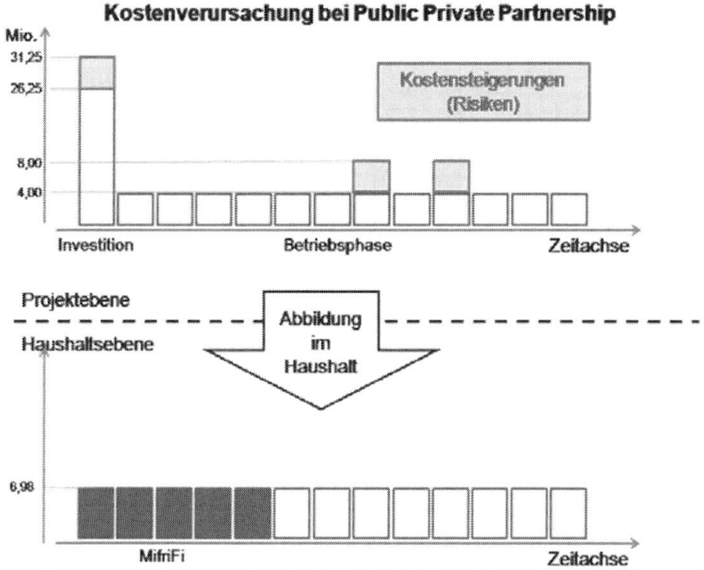

Abb. 5: Prinzip-Schaubild der Risikobehandlung bei Public Private Partnerships

Quelle: Pfnür, A./Schetter, C./Schöbener, H. (2008), S. 36.

4.4 Kritische Würdigung der Ergebnisse

Vergleicht man die Gesamtkosten der Beschaffungsvarianten, zeigt sich das in Tab. 4 dargestellte Bild.

Beschaffungsvariante	Summe Plan	Summe Ist (Haushaltsbelastung)
Konventionelle Beschaffung	85,00 Mio.	105,00 Mio.
Fremdvergabe	86,85 Mio.	86,85 Mio.
PPP	83,76 Mio.	83,76 Mio.

Tab. 4: Haushaltsbelastung unterschiedlicher Beschaffungsvarianten im Vergleich

Quelle: Pfnür, A./Schetter, C./Schöbener, H. (2008), S. 36.

Insgesamt ist in unserem Beispiel die PPP-Beschaffungsvariante die aus Sicht der Kommune günstigste Beschaffungsvariante. Auffällig ist zugleich ein für dieses Gutachten wie auch die betriebliche Praxis der öffentlichen Investitionsentscheidungen sehr wesentlicher Sachverhalt: Das tatsächlich realisierte Ausmaß des Wirtschaftlichkeitsvorteils der Fremdvergabe und insbesondere auch der PPP-Variante wird in der Planungsperspektive gar nicht in vollem Umfang deutlich. Das Beispiel zeigt, dass unter Vernachlässigung der PPP-Variante auf Basis von Planwerten die Investitionsentscheidung gegenüber der Fremdvergabe sogar zugunsten der konventionellen Beschaffung gefallen wäre. Ein Vergleich der Auswirkungen beider Beschaffungsvarianten auf die mittelfristige Finanzplanung zum Zeitpunkt der Investitionsentscheidung verstärkt dieses Bild noch. Einer Haushaltsbelastung von 45,0 Mio. Euro in der konventionellen Beschaffung stehen 46,45 Mio. Euro in der Fremdvergabe gegenüber. Der relative Kostennachteil der Fremdvergabe gegenüber der konventionellen Variante steigt von 2 % auf 3 % an. Ursache dieser Divergenz in Planungs- und Istwerten ist die Berücksichtigung von Risikovorsorge in den Planungswerten der Fremdvergabe-

Variante, wohingegen im Rahmen der konventionellen Beschaffung keine Risikovorsorge in Ansatz gebracht wurde.

Bei der PPP-Variante ist dieser Effekt in derart isolierter Form nicht mehr sichtbar, da hier die Investitionskosten als Bestandteil des Nutzungsentgelts über die Perioden verteilt werden. Gleichwohl zeigt ein Vergleich der Beschaffungsvarianten anhand der Ist-Situation der Haushaltsbelastung, dass hier ein noch stärkerer Hebel durch ein effizientes Risikomanagement entsteht als in der Fremdvergabe-Variante. Das Beispiel zeigt, dass bei einer Vernachlässigung der Risikovorsorge im finanziellen Planungsprozess der öffentlichen Hand Fehlentscheidungen bei Investitionen drohen. Eine Verlagerung riskanter Investitionen in den privatwirtschaftlichen Sektor macht die wahren Risikokosten transparent. Alternative Beschaffungsvarianten, insbesondere in Form einer PPP, schaffen vielfältige Optimierungspotenziale im Risikomanagement. Vom entstandenen Effizienzgewinn wird die öffentliche Hand immer dann in besonderem Maße profitieren, wenn die Privaten im starken Wettbewerb um die Projekte stehen.

5 Resümee

Risiken haben ihre Ursache in der Unsicherheit betriebswirtschaftlicher Werte. Dabei sind Risiken nicht per se als negativ zu bewerten, sondern sie sind unmittelbar immer auch mit Chancen verbunden, die unternehmerische Optionen eröffnen. Derjenige, der Risiken besser beherrscht, kann daraus einen Wettbewerbsvorteil generieren. Studien machen deutlich, dass die Unsicherheit über die Entwicklung der Zahlungsströme und damit auch das Risiko bei Infrastrukturinvestitionen erheblich sind. Die Ursache der Risiken liegt neben der Planungsunsicherheit auch im erheblichen Verlust bei Eintritt des Schadenfalls, der sich durch den langen Investitionszeitraum und den hohen Investitionsbetrag ergeben kann. Der Eintritt des in den Planungen erwarteten Falls stellt eher die Ausnahme, denn die Regel dar. Die Wirtschaftlichkeit von Infrastrukturprojekten hängt deshalb in mindestens eben so hohem Maße von einem effektiven Umgang mit den Risiken wie von niedrigen Projektkosten im wahrscheinlichsten Fall ab.

Die Analyse des Entwicklungsstands des Risikomanagements bei öffentlichen Infrastrukturinvestitionen verdeutlicht, dass dieses nur gering ausgeprägt ist. Anders als bei privaten Unternehmen hat es hier in den letzten Jahren kaum Entwicklungsfortschritte gegeben. Zurückzuführen ist dies darauf, dass es keine rechtlichen Verpflichtungen zur Einführung von Risikomanagementsystemen gibt. Der öffentliche Sektor orientiert sich vornehmlich am Selbstversicherungsprinzip als vorherrschendes Paradigma. Dabei wird schnell übersehen, dass Andere die Risiken möglicherweise besser beherrschen und aus der Übertragung der Risiken Effizienzgewinne entstehen können. Operativ behindert das öffentliche Rechnungswesen ein effizientes Risikomanagement. Das hier dominierende Realisationsprinzip führt zur Vernachlässigung kalkulatorischer Wagnisse. Schließlich ist der Planungshorizont im öffentlichen Sektor sowohl von den politischen als auch administrativen Strukturen maximal mittelfristig ausgelegt. Eine systematische langfristige Planung erfolgt de facto nur selten und ist im Umfang sehr begrenzt.

Der entscheidende Grund für den geringen Entwicklungsstand des Risikomanagements bei öffentlichen Infrastrukturinvestitionen aber ist die unzureichend wahrgenommene unternehmerische Verantwortung der öffentlichen Hand für das ihr zur Verfügung stehende Kapital. Im öffentlichen Sektor fehlt hier im Vergleich zur Privatwirtschaft die hohe Wettbewerbsintensität und darüber hinaus die Identität von Eigentum und Verfügungsrecht.

Summa summarum ist angesichts dieser Hindernisse nicht zu erwarten, dass auf mittlere Sicht große Fortschritte im Risikomanagement von öffentlichen Infrastrukturinvestitionen zu erzielen sind. Der oben dargestellte Fall zeigt exemplarisch, dass durch eine Fremdvergabe der Leistungen ein deutlich effektiveres Risikomanagement erfolgen kann. Durch die Nutzung der besseren Rahmenbedingungen des privatwirtschaftlichen Sektors sowie zusätzlicher Ressourcen und Fähigkeiten können die negativen Folgen von Planungsunsicherheiten für den öffentlichen Sektor abgefangen werden. Die Realisierung der Vorteile setzt naturgemäß eine gut geplante und durchgeführte Vergabe der Leistungen voraus. In Deutschland gibt es hier nicht nur positive Beispiele.

Zukünftig geht es darum, das grundsätzliche Potenzial des Risikomanagements in der effektiven Einbindung privater Partner besser zu nutzen. Public Private Partnerships weisen bei öffentlichen Infrastrukturinvestitionen konzeptionell regelmäßig Vorteile gegenüber der reinen Fremdvergabe auf. Erfolgsentscheidend für die Nutzung von Effizienzvorteilen durch die Allokation der Risiken zwischen den Vertragsparteien ist ein tiefgreifendes Verständnis für die komparativen Vorteile im Management der Risiken. Ein erster, in der Praxis weitgehend positiv aufgenommener Vorschlag zur Risikoallokation wurde vom Arbeitskreis Immobilienmanagement im Bundesverband PPP e.V. erarbeitet.[5] In der effizienten Allokation und vor allem auch in der nachhaltigen Durchsetzung der im Planungsprozess vorgesehenen Risikoallokation über den gesamten Projektlebenszyklus liegt ein erhebliches Potenzial verborgen, welches einer intensivierten Beschäftigung mit dem Thema bedarf.

Literaturverzeichnis

Alfen, H./Fischer, K. (2006): Der PPP-Beschaffungsprozess. In: Weber, M./Schäfer, M./Hausmann, F. (Hrsg.): Praxishandbuch Public Private Partnership. München, S. 1-84.

Arbeitskreis PPP im Management öffentlicher Immobilien im BPPP e.V. (2006): Risiken immobilienwirtschaftlicher PPPs aus Sicht der beteiligten Akteure. In: Pfnür, A. (Hrsg.): Arbeitspapiere zur immobilienwirtschaftlichen Forschung und Praxis, Band Nr. 4. Darmstadt.

5 Vgl. Arbeitskreis PPP im Management öffentlicher Immobilien im BPPP e.V. (2006).

BMVBW (2003): Gutachten – PPP im Öffentlichen Hochbau, Band I: Leitfaden. Berlin.

Budäus, D. (2004): Public Private Partnership - Ansätze, Funktionen, Gestaltungsbedarfe. In: Gesellschaft für öffentliche Wirtschaft (Hrsg.): Public Private Partnership: Formen – Risiken – Chancen. Berlin, S. 9-22.

Buschor, E./Lüder, K. (1994): Thesen zur künftigen Gestaltung des öffentlichen Rechnungswesens. In: Lüder, K. (Hrsg.): Öffentliches Rechnungswesen 2000. Berlin, S. 161-188.

Picot, A. (1984): Verfügungsrechte und Wettbewerb als Determinanten der Entwicklung des Verwaltungsbereichs von Organisationen. In: Boettcher, E./ Herder-Dorneich, P./Schenk, K.-E. (Hrsg.): Jahrbuch für Neue Politische Ökonomie. 3. Band, Tübingen, S. 198-222.

Pfnür, A./Armonat, S. (2001): Immobilienkapitalanlage institutioneller Investoren – Risikomanagement und Portfolioplanung. Arbeitspapier Nr. 26 des Arbeitsbereichs Öffentliche Wirtschaft am Fachbereich Wirtschaftswissenschaften der Universität Hamburg.

Pfnür, A./Schetter, C./Schöbener, H. (2008): Risikomanagement öffentlicher Infrastrukturinvestitionen in Public Private Partnerships. Wissenschaftliches Gutachten im Auftrag der Initiative Finanzstandort Deutschland (IFD). Darmstadt.

Streitferdt, L. (1985): Pathologische Muster (Schwachstellenprofile) von Organisationen (Verwaltungsorganisationen). In: Lüder, K. (Hrsg.): Betriebswirtschaftliche Organisationstheorie und öffentliche Verwaltung. Speyerer Forschungsberichte Nr. 46, Hochschule für Verwaltungswissenschaften Speyer, S. 101-129.

Ordering in Public Private Partnerships: Zur Evolution von Governance-Designs für internationale Transaktionen

Jörg Freiling & Gralf-Peter Calliess

Inhaltsverzeichnis

1 Einleitung und Problemstellung

Der Gedanke der Public Private Partnerships (PPP) ist bislang vor allem im Kontext der Neuordnung der Aufgaben staatlicher Institutionen in Richtung auf die Privatisierung vormals öffentlich erstellter Leistungen diskutiert worden.[1] In diesem Zusammenhang stellt sich nicht nur die Frage, welche Aufgabenfelder staatlicher Tätigkeit seitens privatwirtschaftlicher Träger im Rahmen wirtschaftlicher Überlegungen sinnvoll übernommen werden können, sondern auch und vor allem nach den Möglichkeiten und Grenzen eines Zusammenwirkens staatlicher und privater Akteure. Derartige Gedanken sind selten unabhängig vom Staatsverständnis und den damit verbundenen Vorstellungen von den Aufgaben, die der Staat zu erbringen hat. So stellen etwa GRIMSEY und LEWIS (2004) fest, dass große Teile des staatlichen Sektors als politisches Artefakt zu sehen sind, weniger hingegen als ökonomische Notwendigkeit oder öffentlicher Wille.

Die PPP-Diskussion wird maßgeblich von ökonomischen Rationalitätskalkülen getragen, wobei zum Teil komparativ-statische Optimierungsüberlegungen angestellt werden, zum Teil aber auch evolutorische Betrachtungen, welche die Historizität staatlicher und privater Akteure einschließlich damit verbundener begrenzter Entwicklungskorridore in die Betrachtung aufnehmen. Während im ersten Fall transaktionskostentheoretische Überlegungen und die damit eng verbundene Theorie unvollständiger Verträge eine bedeutende Stellung einnehmen[2], ist im zweiten Fall zum Beispiel der Kernkompetenzenansatz[3] zu beachten.

[1] Zu einem Überblick über die Diskussion: Shleifer, A. (1998); Savas, E. S. (2000); Roentgen, F. (2001).

[2] Vgl. z.B. Schmidt, K. (1996).

[3] Vgl. z.B. Prahalad, C. K./Hamel, G. (1990), allgemeiner: Freiling, J./Gersch, M./Goeke, C. (2008).

Die augenblickliche Diskussion setzt primär folgende Akzente:

- Es werden bewusste, planungsbasierte, zumeist ökonomisch fundierte Entscheidungen in Richtung auf Privatisierung bzw. privatwirtschaftlich-staatliche Kooperation betrachtet. Die zum Teil emergenten Prozesse des Zusammenwirkens sind hingegen unterbelichtet.
- Die Betrachtungsebene ist – je nach Analyseziel – zum Teil einzelwirtschaftlich (bzw. mikroskopisch), zum Teil gesamtwirtschaftlich (bzw. makroskopisch). Es fehlt hingegen an Darstellungen, die das ebenen-übergreifende Zusammenspiel betrachten. So führen einzelwirtschaftliche Entscheidungen zu gesamtwirtschaftlichen Konsequenzen, die wiederum nachfolgendes einzelwirtschaftliches Handeln bedingen (usw.).
- Die Diskussion um PPP konzentriert sich auf die Wirtschaft und dort speziell auf ausgewählte Sektoren, die traditionell durch staatliche Eingriffe in den Marktprozess gekennzeichnet sind (z.B. Gesundheit, Bildung, Versorgung, Verkehr, Umweltschutz). Ein Miteinander staatlicher und privater Akteure ist jedoch bei weitem nicht auf die Wirtschaft selbst beschränkt. So stellt z.B. die Evolution des Rechts im internationalen Raum, die sowohl auf gezielter, aber auch auf ungeplanter Entwicklung beruht, ein Anwendungsfeld für PPP-Überlegungen dar, welches als noch unerschlossen zu gelten vermag.

Der vorliegende Beitrag setzt sich zum Ziel, die PPP-Diskussion durch Erweiterung fortzuführen und die drei o.g. Punkte, die in der bisherigen Diskussion wenig oder keine Beachtung gefunden haben, zu berücksichtigen. Dabei verfügt der Beitrag insofern über einen interdisziplinären Akzent, als er die ökonomisch relevante Frage der rechtlichen Absicherung von wirtschaftlichen Transaktionen in internationalen Handlungskontexten beleuchtet. Hier stellt sich das konkrete Problem der Entwicklung und Anpassung von Recht und Rechtsäquivalenten an die im internationalen Bereich geltenden Kontextbedingungen.

Dieses Problem erweist sich aus folgenden Gründen als nicht trivial:

- Staatliche Rechtsordnungen existieren, verfügen jedoch über einen Geltungsbereich, der an ein nationalstaatliches Hoheitsgebiet gebunden ist. Eine wie auch immer geartete Ausweitung des Geltungsbereichs ist ohne weiteres nicht möglich.
- Erschwerend kommt hinzu, dass ein funktionsfähiges nationenübergreifendes Handelsrecht trotz der immer stärkeren Formierung von überstaatlichen Wirtschaftsgruppen (z.B. EU) nicht existiert und wohl auch in absehbarer Zeit nicht zur Verfügung stehen wird.[4]
- Im Rahmen internationaler Transaktionen ergibt sich somit regelmäßig die Frage, welche Gerichte zuständig sind, welches Recht diese anwenden und ob resultierende Urteile auch im Ausland vollstreckbar sind. Eine besondere Rechtsunsicherheit ergibt sich dadurch, dass selbst bei Vereinbarungen der Geschäftspartner bezüglich der Relevanz eines bestimmten nationalen Rechtssystems für eine Transaktion nicht sichergestellt werden kann, dass diese Vereinbarungen auch eingehalten und somit durchgesetzt werden können. Insofern unterliegt die Verwendung staatlichen Rechts (Public Ordering) bei internationalen Transaktionen erheblichen Einschränkungen.
- Das vorliegende Problem könnte grundsätzlich dadurch gelöst werden, dass durch bilaterale Vereinbarungen wirkungsvolle Absicherungen geschaffen werden (Private Ordering)[5]. Dann tritt privatwirtschaftliche Koordination (zumindest partiell) an die Stelle staatlichen Rechts, wobei offen bleibt, wie etwaige Konflikte im Anschluss an getroffene Vereinbarungen gelöst werden können. Ob hierbei vollständig auf die staatliche Rechtsinfrastruktur verzichtet werden kann, ist zumindest zu bezweifeln.

[4] Vgl. Calliess, G.P. et al. (2008).
[5] Vgl. Williamson, O.E. (2005).

Empirische Studien zur Governance internationaler Transaktionen belegen, dass staatliches Handelsrecht im grenzüberschreitenden Geschäftsverkehr aufgrund der beschriebenen Schwächen eine im Vergleich zu nationalen Transaktionen geringere Bedeutung hat, während privatwirtschaftliche Koordination stärker in die Governance internationaler Transaktionen einbezogen wird.[6] Der Begriff der Governance wird dabei verstanden als ein *institutionenbasiertes Maßnahmenpaket zur Steuerung, Überwachung und Sanktionierung menschlichen Verhaltens im Kontext von Unsicherheit und Arbeitsteilung zum Zwecke des Ausschlusses unerwünschter und der Erhöhung der Wahrscheinlichkeit des Eintretens erwünschter Handlungen.* Vor diesem Hintergrund ergibt sich dann aber ein bislang wenig beachtetes Feld von Public Private Partnerships i.w.S.: nämlich das Miteinander von Public and Private Ordering im internationalen Handel.

Es ist Ziel dieses Beitrags, das Zusammenwirken einzelwirtschaftlicher Akteure und deren gesamtwirtschaftlich-gesellschaftlichen Niederschlag unter Berücksichtigung damit verbundener Evolutionsprozesse vor dem Hintergrund der Reduzierung rechtlicher Unsicherheit näher zu untersuchen. Dazu gliedert sich der Beitrag in folgende Bearbeitungsschritte:

Zunächst erfolgt eine themenspezifische Aufbereitung des PPP-Konzepts (Kapitel 2). Daran schließt sich die Auseinandersetzung um die „Governance-Lücke“ im internationalen Geschäft an, die zur weiteren Entfaltung des Themas grundlegend ist (Kapitel 3). Kapitel 4 behandelt sodann die Möglichkeiten, die das transnationale Recht zur Schließung der Lücke vorhält. Wie durch Kombination zur Verfügung stehender Mittel staatlichen und privaten Rechts Governance-Designs entstehen und sich entwickeln, ist Gegenstand von Kapitel 5. Im letzten Schritt erfolgt ein kurzer Aus- und Überblick (Kapitel 6).

---

6 Vgl. Calliess, G.P. et al. (2008).

2 Das PPP-Konzept im Zusammenhang internationaler Geschäftstätigkeit

Wie lässt sich die oben umrissene Thematik in den PPP-Kontext einpassen? Die Beantwortung der Frage erfordert eine Auseinandersetzung mit dem PPP-Verständnis in engerer und weiterer Interpretation. Grundsätzlich kann bei einer engeren Auslegung des Begriffs zwischen einer funktionalen und institutionellen Sichtweise unterschieden werden. Die funktionale Perspektive zielt auf das (zumeist organisierte) Zusammenwirken privater Akteure bzw. Institutionen und Hoheitsträger zum Zwecke der (vornehmlich durch Synergien) wirtschaftlicheren Erfüllung von Aufgaben des öffentlichen Bedarfs ab. Die zu erfüllende Aufgabe wird dabei von BUDÄUS (2004) als schlecht strukturiert beschrieben, was impliziert, dass dynamik- und komplexitätsbedingt die einzelnen Rechte, Pflichten, Kosten, Leistungen und Risiken der Partner nicht vollständig im Detail festgelegt werden (können). Im Rahmen des Zusammenwirkens erfolgt die Tätigkeit der involvierten Privatwirtschaft unter Zugrundelegung marktlicher Prinzipien. Tendenziell führt dies zu einem Rückzug des Staates aus vormals von ihm (zumeist) allein wahrgenommenen Aufgaben. Die institutionelle Sichtweise hebt demgegenüber auf den für längere Zeit geltenden Kooperationsrahmen von Akteuren des privaten und staatlichen Sektors ab, der mit Blick auf die beteiligten Akteure deren Identität unverändert lässt. Die Zusammenarbeit kann sowohl vertrags- als auch vertrauensbasiert sein.[7] Die Kennzeichnung lässt erkennen, dass im engeren Sinne des PPP-Gedankens vornehmlich geplante Kooperationen zwischen öffentlicher und privater Seite thematisiert werden.

Eine erweiterte Sicht umfasst hingegen auch Tätigkeiten faktischen Zusammenwirkens beider Bereiche, die ohne eine explizite Absichtserklärung zur Kooperation erfolgen und damit tendenziell auch einen weitaus geringeren Institutionalisierungsgrad aufweisen. Erfassbar werden auf diesem Wege unterschiedlichste Formen des öffentlich-privaten Miteinanders, wie z.B. auch die

---

7 Vgl. Budäus, D. (2004).

Kombination rechtssichernder Mechanismen privater und öffentlicher Steuerung, die im Mittelpunkt des vorliegenden Beitrags steht. Auch diese (deutlich gegenüber oben) erweiterte Perspektive, die nicht einmal auf bestimmte Akteure fokussieren muss, sondern auch auf Institutionen wie das staatliche Recht abstellt, schließt den Gedanken ein, dass von staatlicher und privater Seite spezifische, komplementäre Inputs in den Bereich des Zusammenwirkens bei tendenziellem Rückzug des Staates eingebracht werden. Auf diesen Aspekt wird im weiteren Verlauf mit Blick auf die Besonderheiten staatlicher und privater Governance noch ausführlicher einzugehen sein.

Eine derartige Betrachtung soll nicht einer Ausweitung und damit möglicherweise auch Aufweichung des PPP-Gedankens[8] das Wort reden. Vielmehr soll sie dazu führen, bislang unter anderen Gesichtspunkten geführte Debatten – so vor allem um den „kooperativen Staat“ (als geteilte Verantwortung für die Umsetzung von Gesetzen) sowie um die „Co-Regulation“ im Spannungsfeld zwischen Staat, Markt und Zivilgesellschaft – in den PPP-Kontext einzuordnen bzw. auf ihn zu beziehen. Eine solche Betrachtung mag nicht nur dem PPP-Kontext dienen, sondern auch und vor allem für die Auseinandersetzung um die Public versus Private Ordering in internationalen Transaktionen eine weitere Perspektive bieten: das Public Private (Partnership) Ordering, das in unterschiedlichen Konstellationen denkbar ist. Dabei steht die Frage im Vordergrund, welche Aufgaben und welche Rollen privaten Akteuren und staatlichen Institutionen zufallen, wobei zwischen Regelsetzung und Regelanwendung zu differenzieren ist. Schlussendlich resultiert aus der Übertragung von PPP-Gedankengut auf die vorliegende Problematik eine Sichtweise, die offenlegt, dass für die Governance internationaler Transaktionen nicht selten ein Kompositum privater und staatlicher Steuerungsmechanismen zur Anwendung gelangt. So nehmen etwa Schiedsgerichte Aufgaben wahr, die vorher dem Staat zugeordnet waren. Gleichzeitig wird aber auch der Staat aktiv und hat z.B. mit der New York Convention einen „Public Frame für Private Ordering“ gesetzt.

---

8 Vgl. hierzu u.a. Budäus, D. (2004).

Eine solche Perspektive hilft zu verdeutlichen, dass bei allen Verlagerungsprozessen von staatlicher zu privater Governance der Staat – in welcher Form und auf welcher Ebene auch immer – nicht gänzlich wegzudenken ist. Dann aber erscheint das PPP-Denken umso interessanter, um die vorliegende Thematik einordnen und um dessen Potenzial abschätzen zu können. Mit aktuellen Befunden aus der PPP-Forschung scheint diese Perspektive jedenfalls konform zu gehen. So stellt etwa BUDÄUS (2004) fest, „(...) dass die klassische, ordnungspolitisch geprägte Dichotomie von Staat und privatem Sektor kaum mehr zugunsten von Kooperationsstrategien eine Rolle zu spielen scheint. Und daraus wiederum resultiert dann weiterhin, dass praktisch kein öffentliches Handlungsfeld mehr existiert, in dem nicht mehr oder minder intensiv PPP-Ansätze diskutiert und für möglich gehalten werden“[9]. Die nachfolgenden Überlegungen werden untermauern, dass sich die Verquickungsvermutung staatlichen und privaten Agierens auch für die Entwicklung der Governance-Problematik internationaler Transaktionen beobachten lässt. Interessanterweise ergeben sich auch mit Blick auf die Treiber dieser Entwicklung auffällige Parallelen: Während in der gegenwärtigen PPP-Diskussion häufig die Ineffizienz öffentlicher Verwaltung genannt wird, ist – wie Abschnitt 3 zeigen wird – im Bereich der transnationalen Governance von einer fehlenden Anwendbarkeit und damit auch Wirksamkeit nationalstaatlichen Handelsrechts auszugehen.

3 Die Governance-Lücke im internationalen Geschäft

Wie ist das oben beschriebene Defizit staatlicher Steuerung im Bereich internationaler Transaktionen zu erklären und welche Konsequenzen ergeben sich daraus? Zunächst ist festzustellen, dass dem internationalen im Vergleich zum

---

[9] Budäus, D. (2004), S. 312 f.

nationalen Geschäft besondere Risiken zugeschrieben werden.[10] Diese Risiken lassen sich vor allem auf folgende Faktoren zurückführen:[11]

- politische Risiken aufgrund anderer, tendenziell unbekannter politischer Rahmenbedingungen im Zielland in Verbindung mit der Gefahr daraus resultierender konkreter Nachteile (z.B. Bevorzugung heimischer Betriebe im Zielland, politische Instabilität oder Eingriffe des Staates in den Marktprozess – so etwa bei Local-Content-Auflagen),
- ökonomische Risiken vor allem infolge von Marktzugangsbarrieren, etwaigen Wechselkursunsicherheiten, mangelnder Fähigkeit und Verlässlichkeit lokaler Partner sowie Zugang zu kritischen Ressourcen (Personal, Kapital, Vorprodukte),
- soziologisch-kulturelle Risiken durch die Unkenntnis kultureller Besonderheiten im Zielland und die etwaigen Probleme durch mangelnde Sprachkenntnisse,
- rechtliche Risiken durch die Anwendung des nationalstaatlichen Rechtssystems im Zielland, dessen Andersartigkeit sich bei weitem nicht allein auf die Geltung anderer Normensysteme (explizite und implizite Normen) bezieht, sondern auch die Unterschiede in der konkreten Rechtsprechung mit betrifft. In diesem Zusammenhang ist mit Blick auf die vorliegende Thematik bemerkenswert, dass es Länder gibt, in denen staatliches Recht aus unterschiedlichen Gründen (z.B. Korruption, Staatskrisen, Krieg) gar nicht erst zur Anwendung gelangt, was wiederum die Risikosituation in substantieller Weise zuspitzt.

Die Internationalisierungsforschung hat betont, dass allgemeine Aussagen über die Risiken des internationalen Geschäfts problematisch sind, weswegen es

[10] Vgl. z.B. Kulhavy, E. (1993); Backhaus, K./Büschken, J./Voeth, M. (2003).

[11] Vgl. z.B. Bassen, A./Behnam, M./Gilbert, D.U. (2001) mit Blick auf die Relevanz einzelner Risiken im Kontext der Internationalisierung mittelständischer Betriebe.

spezifischer Verfahren zur länderbezogenen Risikoanalyse bedarf.[12] Ungeachtet dessen lässt sich anhand dieser generellen Risikokonstellation des internationalen Geschäfts bereits ein erhöhter Absicherungsbedarf im Falle zunehmender internationaler Geschäftstätigkeit erkennen. Dies gilt nicht nur für Großbetriebe, sondern auch und insbesondere für den durch eine tendenziell geringere Mittelausstattung und einen geringeren Professionalisierungsgrad gekennzeichneten betrieblichen Mittelstand. Damit verbunden steigt somit auch der Bedarf an risikoreduzierenden Maßnahmen, was sich in der oben skizzierten Governance-Problematik niederschlägt, die schlussendlich alle genannten Risikobereiche tangiert.

Ein besonderes Problem ist dabei die Einschränkung von Rechtssicherheit in internationalen Transaktionen, da hier das Recht eines Staates territorial bedingt nicht mehr problemlos angewandt werden kann. Insofern wäre eine den nationalen Transaktionen vergleichbare Rechtssicherheit nur dann herzustellen, wenn ein über Nationengrenzen übergreifendes staatliches Handelsrecht vorläge, das mit einem vergleichbaren Regelungs- und Verbindlichkeitsgrad ausgestattet ist.

Ein solches staatlich basiertes Handelsrecht für den internationalen Raum wäre mit Blick auf Abbildung 1 in unterschiedlicher Weise denkbar. So könnte etwa ein (zumindest annähernd) global verbindliches Recht (z.B. auf Ebene der United Nations oder der OECD) bei internationalen Transaktionen an die Stelle des nationalstaatlichen Rechts treten. Ein derartiges Recht wäre mit CALLIESS (2006) als *internationales Recht* zu bezeichnen und ist als solches als Recht zwischen Staaten zu verstehen (völkerrechtlicher Charakter). Mit Blick auf die weltweit stark unterschiedlichen Staats-, Gesellschafts-, Rechts- und Wirtschaftssysteme erscheint die Vorstellung jedoch fast illusorisch, ein solches Recht könne der Governance-Problematik, die aktuell besteht, wirksam und vor allem schnell abhelfen. Auch auf längere Sicht ist eine derartige Evolution staat-

---

[12] Vgl. z.B. Meyer, M. (1987).

lichen Rechts jenseits des Nationalstaates aufgrund des erheblichen Koordinationsbedarfs kaum absehbar.[13]

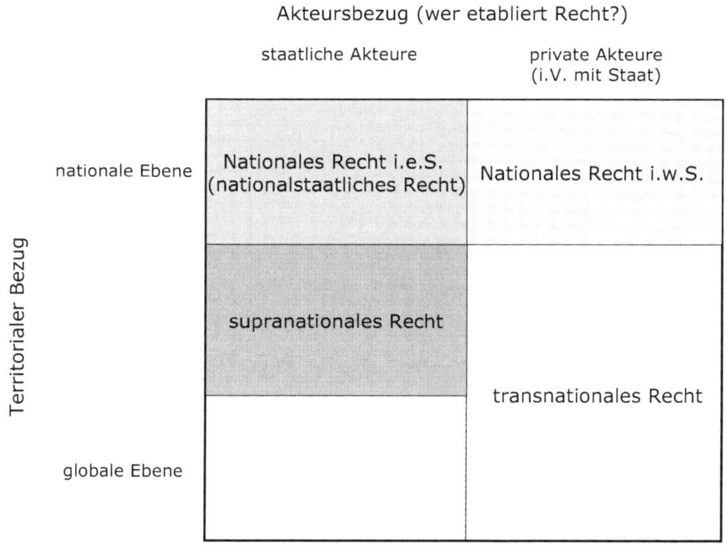

Abb. 1: Handelsrecht im Kontext von Internationalität und Privatisierung
Quelle: eigene Darstellung.

Auf anderer Ebene und mit weitaus kleinerem Anwendungsbereich wäre an ein Recht in institutionalisierten nationenübergreifenden Wirtschaftsräumen zu denken. Die Europäische Union ist ein Beispiel für einen derartigen Wirtschaftsraum, der durch eine Mehrzahl von Gemeinschaftsinstitutionen und durch den Vorrang von Gemeinschaftsrecht vor nationalen Rechtssystemen gekennzeichnet ist. Da hier im materiellen Sinne weder internationales Recht vorliegt noch vom typischen Fall innerstaatlichen Rechts auszugehen ist, bietet es sich an, im Einklang mit Abbildung 1 für derartige Konstellationen den Begriff des *supranationalen Rechts* zu verwenden. Supranationales Recht nimmt also eine

[13] Zu Details siehe Calliess, G. P. et al. (2008).

Zwischenposition im Übergangsbereich von nationalem und internationalem Recht ein und vereinigt Züge von beidem in sich.

Die Europäische Union ist bei der Entwicklung geeigneter Rechtsstrukturen zur Lösung der Governance-Problematik für grenzüberschreitende Transaktionen im Vergleich zu den internationalen Institutionen relativ erfolgreich. Zu nennen sind insbesondere die sog. „Brüssel-Verordnungen", welche die Zuständigkeit der Gerichte und die europaweite Anerkennung und Vollstreckung von Urteilen regeln. Mit den sog. „Rom-Verordnungen" ist jüngst auch die Frage des anwendbaren Rechts geklärt worden. Ein einheitliches europäisches Vertragsrecht wird zwar diskutiert, dem kürzlich von Wissenschaftlern vorgelegten Entwurf wird freilich kaum eine Chance eingeräumt. Problematisch bleibt bei den genannten Maßnahmen aber, dass das supranationale Recht der EU in seiner Wirksamkeit wiederum territorial begrenzt bleibt. Transaktionen, die den europäischen Binnenmarkt überschreiten, profitieren nicht von der so geschaffenen Rechtssicherheit.

Insofern ist im Einklang mit zahlreichen Beiträgen zu den Entwicklungen und Entwicklungsmöglichkeiten eines Handelsrechts auf nationenübergreifender Ebene zu konstatieren, dass sich Fortschritte in dieser Richtung bislang als äußerst bescheiden ausnehmen und darüber hinaus die Evolution eines solchen Rechts mit einer recht mäßigen Geschwindigkeit voranschreitet, die jedenfalls mit der Dynamik internationaler Transaktionen nicht im Ansatz Schritt halten kann.[14]

Setzt man demnach die fortschreitende Tendenz zur Internationalisierung wirtschaftlicher Transaktionen in Relation zur Verfügbarkeit staatlichen Rechts auf internationaler Ebene, so tritt in der Tat die Gefahr einer Regelungslücke hervor, was auch in einschlägigen Forschungsarbeiten so gesehen wird.[15] Dann aber ist es problematisch, anzunehmen, die zur Abwicklung ökonomischer

---

[14] Vgl. Calliess, G. P. (2007).

[15] Vgl. z.B. Bernstein, L. (1992); Dixit, A. K. (2004); Calliess, G. P. et al. (2008).

Transaktionen erforderliche rechtliche Infrastruktur (vor allem staatlicherseits) stehe vollumfänglich zur Verfügung, was eine in der Ökonomie mancherorts vorzufindende Auffassung ist.[16]

Tritt die angeführte „Governance-Lücke" aber faktisch wirklich auf und ist sie nachweisbar? Eine Antwort auf diese Frage ist nur möglich, wenn im Sinne dieses Beitrags und des erweiterten PPP-Gedankens der staatliche Rechtsrahmen im Verbund zu privatwirtschaftlichen Tätigkeiten vor dem Hintergrund betrachtet wird, transaktionsbedingte Unsicherheit zu reduzieren und somit einen stabilen, belastbaren Rahmen für den ökonomischen Vollzug internationaler Tauschakte zu schaffen. Hier setzt eine weitere Kategorie nationenübergreifenden Handelsrechts an, die in der Literatur als *transnationales Recht* beschrieben wird.[17] Dabei bezeichnet Transnationalität in allgemeinster Form Phänomene, die über den Nationalstaat hinausgehen. Transnationales Recht schließt somit Rechtsquellen und Rechtsäquivalente ein, die unabhängig vom nationalstaatlichen Recht (co-)existieren können – aber nicht zwangsläufig müssen. So ist auch in Abbildung 1 angedeutet, dass private Rechtsakteure Recht und Rechtsäquivalente zum Teil mit dem Staat bzw. seiner vorhandenen staatlichen Infrastruktur schaffen. Es erfolgt insoweit eine Art Anlagerung von neuen Rechtsstrukturen an bereits vorhandene. Im Ergebnis wird in diesem Fall Recht durch die Rechtsschöpfungskräfte einer globalen Zivilgesellschaft geschaffen und beruht auf allgemeinen Rechtsprinzipien sowie deren Niederschlag in wirtschaftlichen Transaktionen und deren Anpassung in Verfahren der Konfliktbeilegung. Es ist aufgrund seiner kollektiven Verbindlichkeit Teil des Rechts – zumindest in einem weiter gefassten Sinne.

Die Wirkweise transnationalen Rechts ist durch einen hybriden Governance-Modus gekennzeichnet, in welchem sich staatliche und private Ordnungsleistungen wechselseitig voraussetzen, aufeinander aufbauen oder auch konkurrieren, jedenfalls nicht mehr wie im Nationalstaat in einem Über-

[16] Vgl. Dixit, A. K. (2004).
[17] Vgl. Calliess, G. P. (2006).

Unterordnungsverhältnis zueinander stehen.[18] In diesem Zusammenhang sprechen GENSCHEL und LEIBFRIED (2008) treffend von der „Ko-Produktion" von Staatlichkeit durch private und staatliche Akteure. Aus evolutorischer Perspektive ist das Element der Ko-Produktion freilich in zeitlich-prozesshafter Sicht um den Gedanken des Co-Development von privaten und staatlichen Steuerungselementen in internationalen Transaktionen zu erweitern. Das wiederum belegt die unmittelbare Relevanz transnationalen Rechts für die PPP-Problematik. Die Evolution transnationalen Rechts wird auf diese Weise zum Schlüssel zur Beantwortung der Frage nach der Schaffung von Rechtssicherheit in internationalen Transaktionen und somit zur Kompensation der Governance-Lücke.

Die Co-Evolution staatlichen und privaten Rechts sowie staatlicher und privater Akteure wirft indes Anschlussfragen auf. Sie betreffen die Antriebskräfte und Wirkungsmechanismen, um die Entstehung des für die hier vorliegende PPP-Thematik relevanten transnationalen Rechts nachvollziehen zu können. Der folgende Abschnitt beschäftigt sich mit diesen Fragen.

4 Transnationales Recht als „Füllstoff" der Governance-Lücke internationaler Transaktionen?

Worin besteht und wie entwickelt sich transnationales Recht – insbesondere mit Blick auf den Bereich der „Private Governance"? Privatwirtschaftliche Tätigkeit zur Schließung der Governance-Lücke ist mit Blick auf internationale Transaktionen auf unterschiedliche Weise erkennbar, wobei zur Erfassung zwei unterschiedliche Zugänge sinnvoll erscheinen:

- In den einzelnen *Branchen* haben sich unterschiedliche Gepflogenheiten etabliert, die Unsicherheit internationaler Geschäfte zu reduzieren.

[18] Vgl. Calliess, G. P. (2006).

- Unabhängig von Branchengrenzen erscheint es sinnvoll, vergleichbare *Transaktionssituationen* typischer Art zu erfassen und sie anderen Konstellationen gegenüber abzugrenzen.

Auf beide Punkte ist mit Blick auf privatwirtschaftliche Governance-Tätigkeit nachfolgend kurz einzugehen. CALLIESS et al. (2008) haben einen Überblicksbeitrag vorgelegt, der in unterschiedlichen *Branchen* zeigt, wie wirtschaftliche Akteure durch Maßnahmen der Private Governance zur Verringerung rechtlicher Unsicherheit beitragen:

- Im *internationalen Holzhandel* haben sich durch jahrzehntelange Praxis Konventionen herausgebildet, die innerhalb der Branche ein hohes Maß an Verbindlichkeit erlangt haben. Ihre Entstehung fußt auf zeitstabilen Branchenstrukturen mit netzwerkartigen Beziehungen zwischen den Marktakteuren, aus denen ein vergleichsweise hoher Grad an Markttransparenz resultiert. Diese Ausgangskonstellation ermöglicht den Marktteilnehmern, das Instrument der Selbstregulierung einzusetzen und von formalen Verträgen Abstand zu nehmen. In den entsprechenden Transaktionen des Holzgeschäfts, die üblicherweise in lose Geschäftsbeziehungen eingepasst sind, erfolgt demnach ein regulierender Effekt durch Branchenkonventionen, deren Ausformulierung und Einhaltung nicht zuletzt Branchenverbänden und – im seltenen Streitfall – Schiedsgerichten obliegt. Zusätzliche Stabilisierungswirkungen auf die internationalen Transaktionen gehen überdies von im Markt gesetzten Standards aus. Man kann vor diesem Hintergrund feststellen, dass altbewährte Handelsbräuche und Konventionen eine derart starke Absicherungswirkung zeitigen, dass sie de facto Rechtsstatus erlangt haben. Mit Blick auf diese bewährten und bekannten Gewohnheiten – z.B. der internationalen Kaufmannschaft – wird von der sog. „lex mercatoria“ gesprochen, die als sichtbares Zeichen transnationalen Handelsrechts mit dominanten privaten Regelungsmechanismen aufzufassen ist. Lex mercatoria findet bei weitem nicht nur Anwendung in der internationalen Holzindustrie, sondern z.B. auch im Diamantenhandel oder im Baumwollgeschäft.

- In der *IT-Branche* hingegen wird mit Blick auf das Outsourcing von Softwareentwicklungsleistungen festgestellt, dass bedingt durch die Vielzahl vereinbarungsbedürftiger Leistungsspezifikationen und die vielfältigen Handlungsmöglichkeiten der Softwareentwicklungs-Betriebe ein unter Risikogesichtspunkten besonderes Spannungsfeld besteht. Die Kopplung von Anbietern und Nachfragern ist spätestens nach Auftragserteilung eng und nicht zwangsläufig projektbezogen, sondern in enge Geschäftsbeziehungen mündend. Als Absicherungsmöglichkeit ist in derart engen, relational geprägten Kontexten eine rahmenvertragliche Vereinbarung in Verbindung mit Einzelverträgen üblich. Die Verträge nehmen für sich aber nicht annähernd in Anspruch, vollständig zu sein und somit alle Eventualitäten zu regeln – was in Anbetracht der Ungewissheit der zukünftigen Entwicklung ohnehin unrealistisch wäre. Insofern stellt sich unmittelbar die Frage, wie etwaige Governance-Lücken, die das Vertragswerk allgemeiner und projektspezifischer Art hinterlässt, geschlossen werden können. Die Untersuchungen gemäß CALLIESS et al. (2008) sowie DIETZ und NIESWANDT (2009) lassen erkennen, dass im Gegensatz zu den z.B. im internationalen Holzhandel mehr oder weniger sozial bewährten und anerkannten Normen im Rahmen derart enger bilateraler Kooperation sog. „relationale" Normen und Werte an deren Stelle treten.[19] Relationale Normen entwickeln sich durch die Zusammenarbeit der Transaktionspartner (z.B. in Form von Vertrauen, wie NOOTEBOOM 1996 zeigt, oder Solidarität). Sie erlangen verhaltensbezogene Verbindlichkeit allein schon durch den Umstand vorhandener und nicht ohne weiteres auflösbarer Reziprozität im Sinne gegenseitiger wirtschaftlicher, sozialer, technischer und eben auch rechtlicher Kopplungen, wobei im Geschäfts-

[19] Vgl. Macneil, I. R. (1974).

beziehungskontext das Prinzip der kollektiven Verbindlichkeit durch die relationale Verbindlichkeit ersetzt wird. Dies schließt weder die Bezugnahme auf staatliches Recht noch auf soziale Normen aus, wie die o.g. Vertragsgrundlagen erkennen lassen. Insofern ist auch bei Governance-Lösungen, die auf relationalen Mechanismen beruhen, der Staat mit dem von ihm bereitgestellten Rechtssystem alles andere als irrelevant oder sogar obsolet. Im Gegenteil: Im Falle von relational unlösbaren Konflikten kann der Staat mit seinen Rechtsinstitutionen als „Auffangstation" die notwendige Stabilisierung leisten, die auf anderem Wege nicht mehr denkbar ist. Dies setzt allerdings die Anerkennung staatlicher Rechtsgrundlagen durch beide beteiligten Marktpartner voraus. Darüber hinaus verweisen CALLIESS et al. (2008) auch auf neutrale Drittparteien aus dem privaten Sektor, wie etwa Steuerungs-Komitees im Rahmen größerer Projekte oder die Einschaltung von Kammern oder Schieds- und Schlichtungsparteien. Auch ist die Gründung von Projektgesellschaften im Sinne von Joint Ventures beider Parteien denkbar, um durch vertikale Integration im Sinne einer hierarchischen Steuerung die internationale Transaktion zu stabilisieren.

Die Betrachtung der beiden Branchen lässt erkennen, dass zwar auf unterschiedliche Weise, aber dennoch wirkungsvoll eine unsicherheitsreduzierende Grundlage zur Durchführung internationaler Transaktionen geschaffen werden kann. Dabei kommt dem transnationalen Recht entscheidende Bedeutung zu. Dieses transnationale Recht speist sich zu wesentlichen Teilen aus privaten Ordnungsleistungen. Der Staat hingegen steht eher im Hintergrund und übt dort eine wichtige stabilisierende Funktion aus, etwa wenn er Schiedssprüche als rechtlich verbindlich anerkennt und international vollstreckt. Das Miteinander von staatlichen und privaten Akteuren ist somit erkennbar.

Offenbar nimmt die Transaktionskonstellation selbst Einfluss auf die Governance-Lösung, die es zu finden gilt. Dann aber stellt sich die Frage nach den wichtigsten Bestimmungsfaktoren des transaktionsbezogenen Absicherungsbedarfs. Es ist ein Verdienst der Industrial Marketing and Purchasing Group (IMP Group) um TURNBULL und VALLA (1989), derartige Faktoren innerhalb eines Totalmodells der Anbieter-Nachfrager-Interaktion auf netzwerktheoretischer Basis erfasst zu haben. In diesem Zusammenhang sind folgende Faktorbereiche im Kontext der Rechtssicherheit internationaler Transaktionen von Belang:

- anbieterbezogene Merkmale (v.a. personelle Ziele der Transaktionsbeteiligten, Technologieposition, Erfahrungen und Wissensstand),
- nachfragerbezogene Merkmale (v.a. Beschaffungs-Know-how, Bedarfssituation),
- Interaktionsprozess (v.a. Produktkomplexität, relationaler versus transaktionaler Kontext, Machtverteilung zwischen den Partnern),
- Interaktionsatmosphäre (v.a. kooperative versus konfliktäre Atmosphäre),
- Makro-Umwelt der Interaktion (v.a. Dynamik der Umwelt und internationale Einbettung).

Die Vielfalt transaktionsrelevanter Kriterien lässt zwar Zweifel an jeder Klassifikation von Transaktionssituationen aufkommen, weil es schwierig ist, auf diesem Wege dem Transaktionsprofil gerecht zu werden. Gleichwohl zeigen zahlreiche Typologisierungsversuche[20], dass mit der Unterscheidung in Routine- und Individualtransaktionen sowie (einzel-) transaktionalen und relational eingebetteten Transaktionen eine geeignete Vereinfachung der Vielfalt möglich ist. Ohne alle vier Transaktionssituationen näher vorstellen zu wollen[21], kann festgestellt werden, dass beim Extremtyp der einzelnen Routinetransaktion allgemeinverbindliche Normen die effizienteste Absicherungsmöglichkeit bieten, wobei der Regelungsumfang insgesamt sehr begrenzt ist. Hier kann sowohl staat-

---

[20] Für einen Überblick: Backhaus, K./Voeth, M. (2007).
[21] Vgl. hierzu: Freiling, J. (2009).

liches als auch privates Recht zur Anwendung gelangen. Anders gestaltet sich die Beurteilung bei dem anderen Extremtyp der Individualtransaktion im relationalen Kontext. Bei großem Regelungsbedarf sind allgemeinverbindliche Regelungen zwar möglich und auch sinnvoll einsetzbar, aber niemals in der Lage, eine für internationale Transaktionen annähernd vollständig geeignete Absicherung zu bieten. Insofern sind der Individualität der Transaktion entsprechende relationale Normen zu entwickeln, um den Spezifika der Beziehung mit Blick auf die o.g. fünf Kriterienbereiche gerecht werden zu können. Hierzu bietet sich zunächst bilaterale Governance privater Art an, die – je nach Ausgangslage – durch private trilaterale, multilaterale sowie staatliche Governance arrondiert werden kann. Ist es nicht möglich, dem Regelungsbedarf auf diese Weise zu entsprechen, kommt – mehr oder weniger alternativ zu den genannten Absicherungsformen – die unilaterale Governance in Betracht (z.B. Projektgesellschaften, Arbeitsgemeinschaften, Joint Ventures). Abbildung 2 ist zu entnehmen, mit welchen Besonderheiten bezüglich Rechtsfindung, Rechtsprechung und Vollzug die jeweiligen Governance-Grundmodi einhergehen.

Governance-Modus	Gesetzgebung/ Rechtsfindung	Rechtsprechung	Vollzug/ Umsetzung
Staatlich	Gesetze	Gericht	Rechtliche Sanktionen
Private tri- und multilaterale Governance	Soziale Normen	Schiedsgericht	Soziale Sanktionen
Private bilaterale Governance	Relationale Normen	Verhandlung	Ökonomische Sanktionen
Private unilaterale Governance	Betriebliche Normen	Entscheidung auf formaler inner-betrieblicher Legitimationsbasis	Anweisung und betriebliche Sanktionen

Abb. 2: Staatliche und private Governance bei internationalen Transaktionen
Quelle: in Anlehnung an Calliess, G. P. et al. 2008, S. 111.

Die Übersicht veranschaulicht, dass gerade die Unterschiedlichkeit der für das internationale Geschäft in Frage kommenden Governance-Modi beträchtliche Möglichkeiten einer situativen Anpassung an die Transaktionsbedingungen bietet. Dieser Eindruck gilt vor allem mit Blick auf die Tatsache, dass die einzelnen Governance-Typen eben nur Grundmodi darstellen. Die jeweiligen Elemente der Governance-Typen können nämlich so miteinander kombiniert werden, dass transaktionsspezifisch angepasste Governance-Designs entstehen, in denen unterschiedliche private und staatliche Mechanismen sich wechselseitig abstützen oder zeitlich im Sinne von Auffanglösungen aufeinander aufbauen.[22] Wenn dies aber grundsätzlich der Fall ist, so stellt sich folgende Anschlussfrage, die im nächsten Abschnitt zu klären ist: Wie entwickeln sich spezifische Governance-Lösungen und wie werden sie im Sinne des erweiterten PPP-Gedankens miteinander kombiniert?

[22] Vgl. Calliess, G. P. et al. (2008).

5 PPP-basierte Governance Designs in evolutorischer Betrachtung

Während der Governance-Begriff bereits eingangs geklärt wurde, so ist hier darzulegen, was unter einem Governance-Design zu verstehen ist. Ein Governance-Design stellt die situationsgerechte Kombination einzelner institutioneller Lösungen dar, um den Zielen der Governance (Steuerung, Überwachung und Sanktionierung menschlichen Verhaltens im Kontext von Unsicherheit und Arbeitsteilung) gerecht werden zu können.

Geht man von der Akteursgebundenheit von Handlungen aus, so können neue Governance-Designs von staatlichen und/oder privaten Akteuren geschaffen werden. Während der Gesetzgebungsprozess in vorhersagbarer und eindeutig geregelter Weise verläuft, unterliegt die Entstehung privater bzw. PPP-äquivalenter Governance grundsätzlich anderen Mustern. Folgende Elemente bestimmen den Verlauf:

- Die Entscheidungsprozesse verlaufen überwiegend dezentral.
- Sie folgen im Wesentlichen dem Prinzip des Versuchs und Irrtums. Stellt sich bei internationalen Transaktionen eine neuartige Koordinationsherausforderung, so versuchen die betroffenen Akteure eine Lösung zu finden. Hierzu experimentieren sie unter Zuhilfenahme ihrer bisherigen Erfahrungen und Interpretationsmuster. Dabei sind Irrtümer in Folge von Neuheit und unvollständiger Information „garantiert“.
- Irrtümer sind insofern nützlich, als sie neues Wissen generieren. Getestete Governance-Designs, die sich nicht (vollständig) bewährt haben, vermitteln den Handelnden Eindrücke, wo Probleme aufgetreten sind, wie sie sich nicht lösen lassen und was möglicherweise eher geeignet sein könnte. Der veränderte Wissensstand verbessert die Ausgangslage in der nächsten Entscheidungssituation.

- Aus der Vielzahl von dezentralen, teils geplanten, teils aber auch weniger planvollen Entscheidungen ergibt sich trotz der Verschiedenartigkeit der Handlungen über die Zeit eine Struktur. Bestimmte Governance-Designs bewähren und verfestigen sich. Aus dem Zustand der ehemals nicht erkennbaren Ordnung ergeben sich allmählich Muster.
- Die Entwicklung wird bestimmt durch den Dreiklang dreier Evolutionsmechanismen, die dem evolutionstheoretischen Kontext entstammen[23]: die (blinde, d.h. ungesteuerte) Variation im Sinne des o.g. Trial-and-Error-Prinzips, die Selektion durch Mechanismen im sozialen Raum (v.a. ökonomische Effizienzkriterien, soziale Gerechtigkeitskriterien, juristische Legitimationskriterien) und die sich daran anschließende Retention.
- Wenn demnach eine Bewährung einsetzt, so gehen damit nahezu unweigerlich Informationen einher, die sich über den Kreis der Handelnden ausdehnen. Dieses „Signaling“ geeigneter bzw. überlegener Governance-Designs führt zu einem Prozess zunehmender Beachtung, Beurteilung und ggf. Akzeptanz. Es ergibt sich mit anderen Worten ein Standardisierungsprozess. Die Standardisierung beschreibt dabei die freiwillige Anerkennung einer vereinheitlichten Lösung, beispielsweise auch eines neuen Governance-Designs. Ein Beispiel geben etwa die immer stärkere Akzeptanz findenden Betreibermodelle in der Energieversorgung sowie im Maschinen- und Anlagenbau. Hier wurden Geschäftsbeziehungsstandards im Verbund mit anderen Governance-Grundmodi etabliert, die den früheren Eigentumserwerb einer komplexen technischen Infrastruktur durch den Nachfrager in Frage stellten und in vielen Bereichen ablösten.
- Das Beispiel verdeutlicht zugleich, dass ein Retentionsprozess nicht zwingend unidirektional verlaufen muss, sondern dass auch in der

[23] Vgl. Calliess, G. P./Freiling, J./Renner, M. (2008); Freiling, J. (2009).

Retention neue graduelle Variationen in Folge besseren Wissens nicht ausgeschlossen sind. So wurden die Betreibermodelle immer weiter verfeinert, um ihre Anwendungsnähe zu verbessern.

- Die beschriebenen Prozesse verlaufen nicht voraussetzungsfrei. So sind die Akteure durch ihr Wissen, ihre Ausgangssituation und ihre sonstigen Mittel vorgeprägt. Auch die Entwicklung von Governance-Designs erfolgt nicht „aus dem Nichts heraus". So stellte sich bei der Herausbildung von Betreibermodellen etwa heraus, dass die Nachfrager erstens den Know-how-Verlust bei dieser Form des Outsourcings fürchteten und zweitens einen Verlust an spezifischem Leistungszuschnitt befürchteten – vor allem dann, wenn die technische Infrastruktur nicht nur ihnen, sondern aus Wirtschaftlichkeitsgründen auch der Betreuung anderer Kunden diente. Entsprechend wurden im Sinne eines gleitenden Übergangs für den Kunden Stufenmodelle zum Performance Contracting entwickelt[24]. Die bislang primär zur Anwendung gelangten Theorien im Kontext von Governance-Designs (Transaktionskostentheorie, Agenturtheorie) blenden die Anpassungsprobleme in diesem Bereich aus. GERSCH (2007) zeigt am Beispiel der Spezifität, wie wichtig eine evolutorische Betrachtung transaktionsrelevanter Stellgrößen ist.

Übertragen auf den Kontext der Governance internationaler Transaktionen lässt sich dieser Eindruck nur unterstreichen. Staatliche Akteure erzielen bei der Schaffung internationalen und supranationalen Rechts kaum erkennbare Fortschritte. Dies belegt die erhebliche organisationale Trägheit des Staates bei der Bereitstellung normativer Güter für eine funktionsfähige rechtliche Infrastruktur. Die *Evolution von Governance-Designs im privatwirtschaftlichen Bereich* läuft demgegenüber *weitaus schneller*, aber auch *weitaus ungerichteter*. Das hat zur Konsequenz, dass viele Governance-Designs nach ersten Versuchen verschwinden, ohne überhaupt von einer größeren Zahl wirtschaftlicher Akteure

---

[24] Vgl. Freiling, J. (2004).

bemerkt worden zu sein. Daher kann ohne weiteres von unterschiedlichen Geschwindigkeiten im Vergleich von Public und Private Governance gesprochen werden. Allerdings zeigen die Ausführungen des vorangegangenen Abschnitts, dass Private Governance bei weitem nicht durchweg als „Schnellzug" der Rechtsentwicklung verstanden werden kann. Das Beispiel der Lex mercatoria und die allmähliche Herausbildung von Normen, Gewohnheiten und Konventionen in der privaten Gesellschaft verdeutlicht, dass auch hier ausgesprochen lange Entwicklungskorridore möglich sind. Überdies lässt sich in der Entwicklung privaten und staatlichen Rechts eine interessante Entwicklung erkennen: Nicht alle Governance-Lösungen, die sich etabliert haben, haben sich durch überragende Effektivität und/oder Effizienz bewährt. Vielmehr ist die Realität von Governance in nicht unmaßgeblicher Weise durch Habiti geprägt.

Spezifisch für die Evolution transnationalen Rechts ist dabei das Zusammenwirken von staatlichen, wirtschaftlichen und zivilgesellschaftlichen Akteuren, welches im Kontext von PPP besonders interessant erscheint. Weil staatliche Steuerungsleistungen im transnationalen Raum nicht auf der Grundlage des Rechtsmonopols des Staates erbracht werden, eröffnet sich den Akteuren ein neuartiger Raum für Variationen bei der Entwicklung transaktionsspezifischer Governance-Designs, die ihre Attraktivität gerade aus der innovativen Re-Kombination von staatlichen und privaten Ordnungsleistungen beziehen. Von den nur national wirksamen Schranken des staatlichen Rechtsmonopols befreit, können im transnationalen Raum die Selektionsprozesse für Governance-Designs radikal auf Nachfrage- bzw. Nutzerorientierung umgestellt werden. Schließlich zeigt sich bei der Retention, dass internationale Rechtsinstrumente insbesondere dann wirkkräftig werden, wenn sie im Evolutionsprozess vorselektierte Governance-Modi staatlich absichern und bestärken.

Ein besonders gelungenes Beispiel für PPP-Ordering internationaler Transaktionen ist zum Beispiel das o.g. New Yorker Übereinkommen zur gegenseitigen Anerkennung und Vollstreckung von Schiedssprüchen.[25] Denn dieses

---

[25] Vgl. dazu Calliess, G. P. (2007).

völkerrechtliche Übereinkommen greift eine in der Praxis internationaler Transaktionen vorgefundene Selektion zu Gunsten privater Schiedsgerichte auf und verstärkt diesen Trend zur Privatisierung der Streitschlichtung nochmals, indem der staatliche Sanktionsapparat zur Vollstreckung von Schiedssprüchen zur Verfügung gestellt wird, was als wichtiger staatlicher Beitrag im Prozess der Retention zu verstehen ist. Diese staatliche Steuerungsleistung wird freilich an Bedingungen geknüpft (freier Konsens der Parteien, kein Verstoß gegen das öffentliche Interesse), was den weiteren Selektionsprozess in Richtung auf staatlich anerkannte Schiedsgerichte beeinflusst hat.

6 Ausblick

Alles in allem darf weder der Stellenwert privater noch staatlicher Governance unterschätzt werden. Im internationalen Geschäft vermag die Herausbildung eines transnationalen Rechts augenblicklich die beschriebene Governance-Lücke am ehesten zu schließen. Das allein belegt noch nicht eine augenblickliche Dominanz der Mittel des Private Ordering bei der Schaffung und Weiterentwicklung von Governance-Designs, da auch der Staat im transnationalen Recht eine Rolle spielen kann – und spielt: Er verfügt über eine für private Governance anlagerungsfähige rechtliche Infrastruktur und kann – wie für die Schiedsgerichtsbarkeit gezeigt – über die Festlegung der Bedingungen für eine Verknüpfung staatlicher mit privaten Steuerungsleistungen indirekt die Evolution des transnationalen Rechts beeinflussen. Daneben kann er mit dem Angebot staatlicher Justiz-Dienstleistungen aber auch in Konkurrenz zu privaten Ordnungsleistungen treten. Je wirkungsvoller die rechtliche Infrastruktur des Staates ist, desto größer sind auch die Chancen, dass sich private Akteure freiwillig auf die Nutzung einer solchen einigen. Darin werden zugleich zwei Fälle von „Co-opetition“[26] als Überlappung kooperativer und kompetitiver Effekte

[26] Vgl. Brandenburger, A./Nalebuff, B. (1996).

ersichtlich. Das Co-opetition-Verhältnis bringt die Besonderheiten der hier untersuchten PPP-Ordering für internationale Transaktionen zum Ausdruck.

Literaturverzeichnis

Backhaus, K./Büschken, J./Voeth, M. (2003): Internationales Marketing. 5. Aufl., Stuttgart.

Backhaus, K./Voeth, M. (2007): Industriegütermarketing. 8. Aufl., München.

Bassen, A./Behnam, M./Gilbert, D.U. (2001): Internationalisierung des Mittelstandes. In: Zeitschrift für Betriebswirtschaft, 71. Jg., S. 413-432.

Bernstein, L. (1992): Opting Out of the Legal System: Extralegal Contractual Relations in the Diamond Industry. In: Journal of Legal Studies, 21. Jg., S. 115-157.

Brandenburger, A./Nalebuff, B. (1996): Co-opetition. New York.

Budäus, D. (2004): Public Private Partnerships. Strukturierung eines nicht ganz neuen Problemfeldes. In: ZFO, 73. Jg., S. 312-318.

Calliess, G.P. (2006): Grenzüberschreitende Verbraucherverträge, Rechtssicherheit und Gerechtigkeit auf dem elektronischen Weltmarktplatz. Tübingen.

Calliess, G.P. (2007): The Making of Transnational Contract Law. In: Indiana Journal of Global Legal Studies, 14. Jg., Heft 2, S. 469-483.

Calliess, G.P. et al. (2008): Transformation des Handelsrechts? Neue Formen von Rechtssicherheit in globalen Austauschprozessen. In: Hurrelmann, A. et al. (Hrsg.): Zerfasert der Nationalstaat? Frankfurt/New York 2008, S. 143-175.

Calliess, G.P./Freiling, J./Renner, M. (2008): Law, the State, and Private Ordering: Evolutionary Explanations of Institutional Change. In: German Law Journal, 9. Jg., S. 395-408.

Dietz, T./Nieswandt, H. (2009): The Emergence of Transnational Cooperation in the Software Industry. In: Gessner, V. (Hrsg.): Contractual Certainty in International Trade. Oxford, S. 87-105.

Dixit, A. K. (2004): Lawlessness and Economics. Alternative Modes of Governance. Princeton.

Freiling, J. (2004): Performance Contracting. In: Backhaus, K./Voeth, M. (Hrsg.): Handbuch Industriegütermarketing, Wiesbaden, S. 677-695.

Freiling, J. (2009): Institutional Designs in International Transactions. In: Gessner, V. (Hrsg.): Contractual Certainty in International Trade, Oxford, S. 257-287.

Freiling, J./Gersch, M./Goeke, C. (2008): On the Path Towards a Competence-based Theory of the Firm. In: Organization Studies, 29. Jg., S. 1143-1164.

Genschel, P./Leibfried, S. (2008): Schupperts Staat. Wie beobachtet man den Wandel einer Reformidee? In: Staat, 47, Jg., Heft 3, S. 359-380.

Gersch, M. (2007): Specificity-based Commitments from a Co-evolutionary Perspective – First Conceptual Considerations and Implications for Relationship Management. SSRN Working Paper: http://papers.ssrn.com/sol3/papers.cfm?abstract_id=979789 (Abruf: 26.9.2008).

Grimsey, D./Lewis, M.K. (2004): Public Private Partnerships. Cheltenham.

Hart, O.D. (2003): Incomplete Contracts and Public Ownership: Remarks, and an Application to Public-Private Partnerships. In: Economic Journal, 119. Jg., S. C69-C76.

Kulvavy, E. (1993): Internationales Marketing. 5. Aufl., Linz.

Macneil, I.R. (1974): The Many Futures of Contracts. In: Southern California Law Journal, 47. Jg., S. 691-816.

Meyer, M. (1987): Die Beurteilung der Risiken der internationalen Unternehmung. Berlin.

Nooteboom, B. (1996): Trust, Opportunism and Governance. In: Organization Studies, 17. Jg., S. 985-1010.

Prahalad, C.K./Hamel, G. (1990): The Core Competence of the Corporation. In: Harvard Business Review, 69. Jg., S. 79-91.

Roentgen, F. (2001): Public-Private-Partnership. Eine effizienzorientierte Analyse kommunaler Aufgabenerfüllung unter Einbeziehung erwerbswirtschaftlicher Unternehmungen. Aachen.

Savas, E.S. (2000): Privatization and Public-Private-Partnerships. New York.

Schmidt, K. (1996): The costs and benefits of privatization: An incomplete contracts approach. In: Journal of Law, Economics and Organization, 12. Jg., S. 1-24.

Shleifer, A. (1998): State versus private ownership. In: Journal of Economic Perspectives, 12. Jg., S. 133-150.

Turnbull, P.W./Valla, J.-P. (1989): Strategies for International Industrial Marketing. London.

Williamson, O.E. (2005): The Economics of Governance. In: American Economic Review, 95. Jg., S. 1-18.

Chancen und Risiken von öffentlich-privaten Partnerschaften (Public Private Partnerships) aus Sicht der öffentlichen Hand

Stefan Rufera

Inhaltsverzeichnis

Keywords

Abschlusstechniken, Berufung, Einstellungen, Einstellungsanalyse, Feldanalysen, Geist, Handeln, Körper, Leben, Management, Marktkenntnisse, Postminister, Potentiale, Reserve, Ressourcen, Seele, Seelenamt, Spitzenleistungen, Spitzenverkäufer, Stärke, Untersuchungen, Vision, Ziele, Zielportfolio, Zukunft

1 Ausgangslage

Angesichts des kontinuierlich hohen Bedarfs an öffentlichen Infrastrukturinvestitionen in den verschiedensten Bereichen (Verkehr, Bildung, Gesundheit etc.) bzw. der zunehmenden Komplexität von öffentlichen Aufgaben und der angespannten Haushaltslage stößt der Staat bei der Erfüllung der anstehenden Herausforderungen zunehmend an seine Grenzen. Daher ist die öffentliche Hand gefordert, konsequent zu prüfen, inwieweit die Erfüllung der öffentlichen Aufgaben wie die **Bereitstellung öffentlicher Infrastruktur durch neue Wege** beschritten werden kann. Eine Möglichkeit kann die Zusammenarbeit mit privaten Partnern im Rahmen von sogenannten **öffentlich-privaten Partnerschaften** (Public Private Partnerships, PPPs) sein.

Bei der Umsetzung solcher PPP-Lösungen muss jedoch klar sein, dass PPP-Konzepte nicht für alle Investitionsvorhaben geeignet sind – insbesondere wenn die damit verbundenen Risiken überwiegen. Dass sich mit PPP-Modellen die potentiell möglichen Vorteile auch realisieren lassen, kann somit nicht generell gelten, sondern kann nur im Einzelfall durch spezifische Analysen und Wirtschaftlichkeitsuntersuchungen geprüft und bewertet werden.

PPPs stellen dabei einen möglichen Ansatz dar, privates Kapital und Know-how bei der Beschaffung bzw. Bereitstellung öffentlicher Infrastruktur oder öffentlicher Aufgaben zu nutzen. Bei der Beurteilung dieser öffentlich-privaten Partnerschaften sollte freilich nur auf den ersten Blick die **Nutzung einer privaten Finanzierung** zur Realisierung öffentlicher Aufgaben im Vordergrund stehen. Vielmehr sollten darüber hinaus weitere Vorteile für alle beteiligten Parteien genutzt werden, so beispielweise eine Optimierung der Gesamtkosten eines Projekts durch die **Betrachtung des gesamten Lebenszyklus**, eine mögliche Realisierung von **Effizienzgewinnen** oder eine angemessene **Allokation von Risiken** aus der bestmöglichen Einbringung der Stärken jeweils des öffentlichen und des privaten Partners. Diese Vorteile und Chancen gilt es bewusst zu identifizieren, um sie in weiterer Folge auch gezielt forcieren zu können, um aus Sicht der öffentlichen Hand bzw. des Steuerzahler den Nutzen optimieren zu können.

Im Folgenden sollen nun zum einen genau diese möglichen Vorteile aus Sicht der öffentlichen Hand dargestellt werden, um bei der Bewältigung von neuen komplexen Herausforderungen durch PPP-Lösungen genau diese Potentiale systematisch und gezielt verfolgen zu können. Zum anderen sollen aber auch mögliche damit verbundene **Risiken und Probleme** aufgezeigt werden, um diese frühzeitig identifizieren und entsprechend reflektieren zu können.

Angesichts der überragenden Bedeutung der Infrastruktur für eine Volkswirtschaft ist es verständlich, dass der Staat für die Entwicklung der Infrastruktur sorgt. Der Fokus der folgenden Ausführungen wird sich daher auf die Vorteile und Risiken aus Sicht der öffentlichen Hand bei der **Beschaffung von Infrastruktur** durch PPPs konzentrieren. Dabei tritt im Rahmen von PPP-Lösungen die öffentliche Hand regelmäßig als Besteller, der private Partner zumeist als Errichter und eventuell Betreiber der jeweiligen Infrastruktur auf.

2 Chancen und Risiken von öffentlich-privaten Partnerschaften (Public Private Partnerships) aus Sicht der öffentlichen Hand

2.1 Herausforderungen der öffentlichen Hand im Infrastrukturbereich

Der Bedarf für die Bereitstellung von öffentlicher Infrastruktur ist ungebrochen und stellt die öffentliche Hand insbesondere vor folgende Herausforderungen.

2.1.1 Wachsender Bedarf an der Bereitstellung von Infrastruktur

Durch die Entwicklung der politischen, wirtschaftlichen und sozialen Rahmenbedingungen ist der Neubedarf an (öffentlicher) Infrastruktur in den verschiedensten Bereichen enorm. Ergänzend dazu kommt der wachsende Bedarf an notwendigen Reinvestitionen und Modernisierungen.

So erlebt Europa in der Gegenwart bspw. ein rapides Wachstum des Verkehrsaufkommens im Bereich des Landverkehrs, auf das die Infrastruktur nur teilweise vorbereitet scheint. Angesichts der damit verbundenen Herausforderungen haben die politischen Akteure auf allen Ebenen die Notwendigkeit einer nachhaltigen Verkehrspolitik und ihrer konkreten Umsetzung erkannt.

EU-Verkehrspolitik: Jacques Barrot, EU-Kommissar für Verkehrsfragen in der Halbzeitbilanz zum Verkehrsweißbuch der Europäischen Kommission von 2001

„(...) Ziel der EU-Kommission ist es, eine nachhaltige Mobilität in Europa zu gewährleisten. Nach den derzeitigen Vorausschätzungen steht bis zum Jahr 2020 eine Zunahme des Verkehrs in der Größenordnung von 50 % beim Güterverkehr und von 35 % beim Personenverkehr zu erwarten – Europa kann sich also ein Scheitern bei dieser Aufgabe nicht leisten. Dazu müssen wir die Mobilität von ihren negativen Auswirkungen abkoppeln: Hierzu bedarf es einer Förderung der technologischen Innovation, der Verlagerung des Verkehrs auf die umweltschonendsten und energiesparendsten Verkehrsträger, insbesondere bei langen Strecken und in den Städten, sowie vor allem einer Entwicklung der Komodalität, d. h. der optimalen Kombination verschiedener Verkehrsträger in der Logistikkette, die für den Güterverkehr die Zukunftslösung darstellt. (...)"[1]

Nach Schätzung der Van-Miert-Kommission sind daher über 600 Milliarden Euro notwendig, um alle TEN-Maßnahmen zu realisieren. Es ist augenscheinlich, dass die dafür notwendigen Mittel aus den nationalen Budgets nicht im erforderlichen Ausmaß zur Verfügung stehen.

Ähnlich stellt sich auch die Lage in anderen Infrastrukturbereichen dar. Besonders betroffen ist dabei etwa – auch aufgrund der demographischen Entwicklung – der Gesundheitssektor.

Investitionsbedarf im Krankenhaussektor in Deutschland

„(...) Der die Fördermöglichkeiten der Länder und Gemeinden weit übersteigende Bedarf an Investitionen im Krankenhaussektor hat besorgniserregende Ausmaße angenommen. So schätzen Experten den Investitionsstau inzwischen auf rd. 30 Mrd. € – mit steigender Tendenz. (...)"[2]

Aufgrund der substantiellen Kapitalerfordernisse im Kontext von Infrastrukturausbaumaßnahmen stellt sich vor dem Hintergrund der Finanzmittelknappheit des öffentlichen Sektors die Frage, inwieweit öffentlich-private Partnerschaften als zweckdienliches Instrument einer (rascheren) Realisierung herangezogen werden können.

2.1.2 Dominanz der Betrachtung von Investitionskosten

Investitionskosten stellen nur einen Teil der Gesamtkosten von Infrastrukturprojekten über die gesamte Nutzungsdauer dar. In der öffentlichen Beschaffung besteht eine **Tendenz, jene Planung für das Projekt auszuwählen**, die **geringere,** jedoch sehr augenscheinliche **Kosten im Bau** aufweist, dafür aber teurer in Betrieb und Erhaltung ist. Dabei besteht jedoch ein unmittelbarer Zusammenhang zwischen der betriebswirtschaftlichen Einschätzung des Projekts mit der

---

1 Europäische Kommission (2006).
2 Alfen, H. W. et al. (2005).

Qualität des Bauens und den daraus resultierenden späteren Erhaltungs- und Betriebskosten. Höhere langfristige Erhaltungs- und Betriebskosten liegen häufig jenseits des Horizonts der Finanzplanung von heute. Eine Lebenszyklusbetrachtung wird daher häufig nicht angestellt.

2.1.3 Effiziente Planung und verantwortungsvoller Einsatz von öffentlichen Ressourcen – Optimism Bias

Auch im Fall von Lebenszyklusbetrachtungen besteht die Tendenz, dass die Kosten eines Infrastrukturprojekts von der öffentlichen Hand tendenziell zu gering und der Erträge aus dem Projekt meist zu hoch – in der Literatur als „**Optimism Bias**" bezeichnet – angesetzt werden. Als Grund dafür wird der Druck angeführt, die Umsetzung des jeweiligen Projektes mittels optimistischen Planrechnungen zu unterstützen. Die Probleme durch Kostenüberschreitungen werden dann meist das Problem für den Haushalt in zukünftigen Perioden.

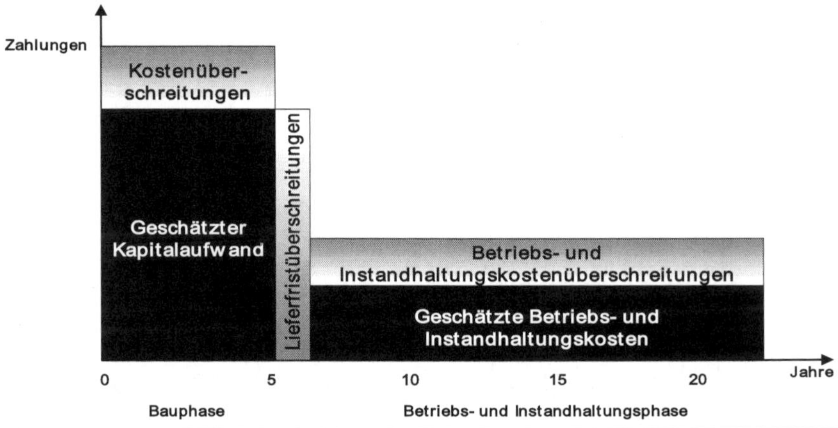

Abb. 1: Optimism Bias – Tendenz zur Unterschätzung von Kosten und Zeit
Quelle: eigene Darstellung.

Der Optimism Bias wird als prozentuelle Differenz der **Abweichung der geschätzten Annahmen zu den tatsächlich ex post zu beobachtenden Größen** ausgedrückt. Dabei werden die Daten aus einem Vergleich eines Planfalls am Beginn der Ausschreibungsphase mit den tatsächlichen Ergebnissen nach Projektrealisierung ermittelt. Folgende Tabelle zeigt durchschnittliche Abweichungen bei öffentlichen Beschaffungen, die als Richtwerte zu Bauzeit bzw. zu den geschätzten Investitionskosten verstanden werden können.

Projekttyp	**Optimism Bias in %**			
	Bauzeit		Investitionskosten	
	obere Grenze	untere Grenze	obere Grenze	untere Grenze
Gebäude (nicht-standard)	39	2	51	4
Gebäude (standard)	4	1	24	2
Hoch- und Tiefbau (nicht standard)	25	3	66	6
Hoch- und Tiefbau (standard)	20	1	44	3
Ausrüstung/Entwicklung	54	10	200	10
Outsourcing	n/a	n/a	41	0

Tab. 1: Bandbreiten des Optimism Bias für Bauzeit und Investitionskosten
Quelle: Mott MacDonald (2002).

Untersuchungen zeigen, dass der Optimism Bias insbesondere durch eine zu kurz greifende Risikoidentifikation und ein ungenügendes Risikomanagement bedingt ist. Dementsprechend kann der Bias durch ein **systematisches Risikomanagement**, eine **ganzheitliche Betrachtung der Projekte**, eine **sorgfältige Planungsphase** und ein **Kostencontrolling** in allen Projektphasen abgefedert werden.

2.1.4 Budgetäre Engpässe

Eine der zentralen Gründe für die zunehmende Bereitschaft, anstehende Infrastrukturprojekte im Rahmen von PPP-Lösungen zu realisieren, sind die **stetig wachsenden Haushalts- und Liquiditätsengpässe auf Bundes-, Landes- und Kommunenebene**. Diese Engpässe verzögern die Erfüllung der traditionellen Aufgaben der öffentlichen Hand oder machen diese in manchen Fällen sogar unmöglich. Viele Städte und Gemeinden können unter den gegebenen Anforderungen ihren Budgethaushalt nicht mehr ausgeglichen halten und verfügen nicht über die notwenigen Mittel, um die Investitionen aus eigener Kraft tätigen zu können.

Im Ergebnis machen diese eben dargestellten Herausforderungen das Dilemma aus Sicht der öffentlichen Hand augenscheinlich, da ein wachsender Investitionsbedarf einer sich ständig verschärfenden budgetären Knappheit und Restriktionen gegenübersteht. Durch die längerfristige Betrachtungsperspektive und die stärkere Einbindung eines privaten Partners stellen PPPs ein Mittel dar, um diesem Dilemma zu begegnen, wobei die im Folgenden dargestellten Chancen und Risiken durch eine solche Beschaffungsmethode ausgelöst werden können.

2.2 Chancen aus PPP-Lösungen für die öffentliche Hand

2.2.1 Kostenoptimierung durch Lebenszyklusbetrachtung

Der Lebenszyklus einer Investition beschreibt die Entwicklungsphasen, die ein Objekt bzw. auch ein Projekt im Rahmen seiner **wirtschaftlichen Nutzungsdauer** durchläuft. Die einfachste Unterteilung des Lebenszyklus ist dabei die Gliederung in zwei Phasen:

- Herstellphase und
- Nutzungsphase.

Im Detail stellen sich die einzelnen Phasen des Lebenszyklus einer Investition wie folgt dar:

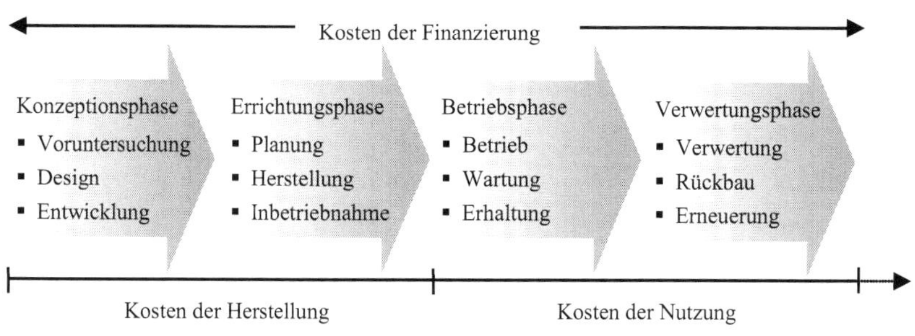

Abb. 2: Phasen im Lebenszyklus einer Investition
Quelle: eigene Darstellung.

Wie aus obiger Abbildung erkennbar, sind für die ganzheitliche betriebswirtschaftliche Einschätzung einer Investition nicht nur die Kosten der Herstellphase relevant, sondern in gleichem Maße auch jene der Nutzungsphase von Bedeutung.

Die **Kosten der Herstellphase** sind zumeist recht gut erfassbar und beinhalten sämtliche Kosten der Planung, Entwicklung und Errichtung der jeweiligen Investition. Die Kosten der Inbetriebnahme (Installation, Übergabe und abschließende Übergabeprüfungen) sind insbesondere bei Infrastrukturprojekten nicht zu vernachlässigen und bilden den Abschluss der Herstellphase der Infrastrukturinvestition. Sie werden daher zumeist der Herstellphase zugerechnet.

Demgegenüber ist die Ermittlung der **Kosten der Nutzungsphase** – auch wenn diese über die Nutzungsphase hinweg häufig ein signifikantes Ausmaß annehmen können – oft nur sehr schwierig möglich. Häufig werden daher diesbezüglich durch Schätzungen ermittelte Näherungswerte herangezogen. Zusätzlich ist die Abgrenzung und Zuordnung der anfallenden Kosten problematischer, da häufig nicht eindeutig. Die relevanten Kostenbestandteile müssen daher genau definiert und abgegrenzt werden. Dabei müssen, wenn möglich und nötig, auch Kosten der Verwertungsphase (bspw. die Kosten einer Stilllegung) als Kostenanteil in Betracht gezogen werden.

Insgesamt werden in den frühen Phasen des Lebenszyklus die Gesamtzykluskosten bereits wesentlich beeinflusst. Nach Abschluss der Konzeptionsphase sind allgemeinen Untersuchungen zufolge bereits bis zu 70 % der Gesamtlebenszykluskosten determiniert. So wird auch die Zuverlässigkeit und Instandhaltung maßgeblich in den Phasen der Projektierung und Bereitstellung beeinflusst. Die Wechselwirkungen zwischen den Anfangs- und Folgekosten sind bei den Betrachtungen der Life-Cycle-Kosten von wesentlicher Bedeutung. Der Zusammenhang wird in nachstehender Abbildung veranschaulicht.

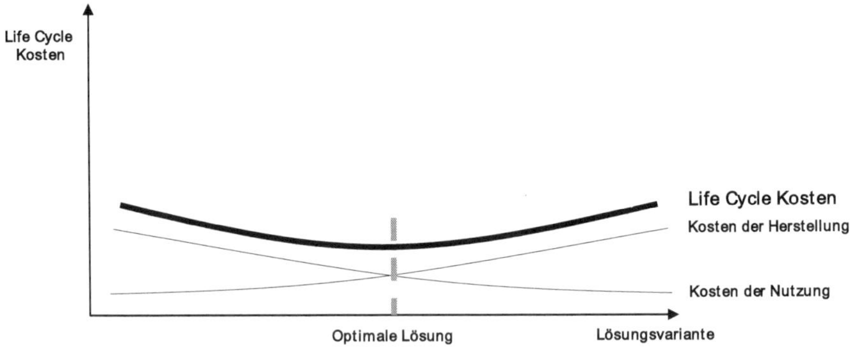

Abb. 3: Kostenoptimum im Lebenszyklus
Quelle: eigene Darstellung.

Die effektivste bzw. optimale Lösung – der **Break-Even-Punkt** – ist dabei der Schnittpunkt des Verlaufs der Herstellungs- und Nutzungskosten bei unterschiedlichen Realisierungsvarianten und gibt jenen Punkt an, ab dem eine Variante kostengünstiger wird als andere.

Es folgt daher, dass durch die Berücksichtigung auch der späteren Nutzungskosten bereits in der Planungsphase das **wirtschaftlichste Verhältnis zwischen Errichtungs- und Nutzungskosten** gefunden werden kann. Ein besonderes Interesse daran, diese wirtschaftlichste Lösung zu finden, hat derjenige, der die Gesamtkosten und -risiken einer solchen Investition zu tragen hat. Insofern stellt der **Lebenszyklus-Ansatz** ein probates Instrument dar, um bereits in einer Frühphase des Projekts dessen Effizienz zu steuern.

Dies kann insbesondere bei Investitionen im Infrastrukturbereich eine zentrale Rolle spielen, da häufig die Kosten der Nutzungsphase einen wesentlichen Anteil der Lebenszykluskosten insgesamt ausmachen.

Durch PPP-Modelle wird erreicht, dass der **Betrachtungshorizont für einzelne Projekte bereits vor deren Realisierung auf deren gesamten Lebenszyklus ausgedehnt** und somit ein **phasenübergreifendes Kostenbewusstsein** erzielt wird, um die effizienteste Lösung hinsichtlich der gesamten Lebenszykluskosten zu finden. Es werden dabei die Phasen von Planung & Design, Finanzierung, Errichtung, Betrieb, Erhaltung & Erneuerung und der Liquidation über einen bestimmten Zeitraum in Betracht gezogen. Da ein und derselbe Betrachter – der private Partner – nun auch für das Projekt während all dieser Phasen verantwortlich ist, wird auch eine phasenübergreifende Analyse der Kosten erreicht. Durch die Integration auch von Erhaltungs- und Betriebskosten entsteht bereits in der Planungsphase eine hohe Kostentransparenz und es werden verschiedenste Alternativen möglich, damit umzugehen. So können etwa auch höhere Errichtungskosten gerechtfertigt sein, wenn diese die Aufwendungen im Rahmen der Erhaltung über den Lebenszyklus des Projekts hinweg erheblich reduzieren zu können.
In der traditionellen Beschaffung werden durch die Dominanz der Betrachtung der Investitionskosten bei diesen häufig Kürzungen angestellt, was vielfach zu erheblichen Mehraufwendungen in Erhaltung und Betrieb des Projekts führen und so die Lebenszykluskosten insgesamt erhöhen kann.

2.2.2 Effizienzen durch eine funktionale Leistungsbeschreibung

Die Beschaffung von Projekten im Rahmen einer PPP-Lösung geht mit einer grundsätzlich **geänderten Herangehensweise** der öffentlichen Hand **hinsichtlich der Beschreibung der zu erbringenden Leistung** im Vergleich zu einer traditionellen Beschaffung einher, um die möglichen Vorteile und Potentiale dieser Beschaffungsvariante optimal nutzen zu können.

In diesem Zusammenhang sollte der Fokus der öffentlichen Hand verstärkt auf dem Ergebnis der Leistung, die sie zu beschaffen gedenkt, d.h. auf ihrem **Output**, liegen. Dies stellt natürlich auch geänderte Anforderungen an die der Beschaffung zugrunde liegende Leistungsbeschreibung, die ihren Schwerpunkt nicht so sehr auf die Detailplanung bzw. die benötigten Einzelleistungen (Input) legen darf, sondern eben das **erwartete Beschaffungs(end)ergebnis in den Vordergrund stellen** sollte. Das inkludiert etwa die Definition der Ziele der Beschaffung oder die Anforderungen an die Qualität und den Umfang der Leistungserbringung. Dabei sollten auch geeignete Messgrößen zu deren Nachweis aufgenommen werden.
Basis dafür ist eine **funktionale, ergebnisbezogene („outputorientierte") Leistungsbeschreibung**, die dem privaten Partner die nötige Flexibilität für Innovation und unternehmerische Entscheidungen darüber offen lässt, wie er das von der öffentlichen Hand erwartete Ergebnis am effizientesten und effektivsten – und damit für die öffentliche Hand am kostengünstigsten – realisieren kann. Durch den Fokus vorrangig auf die funktionalen Anforderungen des zu beschaffenden Projekts wird dem Privaten die Möglichkeit eröffnet, optimale Lösungsansätze über den gesamten Lebenszyklus des Projekts hinweg zu suchen.

Im Ergebnis stellen sich häufig geringere Kosten für Bau, Betrieb und Erhaltung durch die aus der funktionalen Ausschreibung mögliche Flexibilität und die ganzheitliche Übertragung des Projektes an den Privaten dar (**Effizienzgewinn**).

Internationale Studien Erzielung möglicher Effizienzgewinne

„Internationale Vergleichsstudien zur Einschätzung der Vorteilhaftigkeit von PPP-Lösungen zeigen, dass

- etwa 80% der untersuchten PPP-Projekte im vorgegebenen Zeitrahmen oder früher fertig gestellt wurden, jedoch nur etwa 30% im Fall einer herkömmlichen Beschaffung
- die untersuchten PPP-Projekte Kosteneinsparungen im Vergleich zu einer herkömmlichen Beschaffung zwischen 9% und 20% erzielen konnten.“ [3]

Das bedeutet jedoch nicht, dass lediglich nur grobe oder ungefähre Angaben hinsichtlich der Anforderungen der bereitzustellenden Leistung notwendig sind. Ganz im Gegenteil – insbesondere weil diese Anforderungen auch für eine längerfristige vertragliche Bindung gelten sollen – stellt eine outputorientierte Leistungsbeschreibung eine erhebliche Herausforderung an die öffentliche Hand dar. Sie determiniert in einer Frühphase, ob das erwartete Beschaffungsergebnis über die folgende vertragliche Laufzeit auch tatsächlich entsprechend der Erwartungen realisiert werden kann. So ist es etwa von zentraler Bedeutung, die wesentlichen Aufgabenbereiche des künftigen privaten Partners und insbesondere die Behandlung und Regelung von etwaigen Schnittstellen zum Auftraggeber für einen längerfristigen Zeitraum zu erfassen und festzulegen.

Beispielhafte Aufgabenabgrenzung im Krankenhausbereich

Wie die folgende Abbildung schematisch für ein Krankenhaus zeigt, verbleiben dabei die eigentlichen Kernleistungen im Zusammenhang mir der zu beschaffenden Infrastruktur jedoch häufig bei der öffentlichen Hand.

[3] Partnerships UK (2008).

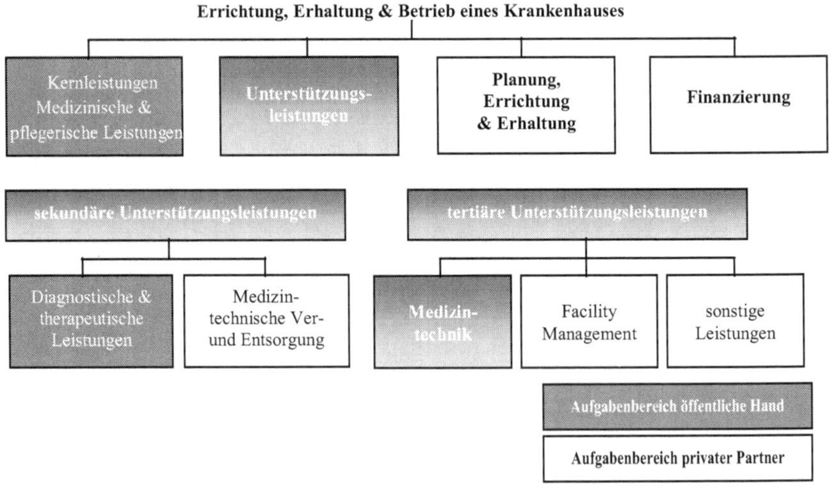

Abb. 4: Beispielhafte Aufgabenabgrenzung für ein Krankenhaus
Quelle: in Anlehnung an Book, R. (2006).

Notwendig ist dafür jedenfalls bereits zu Beginn des jeweiligen Projekts – schon auch aufgrund des Gleichbehandlungs- und Transparenzgebotes – eine **klare Definition**, was denn überhaupt die Erwartung der öffentlichen Hand hinsichtlich **der zu beschaffenden Leistung** ist.

Dabei gilt es aus Sicht der öffentlichen Hand jedoch genau abzuwiegen, welches Leistungsniveau über die vertragliche Laufzeit gewünscht wird und welches auch tatsächlich notwendig ist. Sämtliche zu erbringende Leistungen werden vom Privaten im Rahmen seiner Kalkulation berücksichtigt und können damit Projekte auch – bei etwaigen Mehrleistungen im Vergleich zu den ursprünglichen Planungen – signifikant verteuern.

Eine sorgfältige Formulierung der Anforderungen bereits zu Projektbeginn kann zudem das Risiko von später notwendig werdenden Leistungsänderungen, welche häufig mit erheblichen Zusatzkosten für die öffentliche Hand verbunden sind, mindern. Dadurch wird der öffentliche Auftraggeber von Beginn an dazu angehalten, sich bewusst zu werden, welche Leistungen er erwartet und vor allem auch, welche nicht.

2.2.3 Optimale Risikoverteilung

Die Optimierung der Risikoallokation liefert einen wesentlichen Anteil zu einer eventuellen Vorteilhaftigkeit einer Projektumsetzung als PPP-Lösung aus Sicht der öffentlichen Hand. Dabei werden die mit einem Projekt in Zusammenhang stehenden Risiken im Wesentlichen identifiziert, bewertet und verteilt.

Unter **Risiko** versteht man dabei zumeist die **Möglichkeit einer negativen Zielabweichung**. Ziel des Risikomanagements ist es, Risiken durch geeignete Maßnahmen zu begegnen, um eine Durchführung eines Projekts unter entsprechenden Rahmenbedingungen und mit entsprechendem Nutzen zu gewährleisten. Dazu sind eine Bewertung, Planung/Steuerung sowie Überwachung/Kontrolle der Risiken notwendig, um Gefahren frühzeitig zu erkennen und durch Gegenmaßnahmen abwenden zu können.

Risiken können normalerweise einzelnen Projektphasen zugeordnet werden. Dabei kann eine Aufteilung in **Projekt- und Prozessrisiken** vorgenommen werden. Prozessrisiken sind die weniger augenscheinlichen und oft schwer zu identifizierenden Risiken, können jedoch nichtsdestotrotz erhebliche Auswirkungen haben. Es erfordert ein professionelles Projektmanagement, um ihre Wirkung möglichst weit abzumildern und eine dem Projekt und der Beschaffungsweise (PPP, konventionell, ...) angemessene Risikoverteilung zu erreichen.

Der Tätigkeitsbereich des Risikomanagements für ein Projekt umfasst eine **permanente Evaluierung und Aktualisierung der Risikoeinschätzung über die gesamte weitere Laufzeit des Projekts**. Für eine systematische Abwicklung sind dabei die folgenden Schritte notwendig.

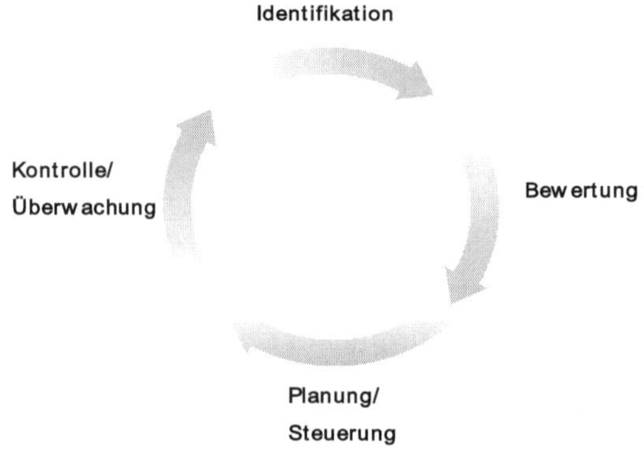

Abb. 5: Phasen im Risikomanagement
Quelle: eigene Darstellung.

1. Risikoidentifikation

Die Risikoidentifikation beinhaltet die Auflistung der möglichen Risiken. Dies wird häufig aufgrund offensichtlicher Sachverhalte sowie durch Erfahrung, Marktkenntnis, Fachwissen und bestehende Referenzprojekte erfolgen. Da davon auszugehen ist, dass bestimmte Risiken in den verschiedenen Projektphasen unterschiedliche Relevanz aufweisen, ist gleichzeitig eine **Zuordnung der Risiken zu den einzelnen Projektphasen** durchzuführen.

2. Risikobewertung

Unter Risikobewertung versteht man die Analyse der einzelnen Risiken im Hinblick auf die **Wahrscheinlichkeit ihres Eintretens**, die **potentielle Auswirkung** (Schadenshöhe) und die **Zeitspanne**, in der die Risiken auftreten können.

3. Risikoplanung/Risikosteuerung

Dabei werden Gegenstrategien entwickelt, welche das Risiko begrenzen sollen.

Grundsätzlich kann man Risiken folgendermaßen behandeln:

- Vermeiden – Verzicht auf risikobehaftete Geschäfte
- Begrenzen – Senken der Eintrittswahrscheinlichkeit oder Schadenshöhe
- Transferieren – auf privaten Partner oder Versicherungen
- Kompensieren – durch Gegengeschäfte (Hedging, Netting)
- Tragen – bewusstes „in Kauf nehmen".

Daraus ergibt sich auch die Zuordnung (**Allokation**) des Risikos, also auf wessen Vermögens- und Wohlfahrtsposition sich das Risiko auswirken soll. Zumeist stellt sich in diesem Zusammenhang die Frage, ob ein Risiko bei der öffentlichen Hand verbleiben oder doch auf den privaten Partner transferiert werden soll, da dieser das Risiko effizienter handhaben kann.

4. Risikokontrolle/Risikoüberwachung

Bei einer effektiven Risikokontrolle werden die **Risiken während des Projektverlaufs** überwacht und neben den reinen Datenvergleichen (Soll–Ist) sowohl eine Ursachenbestimmung als auch eine Maßnahmenerarbeitung bei Fehlläufen durchgeführt.

Bei einer solchen Risikoverteilung sind insbesondere jene Risiken von Bedeutung, die bei klassischer Beschaffung von der öffentlichen Hand getragen werden, im Rahmen eines PPP-Modells jedoch auf den privaten Partner übertragen werden können (transferierte Risiken). In diesem Zusammenhang sollte auch erwähnt werden, dass ein maximaler Risikotransfer nicht zwangsläufig ein Optimum aus Sicht der öffentlichen Hand darstellen muss, sondern viel eher eine **ausgewogene Allokation der Risiken**. Als grundlegende Maxime des Risikotransfers sollte dabei gelten, dass **derjenige Vertragspartner das Risiko tragen soll, der am besten damit umgehen bzw. es am besten beeinflussen kann**. Im Idealfall sollte somit soll ein Optimum der Risikoverteilung zwischen öffentlicher Hand und privatem Partner erreicht werden.

Gewisse Risiken, die vom privaten Partner nur schwer beherrscht werden können, verbleiben dabei zumeist bei der öffentlichen Hand. Dazu zählen etwa das Genehmigungsrisiko oder das Risiko von gesetzlichen Änderungen. Eine Übertragung solcher Risiken könnte häufig – durch die vom Privaten angesetzten Risikoprämien – nicht zu einem optimalen Gesamtergebnis für alle beteiligten Parteien führen.

2.2.4 Hohe Qualität durch anreizorientierte Vergütungssysteme

Die Wahl eines adäquaten Vergütungsmodells stellt eine weitere Möglichkeit für die öffentliche Hand dar, Vorteile aus PPP-Lösungen zu generieren. Dabei sollte ein adäquates Vergütungsmodell folgende Anforderungen erfüllen:

- Übertragung eines angemessenen Risikos an den Privaten
- Finanzierbarkeit über den Kapitalmarkt
- Vertragliche Umsetzbarkeit und überschaubare Komplexität
- Anreizwirkung zur Sicherstellung einer optimalen Verfügbarkeit und eines Qualitätsniveaus.

Im Wesentlichen unterscheidet man für PPP-Lösungen im Infrastrukturbereich zwei unterschiedliche Grundtypen von Vergütungsmodellen:

- nutzungsabhängige Vergütungsmechanismen
- leistungsabhängige Vergütungsmechanismen.

Bei **nutzungsabhängigen Vergütungssystemen** wird auf die Häufigkeit der Nutzung der Infrastruktur durch die Endkunden abgestellt. Dabei wird das Entgelt erhöht, je mehr Nutzer die jeweilige Leistung bzw. das jeweilige Objekt in Anspruch nehmen. Dies schafft für den Privaten einen direkten Anreiz, eine für den Nutzer möglichst attraktive Infrastruktur bereit zu stellen, da sich auch seine Vergütung direkt daran bemisst.

Bei einem **leistungsabhängigen Vergütungsmechanismus** erhält der Private ein Entgelt abhängig von der Verfügbarkeit bzw. vom Zustand der jeweiligen Infrastruktur in einer vorgegebenen Qualität und abhängig von der fristgerechten Erbringung der gewünschten Leistungen. Damit werden die Zahlungen für die erbrachte Leistung vom Nachweis messbarer Vorgaben abhängig gemacht. Dies schafft etwa Anreize,

- den Bau in der vorgegebenen Frist bereits in Hinblick auf zukünftige Instandhaltungserfordernisse so effizient als möglich zu planen und umzusetzen,
- das Instandsetzungs- und Instandhaltungsprogramm sowie den Betrieb auch zeitlich so effizient als möglich zu planen und umzusetzen, um maximale Verfügbarkeit der Infrastruktur für den Nutzer und damit Vergütung für seine Leistungen zu lukrieren, sowie auch
- insgesamt zur Gewährleistung des gewünschten Qualitätsniveaus über die Projektlaufzeit.

2.2.5 Preiskampf durch Wettbewerb

Ein optimales Preis-Leistungsverhältnis ist eher realisierbar, wenn ein effektiver Wettbewerb generiert werden kann. Diese Erzeugung von Wettbewerb kann sich auf zwei Ebenen manifestieren.

Zum einen entsteht **Wettbewerb zwischen den privaten Anbietern** um das Projekt selbst. Da es sich bei Infrastrukturprojekten – noch dazu bei Betrachtung über ihren Lebenszyklus – häufig um signifikante Volumina handelt, wird die Anreizwirkung zur Teilnahme an solchen öffentlichen Ausschreibungs- bzw. Beschaffungsprozessen zusätzlich erhöht.

Zum anderen entsteht implizit auch ein Wettbewerbsdruck auf der Ebene der Subunternehmer, der durch die Komplettvergabe des Projektes – und nicht die Vergabe von Einzelgewerken wie bei einer traditionellen Beschaffung – über den gesamten Lebenszyklus an das private Konsortium erzeugt wird. Da die Vergabe der Einzelgewerke bei PPP-Modellen an den Privaten weitergereicht wird, der **als Generalunternehmer auftritt und mit den diversen Subunternehmen und Lieferanten über Preise verhandeln** wird, kann der dadurch generierte Wettbewerb auch zusätzlich preisliche Vorteile bringen, die idealerweise an die öffentliche Hand im Wettbewerb um das Gesamtprojekt selbst weitergegeben werden.

Zentral ist es daher, einen ausreichend großen Interessentenkreis für ein bestimmtes Projekt zu gewinnen, um die aus einer solchen Wettbewerbssituation entstehenden Vorteile für die öffentliche Hand nutzen zu können.

2.3 Risiken bei PPP-Lösungen für die öffentliche Hand

Im Folgenden werden kritische Faktoren bzw. Risiken bei der Realisierung von PPP-Lösungen aus Sicht der öffentlichen Hand aufgezeigt und erläutert. Auch diese Faktoren haben einen wesentlichen Einfluss auf die effiziente Umsetzung von Projekten dieser Art sowie auf dabei erzielbare Wirtschaftlichkeitsvorteile.

2.3.1 Auswahl und Strukturierung von Projekten

Wie bereits einleitend erwähnt, stellen PPP-Lösungen nur eine mögliche Form der Beschaffung für die öffentliche Hand dar, die auch nur dann zum Einsatz kommen sollen, wenn sich eine **öffentlich-private Partnerschaft für diese bestimmte Aufgabenerfüllung** als **zweckmäßig** erweist.

Einzelne Aufgaben oder Anforderungen werden von der öffentlichen Hand effizienter bewältigt werden können. Werden solche Aufgaben dennoch auf einen privaten Partner übertragen, können diese eventuell nur unter einem Mehraufwand bewältigt werden, der über den Angebotspreis dann wieder an die öffentliche Hand weitergegeben wird. Insbesondere die mit dem Projekt verbundenen Risiken sind dabei dahingehend genau zu analysieren, ob diese tatsächlich vom Privaten effizienter gehandhabt werden können.

Zudem kann auch bereits die Strukturierung von Projekten wesentliche Risiken – beispielsweise hinsichtlich unzureichender vertraglicher Regelungen oder einer ineffizienten Ausgestaltung kommerziell relevanter Bestandteile – mit sich bringen. In diesem Zusammenhang können etwa ineffiziente Anreiz- bzw. Sanktionsmechanismen oder eine übermäßige vertragliche Komplexität genannt werden.

2.3.2 Transaktionskosten

Allein durch ihre Größenordnung, durch die Anzahl der involvierten Parteien sowie durch den damit verbundenen Leistungsumfang weisen **PPP-Projekte häufig einen hohen Komplexitätsgrad** auf. Dieser betrifft

- die Vorbereitung und Strukturierung des Projekts,
- die Erstellung der notwendigen Dokumentation,
- die Auswahl des privaten Partners sowie auch
- die spätere Abwicklung der öffentlich-privaten Partnerschaft.

Dieser Grad an Komplexität wird noch zusätzlich erhöht, wenn es sich dabei aus Sicht der öffentlichen Hand um eine neuartige Konstruktion (Pilotprojekt) handelt.

Aus diesem Grund sind mit der Entwicklung und Umsetzung von PPP-Projekten – vor allem, wenn es sich um solche Pilotprojekte handelt – erhöhte Trans-aktionskosten verbunden, die sich aus

- internen Kosten sowie
- externen Kosten

zusammensetzen.

Diese Kosten entstehen nicht nur bei der öffentlichen Hand sondern auch beim privaten Partner.

Die **internen Kosten** entstehen bei der öffentlichen Hand selbst, da zumeist auch eigene Spezialisten – zumindest zeitweise – für die Realisierung und spätere Betreuung von Projekten dieser Art abgestellt werden. Diese begleiten sowohl die Vorbereitung des Projekts als auch die Auswahl des privaten Partners. Zudem ist auch die Begleitung der Partnerschaft über die vertraglich vorgesehene Laufzeit notwendig, was zu einer langfristigen Bindung von Ressourcen führt.

Die **externen Kosten** werden zumeist durch Beratungsbedarf verursacht, der insbesondere durch die Unterstützung von Spezialisten in vergaberechtlichen, vertragsrechtlichen und finanztechnischen Fragen notwendig wird.

In Zusammenhang mit den Transaktionskosten sind zudem die **vertraglich bedingten möglichen Mehrkosten** zu erwähnen, die sich aufgrund der Charakteristik einer langfristigen vertraglichen Partnerschaft ergeben. Dabei sind zum einen **nachträgliche Änderungen oder Ergänzungen des** ursprünglich gewünschten **Leistungsumfangs** oder auch notwendige Anpassungen aufgrund von geänderten gesetzlichen Rahmenbedingungen zu nennen. Wegen der langfristigen Kalkulation des privaten Partners über den Lebenszyklus des Projekts können solche ungeplanten nachträglichen Änderungen erhebliche Konsequenzen auf die anfänglich geplanten Erhaltungs- und Betriebsaufwendungen haben. Diese nicht vorhersehbaren Änderungen sind dann zumeist auch von der öffentlichen Hand zu tragen.
Zum anderen kann auch die **außerordentliche Vertragsbeendigung** erhebliche Austrittskosten verursachen und damit sogar eine gewisse Austrittsbarriere für die öffentliche Hand darstellen. Daher ist insbesondere auch auf die vertragliche Regelung der Kündigungsfälle und die damit verbundenen Kompensationszahlungen Bedacht zu nehmen.

Wie bereits angemerkt, entstehen diese **Transaktionskosten in noch höherem Ausmaß bei der Realisierung von Pilotprojekten**. Sofern durch wiederholt durchgeführte Transaktionen von vergleichbarer Art Standards in verschiedenen Bereichen – wie beispielsweise durch Vertragsstandardisierung oder verbessertes Ausschreibungsmanagement – etabliert werden können, kann dies die Transaktionskosten signifikant reduzieren.

2.3.3 Rahmenbedingungen

Vor dem Hintergrund des speziellen Anforderungsprofils einer effizienten Umsetzung von PPP-Lösungen wird in vielen Bereichen auch eine entsprechende **Adaptierung der Rahmenbedingungen notwendig**. Dies wird nicht nötig, um PPP-Lösungen überhaupt erst zu ermöglichen, sondern insbesondere deshalb, um aus Sicht der öffentlichen Hand **potentiell realisierbare Wirtschaftlichkeitsvorteile möglichst optimal generieren** zu können. In diesem Zusammenhang können beispielsweise rechtliche, steuerliche oder fördertechnische Rahmenbedingungen eine Hemmschwelle darstellen.

Hinsichtlich der **rechtlichen Rahmenbedingungen** können dabei exemplarisch die Vorgaben bzw. Regelungen im Rahmen des Vergaberechts, dem auch die Vergabe von PPP-Projekten unterliegt, angeführt werden. Dabei kann die Wahl der Verfahrensart schon durch die ausgeschriebene Leistung eingeschränkt oder determiniert werden, weshalb eventuell ein nicht optimales Verfahren zur Vergabe gewählt werden muss. Zudem stellt auch die schon zu Verfahrensbeginn notwendige Festlegung des Bewertungsschemas für erst im Verfahren präsentierte Lösungen oft eine erhebliche Herausforderung dar.

Einen weiteren Bereich betrifft die **Nutzung** von möglichen nationalen oder internationalen **Förderprogrammen**, die häufig explizit zur Forcierung von Infrastrukturprojekten zur Verfügung stehen sollen. Dabei besteht oft die Schwierigkeit, dass diese Programme mit den Charakteristika von PPP-Lösungen – etwa einem damit verbundenen langfristig wirkenden Vergütungsmechanismus – nicht abgestimmt sind, um diese auch tatsächlich bei der Umsetzung solcher Projekte nutzen zu können. So sind beispielsweise Programme, bei denen Mittel nur für einen beschränkten – meist mittelfristigen – Zeitraum zur Verfügung stehen, häufig mit Zahlungsmechanismen bei PPP-Projekten, bei welchen die Zahlungen der öffentlichen Hand über einen Zeitraum von 25 oder 30 Jahren erfolgen, nicht kompatibel.

Die explizite Berücksichtigung von spezifischen, sich aufgrund der besonderen Charakteristik von PPP-Projekten ergebenden Anforderungen bei der Strukturierung der für die Umsetzung von solchen Projekten relevanten Rahmen- und Umfeldbedingungen können daher einen wesentlichen Beitrag leisten, um eventuelle Wirtschaftlichkeitspotentiale aus Sicht der öffentlichen Hand zu optimieren.

2.3.4 Langfristige Partnerschaft

Partnerschaften, insbesondere wenn sie mit einer eher langfristigen Perspektive eingegangen werden, sind nur von Erfolg gekennzeichnet, wenn ein **faires und transparentes Agieren aller Beteiligten** stattfindet. Ein solches Verhalten und Agieren ist insbesondere dann von Bedeutung, wenn sich aufgrund der langfristig zu regelnden komplexen Sachverhalte nicht alle vertraglichen Details im gesamten Verlauf absehen und damit im Voraus abschließend regeln oder vereinbaren lassen. Damit würde eventuell sogar eine vertragliche Flexibilität eingeschränkt werden, die später ein effizienteres Handeln erlaubt.

Damit werden sowohl die Wahl des privaten Partners als auch die Einstellung der öffentlichen Hand zu einer solchen Partnerschaft zu einem Schlüssel für den Erfolg.

Die **Wahl des privaten Partners** ist vor allem daher relevant, weil eine vorzeitige Beendigung der Partnerschaft zu erheblichen zusätzlichen Kosten führen kann. Dies betrifft zum einen die bei der öffentlichen Hand entstehenden internen Kosten, die bei einer nicht funktionierenden Partnerschaft in den meisten Fällen steigen werden, da häufig ein gesteigerter Monitoring- und Abstimmungsbedarf gegeben ist, als auch die mit der eigentlichen Beendigung der vertraglichen Partnerschaft (Kündigung) direkt entstehenden externen Kosten. Daher sollte die Auswahl des privaten Partners etwa durch die **Einholung von Informationen** bereits im Vorfeld unterstützt werden. Dabei kann beispielsweise erhoben werden, ob ein potentieller Partner bereits andere vergleichbare Projekte erfolgreich umgesetzt hat oder ob bereits ein mehrfaches Scheitern in solchen Partnerschaften zu beobachten ist. Zudem sind auch die Relevanz und vor allem die **Durchsetzbarkeit der vertraglich festgelegten Leistungs- und Qualitätskriterien** von Bedeutung, um gegebenenfalls ausreichend Sanktionsmechanismen aus Sicht der öffentlichen Hand zur Verfügung zu haben.

Daneben ist aber auch die **Einstellung der öffentlichen Hand** für das erfolg-reiche Funktionieren der Partnerschaft von Bedeutung. Möglichkeit und Intensität der Einflussnahme der öffentlichen Hand in den einzelnen Phasen des Projekts werden durch den vertraglich festgelegten Rahmen determiniert. Dabei kann eine extensive Festlegung und auch spätere Nutzung dieser Möglichkeiten ein effizientes Agieren des privaten Partners und so die notwenige Flexibilität der Partnerschaft einschränken.

Zentral für die erfolgreiche Umsetzung solcher Partnerschafts-Konzepte ist die Einschätzung von allen beteiligten Parteien – der öffentlichen Hand, der privaten Unternehmungen und auch der Steuerzahler – im Rahmen der Umsetzung eines solchen Projekts, dass jeder Partei mehr Vor- als Nachteile durch die erfolgreiche partnerschaftliche Zusammenarbeit entstehen, d.h. sich im Endeffekt eine sogenannte „Win-Win“-Situation darstellt. Dies wird auch ein langfristiges Funktionieren einer derartigen Partnerschaft fördern.

3 Conclusio

Zusammenfassend lässt sich festhalten, dass das Konzept von öffentlich-privaten Partnerschaften darauf abzielt, aus der gemeinsamen Umsetzung von Projekten Vorteile für alle beteiligten Parteien zu realisieren. Dies soll insbesondere durch eine dauerhafte und langfristige vertragliche Beziehung erreicht werden, welche eine Kostenoptimierung der Projekte durch die Betrachtung über ihren Lebenszyklus sowie auch Effizienzgewinne durch zugelassene Flexibilität und Innovation gegenüber der herkömmlichen Realisierung von Projekten möglich macht.

Diese Ziele können aus Sicht der öffentlichen Hand umso besser und effizienter erreicht werden, wenn die möglichen Vorteile von solchen Konzepten bewusst direkt forciert oder indirekt die notwendigen Rahmenbedingungen geschaffen werden, damit diese Vorteile bestmöglich zur Geltung kommen können.

Daher gilt es, insbesondere eine Lebenszyklusbetrachtung zu fördern, die Leistungsbeschreibung entsprechend funktional zu gestalten, die Risiken angemessen zu verteilen, Anreizsysteme zur Sicherstellung einer konstant hohen Qualität der Leistungserbringung zu schaffen sowie ausreichend Wettbewerb zu generieren, um die Potentiale von PPP-Lösungen für die öffentliche Hand optimal nutzen zu können.

Literaturverzeichnis

Alfen, H. W. et al. (2005): Public Private Partnership im Krankenhausbereich. In: Das Krankenhaus, S. 1083-1088.

Berner, F./Lohmann, T. (2006): Stand Öffentlich Privater Partnerschaftsprojekte – PPP in Deutschland. In: Immobilien-Jahresbericht 2006 der Bündelungsinitiative in der Deutschen Immobilienwirtschaft e. V., S. 181-196.

Bolz, U./Ehrensperger, M./Oetterli, J. (2005): Teil 1: Grundlagen. In: Bolz, U. (Hrsg.): Public Private Partnerships in der Schweiz. Zürich.

Böning, M. (1997): Einsatzmöglichkeiten eines lebenszyklusorientierten Controlling von Produktionsanlagen. Dissertation. München: VVF.

Book, R. (2006): Public Private Partnership – neue Kooperationsmodelle (auch) für kommunale Stiftungen. Herbsttagung AK Kommunale Stiftungen. 9.10.2006.

Brandes, K. (2003): Life-Cycle-Cost Analysis and Design of Civil Infrastructure Systems. In: Stahlbau 72, Heft 7, S. 534 ff. Berlin.

Europäische Kommission (Hrsg.) (2001): Weißbuch: Die europäische Verkehrspolitik bis 2010 – Weichenstellungen für die Zukunft.

Europäische Kommission (Hrsg.) (2003): Hochrangige Gruppe für das Transeuropäische Verkehrsnetz (Leitung: Karel van Miert). Bericht, 27. Juni 2003.

Europäische Kommission (2004): Grünbuch zu öffentlich-privaten Partnerschaften und den gemeinschaftlichen Rechtsvorschriften für öffentliche Aufträge und Konzessionen. Frankfurt am Main.

Europäische Kommission (2006): Nachhaltige Mobilität für unseren Kontinent, Halbzeitbilanz zum Verkehrsweißbuch der Europäischen Kommission von 2001. Luxemburg.

Fitzgerald, P. (2004): Review of Partnerships Victoria Provided Infrastructure: Final Report. Melbourne.

Flyvbjerg, B./Glenting, C./Ronnest, K. A. (2004): Procedures for Dealing with Optimism Bias. In: Transport Planning: Guidance Document, Studie im Auftrag des britischen Verkehrsministeriums (Department for Transport).

Gray, M. (2004): Discounted Cash Flow (DCF). International Benchmark: Australian Public Private Partnership Models. In: Mittendorfer F./S. Weber (Hrsg.): Public Private Partnership Gestaltung aus ökonomischer und juristischer Sicht. Wien.

Harth, C. (2005): Umsetzungsmöglichkeiten von öffentlich-privaten Partnerschaften („Public Private Partnership – PPP“) dargestellt an Bau- und Bewirtschaftungsprojekten. Mainz.

Mott MacDonald (2002): Review of Large Public Procurement in the UK.

Partnerships UK (2008): http://www.partnershipsuk.org.uk/.

The National Audit Office (2008): http://www.nao.org.uk/.

Van Ewijk/Tang, P. (2003): How to price the risk of the public investment? In: De Economist, Vol. 151, No. 3.

Wildemann, H. (1982): Kostenprognosen bei Großprojekten. Stuttgart: C. E. Poeschel Verlag.

Bedeutung von PPP für ein modernes Infrastrukturmanagement im öffentlichen Sektor

Dieter Jacob & Nadine Schröter

Inhaltsverzeichnis

1 Einführung

Der öffentliche Sektor verfolgt mit einem modernen Infrastrukturmanagement Effizienzziele wie die Kostenoptimierung der Erbringung staatlicher Leistungen, die Erschließung von Managementpotenzialen und privatem Know-how, die Verschiebung operativer Verantwortlichkeiten und sogar die Schaffung von neuen Märkten, um bisher ausschließlich öffentliche Leistungserbringungen dem Wettbewerb zu unterstellen. Ein Instrument zur Umsetzung der formulierten Ziele stellt die alternative Beschaffungsvariante Public Private Partnership (PPP) dar. Sie findet in verschiedenen Bereichen der öffentlichen Leistungserbringung Anwendung.

Der folgende Beitrag hat die Zielsetzung, die öffentliche Infrastruktur in ihrer Breite zu umreißen und mit dem PPP-Ansatz zu verschränken. Eine mögliche Umsetzung wird exemplarisch am vermögensstärksten Sektor, der Verkehrsinfrastruktur, unter Berücksichtigung verwaltungstechnischer Randbedingungen an bestehenden Ansätzen dargestellt.

2 Begriffsbestimmung Infrastruktur [1]

In der Literatur zur Theorie der Infrastruktur ist keine allgemein anerkannte Begriffsbestimmung zu finden. Vielmehr werden zur Begriffsbestimmung Aufzählungen, die die Vielfalt des Begriffs wiederspiegeln, verwendet.

Eine umfassende Definition von Infrastruktur, welche auch in der wissenschaftlichen Literatur breite Verwendung gefunden hat, wurde von JOCHIMSEN (1966) geprägt. Infrastruktur wird hier verstanden als die „Summe der materiellen, institutionellen und personalen Einrichtungen und Gegebenheiten [...], die den Wirtschaftseinheiten zur Verfügung stehen und mit beitragen, den Ausgleich der Entgelte für gleiche Faktorbeiträge bei zweckmäßiger Allokation der

---

[1] Vgl. v. a. Blochmann, G./Jacob D./Wolf R. (2003) und Stobbe, A. (1997).

Ressourcen, d.h. vollständige Integration und höchstmögliches Niveau der Wirtschaftstätigkeit, zu ermöglichen."[2]

Infrastruktur kann demnach als Grundlagenfunktion für den arbeitsteiligen Wirtschaftsprozess angesehen werden. Dabei bildet die institutionelle Infrastruktur den Rahmen, innerhalb dessen die Wirtschaftseinheiten eigene Wirtschaftspläne formulieren und durchführen. Sie umfasst die staatliche Rechtsordnung und darüber hinaus das tatsächliche Verhalten und die Einrichtungen und Institutionen von Gruppen oder Individuen. Unter personaler Infrastruktur versteht JOCHIMSEN die Anzahl und die Fähigkeit der Menschen, die zur Erhöhung der Wirtschaftstätigkeit beitragen. Bei der materiellen Infrastruktur wird unterschieden in die Basisinfrastruktur[3], welche die Gesamtheit aller Anlagen, Ausrüstungen und Betriebsmittel zur Energieversorgung, Telekommunikation, Wasserversorgung, Verkehrsbedienung und zum Umweltschutz umfasst, und in die soziale Infrastruktur, die Gebäude und Einrichtungen des Erziehungs- und Forschungs- sowie Gesundheits- und Fürsorgewesens beinhaltet. Darüber hinaus gibt es Gebäude der staatlichen Verwaltung, Wohngebäude und Unterkünfte sowie sonstige Infrastrukturgüter. Somit umfasst die Infrastruktur die Gesamtheit aller staatlichen Einrichtungen zur Daseinsvorsorge[4] und zur wirtschaftlichen Entwicklung des Raumes.

3 Materielle Infrastrukturgüter

Die materielle Infrastruktur als bauliche Anlage im Sinne einer Investition soll Gegenstand der weiteren Betrachtungen sein. Die Gliederung der Sektoren der materiellen Infrastruktur, die zu planen, bauen, betreiben und finanzieren sind, ist

2 Jochimsen, R. (1966).
3 Vgl. Lauwe, P./Riegel, Ch. (2008).
4 Def. Daseinsvorsorge nach Forsthoff, E. (1958): „Dem Staat ist die Aufgabe und die Verantwortung zugefallen, alles das vorzukehren, was für Daseinsermöglichung des modernen Menschen ohne Lebensraum erforderlich ist. Was in der Erfüllung dieser Aufgaben notwendig ist, nenne ich Daseinsvorsorge."

nachfolgend dargelegt. Darüber hinaus wurden für die identifizierten Bereiche die vom Deutschen Institut für Urbanistik (Difu) ermittelten kommunalen Investitionsbedarfe[5] wiedergegeben. Belastbare Aussagen über notwendige Investitionen der Länder und des Bundes sind für die hier durchgeführte detaillierte Aufschlüsselung der Sektoren nicht verfügbar.

3.1 Energieversorgung und Telekommunikation

Zu den Gegenständen der Energieversorgung zählen die Stromversorgungsanlagen, Nah- und Fernwärmeversorgungsanlagen inklusive der zentralen Einrichtungen der Wärmeerzeugung und der Wärmenetze sowie die Gasversorgungsanlagen. Charakteristisch für diesen Bereich ist die Verwendung von physischen Netzen, in der Literatur auch als netzförmige[6] Infrastrukturgüter bezeichnet. Die leitungsgebundene Energieversorgung gehört dabei traditionell zu den Aufgaben der kommunalen Daseinsvorsorge, die wiederum zur öffentlichen Versorgung zählt. Im Bereich der Telekommunikation fand eine vollständige Marktöffnung und Privatisierung statt. Der Investitionsbedarf der kommunalen leistungsgebundenen Energieversorgung liegt für den Zeitraum 2006-2020 bei 60 Mrd. Euro.

3.2 Wasserversorgung und Umweltschutz

Ziel einer nachhaltigen Wasserwirtschaft ist die zweckentsprechende Bereitstellung von Wasser beispielsweise als Trinkwasser oder Brauchwasser sowie eine zielgerichtete Wasseraufbereitung.

---

5 Vgl. Reidenbach, M. et al. (2002) und Reidenbach, M. et al. (2008).

6 Im Bereich der materiellen Infrastruktur kann zwischen punktförmigen und netzförmigen Infrastrukturgütern unterschieden werden. Punktförmige Infrastrukturgüter sind Anlagen, die ihre Leistung von einem bestimmten Ort abgeben, so z.B. Klärwerke. Netzförmige Infrastruktur dagegen verbindet unterschiedliche Standorte miteinander, z.B. Straßen oder Gleise. Vgl. Funck, R./Blum, U. (1984).

Wasserversorgung

Zur Wasserversorgung zählen Anlagen zur Grundwasseranreicherung, Wasserverteilung und Löschwasserversorgung sowie Wassergewinnungs- und -aufbereitungsanlagen. Diese können sowohl den punktförmigen als auch den netzförmigen Infrastrukturgütern zugeordnet werden. Die sparsame Nutzung von Trink- und Betriebswasser und die Erhaltung und Verbesserung der Oberflächen- und Grundwasserqualität sind Ziele der Wasserversorgung, die in den Bereich der kommunalen Selbstverwaltung fällt. Zumeist wird sie von kommunalen Regiebetrieben, Eigenbetrieben oder Eigengesellschaften organisiert oder ist in größeren Städten eine Sparte der Stadtwerke. Gegenwärtig ist im Bereich der Trinkwasserversorgung eine fortschreitende Privatisierung festzustellen. Für die Trinkwasserversorgung liegt der kommunale Investitionsbedarf im Zeitraum 2006-2020 bei 29,0 Mrd. Euro.

Abwasserbeseitigung

Zur Abwasserbeseitigung zählen die Regenwasserbewirtschaftungsanlagen, Regenüberlaufbecken, Versickerungsanlagen, Kläranlagen, die Grubenentleerung und dezentrale Abwasserbeseitigungsanlagen, die der punktförmigen Infrastruktur zuzuordnen sind. Die Kanalisation hingegen stellt eine netzförmige Infrastruktur dar. Ziel der Abwasserbeseitigung ist die Erfassung und Aufbereitung der anfallenden Haushalts-, Industrie- und Gewerbeabwässer. In der Regel besteht ein Anschluss und Benutzungszwang zur Sicherung von angemessenen Abnahmedichten und zur Gewährleistung der Gewässerreinhaltung. Die Einbindung Privater in den Sektor ist bei entsprechender Vorlage von landesrechtlichen Voraussetzungen möglich. Für die Abwasserbeseitigung sind kommunale Investitionen von 58,2 Mrd. Euro im Zeitraum 2006-2020 notwendig.

Abfallwirtschaft

Anlagen zur Abfallsammlung, Deponien, Recyclinganlagen, Kompostierungsanlagen, Zwischenlager und -stationen, Sortierstationen, Thermische Verwertungsanlagen und Tierkörperbeseitigungsanlagen gehören zum Abfallwirtschaftssektor, der abermals den punktförmigen Infrastrukturgütern zuzuordnen ist. Zum Abfall zählen alle beweglichen Sachen, derer sich Besitzer/Eigentümer entledigen. Die Abfälle können entweder verwertet oder müssen beseitigt werden. Die Pflichten und die Aufgabenverteilung sind entsprechend den gesetzlichen Regelungen auf Private und die öffentliche Hand übertragen. Die Abfallbeseitigungsanlagen werden größten Teils von den Kommunen bzw. Landkreisen betrieben, wobei auch hier in den letzten Jahren vermehrt eine Ausgliederung aus dem kommunalen Haushalt stattfand. Dafür wurde vielfach die Rechtsform des Eigenbetriebs bzw. der GmbH, häufig mit Beteiligung privater Unternehmen, gewählt. Die Verwertung von Abfällen gewerblicher Abfallerzeuger erfolgt schon seit Jahren überwiegend privatwirtschaftlich. Für den Zeitraum 2000-2009 lag der kommunale Investitionsbedarf für die Abfallbeseitigung bei 20,5 Mrd. Euro.[7]

Altablagerungen und Altstandorte

Altablagerungen und Altstandorte entstehen dort, wo sich ehemals Mülldeponien, Halden, Betriebsstandorte und Lagerplätze befanden. Zum Schutz des Bodens, des Grundwassers und damit der Gesundheit aller müssen Altlasten beseitigt werden. Für die Sanierung ist grundsätzlich der Verursacher – und sofern nicht auffindbar, der Grundstückseigentümer – zuständig; das sind in vielen Fällen Bund, Länder und Gemeinden. Bei der Sanierung von Altablagerungen kommen oft privatwirtschaftliche Lösungen zum Einsatz, die sich beispielsweise durch die Verwertung der sanierten Grundstücke refinanzieren lassen. Für den Zeitraum 2000-2009 lag der kommunale Investitionsbedarf im Bereich von Altablagerungen bei 12,1 Mrd. Euro.[8]

---

7 Zahlen für den Zeitraum 2006-2020 bei Neufassung der DIFU Studie „Investitionsrückstand und Investitionsbedarf der Kommunen" nicht verfügbar.

8 Zahlen für den Zeitraum 2006-2020 bei Neufassung der DIFU Studie „Investitionsrückstand und Investitionsbedarf der Kommunen" nicht verfügbar.

3.3 Verkehr

In der wirtschaftswissenschaftlichen Literatur wird einzig der Verkehrssektor unumstritten der Infrastruktur zugeordnet. Dieser ist ein Musterbeispiel für netzförmige Infrastruktur, zu dem neben dem straßengebundenen Verkehr auch der Schienenverkehr und der Wasserstraßenverkehr inkl. der Häfen zuzurechnen ist.

Straßen, Wege, Brücken

In diesen Bereich fallen Bundesfernstraßen, Landesstraßen, Gemeindestraßen und Plätze, Parkhäuser, Wirtschaftswege, Privatstraßen der öffentlichen Hand, Ingenieurbauwerke an Verkehrswegen, Straßenbegleitgrün, Straßenbeleuchtung und die Straßenreinigung. Eine moderne und gute ausgebaute Straßeninfrastruktur ist Voraussetzung für die Mobilität der Bevölkerung und sichert damit den wirtschaftlichen und gesellschaftlichen Erfolg einer Region. Im kommunalen Straßenbau liegt der größte, durch das Deutsche Institut für Urbanistik ermittelte Investitionsbedarf. Er beträgt für den Zeitraum 2006-2020 161,6 Mrd. Euro.

Eisenbahnen, SPNV, ÖPNV

Schienenwege inklusive der Oberleitungen, Bahnhöfe, Signalanlagen, Busbahnhöfe und Buslinien werden zum Schienenverkehrssektor gezählt. Die Verantwortung für Bau, Unterhaltung und Betrieb von Schienenwegen unterliegt einem Wirtschaftsunternehmen in privat-rechtlicher Form, welches zu 51 % im Eigentum des Bundes zu stehen hat.[9] Eine Privatisierung der Schienenwege scheint nach Einschätzung der Kommission für Verkehrsinfrastrukturfinanzierung von 2000 aussichtslos, da die Erwirtschaftung der vollen Wegekosten ohne staatliche Subventionierung vermutlich nicht möglich ist. Der Bahnbetrieb dagegen kann nach Meinung der Fachleute dem Wettbewerb unterworfen werden. Für den Öffentlichen Personennahverkehr, der den kommunalen Trägern zugeordnet ist,

[9] Nach Art. 87 e Abs. 3 GG; Aufgrund der Privatisierung der DB wurde für hoheitliche Aufgaben das Eisenbahnbundesamt (EBA) gegründet.

wird ein Investitionsbedarf von 38,4 Mrd. Euro für den Zeitraum 2006-2020 prognostiziert.

Wasserstraßen und Häfen

Zu den Wasserstraßen zählen die Binnenwasserstraßen, die Seeschifffahrtsstraßen (evtl. auch Seestraßen), die Häfen, Schleusen, Hebewerke, Schifffahrtzeichen, Leuchttürme, Radaranlagen, Dücker, Pumpwerke und sonstige Gewässer (z.B. Gewässer III. Ordnung).

Bundeswasserstraßen sind öffentliche Sachen, die nach Art. 89 GG im Eigentum des Bundes stehen, sie besitzen eine doppelte Zweckbestimmung. Zum einen dienen sie Verkehrszwecken[10], zum anderen wasserwirtschaftlichen[11] Belangen. Die Zuständigkeit des Bundes ist auf die Verkehrszwecke beschränkt, er hat hier die Verwaltungskompetenz, während die Länder die Verwaltungszuständigkeit für die Wasserwirtschaft besitzen. Die Unterhaltung von Gewässern III. Ordnung ist oft Aufgabe der Anlieger. Häfen können privatwirtschaftlich betrieben werden. Es liegen keine Angaben zum Investitionsbedarf vor.

3.4 Soziale Infrastruktur

Unter sozialer Infrastruktur wird die Versorgung der Bevölkerung mit sozioökonomischen und soziokulturellen Einrichtungen verstanden. Neben den klassischen Einrichtungen wie zum Beispiel Schule, Kindertagesstätte und Gemeindezentrum werden darunter inzwischen auch Treffpunkte mit unterschiedlichsten Angeboten für spezielle Nutzergruppen verstanden. Die Einrichtungen der sozialen Infrastruktur können den punktförmigen Infrastrukturgütern zugeordnet werden.

---

[10] Vgl. Wasserstraßenrecht (z.B. WStrG- Wasserstraßengesetz).

[11] Vgl. Wasserrecht (z.B. WHG- Wasserhaushaltsgesetz).

Schulen

Folgende Arten von Schulen fallen in diesen Sektor: Grund-, Haupt-, Realschulen und Gymnasien, Integrierte Gesamtschulen, Berufsbildende Schulen, Sonderschulen, Bildungsstätten des öffentlichen Dienstes, Fachoberschulen und nicht zuletzt auch Hochschulen und Universitäten. In Deutschland sind die Länder für das Schulwesen verantwortlich. Die kommunale Ebene als Schulträger schafft die sachlichen Voraussetzungen für die Durchführung des Schulwesens. Die Finanzierung des Systems ist von Land zu Land unterschiedlich geregelt. Von rechtlicher Seite gibt es keine wesentlichen Hindernisse, Schulen privat zu errichten und zu betreiben. Eine Übernahme aller Aufgaben öffentlicher Schulen durch Private ist in den Landesgesetzen jedoch nicht vorgesehen. Der kommunale Investitionsbedarf für Schulen liegt für den Zeitraum 2006-2020 bei 73,0 Mrd. Euro.

Kindertagesstätten, Jugend- und Altenhilfe

Kinderkrippen, Kindergärten, Jugendhäuser, Jugenderholungsheime, Einrichtungen der Jugendfürsorge, Altenheime, Altentageseinrichtungen und Werkstätten für Behinderte fallen unter diese Kategorie. Hierbei handelt es sich um Pflichtaufgaben der kommunalen Selbstverwaltung. Der von der Bundesregierung gesetzlich verankerte Anspruch auf einen Kindergartenplatz für Kinder ab einem Alter von 3 Jahren hat in den letzten Jahren in den alten Bundesländern zu einem erheblichen Nachholbedarf geführt. In den neuen Bundesländern wurde dagegen die Zahl der Einrichtungen reduziert. Immer häufiger werden derzeit staatliche Einrichtungen in private Trägerschaften übergeben. Aufgrund des demografischen Wandels ist abzusehen, dass die Zahl der Altenheime und Altentageseinrichtungen in den kommenden Jahren ansteigen wird. Für den Zeitraum 2000-

2009 lag der kommunale Investitionsbedarf im Bereich Kindertagesstätten bei 7,1 Mrd. Euro.[12]

Sportanlagen, Bäder, Freizeit- und Kultureinrichtungen

Sporthallen, Sportplätze, Stadien, Schwimmhallen, Freibäder, Museen, Theater, Bürgerhäuser, Stadthallen, Tierparks, Zoos, Wanderwege und sonstige touristische Einrichtungen sind freiwillige Aufgaben der kommunalen Selbstverwaltung, bei denen es bzgl. einer privatwirtschaftlichen Realisierung keine Einschränkung gibt. Für Sportstätten in kommunaler Trägerschaft liegt ein Investitionsbedarf von 35,2 Mrd. Euro für den Zeitraum 2006-2020 vor.

Gesundheitswesen

Zum Gesundheitssektor zählen Krankenhäuser, psychiatrische Anstalten, Kureinrichtungen und das Rettungswesen. Als Pflichtaufgabe der kommunalen Selbstverwaltung kann die Gesundheitsfürsorge dennoch an Private übertragen werden. In den letzten Jahren hat die Anzahl und Bettenzahl der Krankenhäuser kontinuierlich abgenommen. Der Investitionsbedarf im kommunalen Krankenhaussektor liegt für den Zeitraum 2006-2020 bei 30,9 Mrd. Euro.

3.5 Verwaltungsgebäude

Rathäuser, Landratsämter, Kfz-Zulassungsstellen, Bundes- und Landesbehördenhäuser, Finanzämter, Ministerien, Arbeitsämter, Polizeistationen, Gerichte, Gefängnisse usw. zählen zu den Verwaltungsgebäuden. Es handelt sich hierbei um punktförmige Infrastrukturgüter. Die Vielfalt und Anzahl der öffentlichen Aufgaben bedingt deutliche Unterschiede in der baulichen Typologie und dem Betrieb der Verwaltungsgebäude. Rechtliche Einschränkungen beim Bau und baulichen Betrieb öffentlicher Gebäude gibt es dort, wo erhöhte Sicherheits-

[12] Zahlen für den Zeitraum 2006-2020 bei Neufassung der DIFU Studie „Investitionsrückstand und Investitionsbedarf der Kommunen“ nicht verfügbar.

vorschriften eingehalten werden müssen (z.B. Verfassungsschutz); ansonsten besteht zudem die Möglichkeit, diese Leistung an Private zu vergeben. Der kommunale Investitionsbedarf für den Zeitraum 2006-2020 liegt hier bei 19,8 Mrd. Euro.

3.6 Wohngebäude, Unterkünfte

Bundes-, Landes- und Gemeindewohnungen, Obdachlosen- und Flüchtlingsunterkünfte gehören zum Komplex der Wohngebäude (punktförmige Infrastrukturgüter). Der Bau von Wohngebäuden ist im Gegensatz zu den Unterkünften für Flüchtlinge und Obdachlose keine öffentliche Aufgabe mehr und auch eine weitergehende Privatisierung des öffentlichen Wohnungsbestandes ist rechtlich möglich. Für den Zeitraum 2000-2009 lag der Investitionsbedarf für den kommunalen Wohnungsbau bei 47,3 Mrd. Euro.[13]

3.7 Sonstiges

Verteidigungsanlagen

Kasernen, Schießstände, Lager, Werkstätten, Hallen und Standortübungsplätze werden militärisch genutzt. Sie gehören zur Gruppe der punktförmigen Infrastrukturgüter. Die Verteidigung ist eine hoheitliche Aufgabe des Bundes, er hat auf diesem Gebiet einschließlich des Zivilbevölkerungsschutzes die ausschließliche Gesetzgebungskompetenz.[14] Die primäre Verteidigungsaufgabe kann nicht privatisiert werden, jedoch können Teilaufgaben, die nicht zum militärischen Kernbereich gehören, unter Beachtung von Sicherheitsaspekten an private Dritte vergeben werden. Die Bundesregierung hat dazu im Jahr 2000 ein entsprechen-

[13] Zahlen für den Zeitraum 2006-2020 bei Neufassung der DIFU Studie „Investitionsrückstand und Investitionsbedarf der Kommunen" nicht verfügbar.

[14] Vgl. Art. 73 Abs. 1 GG.

des Bundeswehrreformkonzept beschlossen. Es liegen keine Angaben zum Investitionsbedarf vor.

Baulandentwicklung, Gesamterschließung, Entwicklungsprojekte

Die Steuerung der baulichen Entwicklung in Städten und Gemeinden ist Aufgabe der kommunalen Selbstverwaltung. Sie findet auf der Grundlage von Flächennutzungs- und Bebauungsplänen statt. Die Einbindung Privater ist rechtlich möglich und zum Teil sogar erwünscht[15]. Hoheitliche Kompetenzen wie Satzungsbeschlüsse allerdings bleiben auch weiterhin bei den Städten und Gemeinden. Der kommunale Investitionsbedarf für den Zeitraum 2006-2020 im Bereich Städtebau wird auf 10,1 Mrd. Euro geschätzt.

4 Infrastruktur, Daseinsvorsorge und Effizienz

Öffentliche Infrastrukturgüter finden sich in allen Sektoren in verschiedensten Ausprägungen hinsichtlich der funktionellen und baulichen Anforderungen wieder. Allen ist gemein, dass sie für die staatliche Aufgabenerfüllung unabdingbar in entsprechender Qualität vorhanden sein müssen, d.h. als notwendiges Daseinsvorsorgeelement zu betrachten sind.

Ein erster Schritt war und ist ein Umdenken in den Köpfen hin zum effizienten Verständnis der Daseinsvorsorge. JAKUBOWSKI (2006) definiert das in seinem Artikel „Stadt ohne Infrastruktur heißt Stadt ohne Zukunft" wie folgt: „Dem Staat fällt die Verantwortung zu, alles das zu gewährleisten, was für die Daseinsermöglichung des modernen Menschen erforderlich ist. Bei der Erfüllung dieser Aufgaben hat der Staat zu organisieren und zu kontrollieren. Produzieren muss der Effizienteste."[16] In Abhängigkeit vom jeweiligen Infrastruktursektor sollten daher verschiedene, alternative Möglichkeiten zur Bewirtschaftung

[15] Vgl. § 12 BauGB: Vorhaben- und Erschließungsplan.
[16] Jakubowski, P. (2006).

jenseits der herkömmlichen Finanzierung in Betracht gezogen werden. Dazu zählen alternative Beschaffungsvarianten wie beispielsweise PPP, Betreiberverträge, Vereinszuschüsse, gemeinschaftliche Betreibung Stadt/Verein, Vereinsbeteiligung, gemeinnützige GmbH, Teilprivatisierung oder die Gründung eines Bürgervereins.

Die im vorangegangenen Kapitel dargestellten Schätzungen der Difu-Studie aus dem Jahr 2008 gehen alleine im Bereich der kommunalen Infrastrukturgüter von einem Investitionsbedarf von insgesamt 704 Mrd. Euro[17] für den Zeitraum 2006-2020 aus. Ein hoher Investitionsbedarf wird bei Schulen und kommunalen Abwasseranlagen erwartet. Der größte Investitionsbedarf von 162 Mrd. Euro wird jedoch im Straßenbau und insbesondere beim Ersatzbedarf für vorhandene Straßen, Brücken und Tunnelanlagen gesehen.[18] Auf Grund dessen wird im Folgenden insbesondere der Straßenverkehrssektor in Hinblick auf den Einsatz von PPP näher betrachtet.

5 PPP und modernes Management

Von der Bundes Task Force wird PPP definiert als „(...) langfristig vertraglich geregelte Zusammenarbeit zwischen öffentlicher Hand und Privatwirtschaft, bei der die erforderlichen Ressourcen von den Partnern zum gegenseitigen Nutzen in einem gemeinsamen Organisationszusammenhang eingestellt und vorhandene Projektrisiken entsprechend der Risikomanagementkompetenz der Projektpartner optimal verteilt werden".

Wir verstehen unter PPP etwas präziser eine öffentliche Projektrealisierung unter privatem Gewinnstreben, die möglichst den gesamten Lebenszyklus eines

[17] Difu Studie „Investitionsrückstand und Investitionsbedarf der Kommunen".

[18] Difu Studie s.o.: 71 Mrd. Euro Ersatzbedarf für vorhandene Straßen, Brücken und Tunnel; 24 Mrd. Euro Erweiterungsbedarf für Erschließungsmaßnahmen; 31 Mrd. Euro Nachholbedarf vor allem in der Umgestaltung von Kommunalstraßen; 36 Mrd. Euro für sonstige Verkehrseinrichtungen (Steuerungssysteme, Lärmschutz etc.).

Bauprojektes umfasst (von Planung über Bau und Betrieb hin zu Erhaltung und evtl. sogar Verwertung). Die öffentliche Hand bleibt, anders als bei einer Privatisierung, i.A. Eigentümer der Grundstücke.

Nicht ein Zinsvorteil steht im Vordergrund, sondern die simultane Optimierung von Planung, Bau, Betrieb und Erhaltung durch Private. Die Zinskosten sind nur eine (mittlere) Komponente der gesamten Lebenszykluskosten.

Es handelt sich also betriebswirtschaftlich um eine spezielle Form des längerfristigen Outsourcing durch die öffentliche Hand und eine Fokussierung auf die Kernkompetenzen der öffentlichen Hand. Die öffentliche Hand verringert demnach mit Hilfe von PPP ihre eigene Fertigungstiefe, es bleibt aber eine öffentliche Infrastruktur.

Im Gegensatz zur Privatisierung bleibt die öffentliche Hand i.A. Eigentümer der Grundstücke, auch im Straßenbau, ebenso bleiben sie ein öffentliches Gut und eine öffentliche Infrastruktur. Dies ist ein wichtiger grundlegender Unterschied zwischen PPP und Privatisierung und ist deshalb so stark zu betonen, weil selbst mancher Politiker oder Journalist glaubt, PPP sei etwas Ähnliches wie Leasing – allerdings liegt bei Leasing die Eigentümerstellung am Grundstück eben bei der Leasinggesellschaft und nicht mehr beim Staat.

Ein weiteres, von Haushältern gerne gepflegtes Vorurteil ist, dass PPP immer teurer sein müsse als eine konventionelle staatliche Realisierung, weil der Staat einfach die günstigste Refinanzierung habe. In der Tat muss der Private einen höheren Zinssatz bezahlen als der Staat. Aber nur dadurch gelingt der Risikotransfer auf die Privatwirtschaft, denn Risiko kann ökonomisch nur über den Zahlungsmechanismus transferiert werden, egal was die Juristen vertraglich fixiert haben. Die Zinskosten sind jedoch nur eine mittlere Komponente der gesamten Lebenszykluskosten eines Bauobjektes, Kosteneinsparungen bei anderen Teilen der Lebenszykluskosten oder eine bessere Leistungserbringung können diesen Zinsnachteil leicht überkompensieren.

6 PPP am Beispiel des Straßenbaus

Das Infrastrukturgut Straße weist hinsichtlich der Aufgabenverantwortung und der Leistungserbringung in Deutschland eine komplexe Verwaltungsstruktur auf. Nachfolgend sollen kurz die Aufgabenträgerschaft sowie die Lebenszyklen eines Straßenkörpers erläutert werden, bevor die durch ein modernes Management erzielbaren Effizienzgewinne dargestellt werden. Im Anschluss werden die derzeit in Umsetzung oder Diskussion befindlichen PPP-Ansätze im Straßenbau beschrieben, um mit der Vision eines effizienten und damit modernen Infrastrukturmanagements abzuschließen.

6.1 Aufgabenträgerschaft des Straßenbaus in Deutschland

Aufgrund der föderalistischen Struktur in Deutschland besitzen Bund, Länder, Kreise und Gemeinden (Städte) jeweils eigene Straßen. Die Zuständigkeiten für die Straßen und Wege sind im GG, den Straßengesetzen des Bundes und der Länder und in den Gemeindeverordnungen geregelt. Die im Eigentum des Bundes stehenden Bundesfernstraßen werden im Rahmen der Auftragsverwaltung durch die Länder verwaltet.[19] Die Eigenständigkeit der Länder ist durch die Regelungen der Auftragsverwaltung begrenzt, der Bund hat die Grundsatzentscheidungskompetenz und ihm obliegt die Finanzverantwortung für den Bau und die Unterhaltung der Bundesfernstraßen sowie dadurch auch die Entscheidung über den Einsatz von PPP.[20] In der Straßenbaulast und somit Entscheidungskompetenz der Länder befinden sich die Landesstraßen. Landkreise und Kreisfreie Städte sind Träger der Straßenbaulast für Kreisstraßen, die Gemeinden wiederum sind Baulastträger für die Gemeindestraßen. Für sonstige öffentliche Straßen sind die Träger der Straßenbaulast in der Widmungs- bzw.

---

19 Vgl. Art. 90 Abs. 2 GG.
20 Vgl. Bauer, K. (2008).

Umstufungsverfügung zu bestimmen.[21] Für den Bereich der Ortsdurchfahrten gibt es gesonderte gesetzliche Regelungen.

Die nachfolgende Abbildung stellt die Aufgabenträgerschaft zwischen Bund, Land und Kommune und den dafür bestellten Aufgabenerbringern, sprich Straßenmeistereien, Autobahnmeistereien und Bauhöfen, dar.

Abb. 1: Aufgabenzuordnung in der Straßenverkehrsinfrastruktur
Quelle: eigene Darstellung.

6.2 Lebenszyklusansatz im Straßenbau

Besteht der (verkehrliche) Bedarf oder eine politische Grundentscheidung, eine Straße neu bzw. auszubauen, muss ein langer Weg beschritten werden, der nachfolgend exemplarisch für Bundesfernstraßen kurz skizziert wird. Voraussetzung ist, dass die Maßnahme im Bundesverkehrswegeplan (BVWP)[22] aufgenommen worden ist. Dieser ist Grundlage für den Bedarfsplan für die Bundesfernstraßen (BPL)[23], der die gesetzliche Grundlage für den Neubau und die Erweiterung der Bundesstraßen darstellt. Fünfjahrespläne[24] als integrale Bestandteile des

21 In Anlehnung an das BbgStrG § 9 Abs. 4.
22 Bundesverkehrswegeplan 2003 (aktuell gültig).
23 Bedarfsplan für Bundesfernstraßen derzeit mit einem Planungshorizont bis 2015.
24 Nach § 5 FStrG.

verkehrsträgerübergreifenden Investitionsrahmenplans bilden schließlich die Grundlage für die jährlichen Straßenbauprogramme. Ist der Bedarf festgestellt, erfolgt zur Beurteilung der Eingriffe in die Natur eine Umweltverträglichkeitsuntersuchung. Das Ergebnis der Umweltverträglichkeitsstudie (UVS) legt die Grenzen der weiteren Planung fest, die bei der Aufstellung des Linienentwurfs berücksichtigt werden. Anschließend kommt es zum Linienbestimmungsverfahren. Für die Bestimmung der Linie wird die Zustimmung des Bundesministeriums für Verkehr, Bauen und Stadtentwicklung (BMVBS) benötigt. Darauf folgt der RE-Entwurf, der neben den technischen Unterlagen auch eine Kostenschätzung, eventuell mit Kostenteilung auf verschiedene Baulastträger, enthält. Durch Prüfung mit anschließendem Sichtvermerk des BMVBS erhält der RE-Entwurf eine fachliche und haushaltsrechtliche Genehmigung. Im Anschluss daran erfolgt die Durchführung eines Planfeststellungsverfahrens, nach Rechtskraft des Planfeststellungsbeschlusses kann mit der baureifen Ausführungsplanung begonnen werden.

Die Komplexität der Verbindungen und Abgrenzungen zwischen Zuständigkeiten und die hoheitlichen Tätigkeiten (z.B. Planfeststellung) in der Planungsphase einer Baumaßnahme eignen sich nicht bzw. nur bedingt zur Übertragung an einen Privaten, vielmehr ist hier innerhalb der Verwaltung Optimierungspotential zu ermitteln. Anders sieht es im Bereich des sich anschließenden Baus, des Betriebs und der Unterhaltung von Straßenbaumaßnahmen aus. Im Bereich des Fernstraßenverkehrs sind hierbei schon zwei PPP-Ansätze zur Umsetzung gebracht worden. Durch die Einführung des FStrPrivFinG[25] wurde Privaten die Möglichkeit eröffnet, Bundesfernstraßen zu bauen, zu betreiben und zu erhalten und dafür eine Mautgebühr zu erheben (das sogenannte F-Modell). Ferner konnten durch die Einführung der wegekostenorientierten Benutzungsentgelte für den Schwerlastverkehr auf Bundesautobahnen privatwirtschaftlich zu realisierende Vorhaben möglich gemacht werden (das sogenannte A-Modell). Beide Modelle sind dem PPP-Konzessionsmodell zuzuordnen. Daneben gibt es

[25] FStrPrivFinG: Fernstraßenbauprivatfinanzierungsgesetz.

weitere PPP-Ansätze im kommunalen und Landesbereich, die ein modernes Infrastrukturmanagement im Straßenverkehrssektor sicherstellen sollen.

Was sind die einzelnen Komponenten der Lebenszyklusbetrachtung im Straßenbau? Hierzu dient die linke Hälfte des nächsten Schaubildes mit den Rubriken Bau, Betrieb und Erhaltung als Erläuterung.

Abb. 2: Elemente eines PPP-Modells
Quelle: Jacob, D. (2008).

Finanziell wird die erbrachte Leistung im Straßenbau dem Privaten entgolten. Im Falle eines PPP-Modells erfolgt die Honorierung durch Mautzahlungen, Abschlagszahlungen oder Verfügbarkeitsentgelte, wie die zweite Spalte desselben Schaubildes näher ausweist.

6.3 Effizienzgewinne durch PPP

Woraus resultieren die Effizienzgewinne durch PPP gegenüber einer konventionellen Realisierung?

Abb. 3: PPP-Effizienzpyramide
Quelle: Jacob, D./Kochendörfer, J. (2002), S. 19.

Zunächst ist die Optimierung des Risikotransfers wichtig – darüber zu einem späteren Zeitpunkt mehr. Weiterhin soll die Aufgabe möglichst nur outputorientiert, sprich funktional beschrieben werden, damit dem Privaten noch genügend Innovationsspielraum verbleibt. Zudem sollte möglichst ein funktionierender Wettbewerb der Ausschreibung zugrunde liegen, denn Effizienz entsteht ökonomisch nur im Wettbewerb. Schließlich sollte möglichst der gesamte Lebenszyklus simultan unter Wettbewerb gestellt werden. Ferner gibt es noch eine ganze Reihe weiterer Faktoren, die die Effizienz beeinflussen, so z.B. Projektüberwachung und Anreize im Vertrag, Qualität der Beratung und Verträge, Transparenz des Prozesses etc.

Entscheidend ist die optimale Risikoverteilung zwischen öffentlicher Hand und Privatem Anbieter. Jeder sollte die Risiken übernehmen, die er am besten managen kann. Hier bleiben bei traditioneller Beschaffung oftmals unnötig viele Risiken bei der öffentlichen Hand. Zu nennen sind hier u.a. die Nachtragsrisiken und die Terminrisiken. Andererseits gibt es Risiken wie Nachfragerisiken, Enteignungsrisiken oder Genehmigungsrisiken, die nicht alleine beim Privaten bleiben sollten. Die Risiken können von der öffentlichen Hand mitbeeinflusst werden; hier sollte es demzufolge zumindest eine Risikoteilung geben. Ansonsten müsste der Private „Angstzuschläge“ einkalkulieren oder die Projekte wären in der heutigen Zeit nicht mehr bankable, d.h. eine Finanzierung käme nicht mehr erfolgreich zustande (siehe dazu die nachfolgenden A- und F-Modelle).

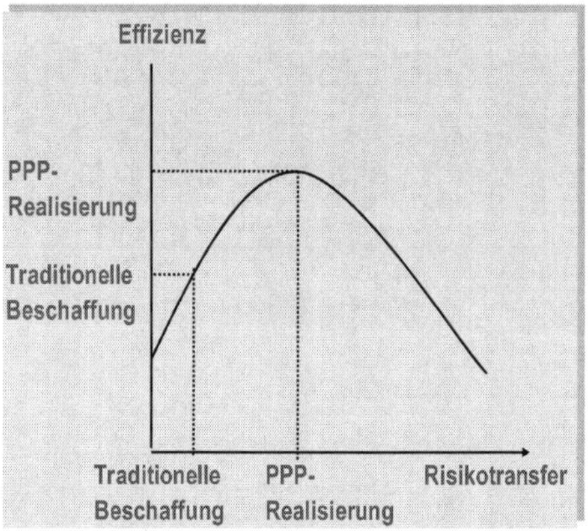

Abb. 4: Einfluss des Risikotransfers auf den Effizienzgewinn
Quelle: Jacob, D./Kochendörfer, J. (2002), S. 21.

6.4 A-Modell

Kommen wir zunächst zum A-Modell, welches sich durch folgende Charakteristika auszeichnet:

- Ausbau einer Bestandsstrecke von 4 auf 6 Spuren
- Planung, Neubau, Finanzierung, Betrieb und Erhaltung
- Durchschnittliche A-Modell-Streckenlänge: 50-70 km
- Laufzeit: 30 Jahre

- Rücküberführung an öffentliche Hand gemäß vertraglich vereinbarter Zustandswerte
- Vergütungselemente:
  - Anschubfinanzierung max. 50 % der Investition
  - indirekte Nutzerfinanzierung durch Weiterleitung der LKW-Maut von diesem Abschnitt
- keine gesonderten gesetzlichen Grundlagen

Bisher sind drei Projekte bezuschlagt worden: A 8 / München – Augsburg, A 4 / Umfahrung Hörselberge und A 1 / Buchholz Bremer Kreuz. Die Entscheidung für die A 5 / Baden-Baden – Offenburg steht noch im Jahr 2008 an.

Im nächsten Jahr sollen die Verlängerung der A8 nach Ulm sowie die A9 hinzukommen. Weitere sechs Projekte sind angekündigt, sie sind in folgendem Schaubild dargestellt.

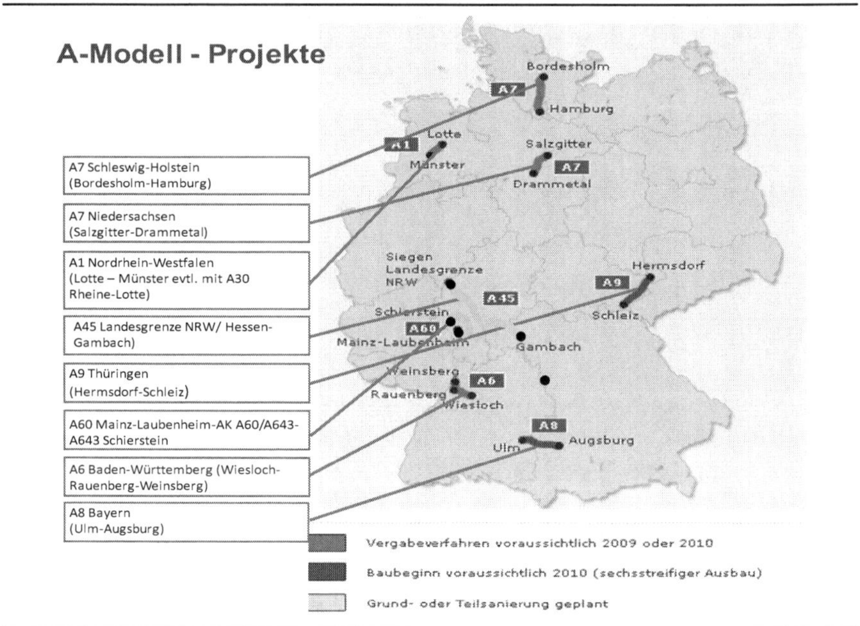

Abb. 5: Weitere A-Modellprojekte 2009-2010
Quelle: Stolle, C.-D. (2008).

Die bisherigen drei bezuschlagten Projekte waren bankable, wenn auch wohl mit gewissen Anfangsschwierigkeiten. Bei den weiteren Projekten wird man sehen. Es handelte sich bisher um Strecken mit hohem LKW-Aufkommen, die mit Blick auf ihren Cash-Flow sehr robust waren. Trotzdem ist die volle Verlagerung des Verkehrsrisikos eine Gefahr für die Finanzierbarkeit der Projekte.

6.5 F-Modell

Während sich bei den A-Modellen von einem gewissen Erfolg sprechen lässt (wenn auch die Vergabezeiten bisher extrem lang waren), kann im Rahmen der F-Modelle von einem Fiasko gesprochen werden.

Grund dafür ist, dass die Strecken über 30 Jahre vollamortisiert werden sollen. Das volle Nachfragerisiko bei Projekten auf der grünen Wiese liegt beim Privaten. Hier ist insbesondere die mangelnde Verkehrswegeplanungssicherheit anzukreiden. Ein Ausweg könnte ein Verfügbarkeitsentgelt sein, wie es im Ausland vermehrt angewendet wird.

Nachdem sowohl das F-Modell Warnowquerung in Rostock wie auch die Travequerung in Lübeck für die Banken zu Verlusten geführt haben, ist das F-Modell in seiner bisherigen Form ökonomisch tot.

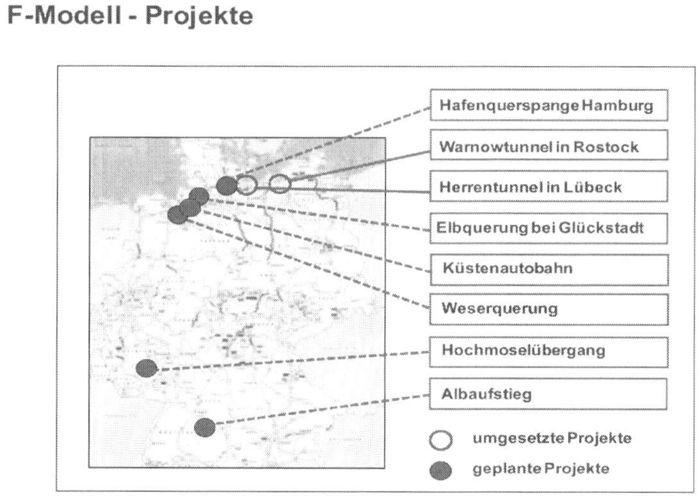

Abb. 6: F-Modell-Projekte
Quelle: in Anlehnung an Schröter, N. (2006), S. 26.

6.6 PPP-Modelle für Kommunal- und Landesstraßen

In diesem Bereich stehen wir noch ganz am Anfang der Entwicklung, sozusagen in der Experimentierphase. Ziel muss der wirtschaftlich optimale Mitteleinsatz bei Planung, Bau und Erhaltung von Verkehrswegen sein.

Ein möglicher Leistungsumfang sollte möglichst viele der Phasen Planung, Neu-, Um- und Ausbau, Finanzierung, Betrieb und Erhaltung umfassen. Es muss sich dabei immer um ein zusammenhängendes Netz handeln, zudem müssen die Zustandswerte sowohl während der PPP-Laufzeit als auch bei Rücküberführung klar im Vorhinein festgelegt werden. Die Laufzeit sollte zwischen 16 und 30 Jahre betragen. Die Leistungsentgelte sollten auf Basis der Verfügbarkeit gezahlt werden. Es sollte weiterhin Leistungsanreize in Form von Bonus-Malus-Systemen geben. Gesonderte gesetzliche Grundlagen gibt es für die Modelle im Kommunal- und Landesstraßenbereich nicht.

Landesstraßenprojekt NRW

Es geht um Bestandsstrecken, die innerhalb von 3 Jahren wieder in einen ordnungsgemäßen Zustand gebracht werden und dann für eine mit 16 Jahren eher kurz bemessene Zeit erhalten werden sollen. Dazu wurde ein bestimmter Zustandswert über die Laufzeit vertraglich vereinbart. Zum Zwecke des Risikotransfers ist auch eine gewisse private Finanzierung vorgesehen, die in wesentlichen Teilen einen Einredeverzicht einschließt, um mittelstandsfreundlich zu sein. Der Einredeverzicht orientiert sich dabei an dem Baufortschritt in den ersten drei Jahren. Die Vergütung erfolgt ab dem ersten Vertragsjahr in konstanten quartalsweise ausgezahlten Raten. Sie umfasst als Basisentgelt die anfänglichen Investitionen sowie die dafür notwendigen Finanzierungskosten und ein Entgelt für die Erhaltung.

Kommunale Projekte

An erfolgreichen kommunalen Projekten ist zunächst die Ortsumgehung Harsewinkel zu nennen. Es handelt sich um Neubau, Erhaltung und Betrieb über 30 Jahre. Der Zuschlag wurde seinerzeit an das Unternehmen Kirchner erteilt. Das Projekt befindet sich bereits in der Betriebsphase.

Bei den Kreisstraßen Lippe geht es um die Erhaltung, ggf. um einen geförderten Neu-, Um- und Ausbau von Straßen mit einer Projektlaufzeit von

25 Jahren. Vorgesehen ist ein Netz von ca. 450 km. Das Finanzierungsvolumen über diese Laufzeit und Netzlänge liegt bei ca. 120 Mio. Euro. Das Projekt befindet sich noch in der Verhandlungsphase, so dass über die konkreten Strukturen noch spekuliert werden muss.

In einer noch früheren Phase steht ebenso das kommunale Erhaltungsmodell der Stadt Brandenburg an der Havel. Als Leistungen könnten Erhaltung, Betrieb, Neu-, Um- und Ausbau an den Privaten vergeben werden. Nach momentanem Stand werden eine Machbarkeitsstudie und eine Wirtschaftlichkeitsuntersuchung durchgeführt werden.

6.7 Funktionsbauvertrag gleich PPP?

Immer wieder wird die Frage gestellt, was es mit dem Funktionsbauvertrag auf sich hat. Der Funktionsbauvertrag schließt weder Betrieb noch längerfristige Finanzierung ein. Es ist im Grunde genommen ein GU-Vertrag mit verlängerter Ansprüchemängelhaftung (früher Gewährleistungsansprüche).

Die verlängerte Gewährleistung beläuft sich auf 15-30 Jahre. Damit der Risikotransfer tatsächlich ökonomisch gelingt, müsste eine entsprechend lang laufende Bürgschaft gefordert werden. Eine solch lang laufende Bürgschaft wäre allerdings nicht mittelstandsfreundlich. Wie soll sich ein Mittelstandskonsortium eine solche Bürgschaft beschaffen können, gerade in der heutigen Zeit der Subprimekrise. Wird eine solche Sicherung nicht verlangt, ist der Risikotransfer der Gewährleistung nicht gelungen, weil sich Firmen dem ökonomisch durch Insolvenz entziehen können. Die Angebote wären letztlich nicht mehr vergleichbar. Insgesamt scheint beim Funktionsbauvertrag auch wenig Innovation von Seiten der Bauwirtschaft möglich zu sein. Man sollte deshalb genau überlegen, ob das der Weisheit letzter Schluss ist.

6.8 Vision

Wir befinden uns mit PPP im Straßenbau noch in der Experimentierphase. Was könnten Kriterien für effiziente PPP-Modelle im Straßenbau sein?

Zunächst sollte wie im Hochbau der Lebenszyklusgedanke Platz greifen. Außerdem sollten Nebenanlagen wie Entwässerung und Verkehrsbeschilderung eingeschlossen sein. Weiterhin wird eine gewisse Größe der Projekte benötigt, damit der Straßenbetriebsdienst wirtschaftlich von statten gehen kann. Die Projekte sollten zugleich jedoch nicht zu groß gewählt werden, damit auch ausreichend Wettbewerb vorhanden ist. Die optimale Losgröße hängt sicher auch von der Komplexität der Maßnahme ab. Hierbei sollte die Zielstellung sein, Schnittstellen zu minimieren und Kosten und Leistung zu optimieren. Dazu zählt auch möglichst ein zusammenhängendes Verkehrsnetz zu wählen, obwohl dies bedeuten kann, dass verschiedene Träger der Straßenlast einzubinden sind. Ferner sollte eine leistungsorientierte Vergütung zu Grunde gelegt werden.

Literaturverzeichnis

Bauer, K. (2008): Die Straßenbauverwaltung in Deutschland. In: Straße und Autobahn.

Blochmann, G./Jacob, D./Wolf, R. (2003): Kooperationen mittelständischer Bauunternehmen – Zur Erschließung neuer Marktfelder bei der Privatisierung öffentlicher Aufgaben. Wiesbaden

Forsthoff, E. (1958): Die Daseinsvorsorge und die Kommune. Köln.

Funck, R./Blum, U. (1984): Zentralörtlicher Status, Verkehrsinfrastruktur und regionales Einkommen. Göttingen.

Jacob, D. (2008): Vortrag „PPP-Modelle für den Straßenbau in Deutschland“. Veranstaltung „PPP im Straßenbau und Hochbau“, Stuttgart.

Jacob, D./Kochendörfer, J. (2002): Effizienzgewinne bei privatwirtschaftlicher Realisierung von Infrastrukturvorhaben. Bundesanzeiger Verlag, Köln.

Jakubowski, P. (2006): Stadt ohne Infrastruktur heißt Stadt ohne Zukunft“. In: Zukunft Städtischer Infrastruktur, Informationen zur Raumentwicklung, Heft 5.

Jochimsen, R. (1966): Theorie der Infrastruktur. Grundlagen der marktwirtschaftlichen Entwicklung. Tübingen.

Lauwe, P./Riegel, Ch. (2008): Schutz Kritischer Infrastrukturen – Konzepte zur Versorgungssicherheit. In: Infrastruktur und Daseinsvorsorge in der Fläche, BBR, Informationen zur Raumentwicklung Heft1/2.

Reidenbach, M. et al. (2002): Der kommunale Investitionsbedarf in Deutschland. Difu-Beiträge zur Stadtforschung, Berlin.

Reidenbach, M. et al. (2008): Investitionsrückstand und Investitionsbedarf der Kommunen. Edition – Stadt Forschung Praxis Bd. 4, Berlin.

Schröter, N. (2006): Buchbeitrag „Umsetzung des PPP-Gedankens im Bundesfernstraßenbau“, S. 26. 17. Treffen der Universitätsassistenten für Bauwirtschaft, Baubetrieb und Bauverfahrenstechnik. Technische Universität Dresden, Dresden.

Stobbe, A. (1997): Zur Leistungsfähigkeit privaten Infrastrukturengagements. Jena.

Stolle, C.-D. (2008): Vortrag „Perspektiven der Bundesfernstraßen“, Veranstaltung „Neuere Entwicklungen in der Straßenverkehrsinfrastruktur und Implikationen für Sachsen“, Freiberg.

Chancen von Public Private Partnership im Bildungssektor

Ergebnisse einer empirischen Analyse zur Zusammenarbeit von Schule und Wirtschaft in der Region Ingolstadt

Monika Bachinger, Harald Pechlaner & Wolf von Holzschuher

Inhaltsverzeichnis

1 Theoretischer Bezugsrahmen

1.1 Die Rolle von regionalem Wissen

Wissensgenerierung ist Ergebnis sozialer Interaktion. Es entsteht durch den Austausch von Information und Erfahrung zwischen Akteuren aus unterschiedlichen gesellschaftlichen und wirtschaftlichen Bereichen. Bedeutsam für die Wettbewerbsfähigkeit einer Region ist daher, welche Akteure an diesem Austausch teilnehmen können – sprich, welchen Erfahrungs- und Wissensstand sie mitbringen, wie sie interagieren und kommunizieren. Gerade den allgemeinbildenden Schulen, aber auch den Fach- und Hochschulen kommt hier eine entscheidende Rolle zu: sie sind es, die Identität vermitteln und Menschen mit unterschiedlichsten Lebenshintergründen eine gemeinsame Sozialisation ermöglichen. Sie sind die Plattform, auf der gemeinsame Denkmuster entwickelt werden und über die eine erfolgreiche Kommunikation im Sinne eines missverständnislosen Zusammenspiels von Sender und Empfänger einer Information[1] entstehen kann. Und nicht zuletzt sind Schulen diejenigen Einrichtungen, die zukünftigen Talenten für Wissenschaft, Forschung und Wirtschaft ein Fundament an Wissen vermitteln. Schulen spielen damit im Kreislauf der regionalen Wissensgenerierung eine wesentliche Rolle, da sie die Chance haben, zum einen flächendeckend wichtige soft skills (z. B. Kommunikationsfähigkeit), zum anderen die Fähigkeit zum Lernen zu vermitteln. Eine Region wird sich daher an der Qualität ihrer Schulen messen lassen müssen.

Umso problematischer erscheint es, wenn Schulen über eine mangelnde Ausstattung oder fehlendes Lehrpersonal klagen und deutsche Schüler im Vergleich zu anderen europäischen Ländern eher mittelmäßig abschneiden.[2] Deutschland gibt in absoluten Zahlen Jahr für Jahr zwar mehr für Bildung aus, 2004 wurde mit 5,2% des BIP jedoch weniger als in anderen OECD-Staaten

1 Vgl. Angerer, Th. (2003), S. 61 ff.

2 Ergebnisse PISA (2000).

(OECD-Mittel 5,8%) in das Bildungssystem investiert. Die absoluten Bildungsausgaben pro Teilnehmer vom Primar- bis Tertiärbereich lagen 2004 in Deutschland allerdings mit 7.800 US-Dollar über dem OECD-Mittel (7.100 US-Dollar), wobei zwischen den Bildungsbereichen deutliche Unterschiede existieren: die Ausgaben je Teilnehmer im Primarbereich und im allgemeinbildenden Sekundarbereich I und II waren niedriger als das OECD-Mittel, während in den beruflichen Bildungsgängen und im Tertiärbereich je Bildungsteilnehmer in Deutschland mehr ausgegeben wurde.[3] Gerade für erstere Schultypen erscheinen demzufolge zusätzliche Finanzierungsformen attraktiv. Im folgenden Artikel soll daher geprüft werden, welche Möglichkeiten es für die verstärkte Zusammenarbeit zwischen Schule und Wirtschaft gibt, welche Motive identifiziert werden können und inwiefern konkrete Handlungsempfehlungen am Beispiel der Region Ingolstadt abgeleitet werden können.

1.2 Das Engagement der Wirtschaft im Schulsystem

Die häufigste Form von unternehmerischem Engagement im Bildungsbereich ist das Schulsponsoring. Sponsoring bezeichnet dabei „die Gewährung von Geld oder geldwerten Vorteilen durch Unternehmen zur Förderung von Personen, Gruppen und/oder Organisationen in sportlichen, kulturellen, kirchlichen, wissenschaftlichen, sozialen, ökologischen oder ähnlich bedeutsamen gesellschaftspolitischen Bereichen… mit der regelmäßig auch einige unternehmensbezogene Ziele der Werbung oder Öffentlichkeitsarbeit verfolgt werden"[4]. Sponsoring wird nicht mehr isoliert, sondern systemisch betrachtet und durch präzise Planung, Organisation und Durchführung gesteuert. Es ist ein gewinnorientiertes Geschäft, welches investierte Budgets wieder einspielen soll und im Idealfall sogar Gewinn abwirft. Ausschlaggebend ist der erzielte Return on Sponsoring Investment (ROSI) in Form einer Steigerung des Kommunikations-, Marken-

---

3 Autorengruppe Bildungsberichterstattung (2008), S. 34.

4 Bundesfinanzministerium Internetlink.

und/oder Unternehmenswertes.[5] Sport- oder Kultursponsoring erreichen mit diesem Ansatz Milliarden-Budgets: das deutsche Sponsoring-Volumen steigt seit Jahren stark an. Lag es im Jahr 2000 noch bei knapp unter 2,5 Mrd. Euro, so werden für 2009 Gesamtausgaben von nahezu 4,5 Mrd. Euro erwartet. Weit über die Hälfte wird dabei für Sport-Sponsoring ausgegeben (2008: ca. 2,7 Mrd. Euro), gefolgt von Medien-Sponsoring (knapp eine Mrd. Euro) und Kultur-Sponsoring (knapp 0,4 Mrd. Euro). Sponsoring-Aktivitäten im Bereich des Public Sponsoring, unter das auch Ausgaben für Bildungseinrichtungen fallen, lagen mit steigendem Trend bei ebenfalls ca. 0,4 Mrd. Euro im Jahre 2008. Für die Zukunft wird dabei gerade den Schulen eine positive Entwicklung bescheinigt: 56% der befragten Unternehmen erwarteten eine positive Entwicklung des Bildungs-Sponsorings.[6]

Dass Schulsponsoring bereits heute einen wichtigen Bestandteil der Vernetzung zwischen Schule und Wirtschaft darstellt, zeigt auch eine Studie, die bei allgemeinbildenden Schulen und Unternehmen in Nordrhein-Westfalen durchgeführt wurde. Demnach erhalten die meisten Schulen bereits durch einen oder sogar mehrere Sponsoren (40,4%) Unterstützung.[7] Hintergrund für diese Verbreitung von Schulsponsoring ist zweifelsohne die zunehmende Wettbewerbssituation, der sich Schulen stellen müssen. Nicht nur abnehmende Schülerzahlen, sondern auch die Möglichkeit, zusätzliche Mittel einzuwerben, führen dazu, dass Schulen sich verstärkt unterscheidbare Profile geben. Sponsoring unterstützt dieses Anliegen und trägt zugleich zum Schulentwicklungsprozess bei, der u.a. durch eine „Öffnung der Schule gegenüber ihrem Umfeld“[8] gekennzeichnet ist. Bildungseinrichtungen vernetzen sich stärker mit Betrieben, Sport- und anderen Vereinen, Kunst- und Musikschulen, kommunalen und kirchlichen Einrichtungen und betreiben Öffentlichkeitsarbeit sowie Profilbildung. Eines der Ziele von Schulsponsoring ist bei Bildungseinrichtungen daher auch die Förderung der

---

5 Müller-Schwemer, Th./Sorg, G. (2006), S. 3.
6 Vgl. Krüger, J./Bacher, J. (2007).
7 Vgl. Heinrich, G./Hüchtermann, M./Nowak, S. (2002), S. 24 f.
8 Bayerische Staatsregierung (2000).

Umsetzung eines Schulprofils (90,0%), gefolgt von Einbindung in das Umfeld (82,9%) und eine Verbesserung der Öffentlichkeitsarbeit (76,7%). Weitere Ziele sind die Verbesserung des außerschulischen Angebots, Schaffung eines Freizeitangebots oder die Einrichtung von Förderkursen. Dabei betrachten die meisten Bildungseinrichtungen die Sponsorenmittel als zusätzliche Ressourcen, die zur qualitativen Verbesserung von Unterricht und Erziehung beitragen können. Abgelehnt wird demgegenüber die Finanzierung der Grundversorgung der Schule durch Sponsorenmittel (97,4% der NRW-Umfrage[9]). Hierbei schwingt die Befürchtung mit, dass sich der Aufwandsträger der Schulen (Kommunen oder Landkreise) aus ihrer finanziellen Verantwortung zurückziehen und mit regelmäßigen Zahlungseingängen aus der Wirtschaft rechnen könnten.[10]

Aus Unternehmenssicht betrachtet stellen Schulen attraktive Partner für Sponsoring-Maßnahmen dar: sie verfügen über weitreichende Kommunikationsstrukturen (Eltern, Schüler, Ehemalige, Politik), vermitteln Jugendlichen Identität und Schlüsselqualifikationen und ermöglichen Kontakt zu einem großen Pool an Begabungen, aus dem eventuell zukünftige Mitarbeiter geworben werden können.[11] Die Zielsetzungen der Unternehmen konzentrieren sich daher auch auf kommunikative Wirkungen der Zusammenarbeit: Imageziele wie Imagepflege bzw. -transfer stehen bei 90% der Befragten einer Studie unter Werbetreibenden im Mittelpunkt des Interesses.[12] Weitere Ziele sind Kontaktpflege zu Geschäftspartnern und potenziellen Partnern/Kunden sowie Meinungsführern, Kundenbindung, Mitarbeitermotivation und gesellschaftliche Verantwortung. Das heißt, es geht auf der einen Seite um ökonomische Motive, auf der anderen Seite um normativ-psychologische.[13] Wesentlich ist, durch Sponsoring den Bekanntheitsgrad und das Image des Unternehmens positiv zu beeinflussen. Es geht um „Awareness“ und einen Kommunikationsvorteil für das Unter-

9 Heinrich, G./Hüchtermann, M./Nowak, S. (2002), S. 28.
10 Lommarzsch, L. (2003), S. 37.
11 Bruhn, M. (2003), S. 229.
12 Vgl. Krüger J./Bacher, J. (2007).
13 Ahlert, D./Vogel, V./Woisetschläger, D. (2007), S. 18.

nehmen im Vergleich zu den Mitbewerbern. Die Auswahl der zu fördernden sozialen Ziele ist dabei mit Bedacht zu treffen: entscheidend für die positive Rückwirkung einer Sponsoring-Maßnahme auf das Unternehmen ist die Glaubwürdigkeit des Engagements. Unternehmen müssen es schaffen, die eigenen unternehmerischen Ziele in einen sinnvollen Kontext zum Bildungsengagement zu stellen.[14] Dann gelingt es auch, bestehende Kunden stärker an sich zu binden oder die Barrieren zu potentiellen neuen Kunden durch Kommunikation in nichtkommerziellen Situationen zu vermindern. In jedem Fall ist entscheidend, dass Unternehmen ihr Engagement widerspruchsfrei begründen können – und zwar ethisch in Bezug auf ihre Verantwortungsbereitschaft für soziale Fragestellungen, sachlich aufgrund der eigenen Betroffenheit von sozialen Problemen oder kommunikativ als Dialogbereitschaft mit wichtigen Anspruchsgruppen.[15] Gelingt dies, so können Sponsoring-Aktivitäten im Sinne eines Frühwarnsystems wichtige Informationen über Umweltveränderungen in das Unternehmen zurückspielen, was der Risikoreduktion dient. Außerdem steigt die Akzeptanz für das Unternehmen in der Gesellschaft. Gleichzeitig bedingen glaubhaft durchgeführte Sponsoring-Commitments eine Anpassung des internen Verhaltens im Unternehmen: das heißt, sie prägen die Unternehmensidentität und können zu einer stärkeren Identifikation der Mitarbeiter beitragen.

Entscheidend für die Dauerhaftigkeit und den Erfolg eines jeden schulischen Engagements der Wirtschaft ist dabei, dass die Lehr- und Methodenfreiheit des Unterrichts respektiert wird und Schulen weder in eine wirtschaftliche noch pädagogische Abhängigkeit vom Sponsor geraten. Gerade hier setzen die größten Befürchtungen von Kritikern an: gesprochen wird von einer Instrumentalisierung der Schule für Belange der Wirtschaft; außerdem bestünde die Gefahr der Kommerzialisierung bzw. dass Schüler zu intensiv werblichen Maßnahmen ausgesetzt würden. Produktwerbung an Schulen ist jedoch grundsätzlich verboten – es geht vielmehr um Imagebildung von Unternehmen und dies in

[14] Vgl. Müller-Schwemer, Th./Sorg, G. (2006), S. 23 f.
[15] Bruhn, M. (1990), S. 64.

einem engen rechtlichen Rahmen. So heißt es im entsprechenden bayerischen Gesetz: „Sponsoring ist in der Schule gestattet, wenn die Schule bei der Erfüllung ihrer Aufgaben unterstützt wird... Auf Antrag... kann ein Hinweis (Plakat usw.) ohne besondere Hervorhebung angebracht werden. Weitergehende Produktwerbung ist unzulässig.“[16] Betont werden muss daher: Sponsoring wird in Schulen nur dann praktiziert, wenn der Werbeeffekt deutlich hinter den pädagogischen Nutzen zurücktritt.[17] Weiterhin wird diskutiert, ob Sponsoring zu einer ungleichen Behandlung von Schulen beiträgt und beispielsweise Schulen in städtischen Brennpunktvierteln benachteiligt würden. Ungeachtet der Frage ob dies wirklich so ist, sind Schulträger daher aufgefordert, über Fonds- oder Pool-Modelle Ausgleich zu schaffen.[18]

Die Anforderungen an Schule und Wirtschaft sind insgesamt nicht gering: auf beiden Seiten müssen gängige Denkmuster aufgebrochen und Verständnis für die jeweils andere Seite entwickelt werden. Auch der Grad der Professionalisierung von Schulsponsoring kann noch ausgebaut werden: benötigt wird von beiden Seiten eine konzeptionelle Ausrichtung der Aktivitäten. Auf schulischer Seite bedarf es einer verlässlichen Durchführung der Sponsoring-Gegenleistung (Pressearbeit), einer soliden internen Abstimmung mit Eltern, Lehrern und dem Schulträger sowie klaren Richtlinien über die eigene Positionierung. Bei Unternehmen geht es um die langfristige Begründbarkeit der Wirkung von Sponsoring-Maßnahmen im Rahmen einer betriebswirtschaftlichen Kosten-Nutzen-Betrachtung. Hier dürfte wesentlich sein, ob schulisches Engagement eher in den Bereich der Corporate Social Responsibility oder einer Public-Private Partnership fällt. Zunächst sollen daher beide Begriffe abgegrenzt werden um sodann zu begründen, warum beide Konzepte Unterschiede für das Bildungssponsoring darstellen.

---

[16] §84 Abs.1,2 BayEUG

[17] Landesinstitut für Erziehung und Unterricht Stuttgart (2001), S. 177.

[18] Vgl. Heinrich, G./Hüchtermann, M./Nowak, S. (2002), S. 17 ff.

1.2.1 Corporate Social Responsibility

Unter Corporate Social Responsibility (CSR) versteht man im Allgemeinen die Wahrnehmung einer gesellschaftlichen Verantwortung durch ein Unternehmen. CSR lässt sich als Konzept definieren, „das den Unternehmen als Grundlage dient, auf freiwilliger Basis soziale Belange und Umweltbelange in ihre Unternehmenstätigkeit und in ihre Wechselbeziehung mit den Stakeholdern zu integrieren…“.[19] Sie ist eine unternehmensstrategische Entscheidung, die darauf abzielt, dass „sowohl das gesellschaftliche Umfeld als auch das engagierte Unternehmen auf vielfältige Weise in unterschiedlichen Bereichen von der Zusammenarbeit profitieren“.[20]

Grundsätzlich ist nicht neu, dass Unternehmen sich für Ziele der Gesellschaft engagieren: bereits das deutsche Grundgesetz bindet Eigentum an eine besondere gesellschaftliche Verpflichtung. Unternehmen haben ebenso wie Privatpersonen bestimmte Rechte und Pflichten. Sie sind „Bürger“ (Corporate Citizens) der Gesellschaft und sind angehalten, das eigene Gewinnstreben mit dem Gemeinwohl zu verbinden. Nur ein Unternehmen, das in einer gesunden und dynamischen Umwelt angesiedelt ist, kann selbst erfolgreich wirtschaften.[21] Aktualität hat die Gemeinwohlorientierung unternehmerischen Handelns dadurch erhalten, dass Konsumenten immer häufiger Produktions- und Vertriebsprozesse kritisch hinterfragen. Die Kaufentscheidung wird nicht mehr alleine aufgrund des Preis-Leistungs-Verhältnisses des Produkts oder des Markennamens getroffen. Zentral sind vielmehr Forderungen in Bezug auf soziale und ökologische Nachhaltigkeit, wobei sich erstere auf die Interaktion des Unternehmens mit der Gesellschaft, sprich den eigenen Mitarbeitern, aber auch Zulieferern und Kunden bezieht. Die ökologische Nachhaltigkeit konzentriert sich wiederum auf den sparsamen und effizienten Einsatz natürlicher Ressourcen bzw. deren Erhalt durch Maßnahmen des Umweltschutzes.

---

[19] Europäische Kommission, in: Wühle, M. (2007), S. 6.
[20] Habisch, A./Wildner, M./Wenzel, F. (2008), S. 13.
[21] Köppl, P./Neureiter, M. (2004), S. 15.

CSR ist in den Kontext der stakeholderorientierten Unternehmenspolitik einzuordnen. In Abgrenzung von einer rein gewinn- und rentabilitätsorientierten Unternehmenspolitik, die eine maximale Wertschöpfung für Shareholder in den Mittelpunkt stellt, betont der Stakeholder-Ansatz die Berücksichtigung der Interessen von weiteren gesellschaftlichen Gruppen, die in Beziehung zu dem Unternehmen stehen.[22] Diese sind z. B. Mitarbeiter, Kunden, Lieferanten und Vertreter der Gesellschaft (Politik, Umweltschutzverbände, etc.). Stakeholder-Orientierung wäre jedoch ebenso wie CSR missverstanden, wenn sie als Abkehr von wirtschaftlichen Erfolgsgrößen ausgelegt würde. Es geht vielmehr darum, diese durch außerökonomische Zielsetzungen zu ergänzen. Im Allgemeinen fußen CSR-Strategien auf der sogenannten Triple-Bottom-Line[23], bei der es um die Koordination von ökonomischen, ökologischen und sozialen Fragestellungen geht. Grundlage dieser mehrdimensionalen Perspektive ist die Überzeugung, dass Unternehmen zunächst gewinnbringend wirtschaften müssen, um überhaupt in der Lage zu sein, gesellschaftliche Ziele zu unterstützen. Die betriebliche Wertschöpfung ist zentral, gleichzeitig soll jedoch das eingesetzte Kapital erhalten bleiben – egal, ob es um finanzielles, natürliches oder soziales Kapital geht.[24]

Unternehmen verfolgen daher mit ihrem Engagement für die Gesellschaft nicht in erster Linie altruistische Ziele, sondern schaffen die Grundlage für den eigenen Erfolg.[25] Gelingt es, die soziale Wertschöpfung zu erhöhen, so profitiert das Unternehmen von qualitativ besseren Ressourcen des Umfelds – wie z. B. qualifizierten Mitarbeitern oder einer anspruchsvollen Nachfrage. Des Weiteren ist das Engagement so zu platzieren, dass weitere Unternehmen einsteigen, was zu einer größeren Wirkung führt, die Last der Einzelnen jedoch senkt. Weitere wichtige Rahmenbedingungen sind: die Effektivität der Leistung beim Empfän-

---

[22] Rühli, E./Sachs, S. (2003), S. 53.
[23] Moon, J./Crane. A./Matten, D. (2008), S. 59.
[24] Vgl. Kirchhoff, K. (2008), S. 114 ff.
[25] Habisch, A. (2003), S. 165.

ger durch direkten Know-How-Transfer verbessern und nicht zuletzt gemeinsame Erarbeitung von neuen Lösungskonzepten für soziale Probleme.

Neben diesen umfeldbezogenen Gründen für soziales Engagement können auch konkrete betriebswirtschaftliche Nutzen festgemacht werden. Zu unterscheiden sind externe und interne Nutzen. Extern ist CSR zuallererst ein Marketing-Tool, das die klassischen Kommunikationsmittel (wie Werbung, Product Placement und Öffentlichkeitsarbeit) ergänzt. CSR trägt über die Zusammenarbeit mit potenziellen neuen Kundengruppen dazu bei, dass ein Unternehmen deren Nutzenerwartungen und Bedürfnisse unmittelbarer kennen lernen kann. Überdies ermöglichen soziale oder ökologische Aktivitäten die Schärfung des eigenen Profils gegenüber konkurrierenden Unternehmen. Auf der anderen Seite steigern CSR-Maßnahmen die Loyalität und Markentreue bestehender Kunden, indem es dem Unternehmen gelingt, Vertrauen und Glaubwürdigkeit aufzubauen. In der Gesellschaft insgesamt verbessern sich das Image und die Reputation des Unternehmens.

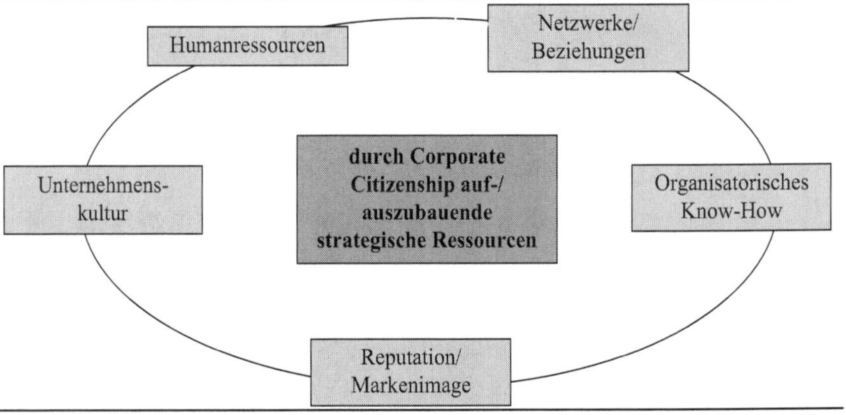

Abb. 1: Durch Corporate Citizenship auf-/auszubauende strategische Ressourcen

Quelle: Habisch, A./Wildner, M./Wenzel, F. (2008), S. 17.

Interne Zielgruppen von CSR-Maßnahmen sind die eigenen Mitarbeiter und die Kapitalgeber. Auf der einen Seite steigert CSR die Identifikation des Mitarbeiters mit seiner Firma. Auf der anderen Seite stellen Betriebe ihre Mitarbeiter zeitweise auch für gemeinwohlorientierte Aufgaben frei, was dem Einzelnen zudem die Möglichkeit der Persönlichkeitsentwicklung eröffnet. Kapitalgeber wiederum schätzen CSR aufgrund ihrer positiven Wirkung auf die Unternehmensbewertung an den Kapitalmärkten. Unternehmen profitieren damit mehrfach von CSR: der Unternehmenswert steigt, qualifiziertes Personal kann gewonnen und gehalten werden, die Abwanderung von Kunden wird verhindert, Boykotte des Unternehmens werden ausgeschlossen. Es entsteht ein stabiles Umfeld, in dem Unternehmen sich durch ein positives Image von ihren Konkurrenten abheben können.[26] Gerade die intangiblen Werte wie Reputation, Image, Vertrauen und Kooperation rechtfertigen in den allermeisten Unternehmen CSR-Aktivitäten: „Reputation stellt also vermutlich das stärkste intangible asset für den ökonomisch motivierten Ansatz der CSR dar…“[27].

Dass CSR trotz dieser Vorteile in Deutschland erst langsam Verbreitung findet, liegt hauptsächlich daran, dass viele ihrer Aktivitäten nur schwer gemessen und damit auf ihre wirtschaftliche Relevanz hin überprüft werden können. Denn die einzelnen CSR-Maßnahmen können harte oder weiche Ausprägung annehmen. Harte Formen der CSR betreffen z. B. den Umweltschutz in einem Unternehmen, dessen Spendenpolitik, Arbeitsbedingungen oder sein Verhalten in Bezug auf geltendes Recht (z. B. Verbot der Korruption). Weiche CSR-Maßnahmen sind in der Regel schwerer zu messen und umfassen Themen wie religiöse und kulturelle Toleranz oder Möglichkeiten der Mitarbeiter, sich weiterzuentwickeln. Tendenziell ist eine zunehmende Bedeutung weicher CSR-Themen zu beobachten.[28]

---

[26] Vgl. Kuhlen, B. (2005), S. 10 ff.
[27] Wühle, M. (2007), S. 23.
[28] Vgl. Schönborn, G. (2008), S. 98 ff.

Des Weiteren fehlt beiden Seiten – sowohl den Unternehmen als auch den Empfängern – häufig die Erfahrung im Umgang miteinander. Empfänger betrachten Firmen meist nur als Geldgeber und sich selbst als passiv Nehmende. Wichtig wäre aber im Sinne einer Professionalisierung von CSR, dass erstens sich beide Seiten auf derselben Kommunikationsebene befinden und Zuwendungsempfänger selbstbewusst den eigenen Wert für die Unternehmenskommunikation im Rahmen von Sponsoring-Aktivitäten ins Blickfeld rücken und zweitens nicht nur finanzielle Mittel herangezogen werden, sondern auch andere Kompetenzen von Unternehmen, die es für sie wiederum leichter machen, die oben beschriebene Kongruenz zwischen CSR und eigenen Geschäftszielen zu erreichen.[29] Wichtig für die Zusammenarbeit ist außerdem, dass kurzfristige Aktivitäten abgelöst werden von einem langfristig wirksamen CSR-Konzept beider Seiten.

1.2.2 Public Private Partnership

Bei Public Private Partnership (PPP) geht es ebenso wie bei CSR um das Engagement der Wirtschaft für gesellschaftliche Ziele. Allerdings sind in den meisten Fällen die Inhalte dieser Zusammenarbeit unterschiedlich. Hintergrund für die Entwicklung von PPP-Modellen ist der Umstand, dass staatliche Einrichtungen zum einen mit einem wachsenden Aufgabenkanon konfrontiert sind, der zum Zweck der wettbewerblichen Differenzierung gegenüber anderen Kommunen durch eine Ausweitung der freiwilligen Aufgaben (z. B. Wirtschaftsförderung und Tourismusarbeit) oder aufgrund der Schwerpunktverlagerung staatlicher Pflichtaufgaben auf untere kommunale Ebenen zustande kommt. Auf der anderen Seite hat sich die öffentliche Einnahmensituation verschlechtert. Um ihren Aufgaben trotzdem auf ausreichendem Niveau nachkommen zu können und in manchen Fällen auch Spielraum für innovative Projekte zu haben, greifen Kommunen immer häufiger auf eine Kooperation mit der Privatwirtschaft zurück. Manche Aufgaben werden dabei im Rahmen einer Privatisierung

[29] Vgl. Taubken, N. (2006), S. 163 f.

komplett ausgegliedert (z. B. städtische Freizeitanlagen), für andere bildet man gemeinsame Projektgesellschaften (z. B. beim Straßenbau) oder eine Tätigkeit wird im Rahmen einer Ausschreibung an einen Privaten vergeben. Immer jedoch steht der „Rückbau des Staates“[30], d. h. eine Verschlankung staatlicher Strukturen und ein damit verbundener Effizienzgewinn der staatlichen Verwaltung, im Vordergrund. Der Staat selbst zieht sich aus der direkten Aufgabenausübung zurück, trägt jedoch weiterhin die Gewährleistungsverantwortung, d. h. dass öffentliche Aufgaben in einer bestimmten Art und Weise erfüllt werden.

PPP kann damit verstanden werden als „Ansatz, öffentliche Leistungen zu produzieren und zu liefern, die den privaten und den öffentlichen Sektor in einer langfristigen Partnerschaft zusammenbringt und bei der jeder seine Identität und bestimmte Verantwortlichkeiten beibehält“[31]. Merkmale von PPP sind ebenso wie bei CSR die Freiwilligkeit der Zusammenarbeit und der Erhalt der institutionellen Eigenständigkeit der Partner. Deren Zielsetzungen müssen nicht notwendigerweise identisch sein, es genügen komplementäre Ziele, die auf lange Sicht das Erreichen einer Win-Win-Situation ermöglichen. Immer bezieht sich die Zusammenarbeit im Rahmen einer PPP auf eine öffentliche Aufgabe – im Kreise der Projektpartner findet sich immer eine staatliche oder kommunale Stelle.[32] Dies unterscheidet PPP von CSR-Ansätzen, die auch die Kooperation zwischen Wirtschaft und gesellschaftlichen (staatsfreien) Gruppen wie z. B. Sportvereinen umfasst. Sind letztere häufig auch nur mündlich vereinbart, so ist die Grundlage einer PPP immer ein Vertrag, der Leistung und Gegenleistung der Vertragsparteien über die gesamte Laufzeit des Projekts festlegt.[33] PPP-Projekte kommen selten ad-hoc zustande, sondern bedürfen einer längeren Vorbereitungszeit und sind gekennzeichnet durch eine längerfristige und auf Dauer angelegte Interaktion. Zwischen beiden Partnern wird daher auch der „Prozess

[30] Fürst, D. (2007), S. 174.
[31] Grüb, B. (2007), S. 27.
[32] Thierstein, A. (2007), S. 167.
[33] Thom, N./Ritz, A. (2008), S. 236.

der Zusammenarbeit und nicht die Form der Struktur"[34] betont. Charakteristisch ist bei PPP-Projekten, dass zu Beginn der Kooperation der Verlauf des Projektes und damit die Anforderungen (Leistung, Gegenleistung und Risiko) an beide Partner vielfach noch nicht abschließend bekannt sind. Die Ausgangssituation ist unstrukturiert und stellt an beide Seiten einen hohen Bedarf an Abstimmung. Gegenseitiges Vertrauen und Kooperationsbereitschaft sind erforderlich, um die Situation allmählich zu ordnen. Je größer die Fähigkeit der Vertragspartner zu Vertrauen und Kooperation, desto geringer sind die Transaktionskosten im Projekt. Vertragliche Beziehungen zwischen öffentlichen und privaten Partnern, die von Anfang klar definiert werden können und keinen Abstimmungsbedarf beinhalten, sind nach BUDÄUS (2006) keine PPP-Projekte, deren Charakteristikum eben der starke Kommunikations- und Klärungsbedarf im Rahmen eines aus Teilmodulen bestehenden Gesamtprozesses ist.[35]

Gelingt es, sich aneinander anzupassen und gemeinsam an einem Strang zu ziehen, erzeugen PPPs eine Vielzahl an positiven Wirkungsweisen. Am deutlichsten sind Synergieeffekte bzw. Effizienzvorteile wie z. B. Kosten- und Zeiteinsparung sichtbar. Bei PPP-Projekten übernimmt jede Seite die Verantwortung für diejenigen Aufgaben, für die sie am besten qualifiziert ist. Fortschritte werden damit schneller und kostensparend erzielt. Damit verbunden ist der Vorteil der Risikostreuung.[36] Die staatliche Seite zeichnet meist für gesetzgeberische und politische Risiken verantwortlich, während der private Partner die Risiken aus Planung, Bau, Betrieb und/oder Markt sowie jene der Finanzierung trägt.[37] Ein weiterer Nutzen aus der Zusammenarbeit ist der gegenseitige Wissenstransfer. Öffentliche Einrichtungen profitieren meist von der betriebswirtschaftlichen Management-Kompetenz der Privatwirtschaft. Aber auch jenen erschließen sich neue Erfahrungen: öffentliche Einrichtungen funktionieren nach ganz eigenen Gesetzen. Entscheidungsfindung und Mittelallokation sind häufig noch

---

[34] Grüb, B. (2007), S. 18.
[35] Vgl. Budäus, D. (2006), S. 16 f.
[36] Thierstein, A. (2007), S. 167.
[37] Napp, H.-G./Walter, P. (2007), S. 152.

politisch geprägt. Die enge Zusammenarbeit ermöglicht privaten Partnern die politische Einflussnahme (Gatekeeper-Strategie) bzw. eine frühe Kenntnisnahme über politische Entwicklungen.[38] Große staatliche Aufträge sind außerdem meist öffentlichkeitsrelevant. Das heißt, beteiligte private Unternehmen können positive Image-Effekte aus der Kooperation mitnehmen. Image bzw. der Beweis, betriebswirtschaftlich zu denken, motiviert außerdem auch staatliche Einrichtungen, auf PPP-Modelle zurück zu greifen. Nicht zuletzt geht es bei PPP jedoch auf beiden Seiten um Ressourcen bzw. um Rentabilität und Gewinn. Die Leistungsfähigkeit einer PPP muss höher sein als jene des Staates allein. Auf unternehmerischer Seite steht der Rückfluss aus den eingesetzten Mitteln im Vordergrund. Es geht um rentable Investitionen – wobei in Projekten, die eher in den Bereich der CSR hineinwachsen (z. B. PPP bei Wirtschaftsförderung) durchaus auch Nutzenerwartungen mit einfließen, die außerhalb des monetären Gewinns liegen. Unter dem Aspekt der Umwegrentabilität spielen daher auch Gesichtspunkte wie die Entwicklung des regionalen Absatzmarktes oder die Qualifikation potenzieller Arbeitnehmer eine Rolle[39], welche die Wettbewerbsfähigkeit des Standortes positiv beeinflussen.

Zu unterscheiden sind daher klassische harte PPPs von weicheren Formen, die sich dem CSR annähern. FÜRST (2007) bezeichnet erstere als PPPs in Form des Projektmanagements. Gemeint sind Aktivitäten, in denen ein Privater auf Vertragsbasis und für eine Gegenleistungen Infrastruktur-, Bau- oder Dienstleistungen unter Übernahme leistungstypischer Risiken übernimmt. Weiche PPPs werden demgegenüber als Kooperations-PPPs charakterisiert, bei denen Themen wie soziale Sicherheit, Umweltschutz sowie wirtschaftliche Wettbewerbsfähigkeit der Kommune über Verhandlung und Diskussion gesteuert werden. Typisch für diese Form der PPP ist die Organisation z. B. von regionalen Zukunftsforen und Expertenkreisen der Regionalentwicklung, in denen Vertreter der Wirtschaft und Sozialpartner eingebunden sind.[40] Auf die Organi-

[38] Brandt, A. (2007), S. 38.
[39] Brandt, A. (2007), S. 38.
[40] Fürst, D. (2007), S. 174.

sationsform der PPP bezogen lassen sich außerdem Tausch- und Poolmodelle unterscheiden. Beim Tauschmodell geht es um die Aufrechnung einer Leistung mit einer Gegenleistung. Grundlage ist wiederum ein Vertrag, der sich auf ein konkretes Projekt bezieht (projektbezogene PPP). Demgegenüber sind Poolmodelle durch eine Zusammenlegung von Ressourcen beider Partner gekennzeichnet, um eine gemeinsame Aufgabe zu lösen. Dieses Modell ist meist auf Dauer angelegt und entwickelt eigene organisatorische Strukturen (Organisations-PPP).[41] Die Dauerhaftigkeit der Beziehung zwischen Staat und Privatwirtschaft ist daher auch Merkmal einer weiteren Differenzierung von PPP-Formen.

Von PPPs der ersten Generation spricht man hingegen, wenn es sich um eine einfache Vergabe öffentlicher Aufgaben an Dritte handelt und das Risiko der korrekten Aufgabenerfüllung im Rahmen dieser Auftraggeber-Auftragnehmer-Beziehung größtenteils beim Staat verbleibt. Die zweite Generation von PPP ist längerfristig angelegt. Bei ihr übernehmen Private die operativen Aufgaben eines Projekts bereits weitestgehend eigenverantwortlich. Der Staat hat hauptsächlich koordinierende Aufgaben. Zur Berechnung von Rentabilitäten wird der gesamte Lebenszyklus eines Projekts zugrunde gelegt. Die dritte Generation von PPP definiert sich über die Verknüpfung von CSR-Themen mit PPP.[42] Hier scheint die Initiative von der Privatwirtschaft auszugehen, auf jeden Fall hat sie aber großen Einfluss auf Ausgestaltung und Inhalt des eigenen Engagements.

---

[41] Budäus, D. (2006), S. 17.
[42] Budäus, D. (2006), S. 25.

2 Empirische Ergebnisse

CSR und PPP sind keine Begriffe, die sich gegenseitig ausschließen. Vielmehr gibt es zahlreiche Überschneidungsbereiche – vor allem bei Themen, die weniger investitionsorientiert, sondern stärker gesellschaftspolitisch zentriert sind. CSR scheint dort die unternehmerische Perspektive für Aktivitäten zu sein, die von staatlicher Seite eventuell schon als PPP bezeichnet werden. Beispiele hierfür sind Projekte im Bereich des Jugendschutzes wie die Ausstattung eines Jugendzentrums mit moderner EDV-Infrastruktur. CSR wie PPP entspringen einem neuen Verständnis von Zusammenwirken zwischen Staat, Gesellschaft und Wirtschaft. Nicht mehr Hierarchie und Marktmechanismen allein steuern deren Interaktion, sondern das Netzwerk wird zum prägenden Steuerungsmuster. Häufig bezieht sich die Kooperation auf einen regionalen Kontext und wird dann als Regional Governance bezeichnet. Deren Merkmale sind „komplexe Steuerungs- und Koordinationsstrukturen, die formelle und informelle Elemente, staatliche und nicht-staatliche Akteure sowie hierarchische, kompetitive und kooperative Akteursbeziehungen“ [43] umfassen.

Insgesamt ergibt sich gedanklich ein Kontinuum an Aktivitäten zwischen Staat und Gesellschaft, das auf der einen Seite auf das Konzept CSR fokussiert ist, auf der anderen Seite härtere Formen der PPP aufweist. Wichtig an dieser Gegenüberstellung ist, zu verstehen, dass sich beide Konzepte nicht ausschließen, sondern vielmehr zwei strategisch unterschiedliche Ansätze sind, über die unternehmerisches Engagement für öffentliche Aufgaben begründet werden kann. Im Mittelpunkt steht immer die Erfüllung einer öffentlichen Aufgabe, die auf der einen Seite aus strategischen Überlegungen in Richtung CSR oder eben über ein PPP-Modell realisiert werden kann. Häufig finden sich auch beide Ansätze parallel oder Mischformen aus beiden in einem Unternehmen.

Weniger zur Trennung von beiden Ansätzen als vielmehr zum besseren Verständnis ihrer unterschiedlichen Schwerpunktsetzungen sollen einige charak-

[43] Benz, A. (2001), S. 55.

teristische Merkmale herausgearbeitet werden: in Bezug auf die Kooperationspartner ist festzustellen, dass PPPs meist in einer Zweierbeziehung zwischen Staat und Wirtschaft ausgestaltet sind. CSR-Maßnahmen hingegen finden häufig ohne Beteiligung staatlicher Stellen statt, sondern umfassen Privatwirtschaft und gesellschaftliche Gruppen z. B. Umweltschutzgruppen oder kirchliche Einrichtungen. Ebenso ist der Formalisierungsgrad und damit verbunden auch der Zeithorizont beider Konzepte unterschiedlich: CSR-Maßnahmen werden zwar immer häufiger von (vor allem größeren) Unternehmen strategisch geplant, die überwiegende Mehrheit dürfte jedoch auf Ad-hoc-Entscheidungen beruhen, die mündlich kommuniziert werden und eine eher kurzfristige Reichweite haben. PPPs fußen hingegen fast ausschließlich auf vertraglichen Vereinbarungen. Ihr Trend geht zu langen Laufzeiten (Lebenszyklus-Ansatz) und bindet die Vertragspartner auf Dauer aneinander.

Die Ziele bei PPPs bestehen hauptsächlich in der Realisierung von Effizienzvorteilen, der Wissensgenerierung und Risikostreuung. Es stehen Investments im Mittelpunkt, die sich rentieren müssen. Unternehmen bringen meist eigenes Kapital sowie ihre Managementkompetenz in das PPP-Projekt ein und erhalten dafür vom Staat eine definierte Leistungsvergütung sowie Planungssicherheit und Zugang zu öffentlichen Fördermitteln. Betriebswirtschaftliche Grundsätze sind der Nährboden für erfolgreiche PPPs. Es ist ein Geschäftsmodell zwischen Staat und Wirtschaft, das auf Leistung und Gewinnorientierung basiert. CSR-Maßnahmen werden zwar auch mit Hinweis auf ökonomische Rentabilitäten (Imagegewinne, Entwicklung des unternehmerischen Umfelds) durchgeführt, diese lassen sich jedoch kaum messen. CSR ist somit weniger an Zahlen orientiert. Sie fußt nicht auf dem Prinzip von Leistung und Gegenleistung. CSR-Maßnahmen werden auch dann durchgeführt, wenn der Empfänger zu keiner Leistung fähig ist. Werden bei CSR Aktivitäten auf Grundlage der Triple-bottom-line (Einklang von sozialen, ökologischen und ökonomischen Zielen) durchgeführt, so stehen bei harten PPPs rein ökonomische Gesichtspunkte im Vordergrund und es wird sogar angenommen, dass aufgrund der Effizienzkriterien und der Projektorganisation unter Ausschluss betroffener Sozialpartner entsprechende soziale oder umweltbezogene Belange in den Hintergrund gedrängt werden. Bei CSR hingegen geht es fast ausschließlich um die Lösung sozialer und ökologischer Problemstellungen. Die Erwartungen der Unternehmen beziehen sich hier nicht auf Renditeziele, sondern auf Reputationsgewinne – ökonomisch messbaren Zielen bei PPPs stehen intangible Werte bei CSR-Aktivitäten gegenüber.

Bringt man die so definierten Begriffe CSR und PPP in Bezug zum Bildungssponsoring, so zeigt sich, dass unternehmerisches Engagement in Schulen sowohl CSR-orientiert (Unterstützung von Schulveranstaltungen) als auch PPP-zentriert (Sanierung eines Schulgebäudes) sein kann. Diesen Zusammenhang verdeutlicht die nachstehende Graphik:

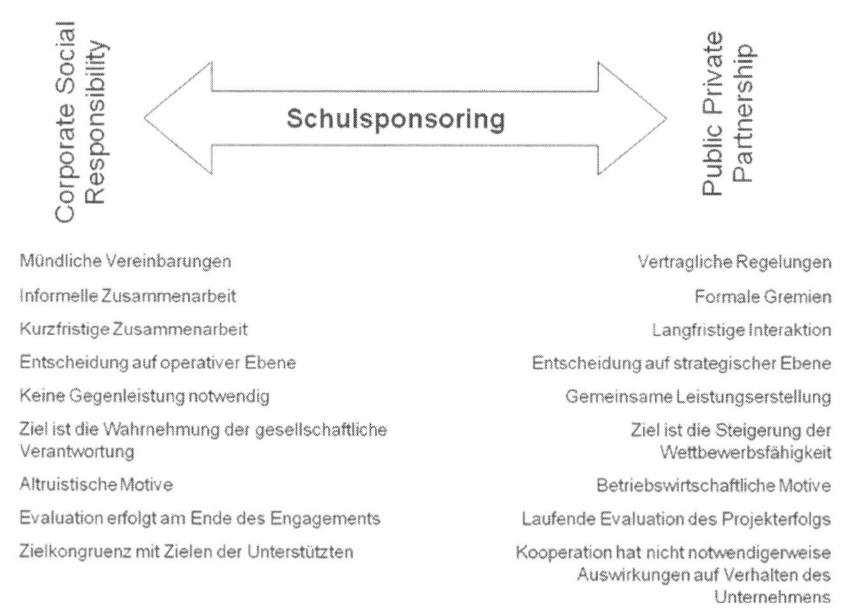

Abb. 2: Untersuchungsrahmen der empirischen Erhebung
Quelle: eigene Darstellung.

Ob sich Unternehmen dieses Unterschieds bewusst sind bzw. aus welchem Blickwinkel sie ihr schulisches Engagement begründen, zeigt die empirische Analyse in der Region Ingolstadt, die im November und Dezember 2008 bei 96 Unternehmen und 160 Schulen mit Hilfe eines Online-Fragebogens durchgeführt wurde. Angemerkt werden kann, dass der Rücklauf bei beiden Gruppen mit 42% (Unternehmen) bzw. 46% (Schulen) gut ausfiel. Beteiligt haben sich auf beiden Seiten hauptsächlich größere Einrichtungen. Auf schulischer Seite stammen über die Hälfte der Antworten von Grundschulen und Hauptschulen, insgesamt haben die Hälfte aller teilnehmenden Schulen zwischen 300 und 1000 Schüler. Auf unternehmerischer Seite kam der Rücklauf vornehmlich von Industrie- und Dienstleistungsbetrieben. Hier ist eine Häufung bei Unternehmen mit einer Mitarbeiterzahl zwischen 201 und 300 festzustellen, das heißt, es kann eine rege Beteiligung des Mittelstands verzeichnet werden. Besonders hervorzuheben ist in diesem Kontext auch die hierarchische Stellung der Antwortenden: bei Schulen waren dies zu überwiegender Mehrheit (82%) die Schulleiter, bei Unternehmen hauptsächlich Mitglieder der Geschäftsführung oder aber Abteilungsleiter, die mehrheitlich aus dem Personalbereich stammen. Insgesamt legt dies den Schluss nahe, dass die Kooperation zwischen Schule und Wirtschaft bei beiden Partnern Chefsache ist – jedenfalls vorwiegend auf Leitungsebene koordiniert wird. Dies deutet bereits auf einen hohen Professionalisierungsgrad hin und weist daher in Richtung PPP-Konzept. Ob sich diese Vermutung durch die weiteren empirischen Daten festigen lässt, zeigen die nächsten Abschnitte.

Zunächst soll festgehalten werden, dass die generelle Zufriedenheit mit der Zusammenarbeit sowohl bei Schulen als auch in Unternehmen sehr hoch ist. Beide beantworteten eine entsprechende Frage auf einer 5-teiligen Skala mit durchschnittlich 4 Punkten. Schulen sind etwas zufriedener mit der Zusammenarbeit (4,07 Punkte) als Unternehmen (3,97 Punkte). Die Unterschiede sind allerdings nicht groß. Wichtiger ist es zu erkennen, dass kein einziges Unternehmen mit der vollen Punktzahl geantwortet hat – sprich keines ist mit der

Zusammenarbeit vollkommen zufrieden, was auf ein Verbesserungspotenzial schließen lässt. Dabei sollte allerdings erwähnt werden, dass Unternehmen die Kooperation nicht so bedeutsam für den eigenen Erfolg einstufen wie Schulen. Während jene im Durchschnitt mit 3,82 Punkten aussagten, dass die Kooperation wesentlichen Einfluss auf den Erfolg der schulischen Einrichtung hat, bewerten Unternehmen diesen ein wenig niedriger: sie vergaben hier durchschnittlich nur 3,32 Punkte, was auf der 5-teiligen Skala einem mittleren Platz entspricht. Dieses Ergebnis geht einher mit praktischen Erfahrungen und den Ausführungen im vorausgehenden Teil dieses Artikels. Dort wurde bereits festgehalten, dass Schulen aufgrund finanzieller Engpässe der Aufwandsträger immer häufiger auf Mittel aus der Privatwirtschaft angewiesen sind. Desweiteren sind sie bemüht, ihren Abgängern gute berufliche Perspektiven zu verschaffen. Beides könnten Gründe sein, warum Schulen die Kooperation für ihren Erfolg bedeutsamer einstufen als Unternehmen es tun. Dies belegt auch ein weiteres Faktum der Studie: Schulen kooperieren im Durchschnitt häufiger mit Unternehmen als umgekehrt. Über 40% der an der Befragung teilnehmenden Schulen hatten 10 und mehr privatwirtschaftliche Partner. Bei den Unternehmen ist in der Mehrheit eine Zahl von 3 bis 5 schulischen Kooperationspartnern gegeben.

Was jedoch macht eine Kooperation erfolgreich? Insgesamt konnten anhand der Rückläufe sieben Handlungsbereiche für Akteure in Unternehmen und Schulen identifiziert werden, die eine Zusammenarbeit erleichtern:

1. **Förderschulen** erzielen mit Unternehmen besonders häufig erfolgreiche Kooperationen. Dieser Schultyp sorgt auch für die höchste Zufriedenheit und könnte daher als Best-Practice-Beispiel dienen, um die Zusammenarbeit zwischen Unternehmen und anderen Schultypen zu verbessern. Aus unserer Erhebung wurde deutlich, dass Unternehmen, die ihre Zusammenarbeit mit Schulen in hohem Maße in Bezug zum eigenen Erfolg setzen, besonders häufig mit Förderschulen zusammenarbeiten. Es gibt somit einen positiven Zusammenhang zwischen Unternehmenserfolg und Kooperation mit Förder-

schulen. Für Akteure auf beiden Seiten kann daher ein Blick in Förderschulen hilfreich sein, die eigenen Projekte noch erfolgreicher zu machen.

2. Das **Personalwesen** ist der Kooperationspartner von Schulen, die mit der Zusammenarbeit besonders zufrieden sind. Für die Schulen wurden in der Erhebung insgesamt acht Unternehmensfunktionen zur Auswahl gestellt mit der Frage, welche davon überwiegend mit der Umsetzung der Kooperation befasst sei. Vor der Geschäftsführung mit 17% wurde hierbei das Personalwesen (32%) genannt. Setzt man dieses Ergebnis in Bezug zur generellen Zufriedenheit der Schulen mit der Zusammenarbeit, so ergab sich außerdem, dass diese Unternehmensfunktion auch diejenige ist, die den Schulen die größte Zufriedenheit stiftet. Umgekehrt ist die Zusammenarbeit auch für die Unternehmen zufriedenstellend, wenn die Personalstelle involviert ist. Insgesamt lässt sich daher der Rückschluss ziehen, dass positiv beurteilte Kooperationen rund um die Unternehmensfunktion „Personal" entstehen. Schulen und Unternehmen mit weniger gut laufenden Projekten könnten hier Hinweise auf Erfolgsvariablen finden. Für ein Regionalmanagement ließe sich der Ansatz ableiten, aktive Wissensplattformen zwischen Mitarbeitern in Personalabteilungen, die erfolgreiche Kooperationen durchführen, und solchen in – eventuell auch kleineren – Betrieben zu schaffen, denen die entsprechende Erfahrung noch fehlt.

3. **Schüler** haben aus Sicht der Unternehmen die größte Bedeutung für den Erfolg der Kooperation. Ruft man sich die oben dargestellten Motive von Unternehmen in Bezug auf ein Schul-Sponsoring wieder ins Gedächtnis, so wird deutlich, dass das frühzeitige Einbinden und Kennenlernen von zukünftigen Mitarbeitern ein wichtiger Grund für ihr Engagement ist. Die Erhebung des Zentrums für Entrepreneursh!p der Katholischen Universität Eichstätt-Ingolstadt ergab jedoch, dass Schüler nur zu einem geringen Grad (5% der Kontakte) in die Umsetzung der Zusammenarbeit einbezogen wurden. Ist dies jedoch der Fall, so stufen Unternehmen die Kooperation als sehr erfolg-

reich ein. Kurz gesagt erscheint die direkte Beteiligung von Schülern in Kooperationsprojekten für die unternehmerische Seite ein wesentlicher Schlüssel für den Erfolg. Für die Schulen jedoch sind andere Personen erfolgsrelevant. Hier werden vor allem die Schulleitung und Eltern genannt. Festzuhalten bleibt daher: um die Kooperation für Unternehmen attraktiv zu gestalten, könnte eine stärkere Einbindung von Schülern in die Zusammenarbeit sinnvoll sein.

4. Die **Nachmittagsbetreuung** sollte stärker in die Zusammenarbeit einbezogen werden. Insgesamt beinhaltete die Untersuchung sechs schulische Bereiche, die von der Kooperation betroffen sein könnten. Diese reichten von der Ausstattung der Schule über eine Verbreiterung des Lehrangebots und der Bereitstellung von Beratungsleistungen z. B. zu Organisationsfragen an die Schule bis hin zur Übernahme von Personal- oder Sachkosten und der Organisation von Nachmittagsbetreuung. Insgesamt am häufigsten genannt wurde von den Unternehmen ein Engagement bei den beiden ersten Punkten (Ausstattung, Lehrangebot). Interessant war jedoch die Inbezugnahme von Erfolg und Zufriedenheit der Betriebe und der Schulen mit der Kooperation. Dann nämlich punktet die Nachmittagsbetreuung. Sie korreliert deutlich positiv bei beiden Partnern sowohl hinsichtlich Erfolg als auch Zufriedenheit. Sie ist also derjenige Kooperationsbereich, der beide Seiten sowohl zufriedenstellt als auch positiv auf die Erfolgsbeurteilung wirkt. Sie sollte daher bewusst zum Gegenstand der Zusammenarbeit gemacht werden.

5. Für Unternehmen ist der Erhalt von **Gegenleistungen** für die Kooperationszufriedenheit bestimmend. Ein großes Thema bei der Zusammenarbeit zwischen Schule und Wirtschaft ist immer die Frage, ob und in welchem Ausmaß das unternehmerische Engagement von den Schulen honoriert werden soll und kann. Die Studie bot mehrere mögliche schulische Gegenleistungen zur Auswahl an und fragte deren Einsatz auf beiden Seiten ab. Knapp die Hälfte aller Schulen gewähren demnach Gegenleistungen in Form

eines Hinweises auf das Unternehmen auf dem geförderten schulischen Gegenstand (z. B. Computer) oder durch Nennung in der Öffentlichkeit. Weniger praktiziert werden Gegenleistungen wie die Änderung des Schulnamens, Logo des Unternehmens auf dem schulischen Briefbogen oder der Webpage sowie Teilnahme von Schulvertretern an Unternehmensveranstaltungen. Auch hier ist die Zusammenschau zwischen Gegenleistung und Erfolg bzw. Zufriedenheit mit der Kooperation aufschlussreich. Unternehmen honorieren demnach die Gegenleistung als solche – ihnen ist es nicht primär wichtig, welche Leistung dies ist, aber es muss eine Leistung fließen. Dann steigt auch deren Kooperationszufriedenheit. Für Schulen wiederum ist die Gegenleistung (außer, wenn das Unternehmen in der Öffentlichkeit genannt wird) kaum ausschlaggebend für ihre Zufriedenheit.

6. Einen weiteren Hinweis auf die erfolgreiche Gestaltung von Kooperationen zwischen Schule und Wirtschaft liefern die **Motive** der beiden Partner zur Zusammenarbeit. Für die Unternehmen lassen sich vor allem vier Beweggründe identifizieren. Diese sind – ganz im Einklang mit den theoretischen Erkenntnissen – Imagepflege, Gewinnung von Personal, Wahrnehmung gesellschaftlicher Verantwortung und Mitarbeitermotivation. Auf schulischer Seite wiederum dominiert der Wunsch, den Unterricht praxisnäher zu gestalten, das Praktikumsangebot auszuweiten und die Schule stärker ins gesellschaftliche Umfeld integrieren zu können. Weitere Motive betreffen die Schärfung des Schulprofils sowie die Verbesserung der Öffentlichkeitsarbeit der Schule. Besonders interessant erscheint nun, dass Unternehmen, die besonders zufrieden mit der Zusammenarbeit sind, großen Wert darauf legen, die Lehrinhalte an den Schulen mitbestimmen zu können. Bedenkt man, dass dies eben jener Umstand ist, der manche Schule kritisch über Kooperationen mit der Wirtschaft denken lässt, so wird das entstehende Konfliktpotenzial deutlich. Auf der einen Seite steht der intensive Wunsch von Schulen und den zuständigen Landesbehörden auf Freiheit des Unterrichts von Unternehmensinteressen, auf der anderen Seite würde eine

Kooperation bei den Lehrinhalten den Unternehmen jedoch entgegenkommen. Abgesehen von diesem Umstand lassen sich jedoch zwei konkrete Handlungsempfehlungen formulieren: da erstens Unternehmen ein Hauptmotiv ihres Engagements in der Personalgewinnung sehen, sollten ein weiteres Mal die Kooperationen unter intensiver Beteiligung der Schüler konzipiert und umgesetzt werden. Zweitens könnten davon auch die Schulen profitieren, denn sie könnten über vermehrte Praktika das Ziel eines erfolgreichen Einstiegs ihrer Schüler ins Berufsleben verfolgen.

7. Der **Kooperationsmarkt** für Schulen und Unternehmen ist intransparent. Bei Weitem nicht alle befragten Einrichtungen konnten auf aktuell bestehende Kooperationsprojekte verweisen. Der Hauptgrund liegt ihren Angaben entsprechend darin, dass sie keinen geeigneten Partner kennen. Hier würde sich ein lohnendes Tätigkeitsfeld für vermittelnde Akteure anbieten. Es sollte möglich sein, über virtuelle oder persönliche Kontaktplattformen interessierte Unternehmen und Schule aufeinander aufmerksam zu machen.

Festzuhalten bleibt damit, dass die Zusammenarbeit zwischen Schule und Wirtschaft in der Region Ingolstadt durch vielfältige Weise gefördert werden könnte. Beide Seiten sind konzeptionell nicht weit voneinander entfernt. Beide bevorzugen Arrangements, die eher in Richtung Public Private Partnership-Modell gehen und damit gekennzeichnet sind von einer langfristigen Zusammenarbeit, die auf oberster Ebene der Schule oder des Unternehmens koordiniert wird.

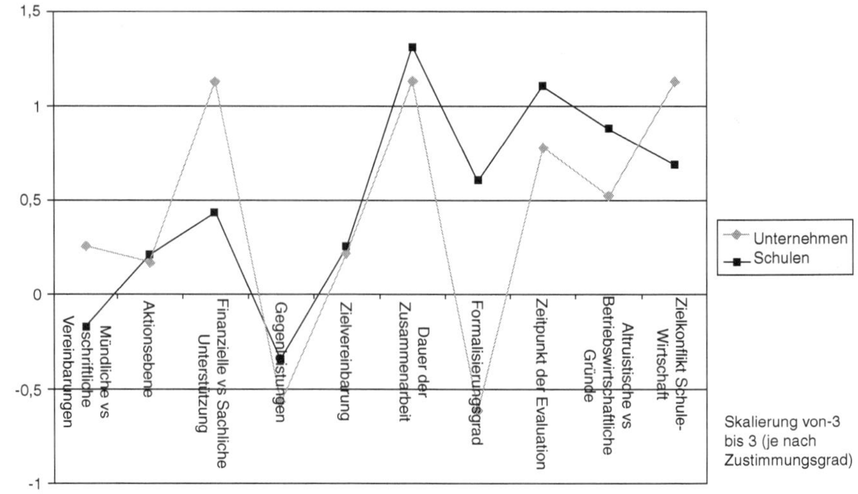

Abb. 3: Grundhaltungen von Schulen und Firmen in Hinblick auf CSR- und PPP-Modelle

Quelle: eigene Darstellung.

Beide Seiten möchten in der Zusammenarbeit von einer Wettbewerbssteigerung profitieren und setzen dafür einen hohen Professionalitätsgrad der Kooperation voraus. Dieser manifestiert sich z. B. durch den Wunsch nach einer laufenden Erfolgskontrolle. Auf der anderen Seite lassen sich in der operativen Umsetzung der Zusammenarbeit unterschiedliche Auffassungen erkennen. Schulen bevorzugen eher finanzielle Leistungen der Unternehmen, während jene lieber sachliche Unterstützung einbringen. Unternehmen bevorzugen schlanke, formlose Strukturen, während Schulen mündliche Vereinbarungen wertschätzen. Insgesamt ist der Unterschied in der Herangehensweise jedoch nicht groß und, wie oben gezeigt werden konnte, gibt es konkrete Handlungsansätze, die Schulen und Unternehmen noch näher aneinander heranrücken lassen. Weiche Formen von PPP-Modellen im Sinne von Kooperations-PPPs, die Entscheidungen weniger über Verträge als mehr über Verhandlung und Diskussion steuern, erscheinen damit geeignet, die Zusammenarbeit zwischen Schule und Wirtschaft zu fördern. Sicherlich ist dabei auf beiden Seiten, aber auch auf übergeordneter behördlicher Seite, das Wissen um die Möglichkeiten und Grenzen dieser Zusammenarbeit auszubauen. Dieser Beitrag hat versucht, eine Grundlage dafür zu schaffen.

3 Literaturverzeichnis

Ahlert, D./Vogel, V./Woisetschläger, D. (2007): Ist Sponsoring der Zaubertrank einer starken Marke? In: Ahlert, D./Vogel, V./Woisetschläger, D. (Hrsg.) (2007): Exzellentes Sponsoring. Innovative Ansätze und Best Practices für das Markenmanagement. DUV, Wiesbaden, S. 5-29.

Angerer, Th. (2003): Management von Kundenfeedback : integrative Konzeption und empirische Transaktionsanalyse der Erfolgswirksamkeit, Wiesbaden.

Autorengruppe Bildungsberichterstattung im Auftrag der Ständigen Konferenz der Kultusminister der Länder in der Bundesrepublik Deutschland und des Bundesministeriums für Bildung und Forschung (2008): Bildung in Deutschland 2008. Ein indikatorengestützter Bericht mit einer Analyse zu Übergängen im Anschluss an den Sekundarbereich I. W. Bertelsmann Verlag GmbH & Co. KG, Bielefeld.

Benz, A. (2001): Vom Stadt-Umland-Verband zu „regional governance" in Stadtregionen. In: Deutsche Zeitschrift für Kommunalwissenschaften, Jg. 40, H. 2, S. 55-71.

Brandt, A. (2007): Was heißt PPP in der Wirtschaftsförderung? In: Brandt, A. et al. (Hrsg.): Public Private Partnership in der Wirtschaftsförderung. Herausforderungen, Chancen und Grenzen. Deutscher Sparkassenverlag, Stuttgart, S. 32-41.

Bruhn, M. (2003): Sponsoring. Systematische Planung und integrativer Einsatz. GWV Fachverlage GmbH, Wiesbaden.

Bruhn, M. (1990): Sozio- und Umweltsponsoring. Engagements von Unternehmen für soziale und ökologische Aufgaben. Vahlen, München.

Budäus, D. (2006): Public Private Partnership – Kooperationsbedarfe, Grundkategorien und Entwicklungsperspektiven. In: Budäus, D. (Hrsg.) (2006): Kooperationsformen zwischen Staat und Markt. Theoretische Grundlagen und praktische Ausprägungen von Public Private Partnership. Schriftenreihe der Gesellschaft für öffentliche Wirtschaft, Heft 54, Nomos, S. 11-28.

Fürst, D. (2007): PPP, New Regional Governance und Probleme der Legitimation. In: Brandt, A. et al. (Hrsg.) (2007): Public Private Partnership in der Wirtschaftsförderung. Herausforderungen, Chancen und Grenzen. Deutscher Sparkassenverlag, Stuttgart, S. 174-185.

Fürst, D. (2006): Regional Governance – ein Überblick. In: Kleinfeld, R./Plamper, H./Huber, A. (Hrsg.) (2006): Regional Governance Band 1. Steuerung, Koordination und Kommunikation in regionalen Netzwerken als neue Formen des Regierens. V&R unipress, Osnabrück, S. 37-59.

Grüb, B. (2007): Sozialkapital als Erfolgsfaktor von Public Private Partnership. Schriften zur öffentlichen Verwaltung und öffentlichen Wirtschaft, Band 206, BWV, Berlin.

Habisch, A./Wildner, M./Wenzel, F. (2008): Corporate Citizenship (CC) als Bestandteil der Unternehmensstrategie. In: Habisch, A./Schmidpeter, R./ Neureiter M. (Hrsg.) (2008): Handbuch Corporate Citizenship, Berlin, S. 3-43.

Habisch, A. (2003): Corporate Citizenship: gesellschaftliches Engagement von Unternehmen in Deutschland. Berlin.

Habisch, A./Meister, H.P./Schmidpeter, R. (2001): Corporate Citizenship as Investing in Social Capital. Logos Verlag, Berlin.

Heinrich, G./Hüchtermann, M./Nowak, S. (2002): Macht Sponsoring Schule? Deutscher Instituts-Verlag, Köln.

Kirchhoff, K. (2008): Investor Relations. In: Habisch, A./Schmidpeter, R./ Neureiter M. (Hrsg.) (2008): Handbuch Corporate Citizenship, Berlin, S. 109-116.

Köppl, P./Neureiter, M. (Hrsg.) (2004): Corporate Social Responsibility. Wien.

Kuhlen, B. (2005): Corporate Social Responsibility (CSR). Die ethische Verantwortung von Unternehmen für Ökologie, Ökonomie und Soziales. Entwicklung – Initiativen – Berichterstattung – Bewertung. DWV, Baden-Baden.

Lommarzsch, L. (2003): Schulsponsoring. Grundlage, Praxis, Chancen, Risiken für Unternehmen und Schulen. VDM Verlag Dr. Müller, Düsseldorf.

Moon, J./Crane. A./Matten, D. (2008): Citizenship als Bezugsrahmen für politische Macht und Verantwortung der Unternehmen. In: Backhaus-Maul, H. et al. (2008): Corporate Citizenship in Deutschland, Bilanz und Perspektiven. Wiesbaden, S. 45-67.

Müller-Schwemer, Th./Sorg, G. (2006): Was Sie schon immer über Sponsoring wissen wollten. In: Braun, K. et al. (Hrsg.) (2006): Marketing- und Vertriebspower durch Sponsoring. Sponsoringbudgets strategisch managen und refinanzieren. Springer, Berlin, S. 1-38.

Napp, H.-G./Walter, P. (2007): Public Private Partnership im Bildungssektor – Investitionsoffensive statt Sanierungsstau: In: Brandt, A. et al. (Hrsg.) (2007): Public Private Partnership in der Wirtschaftsförderung. Herausforderungen, Chancen und Grenzen. Deutscher Sparkassenverlag, Stuttgart, S. 145-156.

Rühli, E./Sachs, S. (2003): Der Stakeholder Ansatz – Ein umfassendes Framework des strategischen Managements. In: Matzler, K./Pechlaner, H./Renzl, B. (Hrsg.) (2003): Werte schaffen. Perspektiven einer stakeholderorientierten Unternehmensführung. Wiesbaden.

Schönborn, G. (2008): Corporate Citizenship und Wertemanagement im Unternehmen. In: Habisch, A./Schmidpeter, R./Neureiter M. (Hrsg.) (2008): Handbuch Corporate Citizenship. Berlin, S. 97-105.

Taubken, N. (2006): Corporate Social Responsibility und Regional Governance – Ein Zusammenhang? In: Kleinfeld, R./Plamper, H./Huber, A. (Hrsg.) (2006): Regional Governance Band 1. Steuerung, Koordination und Kommunikation in regionalen Netzwerken als neue Formen des Regierens. V&R unipress, Osnabrück, S. 153-166.

Thierstein, A./Schedler, K./Bieger, Th. (Hrsg.) (2000): Die lernende Region. Regionale Entwicklung durch Bildung. Rüegger, Zürich.

Thierstein, A. (2007): Public Private Partnerships für Wirtschaftsförderung unter dem Blickwinkel der Raumentwicklung. In: Brandt, A. et al. (Hrsg.) (2007): Public Private Partnership in der Wirtschaftsförderung. Herausforderungen, Chancen und Grenzen. Deutscher Sparkassenverlag, Stuttgart, S. 167-173.

Thom, N./Ritz, A. (2008): Public Management. Innovative Konzepte zur Führung im öffentlichen Sektor. Wiesbaden.

Wühle, M. (2007): Mit CSR zum Unternehmenserfolg. VDM Verlag, Saarbrücken.

Internetquellen

Krüger, J./Bacher, J. (2007): Sponsoring im Fokus der Unternehmen und Agenturen. In: TNS Infratest und IPSOS (Hrsg.): Sponsor Visions 2007, unter http://www.sponsors.de/uploads/tx_svsstudiengaenge/Sponsor_Visions_2007_323767.pdf (Stand vom 9.9.08)

Deutscher Bundestag: Grundgesetz der Bundesrepublik Deutschland, unter: http://www.bundestag.de/parlament/funktion/gesetze/gg_jan2007.pdf (Stand vom 9.9.08)

Bayerische Staatsregierung: Bayerisches Gesetz über das Erziehungs- und Unterrichtswesen (BAYEUG) in der Fassung der Bekanntmachung vom 31. Mai 2000 unter http://www.verwaltung.bayern.de/Titelsuche-.116.htm?purl= http://by.juris.de/by/EUG_BY_2000_rahmen.htm (Stand vom 9.9.08)

Bundesfinanzministerium: Anwendungserlass zur Abgabenordnung (AEAO), unter: http://www.bundesfinanzministerium.de/nn_92/DE/BMF__Startseite/ Service/Downloads/pp/AEAO__1,templateId=raw,property=publicationFile. pdf (Stand vom 9.9.08)

Landesinstitut für Erziehung und Unterricht: Förderalmanach. Ein Handbuch zum Bildungssponsoring, Stuttgart 2001, unter: http://www.leu.bw.schule.de/ 1/data/sponsoring/foerderalmanach.pdf (Stand vom 9.9.08)

Job Creation and Lifelong Employment – Innovative Solutions from Public Private Partnerships in Europe

Germana Di Domenico & Marco Meneguzzo

Inhaltsverzeichnis

1 Introduction

The overall objective of the paper is to explore the rationale behind Public Private Partnerships in labour market, therefore it is mainly intended to:

- Clarify the roles of PES and PRES, as a precondition for successful partnerships, in a dynamic perspective while avoiding possible segmentation of the market
- Explore the scope for PES-PRES[1] cooperation according to different contexts and variables

There are indeed remarkable differences in shaping public-private relationships, from the institutional and organisational point of view, thus showing various typical features in the labour market systems of EU Member States. Therefore, there is a constant need to take into account the diversity of national situations regarding PES and PRES as well as their institutional interactions.

2 The reference framework behind Public Private Partnerships

The Public Private Partnership (PPP) is defined as any agreement between the public sector and private entities (both defined in a broad sense) to achieve an objective.

The objective and initiative of PPPs usually come from public entities; however, the private entity aim to maximize profits and objectives may not be in line with those of the public sector. Moreover, the incentives for private and public agents may change during the relationship. The reasons why public entities foster this kind of relationship are multiple; among the most common factors

[1] PES = Public Employment Services; PRES = Private Employment Services

are managerial practices, problem conversion, morale regeneration, risk- and power-sharing and restructuring the public service.

The various types of PPP can find applications in the different functions carried out by public administrations and agencies, such as the realisation of infrastructure projects and public works, from investments in the network services sector to the formulation of policies and delivery of services.

There are in fact various types of PPP which, as figure 1 shows, show the involvement of private subjects, both for-profit and non-profit, in planning policies for intervention and in the design of the system for supply of services (co-formulation), in the decision-making process (co-decision making), through processes of stakeholder engagement, in co-financing of investments and interventions. This latter modality is appropriate to private finance initiatives, as experienced in the United Kingdom since the 1990s, and to project finance. Finally, other types may be associated with an offer of services (co-production) and the evaluation of the impact and the results (co- evaluation).

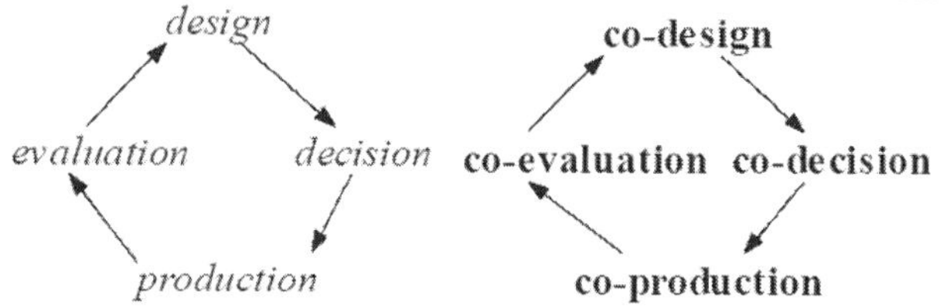

Fig. 1: The evolution towards co-design, co-decision, co-production and co-evaluation

Source: http://www.4qconference.org.

PPP is linked closely to processes of modernisation, innovation and managerial development of public administration. Particularly interesting in this sense are the indications from a recent initiative developed at the European level – the European Public Sector Award (EPSA). The EPSA, activated since 2007, has the goal of rewarding innovative and excellent experiences in public administration, so as to facilitate the spread and transfer of knowledge.[2]

The areas of innovation taken into consideration by EPSA are: i) collaborative governance; ii) efficient and effective management of resources; iii) management of demographic changes.

In particular, collaborative governance, developed through co-operation with other public and private actors, citizens and users, is considered as an effective solution to confront the scarcity of resources available to public administration.

Table 2 summarizes by thematic area the projects presented by the various European public administrations for the first competition in 2007.

PPP experiences and projects are presented in various areas: from co-operation (27 projects), to PPP itself (4; for EPSA PPP is understood as project finance), to the co-involvement of stakeholders and the community (37 projects), to financial innovation and co-financing (13 projects).

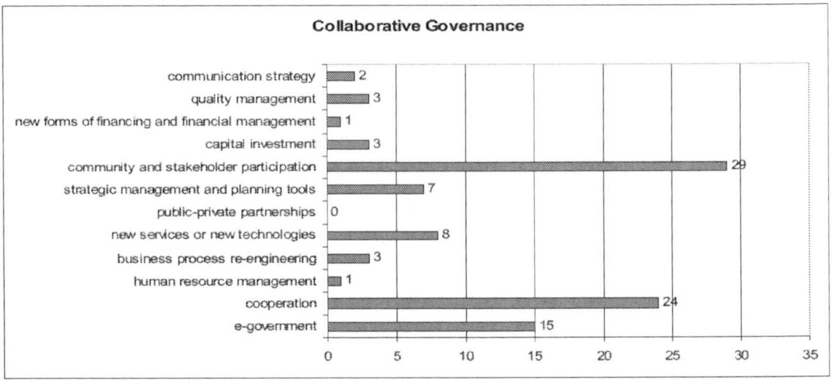

Table 1: The 2007 EPSA: applicants and domain of intervention
Source: own graphics.

2 The promoters of the prize are the European Group of Public Administration (EGPA), the University of Speyer (DHV) and the Bertelsmann Foundation. Cf. www.eps-award.eu.

Other relevant indications for the relevance of PPP emerge from the last conference on the quality of public administrations in the European Union.[3]

The challenges around us – for example the growing weight of economic and digital inequalities in modern societies, the financial crisis triggered by the sub-prime phenomenon, demographic ageing or immigration – require co-operative solutions involving different levels of government between public administrations and civil society organisations and other stakeholders (media and businesses).[4]

Strategies of participation and co-involvement assume centre stage, as does adequate knowledge of needs and performances.

The PPPs are broadly used in many areas, such as healthcare, education, infrastructure and research. However, governments have not found the same need for PPPs in the labor market as they have in other matters. As with education, PPPs in labor affairs focus on offering services, so do not cany the risks derived from owning and recording assets.

Interesting indications on the potential of PPP are contained in the report prepared by Business Europe (Business Europe 2008) which groups together 40 associations and federations of private businesses at the European level and which synthesises the 'point of view' of the private side of the partnership.

In this report the volume of public investments which saw the adoption of the logic of PPP in the period 1990-2006 was estimated at 200 billion Euros; the most dynamic countries were indicated as the United Kingdom, followed by Spain, France and Germany. Businesseurope indicates that the value added linked to the choice to turn to PPP leads to better value for money, to innovation in sources of financing for public investments, to better performance, to a faster and flexible public services delivery, to effective support for environmental and

3 See Pollitt, Ch./Bouckaert, G./Löffler, E. (2006).

4 "The achievement of continuing stakeholder participation is a prerequisite for the achievement of sustainable solutions". Cf. Pollitt, Ch./Bouckaert, G./Löffler, E. (2006).

societal goals and lastly to an improvement in EU competitiveness and global economic opportunities. Among the numerous case studies of success discussed by Businesseurope, one (progress2work Working links Wales UK) concerns public partnership with private for profit and private not for profit bodies, and looks at social services and job creation.

3 Key variables for development of PPP in public policies for the employments

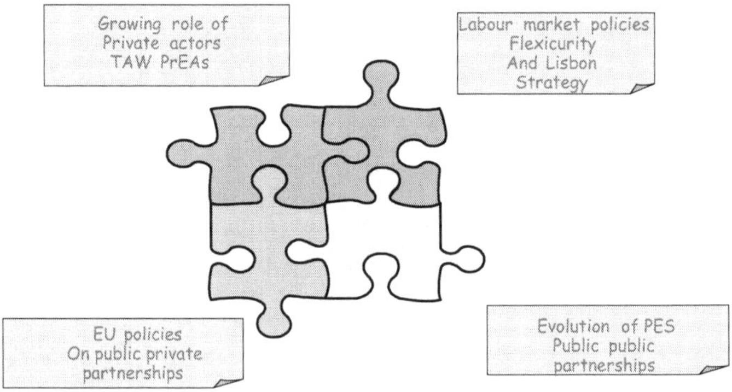

Fig. 2: Key variables for development of PPP in public policies for the labour market

Source: our elaboration.

In figure 2 the principal variables which can play a relevant role in the introduction and above all in the spread of PPP in the sector of policies for public intervention in the labour market are set out.

The most important variable is represented by the **EU level policies**.

The European Commission has been exploring the key issue of public and private partnerships (PPPs) mainly in response to the market trends that took place in Europe over the last decade concerning all public services in a broad sense, in particular the decentralisation of service delivery to local government and the opening-up of the market to private providers. The Commission adopted in November 2005 a Communication on PPPs to clarify how public authorities can choose their private partners on a more competitive basis and how to improve public procurement practices and procedures. Given the continuance of the trend, a more specific Communication, dealing with operational issues was published in February 2008.

When it comes specifically to Employment Services, this issue started to be addressed a few years ago by the European Commission. In September 2004 a seminar on PES-PRES cooperation took place with the main aim of identifying effective ways of interaction between public and private services, and related opportunities, disadvantages or limitations. Furthermore, in the context of the modernisation of Public Employment Services the Commission co-financed a project in 2005 concerning "Guidelines for quality assurance in public and private employment services" that was implemented by several national PES.

ILO Convention on "private employment agencies": The General Conference of the International Labour Organisation adopted the Convention on Private Employment Agencies on 19 June 1997, one of the aims of which is to protect temporary workers. The Convention, which has replaced the previous ILO one No. 96/1949, is an attempt to modernize the law related to temporary work agencies in order to promote flexibility in the functioning of the labour markets. It also specifies the type of measures which States must take in order to guarantee adequate protection of temporary workers. The aim of Art. 2 of the Convention is indeed "to allow the operation of private employment agencies as well as the protection of the workers using their services (...)".

European Commission Communication on *Public-Private Partnerships and Community Law on Public Procurement and Concession* (COM/2005/0569 final) and on the *application of Community law on Public Procurement and Concessions to Institutionalised Public-Private Partnerships* (C(2007)6661).

The recently (2008) adopted Interpretative Communication on the application of Community law on Public Procurement and Concessions to Institutionalised Public-Private Partnerships (IPPP) explains the EC rules to comply with when private partners are chosen for IPPP. Depending on the nature of the task (public contract or concession) to be attributed to the IPPP, either the Public Procurement Directives or the general EC Treaty principles apply to the selection procedure of the private partner. The Communication expresses the view of the Commission that under Community law one tendering procedure suffices when IPPP are set up. Accordingly, Community law does not require a double tendering – one for selecting the private partner to the IPPP and another one for awarding public contracts or concessions to the public-private entity – when IPPP are established. The Communication also states that as a matter of principle IPPP must remain within the scope of their initial object and cannot obtain any further public contracts or concessions without a procedure respecting Community law on public contracts and concessions. However, it is acknowledged that IPPP are usually set up to provide services over a fairly long period and must, thus, be able to adjust to certain changes in the economic, legal or technical environment. (...)

Secondly a relevant variable is represented by the **growing role of private actors** from TWA (Temporary Work Agencies) to PREAS (Private Employment Agencies).

During the past two decades private employment services (PRES) have spread in European national labour markets at a gradually accelerating pace. Propelled by market forces and recently profiting from a more liberal public regulation, their proliferation is expected to continue in the near future. PRES offer a range of services: various kinds of assistance in search, selection and recruitment, outplacement services, and the hiring out of workers under a multitude of contractual formats. Adjustment services, like training and retraining, are also provided. Such training may be organised as an additional activity of placement agencies, but it may also be the main activity of specialised enterprises. Since then, quite a number of changes have affected the European labour market, like the growing use of atypical employment contracts to meet flexibility needs and the increasing share of temporary work in particular. According to a 2005 Eurofound report[5], temporary agency work (TWA) was the most rapidly growing form of atypical employment in the European Union since the 1990s. The regulation of temporary work at European level has been contentious for over twenty years and there is still room for a European regulatory framework in the concerned field. This basically relates to the different regulatory frameworks and socio-economic contexts at national level, which is a crucial variable to be taken into due account and adequately respected especially when dealing with such delicate issues as shaping public-private relationships.

The importance of developing functional networks with all involved actors in the labour market should also be stressed. Partnerships between PES and PREA play a key role in terms of "**labour market governance**". For example, in operational terms joint projects between PES and PREAS seem to be very successful with regard to "outplacement and relocation services", which also involves new forms of negotiation and sharing responsibilities between workers, employers and public administration.

TWAs themselves co-operate through an international association, the *Confédération Internationale des Entreprises de Travail Temporaire (CIETT)*, to advocate their trade and to lobby with public authorities and trade-unions for less restrictive regulations. They also fight restrictive regulation and (what they regard as) unfair competition by appealing to the official procedures of European competition law (delivering official complaints at Commission level and taking cases to national and European court). In doing this they proved indeed able to influence case law.

---

[5] European Foundation for the Improvement of Living and Working Conditions, "*Temporary agency work in an enlarged European Union*", ISBN 92-897-0927-8, of 8/03/2006.

Other kinds of PRES (outplacement agencies, agencies for selection and recruitment services) have also established international associations. These have developed specific branch 'codes of practice'.

Third crucial variable is represented by the **public policies on labour market**.

The type of collaboration in labour markets depends on the nature of the policies. The OECD splits labour market policies into so-called ***active*** **and** ***passive*** **labour market measures**. The active measures comprise a wide range of policies aimed at improving unemployed workers' access to the labour market and jobs, job-related skills and the functioning of the labour market. The passive measures relate to spending on income transfers. The measures included in the Active Labor Market Policy (ALMP) are broken down into five main program categories[6]: (i) public employment services and administration; (ii) youth measures; (iii) subsidized employment focused on hiring, assistance in starting a business and direct job creation; (iv) measures for the disabled; and (v) labour market training programs. The development of the ALMP comprises the initial framework for the collaboration between public and private agents.

Moreover one of the main priority areas for the next cycle of Lisbon and the European Employment Strategy is **flexicurity**, both internal (within the enterprise) and external (from one enterprise to another), alongside which Member States are expected to develop such policies. Flexicurity has four components[7]: flexible and reliable contractual arrangements (from the perspective of the employer and the employee, of insiders and outsiders); comprehensive lifelong learning strategies; effective active labour market policies; and modern social security systems.

---

6 See Martin (2000).

7 Communication from the Commission to the European Parliament, the Council, the European Economic and Social Committee and the Committee of the Regions on *Towards Common Principles of Flexicurity: More and better jobs through flexibility and security* (Brussels, 26 June 2007).

It seems indeed possible to have flexible labour markets and workers' security if certain conditions are observed. Examples are some investment in active labour market policies and social rights; balancing of employer and worker oriented flexibility, internal and external flexibility and a genuine social dialogue. Several configurations are possible and a cross-country analysis of selected EU member states shows that some countries have succeeded in organizing their labour markets in a manner that combines flexibility with security with beneficial effects on decent work. Such pathways stress the importance of developing the role of PES in active labour market policies[8] in a complementary way with passive ones, and in some contexts the importance of their cooperation with PRES[9] and the private sector in a broader sense[10].

There are although remarkable differences in shaping public-private relationships, from the institutional and organisational point of view, thus showing various typical features in the labour market systems of EU Member States. Therefore, there is a constant need to take into account the diversity of national situations regarding PES and PRES as well as their institutional inter-actions.

Lastly a relevant variable is the process of redefining strategy and operation management of PES in the different EU countries. Despite cross-countries diversity, a number of common trends in the modernisation process of PES may be observed in the EU, namely:

- Decentralisation of the services provision to local authorities with related governance issues (i.e. coordination and cooperation among

8 "*Cooperation with market partners, such as temporary work agencies, would be considered. Active labour market policies would be designed to support not only (long-term) unemployed but also those who are experiencing frequent intervals of Unemployment*" (Commission Communication on Flexicurity, pag. 15)

9 Ref. to the Eurociett/Uni-Europa Joint Declaration on 28/02/2007.

10 "*Public-private partnership of all stakeholders (public authorities at all levels, education and training providers, social partners, companies, NGOs, private employment agencies) could contribute to effectiveness of active labour market policies*" (Commission Communication on Flexicurity, pag. 19).

institutions, territorial levels and different, profit and non-profit, stakeholders);

- Opening up of the market to private players;
- Diversification of services providers.

Such changes have also implied internal re-organisation of PES, that are now more deeply looking for new constructive ways to interact with private agencies[11]. In particular some questions remain open: how to conclude successful partnerships, what form a good contracting with the private sector should take, which role and tasks should the public have in orienting the services of partners, how should this be done, through incentives, monitoring, control mechanisms[12].

Moreover new actors are entering in labour market arena between PES and PRES, next to private employment services. Therefore, various institutional interests tend to become more involved in organising employment services: these new actors are:

- Schools and universities more often make special efforts to assist their pupils/students in finding their way into the labour market.
- Increasingly municipal, sector-bound and national agencies for the administration of unemployment benefits, disability benefits and social

[11] The ILO has recently delivered a "Guide to private employment agencies" for a better regulation and monitoring of the market, which is another indicator of the huge potential of the private market)

[12] Commission Communication on Services of General Interest, including social services of general interest: a new European commitment (COM(2007) 725 final of 20 November 2007), as part of a larger package including the Communication "A single market for 21st century Europe" aiming at improving general awareness and understanding of the EU rules mainly on public procurement: it distinguishes between economic services of general interest (such as electricity, gas, transport) and non-economic (traditional state prerogatives such as police, justice and statutory social security schemes). Such distinction turns to be very relevant to PES since "social services" can be of an economic (e.g. social assistance services, training) and non-economic (e.g. statutory and complementary social security schemes) nature depending on the activity under consideration.

welfare feel inclined to add active employment services to their income replacement services.

- Local and regional public authorities, who have acquired a stronger stake in employment policies, develop a growing interest in the organisation of employment services.
- Market associations of workers and employers or of social partners together, more often seek to use employment services within the framework of human resource management and enterprise restructuring.

All these organizations and bodies may use the PES as a delivery mechanism, but a second option is to create intermediary agencies of their own. They may also adopt a third option purchasing e-services from PRES. And they may choose for a combination of these options.

With an increasing variety of PRES in the market and with a growing number of institutions interested in the organisation of employment services, the Ministry of Employment itself may start to use other agencies for service delivery as well, next to the PES.
Certainly these developments have much more advanced in some countries than in others. But it holds true for every PES, if not with an eye to the present than anticipating the future, that it can no longer regard itself as the natural and sole service provider. It has to define its position among other agencies in the market and has to deal with them in two directions:

a) towards the final customers, jobseekers and employers,
b) towards several public and other collective bodies with an interest in employment services, who have become more numerous and who may choose to work with other delivery agencies.

To justify funding of the PES two criteria tend to become increasingly important for the Ministry of Employment:

a) Intermediary services no longer necessarily require public initiative. Therefore, such public activities should be more precisely defined in terms of added social and/or economic value to the labour market (principle of additionality).

b) When public initiative is needed, then the PES should only be used if it works at least as cost-effective as other delivery mechanisms (principle of efficiency).

These criteria may seem simple and clear, but actually they are not. It is not easy to define a market optimum in which all legitimate private and public needs for employment services are served at best. Therefore, it remains open for debate in what kind of activities PES should engage and to what extent. Some key questions are:

– What general infrastructure for employment services should PES establish?

– What services should PES perform itself and what services can be outsourced?

The challenge of defining new PES roles is linked to other changes in the labour market as well, such as a spread of more flexible employment relations, a revolution in communication technology, and so on.

4 Public and private partnership; alternative approaches

As stated in the so called "Kok Report" from the High Level Group on Employment of the European Commission ("*Jobs, Jobs, Jobs*", 2004), "Public-private partnerships should be facilitated and encouraged as a means of boosting investment. (…) Public-private partnership of all stakeholders (public authorities at all levels, education and training providers, social partners, companies, NGOs, private employment agencies) could contribute to effectiveness of active labour market policies".

It is anyway quite complex to make a systematic and exhaustive inventory of the ways in which PESs develop a relationship with PRES. Some quick observations are following. They are arranged under three headings: co-operation, complementarity, competition.

Cooperation – Information and Basic Matching Services – PESs have started to develop self-service systems, both within the local employment offices and on the Internet. Linked to these systems new patterns of co-operation with PRES develop. The nature of it is determined by answers to three questions:

- Should PRES have access to PES registrations of vacancies and jobseekers?
- Should PRES be offered the opportunity of advertising their vacancies within the PES offices and/or the PES jobsbank on the Internet?

Member state PESs experiment with different modalities. Interesting cases seem to be the ***United Kingdom, the Netherlands, Sweden and Belgium***.
Another example of more intensive services which may also entail co-operation is **active brokerage**.
PES may actively refer some clients to PRES. Jobseekers may be left free to accept such referral or not; they may also be obliged if benefit entitlement requires search behaviour that includes looking for jobs via PRES.
For certain clients PES may outsource some parts of the individual case management. In principle this may involve any particular service, from information and guidance up to training and other adjustment services. PES may outsource to PRES the complete case-management of particular (groups of) clients.

To some extent outsourcing is common practice in almost all PESs. But practices show a wide variety across member states. Sometimes outsourcing is proceeded by cutting off specialised business units from PES. These are then made independent organisations who are henceforth expected to sell their services on the open market (facilities for vocational training and facilities for vocational guidance are examples). Some PESs experiment with co-location, offering PRES the opportunity to establish a branch within their premises. **Arbeidsvoorziening in the Netherlands** is one example.

PES may also seek to establish and develop specific joint ventures with some PRES, for instance to organise 'full-service' to employers and thus becoming more attractive to them. In such joint ventures PES may seek to create extra opportunities for disadvantaged jobseekers. On a large scale this approach is now being pursued **in the Netherlands**.

Complementarity – With other service providers proliferating, PES may decide either to stay out of particular market areas, or not to engage in particular kinds of services, or not to extend its services to particular groups of jobseekers and employers. This leads to a division of labour with others. Often the Ministry of Employment is involved in such decisions.

In many countries one early example was vocational guidance for youngsters who still follow full-day education in schools. Re-adjustment services for workers within enterprises are a more recent example in many countries. Up-market activities, like selection and recruitment of managers and of highly specialised staff, may also be left to specialised private agencies. An interesting example is at present to be found in **Ireland and Denmark**, where re-integration services for unemployed workers without unemployment insurance benefit tend to be made a task for separate offices under authority of special regional or local bodies.

Competition – In many market segments PES will anyway be keen to keep sufficient business with employers in order to have sufficient placement opportunities for jobseeking clients. Competing with PRES PES will seek to improve its services to employers through many innovations. In that case two questions tend to be asked by public authorities (and PRES):

- Is such competition really necessary for achieving the public objectives of the PES?
- Is such competition organised with acceptable means? Is it not distorting markets by providing cheap services financed by public money, that PRES could provide as well at a reasonable fee.

Recently there were interesting discussions on the latter issue **in Belgium**.

Probably the most revolutionary reshaping of public intervention in employment services is nowadays happening in Australia. There the PES, as a public enterprise for reintegrating unemployed jobseekers through case management, is abolished since May 1998. The former PES has been transformed into a government owned enterprise (Employment National) that henceforth must compete with PRES for public case-load assignments. This is a rather radical way of giving substance to the more widely discussed idea of inserting market signals in the relationship between the government and the PES. In a less radical way this option is also considered and experimented with in some EU member states, **like United Kingdom** (private employment services implementing the 'Welfare to Work' programme in a number of city districts) **and the Netherlands** (leaving unemployment insurance and welfare agencies free to purchase services either from PES or from other service providers).

Without being exhaustive the above listing of co-operation, complementarity and competition already shows a wild array of initiatives. It is a rich source of new experiences that should be analysed more deeply.

5 Public Private Partnerships: Final remarks and possible recommendations

Public Private Partnerships have, as you know, been developed in several areas of the public sector and are widely used within the EU. In times of tight public budgets their importance for the European Economy can hardly be underestimated. Value for money in the context of PPPs can obviously best be achieved if private partners are chosen on the basis of fair competition.

Public-private partnerships can, if managed correctly, improve the quality of services, provide greater choice for citizens, allow for faster delivery and improve control of public spending. In this context, for instance, the EU and other European public authorities are called to remove barriers that restrict partnership between the public and private sectors and calls for the wider promotion and use of PPPs as a key way to improve public service innovation[13].

Against this background, moving specifically to the field of labour market as our core business, a number of issues still seem to be open and need to be faced – namely concerning the role of the public administration when service provision is outsourced to private providers. From this viewpoint, there is a clear need to define the conditions under which the outsourcing should be carried out, in order to ensure that certain objectives of general interest are met (e.g. through authorisation regimes, public service obligations, selection criteria in the context of a public procurement procedure). Room is also for such relevant questions as:

1. To what extent do public procurement rules apply to Public Private Partnerships?
2. How long should a "convenient" contracting-out (from PES to PRES) last?
3. Which degree of autonomy and level of responsibility are on PRES?

[13] Business Europe, 2008

4. How to ensure efficiency and *cost-consciousness* of PRES?

5. How to measure the results and effects of PRES also in comparisons with those of PES?

6. Should the *criteria for selecting* the service provider (and the related procedure) be defined in a "common (European level) framework"?

7. How to *avoid service segmentation* and to *preserve the "holistic" approach behind the integrated service delivery*? In other terms: is it better/suitable/convenient/effective/sustainable to outsource the whole package of services to one private provider only and/or to outsource each service to a different provider (service segmentation)?

Many of these problems result from uncertainty about the applicable rules at European level. What should anyway always be highlighted is that there is no "one size fits all" solution to the problems in question.

However, literature dealing with PPPs shows several common success factors that those involved in labour markets should also share:

- Availability of resources: Quantity, quality and duration of any kind of resources should be guaranteed for all members of the partnership to undertake the project.

- Advertisement effort: In addition to guaranteed resources, clear public support of labor market projects by leading politicians is recommended, obtaining significant commitment in favor of these activities.

- Full confidence among the members of the partnership: The objectives of the partnership must be clearly defined, as well as reporting and monitoring systems. When the interests of the public and private agents are aligned and they share objectives, the evolution of the partnership goes more smoothly than when the opposite is true. Furthermore, both risk and uncertainty interfere with the optimal performance of PPPs.

The identification and sharing of risks of the partnership lead to responsible participation of private agents in the project.

- Monitoring: the PPP "must be accountable." Monitoring of PPPs is twofold. First, the accountability of partners to perform their responsibilities is undertaken through internal control. Second, new processes of partnerships should be fostered to find the best response to new demands for society. The use of experiments produces valuable databases to analyze the evolution of the project and improve a partnership's performance.

By accurately taking into account all the relevant above mentioned aspects a tailor-made solution to single cases can realistically be designed to effectively manage a PPP approach to labour market issues.

References

Ambrosanio M.F./Bordignon M./Etro F. (2004): Investimenti in infrastrutture.

Balduzzi, P. (2006): Models of Partnerships. Working Paper N. 96, Economics Department, University of Milan-Bicocca.

Business Europe (2008): Public-private partnerships: Adding value to Europe's public services. Brussels.

Canadian Council for Public-Private Partnerships – Publications – http://www.pppcouncil.ca/publications.asp.

Colman, J. (2002): Mumbo jumbo…and other pitfalls: Evaluating PFI/PPP projects. National Audit Office PFI / PPP Conference "Bringing about beneficial change. London.

C.R.E.A.M. Europe – Public Private Partnerships in the EU Enlargement http://www.cream-europe.eu

Di Domenico G./Gilli D. (2005): Public and Private Employment Services: co-operation or competition? In: Rivista SPINN 05-2005 (09-02-2006).

Di Domenico G./Gilli D. (2006): Governance e modelli di policy sul mercato del lavoro. Riflessioni comparate sui sistemi europei di Servizi all'impiego.

Di Domenico G./Spattini, S. (Eds.) (2008): New European Approaches to Long-term Unemployment. What Role for Public Employment Services and What Market for Private Stakeholders? Kluwer Law International Ed.

European Commission – Public-Private Partnerships and Community Law on Public Procurement and Concession (COM/2005/0569 final): http://europa.eu.int/eur-lex/lex/LexUriServ/site/en/com/2005/com2005_0569 en01.pdf

European Commission – Interpretative Communication on the application of Community law on Public Procurement and Concessions to Institutionalised Public-Private Partnerships (IPPP), C(2007)6661:http://ec.europa.eu/internal_market/publicprocurement/docs/ppp/comm_2007_6661_en.pdf

European Commission – A single market for 21st century Europe (COM(2007)0724): http://eur-lex.europa.eu/LexUriServ/site/en/com/2007/com2007_0724en01.pdf

European Commission – Towards Common Principles of Flexicurity: More and better jobs through flexibility and security (COM(2007359): http://eur-lex.europa.eu/LexUriServ/LexUriServ.do?uri=COM:2007:0359:FIN:EN:PDF

Harris, A.C. (1996): Financing infrastructure: private profits from public losses. Audit Office of NSW, Public Accounts Committee, Parliament of NSW, Conference, Public/Private infrastructure financing: Still feasible? Sydney.

Hart O. (2002): Incomplete contracts and Public Ownership: Remarks and an Application to Public-Private Partnerships. mimeo, Harvard.

ILO (2004): Public-Private Partnerships in Employment Services. Working Paper, No. 17, Geneva.

ILO: Guide to private employment agencies: http://www.ilo.org/public/english/employment/skills/download/peaguide.pdf

Kok, W. (2004): Facing the challenge. The Lisbon strategy for growth and employment. Brussels. http://ec.europa.eu/growthandjobs/pdf/kok_report_en.pdf

Linotte, D. (2005): Un cadre juridique désormais sécurisé pour les contrats de partenariat. In: AJDA, n° 1/2005 du 10 janvier 2005.

Monbiot, G. (2000), 'Captive State, The Corporate Takeover of Britain', Macmillan.

Monera, F. (2005): Les financements innovants de services et de projets publics. In: Revue de la Recherche Juridique – Droit prospectif, PUAM, 2005-1, p. 337 & s.

OECD (2005): Employment Outlook 2005 Chapter 5: "Public Employment Services: Managing Performance". http://www.oecd.org/dataoecd/2/40/36780883.pdf

OECD (2008): Public-Private Partnerships: In Pursuit of Risk Sharing and Value for Money. Paris, June 2008.

Pollitt, Ch./Bouckaert, G./Löffler, E. (2006): Making quality sustainable: co-design, co-decide, co-produce, co-evaluate. 4QC Conference, Tampere.

Shleifer A. (1998): State versus Private Ownership. In: Journal of Economic Perspectives, 12, 4, p. 133-50.

Spackman, M. (2002): Public-private partnerships: lessons from the British approach. In: Economic Systems, 26(3), 283-301.

United States PPP lobby – National Council for Public-Private Partnerships http://www.ncppp.org

UK – Flexible New Deal: http://www.dwp.gov.uk/welfarereform/in-work-better-off/annex.pdf

Ökonomische Grundlagen von Public Private Partnership in Österreich

Kurt Promberger

Inhaltsverzeichnis

Abkürzungsverzeichnis

ASFINAG	Autobahnen- und Schnellstraßen-Finanzierungs-Aktiengesellschaft
BMI	Bundesministerium für Inneres
BMVIT	Bundesministerium für Verkehr, Innovation und Technologie
BMF	Bundesministerium für Finanzen
BMWF	Bundesministerium für Wissenschaft und Forschung
BMWA	Bundesministerium für Wirtschaft und Arbeit
BMLV	Bundesministerium für Landesverteidigung
BOO	Build-Own-Operate
BOT	Build-Operate-Transfer
DBFO	Design-Build-Finance-Operate
Eurostat	Statistisches Amt der Europäischen Gemeinschaften
GVP-Ö	Generalverkehrsplan – Österreich
MbO	Management by Objectives
NGO	Nicht-Regierungsorganisation
NPM	New Public Management
ÖPP	Öffentlich-Private Partnerschaft
PFI	Private Finance Initiative
PPP	Public Private Partnership
SCHIG	Schieneninfrastruktur-Dienstleistungsgesellschaft mbH

1 Public Private Partnership (PPP) – ein mehrdeutiges Konzept!

Public Private Partnerships[1] (PPP) sind weltweit zu einem beliebten Instrument der Politik geworden. Regierungen, insbesondere die, die sich dem dritten Weg[2] verschrieben haben, betonen mit Nachdruck, dass Öffentlich-Private Partnerschaften ein wichtiges Mittel zur Modernisierung unserer Gesellschaft darstellen und dass die Einbeziehung von privaten Akteuren in die Bereitstellung von öffentlichen Diensten einen essentiellen Beitrag zur Erreichung politischer Ziele leisten können und damit einen gesellschaftlichen Mehrwert schaffen. PPPs sind aber auch ein Ausdruck des herrschenden Zeitgeistes, der von Modeworten mit Symbolkraft geprägt ist. Die zunehmende Popularität wird vielleicht auch dadurch gefördert, dass das PPP-Konzept sehr projektionsoffen formuliert ist und die Entscheidungsträger – ganz gleich, ob Politiker, Spitzenbeamte, Unter-

1 Anstelle des Anglizismus „Public Private Partnership" (PPP) wird häufig der deutschsprachige Ausdruck „Öffentlich-Private Partnerschaft" (ÖPP) verwendet.

2 Vgl. Giddens, A. (1997).

nehmer, Interessensvertreter, Bürger, etc. – ihre Vorstellungen von Partnerschaft (Kooperation, Kollaboration, Interaktion) zwischen öffentlichem und privatem Sektor darunter subsumieren können. Gerade dieser Umstand – so die kritischen Stimmen – soll von der wahren Absicht der Politik ablenken, den öffentlichen Sektor durch Privatisierungen und Contracting Out weiter auszuhöhlen. In der politischen Auseinandersetzung ist es manchmal erfolgversprechend, abgenützte Namen (wie Privatisierung, Ausgliederung etc.) gegen neue auszutauschen. Dadurch kann die gleiche Politik unter einem neuen, weniger verfänglicheren Namen fortgesetzt werden.

Am Beispiel einer in der PPP-Fachliteratur häufig verwendeten Definition lässt sich diese Projektionsoffenheit des PPP-Konzepts anschaulich demonstrieren:

> *PPP bezeichnet eine mehr oder weniger nachhaltige Kooperation zwischen öffentlichen und privaten Akteuren zur gemeinsamen Entwicklung von Diensten (Sach- u./o. Dienstleistungen), bei denen die Risiken, die Kosten und die Gewinne partnerschaftlich geteilt werden.*[3]

Obwohl diese Definition sehr breit angelegt ist, ist sie doch in der Lage, einige wichtige Aspekte hervorzuheben:

- Die Kooperation muss eine bestimmte Dauerhaftigkeit aufweisen und darf sich nicht in einer kurzfristigen Zusammenarbeit erschöpfen.
- Die Teilung der Risiken, Kosten und Gewinne zwischen den Partnern wird als konstituierendes Merkmal gesehen, wobei die Risiken vielfältiger Natur sein können. Der private Partner kann Risiken übernehmen, die traditionell der öffentliche Sektor getragen hat. Risikoübertragung bedeutet aber nicht automatisch, dass der private Partner sämtliche oder den größeren Teil der Risiken zu tragen hat. Die Teilung des Risikos ist projektspezifisch festzulegen und hängt von den Fähigkeiten der Beteiligten ab, diese zu beurteilen und zu kontrollieren.

---

3 Klijn, E. H./Teisman, G. R. (2000), S. 85.

- Die Dienste werden derart entwickelt bzw. bereitgestellt, dass beide Partner davon profitieren können. Die Akteure aus dem öffentlichen und dem privaten Sektor verfügen über spezifische Fähigkeiten, die – richtig miteinander verknüpft – zu einem beiderseitigen Mehrwert führen.

Diese Definition ist sehr allgemein gehalten und daher auch nicht sehr präzise. Sie erlaubt eine große Streuung in den Ausprägungen wichtiger Parameter wie Zeitdauer, Enge der Kooperation, Art der Produkte/Dienstleistungen, Form der Zusammenarbeit, Kosten, Komplexität, Ebene der Institutionalisierung und Anzahl der einbezogenen Akteure.

HODGE und GREVE (2007) haben eine Typologie Öffentlich-Privater Partnerschaften entwickelt, die versucht, die Form und die Intensität der Beziehungen zwischen den Akteuren als Differenzierungsmerkmale zu verwenden. Hinsichtlich der Form unterscheiden sie zwischen finanziellen und organisationalen Verflechtungen, die – je nach Intensität – entweder eng oder lose sein können. Mit Hilfe der beiden Dimensionen und ihren Ausprägungen können verschiedene PPP-Typen abgeleitet werden. [4]

Organisation/ Finanzierung	enge organisationale Verflechtung	lose organisationale Verflechtung
enge finanzielle Verflechtung	Joint Venture Unternehmen	DBFO, BTO, BOT, BOO
lose finanzielle Verflechtung	Policy Network	Issue Network

Abb. 1: Typologie von Öffentlich-Privaten Partnerschaften
Quelle: eigene Darstellung, in Anlehnung an Hodge, G./Greve, C. (2007), S. 545.

[4] Vgl. Hodge, G./Greve, C. (2007), S. 545.

Entsprechend Abbildung 1 gibt es PPPs, in denen die öffentlichen und privaten Akteure finanziell sehr eng miteinander verflochten sind, jedoch nicht in organisationaler Hinsicht. Diese Formen findet man vorwiegend im Bereich von öffentlichen Infrastrukturprojekten, in denen die Beziehungen zwischen den öffentlichen und privaten Akteuren durch detaillierte marktorientierte Verträge mit Laufzeiten zwischen 20 und 30 Jahren geregelt sind. Für die rechtliche Ausgestaltung dieser Partnerschaften stehen verschiedene Formen von vertraglichen Arrangements zur Verfügung, die international unter Bezeichnungen wie DBFO (Design-Build-Finance-Operate), BOT (Build-Operate-Transfer), BOO (Build-Own-Operate), etc. firmieren. Es gibt Autoren, die die Bezeichnung PPP auf diese Erscheinungsformen einschränken und nur dann von PPP sprechen, wenn folgende Bedingungen erfüllt sind:[5]

- langfristiger Vertrag zwischen einem öffentlichen und einem privaten Partner;
- Planung, Errichtung, Finanzierung und Betrieb einer öffentlichen Infrastruktur durch den privaten Partner;
- Zahlungen über die Vertragslaufzeit an den privaten Partner für die Nutzung der Infrastruktur, entweder durch den öffentlichen Partner oder durch die privaten Nutzer;
- Infrastruktur bleibt in öffentlichem Eigentum oder geht am Ende der Vertragslaufzeit in privates Eigentum über.

Eine weiter gefasste Interpretation von Partnerschaft findet man dort, wo vertragliche und damit finanzielle Faktoren eine geringe bis gar keine Rolle spielen, sondern interorganisationale Verflechtungen im Vordergrund stehen. Beispielsweise können verschiedene Akteure im Bereich der Landwirtschaftspolitik (Landwirtschaftsministerium, Landwirte, Interessensvertretungen der Landwirte und andere Interessensvertretungen) zur Verfolgung bestimmter gesellschafts-

[5] Vgl. Yescombe, E. R. (2007), S. 3.

politischer Ziele zusammenarbeiten. Ein derartiges Policy Network kann dann ein PPP darstellen, wenn eine entsprechende Nachhaltigkeit in der Interaktion besteht.[6]

In ähnlicher Weise unterscheiden KLIJN et al. (2007) zwischen Partnerschaften, die auf Grundlage von (langfristigen) Verträgen geschlossen werden und jenen, die in einer interorganisationalen Verflechtung bestehen.[7]

Bei vertragsbasierten PPPs ist die Intensität der Kooperation zwischen den öffentlichen und privaten Akteuren gering. Sie besteht hauptsächlich aus der Interaktion in der Startphase des PPP-Projekts und erstreckt sich auf die Definition des Projekts, das zur öffentlichen Ausschreibung gelangt. Diese Art der Kooperation stellt eine Variation der klassischen Methode der Auftragsvergabe im öffentlichen Beschaffungswesen dar. Durch „neue" Formen der Vertragsgestaltung wird versucht, den Mehrwert für beide Parteien zu steigern. Die Voraussetzung für den Erfolg ist dabei, dass der öffentliche Partner in der Lage ist, das Problem (allerdings nicht die Lösung, was der Fall in einem traditionellen Vertragsarrangement wäre) zu definieren und dass klare Regeln für das Ausschreibungsverfahren existieren.

Interorganisationale Kooperationen zeichnen sich durch intensivere Austauschprozesse aus, da die verschiedenen Projektkomponenten, die sich im Kompetenzbereich verschiedener privater und öffentlicher Akteure befinden, koordiniert werden müssen. Darüber hinaus ist es schwieriger, vorweg den Inhalt und die Ziele der Kooperation klar abzugrenzen.

In einer Vertragsbeziehung gibt es eine klare Abgrenzung der Verantwortung und des Risikos. Sowohl durch ex ante- als auch durch ex post-Verhandlungen wird diese Abgrenzung auf den Prüfstand gestellt. Der öffentliche Partner (Vergabestelle) ist für die Spezifikation des Problems bzw. des Projekts verantwortlich. Nach einer Zusammenarbeit in der frühen Phase

---

6 Vgl. Hodge, G./Greve, C. (2007), S. 545.
7 Vgl. Klijn, E. H./Edelenbos, J./Hughes, M. (2007), S. 752.

(Phase der vorvertraglichen Verhandlungen), sind die Aufgaben zwischen den öffentlichen und privaten Parteien genau aufgeteilt. Sobald das Ausschreibungsverfahren abgeschlossen ist, überwacht der Prinzipal (öffentlicher Akteur) das Verhalten und die Handlungen des Agenten (privater Akteur).

In einer „echten" Partnerschaft ist jedoch die Koproduktion langfristig angelegt und intensiver, da die involvierten Parteien gemeinsam für die Implementierung verantwortlich sind. Zumindest ist Koordination notwendig, da die Beiträge der beteiligten Parteien aufeinander abgestimmt werden müssen und eine gemeinsame Produktentwicklung stattfindet.

Die Art der partnerschaftlichen Beziehung zwischen den öffentlichen und privaten Akteuren kann auch vor dem Hintergrund der Agentur-Theorie betrachtet werden. In PPPs, die auf (langfristigen) Verträgen fußen, findet man eine klassische „Principal-Agent"-Beziehung, während in interorganisationalen PPPs eine „Principal-Principal"-Relation vorherrscht.

Eine ähnliche Einteilung findet sich auch im Grünbuch[8] der Kommission der Europäischen Gemeinschaften, das sich mit öffentlich-privaten Partnerschaften vor allem vor dem Hintergrund der gemeinschaftlichen Rechtsvorschriften für öffentliche Aufträge und Konzessionen beschäftigt. Es unterscheidet zwischen ÖPP auf Vertragsbasis und institutionalisierter ÖPP. Bei ersterer gründet sich die Partnerschaft zwischen öffentlichem und privatem Sektor nur auf einer vertraglichen Beziehung, bei letzterer erfolgt die Zusammenarbeit zwischen dem öffentlichen und privaten Partner innerhalb eines eigenständigen Rechtsubjekts (Wirtschaftsgebilde mit gemischtem Kapital oder Übernahme der Kontrolle über ein öffentliches Unternehmen durch einen privaten Akteur). Bei einer institutionalisierten ÖPP besteht der private Beitrag neben der Einbringung von Kapital oder anderer Vermögensgegenstände in der aktiven Teilnahme an der Ausführung der Aufgabe, die dem gemischtwirtschaftlichen Unternehmen

8 Grünbuch der Kommission zu Öffentlich-Privaten Partnerschaften und den gemeinschaftlichen Rechtsvorschriften für öffentliche Aufträge und Konzessionen vom 30. April 2004, KOM (2004), S. 327.

übertragen wurde und/oder in der Geschäftsführung der Gesellschaft. Eine reine Kapitalbeteiligung eines privaten Investors an einem öffentlichen Unternehmen stellt keine ÖPP dar.

2 Traditionen der PPP-Forschung

Die bisherigen Ausführungen lassen erkennen, dass sehr unterschiedliche Formen der Zusammenarbeit von öffentlichen und privaten Institutionen mit dem Etikett Public Private Partnership versehen werden können. Die mittlerweile schon sehr umfangreiche und von den verschiedensten Wissenschaftsdisziplinen gespeiste PPP-Forschungsliteratur spiegelt diese Vielfalt in begrifflicher und konzeptioneller Weise wieder. Diese Diversität kann möglicherweise dadurch erklärt werden, dass die PPP-Forschung aus qualitativ unterschiedlichen Traditionen besteht und jede Forschungstradition eine mehr oder weniger eigenständige Betrachtungsweise von öffentlich-privaten Partnerschaften entwickelt hat. WEIHE (2006) unterscheidet folgende PPP-Ansätze in der PPP-Forschung[9]:

(1) Ansatz der Orts-, Stadt- und Regionalentwicklung

Die Entwicklung urbaner und ruraler Räume erfordert gemeinschaftliches Handeln und die Zusammenarbeit verschiedenster Institutionen und Personen eines Territoriums, bestehend aus öffentlicher Verwaltung, privater Wirtschaft und Bürgerschaft bzw. deren Einbindung in regionale Netzwerke. Diese Form der Kooperation findet man gewöhnlich bei Projekten im Bereich Städtebau und Stadt- bzw. Dorferneuerung, in denen Maßnahmen zur Lösung von Verkehrsproblemen mit Maßnahmen zur Stärkung des Wirtschaftsraumes verknüpft werden. Der Mehrwert entsteht durch die Kombination von substanziellen Aktivitäten und Projekten, die sich gegenseitig verstärken. Dies ermöglicht auch einen finanziellen Ausgleich zwischen profitablen und weniger profitablen, aber gesellschaftlich

9 Vgl. Weihe, G. (2006).

interessanten Komponenten. Dieser Ansatz existiert schon seit mehreren Jahrzehnten und hat seine Wurzeln primär in der US-amerikanischen Urban Governance-Literatur. Solche Kooperationen können wiederum die unterschiedlichsten Formen annehmen. Charakteristisch für dieses PPP-Verständnis ist, dass die Austauschbeziehungen zwischen den Partnern auf Freiwilligkeit beruhen, aus eigenem Antrieb und gegenseitigem Interesse entstehen, nicht aber durch Zwang oder Anordnung.

(2) ***Policy-Ansatz***

Dieser Strang der PPP-Literatur[10] hat seine Ursprünge in der US-amerikanischen Policy-Forschung (auch als Politikfeldanalyse bezeichnet). Im Policy-Ansatz ist das PPP-Konzept sehr offen formuliert. Im Mittelpunkt stehen dabei nicht bestimmte Formen der Partnerschaft, sondern die Analyse der Interaktionen zwischen öffentlichen und privaten Akteuren innerhalb eines bestimmten Politikfeldes, wie beispielsweise Verkehr, Bildung, innere und äußere Sicherheit oder auch Gesundheit. Es wird dabei auch der Frage nachgegangen, wie die Erstellung und Bereitstellung von öffentlichen Diensten im Zusammenspiel zwischen öffentlichen und privaten Akteuren gestaltet ist und welche gesellschaftlichen Wirkungen daraus resultieren. Im Policy-Ansatz ist das PPP-Verständnis sehr breit und umfasst alle denkbaren Konstellationen öffentlich-privater Kooperation in einem bestimmten Politikfeld. Wichtig ist in diesem Zusammenhang die Identifizierung und Untersuchung der Rollen, die von öffentlichen und privaten Akteuren in verschiedenen Politikfeldern eingenommen werden. Verdeutlichen lässt sich dieser Ansatz am Beispiel einer Studie zu Öffentlich-Privaten Partnerschaften im US-amerikanischen Strafvollzug[11], in welcher die Eigenschaften solcher Partnerschaften, die Gründe für die Einbeziehung des privaten Sektors und die Auswirkungen

[10] Vgl. Rosenau, P. (2000).
[11] Vgl. Schneider, A. L. (2000).

der spezifischen Eigenschaften des Politikfeldes „Strafvollzug bzw. Strafanstalten“ auf die Involvierung des privaten Sektors untersucht werden.

(3) ***Infrastruktur-Ansatz***

Hier werden PPPs aus der Perspektive von öffentlichen Infrastrukturprojekten betrachtet, die mit privaten Mitteln finanziert werden. Der Großteil der Fachliteratur beschäftigt sich mit Typen von PPPs, die im Kontext von großen Infrastrukturprojekten zu beobachten sind. In der Welt der Infrastrukturprojekte handelt es sich um Finanzierungsmodelle, die es dem öffentlichen Sektor ermöglichen, privates Eigen- und Fremdkapital zum Nutzen der Politik und der Unternehmen einzusetzen. Weltweit beziehen sich viele offizielle Web-Seiten auf solche Partnerschaften bei Infrastrukturprojekten und nicht auf die weicheren, lockereren und informaleren. Auch in der österreichischen Bundesverwaltung dominiert im PPP-Verständnis dieser Infrastruktur-Ansatz. Dieser Umstand trifft auf viele andere Länder (Vereinigtes Königreich, USA, Kanada, Australien, Niederlande, Dänemark, Deutschland) zu. Auch die Kommission der Europäischen Gemeinschaften, die sich in mehreren Publikationen mit dem Thema ÖPP beschäftigt hat, sieht diese vor allem im Bereich öffentlicher Infrastrukturprojekte in den Sektoren Verkehr, öffentliche Gesundheit, Bildung und öffentliche Sicherheit vor. Die wichtigsten Vertreter des Infrastrukturansatzes sind PPPs, wie sie im Rahmen der Public Finance Iniative (PIF) des Vereinigten Königreichs entstanden sind, um den beträchtlichen Investitionsrückstand im Infrastrukturbereich auf marktorientierte Weise zu verringern.[12]

---

[12] Vgl. Clark, G. L./ Root A. (1999).

(4) Governance-Ansatz

Diese Sichtweise, die sich in den letzten Jahren herausgebildet hat, gewinnt mittlerweile immer mehr an Konturen und entstand als Reaktion auf die Auswirkungen der New Public Management Reformen, die in einigen Ländern zu umfangreichen Verwerfungen im Gefüge öffentlicher Institutionen geführt haben. Die einst monolithisch und monopolistisch aufgebaute öffentliche Verwaltung wurde in ein komplexes Gebilde aus quasi-autonomen Organisationen mit stark ausgeprägter Einbindung privater Unternehmen in die Bereitstellung öffentlicher Leistungen transformiert – mit der Folge, dass sich die Grenzen zwischen öffentlichem und privatem Sektor verschoben oder aufgehoben haben.

Governance beschäftigt sich mit der Koordination kollektiver Handlungen und stellt eine Art Gegenmodell zu „Government" dar, dem klassisch hierarchischen Steuerungsverhältnis zwischen Staat und Gesellschaft. Governance bezeichnet die Gesamtheit aller nebeneinander bestehenden Formen der kollektiven Regelung von gesellschaftlich relevanten Sachverhalten, die von der zivilgesellschaftlichen Selbstregelung über verschiedene Formen des Zusammenwirkens staatlicher und privater Akteure bis hin zu hoheitlichem Handeln staatlicher Akteure reicht.[13] In diesem Kontext bedeutet Governance auch die (regierungslose) Selbststeuerung von unterschiedlichen Organisationen, die zusammen ein interorganisationales Netzwerk[14] bilden. Besonders wichtig im Government-Ansatz ist, dass „privat" hierbei nicht nur privatwirtschaftliche, sondern auch zivilgesellschaftliche Akteure bezeichnet. Im Gegensatz zum Infrastruktur-Ansatz lässt der Governance-Ansatz finanziellen Arrangements und rechtlichen Fragen wenig Beachtung zukommen und betont weichere Formen des PPP, bei denen die kooperativen Austauschprozesse den Schwerpunkt der Analyse bilden.

---

13 Vgl. Mayntz, R. (2004).

14 Vgl. Rhodes, R. A. W. (1996).

(5) Entwicklungs-Ansatz

Dieser Ansatz knüpft an die Aktionsprogramme internationaler NGO's, wie der Weltbank oder den Vereinigten Nationen im Rahmen von Entwicklungshilfeprogrammen und der internationalen Entwicklungspolitik, an. Die inhaltlichen Schwerpunkte derartiger PPP-Projekte können beispielsweise in der Bekämpfung von Korruption, in der Förderung des nationalen Zusammengehörigkeitsgefühls, in der Verminderung von Armut und sozialer Ausgrenzung, in der Eindämmung von Umweltverschmutzung oder im Aufbau einer nachhaltigen Infrastruktur liegen. PPP steht im Zusammenhang mit Entwicklung und dem Aufbau von Institutionen in Schwellenländern.

Natürlich ist es nicht möglich, alle Autoren und wissenschaftlichen Beiträge diesen fünf Ansätzen eindeutig zuzuordnen, da die Übergänge zwischen ihnen fließend sind. Nichtsdestotrotz stellen sie eine brauchbare Orientierungshilfe im PPP-Dschungel dar. Im Lichte dieser Argumentation bildet auch die Suche nach einer umfassenden und allgemein akzeptierten Begriffsdefinition kein mit Erkenntnisgewinn verbundenes wissenschaftliches Ziel.

3 PPP im Kontext des New Public Management

Betrachtet man PPPs aus der Perspektive der öffentlichen Verwaltung, so sind sie auch Ausdruck eines veränderten Verständnisses von Staat, Bürokratie und Markt. Diese Entwicklung wurde wesentlich vom New Public Management geprägt.

3.1 New Public Management (NPM)

Im Jahre 1979 begann mit der Wahl von Margaret Thatcher zur Premierministerin des Vereinigten Königreiches von Großbritannien und Nordirland ein großflächiger Umbau der öffentlichen Verwaltung, um diese effektiver und effizienter zu gestalten. Diese Reformbewegung hat unter der Bezeichnung „New Public Management (NPM)“ weltweite Nachahmer unter den Regierungen gefunden. Das NPM ruht auf zwei wichtigen Pfeilern.

Der erste Pfeiler besteht in der Einführung von privatwirtschaftlichen Management-Methoden in der öffentlichen Verwaltung. Dieser Aspekt wird auch als „Managerialismus“ bezeichnet und legt den Schwerpunkt auf die Anwendung in der Wirtschaft bewährter Managementpraktiken, wie Führen mit Zielen im Sinne eines Management by Objectives (MbO), Geschäftsprozess-optimierung, Qualitätsmanagement, Steuerung mit Kennzahlen, Controlling, Kundenorientierung, etc.

Den zweiten Pfeiler des NPM bilden volkswirtschaftliche Ansätze, zu denen vor allem die Public Choice Theorie und die Neue Institutionenökonomie (Theorie der Verfügungsrechte, Agentur-Theorie, Transaktionskostenansatz) zählen. Sie empfehlen die Privatisierung öffentlichen Vermögens (Motto: „Der Staat ist ein schlechter Unternehmer!“), die Förderung des Wettbewerbs zwischen den Produzenten öffentlicher Leistungen durch die Einführung von Marktmechanismen sowie eine verstärkte Orientierung an den Bedürfnissen und Erwartungen der Bürger als Kunden. Mittels wettbewerblicher Ausschreibungsverfahren werden jene Produzenten gesucht, die in der Lage sind, die öffentlichen Dienste mit dem größten Mehrwert (Value for Money) im Sinne von Effektivität und Effizienz bereit zu stellen. An der Ausschreibung können sich hierbei öffentliche Verwaltungen (die bisher die Dienste erbracht haben), privatwirtschaftliche Unternehmen und private Non-Profit-Organisationen beteiligen. Die Fremdvergabe von verwaltungsinternen Leistungen (z. B. Gebäudereinigung, Fuhrpark) wird auch häufig als Outsourcing, die Auslagerung von verwaltungsexternen Leistungen (z. B. Bereitstellung von Kindergartenplätzen) als Contracting Out bezeichnet. Dadurch kommt es zu einer vertraglich gestalteten „Auftraggeber (Besteller)-Auftragnehmer (Lieferant)“ Beziehung, die in der Regel eine Laufzeit zwischen drei und fünf Jahren aufweist.

Verträge[15] (Kontrakte) spielen im NPM eine wichtige Rolle, da sie Instrumente darstellen, mit deren Hilfe man in der Lage ist, Rechte und Pflichten von Parteien zu regeln. Darüber hinaus bieten sie Anreize für eine effiziente Teilung der Risiken und der Informationen. Im Einklang damit steht auch die Forderung nach einer Trennung von Politik und Verwaltung (Motto: „Die Politik soll steuern und nicht rudern!") wie auch die Empfehlung, dass sich öffentliche Verwaltungen auf ihre Kernkompetenzen beschränken sollen.

Im Zuge der NPM-Reformen haben sich die Grenzen zwischen öffentlichem und privatem Sektor in vielen westlichen Industrieländern beträchtlich verschoben.

3.2 PPP-Verständnis der Private Finance Initiative (PFI)

Der Infrastruktur-Ansatz entwickelte sich in den 80er und 90er Jahren des letzten Jahrhunderts und findet seine ideologische und theoretische Begründung in der Reformbewegung des New Public Management. Das Vereinigte Königreich von Großbritannien und Nordirland ist als Mutterland des NPM zugleich Erfinder der Public Finance Initiative (PFI), welche zum weltweiten Vorbild für privat finanzierte Infrastrukturprojekte geworden ist.

Die Einbeziehung von privaten Akteuren zur Erstellung bzw. Bereitstellung öffentlicher Dienste spielt im NPM eine wichtige Rolle. Beispielsweise ist das Vereinigte Königreich eines jener Länder, in denen großflächige Privatisierungen in den Bereichen Telekommunikation, Energiewirtschaft, Wasserversorgung und Verkehrsinfrastruktur durchgeführt wurden. Diese Privatisierungen haben zu einer Modernisierung der Infrastruktur geführt, die ansonsten nicht möglich gewesen wäre. Es gibt eine Reihe von öffentlichen Diensten, die hohe Investitionen in die Infrastruktur erfordern, aber nicht vollständig privatisiert werden können, so beispielsweise Gesundheitsdienste, Strafvollzug, Landesverteidigung, Straßennetz, Bildung, etc. Diese öffentlichen Aufgabenfelder stehen vor der

[15] Vgl. Froud, J. (2003).

Notwendigkeit der Modernisierung ihrer Infrastruktur unter den restriktiven budgetären Rahmenbedingungen (Obergrenzen für das Haushaltsdefizit und Staatsverschuldung).

Die Private Finance Initiative (PFI) versucht dieses Problem zu lösen, indem das grundlegende Modell der Bereitstellung öffentlicher Dienste geändert wird. Das traditionelle Modell besteht darin, dass die öffentliche Verwaltung im Rahmen eines Vergabeverfahrens Akteure aus dem privaten Sektor mit der Errichtung einer Infrastruktur beauftragt. Die Infrastruktureinrichtung befindet sich im öffentlichen Eigentum und die öffentliche Verwaltung bietet die sich daraus resultierenden Dienste an. Diese Investitionen müssen im Voraus finanziert werden, belasten so das Budget und haben entsprechend Auswirkungen auf die öffentliche Verschuldung. Das PFI-Modell besteht darin, dass der private Sektor die Infrastruktur finanziert, errichtet und betreibt. Der öffentliche Sektor kauft nur die aus Infrastruktur resultierenden Dienste auf der Grundlage eines langfristigen Vertrages, der bereits vor Errichtung der Infrastruktur abgeschlossen wurde. Es handelt sich hier um eine außerbudgetäre Finanzierung ohne Auswirkungen auf den Maastricht-relevanten Schuldenstand. PPPs vom Typ PIF sind die bekanntesten Vertreter des Infrastruktur-Ansatzes.

Im Jahre 1992 wurde die Private Finance Initiative (PFI) von der konservativen Regierung unter John Major gestartet, um die Anzahl von Projekten zu erhöhen, die mit Mitteln aus der Privatwirtschaft finanziert werden. Sie wurde ins Leben gerufen, um den Investitionsstau im Bereich der öffentlichen Infrastruktur zur langfristigen Absicherung der öffentlichen Dienste zu verringern. PFI ermächtigt private Vertragspartner zur Planung, zur Errichtung, zum Betrieb und zum Besitz (Eigentum) von Einrichtungen des öffentlichen Sektors wie Schulen, Krankenhäuser, Tunnels, Straßen, Brücken, Gefängnisse. Die Vertragsdauer beträgt normalerweise zwischen 25 und 30 Jahre und beinhaltet die Finanzierung aus privaten Mitteln. Abbildung 2 zeigt die Aufgabenteilung zwischen einem öffentlichen und privaten Partner in einem typischen Infrastrukturprojekt.

Öffentlicher Partner	Privater Partner
1. Bedarfserhebung und Auftragsvergabe	
	2. Definition des Projekts und Festlegung des Projektdesigns
	3. Finanzierung der Investition
	4. Errichtung der Infrastruktur
	5. Betrieb (inklusive Erhaltung) der Infrastruktur und Bereitstellung der Dienstleistung
6. Projektcontrolling, Zahlung des Entgelts und Erhebung des zukünftigen Bedarfes	

Abb. 2: Aufgabenteilung in einem PFI-Projekt
Quelle: Klijn, E. H./Edebbos, J./Hughes, M. (2007), S. 81.

Für die Involvierung von privaten Akteuren in die Bereitstellung von infrastrukturgebundenen öffentlichen Diensten sprechen letztlich nicht nur makroökonomische, sondern auch mikroökonomische Überlegungen. Das bedeutet, dass PFI-Projekte einen Mehrwert[16] (Value for Money) im Vergleich zur traditionellen Beschaffung aufweisen müssen. Dieser ist im Rahmen einer Wirtschaftlichkeitsvergleichrechnung (Vorteilhaftigkeitsanalyse) nachzuweisen. Zu diesem Zweck wurde als Benchmark der sogenannte Public Sector Comparator (PSC) eingeführt, der durch den Barwert aller mit der Eigenerstellung durch öffentliche Hand verbundenen Auszahlungen, Einzahlungen und Risiken

16 Vgl. Coulson, A. (2008).

repräsentiert wird. Von einem Value for Money spricht man dann, wenn der Barwert der PFI-Variante geringer ist als der Barwert des PSC.[17]

Seit 1992 wurden über 510 PFI-Infrastrukturprojekte in den unterschiedlichsten Sektoren (Gesundheitswesen, Bildung, Verkehr, Landesverteidigung, Wohnbau, Freizeit etc.) gestartet. Die privaten Investitionen beliefen sich im Jahre 2007 auf 5,3 Mrd. Pfund. Für die nächsten fünf Jahre sind bereits Projekte in der Größenordnung von 23,3 Mrd. Pfund in Planung. Diese machen ungefähr 10 Prozent der öffentlichen Gesamtinvestitionen aus.[18]

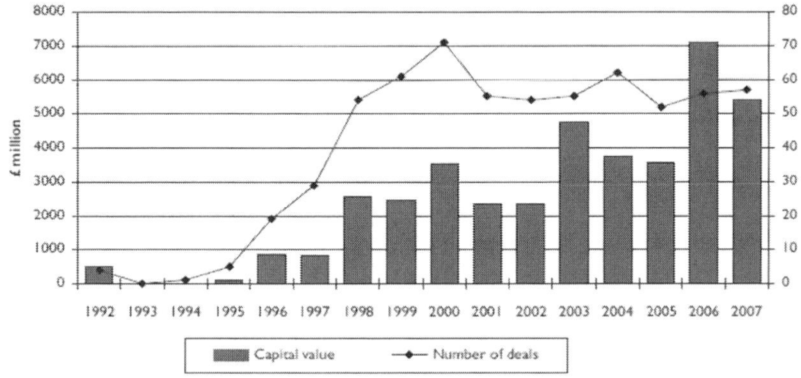

Abb. 3: Entwicklung der PFI-Projekte (Anzahl, Investitionssumme)
Quelle: HM Treasury (2008), S. 7.

Mit der Übernahme der Regierungsgeschäfte durch die Labour Party unter Tony Blair wurde die Private Finance Initiative – trotz der Bedenken der Gewerkschaften, die PFI als eine Privatisierung durch die Hintertür betrachten – weitergeführt. Im Rahmen der Modernisierungsagenda der Labour Party wurde PFI Bestandteil einer breiter angelegten PPP-Initiative der Regierung.

[17] Vgl. Bauer, F. (2004).
[18] Vgl. Flinders, M. *(2005).*

4 Public Private Partnership in Österreich

Österreich ist eines der wenigen westlichen Industrieländer, denen es weitgehend gelungen ist, den öffentlichen Sektor vor den Auswirkungen der NPM-Reformwelle zu schützen. Im Vergleich zu NPM-Musterschülern (wie Vereinigtes Königreich, Neuseeland, Australien und Kanada) sind die NPM-Reformen in Österreich nicht flächendeckend, sondern nur punktuell durchgeführt worden. Auch haben sich hier die Grenzen zwischen öffentlichem und privatem Sektor nicht wesentlich verschoben. Darüber hinaus wirkt die föderale Struktur Österreichs vielfach als Bremse bei der Modernisierung der öffentlichen Verwaltung.

4.1 Politischer Stellenwert von PPPs in der Bundesverwaltung

Erste Anhaltspunkte zum politischen Stellenwert von PPPs findet man im Regierungsprogramm für die XXII. Gesetzgebungsperiode (Regierung Schüssel II - 28. Februar 2003 bis 11. Januar 2007). PPPs werden als Instrument zur Bereitstellung von Infrastruktur gesehen. So findet sich der Hinweis, dass der Generalverkehrsplan-Österreich (GVP-Ö) unter Einsatz von PPP-Modellen zügig vorangetrieben werden soll. Der GVP-Ö wurde gemeinsam mit den Bundesländern, den Infrastrukturgesellschaften des Bundes und den gesetzlichen Interessensvertretungen erstellt und am 25. Januar 2002 der Öffentlichkeit vorgelegt. Es wurde jedoch keine darüber hinaus gehende rechtliche Verankerung des GVP-Ö vorgenommen. Es handelt sich dabei um ein langfristiges strategisches Ausbauprogramm für die Verkehrsinfrastruktur des Bundes, also die Autobahnen und Schnellstraßen, das Schienennetz sowie die Donau als Wasserstraße. PPPs im Kontext des GVP-Ö werden als Instrument zur privaten Vorfinanzierung der Verkehrsinfrastruktur gesehen, die darüber hinaus von den Synergien (Know-How-Transfer zwischen öffentlicher Hand und privaten Organisationen) profitieren sollten. Für die Investitionspakete des GVP-Ö

Infrastrukturprogramms wird das PPP-Potential mit höchstens fünf Prozent der Gesamtinvestitionssumme (ca. 870 Mio. €) geschätzt.[19] Der Bau des Brenner-Basistunnels in einem PPP-Modell unter Beteiligung der Europäischen Union und Italiens ist Ziel der Bundesregierung. Weiterhin soll aus Teilen der Radio- und TV-Gebühren die Digitalisierungsoffensive im Rundfunkbereich sowie die Film- und Produktionswirtschaft auf Basis eines PPP-Modells finanziert werden.

Im Regierungsprogramm für die XXIII. Gesetzgebungsperiode (Regierung Gusenbauer ab 11. Januar 2007) werden PPP-Modelle als Instrumente der Wachstums- und Konjunkturpolitik gesehen. Um PPP-Modelle leichter anwenden zu können, sollen die relevanten vergaberechtlichen Bestimmungen für Ausschreibungen angepasst werden. Um die Innovationskraft und Effizienz der Privatwirtschaft und die Kontrolle der öffentlichen Hand optimal zu nutzen, soll nach dem Vorbild beispielsweise von Deutschland, den Niederlanden oder Großbritannien ein Kompetenzzentrum für PPP-Projekte eingerichtet werden.

4.2 Kompetenzzentrum für PPP-Projekte

Mittlerweile haben das Bundesministerium für Verkehr, Innovation und Technologie (BMVIT) und das Bundesministerium für Finanzen (BMF) in Umsetzung des Regierungsprogrammes eine Plattform zur Erfassung der PPP-Projekte in der österreichischen Bundesverwaltung eingerichtet. Einbezogen wurden auch alle anderen Bundesministerien und ausgegliederten Bundesgesellschaften, die bereits PPP-Projekterfahrungen gesammelt haben.

Das „PPP-Kompetenzzentrum" zielt auf eine Vernetzung aller an PPPs interessierten öffentlichen Einrichtungen unter Einbeziehung der Wirtschaft ab. Weiters sollen die bisherigen PPP-Erfahrungen zur Sicherstellung des Wissens-

---

[19] Vgl. Generalverkehrsplan (2002), S. 37.

transfers für zukünftige Vorhaben gebündelt werden. Angestrebt wird zudem eine Beschleunigung der Durchführung von PPP-Projekten.[20]

Mit der Errichtung eines Kompetenzzentrums folgt die österreichische Bundesregierung internationalen Beispielen und wird zu einem wichtigen Promoter für den Einsatz von PPPs. Die organisatorische Verankerung im Bundesministerium für Verkehr, Innovation und Technologie (BMVIT) zeigt auch, dass PPPs einen Beitrag zur Modernisierung der Infrastruktur leisten sollen. Dieses Kompetenzzentrum ist – der föderalen Struktur entsprechend – auf die Bundesverwaltung beschränkt.

4.3 Stand in der österreichischen Bundesverwaltung

Das PPP-Kompetenzzentrum hat in Kooperation mit den Bundesministerien und den ausgegliederten Bundesgesellschaften überblicksartig die PPP-Projekte auf Bundesebene analysiert. Der daraus entstandene Bericht gibt Auskunft über konkrete PPP-Projekte der einzelnen Bundesministerien und Gesellschaften und zeigt darüber hinaus, wie unterschiedlich solche Vorhaben gestaltet werden können.[21]

[20] Vgl. Bundesministerium für Verkehr, Innovation und Technologie, online vom 18.07.2008.
[21] Vgl. BMVIT (2008).

	Inhaltlicher Projektumfang	Projektdauer	Projekt-volumen in €
ASFINAG – LKW Maut	Planung, Errichtung, Finanzierung und Betrieb der fahrleistungsabhängigen Bemautung von LKW auf allen Autobahnen und Schnellstraßen	Konzessionsdauer: 10 Jahre	Jährliche Vergütungszahlung ca. 100 Mio. € (inkl. variabler Anteile)
ASFINAG – Nordautobahn A5	Detailplanung, Errichtung, Finanzierung und Betrieb von ca. 52 km Autobahn	Konzessionsdauer: Bauzeit plus 30 Jahre	Barwert der Vergütungszahlung 933 Mio. €
SCHIG – Güterterminal Graz/ Werndorf	Planung, Errichtung, (Vor-)Finanzierung und Betrieb einer Anlage für den kombinierten Ladungsverkehr, Lagerhalten, Einrichtungen für die rollende Landstraße auf einer Fläche von ca. 50 ha	Konzessionsdauer: ca. 34 Jahre	Barwert der Errichtungskosten: 64 Mio. €
SCHIG – Klima Windkanal	Planung, Errichtung, (Vor-)Finanzierung und Betrieb von zwei Testkammern, zwei Sonnenfeldern, Rollenprüfstände für Schienenfahrzeuge, LKW, Busse	Konzessionsdauer: ca. 37 Jahre	Barwert der Errichtungskosten: ca. 59 Mio. €
SCHIG – Rollende Landstraße Regensburg	Planung, Errichtung, (Vor-)Finanzierung und Betrieb eines Verladeterminals im Hafen Regensburg auf etwa 2,4 ha	Konzessionsdauer: ca. 21 Jahre	Barwert der Errichtungskosten: 2,4 Mio. €

BMI – Digitalfunk BOS Austria	Planung, Errichtung und Betrieb von ca. 1600 Standorten, 6 Switches und 2 Netzmanagementcentern	Konzessionsdauer: 25 Jahre nach Vollausbau	Barwert der Vergütungszahlung: ca. 35 Mio. €
BMWF – IMC Fachhochschule Krems GmbH	Studienjahr 2006/07 1.477 Studierende; Studienjahr 2007/08 ca. 1.600 Studierende	Konzessionsdauer: Reakkreditierung alle 5 Jahre pro Studiengang	Jährliche Gesamterlöse: 2005: 9,66 Mio. € 2006: 10,78 Mio. €
BMWA – Bundescontracting 500	Umsetzung von Energiesparmaßnahmen in rund 500 Bundesgebäuden mit einem Projektvolumen von ca. 15,3 Mio. €	Konzessionsdauer: ca. 10 Jahre	Barwert der Vergütungszahlung: keine Angabe
BMLV – Akademiebad Wiener Neustadt	Betrieb des Akademiebades		Barwert der Vergütungszahlung: 70.000,00 €

Tab. 1: Überblick über die PPPs in der österreichischen Bundesverwaltung
Quelle: eigene Darstellung, in Anlehnung an BMVIT (2008).

Die in Tabelle 1 aufgelisteten Projekte zeigen die Bandbreite des PPP-Verständnisses in der österreichischen Bundesverwaltung. Die PPP-Projekte wurden unabhängig voneinander entwickelt und sind dementsprechend in der inhaltlichen Ausgestaltung unterschiedlich. Fünf dieser PPP-Beispiele betreffen die aus der Bundesverwaltung ausgegliederten Rechtsträger ASFINAG (Autobahnen- und Schnellstraßen-Finanzierungs-Aktiengesellschaft) und die SCHIG (Schieneninfrastruktur-Dienstleistungs GmbH). Zu den gesetzlichen Aufgaben der SCHIG zählt explizit der Abschluss von PPP-Verträgen mit Dritten über die Mitfinanzierung, die Errichtung einschließlich der Verwertung von Schieneninfrastruktur sowie die Abwicklung von damit verbunden Projekten.

4.3.1 Charakterisierung der PPP-Projekte

Die ersten drei in Tabelle 1 genannten Projekte stellen PPPs vom Typ PFI dar. Bei ihnen erfolgt neben einer privaten Finanzierung auch ein Transfer von beträchtlichen Risiken auf den privaten Kontraktor. Generell macht ein solcher Transfer von Risiken auf den privaten Partner nur dann Sinn, wenn dieser in der Lage ist die Risiken besser zu beherrschen, denn nur so kann ein Mehrwert für alle Beteiligten geschaffen werden.

Beim Projekt Nordautobahn A 5 übernimmt der Konzessionär neben dem Betrieb auch die Errichtung und Finanzierung. Sollte bei der Autobahn die Nachfrage geringer als angenommen sein, werden seine Errichtungs- und Finanzierungskosten nur zum Teil refundiert. Bei der LKW-Maut und Digitalfunk BOS Austria verringert sich das Entgelt bei eingeschränkter Verfügbarkeit und geringerer Nachfrage.

Die drei Projekte der SCHIG stellen keine PPP-Projekte vom Typ PFI dar, da wesentliche Risiken beim öffentlichen Partner verbleiben. Im Rahmen eines Pachtvertrages übernimmt der private Partner den Betrieb, jedoch verbleibt das Risiko des finanziellen Ausfalls des Pächters (Refinanzierungsrisiko) bei der im öffentlichen Eigentum stehenden Besitzgesellschaft.

Das Projekt „IMC Fachhochschule Krems GmbH" ist ebenso nicht als PFI-PPP zu qualifizieren. Die IMC Fachhochschule Krems wird seit ihrer Gründung als Gesellschaft mit beschränkter Haftung geführt, bei der die Gesellschafter, das private Bildungsinstitut ITM GmbH (70 Prozent) und die Stadt Krems (30 Prozent), Mitinitiator und Fördergeber sind. Sie bietet auf Grundlage des Fachhochschulstudiengesetzes gegenwärtig sieben berufsorientierte Fachhochschulstudiengängen an, die von ca. 1600 Studierenden besucht werden. Die Finanzierung setzt sich aus öffentlichen und privaten Mitteln zusammen. So fördert beispielsweise der Bund basierend auf einem Normkostenmodell nur die laufenden Kosten des Betriebes der Fachhochschulstudiengänge (insbesondere Personalaufwand und laufender Betriebsaufwand). Die Aufwendungen für die

Gebäude und die sonstige Infrastruktur hat der Erhalter aus anderen Finanzquellen (Land, Stadt, Studienbeiträge, Sponsorengelder, Drittmittel) zu decken. Das Projekt beruht auf keinem vergaberechtlichen Verfahren, sondern auf einem Akkreditierungsverfahren. Bundesmittel fließen nur dann, wenn die beantragten Fachhochschulstudiengänge vom Fachhochschulrat akkreditiert werden, die im Wettbewerb mit anderen Bietern stehen. Im Vergleich zu den vorhergehenden PPP-Projekten basiert dieses auf einer Kooperation von Organisationen (Joint Venture), die ein finanzielles Risiko tragen.

4.3.2 PPP-Projekte aus der Sicht des Maastricht-Vertrages

In vielen Ländern besteht das Hauptmotiv für die Durchführung von PPP-Projekten im öffentlichen Infrastrukturbereich in der Entlastung öffentlicher Budgets durch außerbudgetäre (private) Finanzierung. Diese Überlegungen spielen in der österreichischen Bundesverwaltung – wenn überhaupt – eine zumindest untergeordnete Rolle. Beispielsweise ist die ASFINAG[22] eine aus der Bundesverwaltung und somit auch aus dem Bundesbudget ausgegliederte Aktiengesellschaft, die nach den Kriterien des Statistischen Amtes der Europäischen Gemeinschaft (Eurostat)[23] als Unternehmen mit marktbestimmter Tätigkeit gilt, da sie sich über die von ihr eingehobenen Mauteinnahmen (LKW-Maut, PKW-Autobahnvignette sowie Sondermauten) finanziert. Somit werden die Schulden der ASFINAG bei der Überprüfung der Einhaltung der Regelungen des Europäischen Stabilitäts- und Wachstumspaktes gemäß Artikel 104 EG-Vertrag nicht berücksichtigt.

Für die Maastricht-konforme Gestaltung von PPP-Projekten spielt die Risikoübertragung eine wichtige Rolle. Eurostat hat eine Entscheidung getroffen,

---

[22] Die Zuständigkeit für das hochrangige Straßennetz (Autobahnen und Schnellstraßen) wird für den Bund von der ASFINAG wahrgenommen. Sie plant, finanziert, baut, erhält, betreibt und bemautet das gesamte österreichische Autobahnen- und Schnellstraßennetz mit einer Straßenlänge von etwa 2100 Kilometern.

[23] Verordnung (EG) Nr. 2223/96 des Rates vom 25. Juni 1996 zum Europäischen System Volkswirt schaftlicher Gesamtrechnungen auf nationaler und regionaler Ebene in der Europäischen Gemeinschaft.

wie Verträge staatlicher Einheiten, welche mit nicht-staatlichen Einheiten geschlossen werden, in den Volkswirtschaftlichen Gesamtrechnungen zu verbuchen sind. Werden im Rahmen eines PPP-Projekts Investitionen getätigt, so können sie nur dann als nicht-staatliche Vermögenswerte behandelt werden, wenn es eindeutige Indizien dafür gibt, dass der private Partner einen Großteil der aus der Partnerschaft resultierenden Risiken trägt.[24]

Eurostat teilt die Risiken in die Kategorien Baurisiko, Ausfallsrisiko und Nachfragerisiko ein. Zum Baurisiko zählen dabei insbesondere eine verspätete Lieferung, Nichteinhaltung vorgegebener Standards, zusätzliche Kosten und technische Mängel. Verpflichtet sich der Staat, mit der Leistung regelmäßiger Zahlungen an einen Partner zu beginnen, ohne den tatsächlichen Zustand der Vermögenswerte zu berücksichtigen, so wäre dies ein Zeichen dafür, dass der Staat den Großteil der Baurisiken trägt. Ein Ausfallsrisiko liegt vor, wenn die vertraglich vereinbarte Menge nicht geliefert oder die Sicherheitsnormen (Zertifizierungsstandards) bei der Dienstleistungserbringung an den Endkunden nicht eingehalten werden können. Wenn der öffentliche Vertragspartner berechtigt ist, seine regelmäßigen Zahlungen erheblich zu kürzen, trägt er auch nicht das Ausfallsrisiko. Das Nachfragerisiko betrifft schließlich Schwankungen in der Inanspruchnahme des Dienstes (tatsächliche Nachfrage höher oder geringer als die erwartete), die nicht dem Verhalten des privaten Partners zuzuschreiben sind. Wenn die Nachfrageschwankungen keinen Einfluss auf die Rentabilität des privaten Partners haben, dann trägt der öffentliche Vertragspartner das Risiko.

Zusammenfassend empfiehlt Eurostat, Vermögenswerte, die im Rahmen von PPP-Projekten entstehen, nicht als Vermögenswerte des Staates zu klassifizieren und folglich nicht in der Bilanz des Sektors Staat zu verbuchen, wenn der private Partner sowohl das Baurisiko als auch das Ausfalls- oder das Nachfragerisiko trägt. Wenn das Baurisiko vom Staat getragen wird oder wenn der private Partner nur das Baurisiko und kein anderes Risiko trägt, so werden die

[24] Vgl. EUROSTAT-Pressemitteilung 18/2004 vom 11. Februar 2004 über die Behandlung von Öffentlich-Privaten Partnerschaften. Fleischmann, E. (2004), S. 115 ff.

Vermögenswerte dem öffentlichen Partner zugerechnet. Damit verbunden sind negative Auswirkungen für das Budgetdefizit und den Schuldenstand. Die ursprünglichen Investitionsausgaben für die Vermögenswerte werden als Anlageninvestition des Staates verbucht. Im Gegenzug erhöht sich der öffentliche Schuldenstand durch die Unterstellung eines „fiktiven Kredits" durch den privaten Partner. Die regelmäßigen Zahlungen des Staates an den Partner wirken sich nur insoweit auf das Defizit bzw. den Überschuss aus, als sie sich auf Dienstleistungskäufe und unterstellte Zinsen beziehen.

Tabelle 2 zeigt am Beispiel des PPP-Projekts „Digitalfunk BOS Austria" die Teilung der Risiken zwischen dem Auftraggeber (Konzessionsgeber) und dem Auftragnehmer (Konzessionsnehmer).

Art der Risiken	Risiko wird vom Auftraggeber getragen	Risiko wird geteilt	Risiko wird vom Auftragnehmer getragen
Genehmigungsrisiko		x	
Änderungen in gesetzlichen Auflagen und Vorschriften			x
Änderungen im Stand der Technik			x
Baukostenüberschreitung		x	
Bauzeitüberschreitung		x	
Höhere Gewalt (Krieg, Unruhen, Generalstreik, etc.)	x		
Betriebsrisiko (u. a. Betriebskosten)		x	
Instandhaltungsrisiko		x	
Nachfragerisiko		x	
Verfügbarkeitsrisiko		x	
Zinsänderungsrisiko	x		
Steuern			x

Tab. 2: Risikoaufteilung zwischen den Partnern
Quelle: eigene Darstellung, in Anlehnung an BMVIT (2008), S. 35.

Wendet man die Eurostat-Kriterien an, so deutet die in Tabelle 2 dargestellte Risikoaufteilung darauf hin, dass dieses PPP-Projekt eher dem staatlichen Sektor zuzurechnen ist.

4.3.3 Rechtliche Dimension der PPP-Projekte

Im Gegensatz zur Bundesrepublik Deutschland[25] gibt es in Österreich keine spezifischen gesetzlichen Regelungen für PPPs. Sie können auf der Grundlage der allgemeinen zivil- und haushaltsrechtlichen Normen unter Beachtung vergabe-, beihilfen-, gesellschafts-, steuer-, verfassungs- und arbeitsrechtlicher Regelungen und des gemeinschaftlichen Rechtsrahmens errichtet werden. Eine große Bedeutung bei der Durchführung von PPP-Projekten im Infrastrukturbereich spielt das Vergaberecht. Dabei muss eine Zuordnung zu den von den Richtlinien definierten Vertragstypen (Bau-, Liefer- und Dienstleistungsauftrag sowie Bau- und Dienstleistungskonzessionen) erfolgen, wodurch die Einordnung des Projekts in die vergaberechtlichen Kategorien problematisch werden kann. PPP als Begriff ist dem österreichischen Vergaberecht bislang unbekannt und es enthält keine speziellen Bestimmungen. Bei großen Bauprojekten ist es zudem wichtig, dass das Bundesvergabeamt im Rahmen von Nachprüfungsverfahren rasch entscheidet. Das Ausschreibungsverfahren bei Infrastruktur-PPPs ist außerdem viel komplexer und langwieriger als bei traditionellen Beschaffungsformen und stellt größere Anforderungen an die öffentliche Verwaltung, so dass sich die damit verbundenen Transaktionskosten nur bei größeren Projekten rechnen.

[25] Der deutsche Bundestag hat am 30. Juni 2005 zur Verbesserung der gesetzlichen Rahmenbedingungen ein „Gesetz zur Beschleunigung der Umsetzung von Öffentlich Privaten Partnerschaften und zur Verbesserung gesetzlicher Rahmenbedingungen für Öffentlich Private Partnerschaften“ (kurz: „ÖPP-Beschleunigungsgesetz“) verabschiedet (BGB l. 2005 I, 2676). Dieses Gesetz änderte neben vergaberecht-rechtlichen und steuerrechtlichen Vorschriften auch die Bundeshaushaltsordnung. Im Haushaltsrecht wird jetzt zur Forcierung der ÖPPs auch vorgesehen, dass der Wirtschaftlichkeitsvergleich die mit der Maßnahme verbundene Risikoverteilung zu berücksichtigen hat.

Auf europäischer Gemeinschaftsebene gibt es kein spezifisches Regelwerk für ÖPP-Konstruktionen; auch ist ein derartiges nicht geplant. Gemäß Gemeinschaftsrecht steht es öffentlichen Stellen frei, eine Wirtschaftstätigkeit selbst auszuüben oder sie Dritten zu übertragen. Bei der Einbindung Dritter müssen jedoch die gemeinschaftlichen Rechtsvorschriften für das öffentliche Beschaffungswesen sowie Konzessionen beachtet werden. Sie dienen in erster Linie der Schaffung eines Binnenmarktes, in dem neben dem freien Warenverkehr, der Dienstleistungs- und Niederlassungsfreiheit zugleich die Wahrung der Grundsätze der Gleichbehandlung, der Transparenz und der gegenseitigen Anerkennung gewährleistet ist.[26]

4.4 Schlussfolgerungen

Verglichen mit dem Vereinigten Königreich und den Niederlanden, aber auch mit der Bundesrepublik Deutschland und Frankreich spielen PPP-Projekte in Österreich noch eine untergeordnete Rolle. Die ersten Erfahrungen mit den ausgeschriebenen Infrastrukturprojekten werden insofern für die weitere Entwicklung von großer Bedeutung sein. Auch wird das eingerichtete PPP-Kompetenzzentrum einen Beitrag zur Verbreitung von PPP bei den österreichischen Gebietskörperschaften leisten können.

[26] Vgl. Grünbuch der Kommission zu Öffentlich-Privaten Partnerschaften und den gemeinschaftlichen Rechtsvorschriften für öffentliche Aufträge und Konzessionen vom 30. April 2004, KOM (2004), S. 327.

Literaturverzeichnis

Bauer, F. (2004): Wie ist die Wirtschaftlichkeit von Public Private Partnership zu beurteilen? In: Das öffentliche Haushaltswesen in Österreich. Jahrgang 45, Heft 3-4, S. 121-132.

Bundesministerium für Verkehr, Innovation und Technologie (2008): Online im Internet: http://www.bmvit.gv.at/ministerium/ppp.html, 18.07.2008.

BMVIT (2008): Ergebnisbericht über die PPP-Projekte der Bundesministerien sowie der ausgegliederten Bundesgesellschaften.

Bundeskanzleramt: Regierungsprogramm für die XXII. Gesetzgebungsperiode 2002-2006.

Bundeskanzleramt: Regierungsprogramm für die XXIII. Gesetzgebungsperiode 2007-2010.

Clark, G. L./Root A. (1999): Infrastructure shortfall in the United Kingdom: the private finance initiative and government policy. In: Political Geography 18, S. 341-365.

Coulson, A. (2008): Value for Money in PFI Proposals: A Commentary on the UK Treasury Guidlines for Public Sector Comparators. In: Public Administration, Vol. 86, No. 2, S. 483-498.

EUROSTAT – Pressemitteilung vom 11. Februar 2004 über die Behandlung von Öffentlich-Privaten Partnerschaften.

Fleischmann, E. (2004): PPP und Maastricht. Wie sind öffentlich-private Partnerschaften bei der Berechnung des öffentlichen Defizits und der öffentlichen Schulden zu behandeln? In: Das öffentliche Haushaltswesen in Österreich. Heft 3-4, Jg. 45, S. 112-120.

Flinders, M. (2005): The Politics of Public-Private Partnerships. In: British Journal of Politics and International Relations, Vol. 7, S. 215-239.

Froud, J. (2003): The Private Finance Initiative: risk, uncertainty and the state. In: Accounting, Organisations and Society 28, S. 567-589.

Generalverkehrsplan (2002): S. 37.

Giddens, A. (1997): The third Way. Cambridge: Polity Press.

Grünbuch der Kommission zu öffentlich-rechtlichen Partnerschaften und den gemeinschaftlichen Rechtsvorschriften für öffentliche Aufträge und Konzessionen vom 30. April 2004, KOM (2004) 327.

HM Treasury (2008): Infrastructure procurement: delivering long-term value.

Hodge, G./Greve, C. (2007): Public-Private Partnerships. An International Performance Review. In: Public Administration Review, S. 545-558.

Klijn, E.-H./Edelenbos, J./Hughes, M. (2007): Public-Private Partership: a Two-Headed Reform. A Comparison of PPP in England and the Netherlands. In: Pollitt, Ch./van Thiel, S./Homburg,V. (Hrsg.) (2007): New Public Management in Europe. Adaptation and Alternatives. Palgrave MacMillian, S. 71-89.

Klijn, E. H./Teisman G. R. (2000): Governing public-private partnerships: analysing and managing the processes and institutional characteristics of public-private partnerships. In: Osborne S. P. (ed.): Public-Private Partnerships: Theory and Practice in International Perspective. London: Routledge, S. 84-102.

Mayntz, R. (2004): Governance Theory als fortentwickelte Steuerungstheorie? Max Plank Institut für Gesellschaftsforschung, Working Paper No. 04/1.

Mitteilung der Kommission für das Europäische Parlament, den Rat, den Europäischen Wirtschafts- und Sozialausschuss und den Ausschuss der Regionen zu öffentlich-privaten Partnerschaften und den gemeinschaftlichen Rechtsvorschriften für das öffentliche Beschaffungswesen und Konzessionen vom 15.11.2005, KOM (2005), S. 569.

Rhodes, R. A. W. (1996): The New Governance: Governing without Government. In: Political Studies (1996), S. 652-667.

Schneider, A. L. (2000): Public Private Partnerships in the U.S. Prison System. In: Rosenau, P. (ed.): Public-Private Policy Partnership. Westwood, MA: Massachusetts Institute of Technology.

Verordnung (EG) Nr. 2223/96 des Rates vom 25. Juni 1996 zum Europäischen System Volkswirtschaftlicher Gesamtrechnungen auf nationaler und regionaler Ebene in der Europäischen Gemeinschaft.

Weihe, G. (2006): Public Private Partnerships: Adressing a nebulous concept. Paper presented at the 10th International Research Symposium on Public Management (Glasgow, Scotland).

Yescombe, E. R. (2007): Public-private Partnerships. Principles of Policy and Finance. Elsevier.

Öffentlich – Private Partnerschaften: Eine erste Gegenüberstellung der aktuellen Erfahrungen in Italien und der Schweiz

Tobiolo Gianella, Marco Meneguzzo & Josef Bernhart

Inhaltsverzeichnis

1 Strategisches Benchmarking der Erfahrungen mit öffentlich-privaten Partnerschaften in Italien und der Schweiz

Ziel dieses Beitrages ist die Darstellung der Ergebnisse eines ersten „strategischen Benchmarking“ zwischen Italien und der Schweiz zu Erfahrungen mit Projektfinanzierungen und Public Private Partnerships (PPPs). [1]

Das strategische Benchmarking beinhaltet die Initiierung systematischer Vergleiche in Bezug auf:

- Prozesse der Formulierung und Umsetzung politischer Programme;
- Prozesse des strategischen und organisationalen Wandels sowie der Managemententwicklung in den verschiedenen öffentlichen Verwaltungen (Ebene des Zentralstaates, des Bundes, der Regionen, der Kantone, der Gemeinden und deren Verbände).

Das strategische Benchmarking soll dem – in der öffentlichen Verwaltung seit geraumer Zeit bekannten und schon länger auf europäischer und internationaler

[1] Die Analyse wurde möglich, da die Autoren als Mitglieder einer Forschergruppe an der Universität der Italienischen Schweiz (USI) seit dem Jahre 2004 an einem Vergleich zur Verwaltungsmodernisierung in Italien, der Schweiz und Österreich arbeiten. Der Vergleich basiert auf „grenzüberschreitenden“ Projekten zwischen Italien und der Schweiz sowie zwischen Italien und Österreich, gefördert von der Europäischen Union (Interreg III) und durch die Teilnahme am Projekt „Polo nazionale in amministrazione pubblica (progetto 2008 – 2011)“. Ziel dieses Projektes, an dem das Hochschulinstitut für öffentliche Verwaltung (IDHEAP) in Lausanne und die Universitäten von Bern, Lausanne und der Italienischen Schweiz (Lugano) beteiligt sind, ist der Aufbau eines Netzwerkes von Kompetenzzentren der Ausbildung (universitär und berufsbegleitend – Master of advanced Studies), der wissenschaftlichen Forschung (Koordination der Doktoratsstudien) und der wissenschaftlichen Beratung von öffentlichen Verwaltungen mit dem Fokus Schweiz sowie einer Öffnung für Forschungsnetzwerke in den Bereichen Public Management und Administration in Europa. Dazu zählen insbesondere EGPA (European Group of Public Administration) und IRSPM (International Research Society in Public Management). Auf der Konferenz der IRSPM (Queensland University of Technology) in Brisbane/Australien 2008 wurde ein Paper von Josef Bernhart, Denita Cepiku, Marco Meneguzzo und Kurt Promberger „Strategic Management in the cities and Local Governance: recent trends in some European Countries“ präsentiert, in dem die Erfahrungen im Bereich der strategischen Stadtentwicklungsplanung in Italien, der Schweiz und Österreich verglichen wurden.

Ebene angewandten – „operativen" Benchmarking zur Seite gestellt werden, das in folgenden Formen in Erscheinung tritt:

- als Benchmarking von Kennzahlen (bezogen auf Budgets, Aktivitäten, etc.),
- als Benchmarking von Prozessen der einzelnen öffentlichen Verwaltungen im Rahmen der Bereitstellung von öffentlichen Diensten für die Bürger (Nutzer, Klienten).

Das Benchmarking von Kennzahlen bei Projektfinanzierungen konzentriert sich auf den Auftragswert, die Rückzahlungsdauer und den Projektrealisierungszeitraum. Das Benchmarking von Prozessen umfasst das institutionelle Modell, die einbezogenen Stakeholder und die verwendeten Risikomanagementsysteme.

Die beiden Systeme der öffentlichen Verwaltung, das föderale der Schweiz und das zur Zeit zentralistische Italiens haben seit Langem Erfahrungen mit beiden Formen des Benchmarking auch auf strategischer Ebene[2].

Für Italien hat die von der Abteilung für den öffentlichen Dienst (Amt für Innovation in den öffentlichen Verwaltungen) im Ministerratspräsidium in Zusammenarbeit mit der Universität Rom (Tor Vergata) im Jahre 2002 durchgeführte Erhebung zu Erfahrungen in den 1990er Jahren gezeigt, dass im Laufe der 2000er Jahre zahlreiche und beachtliche Initiativen entwickelt, bestätigt und fortgeführt wurden. Die Bedeutendste davon ist das Projekt „Good Practices" (www.buoniesempi.it), das auch vom Amt für Innovation in den öffentlichen Verwaltungen initiiert wurde und eine Identifikation der Best Practices in der italienischen Verwaltung zum Gegenstand hat. Bis dato sind auf der Webseite ca. 2300 Innovationsprojekte verfügbar, die nach Sachthemen und Politikfeldern geordnet sind.

---

[2] Hier kann daran erinnert werden, dass Italien aktiv an der internationalen „public sector benchmarking group" teilnimmt, die von den öffentlichen Verwaltungen der EU-Mitgliedsländer initiiert wurde.

Das strategische Benchmarking nimmt in der Schweiz an Bedeutung zu, wie die Schaffung eines Web-Portales (www.sgvw.ch) zeigt, auf dem die wichtigsten Verwaltungsinnovationen in systematischer Weise gesammelt und veröffentlicht werden. Die Initiative ging von der Schweizer Gesellschaft für Verwaltungswissenschaften (SGVW) und vom Kompetenzzentrum für Public Management (KPM) der Universität Bern aus.

Jüngstes und interessantes Beispiel des strategischen Benchmarking ist der „European Public Sector Award" (EPSA), der 2007 in Luzern vergeben wurde und in erster Linie von der Deutschen Hochschule für Verwaltungswissenschaften in Speyer (Bundesrepublik Deutschland) gemeinsam mit anderen Institutionen getragen wurde und die folgenden drei Innovationsbereiche umfasste: (a) Gemeinsam Handeln (Collaborative Governance), (b) Zielerreichung mit knappen Mitteln und (c) den demographischen Wandel steuern.

In Tabelle 1 werden die Innovationsbereiche und die eingereichten Projekte der jeweiligen europäischen öffentlichen Verwaltungen dargestellt.

Wie die Tabelle zeigt, sind in Europa die PPP-Projekte unterrepräsentiert (nur vier Projekte). Dieser erste Eindruck ist sicherlich zu modifizieren, wenn die Anzahl der Projekte berücksichtigt wird, die eine Einbindung der Stakeholder, der lokalen Gemeinschaft, neue Formen des Finanzmanagements und Investitionen in das öffentliche Vermögen vorsehen.

	Gemeinsam Handeln	Zielerreichung mit knappen Mitteln	Steuerung des demographischen Wandels
E-Government	15	64	0
Kooperationen	24	1	2
Personalmanagement	1	5	9
Geschäftsprozessmanagement	3	25	2
Neue Dienstleistungen und Technologien	8	11	5
Public Private Partnership	0	4	0
Systeme und Instrumente der strategischen Planung	7	13	8
Involvierung der Stakeholder und der lokalen Gemeinschaft	29	1	7
Vermögensinvestitionen	3	5	0
Neue Instrumente der Finanzierung und im Finanzmanagement	1	11	1
Qualitätsmanagement	3	14	0
Kommunikationsstrategien	2	0	1

Tab. 1: Bewerbungen um den European Public Sector Award (EPSA) Luzern 2007

Quelle: EPSA – How to innovate public sector innovation? Fact Sheet Booklet, 2007, S. 8.

2 PPP, New Public Management und Public Governance

Wie allgemein bekannt, wurden seit Beginn der 1980er Jahre in vielen Staaten auf der Grundlage der Prinzipien des New Public Management (NPM) tiefe und radikale Reformen des öffentlichen Sektors durchgeführt.[3]

In Abbildung 1 sind die wichtigsten Reformansätze des öffentlichen Sektors dargestellt, die in einem engen Zusammenhang mit PPPs stehen. Dazu zählen Finanzinnovationen, wie die Projektfinanzierung und die private Kofinanzierung von öffentlichen Investitionen und vor allem die Einführung von Marktmechanismen, die zu einer Dezentralisierung der Aufgaben und der Verantwortlichkeiten geführt haben, das Contracting Out und das Contracting In von Dienstleistungen sowie die Partnerschaft zwischen Staat und privatem Sektor.[4]

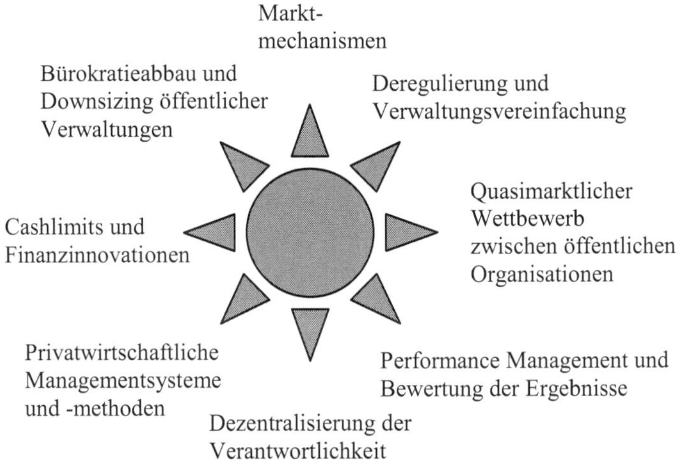

Abb. 1: Aktionshebel des New Public Management im Zeitraum von 1980 bis 1999

Quelle: eigene Darstellung.

3 Vgl. OECD (1990).

4 Vgl. Drewry, G. (2000).

Das PPP hat sich seit Beginn der 1990er Jahre entwickelt, um den Anforderungen der öffentlichen Verwaltung gerecht zu werden. Dabei wurden neue Finanzierungsformen für Infrastrukturinvestitionen entwickelt, um eine maximale Flexibilität und unternehmerische Orientierung bei der Planung, Umsetzung und Steuerung der öffentlichen Investitionen zu ermöglichen. In der Folge wurde versucht, ein Gleichgewicht herzustellen zwischen der Notwendigkeit für die verschiedenen öffentlichen Verwaltungen, die Steuerung und die strategische Koordinierung von Investitionsprozessen zu erhalten sowie eine maximale Einbeziehung von privaten Akteuren (Entwicklungs- und Projektierungsgesellschaften, Bauunternehmen, Dienstleistungsunternehmen und Banken) bei der Finanzierung und Realisierung von Infrastrukturen zu finden. Im Jahre 1991 übernahm das Vereinigte Königreich mit der „Private Finance Initiative" (PFI) eine Pionierrolle, die 1997 in der eigentlichen PPP-Initiative aufging.

Dank dieser beiden englischen Initiativen und jener weiterer europäischer Länder wurde die öffentlich-private Kofinanzierung von größeren und kleineren Investitionsprojekten in Bereichen wie Strom- und Gasversorgung, verschiedener Infrastrukturprojekte, Brücken, Galerien, Krankenhäuser, Universitäten und Gefängnisse eingeführt.

Jüngste Studien zum Thema PPP der OECD, des Internationalen Währungsfonds und der großen internationalen Finanzinstitutionen (Weltbank, Europäische Investmentbank) zeigen, dass PPP und die Projektfinanzierung vermehrt angenommen werden, nicht nur in den öffentlichen Verwaltungen der entwickelten Länder, sondern auch in den BRIC-Staaten, Schwellenländern, wirtschaftlichen Transitionsländern und Entwicklungsländern.

PPP stellt somit einen „Dritten Weg" dar.[5] Traditionell werden die Güter/Dienstleistungen entweder ausschließlich von Seiten des privaten Sektors oder des öffentlichen Sektors erbracht. Im dritten Weg arbeiten der Staat und die

[5] Vgl. Klijn, E. H./Teisman, G. R. (2000).

privaten Unternehmen (unabhängig davon, ob sie gewinnorientiert sind oder nicht) zusammen, um die Bürger mit öffentlichen Sach- und Dienstleistungen zu versorgen. Der dritte Weg kann als Versuch verstanden werden, die Kernkompetenzen des öffentlichen Sektors mit jenen des Marktes zu kombinieren. KLIJN und TEISMAN (2004) definieren PPP als eine nachhaltige Zusammenarbeit zwischen öffentlichen und privaten Akteuren, bei der die Akteure gemeinsam Produkte und Dienstleistungen entwickeln und die Risiken, Kosten und Gewinne partnerschaftlich teilen.

Dabei erfolgt der Übergang vom Modell des Staates als „Unternehmer“, der unmittelbar zur Produktion und zur Bereitstellung von Gütern und Dienstleistungen verpflichtet ist, hin zum Modell des Staates als „Gewährleister“ einer Versorgung der Bürger mit Sach- und Dienstleistungen. Innerhalb dieses Modelles entscheidet der Staat, welche Dienste er garantiert, wer die Dienste produziert (make or buy-Entscheidung) und vor allem, wer den Bereitstellungsprozess überwacht und kontrolliert. Die öffentliche Verwaltung auf den verschiedenen institutionellen Ebenen (national, regional und lokal) muss demnach in der Lage sein, folgende Aufgaben zu erfüllen: Formulierung und Implementierung von Strategien; Koordination der Netzwerke; Leitung des Ausschreibungsverfahrens und der Auswahl der Lieferanten; Führung der Vertragsverhandlungen; Überwachung und Evaluierung der Leistungen der Lieferanten und direkter Eingriff im Falle der Nichterfüllung des Vertrages durch den Lieferanten[6].

3 Projektfinanzierung und PPP in Italien

Italien stellt bei der Umsetzung der Projektfinanzierung und der Anwendung der Logik des PPP einen Sonderfall dar. Dies zeigt sich in der unterschiedlichen Fähigkeit der Entwicklung und Umsetzung dieser Konzepte auf den verschiedenen Ebenen der öffentlichen Verwaltung (national, regional, lokal), in den

[6] Vgl. Reichard, C. (2006).

verschiedenen Landesteilen (Ober-/Mittelitalien versus Süditalien) und in den verschiedenen Sektoren der öffentlichen Verwaltung (Netzdienste, öffentliche Infrastrukturen, Gesundheit, Bildung, etc.).

Im Jahre 2006 belief sich in Italien die Gesamtsumme der im Rahmen von PPP-Projekten und Projektfinanzierungen durchgeführten Investitionen auf ca. 58 Mrd. Euro, von denen gut 32 Mrd. Euro im Jahre 2006 realisiert wurden (Quelle: Osservatorio nazionale sul PPP).

Die durchschnittliche Wachstumsrate in den 2000er Jahren nach Anwendung dieser innovativen Arten der Finanzierung betrug 19 Prozent pro Jahr. Die Finanzierung über PPPs beträgt 30 Prozent des nationalen Marktes für öffentliche Arbeiten.

Die fünf wichtigsten Bereiche der Anwendung von PPP und Projektfinanzierung sind: Netzgebundene Dienste (Wasser, Gas, Energie und Telekommunikation) 48 Prozent; Verkehr 21 Prozent; Gesundheit 9 Prozent; Parkplätze 4 Prozent und Stadterneuerung 4 Prozent.

Zum besseren Verständnis dieser Daten sei vor allem daran erinnert, dass Italien – hinsichtlich Wert und Anzahl – hinter dem Vereinigten Königreich der zweitgrößte europäische PPP-Anwender im Gesundheitswesen ist und eine steigende Tendenz in der Anwendung in den Bereichen der netzgebundenen Dienste (Energie, Gas, Wärme, Telekommunikation) von Seiten der nationalen und lokalen Versorger aufweist. Die letzteren und insbesondere die öffentlichen lokalen Unternehmen haben bereits Mitte der 1990er Jahre vielfach auf spezielle „Zweckgesellschaften" (Special Purpose Vehicle, SPV) und die verschiedenen Formen, so beispielsweise BOT (Build-Operate-Transfer) und BOO (Build-Own-Operate), zurückgegriffen.

Diesen positiven Ergebnissen stehen einige Schwachstellen gegenüber. Auf zentralstaatlicher Ebene zeigten sich große Schwierigkeiten bei der Anwendung der Projektfinanzierung bei einigen großen Projekten insbesondere im Bereich des Ausbaues des höherrangigen Straßennetzes (Autobahn Pedemontana in der

Lombardei, Passante Straßenabschnitt Mestre Venezia, dritte Fahrbahnspur Napoli – Salerno).

Diese Schwierigkeiten sind trotz der Schaffung einer auf Projektfinanzierung spezialisierten Organisationseinheit (ähnlich dem Modell der englischen PFI-Task Force) im Ministerium für das Staatsvermögen zum Ende der 1990er Jahre aufgetreten. Dieser Struktur wurden im Jahre 2000 Organisationseinheiten zur Projektfinanzierung in sechs Regionen – unter ihnen Lombardei und Latium – zur Seite gestellt.

Die regionalen Organisationseinheiten haben dabei immer eng mit den regionalen Entwicklungs- und Finanzierungsagenturen zusammengearbeitet. Diese „Partnerschaft" bewirkte, dass die Projektfinanzierung und PPP bei den lokalen Verwaltungen, wenn auch sehr vorsichtig, zunahmen.

Die zögerliche Verbreitung bei den Gemeinden kann auf Gründe zurückgeführt werden wie die ständige Veränderung der rechtlichen Rahmenbedingungen, die Unsicherheit bei der Nachfrage nach den Dienstleistungen, Finanzierungsengpässe von Seiten der Zwischenfinanzierer und der Bauunternehmen und das Fehlen von institutionalisierten Beratungszentren, die auf regionaler Ebene arbeiten.

Tabelle 2 stellt den Rückgriff auf die Projektfinanzierung bei den lokalen Verwaltungen (Provinzen, Gemeinden und Gemeindekonsortien) dar, unterschieden nach direkten Tätigkeiten der privaten Akteure (Artikel 37 bis) und Tätigkeiten, die unmittelbar von den öffentlichen Akteuren (Konzession zur Umsetzung und Verwaltung) eingeleitet wurden.

Die beiden Verfahren wurden bereits 1994 durch eine nationale Rechtsnorm eingeführt; mit jener der Aktivierung einer speziellen „Zweckgesellschaft" („società veicolo") in Form einer Aktiengesellschaft mit öffentlichem Kapital besteht zudem eine dritte Möglichkeit.

Jahr	Anzahl der Vergaben gem. Art. 37 bis	Vergabewert gem. Art 37 bis	Anzahl der Bewerber um eine Konzession	Wert der Konzessionen
2000	6	99.263.016	24	157.327.602
2001	10	100.605.798	110	853.264.424
2002	20	275.317.224	128	733.357.456
2003	60	1.899.560.435	141	3.143.772.976
2004	86	1.215.094.657	198	1.361.074.740
2005	115	1.120.973.804	117	615.363.583
2006	47	2.761.496.961	148	4.059.057.166
Gesamt	344	7.472.311.895,00	866	10.923.217.947,00

Tab. 2: Von den Lokalverwaltungen in Italien getätigte Projektfinanzierungen
Quelle: Daten OICE (Zahlen in €).

Das Jahr 2002 stellt mit einem raschen Ansteigen der Anzahl realisierter Projekte und der Investitionshöhe den Wendepunkt bei der Verbreitung der Projektfinanzierung dar.

Für ein besseres Verständnis der Dynamiken bei der Umsetzung von PPP in Italien in der hier vorgenommenen Perspektive eines strategischen Benchmarking zwischen Italien und der Schweiz, zeigen sich zwei Bezugspunkte gemeinsamer Betrachtung:

- die möglichen Determinanten, die die Anwendung des PPP erklären, wobei auf die Entwicklung der Finanzfunktion (finanzwirtschaftliche Handlungsfelder) in den lokalen Verwaltungen abgestellt wird;
- eine jüngst durchgeführte Studie der Region Lombardei (2007) über PPP in den Gemeinden und Provinzen, welche sinnvoll für die Gegenüberstellung der Ergebnisse im nächsten Kapitel zu den Gemeinden der

Schweiz ist (hier sei daran erinnert, dass die Region Lombardei mehr Einwohner hat als die gesamte Schweiz).

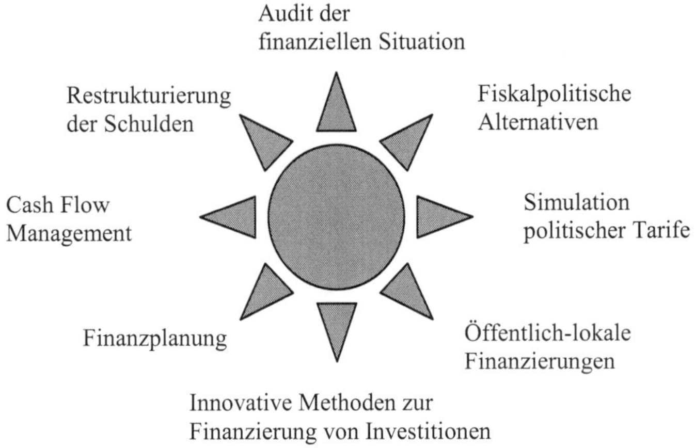

Abb. 2: Überblick über verschiedene finanzwirtschaftliche Handlungsfelder einer Gemeinde
Quelle: eigene Darstellung.

Von besonderer Relevanz ist eine Beurteilung der finanziellen Lage der lokalen Verwaltung (Audit der finanziellen Situation), wobei laufend die Zahlungsströme und der Kassenstand (Überschuss bzw. Defizit) überwacht und bereits im Rahmen der Haushaltsplanung Ressourcen vorgesehen werden müssen, um die benötigten Investitionen finanzieren zu können. Das Audit bildet die Grundlage für das Rating und liefert daher wichtige Informationen für die Ratingagenturen. Das Rating ist insofern von Bedeutung, da es den Gemeinden den Zugang zu innovativen Finanzierungsmethoden eröffnet und einen großen Einfluss auf die Finanzierungskosten hat.

Andere Handlungsfelder betreffen die Planung und Simulation der Auswirkungen politischer Entscheidungsalternativen auf die Eigenmittel der lokalen Körperschaften, von den Tarifpolitiken bis hin zu den Steuer- und Abgabenpolitiken, die einen Rahmen von möglichen Finanzierungsquellen für Projektfinanzierungen anbieten; beispielsweise sei an die Möglichkeit der Gemeinden erinnert, Steuern einzuheben, um öffentliche Bauten zu finanzieren.

Des Weiteren werden Aktivitätspakete berücksichtigt, die mit der Bewertung und den Alternativen der Erhaltung/Ablegung der Vermögenswerte der lokalen Körperschaften verbunden sind.

Das kommunale Finanzwesen stellt ein Aktivitätspaket von beträchtlichem Interesse und großer Potentialität dar, was die Realisierung eines Pools von Tätigkeiten der Projektfinanzierung betrifft. Diese Operationen können die Gemeinden, öffentliche Unternehmen für Netzdienste mit Beteiligungen, lokale Stiftungen in den Bereichen Kultur, Bildung, Sport und die anderen Kommunalbetriebe (z.B. Grünanlagenerhaltung, Abfallwirtschaft) vereinen.

Im Paket der innovativen Methoden der Investitionsfinanzierung sind weiterhin vor allem die Bewertung der finanzwirtschaftlichen Vorteilhaftigkeit und der rechtlich-institutionellen sowie organisatorischen Machbarkeit folgender Alternativen inkludiert:

- Ausgabe von Schuldverschreibungen,
- mittel-/langfristige Verschuldung,
- Leasing zur Realisierung von öffentlichem Bauen,
- öffentlich-private Formen der Kofinanzierung, gewinnorientiert und nicht gewinnorientiert, wie das PPP und die Projektfinanzierung.

Lokale Körperschaften finden immer größeres Interesse an der Neuverhandlung der mittel- bis langfristigen Verschuldung über die Zinssätze oder die unmittelbare Neuaushandlung der Zinssätze, die Laufzeitänderung und in einigen Fällen die Verlängerung der Kreditdauer und den Rückgriff auf derivative Instrumente (Swap, Optionen, Futures).

Folglich wird die Bandbreite der möglichen Aktivitätspakete durch die aktive Liquiditätsverwaltung und durch die Finanzprogrammierung vervollständigt.

Die verschiedenen Aktivitätspakete bilden somit den Kreis der möglichen Interventionsalternativen, die den lokalen Körperschaften offen stehen; es ist in der Folge Aufgabe der Gemeinden und Provinzen, die Aktivitätspakete auszuwählen, auf die sie sich konzentrieren, abhängig von den eigenen Interventionsstrategien und den jeweiligen entscheidungs-, organisations- und verwaltungsmäßigen sowie finanzwirtschaftlichen Besonderheiten.

4 PPP in der Schweiz

Auch in der Schweiz hat sich in den letzten Jahren die Auffassung durchgesetzt, dass es zur Bewältigung der Herausforderungen in der öffentlichen Verwaltung notwendig ist, sehr intensiv mit privaten gewinnorientierten Unternehmen im Rahmen von PPPs zu kooperieren.

Die Anwendung des PPP-Konzeptes setzt für die öffentlichen Verwaltungen die Fähigkeit voraus, folgende geänderte Bedingungen mit Erfolg zu steuern:[7]

- die Aufnahme der Phase des Betriebes der Infrastruktur direkt in den Vertrag,
- die Übertragung der Konzession am Eigentum an den privaten Partner,
- PPP umfasst die gesamte Projektlaufzeit,
- die immer wichtiger werdende Rolle von Investoren und Finanzzwischenhändlern.

PPP ist für jene öffentlichen Körperschaften nützlich, die sich in finanziellen Schwierigkeiten befinden, während es eine Chance darstellt, sowohl für private

[7] Vgl. Bolz, U. (2005).

Unternehmen (diese können ihren Gewinn und ihre Synergien mit dem öffentlichen Sektor erhöhen) als auch für Gemeinden, die beabsichtigen, die eigenen Kompetenzen zu erhöhen und voll von der Partnerschaft mit dem öffentlichen Sektor zu profitieren.

BOLZ (2005) unterscheidet zwei Typen von PPPs, nämlich den Typ Beschaffungs-PPP und den Typ Aufgabenerfüllungs-PPP. Beim Beschaffungs-PPP tritt der Staat als Besteller auf, der Private als Ersteller und Betreiber einer Infrastruktur oder als Erbringer einer längerfristig ausgerichteten Dienstleistung. Diese Variante dominiert vor allem in den Bereichen Hochbau, öffentlicher Verkehr und Straßeninfrastruktur. Beim Aufgabenerfüllungs-PPP ist der Ausgangspunkt die Erkenntnis, dass eine bestimmte öffentliche Aufgabe vom Staat allein nicht mehr oder nicht mehr optimal erfüllt werden kann. Die Zusammenarbeit mit einem privaten Partner verspricht Vorteile bezüglich Zielerreichung, Effizienz und Effektivität. Als Beispiel kann die Stiftung Greater Zürich Area angeführt werden, die 1998 in Zürich mit der Überzeugung gegründet wurde, dass die Förderung und Entwicklung eines Wirtschaftsraumes viel wirksamer und rentabler gestaltet werden kann, wenn die öffentlichen und privaten Fähigkeiten bzw. Kräfte vereint werden. Zu den Mitgliedern dieser Stiftung zählen die Kantone, die Gemeinden, private Unternehmen und einige Banken.

In der Schweiz war der private Sektor immer in den Bau und Betrieb von öffentlichen Infrastrukturen involviert (z.B. Abfallwirtschaft und Alptransit AG). Auf jeder Ebene der Verwaltung (föderal, kantonal und kommunal) ist die Zusammenarbeit zwischen öffentlichen und privaten Akteuren sehr intensiv. Ungeachtet dessen konnte sich das PPP in der Schweiz im Gegensatz zu anderen europäischen Ländern bis jetzt nicht durchsetzen.

Zu den Gründen, die diesen Rückstand erklären, zählt zweifelsohne die Fähigkeit der territorialen Schweizer Gemeinschaften, von den sehr günstigen Finanzierungsmöglichkeiten in der Gesamtheit zu profitieren. Hinzu kommt die Tatsache, dass die Schweiz im öffentlichen Infrastrukturbereich keinen akuten

Nachholbedarf aufweist. Weiters zu nennen sind die Sonder- (z.B. für die Straßen und den öffentlichen Verkehr) und Mischfinanzierungen (der Bundesstaat und die Kantone beteiligen sich an der Finanzierung von städtischen Infrastrukturprojekten), die keine Anreize für PPP ausüben. Als weitere Gründe können die Verwaltungskultur, die direkte Demokratie (mit Auswirkungen wie im Falle des NPM auf die Entscheidungsprozesse) und die fehlenden schweizerischen Größenverhältnisse angeführt werden, die derartige Handlungen weder lohnend noch interessant erscheinen lassen.

Die schweizerische Tradition der vielfältigen Kooperationen zwischen öffentlicher Hand und Privatwirtschaft kann jedoch als gute Voraussetzung für die Entwicklung von weiterführenden PPPs eingestuft werden. Einige internationale PPP-Beispiele lassen sich somit auf die Schweiz übertragen. Andere hingegen müssen vor dem Hintergrund der "nationalen" Besonderheiten relativiert werden, da jeder Staat seine eigene PPP-Strategie entwickeln muss, welche im Einklang mit den nationalen Rahmenbedingungen (Recht, Kultur etc.) steht.

Was die Schweiz betrifft, sprechen folgende Gründe für einen verstärkten Einsatz von PPP: [8]

- PPP stellt für die öffentliche Verwaltung eine wichtige Alternative dar, um neue Herausforderungen zu bewältigen,
- PPP kann einen wichtigen Beitrag für eine effiziente Erfüllung öffentlicher Aufgaben leisten,
- PPP ist zudem eine Chance für die weitere Modernisierung der öffentlichen Verwaltung.

[8] Vgl. Bolz, U. (2005).

Die Zusammenarbeit mit dem privaten Sektor bietet in folgenden Bereichen eine Vielzahl an Möglichkeiten:

1. Hochbau: Das Potential ist sehr groß, vor allem in den Bereichen Instandhaltung und Instandsetzung von Verwaltungsgebäuden, Gebäudeverwaltung, Schaffung von neuen Stadtteilen sowie Sport- und Freizeiteinrichtungen.
2. Verkehr: Hier lassen sich Beispiele aus dem Schienenverkehr und des nationalen, kantonalen und kommunalen Straßennetzes anführen.
3. Wirtschaftsförderung.
4. E-Government: In diesem Fall ist es notwendig, eine Kofinanzierung von IT-Projekten zu initiieren.

Weitere Bereiche, die für PPP interessant sein können, sind Bildung, Kultur, Sport, Landesverteidigung, Gesundheit und Sozialwesen.

In den letzten Jahren wurden in der Schweiz einige PPP-Projekte initiiert. Insbesondere können hier folgende Beispiele angeführt werden: Neues Kongresszentrum Zürich, Kultur- und Kongresszentrum Luzern (KKL), International Packaging Institute (IPI) Genf, Greater Zürich Area, Schule im Netz und Parkhaus AG Zürich.

Das PPP-Projekt „Schule im Netz" lässt sich als Vorzeigeprojekt bezeichnen. Private Unternehmen stellen den Schweizer Schulen Hardware und Software-Dienstleistungen zu Sonderkonditionen zur Verfügung. Die Kantone und die Gemeinden übernehmen die Kosten für Lehrkräfte und Räumlichkeiten und der Bund unterstützt die Ausbildung der Lehrkräfte.

Verschiedene Organisationen der Bundesverwaltung haben zudem die Möglichkeit einer PPP-Finanzierung von Infrastrukturprojekten abgeklärt (zum Beispiel das Departement für Umwelt, Verkehr, Energie und Kommunikation und die Eidgenössische Finanzverwaltung) oder unterstützen im Rahmen der wirtschaftlichen Entwicklungszusammenarbeit diverse PPP-Projekte in osteuropäischen Ländern (Staatssekretariat für Wirtschaft). Insbesondere in der Eidgenössischen Finanzverwaltung und im Departement für Verteidigung, Bevölkerungsschutz und Sport wird gegenwärtig aktiv PPP-Wissen aufgebaut.

5 PPP und die Schweizer Gemeinden

Auch auf kommunaler Ebene ist es möglich und wünschenswert, PPP als alternative Form der direkten Verwaltung einzuführen. Im Jahre 2008 wurde eine repräsentative empirische Untersuchung unter den 2.732 Schweizer Gemeinden durchgeführt, um besser zu verstehen, wie der aktuelle Stand der Einführung von PPP in der lokalen Verwaltung ist.

Hierzu wurden Gemeinden mit über 5.000 Einwohnern (insgesamt 311 Gemeinden) ausgewählt, die auch die drei wichtigsten Sprachgruppen repräsentieren. Die Stichprobe setzte sich aus 77 Prozent deutschsprachigen Gemeinden, 19 Prozent französischsprachigen Gemeinden und 4 Prozent italienischsprachigen Gemeinden zusammen. Von den 104 Gemeinden, die auf den Fragebogen antworteten (das sind 32,4 Prozent), haben 56 keine PPP-Projekte, während 48 Prozent zumindest eines vorweisen können. Insgesamt wurden 315 PPP-Projekte gezählt und es lässt sich interessanterweise feststellen, dass die durchschnittliche Anzahl der PPP-Projekte je Gemeinde in den drei Sprachregionen sehr variiert. Im Kanton Tessin beträgt dieser Wert pro Gemeinde 4,67, in der französischsprachigen Schweiz 3,87 und in der deutschsprachigen Schweiz 2,76. Der gewogene Mittelwert auf nationaler Ebene beträgt hingegen 3,03 PPP-Projekte je Gemeinde.

Nachfolgend werden einige Hinweise aus der Praxis gegeben, welche Typologie von Rechtsformen zur Etablierung und Verwaltung von PPP eingesetzt wird und in welchem öffentlichen Rahmen diese verwendet werden.

Der erste interessante Aspekt betrifft die Einschätzung der Bedeutung von PPP für die lokalen öffentlichen Körperschaften. Zu diesem Zweck wurden die Generaldirektoren und Gemeindesekretäre zur Wichtigkeit von PPP für die eigene Gemeinde befragt. Auf nationaler Ebene gaben gut 89 Prozent der Befragten an, dass das PPP „sehr/ziemlich“ wichtig ist, nur 11 Prozent antworteten, dass das PPP von geringer Bedeutung ist. Im Tessin und in der französischsprachigen Schweiz haben 100 Prozent mit „sehr/ziemlich“ geantwortet, während in der deutschsprachigen Schweiz dies nur 85 Prozent taten.

Als nächstes werden die unterschiedlichen Rechtsformen vorgestellt, welche die lokalen Körperschaften für die Etablierung ihrer PPPs verwenden. Auf nationaler Ebene ist die am häufigsten verwendete Rechtsform der Leistungsauftrag (22,5 Prozent), gefolgt von der Aktiengesellschaft (21,3 Prozent), der Stiftung (18,1 Prozent) und dem Verein (14,6 Prozent). In geringerer Anzahl bestehen Genossenschaften (7 Prozent) und Konzessionen (4,4 Prozent). In den drei Sprachregionen lassen sich dabei einige interessante und bemerkenswerte Unterschiede feststellen. Im Tessin sind die Aktiengesellschaft (46,4 Prozent) und die Konzession (14,3 Prozent) am beliebtesten. Es ist zu beobachten, dass bei 18 Prozent der Gemeindeprojekte noch nicht klar ist, welche Rechtsform verwendet werden soll. In der französischsprachigen Schweiz ist der Verein die bevorzugte Rechtsform (32,8 Prozent), gefolgt vom Leistungsauftrag (22,4 Prozent), der Aktiengesellschaft (12 Prozent) und der Stiftung (10,3 Prozent). In der deutschsprachigen Schweiz hingegen ist der Leistungsauftrag von größter Bedeutung (24,4 Prozent), gefolgt von der Stiftung (21,8 Prozent) und der Aktiengesellschaft (20,5 Prozent). Mit einigem Abstand folgen die Konzessionen (11,8 Prozent) und die Genossenschaften (7,4 Prozent).

Der Tessin favorisiert folglich die Aktiengesellschaft, wohingegen die deutsch- und vor allem die französischsprachige Schweiz dazu tendieren, mit Vereinen, Stiftungen und Leistungsaufträgen zu arbeiten. Im Tessin und in Teilen der deutschsprachigen Schweiz werden privatwirtschaftliche Rechtsformen gewählt, in der französischsprachigen Schweiz hingegen bevorzugt PPP-

Formen, bei denen der öffentliche Sektor stärker in die Leistungserstellung eingebunden ist.

Werden die öffentlichen Verwaltungen analysiert, die an PPP interessiert sind, so zeigt sich, dass die lokalen Körperschaften in der Schweiz hauptsächlich PPP-Projekte in den folgenden Sektoren etablieren: Sozialdienste (14 Prozent), Transportwesen (11,5 Prozent), Kulturgüter (10,8 Prozent), Wasser und Strom (10,5 Prozent) sowie Sportförderung (10,2 Prozent). Weitere relevante Sektoren sind Umwelt (7,6 Prozent), Tourismus (7,3 Prozent) und Bildungswesen (7 Prozent). Auch hier zeigen sich Unterschiede zwischen dem Tessin, der französisch- und der deutschsprachigen Schweiz. Im Tessin ist der am meisten an PPP interessierte Sektor das Verkehrswesen (21,4 Prozent), gefolgt von Wasser und Strom (17,9 Prozent), Tourismus (17,9 Prozent) und Sportförderung (14,3 Prozent). In der französischsprachigen Schweiz zeigt sich eine homogenere Situation in dem Sinne, als dass PPP-Projekte in vielen Bereichen in einem mehr oder weniger gleich hohen Prozentsatz vorzufinden sind. Im Kontext der kommunalen Verwaltung beträgt dieser Wert 13,8 Prozent, 12 Prozent im Bereich Verkehr, Sozialwesen, Bildungswesen und im Bereich Umwelt. 10 Prozent sind es für den Bereich Wasser und Strom sowie Kulturgüter. In der deutschsprachigen Schweiz sind folgende Verwaltungsbereiche an PPP interessiert: das Sozialwesen (16,1 Prozent) an erster Stelle, gefolgt von der Sportförderung (11,8 Prozent), dem Bereich Kulturgüter (11,4 Prozent), Transportwesen (10 Prozent) sowie Wasser und Strom (9,6 Prozent).

Auch im Zusammenhang mit den an PPP interessierten Sektoren der öffentlichen Verwaltung gibt es Unterschiede und Analogien. Einerseits wird im Tessin und in der deutschsprachigen Schweiz versucht, sich auf spezifische Sektoren zu fokussieren (Tourismus, Transportwesen, Mobilität, Sportförderung, Wasser, Strom und Sozialwesen), während auf der anderen Seite die französischsprachige Schweiz eine einförmigere und auf mehrere Sektoren ausgedehnte Ausrichtung aufweist (Wasser und Strom, Sozialdienste, Bildung, Umwelt, Kulturgüter, Kommunalverwaltung, Transportwesen). Zusammenfassend kann festgestellt werden, dass die französischsprachige Schweiz hauptsächlich dazu tendiert, PPPs mit einem ausgeprägten Sozial- und Umweltinteresse (Sozialwesen, Ausbildung, Kulturgüter und Umwelt) zu entwickeln, während das Tessin und die deutschsprachige Schweiz die sogenannten netzgebundenen Dienste bevorzugen (Wasser und Strom, Transport und Verkehr).

Literaturverzeichnis

Bolz, U. (2005): Public Private Partnership in der Schweiz. Zürich, Schulthess.

Drewry, G. (2000): In: Osborne, S. P. (Hrsg.) (2000): Public-private partnerships: rethinking the boundary between public and private law. London, Routledge.

Gianella, T. (2008): Pubblico e privato, un partenariato possibile. Bellinzona, La Regione Ticino.

Klijn, E.H./Teisman, G.R. (2000): In: Osborne, S.P. (Hrsg.) (2000): Governing public-private partnerships: analysing and managing the processes and institutional characteristics of public-private partnerships. London, Routledge.

Klijn, E.H./Teisman, G.R. (2004): Public-Private Partnership: The Right Form at the Wrong Moment? An Analysis of Institutional and Strategic Obstacles. In: Ghobadian, A. et al. (Hrsg.) (2007): Public-Private Partnerships. Policy and Experience, Palgrave Macmillan.

Meneguzzo, M./Gianella, T. (2007): Lo sviluppo del NPM in Svizzera: le "culture", le reti e i centri di competenza, il Partenariato pubblico-privato. In: Meneguzzo, M. et al. (Hrsg.) (2007): Contributi di management pubblico. Mailand, McGraw-Hill.

OECD (1990): Survey of Public Management Reforms. Paris, OECD.

Reichard, C. (2006): New Institutional Arrangements of Public Service Delivery. In: Reichard, C./Mussari, R./Kupke, S. (Hrsg.): The Governance of Services of General Interest between State, Market and Society. Berlin.

Die Bedeutung von PPP für die regionale wirtschaftliche Entwicklung in Estland

Sulev Mäeltsemees

Inhaltsverzeichnis

1 Einleitung

Wie auch in anderen ehemaligen sozialistischen Ländern Europas begann Ende der 1980er Jahre in Estland der Übergang von der zentralen Planwirtschaft zur Marktwirtschaft. Im Gegensatz zu vielen anderen Ländern wurde in Estland aber sogleich der Kurs hin zu ultraliberaler Marktwirtschaft und damit auch zu schneller Privatisierung der Wirtschaft des öffentlichen Sektors eingeschlagen. Im darauffolgenden nächsten Jahrzehnt hatte man inhaltlich betrachtet praktisch in jedem Industriezweig mit schneller Bedeutungszunahme des Privatsektors zu tun, wobei der öffentliche Sektor als uneffektiv und wenig perspektivisch eingeschätzt wurde. Oftmals waren Aussagen zu hören, wonach jede Gemeinde und Stadt, ja sogar der ganze Staat wie Aktiengesellschaften zu managen wären, ohne dabei daran zu denken, dass Staat und Kommunalverwaltungen als solche eigentlich als soziale Modelle gelten. Die zuletzt genannte Erkenntnis ist von wesentlicher Bedeutung unter anderem bei der Umsetzung von PPP-Projekten.

Alle Meinungen, wonach zur Gewährleistung der Stabilität der Gesellschaft doch auch der öffentliche Sektor in wesentlichem Umfang zu fördern sei, wurden ernsthafter Kritik unterzogen. Von in Estland an der Macht gewesenen politischen Kräften sind bereits einige Jahrzehnte lang mit ziemlicher Hartnäckigkeit die Prinzipien ultraliberaler Marktwirtschaft verfolgt worden. Der Kurs hin zur Umsetzung liberaler Marktwirtschaft wird auch durch die Tatsache bestätigt, dass vom Parlament eine stufenweise Reduzierung der Lohnsteuer von 26% im Jahr 2002 bis auf 18% in 2011 verabschiedet wurde. Um die Jahrhundertwende wurden strategische und als Monopol geltende Unternehmen wie die Estnische Eisenbahn AG (AS Eesti Raudtee), die im ganzen Land für die Organisation von Eisenbahnbeförderungen zuständig war, und die Tallinner Wasser AG (AS Tallinna Vesi), die für die Wasserversorgung der Hauptstadt zu sorgen hatte, an ausländische Investoren verkauft.

In den letzten Jahren haben Politiker zunehmend angefangen, zu begreifen, dass auch der öffentliche Sektor gefördert werden muss. So kaufte der Staat 2006 seine frühere Mehrheitsbeteiligung (2/3) an der Estnischen Eisenbahn AG vom Privatunternehmen zurück, wobei der Rückkaufpreis das 2,5-fache des vor fünf Jahren für den Verkauf erhaltenen Betrags betrug. Zugleich wurde beispielsweise auch der Rückkauf der Tallinner Wasser AG bereits in Erwägung gezogen.

Leider hatte die Verfolgung der Theorie eines ausgedünnten Staates (vor allem bezogen auf Steuerreduzierung) große Probleme im Bereich der Investitionsmöglichkeiten im öffentlichen Sektor zur Folge. Die Bedürfnisse der Wirtschaft und der gesamten Gesellschaft sind größer als die dafür notwendigen und momentan dem öffentlichen Sektor zur Verfügung stehenden Mittel, um die Infrastruktur, die größtenteils aus der sowjetischen Zeit stammt, zu erweitern oder gar zu modernisieren.

Viele sozialwirtschaftliche Aufgaben im Bildungswesen, im öffentlichen Transport, etc. gehören in Estland mit seiner einstufigen Kommunalverwaltung zum Zuständigkeitsbereich von Kommunalverwaltungen. Folglich sind es Gemeinden und Städte, die nach Lösungen für die Weiterentwicklung der Infrastruktur dieser Wirtschaftszweige zu suchen haben. Als einer der aussichtsreichsten Wege, insbesondere in der Hauptstadt Tallinn, hat sich die Zusammenarbeit des öffentlichen und privaten Sektors in der Form von PPP-Projekten erwiesen. Leider handelt es sich bei diesen Problemen in Estland noch um eine derart junge Thematik, dass es kaum Forschungsarbeiten und wissenschaftliche Publikationen gibt, welche an dieser Stelle einbezogen werden könnten. Zwar gibt es diesbezüglich einige in der Presse publizierte Artikel, sie dienen jedoch meist politischen Zwecken.

2 PPP-Projekte in der estnischen Politik und Wirtschaftspolitik

Gesetze und andere staatliche Rechtsbeschlüsse haben sich bisher nicht mit der Lösung von mit PPP-Projekten verbundenen Problemen befasst. PPP-Projekte wurden jedoch zumindest einmal im Programm der Regierung der Republik Estland genannt: im Koalitionsvertrag der Estnischen Reformpartei, der Estnischen Zentralpartei und der Volksunion Estlands aus dem Jahre 2005 wurde unter Punkt "Staatlichkeit. Rechtspolitik" erwähnt, dass *"(...) von der Regierungskoalition eine rechtliche Umwelt für die Benutzung der Investitionen des privaten Sektors zwecks Erweisen öffentlicher Dienste geschaffen wird (PPP-Modell)."*[1]

Angesprochen werden PPP-Projekte weiterhin im Entwicklungsplan des Wohnungsbaubereichs für die Jahre 2008-2013, wonach die Vision und das Hauptziel des Vorhabens darin bestehen, dass die Anschaffung einer Wohnung für jeden Einwohner Estlands möglich gemacht werden muss. Man ist bemüht, den bisherigen geringen Anteil von kommunalen und Privatwohnungen am gesamten Wohnungsfonds zu erhöhen. In diesem Zusammenhang setzte man sich zum Ziel, die Zahl kommunaler Mietwohnungen bis zum Jahr 2013 um 6000 Einheiten zu erhöhen und im Rahmen von PPP 700 neue Wohnungen zu schaffen.[2]

Die Tatsache, dass die Investitionen des öffentlichen Sektors merkbar gestiegen sind, weist auf den Wunsch nach einer Umsetzung unterschiedlicher Investitionsschemata und unter anderem nach einer Vergrößerung des Umfanges der PPP-Projekte hin. Während der monetäre Umfang aller öffentlichen Ausschreibungen im Jahre 2000 insgesamt 4,7 Milliarden EEK (300 Millionen EUR) betrug, ist dieser Betrag mit 22,4 Milliarden EEK (1,43 Milliarden EUR) im Jahr

---

1 Koalitionsvertrag der Estnischen Reformpartei, der Estnischen Zentralpartei und der Volksunion Estlands von 2005.

2 Vgl. Entwicklungsplan der Wohnungsbranche Estlands für die Jahre 2008-2013.

2006 um beinahe das 5-fache gestiegen. 2006 wurden von Kommunalverwaltungen fast genau so viele Investitionen getätigt (4 Milliarden EEK oder 255 Millionen EUR) wie vom Staat im Jahr 2000 insgesamt. Die Zahl öffentlicher Ausschreibungen stieg in der gleichen Periode von 1800 auf 8800. Im Jahr 2007 schließlich wurden 7408 öffentliche Ausschreibungen mit einem Gesamtvolumen von 21,6 Milliarden EEK (1,38 Milliarden EUR) umgesetzt, wobei Bauarbeiten 53% bzw. 39% des Gesamtumfangs aller öffentlichen Ausschreibungen in den Jahren 2006/2007 ausmachten.

In Tallinn begann die Planung von PPP-Projekten im Jahre 2001, wobei das Hauptaugenmerk dem Ausbau des Straßen- bzw. Wegenetzes galt. In den Rechtsakten der Stadt erschien das Stichwort PPP-Projekt 2002, als von der Stadtversammlung die Haushaltsstrategie der Stadt Tallinn für die Jahre 2003-2005 genehmigt wurde.[3]

Unter anderem wurde als eines der Hauptziele der Haushaltspolitik der Stadt festgelegt: "*die Einnahmebasis der Stadt ist zu erweitern und zu vergrößern – für die Entwicklung der Stadt wichtigen Investitionen sind in größerem Umfang Mittel unterschiedlicher außer-städtischer Fonds und des privaten Sektors einzubeziehen. (...) die Umsetzung von PPP-Mitteln für die Finanzierung des Straßen- bzw. Wegenetzes gilt als eine der Prioritäten des städtischen Haushalts für 2003.*" Kurz nach der Genehmigung der Haushaltsstrategie der Stadt wurde von der Tallinner Stadtversammlung auch der Entwicklungsplan der größeren Straßen der Stadt verabschiedet[4], in welchem bei zwei großen Objekten – (a) Ausbau einer verkehrsbelasteten Kreuzung zur Kreuzung mit mehreren Ebenen und (b) Ausbau einer neuen Hauptstraße für die Umleitung des Verkehrs um das Stadtzentrum – eine konkrete Umsetzung der Grundsätze der Zusammenarbeit des öffentlichen und privaten Sektors (PPP) vorgesehen wurde. Unglücklicherweise teilte das Finanzministerium daraufhin der Stadt mit, dass die PPP-Projekte zur Kreditbelastung der Stadt zu rechnen sind, weswegen es für

---

3 Vgl. Verordnung der Tallinner Stadtversammlung Nr. 36 (2002).
4 Vgl. Verordnung der Tallinner Stadtversammlung Nr. 43 (2002).

die Stadt unmöglich wurde, diese Objekte auf die geplante Art und Weise auszubauen – und dies trotz der Tatsache, dass (bisher) keine gesetzlichen Einschränkungen bezüglich PPP-Projekten festgelegt worden sind.

Von da an ist eines der größten Streitprobleme zwischen der staatlichen Zentralmacht und den Kommunalverwaltungen die Frage gewesen, ob der Umfang von PPP zur gesetzlich eingeschränkten Kreditbelastung der Gemeinde oder der Stadt zu rechnen sei oder nicht. Laut Gesetz über den Gemeinde- und Stadthaushalt[5] darf eine Einheit der Kommunalverwaltung in Estland einen Kredit aufnehmen, dessen Höhe keine 60% des Haushaltes des laufenden Jahres dieser Einheit übersteigt und für deren Rückzahlung in keinem der Rückzahlungsjahre mehr als 20% des Haushaltes der Einheit benötigt werden. Der Haushalt der Stadt Tallinn für 2008 beträgt gut 7 Milliarden EEK (447 Millionen EUR), die gesamte Kreditbelastung mit ca. 3 Milliarden EEK (192 Millionen EUR) weniger als die Hälfte des Haushalts des betreffenden Jahres[6]. Bisher sind die Kosten der PPP-Projekte von der Stadt Tallinn nur als jährliche Zahlungen an den Privatsektor berechnet worden, nicht als Kredit. Gemäß den neuen Berechnungsregeln buchhalterischer Kreditverbindlichkeiten, die ab 2009 in Kraft treten, ist fortan auch das Volumen der PPP-Projekte zu den Schulden der Kommunalverwaltungen zu rechnen.

2.1 Aktuelle Diskussionen um PPPs in Estland

PPP-Projekte gelten in Estland als Auslöser von diametral entgegengesetzten Meinungen sowohl unter Politikern als auch in den Medien. Einerseits ist zu lesen und zu hören, dass der öffentliche Sektor in Estland zukünftig mehr

5 Vgl. Gesetz über Gemeinde- und Stadthaushalt (RT I 1993, 42, 615; 2003, 88, 588).

6 Der Finanzminister bestätigte am 30. Mai 2008 vor dem Parlament, dass die Kreditbelastung von Tallinn innerhalb der durch die momentan gültigen Gesetzen vorgeschriebenen Grenzen liegt. Laut Angaben der Tallinner Stadtverwaltung betrug die Kreditbelastung der Stadt Ende 2007 49,4%; gemäß der Haushaltsplanstrategie der Stadt sollte sich diese Zahl bis Ende 2008 deutlich reduzieren, bis Ende 2012 sogar auf 43,5% reduzieren.

Investitionen und Know-how bräuchte, um den Staat effektiver verwalten zu können. Über PPP könne der öffentliche Sektor die Innovationskapazität des Privatsektors ausnutzen, optimale Bau- und Nutzungskosten der Objekte gewährleisten, Aufgaben zwischen dem öffentlichen und privaten Sektor je nach ihrer Zuständigkeit verteilen, zur Entstehung von Wettbewerb beitragen, die Qualität der Dienstleistungen sichern und noch vieles mehr. Für den privaten Sektor sei PPP aber eine zusätzliche Möglichkeit für Geschäfte und das Schaffen zusätzlicher Arbeitsplätze.

Es gibt aber auch diametral entgegengesetzte Stellungnahmen. In der Presse sind Artikel zu PPP-Projekten wie „Tallinn ins Schuldgefängnis – wird gemacht"[7] oder „Partei vergoldet ihre Goldsponsoren"[8] erschienen, in denen die PPP-Projekte der Hauptstadt kritisiert werden, alle Ausschreibungen dieser Projekte würden von Unterstützern der in der Stadt regierenden Partei (der Estnischen Zentralpartei) gewonnen.

Im Artikel „PPP in Tallinn – Mythos und Wirklichkeit"[9] steht geschrieben, dass bei gutem Management von PPP-Projekten sowohl der bzw. die Unternehmer als auch die Stadtbevölkerung einen Nutzen daraus ziehen werden, es im negativen Falle aber in der Regel so ende, dass die Kosten von der Stadt getragen und die Einnahmen von Geschäftsleuten in ihre eigenen Taschen gesteckt würden. Gerade der Immobilienmarkt sollte ein besonderes Interesse an PPP-Projekten haben, weil ab 2008 ein gewisser Rückgang auf diesem Markt eingetreten ist, was für Unternehmen dieser Branche besonders schwer zu überleben ist, weil man bis dahin nur die Früchte der extrem schnellen Wachstumsperiode genossen hatte[10]. Natürlich muss man zugeben, dass die Firmen, die mit der Stadt (insbesondere mit der Hauptstadt) ein großes PPP-Projekt abschließen,

7 „Tallinn ins Schuldgefängnis – wird gemacht", Tageszeitung Eesti Päevaleht, 30.04.2008.
8 „Partei vergoldet ihre Großsponsoren", Wochenzeitung Eesti Ekspress, 05.07.2007.
9 „PPP in Tallinn – Mythos oder Wirklichkeit", Wochenzeitung Eesti Ekspress, 05.07.2007.
10 Laut Angaben (2006) von *Global Property Guide* erlebten die Immobilienpreise in Estland den höchsten Anstieg (54%) weltweit, es folgen Dänemark mit 23% und Norwegen mit 14% (vgl. Mäeltsemees, S. (2006), S. 23).

sicherlich ein glückliches Los gezogen haben. Für diese Firmen sind Geschäfte über einen längeren Zeitraum garantiert. Ein langfristiger Vertrag und Geldflüsse der Stadt mit ihren (niedrigen) Risiken sollten auch Privatpartner von der Attraktivität des Projektes, deren Notwendigkeit kaum ignoriert werden kann, überzeugen. Im Entwicklungsplan der Stadt Tallinn für die Jahre 2006-2015[11] wird bei Förderung der Zusammenarbeit mit dem Privatsektor eine Qualitätskontrolle über die Erfüllung der PPP-Projekte vorgeschrieben, um eine höhere Qualität der zu erweisenden Leistungen zu garantieren.

Das Verhalten seitens der Medien hinsichtlich PPP-Projekten der Kommunalverwaltungen hängt offensichtlich davon ab, welche politische Kraft in der betreffenden Kommunalverwaltung an der Macht ist. So ist es in Tallinn ziemlich gewöhnlich, dass zur Koalition diejenigen Parteien gehören, die im Parlament (Riigikogu) in der Opposition sind. Dementsprechend brachte fast jede Aktivität der Tallinner Stadtverwaltung bezüglich der Umsetzung von PPP-Projekten Warnungen seitens der Oppositionspolitiker mit sich, in dem Stile, Tallinn befinde sich am Rande einer Finanzkrise oder Tallinn leihe sich zu Tode, etc. – dies trotz der Bestätigung des Finanzministers im Mai 2008, dass die Kreditbelastung von Tallinn durchaus innerhalb der gesetzlichen Grenzen liege (s. auch die Anmerkung unten). Dieser auf den Staatshaushalt bezogene Streit zwischen staatlicher Zentralmacht und der Hauptstadt verschärfte sich insbesondere im Winter 2008, als die Estnische Wirtschaft, die sich seit Ende der 1990er Jahre schnell entwickelt hatte (Wachstum des BIP zum Teil sogar bis zu 11%), plötzlich in eine Depressionsperiode geriet. In diesem Zusammenhang wurde Tallinn wegen seiner großen Kreditaufnahmen und konsequenten Umsetzung der PPP-Projekte, u.a. wegen der Einleitung neuer Projekte, scharfer Kritik unterzogen.

Im Mai 2008 wurde dem Parlament vom Rechnungshof der Bericht „Über die Organisation von Ausschreibungen für Bauvorhaben in Gemeinden und

[11] Vgl. Verordnung der Tallinner Stadtversammlung Nr. 64 (2006).

Städten“[12] vorgelegt, worin unter anderem bekannt gegeben wurde, dass im Fall von Partnerschaftsprojekten des öffentlichen und privaten Sektors das Gesetz über staatliche Ausschreibungen den Partnern breite Möglichkeiten zur selbständigen Deutung des Gesetzes gewährt, und dass diese Projekte deshalb für die Öffentlichkeit nicht unbedingt transparent sein müssen. Bei allen Finanzierungsschemata der Bauprojekte sollte die Kommunalverwaltung darauf achten, dass Gelder sparsam und zielgebunden genutzt werden, dass von vorhandener Konkurrenz ausgegangen und dass das prinzipiell bestmögliche Verhältnis von Preis und Qualität gewährleistet wird.

Auf die Notwendigkeit einer Ergänzung der mit PPP-Projekten verbundenen Anleitungen und Instruktionen weist gemäß der Einschätzung des Rechnungshofes der Umstand hin, dass trotz der Tatsache, dass unterschiedliche Kooperationsprojekte des öffentlichen und privaten Sektors vom Finanzminister als Konzessionen gedeutet werden, Gemeinden und Städte bei der Planung dieser Projekte doch nicht aus Anweisungen des Ministeriums hervorgegangen sind. Erst im März 2008 wurde im estnischen staatlichen Ausschreibungsregister eine Mitteilung über die Vergabe der ersten Berechtigung veröffentlicht.

2.2 PPP-Verständnis in Estland

Die in Estland bestehenden widersprüchlichen Meinungen zur Frage, was denn überhaupt als PPP-Projekt betrachtet werden kann, sind anscheinend in so mancher Hinsicht dadurch bedingt, dass PPP-Projekte nicht durch Gesetze geregelt werden. Und bestimmt kann auch nicht jede Zusammenarbeit zwischen öffentlichem und privatem Sektor bei der Entwicklung der Infrastruktur als PPP-Projekt bezeichnet werden.

---

[12] Vgl. Organisation von Bauausschreibungen in Gemeinden und Städten. Bericht des Rechnungshofes an das Parlament (Riigikogu) 2008.

Die von der Buchhaltungsarbeitsgruppe des Estnischen Finanzministeriums 2006 ausgearbeitete Anleitung setzt folgende Grundsätze für PPP-Projekte fest[13]:

1. PPP-Projekte werden meistens in solchen Bereichen öffentlicher Dienste umgesetzt, die traditionell vom Staat oder von Kommunalverwaltungen geregelt werden und für die große Startinvestitionen notwendig sind, wie z. B. beim Bau von Wegen bzw. Straßen, Brücken, Krankenhäusern, Schulen und Gefängnissen sowie ihr weiteres Betreiben während der vertraglich festgesetzten Zeiträume. Als Ziele der Umsetzung eines PPP-Projektes können Benutzung der Kompetenzen des privaten Sektors, Erhöhung der Qualität der Dienstleistung, Kosteneinsparung, Verteilung von Risiken oder andere Gründe gelten.
2. Die Hauptfrage eines PPP-Projektes besteht darin, in welcher Bilanz (der des öffentlichen oder des privaten Sektors) das durch Einbeziehung des PPP-Projektes geschaffene Vermögen widergespiegelt werden muss. Das im Rahmen eines PPP-Projektes geschaffene Vermögen wird in der Bilanz jener Einheit aufgeführt, von der die hauptsächlichen, sich aus dem Vertrag des PPP-Projektes ergebenden Risiken getragen werden. Falls als Träger von hauptsächlichen, sich aus dem Vertrag des PPP-Projektes ergebenden Risiken der öffentliche Sektor gilt, werden PPP-Vermögen und PPP-Verbindlichkeiten in der Bilanz der entsprechenden Einheit des öffentlichen Sektors aufgeführt, im entgegengesetzten Fall in der Bilanz der Einheit des privaten Sektors. Für die Einschätzung der Risiken eines PPP-Projektes ist eine detaillierte Risikoanalyse durchzuführen, wobei eventuelle Aspekte berücksichtigt werden müssen.

[13] Vgl. Partnerschaftsprojekte des öffentlichen und privaten Sektors (RTJ 17, 20. März 2006).

Als die wichtigsten Risiken gelten meist:

a) das Baurisiko,

b) das Risiko der Nutzungsbereitschaft und

c) das Nachfragerisiko.

Wird der größte Teil des Baurisikos von der Einheit des öffentlichen Sektors getragen, wird das PPP-Vermögen im allgemeinen Fall in der Bilanz der Einheit des öffentlichen Sektors aufgeführt – das PPP-Vermögen wird hier in der Regel zudem auch dann aufgenommen, wenn dieser Sektor zwar keinen wesentlichen Teil des Baurisikos trägt, jedoch das Risiko sowohl der Benutzungsbereitschaft als auch der Nachfrage in den Zuständigkeitsbereich des Sektors fallen.
Bei der Einschätzung des Bau-, Nutzungsbereitschafts- und Nachfragerisikos müssen weiterhin beiderseits die Bedeutungsstufe und die Eintrittswahrscheinlichkeit (oder der eventuelle Einfluss dieser Komponenten auf aus PPP-Projekten stammende zukünftige Geldflüsse) berücksichtigt werden. Verstärktes Augenmerk sollte denjenigen Risikokomponenten gelten, deren eventueller Einfluss auf sich aus PPP-Projekten ergebende Geldflüsse als größer einzuschätzen ist. Jene Risikokomponenten, deren potentieller Einfluss auf Geldflüsse des gesamten PPP-Projektes unbedeutend oder deren Eintrittswahrscheinlichkeit äußerst klein ist, sind auch bei der Risikoanalyse zu einem geringeren Anteil zu berücksichtigen.

3. PPP-Projekte unterscheiden sich von Pachtverträgen dadurch, dass außer des Einsatzes von Vermögen von der privaten Seite auch damit verbundene Dienstleistungen innerhalb einer vertragsmäßig festgelegten Zeit, gemäß entsprechendem Umfang und mit geforderter Qualität eingebracht werden. PPP-Projekte sind durch den Umstand charakterisiert, dass im Allgemeinen der Ausbau oder eine Anschaffung des für das konkrete Projekt notwendigen Vermögens durch den privaten Partner vorausgesetzt wird.

Zweifellos kann man sich mit dem ersten und dritten Prinzip einverstanden erklären. Doch muss darauf hingewiesen werden, dass die im zweiten Prinzip enthaltene Forderung, wonach das vom privaten Sektor errichtete Objekt in der Bilanz der Gemeinde oder der Stadt aufzuführen ist, zweifellos hemmend auf die regionale Wirtschaftsentwicklung wirkt. Der Bürgermeister der Gemeinde Viimsi (der größten Gemeinde Estlands mit 15000 Einwohnern, die unmittelbar an Tallinn grenzt) behauptete im August 2008, dass dadurch sogar die Zusammenarbeit des öffentlichen Sektors mit dem privaten Sektor (PPP) ausgeschlossen wird.[14] Der Hauptgrund dafür besteht darin, dass die Möglichkeiten der Kreditaufnahme abrupt eingeschränkt werden und, wie bereits erwähnt, der Vorgang der PPP-Projekte ab 2009 innerhalb der Kreditbelastung der Gemeinde oder Stadt (in 20% und 60%) berechnet werden muss. Von ebenso großer Bedeutung (vor allem bezüglich Tallinn, das PPP-Projekte bisher in größerem Umfang umgesetzt hat) ist die Frage über die rückwirkende Kraft dieser Forderung bezüglich der schon sich im Umsetzungsprozess befindenden PPP-Projekte.

Laut Verfasser dieses Artikels können ohne jedwede Zweifel als PPP-Projekte solche Vorhaben bezeichnet werden, wie z. B. die eingeleiteten Projekte der Renovierung der Tallinner allgemeinbildenden Schulen sowie die des Wohnungsbaus, bei denen man sich nicht nur auf die Renovierung oder den Bau beschränkt, sondern auch eine langfristige Instandhaltung und Wartung des Objektes folgt.

3 Die größten PPP-Projekte in Tallinn

Bei der Umsetzung von PPP-Projekten ist zu berücksichtigen, dass die Einheiten der Kommunalverwaltung über einen ausreichenden Umfang sozialwirtschaftlicher Dienstleistungen und *last but not least* über eine ausreichende Ver-

[14] Vgl. Arumäe, U. (2008).

waltungskompetenz verfügen müssen[15]. Um es anschaulicher auszudrücken: es ist wichtig, dass der öffentliche Sektor nicht in die „Falle“ des privaten Sektors gerät. Da es in Estland bisher keine gesetzlichen PPP-Regelungen gegeben hat, ist es ganz besonders wichtig, zu gewährleisten, dass Kommunalbeamte und Politiker, die Schlussentscheidungen zu treffen haben, nicht Opfer der Desinformation des Privatsektors mit seinen tatkräftigen Juristen werden. In dem Zusammenhang sei erwähnt, dass sogar Tallinn mit seiner starken rechtswissenschaftlichen Kompetenz vor der Annahme von PPP-Projekten juristische Gutachten bestellte.

Zu den größten PPP-Projekten in Tallinn gehören das Projekt zur Renovierung von allgemeinbildenden Schulen und das Projekt für den Bau von kommunalen Wohnhäusern – welche auch bereits eingeleitet wurden.

Bei Schulhäusern hat sich die Stadt zum Ziel gesetzt, innerhalb kürzester Zeit eine moderne Lernumwelt für Schüler und für Lehrer eine motivierende Arbeitsbedingungen zu schaffen.

Im Wohnungsbauwesen hatte und hat man mit einem Bedarf anderer Art zu tun – nämlich schnell und zu niedrigen Kosten Mietwohnungen zu bauen.

[15] Als einer der wichtigsten Einflussfaktoren auf die Verwaltungskompetenz gilt zweifellos die Bevölkerungszahl der kommunalen Einheit. Davon sind abhängig sowohl die Höhe des lokalen Haushalts, die Möglichkeiten der Anstellung von zuständigen Beamten, die Umsetzung von PPP als auch der ganze Bedarf an Investitionen überhaupt. Die Einheiten der Kommunalverwaltungen in Estland sind relativ klein. In diesem Land mit einer Fläche von 45000 km^2 und einer Einwohnerzahl von 1,35 Millionen Menschen gibt es 194 Gemeinden und 33 Städte, also insgesamt 227 Kommunalverwaltungen. Die Hauptstadt Tallinn zählt 400 000 Einwohner (1/3 der Bevölkerungszahl des ganzen Landes). Die relative Bedeutung der estnischen Hauptstadt bzgl. der Gesamtbevölkerungszahl zählt zu den größten auf dem europäischen Festland (nur in Lettland ist dieser Index noch höher). In der zweitgrößten Stadt von Estland (Tartu) gibt es 100 000 Einwohner. 80% aller Einheiten der Kommunalverwaltungen in Estland haben unter 5000 Einwohner, für die Umsetzung von PPP-Projekten haben sie praktisch keinerlei Perspektive. Mindestens zehn Jahre lang wurde in Estland über die verwaltungsterritoriale Reform gesprochen. Ergebnisse (d.h. Zusammenschlüsse von Gemeinden und Städten) gab es aber relativ wenige.

3.1 Schulen

Das größte PPP-Projekt, das unter Politikern und in der Öffentlichkeit am meisten Aufsehen erregt hat, wurde 2006 zwischen der Tallinner Stadtverwaltung und zwei Privatfirmen über die Renovierung von allgemein-bildenden Schulen der Hauptstadt und deren spätere technische Instandhaltung vereinbart.

Von der Stadt wurde beschlossen, dieses PPP-Projekt umzusetzen, weil es die Chance bot:

– die Renovierung von Schulen unter den Bedingungen eingeschränkter Finanz- und Verwaltungsressourcen zu beschleunigen;
– die mit der Renovierung und der Verwaltung von Schulen verbundenen Handlungen und die größten Risiken (wie z.B. das Finanzierungs-, Bau-, Verwaltungs- und Instandhaltungsrisiko sowie andere Risiken) an professionelle Partner zu übertragen, von denen gewisse Risiken besser verwaltet werden können als von der Stadt;
– die Renovierungs- und Verwaltungsarbeiten effektiver auszuführen als die Stadt es tun könnte, weil die Mehrheit der im Laufe der Lebensdauer des Projektes anfallenden Kosten vom privaten Partner getragen werden und diese Kosten deshalb zeitlich besser geplant und ausgeglichen werden können.

Durch die Rolle der Stadt als Pächter und die Übertragung wesentlicher Risiken auf den privaten Partner ergibt sich für die Stadt die Möglichkeit, eine Erhöhung der Verschuldung der Stadt über die im Gesetz über den Haushalt der Gemeinden und der Stadt vorgeschriebene Obergrenze zu vermeiden.

Zwecks Lösung komplizierter rechtlicher Fragen und unter anderem auch, um eine Wiederholung der Diskussion um die PPP-Projekte seitens des Finanzministeriums auszuschließen (wie es 2002 beim Entwicklungsprojekt des Tallinner Straßennetzes der Fall war), wurden dem Tallinner Bildungsamt aus dem städtischen Haushalt 1,6 Millionen EEK (100000 EUR) *"für den Einkauf von Rechtshilfe und Finanzberatung im Zusammenhang mit der Renovierung und Verwaltung der Schulen im Rahmen des PPP-Projektes*"[16] bereitgestellt. Mit nachfolgendem Beschluss der Stadtversammlung[17] erhielten Privatfirmen den Zuschlag zur Renovierung von insgesamt zehn Schulen und auf deren Verpachtung an die Stadt für die nächsten 30 Jahre.

Um die Umfänge der Renovierungsarbeiten und ihren Stellenwert im städtischen Bildungssystem einschätzen zu können, muss erwähnt werden, dass es in Tallinn 55 kommunale Gymnasien mit (im Jahr 2007) 39 000 Schülern gibt, in denen in den Jahrgangsstufen 1-12 unterrichtet wird, sowie elf sich im kommunalen Eigentum befindende Grundschulen (3000 Schüler in 2007) mit den Jahrgangsstufen 1-9[18]. Mit Ausnahme von einigen wenigen Schulen im Stadtzentrum, die schon vor den 1940er Jahren und damit vor der sozialistischen Periode gebaut wurden, stammt die absolute Mehrheit der Schulen aus der sowjetischen Zeit und ist, wie für diese Zeit üblich, von relativ schlechter Bauqualität. Obwohl viele dieser Schulen vor Jahrzehnten errichtet worden sind, d.h. während des extensiven Stadtwachstums in den 1960er und 1970er Jahren oder sogar früher, wurde dort bis zuletzt keine Grundrenovierung durchgeführt. In der später wieder selbständigen Republik Estland hatten Kommunalverwaltungen, einschließlich der Stadt Tallinn, keine Mittel, um mit der Sanierung dieser oftmals stark amortisierten Gebäude zu beginnen.

Um die Ergebnisse von PPP deutlicher zu machen, kann in diesem Zusammenhang erwähnt werden, dass allein im Herbst 2008 ganze 5 800 oder 15% aller Schüler der Tallinner Kommunalschulen ihr Schuljahr in neurenovierten Schulen und Gebäuden beginnen konnten.

---

[16] Anordnung der Tallinner Stadtverwaltung Nr. 614-k (2006).

[17] Vgl. Beschluss der Tallinner Stadtversammlung Nr. 184 (2006).

[18] Neben kommunalen Schulen gibt es in Tallinn auch 11 allgemeinbildende Privatschulen mit insgesamt 2200 Schülern; bei diesen Schulen handelt es sich in der Regel um neue oder innerhalb der letzten 10-15 Jahre renovierte Gebäude.

Von Bedingungen der PPP-Projekte für Renovierung der Tallinner allgemeinbildenden Schulen können folgende wichtige Grundsätze hervorgehoben werden. Zu Gunsten als Ergebnis der von der Stadt durchgeführten öffentlichen Ausschreibung zum Projekt einbezogener Privatfirma wird ein entgeltliches und auf 30 Jahre terminiertes Erbbaurecht bestellt, und für jede Schule wird ein separater Vertrag geschlossen. Die privatrechtliche Firma übernimmt als ihre Verpflichtung den wesentlichen Teil der mit den Renovierungsarbeiten des Schulgebäudes verbundenen Tätigkeiten (Beschaffung der Baugenehmigungen, Projektierung, Untersuchung von Grund und Boden, Bauarbeiten). Zu den Aufgaben der Privatfirma als Verpächter der Schule zählt die Verwaltung des Schulgebäudes während der gesamten Vertragsperiode. Innerhalb dieser Zeit ist die Privatfirma verpflichtet, notwendige Renovierungsarbeiten durchzuführen und die Erhaltung des Gebäudes in gutem Zustand zu gewährleisten.

Das Unternehmen hat das Schulgebäude gegen die wichtigsten Risiken (Brand, Vandalismus, Naturkatastrophen) zu versichern und eine technische Überwachung während der Zeit, in der das Gebäude nicht benutzt wird, zu organisieren. Auch ist die Firma verpflichtet, Vorschriften für die Instandhaltung einschließlich der Reinigung und Ordnung der Gebäude zusammenzustellen und diese der Stadt bekannt zu geben. In den Zuständigkeitsbereich der Privatfirma fällt zudem die Pflege des außerschulischen Territoriums, mit Ausnahme des Schneeräumens auf Sportstätten. Die Stadt pachtet die Schulen in deren vollen Umfang und organisiert bei Bedarf ihre Unterpacht an Dritte.

Im PPP-Projekt werden hauptsächlich drei Typen von Gebühren vorgesehen: Pachtgebühren, Nebenkosten und Gebühren im Zusammenhang mit eigentümerbezogenen Verpflichtungen (Gebühr für Erbbaurecht und Grundsteuer). Von der Stadt wird an die Privatfirma monatlich ein Pachtbetrag bezahlt, dessen Änderung an den Verbraucherpreisindex gebunden ist. Die Stadt hat weiterhin alle Nebenkosten zu zahlen und Verträge mit Trägern kommunaler Dienst-leistungen abgeschlossen. Von der Stadt werden auch die Risiken im

Zusammenhang mit eventuellen Änderungen des Euro-Wechselkurses sowie Änderungen des Verbraucherpreisindexes übernommen. Nach Auslaufen des Erbbau-rechtes wird das Schulgebäude in das Eigentum der Stadt übertragen und die Stadt hat der Privatfirma eine Entschädigung in einer Höhe, die sich als Ergebnis aus einem bei Beendigung des Vertrags (Auslaufen des Erbbaurechts) durchzuführenden Gutachtens herausstellt, zu bezahlen. Die Schulen müssen sich während der gesamten Vertragsperiode in einem für ihre Benutzung geeigneten Zustand befinden. Die Stadt ist berechtigt, das Erbbaurecht vor Ablauf der Frist von der Privatfirma zurückzukaufen.

3.2 Wohnungsbau

Das zweite große Tallinner PPP-Projekt befasst sich mit dem Wohnungsbau. Als Hintergrund und Erläuterung der Notwendigkeit dieses Projektes muss erwähnt werden, dass im Laufe der Wohnungsreform der 1990er Jahre in Estland und damit in Tallinn fast alle Wohnungen privatisiert wurden. Damit wurde Estland im Vergleich zu anderen Ländern Europas zu einem der Länder, die im Wohnungssektor einen sehr hohen Anteil vom Privatsektor (über 90%) haben. Außerdem kamen auch sog. Zwangsmieter in den an ehemalige Eigentümer zurückgegebenen Wohnhäusern hinzu, mit denen der Eigentümer den Mietvertrag relativ schnell auflösen konnte. In Tallinn gab es 5000 Familien, die als Ergebnis der Restitution gefährdet waren, auf die Straße gesetzt zu werden. Es gab praktisch keine kommunalen Wohnungen; bei den wenigen vorhandenen kommunalen Wohnungen handelte es sich um in den Jahren 1945-1990 gebaute und aus verschiedenen Gründen nicht privatisierte Wohnungen. So bildete die im Jahr 2005 sich in städtischem Eigentum befindliche Wohnfläche in Tallinn nur 2,5% der gesamten in der Stadt vorhandenen Wohnfläche. In den ersten zehn Jahren nach der Wiederherstellung der Selbständigkeit wurde nirgendwo – weder in Tallinn noch anderswo – eine Kommunalwohnung gebaut. Erst 2002 wurde von Tallinner Stadtversammlung das erste Programm des kommunalen Wohnungsbaus „5 000 Wohnungen in Tallinn“ verabschiedet[19].

Wie die ganze Wirtschaftspolitik Estlands gilt auch hiesige Wohnpolitik als äußerst liberal; dementsprechend dominieren hier Mechanismen des freien Marktes, d.h. dass sich für viele Menschen (Bevölkerungsgruppen) die Möglichkeiten der Beschaffung einer Wohnung trotz des schnellen Zuwachstempos in der Wohnungsbaubranche sogar verschlechtert haben. Insbesondere betroffen sind davon junge Familien und aus dem Kommunalhaushalt bezahlte Lehrer, Kulturarbeiter, etc., deren Vermögensstand und Einnahmen es nicht ermöglichen, sich auf freiem Markt eine Wohnung zu beschaffen oder zu mieten. Um für diese Bevölkerungsgruppen Wohnungen bereitzustellen, wurde von der Tallinner Stadtversammlung am 6. Oktober 2005 das Wohnungsbauprogramm „Jeder jungen Familie ein eigenes Heim“ eingeleitet[20] und am 12. Juni 2008 das zweite Tallinner Wohnungsbauprogramm verabschiedet[21]. Im Rahmen des PPP-Projektes "Jeder jungen Familie ein eigenes Heim" werden in einem der in der sowjetischen Zeit entstandenen Wohnbezirke noch weitere 650 Wohnungen gebaut und diese für 30 Jahre an die Stadt verpachtet. Die Stadt hat ihrerseits dort einige Beziehungen auszubauen und den Eingang der Mietgebühren zu sichern. Gemäß der Haushaltsstrategie kostet dieses Projekt der Stadt um die 1,2 Milliarden EEK (77 Millionen EUR).

Mit dem PPP-Projekt der Wohnwirtschaft ist die Schaffung eines Systems für den Bau von privaten Wohnungen und ihrer Vermietung eingeleitet worden. Es handelt sich um Wohnungen, in denen alle direkten Kosten durch Mietpreise gedeckt werden. Mit solch einem System werden im Vergleich zu Marktmieten niedrigere Mietpreise erreicht, und dies vor allem durch folgende Maßnahmen:

---

[19] Vgl. Verordnung der Tallinner Stadtversammlung Nr. 175 (2002).
[20] Vgl. Beschluss der Tallinner Stadtversammlung Nr. 253 (2005).
[21] Vgl. Beschluss der Tallinner Stadtversammlung Nr. 116 (2008).

- die Stadt kann im Vergleich zu einer Privatfirma Kredite für eine beträchtlich längere Periode und auch zu niedrigeren Kreditzinsen aufnehmen;
- in Mietpreisen ist weder der Entwicklungsgewinn noch der spekulative Preis für Grund und Boden enthalten (bei der Berechnung des städtischen Mietpreises wird als Grundlage für den Preis von Grund und Boden dessen Besteuerungspreis genommen);
- durch langfristige Bauprogramme werden niedrigere Baukosten gewährleistet;
- teure Lösungen und Angebote werden vermieden, gleichzeitig wird aber von möglichst niedrigen Nutzungskosten während der Lebensdauer des Gebäudes ausgegangen.

Eine Festlegung von diesen Kosten ist bei PPP-Projekten zweifelsohne kompliziert und auch umstritten vor allem wegen der Tatsache, dass zukünftige Preise für Dienstleistungen (Nutzungskosten) mit dem heutigen Stand der Dinge sehr schwer vorauszusagen sind. Dieser Umstand bietet für Kritiker solcher Projekte gute Chancen.

Das zweite wichtige Argument für Kritiker der Projekte bezieht sich auf die schon erwähnte ab 2009 in Kraft tretende Änderung, wonach der Umfang der PPP-Projekte zur Kreditbelastung der Kommunalverwaltung gerechnet wird. Gemäß dieser neuen Regelung sollte Tallinn den Gesamtbetrag der an Privatunternehmen für den Bau von Schulen und Kommunalwohnungen geleisteten Zahlungen zu den eigenen Darlehen hinzufügen.

Nach dieser Formel können wir eine vereinfachte Berechnung machen, wonach Tallinn nur aufgrund vorhandener PPP-Projekte seiner bisherigen Kreditbelastung, die 3 Milliarden EEK (172 Millionen EUR) beträgt, noch weitere mindestens 7-8 Milliarden EEK (440-510 Millionen EUR) hinzufügen muss. In diesem Fall würde die Kreditbelastung von Tallinn anstatt der jetzigen

45% des Haushaltes ganze 150% ausmachen. Aber wie bereits oben erwähnt, ist die rückwirkende Kraft der ab 2009 geltenden Vorschrift fraglich; außerdem antwortete auf diese Frage auch der Estnische Rechtskanzler, dessen Aufgabe es ist, Aufsicht über Rechtsakten auszuüben und die Verfassungsmäßigkeit der verabschiedeten Rechtsbeschlüsse zu überprüfen, nicht. Eine Inanspruchnahme neuer PPP-Projekte wird aber für Tallinn bald in jedem Fall praktisch unmöglich sein, obwohl die bisher umgesetzte Zusammenarbeit zwischen dem öffentlichen und privaten Sektor erfolgreich gewesen ist.

In diesem Zusammenhang ist es gar nicht bedeutungslos, zu erwähnen, dass Tallinn die einzige Einheit der Kommunalverwaltungen Estlands ist, die sich auch internationale Beachtung (Rating) eingeholt hat. Gemäß der Beurteilung der Agentur Moody's ist die Kreditbelastung von Tallinn mäßig und die Struktur des Kreditportfolios gut. Als Kritik wurde von der Agentur angemerkt, dass die Kostenseite der Stadt nicht flexibel genug sei. Diese Feststellung muss wohl tatsächlich akzeptiert werden, obwohl die Einnahmequellen von Kommunalverwaltungen nur durch Gesetze festgelegt werden. Die Einnahmenbasis einer estnischen Kommunalverwaltung ist stark auf die Lohnsteuer konzentriert, weil 11,9% dieser Einnahmen (in 2008 beträgt der Lohnsteuersatz 21%) in den Haushalt der Kommunalverwaltung laufen. Im ganzen Land bildet dies durchschnittlich mehr als 90% aller Steuereinnahmen der Kommunalverwaltungen. Kommunalen Selbstverwaltungen ist dabei kaum die Möglichkeit gegeben, Steuersätze zu ändern. Die einzige Ausnahme diesbezüglich ist die Grundsteuer, welche 6% der Einnahmen des lokalen Haushalts ausmacht und hinsichtlich derer die lokale Abgeordnetenversammlung das Recht hat, den Steuersatz in der Spanne 0,1-2,5% des Preises von Grund und Boden zu ändern.

Lokale Steuern, die als finanzwirtschaftliche Drehscheibe für die Kommunalverwaltung gelten könnten, bilden in Estland nur 1% aller Steuereinnahmen der lokalen Haushalte; damit ist dieser Anteil einer der niedrigsten unter den europäischen Ländern, was auch in Berichten des Europäischen Rates erwähnt wurde.

4 Zusammenfassung

Die Einheiten der Kommunalverwaltungen sind gezwungen, bei PPP-Projekten nach Hilfe zu suchen, unter anderem aufgrund der Tatsache, dass den Kommunalverwaltungen von der staatlichen Zentralmacht immer weitere Aufgaben auferlegt werden, die nicht aus dem Staatshaushalt finanziert werden – und dies trotz der Tatsache, dass gemäß dem Grundgesetz Estlands auf Kommunalverwaltungen auferlegte Aufgaben vom Staatshaushalt zu finanzieren sind. Die Einheiten der Kommunalverwaltungen müssen mit dem privaten Sektor noch viel mehr in Kooperation leisten, wenn sie sich vorgenommen haben, auf freiwilliger Initiative entstandene Aufgaben zu lösen und in der Stadt oder Gemeinde Infrastruktur für Freizeitgestaltung oder Sport zu entwickeln. Einmalige PPP-Projekte oder Projekte von kleinerem Umfang sind für diese Zwecke auch außerhalb Tallinns umgesetzt worden. So wurde z. B. in der Stadt Haapsalu von der Stadt-verwaltung in Zusammenarbeit mit dem privaten Sektor 2003 der Wasserpark mit einer Schwimmhalle mit einem 25-Meter-Becken gebaut, von der Stadt-verwaltung Rakvere 2004 ein Sportzentrum mit 2400 Sitzplätzen errichtet, wo auch Konzerte veranstaltet werden können; die Stadtverwaltung Pärnu war Initiator für den Bau der Sporthalle mit einer Fläche von 3300 m^2 im Jahre 2006 usw.[22]

Damit sozialwirtschaftliche Dienstleistungen auf eine effektivere Art und Weise sowie mit höherer Qualität geleistet und dabei auch PPP-Projekte umgesetzt werden könnten, müssten sich die Einheiten der Kommunalverwaltungen in Estland entweder zu einem Zusammenschluss entscheiden oder aber kooperativ vorgehen, doch sind bei diesen beiden Prozessen bisher nur bescheidene Fortschritte gemacht worden. Außerdem kann man hier wohl behaupten, dass für den Fall, dass die Volumina der PPP-Projekte ab 2009 zur Kreditbelastung der Kommunalverwaltung gerechnet werden müssen, die Zusammenarbeit von Gemeinden und Städten in diesem Bereich kaum weiter möglich sein wird.

---

[22] Vgl. Public Private Partnership Projects: http://english.yit.ee.

Zusammenfassend kann festgehalten werden, dass PPP-Projekte in Estland erst seit einigen Jahren umgesetzt wurden, und dies nur zum Zwecke der Renovierung von Objekten sozialer Infrastruktur (Schulgebäude) oder Bautätigkeit (Wohnhäuser, Sportanlagen) geschah. Obwohl PPP-Projekte auch für die Entwicklung technischer Infrastruktur (des Straßennetzes) geplant wurden, sind sie bisher nicht umgesetzt worden. Die bisherigen PPP-Projekte haben sich auf Tallinn konzentriert; einer der Gründe dafür liegt darin, dass Tallinn im Vergleich zu anderen Städten über ein größeres Potential zur Verwaltung und Finanzierung komplizierter PPP-Projekte verfügt. Die Umsetzung von PPP-Projekten wurde wegen des Fehlens staatlicher Regelungen bisher erschwert. Gleichzeitig besteht auch die Gefahr, dass die ab 2009 in Kraft tretende diesbezügliche Regelung, wonach die Volumina der PPP-Projekte zur Kreditbelastung der Kommunalverwaltung gerechnet werden, eine hindernde Wirkung auch auf die in Tallinn sich erst in der Anfangsphase befindende Zusammenarbeit zwischen dem öffentlichen und privaten Sektor haben wird.

Die Tallinner Stadtverwaltung unterbreitete im August 2008[23]der Stadtversammlung den Vorschlag, sich an den Obersten Gerichtshof zu wenden, um die verabschiedeten und ab 1. Januar 2009 in Kraft tretenden Änderungen im Buchhaltungsgesetz und in anderen Rechtsakten der Buchführung (vor allem die Änderungen in der Instruktion der Buchhaltungsarbeitsgruppe beim Finanzministerium „*Konzessionsvereinbarungen der Dienstleistungen*") als nichtig zu erklären, „*weil sie im Widerspruch zu verfassungsmäßigen Garantien der Kommunal-verwaltungen und Prinzipien der Rechtsklarheit stehen*". Im Fall der Umsetzung dieser Grundsätze werden die Möglichkeiten der Kommunalverwaltungen, sich an PPP-Projekten zu beteiligen, eingeschränkt. Eine rückwirkende Anpassung entsprechender Regelungen wird die Situation für Kommunalverwaltungen äußerst kompliziert machen. Gemäß der Tallinner Stadtverwaltung wird das Recht der Kommunalverwaltung auf Umsetzung

[23] Tallinn verlangt eine Aufhebung von einschränkenden Buchhaltungsregeln; vgl. www.tallinn.ee/est/uudised

eigener Entwicklungspläne durch Partnerschaftsprojekte des öffentlichen und privaten Sektors und dementsprechend das Recht auf die Wahl einer passenderen und effektiveren Art und Weise der Erfüllung kommunaler Aufgaben durch die neue Ordnung wesentlich eingeschränkt.

Literaturverzeichnis

Anordnung der Tallinner Stadtverwaltung Nr. 614-k vom 29. März 2006 über die Bereitstellung von Mitteln an das Tallinner Bildungsamt für den Einkauf von Rechtshilfe und Finanzberatung im Zusammenhang mit der Renovierung und Verwaltung der Schulen im Rahmen des PPP-Projektes.

Arumäe, U. (2008): Kommunalverwaltungen in Erwartung harter Zeiten. Zeitung der Parteien Isamaa und ResPublica Liit, 7. August 2008.

Beschluss der Tallinner Stadtversammlung Nr. 253 vom 6. Oktober 2005 „Initiierung des Wohnbauprogramms – Jeder jungen Familie ein eigenes Heim".

Beschluss der Tallinner Stadtversammlung Nr. 184 vom 1. Juni 2006 „Über die Renovierung und Verwaltung sowie Instandhaltung Tallinner Schulen auf Grund der PPP-Projekte".

Beschluss der Tallinner Stadtversammlung Nr. 116 vom 12. Juni 2008 „Genehmigung des zweiten Tallinner Wohnbauprogramms".

Entwicklungsplan der Wohnungsbranche Estlands für 2008-2013: www.mkm.ee.

Gesetz über den Gemeinde- und Stadthaushalt (RT I 1993, 42, 615; 2003, 88, 588).

Koalitionsvertrag der Estnischen Reformpartei, der Estnischen Zentralpartei und der Volksunion Estlands vom 2005: www.valitsus.ee.

Mäeltsemees, S. (2006): Wirtschaftlicher Erfolg und sozialer Preis. Ost-West Gegeninformationen. Nr. 4/2006, S. 23.

Organisation von Bauausschreibungen in Gemeinden und Städten. Bericht des Rechnungshofes an das Parlament (Riigikogu) 2008: www.riigikontroll.ee.

„Partei vergoldet ihre Großsponsoren", Wochenzeitung Eesti Ekspress, 05.07.2007.

Partnerschaftsprojekte des öffentlichen und privaten Sektors (RTJ 17, 20. März 2006).

„PPP in Tallinn – Mythos oder Wirklichkeit", Wochenzeitung Eesti Ekspress, 05.07.2007.

Public Private Partnership Projects: http://english.yit.ee.

„Tallinn ins Schuldgefängnis – wird gemacht", Tageszeitung Eesti Päevaleht, 30.04.2008.

Tallinn verlangt Aufhebung von einschränkenden Buchhaltungsregeln: www.tallinn.ee/est/uudised.

Verordnung der Tallinner Stadtversammlung Nr. 175 vom 18. April 2002 „Tallinner Wohnbauprogramm – 5000 Wohnungen in Tallinn".

Verordnung der Tallinner Stadtversammlung Nr. 36 vom 13. Juni 2002 „Haushaltsstrategie der Stadt Tallinn 2003-2005": www.tallinn.andmevara.ee.

Verordnung der Tallinner Stadtversammlung Nr. 43 vom 20. Juni 2002 „Genehmigung der ersten und zweiten Etappe des Entwicklungsplanes des Tallinner Hauptstraßennetzes": www.tallinn.andmevara.ee.

Verordnung der Tallinner Stadtversammlung Nr. 64 vom 16. November 2006 „Änderung des Tallinner Entwicklungsplanes 2006-2015".

Teil II

Praktische Erfahrungen

Wirtschaftlichkeit von PPP-Projekten: Unter welchen Rahmenbedingungen ist PPP vorteilhafter als die Eigenrealisierung?

Frank Littwin

Inhaltsverzeichnis

1 Einführung

Die Realisierung von Öffentlich-Privaten Partnerschaften (ÖPP bzw. PPP) sollte Teil des Portfoliomanagements der öffentlichen Hand und damit einer Nachhaltigkeits- und Werterhaltungsstrategie sein. ÖPP dient dem Ziel, die Verwaltung zu modernisieren, privates Kapital zu mobilisieren und die Effizienz der öffentlichen Aufgabenwahrnehmung zu erhöhen. Der Staat soll sich auf seine Kernkompetenzen konzentrieren und unterstützende Prozesse auf Private übertragen, soweit dadurch die Effizienz der Aufgabenwahrnehmung gesteigert wird. Das Instrument ÖPP findet in unterschiedlichen öffentlichen Handlungsfeldern Anwendung. Dies umfasst insbesondere den öffentlichen Hochbau, die Verkehrsinfrastruktur, Entsorgung und Versorgung sowie den IT-Sektor. Die nachfolgenden Betrachtungen konzentrieren sich auf den Bereich des öffentlichen Hochbaus und legen einen engen ÖPP-Begriff zu Grunde.

ÖPP soll durch eine langfristig angelegte Zusammenarbeit zwischen Öffentlicher Hand und privater Wirtschaft zu einer wirtschaftlicheren Realisierung öffentlicher Hochbau- und Infrastrukturprojekte führen. Durch die Berücksichtigung des Lebenszyklusansatzes, anreizorientierte Vertragsgestaltung und sachgerechte Risikoverteilung soll eine Optimierung von Planung, Bau, Betrieb, Finanzierung und ggf. Verwertung bei öffentlichen Investitionsvorhaben erreicht werden. Eine ganzheitliche Betrachtung soll zudem eine wirtschaftlichere, nicht zwingend eine preisgünstigere, Erbringung von Dienstleistungen ermöglichen.[1]

ÖPP ist damit weit mehr als eine Finanzierungsvariante – es ist vielmehr eine alternative Beschaffungsvariante, die Private in die öffentliche Aufgabenwahrnehmung einbindet und einen wesentlichen Baustein zur Verwaltungsmodernisierung darstellt. ÖPPs können als sog. Institutionelle ÖPPs ausgestaltet sein, d.h. der Private und die öffentliche Hand gründen zur Aufgabenwahrnehmung eine gemeinsame Gesellschaft, in welcher der private Anteilseigner in der Regel die Mehrheit und damit die unternehmerische Führung übernimmt.

[1] Vgl. hierzu Littwin, F. (2006), S. 1 ff.; Littwin. F. (2008), S. 1 ff.; Christen, J. (2008), S. 9 ff.

Aufgrund steuerlicher Überlegungen finden sich insbesondere im Rahmen der umsatz- und/oder körperschaftsteuerlichen Organschaft auch Mehrheitsbeteiligungen der öffentlichen Hand. Dies gilt vor allem in personalintensiven Bereichen, in denen die öffentlichen Bediensteten längerfristig in ihrem Status gesichert werden sollen.
Beide Gestaltungsformen sind nicht unproblematisch, da die Risikosphären und damit die Verantwortlichkeiten zwischen der öffentlichen und der privaten Seite nicht immer klar zu trennen sind. Eine anreizorientierte Vertragsgestaltung und Betriebsführung ist nur sehr eingeschränkt umsetzbar. Ein ökonomisch sinnvoller Risikotransfer auf den privaten Sektor kann durch diese Gestaltung daher erheblich beeinträchtigt werden. Steuergetriebene Gestaltungformen sind dabei besonders problematisch, da der Effizienzgedanke in den Hintergrund tritt.

In der Praxis, vor allem im Hochbaubereich, sind das sog. Inhaber- und z.T. auch das Erwerbermodell anzutreffen. Beim Erwerbermodell werden die baulichen Anlagen durch den ÖPP-Partner auf dessen eigenem Grundstück errichtet und betrieben und nach Fertigstellung dem öffentlichen Auftraggeber zur Nutzung überlassen. Der ÖPP-Partner wird mit der Erstellung, der Planung und dem Betrieb (Instandhaltung, Instandsetzung, Energiemanagement, Hausmeister- und Reinigungsdienstleistungen) beauftragt. Ebenso ist die Finanzierung des Vorhabens bis zur Nutzungsübergabe an den öffentlichen Auftraggeber sowie die Übertragung des Eigentums an den baulichen Anlagen samt Grundstück auf den öffentlichen Auftraggeber am Ende der Vertragslaufzeit Inhalt des Vertrages. Während der Vertragslaufzeit hat der öffentliche Auftraggeber somit kein zivilrechtliches Eigentum. Er zahlt währenddessen ein festes (gewissen Indexierungen und Anpassungen unterliegendes) Entgelt.[2]

Das Inhabermodell entspricht grundsätzlich dem Erwerbermodell. Der wesentliche Unterschied besteht darin, dass es sich um ein Grundstück des öffentlichen Auftraggebers handelt. Die baulichen Anlagen werden durch den ÖPP-Partner auf dem Grundstück des öffentlichen Auftraggebers errichtet und

[2] Vgl. Littwin, F. (2006), S. 5.

betrieben und ihm nach der Fertigstellung der Baumaßnahme zur Nutzung überlassen.[3]

Erfahrungen zeigen, dass z.B. im öffentlichen Hochbau mindestens zwei Drittel der Kosten über den gesamten Lebenszyklus auf die Betriebsphase entfallen. Demzufolge ist für diesen Sektor die Übertragung der Betriebsleistungen für ÖPP begriffsbestimmend. Bisherige Evaluierungen machen zudem deutlich, dass sich Effizienzvorteile im Wesentlichen aus folgenden Effekten von ÖPP ableiten lassen:

– Einsparungen bei den Baukosten durch Einhaltung von vorher definierten Qualitäten und höhere Kostensicherheit durch Reduktion von Nachtragsrisiken,

– Einsparungen durch optimierte Planungs- und Bauzeiten bei hoher Terminsicherheit; der Private hat einen erheblichen Anreiz zur früheren Fertigstellung des Projektes, da er sein Entgelt erst ab Nutzungsbeginn erhält,

– Einsparungen bei den Betriebskosten durch den Lebenszyklusansatz; Sicherstellung der Werterhaltung der Immobilie und damit Vermeidung von Instandhaltungsrisiken,

– vertraglich geregelte Anreizmechanismen, z.B. durch leistungsorientierte Vergütungen (Reduzierung des Entgeltes bei Schlechtleistungen, ggf. Zahlungen von Boni bei zusätzlichen Einsparungen),

– private Eigenkapitalbeteiligung (ausgeprägtes Interesse der Investoren am Erfolg des Projektes),

– optimale Risikoverteilung zwischen dem privaten Sektor und der öffentlichen Hand und damit besseres Risikomanagement,

[3] Ebd.

- Nutzung der Innovationspotenziale des Privaten, z.B. durch den Know-How-Transfer aus vergleichbaren Projekten im In- und Ausland sowie
- Generierung von Erträgen und Synergie-Effekten: ggf. optimale Auslastung des Grundstücks durch öffentlich-private Mischnutzung und aufeinander abgestimmte Planungs- und Nutzungskonzepte.

ÖPP eröffnet die Möglichkeit, im Rahmen eines Verhandlungsverfahrens bzw. wettbewerblichen Dialogs Planungs- und Betriebskonzepte zu optimieren. Die Vorteile einer Realisierung von ÖPP-Projekten können sich neben einer positiven Wirtschaftlichkeit aus einer Nutzwertanalyse ergeben. Ziel ist die sachgerechte und ökonomisch sinnvolle Zuordnung und Einschätzung von Chancen und Risiken. Eine dynamische Entwicklung des ÖPP-Marktes erschließt Wachstumschancen und verbessert die Voraussetzungen zur Erhaltung und Schaffung von neuen Arbeitsplätzen.

Es hat sich weiterhin gezeigt, dass zur Umsetzung von ÖPP insbesondere folgende Rahmenbedingungen erfüllt sein müssen:

- Der politische Wille sowie die Bereitschaft der öffentlichen Verwaltung, innovative Beschaffungsalternativen zur Realisierung anstehender Investitionen zu nutzen, sind eine Grundvoraussetzung für ein erfolgreiches Projekt und damit wichtiger Bestandteil des ÖPP-Eignungstests;
- gesetzliche und institutionelle Rahmenbedingungen, wie z.B. eine modellneutrale Gesetzgebung, insbesondere im Förder- und Steuerrecht;
- die Einhaltung ÖPP-spezifischer Verfahrensregeln: Klare Organisationsstrukturen beim öffentlichen Auftraggeber, interdisziplinäre Projektvorbereitung, Durchführung von Machbarkeits- und Wirtschaftlichkeitsuntersuchungen, output-orientierte Ausschreibungsunterlagen,

Integration des Lebenszyklusansatzes in die Leistungsbeschreibung, hinreichende Anreizstrukturen im Vertragswerk.

Nur ein Teil der Beschaffungsprojekte der öffentlichen Hand ist zur Umsetzung als ÖPP-Projekt geeignet, d.h. der überwiegende Anteil wird mittel- bis langfristig weiterhin konventionell realisiert werden. Die ÖPP-Eignung ist sektorenspezifisch und projektbezogen zu prüfen. Bundesweit werden mittlerweile **ca. 4,5 Prozent** der Investitionsvorhaben im Rahmen von ÖPP-Strukturen umgesetzt. Bis März 2008 sind nach den Feststellungen der Bundesregierung bundesweit 86 ÖPP-Verträge abgeschlossen worden, die sich auf die Sektoren Schulen, Sportstätten, Schwimmbäder, Verwaltungsgebäude, Justizvollzugsanstalten, Krankenhäuser und Verkehrsinfrastruktur verteilen. Bei den ÖPP-Modellen überwiegen Forfaitierungskonzepte mit einem eingeschränkten Risikotransfer auf den Privaten. Bei großen komplexen Projekten sind dagegen echte Projektfinanzierungsstrukturen zu präferieren. Durch Entwicklung eines ausgewogenen Sicherheitenkonzeptes ist zu gewährleisten, dass die Risiken ökonomisch sinnvoll zwischen dem öffentlichen und privaten Sektor verteilt werden und das Risikomanagement optimiert wird.
ÖPP ist kein Allheilmittel zur Bedarfsdeckung und setzt ebenso wie konventionelle Projekte eine gesicherte Finanzierungsgrundlage und Bedarfssituation voraus.

2 Die Wirtschaftlichkeitsuntersuchung

Der ÖPP-Beschaffungsprozess gliedert sich nach dem Leitfaden der Finanzministerkonferenz vom 7. September 2006 zur Wirtschaftlichkeitsuntersuchung bei ÖPP-Projekten in folgende Phasen:

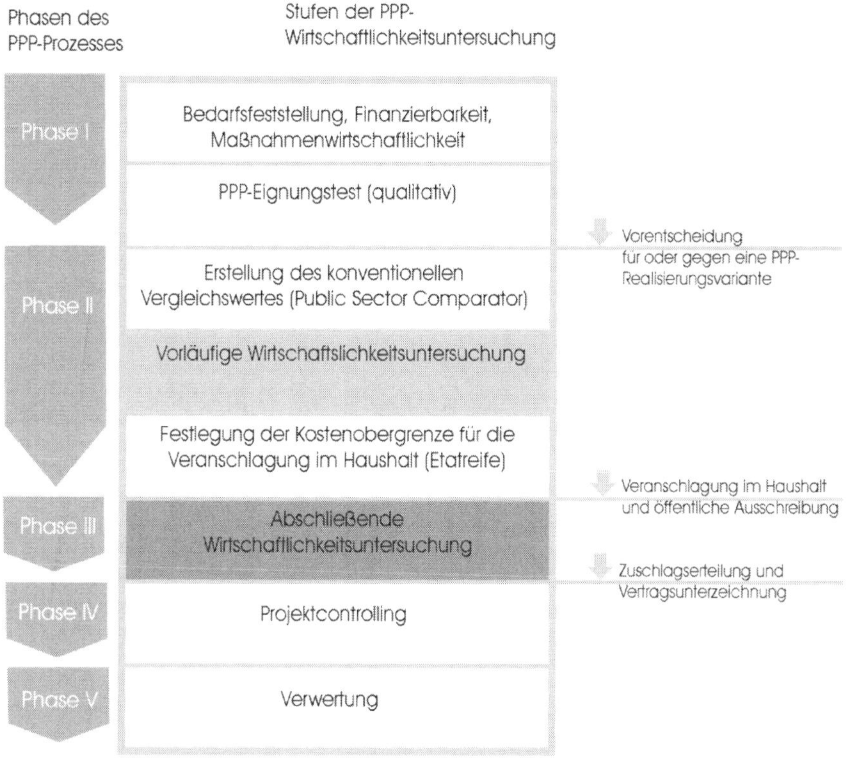

Abb. 1: PPP-Prozess und Wirtschaftlichkeitsuntersuchungen

Quelle: (o. A.) (2006).

Nach §7 der Bundeshaushaltsordnung und den entsprechenden Vorschriften in den Landeshaushaltsordnungen hat die öffentliche Hand bei der Realisierung ihrer Investitionsvorhaben den Grundsatz der Wirtschaftlichkeit und Sparsamkeit zu beachten. Bei einer Wirtschaftlichkeitsuntersuchung handelt es sich um einen mehrstufigen Prozess, bei dem unter Berücksichtigung aller Kosten einschließlich sog. Risikokosten und ggf. Erlöse die wirtschaftlichste Realisierungsvariante ermittelt werden soll.[4]

Die Komplexität und die langfristige Vertragsgestaltung stellen besondere Anforderungen an die Analyse der Wirtschaftlichkeit und die Prüfungspflichten, z.B. der Rechnungshöfe, Rechnungsprüfungsämter und Kommunalaufsichten. Das Innen- und das Finanzministerium in Nordrhein-Westfalen haben daher eine „Anleitung zur Prüfung von Wirtschaftlichkeitsuntersuchungen bei PPP-Projekten im öffentlichen Hochbau" erarbeitet, die als Hilfestellung für Kommunalaufsichten im Lande dienen soll und grundsätzlich auch auf andere Sektoren übertragbar ist.[5]
Zur Unterstützung der praktischen Anwendung durch die Aufsichtsbehörden werden in dem Leitfaden Auslegungshilfen für die einschlägigen Vorschriften des gemeindlichen Haushaltsrechts und Checklisten zur Verfügung gestellt, die wesentliche Prüfkriterien zur Untersuchung der Plausibilität des PPP-Vertragswerkes, dessen Finanzierung und insbesondere der durchgeführten Wirtschaftlichkeitsuntersuchung beinhalten.[6]

Die **vorläufige Wirtschaftlichkeitsuntersuchung** umfasst die Ermittlung der bevorzugten Beschaffungsvariante vor Eröffnung des Vergabeverfahrens. Mit der **abschließenden Wirtschaftlichkeitsuntersuchung** wird die wirtschaftliche Vorteilhaftigkeit des PPP-Angebotes des bevorzugten Bieters gegenüber dem konventionellen Vergleichswert (PSC) ermittelt.[7]

---

4 Vgl. Alfen, H.-W./Daube, D. (2006), S. 175 ff.; Rauschenbach, J./Gottschling, I. (2008), S. 253.

5 Vgl. PPP Task Force NRW (Hrsg.) (2007).

6 Zu weiteren Informationen bzgl. der Struktur und Durchführung des PPP-Eignungstests vgl. PPP Task Force NRW (Hrsg.) (2004); Littwin, F.(2006), S. 13 f.

7 Für weitere Informationen zu diesem Thema vgl. (o. A.) (2006); Alfen, H.-W./ Daube, D. (2006), S. 251 ff.

3 Aufgaben und Prüfungspflichten der Kommunalaufsicht am Beispiel NRW

Nach § 11 GO NRW ist es Aufgabe der Kommunalaufsicht, die Erfüllung der gesetzlichen Pflichten durch die Gemeinden zu sichern und die Kommunen in ihren Rechten zu schützen. In diesem Rahmen hat die Kommunalaufsicht eine beratende Funktion. Damit die Kommunalaufsicht diese Aufgabe sachgerecht erfüllen kann, bestehen für die Kommunen bei bestimmten Sachverhalten Anzeige- und Informationspflichten. Handelt es sich um einen genehmigungsbedürftigen Tatbestand (z.B. Investitionen, die Bestandteil eines Haushaltssicherungskonzeptes sind), werden die entsprechenden Maßnahmen erst mit der Genehmigung wirksam. Demgegenüber versetzt die Anzeige die Aufsichtsbehörde lediglich in die Lage, ggf. ihre Aufsichtstätigkeit rechtzeitig vor Eintritt der Wirksamkeit durchführen zu können.

Verpflichtet sich eine Kommune, wie bei PPP-Projekten üblich, gegenüber dem privaten Partner zur Leistung von Entgelten über die gesamte Laufzeit der Nutzung des Objektes, so handelt es sich um ein kreditähnliches Rechtsgeschäft i.S.d. § 86 Abs.4 GO NRW, welches anzeigepflichtig ist. Auch in den anderen Bundesländern werden ÖPP-Verträge als kreditähnliches Rechtsgeschäft eingestuft, die – mit Ausnahme von NRW – auch als Einzelmaßnahmen grundsätzlich genehmigungspflichtig sind. D.h. es ist eine Wirtschaftlichkeitsuntersuchung vorzulegen, aus der die Vorteilhaftigkeit der geplanten PPP-Realisierung gegenüber der konventionellen Beschaffung hervorgeht. Die Kommunalaufsicht wird sich regelmäßig darauf beschränken, die Darlegungen unter dem Gesichtspunkt der Plausibilität zu prüfen.

Nach Maßgabe des § 86 Abs. 4 GO NRW i.V.m. Ziffer 3 des Krediterlasses vom 9. Oktober 2006[8] sind bei Anzeige des Rechtsgeschäfts die speziellen, das kreditähnliche Geschäft kennzeichnenden Merkmale darzustellen und zu erläutern. Da Mietverträge demgegenüber nicht anzeigepflichtig sind, muss der

[8] Abgedruckt in: PPP Task Force NRW (Hrsg.) (2007).

krediähnliche PPP-Vertrag unter Heranziehung der Vertragstypenregelungen des BGB abgegrenzt werden. Ein wesentliches Kriterium ist insoweit die Einbeziehung der Investitions- und Finanzierungskosten in die Entgeltzahlungen. Diese sind im Gegensatz zur Miete im Vermögenshaushalt zu veranschlagen, soweit noch das kamerale Rechnungswesen Anwendung findet. Im Rahmen des Neuen Kommunalen Finanzmanagements ist zwischen konsumtiven, investiven und Zinszahlungen zu differenzieren. Beim sog. Inhabermodell, das keinen Eigentumsübergang bzw. Eigentumserwerb beim Privaten vorsieht, ist das Investitionsobjekt in der öffentlichen Bilanz zu aktivieren und abzuschreiben.

Nach § 75 Abs.1 Satz 2 GO NRW ist die kommunale Haushaltswirtschaft wirtschaftlich, effizient und sparsam zu führen; dies entspricht grundsätzlich den Regelungen in anderen Bundesländern. Der Grundsatz der Sparsamkeit bedeutet, dass nur solche Aufgaben wahrgenommen und finanziert werden sollen, die bei vernünftiger Betrachtung als angemessen angesehen werden. Der Grundsatz der Wirtschaftlichkeit ist dann gewahrt, wenn mit möglichst geringem Aufwand der größtmögliche Nutzen erzielt wird. Bei PPP-Projekten kommt i.d.R. das Sparsamkeits-/Minimalprinzip zur Anwendung, d.h. bei einem vorgegebenen Ergebnis wird ein möglichst geringer Mitteleinsatz angestrebt.

Beabsichtigt eine Kommune, ein Projekt im Rahmen einer PPP-Struktur zu realisieren, sind nach § 14 Abs. 1 GemHVO NRW die anstehenden Investitionsvorhaben unter Berücksichtigung der in Betracht kommenden Handlungsalternativen im Rahmen einer Wirtschaftlichkeitsuntersuchung zu prüfen. Es ist die wirtschaftlichste Lösung unter Beachtung der Anschaffungs- und Herstellungskosten sowie der Folgekosten zu ermitteln. Bei einem PPP-Projekt sind die an den Privaten zu entrichtenden Gesamtentgelte zu berücksichtigen.
Die zuständige Kommunalaufsicht hat die im Rahmen des Anzeigeverfahrens nach § 86 Abs. 4 GO NRW erstellte Wirtschaftlichkeitsuntersuchung einer Plausibilitätsprüfung zu unterziehen. Die Methodik der Wirtschaftlichkeitsuntersuchung hat sich an den Empfehlungen der Finanzministerkonferenz vom 07.09.2006 zu orientieren, nach der bestimmte Mindeststandards festgelegt

worden sind. Unabhängig von der abschließenden Wirtschaftlichkeitsuntersuchung prüft die Kommunalaufsicht, ob die Gesamtfinanzierung des Vorhabens haushaltsverträglich ist. Es können sich weitere haushaltsrechtliche Anforderungen ergeben, wenn die Kommune zur Aufstellung eines Haushaltssicherungskonzeptes (HSK) nach § 76 GO NRW verpflichtet ist. Kann dieses finanzaufsichtlich nicht genehmigt werden, unterliegt die Kommune den noch strengeren Einschränkungen der vorläufigen Haushaltsführung nach § 82 GO NRW.

Die Kommunalaufsicht nimmt die prüfende Tätigkeit mit **Erhalt der abschließenden Wirtschaftlichkeitsuntersuchung** auf. Zuvor eingereichte vorläufige Abschätzungen der Projektwirtschaftlichkeit (wie die vorläufige Wirtschaftlichkeitsuntersuchung) unterliegen keiner (Neu-)Bewertung durch die Kommunalaufsicht.

Im Vorfeld der Prüfung der abschließenden Wirtschaftlichkeitsuntersuchung empfiehlt es sich nach den Erfahrungen der Praxis, **Informationsgespräche** zwischen Kommune und Kommunalaufsichtsbehörde zu führen. Sie sind jedenfalls dann sinnvoll, wenn sie der frühzeitigen, noch unverbindlichen Information über die aufsichtsrelevanten Sachverhalte dienen, insbesondere im Austausch über die Haushaltsverträglichkeit sowie rechtlichen und tatsächlichen Zweifelsfragen. Dabei ist anzustreben, dass die Kommunalaufsicht die grundlegenden Projektdaten **spätestens nach Abschluss der vorläufigen Wirtschaftlichkeitsuntersuchung** von der Kommune erhält, damit sie ggf. im Rahmen der Beratung Hinweise geben kann.

In den Phasen I bis III im Vorfeld der abschließenden Wirtschaftlichkeitsuntersuchung erfolgt grundsätzlich keine verbindliche Entscheidung durch die Kommunalaufsicht (Ausnahme: Nothaushaltsrecht). Allerdings kann die Kommunalaufsicht wichtige Hinweise für eine erfolgreiche Projektgestaltung geben sowie Bedingungen und Voraussetzungen einer Genehmigung bzw. zustimmenden Kenntnisnahme aufzeigen.

Bei Ausschreibung des Projektes geht die Kommune eine Verpflichtung zur Vergabe von Leistungen ein, wenn nach positiver vorläufiger Wirtschaftlichkeitsuntersuchung die Ausschreibung bekannt gemacht wird. Wird die Ausschreibung ohne triftigen Grund aufgehoben, kann die Kommune gegenüber den Bietern zu **Schadensersatz** verpflichtet sein. Um mögliche Schadensersatzansprüche auszuschließen, reicht es dabei nicht aus, die Bieter erst bei Zuschlag darüber zu informieren, dass die Wirksamkeit des Vertrags von der Zustimmung der Kommunalaufsicht abhängt. Allerdings können Schadensersatzansprüche der Bieter vermieden werden, wenn bereits in den Ausschreibungsunterlagen ausdrücklich auf die Anzeige- bzw. Genehmigungspflicht des Vorhabens hingewiesen wird.[9]

Die in den Informationsgesprächen erfolgende Auskunft der Kommunalaufsicht hat beratenden Charakter. Die Aufsichtsbehörde kann, falls notwendig, die Genehmigung bzw. zustimmende Kenntnisnahme der endverhandelten Verträge eines geplanten ÖPP-Projektes verweigern. Durch frühzeitige Einbindung der Kommunalaufsichtsbehörden kann und sollte dieses Risiko minimiert werden.

---

[9] Vgl. OLG Rostock, v. 07.12.2000 - 1 U 12/99 (OLG Report Rostock 2001, 213, WM 2001, 2206); BGH, Urt. V. 26.10.2000 – III ZR 53/99 (NJW 2001, 2402 L) und BGH, Urt. v. 06.06.2000 – XI ZR 235/99 (MDR 2000, S. 1247).

Checkliste für Informationsgespräche		
Zeitpunkt der Anfrage an die Kommunalaufsicht vor Ausschreibung		Maßnahmen der Kommunalaufsicht
Phase I	Ausarbeitung der Bedarfsfeststellung, Wirtschaftlichkeit der Maßnahme und Finanzierbarkeit liegt vor	• Kenntnisnahme des Projektes • Unverbindliche Einschätzung zur Wirtschaftlichkeit der Maßnahme und • **Unverbindliche Einschätzung** der Haushaltsverträglichkeit
Phase I	Fertigstellung des PPP-Eignungstests	• Kenntnisnahme des konkretisierten Projektes • **Unverbindliche Einschätzung** der Ergebnisse des PPP-Eignungstests (ggf. Vorlage des Ratsbeschlusses zur Information)
Phase II	Fertigstellung der vorläufigen Wirtschaftlichkeitsuntersuchung	• Kenntnisnahme der detaillierten Projektplanungen und der vorläufigen Wirtschaftlichkeitsuntersuchung • **Unverbindliche Einschätzung** der Ergebnisse der vorläufigen Wirtschaftlichkeitsuntersuchung • (ggf. Vorlage des Ratsbeschlusses zur Information)

Tab. 1: Checkliste für die Informationsgespräche

Quelle: PPP Task Force NRW (Hrsg.) (2007).

Grundlegende Zweifel an der **Haushaltsverträglichkeit** des Projektes anhand der haushaltswirtschaftlichen Situation der Kommune sollten so früh wie möglich ausgeräumt werden. Dies gilt auch für die **Zuwendungsfähigkeit** und **Fachplanung**.[10]

Vor Beauftragung externer Berater und dem Erstellen einer vorläufigen Wirtschaftlichkeitsuntersuchung muss vor dem Hintergrund der finanzwirtschaftlichen Situation einer Kommune die Finanzierbarkeit des Projektes gegeben sein. Das heißt, es muss deutlich gemacht werden, dass sich die Kommune das Projekt "leisten" kann. Auch sollte die Bedarfssituation geklärt sein. Die Zahl der in Betracht kommenden Handlungsalternativen (z.B. Neubau, Sanierung, Bündelung von Projekten, Standortauswahl) sollte möglichst überschaubar sein, um die Transaktionskosten zu reduzieren.

Hat die Kommune bereits einen **ÖPP-Eignungstest** durchgeführt, sollten die Ergebnisse der Kommunalaufsicht zur Information zugeleitet und diese über das geplante Projekt in Kenntnis gesetzt werden. Liegen bereits die Ergebnisse einer **vorläufigen Wirtschaftlichkeitsuntersuchung** vor, so sollten diese unbedingt auch an die Kommunalaufsicht weitergeleitet und ggf. mit ihr abgestimmt werden.

Im Folgenden sind die im Rahmen der vorläufigen Wirtschaftlichkeitsuntersuchung bei der Kommunalaufsicht einzureichenden Unterlagen aufgeführt:

[10] Bei der Schlüssigkeitsprüfung der Fachplanung geht es beispielsweise um die Vereinbarkeit des PPP-Projektes mit der Schulentwicklungsplanung.

- Allgemeines zum Vorhaben
- Aktuelle Projektdaten:
  - Umfang
  - Laufzeit
  - Investitionsvolumen
  - weitere Informationen, wenn essentiell
- Ergebnis der Berechnungen der vorläufigen Wirtschaftlichkeitsuntersuchung
  - Annahmen und Ableitungen
  - Berechnungsmethodik und nachvollziehbare Darstellung der Berechnungsschritte
  - Zusammenfassung der Eingangsdaten
  - Zusammenstellung der Ergebnisse

Abb. 2: Einzureichende Unterlagen bei der vorläufigen Wirtschaftlichkeitsuntersuchung

Quelle: PPP Task Force NRW (Hrsg.) (2007).

Die Voruntersuchungen für eine angestrebte ÖPP-Realisierung sollten in diesem Stadium in jedem Fall die Ermittlung eines ersten **Vergleichswertes der konventionellen Eigenrealisierung** sowie die **qualitativen Vorteile einer ÖPP-Realisierung** enthalten. Zusätzlich kann ein ÖPP-Referenzprojekt abgeleitet, dem konventionellen Vergleichswert gegenübergestellt und dadurch der ÖPP-Effizienzvorteil oder -nachteil prognostiziert werden. In einem ÖPP-Referenzmodell wird in vorausschauender Sicht des öffentlichen Projektträgers die als bestmöglich angenommene Projektlösung des Privaten wiedergegeben.[11] Wird eine vorläufige Wirtschaftlichkeitsuntersuchung mit ÖPP-Referenzprojekt erstellt, so muss die Vergleichbarkeit der Höhe der Gesamtkosten beider Realisierungsvarianten und der ÖPP-Variante gegeben sein.

---

[11] Zu weiteren Informationen zum Ablauf und zur Strukturierung der Wirtschaftlichkeitsuntersuchung bei ÖPP-Projekten vgl. PPP-Task Force NRW (Hrsg.) (2007).

Die eigentliche Prüfung eines Vorhabens erfolgt durch die Kommunalaufsicht auf Basis der **abschließenden Wirtschaftlichkeitsuntersuchung**. In dieser Phase befindet sich das Projekt in der Ausschreibung. Der Schritt erfolgt erst, wenn die Verhandlungen mit dem bevorzugten Bieter abgeschlossen sind und die endverhandelten Verträge vorliegen.

Zunächst wird in einer Übersicht dargelegt, welche Unterlagen und Dokumente von der Kommune aufbereitet und eingereicht werden sollten und zu welchen Inhalten darin Stellung zu nehmen ist.

Abschließende Wirtschaftlichkeitsuntersuchung (ggf. Cash-Flow Tabellen)

- Höhe und Zusammensetzung des Leistungsentgeltes und bestehende Anpassungsmechanismen
- Vertragsentwürfe/-eckpunkte mit Informationen zu:
  - Gestaltung der Endschaftsregelung
  - Sicherheitenmodell
  - Bindungswirkungen, Belastungen der Haushalte
  - Laufzeit der Verträge
- Berechnungsmethodik
- Gutachten/Zusammenfassung der Berater mit den wesentlichen Ergebnissen der Wirtschaftlichkeitsuntersuchung
- Risikobewertung und -verteilung
- (Die vertragliche Risikoverteilung ist ggf. durch eine Risikomatrix transparent zu machen.)
- Eckpunkte der Finanzierung

Abb. 3: Einzureichende Unterlagen bei der abschließenden Wirtschaftlichkeitsuntersuchung

Quelle: PPP Task Force NRW (Hrsg.) (2007).

Die Kommunalaufsicht prüft anhand der Eingangsdaten, ob die Kommune eine Wirtschaftlichkeitsuntersuchung vorgenommen hat, die den Anforderungen des Krediterlasses sowie den allgemein anerkannten Standards für Wirtschaftlichkeitsuntersuchungen entspricht. Dabei wird regelmäßig die **Vollständigkeit** und **Plausibilität** der bei der Kommunalaufsicht eingereichten Daten überprüft.

Als Entscheidungsgrundlage für die Einschätzung der PPP-Vorteilhaftigkeit können zwei Ansätze unterschieden werden, die beide in der Praxis Anwendung finden.
Zum einen können die **Gesamtbarwerte aller Zahlungen** des konventionellen Vergleichswertes (PSC) und des bevorzugten ÖPP-Angebotes gegenübergestellt werden. Alle anfallenden Zahlungen werden dabei durch die Diskontierung im Rahmen der Barwertberechnung auf den Investitionszeitpunkt bezogen. Die erwartete Preisentwicklung, die angenommenen Finanzierungskonditionen, etc., fließen bei der vorläufigen Wirtschaftlichkeitsuntersuchung in die Berechnung der Barwerte ein. Den Gesamtbarwerten sollte stets die Summe aller Zeitwerte der Zahlungen zur Seite gestellt werden. Der Zeitwert ist die Höhe des Leistungsentgelts in den Jahren, in denen sie anfallen. Dies ist sinnvoll, da die Barwerte nur einen Vergleichswert und keine realen Zahlungen oder Vermögenswerte darstellen.
Zum anderen kann auch ein Vergleich des **Entgeltes im ersten Monat** bzw. Quartal herangezogen werden. Für diese Option gilt die Voraussetzung, dass für das Projekt ein über die Vertragslaufzeit real konstantes Leistungsentgelt[12] festgelegt wurde. Das heißt, der Private erhält – abgesehen von Preissteigerungen, Abzügen durch Schlechtleistungen, etc. – jede Periode einen feststehenden Betrag als Leistungsentgelt ausgezahlt. Bei dem als Vergleichsgröße herangezogenen Leistungsentgelt handelt es sich um eine konkrete Zahlung und nicht (wie beim Gesamtbarwert der Zahlungen) um eine reine Vergleichsgröße. Das in der ersten Periode zu zahlende Leistungsentgelt ist zudem Vertragsbestandteil, es wird in dem zu schließenden ÖPP-Vertrag festgeschrieben.

Die Bewertung erfolgt durch die Festlegung von Eintrittswahrscheinlichkeit und Schadenshöhe der betrachteten Risiken. Zum konkreten Vorgehen der

12 Zu dem real konstanten Leistungsentgelt ist der jährliche Preisanstieg durch Inflation zu berücksichtigen, wodurch das nominale Entgelt langfristig ansteigt.

Risikobewertung bestehen keine einheitlichen Standards. Die Vorgehensweise bei der Risikobewertung ist der Kommunalaufsicht gegenüber transparent zu dokumentieren. Des Weiteren sollte deutlich gemacht werden, welche Risiken aus der erstellten Risikoliste einen besonders hohen Einfluss auf das Projektergebnis haben. Diese Risiken sollten daher in jedem Fall in die Risikobewertung einfließen.

Die Kosten für zurückbehaltene Risiken werden vereinfachend bei konventioneller und ÖPP-Realisierung als gleich hoch angenommen und können daher für die abschließende Wirtschaftlichkeitsuntersuchung vernachlässigt werden. Die Bezugsgröße beschreibt, auf welche Kosten der ermittelte Risikowert bezogen wird, um die Risikokosten durch Multiplikation von Risikowert und Bezugsgröße ermitteln zu können.

4 Finanzierungsmodelle

Im Rahmen der Wirtschaftlichkeitsbetrachtung werden i.d.R. zwei unterschiedliche Finanzierungsmodelle zugrunde gelegt. Der Projektfinanzierung und der Forfaitierung mit Einredeverzicht liegen grundsätzlich unterschiedliche Sicherungskonzepte zugrunde. Während bei einer Projektfinanzierung für die öffentliche Hand die Möglichkeit besteht, ihre eigenen Schadenspositionen mit noch ausstehenden Zahlungspflichten zu verrechnen, gibt sie gerade dieses Recht mit der Erklärung eines Einredeverzichts auf. Aus diesem Grund ist die Erklärung des Einredeverzichts durch den kommunalen Auftraggeber als Sicherheit zugunsten Dritter gemäß § 87 Abs. 1 GO NRW zu interpretieren, falls sich die wirtschaftliche Position der öffentlichen Hand gegenüber einer konventionellen Eigenrealisierung verschlechtern sollte. Im Landes- wie im kommunalen Bereich bedarf es keiner ausdrücklichen Haushaltsermächtigung bzw. einer Rückstellung, um einen Einredeverzicht zu erklären, da haushaltsrechtlich weder eine Bürgschaft noch eine Garantie vorliegt. Die Zulässigkeit einer solchen Vereinbarung ist im kommunalen Bereich (NRW) nur dann gegeben, wenn im ÖPP-Modell mindestens eine Absicherung analog zur Eigenrealisierung sichergestellt ist.

Im Fall der **Eigenrealisierung** (Sicherheit bei Kommunalkreditfinanzierung) besteht die Absicherung der öffentlichen Hand in den bei Bauvorhaben üblichen Vertragserfüllungs- sowie den anschließenden Gewährleistungsbürgschaften. Als generell zulässig wird bei Bauvorhaben die Forderung von Bürgschaften bis zu einer Höhe von 10% der Auftragssumme erachtet.

Die Sicherungseffekte bei einer Projektfinanzierung gehen deutlich über die sonst üblichen Sicherheiten bei einer konventionellen Eigenrealisierung hinaus, so dass insoweit keine rechtlichen Bedenken bestehen (§ 87 I GO)

Demgegenüber wird eine Finanzierung mittels Einredeverzicht durch die Kommunalaufsicht eingehender geprüft. Zum einen sollten die Sicherheiten mindestens in der Höhe der bei Eigenrealisierung üblichen Vertragserfüllungs- und Gewährleistungsbürgschaften bestehen. Zum anderen kommt der inhaltlichen und zeitlichen Gestaltung der Einredeverzichtserklärung eine wesentliche Bedeutung zu. Gemäß dem Grundsatz, dass die Leistungserbringung „Zug um Zug“ erfolgen sollte, was auch bei der Eigenrealisierung gilt, sollte der Einredeverzicht im Sinne einer ausgewogenen Risikoverteilung ausschließlich über bereits fertiggestellte und vom öffentlichen Auftraggeber anerkannte Leistungen erklärt werden. Würde dieser Grundsatz nicht gewahrt, bestünde für die öffentliche Hand im Schadensfall die Gefahr, Zahlungen für nicht erhaltene Leistungen tätigen zu müssen.

Im Ergebnis bestehen gegen eine Projektfinanzierung grundsätzlich keine Bedenken. Dagegen ist bei einer Forfaitierung mit Einredeverzicht zu prüfen, ob

- die Wirksamkeit der Erklärung erst nach Fertigstellung der Bauleistung eintritt,
- diese ausschließlich auf investive Leistungen beschränkt ist und

- die vorgesehenen öffentlichen Sicherheiten mindestens der Eigenrealisierung entsprechen.

5 Fazit

Auf Grundlage der bisherigen Erfahrungen, die allerdings nur drei bis vier Jahre der Betriebsphase eines ÖPP-Projektes umfassen, haben sich Effizienzvorteile bei den ÖPP-Projekten von 5 bis 25 Prozent gezeigt. Dies liegt nicht zuletzt daran, dass im Rahmen des Eignungstestes und der vorläufigen Wirtschaftlichkeitsuntersuchung bei den Projekten, die für eine ÖPP-Realisierung nicht hinreichend geeignet erschienen bzw. bei denen keine Effizienzvorteile zu erwarten waren, der ÖPP-Beschaffungsweg nicht weiter verfolgt wurde. Eine sorgfältige Anwendung der vorhandenen Instrumente im Rahmen der mehrstufigen Wirtschaftlichkeitsuntersuchung hat sich insoweit in der Praxis bewährt und dazu geführt, dass grundsätzlich ungeeignete Projektstrukturen nicht realisiert wurden. Trotzdem hat sich im Einzelfall – insbesondere aufgrund geänderter politischer Beschlusslagen, Bürgerbegehren sowie nachträglich auftretender Finanzierungs- und Sicherheitenprobleme – gezeigt, dass auch ÖPP-geeignete Projekte noch scheitern können.

Literaturverzeichnis

Alfen, H.-W./Daube, D. (2006): Der Wirtschaftlichkeitsvergleich. In: Littwin, F./Schöne, F.-J. (Hrsg.) (2006): Public Private Partnership im öffentlichen Hochbau. Stuttgart. S. 175-262.

PPP Task Force NRW (Hrsg.) (2007): Leitfaden „Public Private Partnership im öffentlichen Hochbau – Anleitung zur Prüfung der Wirtschaftlichkeitsuntersuchung von PPP-Projekten im öffentlichen Hochbau". April 2007. Düsseldorf.

BGH, Urt. V. 26.10.2000 – III ZR 53/99 (NJW 2001, 2402 L).

BGH, Urt. v. 06.06.2000 – XI ZR 235/99 (MDR 2000, S. 1247).

Christen, J. (2008): PPP-Handbuch. Bad-Homburg.

Littwin, F. (2006): Allgemeiner Teil. In: Littwin, F./Schöne, F.-J. (2006): Public Private Partnership im öffentlichen Hochbau. Stuttgart .

Littwin, F. (2008): Public Private Partnership aus Sicht der PPP-Task Force NRW. In: Meyer-Hofmann, B./Riemenschneider, F./Weihrauch, O. (2008): Public Private Partnership. 2. Auflage. Köln/München, S. 1-31.

OLG Rostock, v. 07.12.2000 - 1 U 12/99 (OLG Report Rostock 2001, 213, WM 2001, 2206);

PPP Task Force NRW (Hrsg.) (2004): Leitfaden „Public Private Partnership im Hochbau – Erste Schritte: Der PPP-Eignungstest". Oktober 2004. Düsseldorf.

Rauschenbach, J./Gottschling, I. (2008): Wirtschaftlichkeitsuntersuchung. In: Bundesministerium für Verkehr, Bau und Stadtentwicklung/Deutscher Sparkassen und Giroverband (Hrsg.) (2008): PPP-Handbuch. Leitfaden für Öffentlich-Private-Partnerschaften. Bad-Homburg, S. 249-281.

o. A. (2006): FMK-Leitfaden vom 7.9. 2006, abrufbar unter www.ppp.nrw.de

PPP-Projekte bei öffentlichen Baumaßnahmen in Bayern – alte Herausforderungen und neue Perspektiven

Detlef Lupp

Inhaltsverzeichnis

1 Verstoß gegen das Nachhaltigkeitsgebot

Ein Grundproblem in Deutschland – und mit Sicherheit auch in vielen anderen Ländern – ist, dass permanent gegen das Gebot der Nachhaltigkeit verstoßen wird. Nachhaltigkeit – das bedeutet weit mehr als nur Schutz von Wald, Feuchtbiotopen und seltenen Tierarten. Es bedeutet auch, dass wir unser Land so entwickeln müssen, dass unsere Kinder genauso gut leben können, wie uns das heute möglich ist. Nachfolgende Generationen werden in Deutschland nicht gut leben können, wenn die Bauten marode sind und die gesamte Infrastruktur – Straßen, Schienen, Wasser- und Abwasserkanäle, Schulen, Verwaltungsgebäude oder Bäder – dramatisch zu verfallen droht. Der Begriff Nachhaltigkeit sollte damit Leitlinie und Maßstab gerade auch für die Notwendigkeit von Bauinvestitionen sein.

2 Enormer Investitionsbedarf bei öffentlichen Baumaßnahmen

In Deutschland besteht im Zeitraum 2006 bis 2020 allein ein kommunaler Investitionsbedarf von 704 Mrd. Euro, was auf das Jahr umgerechnet Investitionen in Höhe von knapp 47 Mrd. Euro entspricht. Das ist das Ergebnis einer Studie des Deutschen Instituts für Urbanistik (Difu), die gemeinsam vom Bundesministerium für Verkehr, Bau und Stadtentwicklung, dem Hauptverband der Deutschen Bauindustrie und dem Bundesverband der Deutschen Zementindustrie gefördert wurde.

Nach Einzelbereichen untergliedert besteht der größte Investitionsbedarf mit rund 162 Mrd. Euro im Straßenbau, gefolgt von Schulen mit 73 Mrd. Euro und Abwasseranlagen mit rund 58 Mrd. Euro. In der zahlenmäßig größten Position "Sonstige Bereiche", die nur pauschal geschätzt wurde, ist u. a. der Investitionsbedarf für die Bereiche Energieversorgung, Abfallwirtschaft, Kindertageseinrichtungen, Feuerwehr sowie Kultur enthalten.

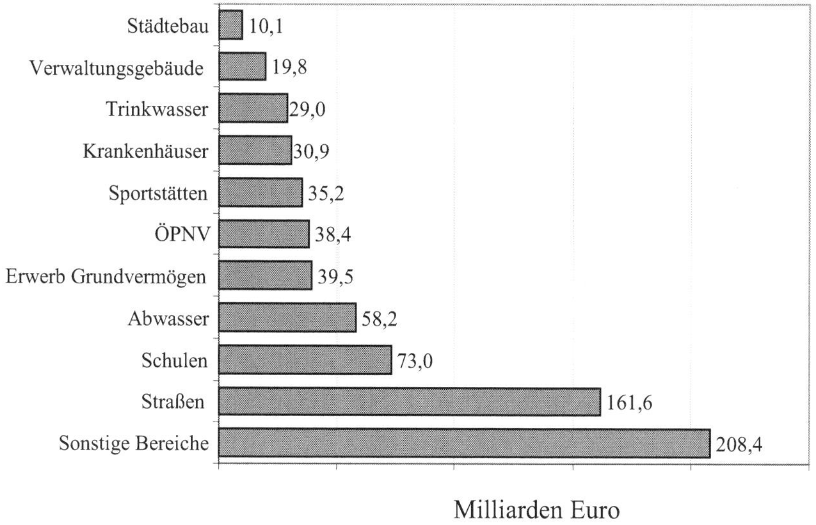

Abb. 1: Kommunaler Investitionsbedarf nach Einzelbereichen
Quelle: Deutsches Institut für Urbanistik.

3 Zukunftsweisender Lösungsansatz: Public Private Partnership (PPP)

Ein Lösungsansatz, der helfen kann, diesem Investitionsdilemma zu entgehen, ist Public Private Partnership (PPP).

Auch wenn man davon ausgeht, dass PPP nur für ca. 20 Prozent aller Investitionen der öffentlichen Hand im Bau- und Immobilienbereich geeignet ist, kann diese alternative Beschaffungsvariante einen erheblichen Beitrag zum Abbau des dramatischen Investitionsstaus bei Bund, Ländern und Kommunen leisten.

Dies hat auch die Bundesregierung erkannt, denn sie will die PPP-Quote in Deutschland – also den Anteil von PPP-Projekten an den öffentlichen Investitionen – an das Niveau anderer Industrieländer heranführen. Als Orientierungsgröße wird eine Quote von 15 % genannt, wie sie sich z.B. in Großbritannien eingependelt hat.

Dabei ist zudem ganz klar: Traditionelle Haushaltsfinanzierung öffentlicher Bauten wird auch weiterhin die bedeutende Rolle spielen, doch in geeigneten Fällen sollten PPP-Konzepte verstärkt neben die herkömmliche Haushaltsfinanzierung treten. Bei den öffentlichen Haushalten müssen damit auch eine spürbare Senkung der Sozialausgaben und eine Anhebung der Investitionsquote auf wieder mindestens 15 % einhergehen.

3.1 Begriffsverständnis von PPP

Wichtig ist, bei Public Private Partnership von einem richtigen Begriffsverständnis auszugehen. Um ein echtes PPP-Projekt handelt es sich nur dann, wenn eine langfristige, vertraglich geregelte und entgeltliche Zusammenarbeit zwischen einem öffentlichen Auftraggeber und einem privaten Partner über den gesamten Lebenszyklus eines Bauwerks vorliegt. Der Private muss bereit sein, die Projektphasen Planung, Bau, Finanzierung, Bauunterhalt, Betrieb und ggf. Verwertung eines Bauwerks, verbunden mit entsprechenden wirtschaftlichen Risiken zu übernehmen. Ferner gilt, dass ein Projektrisiko derjenige der beiden Vertragspartner übernehmen soll, welcher es am besten handhaben kann.

3.2 Was kann PPP gesamtwirtschaftlich leisten?

Eines ist sicher – PPP ist kein Bauen ohne Geld. Eine z.B. völlig verschuldete Kommune wird auch kein PPP-Projekt schultern können, spätestens die Rechtsaufsichtsbehörde wird hier einen Riegel vorschieben.

PPP ermöglicht einen wirtschaftlichen Umgang mit öffentlichen Vermögenswerten, was durch öffentliche Verwaltungsstrukturen bisher erschwert wird. Dem Stop and Go und dem Kurzfristdenken öffentlicher Investitionspolitik wird der Lebenszyklusgedanke mit Erhaltung der Vermögenssubstanz und verlässlicher Finanzplanung gegenübergestellt.

PPP stellt weniger einen Finanzierungsbeitrag für desolate öffentliche Haushalte als immer mehr einen neuen Beschaffungsansatz für bessere Bau- und Dienstleistungen zu niedrigeren Kosten dank privatwirtschaftlicher Realisierung dar.

3.3 Konzeptionelle Ansätze und Wirkungsmechanismen von PPP

Ein zentrales Anliegen von PPP ist, die in Wettbewerbs- und Marktmechanismen verankerten Innovations- und Anreizpotentiale freizusetzen. Schon bei der ersten Konzipierung eines öffentlichen Bauanliegens sollten die Möglichkeiten für eine weitreichende Ideenfindung durch die Privatwirtschaft eröffnet werden.

Man darf PPP nicht als reine Finanzierungsalternative missverstehen, sondern muss diese als umfassenden alternativen Beschaffungsansatz unter Lebenszyklusgesichtspunkten sehen mit dem Ziel, Effizienzvorteile zu erreichen.

Bereits bei Planung und Bau einen Wettbewerb der Ideen für die Nutzungsphase organisieren

Bei der herkömmlichen Umsetzung eines Bauanliegens der öffentlichen Hand (z.B. Verwaltungsgebäude, Schule, Kindergarten, Kläranlage, Wasserver-/ Abwasserentsorgung, Straßen) wird die Bauleistung vorweg „zementiert“ und nur diese ausgeschrieben und damit einem Bieterwettbewerb unterworfen. Für die langjährigen und finanziell wesentlich mehr ins Gewicht fallenden Unterhalts- und Betriebsleistungen wird jedoch ein Ideenwettbewerb um vielfältige Lösungsmöglichkeiten ausgeblendet.

Bei einem PPP-Konzept dagegen werden sämtliche Folgekosten des Unterhalts und Betriebs einer Bauinvestition zum Gegenstand eines Bieterwettbewerbs gemacht. Somit müssen sich die privaten Unternehmen einem Wettbewerb der Ideen für das wirtschaftlichste Gesamtkonzept – also für eine wirtschaftliche Lösung der Bauinvestition einschließlich sämtlicher Folgekosten – stellen. Bereits dies trägt maßgeblich zur Erzielung erheblicher Kostenvorteile bei.

Lebenszyklusbetrachtung – Gesamtoptimierung statt Einzeloptimierung

Bei einem „echten" PPP-Projekt übernimmt der private Vertragspartner i.d.R. die Projektphasen Planung, Bau, Finanzierung, Bauunterhalt, Betrieb und ggf. Folgenutzung/Verwertung einer Immobilie. Dadurch wird gewährleistet, dass schon bei Planung und Errichtung des Bauwerks, also in den frühen Phasen des Lebenszyklus, auf langfristig kostengünstige Instandhaltung und möglichst wirtschaftlichen Betrieb geachtet wird. Alle Leistungen, die über den gesamten Projektlebenszyklus zu erbringen sind, werden in einem gemeinsamen Ausschreibungsverfahren vergeben. Damit werden für die vereinbarte Vertragslaufzeit – u.U. bis zu 30 Jahren – sämtliche Kosten einer öffentlichen Einrichtung kalkuliert und in das PPP-Entgelt eingerechnet. Demzufolge fließen alle voraussichtlichen Kosten von den Planungs- über die Baukosten bis hin zu den Kosten für Bauunterhalt und Betrieb in die Gesamtprojektrechnung ein. Damit werden die Gesamtkosten und -risiken eines öffentlichen Investitionsprojekts auf Dauer transparent und nachprüfbar.

Ergebnisorientierte (funktionale) Ausschreibung fördert privatwirtschaftliches Know-how und Innovationspotential

Bei herkömmlichen Bauvergaben werden die zu erbringenden Bauleistungen in einem Leistungsverzeichnis bis ins kleinste Detail beschrieben. Die Bieter haben hier nur die Möglichkeit, diese detaillierten LV-Positionen zu bepreisen, was in der Regel nur einen Wettbewerb um den billigsten Angebotspreis, nicht aber um das insgesamt wirtschaftlichste Angebot auslöst. Die Suche nach Wettbewerbslösungen und Innovationspotential bleibt hier ausgeschaltet.

Im Rahmen eines PPP-Projekts gibt der öffentliche Auftraggeber in einer ergebnisorientierten (funktionalen) Ausschreibung nur die Ziel- und Rahmenanforderungen (Funktionen, Standards, Qualitäten, etc.) vor. Auf welche Weise der PPP-Vertragspartner diese Anforderungen (z.B. nur die Vorgabe einer konkreten Mindestraumtemperatur in Klassenzimmern einer Schule während der Heizperiode) erfüllt, bleibt weitgehend diesem überlassen. Entscheidend ist also nur das „was", das der PPP-Partner erbringen muss, nicht, „wie" er zu diesem Ergebnis gelangt.

Interessengerechte Risikoaufteilung sichert die Wirtschaftlichkeit des PPP-Konzepts

Von wesentlicher Bedeutung für die Wirtschaftlichkeit eines PPP-Projekts ist eine optimale Risikoaufteilung zwischen dem öffentlichen und privaten Partner. Diese Risikoaufteilung zwischen öffentlicher Hand und Privaten darf nicht einseitig durch den öffentlichen Auftraggeber in einem Über- und Unterordnungsverhältnis, sondern muss partnerschaftlich im Gleichrangverhältnis nur nach Kompetenz- und Effizienzgesichtspunkten erfolgen. Deshalb gilt als Risikoaufteilungsgrundsatz, dass derjenige Partner ein Risiko übernehmen soll, der es am besten beeinflussen und damit auch am kostengünstigsten umgehen kann. Vor diesem Hintergrund sollte die öffentliche Hand nicht versuchen, dem PPP-Partner möglichst alle denkbaren Risiken zu überbürden, sondern an einem intelligenten Risikoaufteilungskonzept mitwirken, das beide Vertragspartner vernünftig in die Pflicht nimmt. Der PPP-Vertragspartner sollte beispielsweise das Planungsrisiko und das Baufertigstellungsrisiko tragen, während bei dem öffentlichen Partner in der Regel das Auslastungsrisiko einer öffentlichen Einrichtung oder auch das Gesetzesänderungsrisiko verbleiben sollte.

Leistungsorientierte Vergütungsmechanismen sichern die Qualitätsstandards über die gesamte Vertragslaufzeit

Dadurch, dass der PPP-Projektpartner in der Regel während der gesamten Vertragslaufzeit für Bauunterhalt und Betrieb der öffentlichen Einrichtung verantwortlich ist, besteht die Möglichkeit, hierfür leistungsorientierte Vergütungsmechanismen zu vereinbaren. Der PPP-Vertragspartner erhält seine Vergütung regelmäßig qualitäts-, nutzungs- bzw. verfügbarkeitsabhängig. Werden auftretende Baumängel oder Betriebsstörungen nicht innerhalb konkret vereinbarter Reaktionszeiten beseitigt, kommt es zu vertraglich geregelten Entgeltkürzungen. Um einen Anreiz für weitergehende Optimierungen zu schaffen, können z.B. auch Bonus-/Malus-Regelungen zum Einsatz kommen.

3.4 Vorteile von PPP-Konzepten für die öffentliche Hand

Vorteile von PPP-Konzepten für die öffentliche Hand bestehen demnach in der

- Senkung der Gesamtkosten einer öffentlichen Immobilie über den gesamten Lebenszyklus,
- Transparenz und Nachprüfbarkeit sämtlicher Projektkosten über die komplette Vertragslaufzeit,
- zeitnahen Realisierung von öffentlichen Investitionsvorhaben gegen periodisch zu entrichtendes Entgelt, ohne den sofortigen Einsatz der gesamten (Bau-) Investitionsmittel,
- langfristigen Instandhaltung/Qualitätssicherung von öffentlichen Einrichtungen über konkret vereinbarte Qualitätsstandards (Service Level Agreements) während der gesamten Vertragslaufzeit,
- Begrenzung des Risikos von notwendigen Nutzungsänderungen zum Vertragsende (z.B. PPP-Partner übernimmt Folgenutzung eines wegen rückläufigen Schülerzahlen nicht mehr benötigten Schulgebäudes),

– Möglichkeit für den öffentlichen Auftraggeber, sich zukünftig nur auf seine Kernaufgaben zu konzentrieren, womit ggf. eine Verschlankung der öffentlichen Verwaltung einhergehen kann.

3.5 Skepsis von öffentlicher Hand gegenüber PPP-Konzepten unbegründet

PPP-Modell keine verschleierte Verschuldung – Kommunalkreditaufnahme ist auch Verschuldung

Sollte das PPP-Konzept auch die Finanzierung des Projekts umfassen, wird immer wieder angebracht, dass dies zu einer verschleierten Verschuldung („Schattenhaushalt“) neben dem offiziellen öffentlichen Haushalt führe. Hierbei wird aber außer Acht gelassen, dass auch bei herkömmlicher Haushaltsfinanzierung einer öffentlichen Investitionsmaßnahme ein öffentlicher Kredit aufgenommen werden muss, bei dem es sich ebenfalls um eine Schuldenaufnahme des öffentlichen Auftraggebers handelt.

Ggf. höhere Finanzierungskosten werden bei einem PPP-Konzept mehr als ausgeglichen, da sonst nicht wirtschaftlicher

Gegen PPP-Projekte wird oft das Argument höherer Finanzierungskosten vorgebracht, da der PPP-Vertragspartner keine Kommunalkreditkonditionen erhalte. Unabhängig davon, dass es mittlerweile PPP-Finanzierungskonzepte gibt, die Kommunalkreditkonditionen erreichen, fließen ggf. erhöhte Finanzierungskosten in die Gesamtkalkulation der PPP-Variante ein, die beim abschließenden Wirtschaftlichkeitsvergleich insgesamt günstiger sein muss als die herkömmliche Haushaltsfinanzierung. Darüber hinaus wird die positive Anreizfunktion der vom PPP-Vertragspartner zu tragenden Zinsen für die Zwischenfinanzierung, nämlich ein Beschleunigungsanliegen, auf Bauablauf und Bauzeit vielfach unterschätzt.

Risiko aus Insolvenz des PPP-Vertragspartners überschaubar und absicherbar

Gerät tatsächlich der PPP-Projektpartner während der Bauunterhalts-/Betriebsphase in Insolvenz, besteht das Risiko für die öffentliche Hand lediglich in den Mehrkosten für die Suche eines neuen Vertragspartners oder für die Eigenübernahme seitens des öffentlichen Auftraggebers. Dieses Risiko kann im PPP-Projektvertrag entsprechend abgesichert werden (insbesondere durch Bürgschaften oder durch den Abschluss einer Betreiberausfallversicherung).

Zukünftige Einflussnahmemöglichkeit des öffentlichen Partners vertraglich regelbar

Gegen PPP-Konzepte wird auch eingewendet, dass sich die öffentliche Hand auf Jahre ihrer Einflussmöglichkeiten auf Bauunterhalt und Betrieb eines Bauwerks begebe. Auch hier besteht die Möglichkeit, durch Vertragsgestaltung dem öffentlichen Auftraggeber entsprechende Einflussmöglichkeiten (z.B. durch einen Beirat) einzuräumen bzw. zu erhalten. Erhöhte Einflussnahmemöglichkeiten des öffentlichen Partners können aber zu einer Verteuerung des Projekts führen.

Derzeit noch erhöhte Transaktionskosten werden durch Standardisierung etc. gesenkt

Zutreffend ist, dass die Komplexität von PPP-Projekten derzeit noch erhöhte Transaktionskosten auslöst. Diese sollen jedoch durch Leitfäden, weitere Informationsbroschüren, entsprechende Vereinheitlichung und Standardisierung, z.B. von Vergabe- und Vertragsunterlagen, weiter gesenkt werden.

3.6 Abschaffung der Kameralistik zugunsten eines kaufmännischen Rechnungswesens mit doppelter Buchführung und Vermögensbewertung dringend erforderlich

Die Kameralistik ist überholt.

Sie ist nicht mehr als ein „erweitertes Kassenbuch". Früher war es nicht notwendig, Vermögen den Schulden gegenüber zu stellen und einen Saldo zu bilden. Das Netto-Vermögen (Vermögen minus Schulden) konnte immer nur positiv – also verantwortbar – sein. Das Nachhaltigkeitsgebot ist dann erfüllt, wenn die öffentliche Hand nachweisen kann, dass ihr Vermögen gestiegen oder zumindest gleich geblieben ist. Das ist exakt die gleiche Aussage wie Gewinn oder Verlust, also nichts anderes als das Bilanzergebnis in einem Unternehmen.

Kaufmännisches Rechnungswesen erleichtert die Zusammenarbeit zwischen öffentlicher Hand und Privatwirtschaft (PPP)

Nur eine kaufmännische Rechnung vergleicht sinnvoll die Kosten privater Zurverfügungstellung öffentlicher Infrastruktur mit den Kosten der Bereitstellung durch die öffentliche Hand selbst. Bei PPP-Modellen z.B. wird immer wieder bemerkt, die öffentliche Hand könne das billiger. Solange die öffentliche Hand kameralistisch Rechnung legt, ist diese Aussage richtig. Wenn die öffentliche Hand Abschreibungen, Rückstellungen für künftige Reparaturen und echte Zinskosten nicht rechnet, ist sie im Vergleich zur Privatwirtschaft auf dem Papier tatsächlich billiger. Hätte die öffentliche Hand gleiche Rechnungslegungsmethoden wie Unternehmen, müsste sie sich einem ehrlichen Vergleich stellen. Die private Wirtschaft glaubt, die öffentliche Hand würde den Wirtschaftlichkeitsvergleich von herkömmlicher Haushaltsrealisierung und PPP-Konzept meistens verlieren, aber letztlich zum Gewinner werden, weil sie die Bereitstellung öffentlicher Einrichtungen/Infrastruktur vom Privaten insgesamt kostengünstiger erhält als bei herkömmlicher Eigenrealisierung.

4 Chancen von PPP für die Bauwirtschaft

Wird eine öffentliche Investitionsmaßnahme im Wege eines PPP-Konzepts in Angriff genommen, die bei herkömmlicher Haushaltsfinanzierung derzeit keine Chance auf Realisierung hätte, wird damit zusätzliches Bauvolumen generiert. Hiervon profitiert der Bieter, der sich im Vergabeverfahren erfolgreich durchsetzt und den Zuschlag für dieses PPP-Projekt erhält. Wenn sich dann dieser erfolgreiche Unternehmer aufgrund entsprechender Kapazitätsauslastung an weiteren „normalen“ Ausschreibungsverfahren für gewisse Zeit nicht beteiligt, profitieren hiervon auch Bauunternehmen, die sich an PPP-Projekten nicht beteiligen.

Ist ein Bauunternehmen in ein PPP-Projekt eingebunden – auf der ersten Ebene i.d.R. innerhalb einer Arbeitsgemeinschaft von mehreren Unternehmen oder auf der zweiten Ebene als Nachunternehmer – trägt das PPP-Projekt zur Stärkung bestehender Geschäftsfelder vor allem hinsichtlich der Kernkompetenz „Bauen“ bei. Im Rahmen von PPP-Projekten besteht aber gerade auch die Möglichkeit, sich neue strategische Geschäftsfelder (z.B. Planungsaufgaben, Facility Management) zu erschließen und in diesen Tätigkeitsbereichen neue Kompetenzen aufzubauen.

Da für PPP-Maßnahmen i.d.R. sehr langfristige Projektverträge (von zehn bis zu dreißig Jahren) abgeschlossen werden, ist damit für den PPP-Vertragspartner die Generierung konstanter Cashflows und eine Verstetigung von Erträgen – auch in Krisenzeiten – verbunden.

Im Bereich der Vergabe öffentlicher Bauaufträge leidet die Bauwirtschaft seit Jahrzehnten unter der fast regelmäßigen Billigstpreisvergabe, die zu den bekannten ruinösen Wettbewerbsverhältnissen im Baubereich geführt hat. Branchenpolitisch bietet PPP die Chance, den bisherigen reinen Preiswettbewerb in einen Qualitätswettbewerb zu überführen, bei dem die Bietereignung (Fachkunde, Leistungsfähigkeit und Zuverlässigkeit) und die Zuschlagserteilung auf das unter Lebenszykluskosten letztendlich wirtschaftlichste Angebot die entscheidenden Wettbewerbskriterien sind. Mittelfristig kann sich die Bauwirtschaft von einer rein nachfrage- zu einer stärker angebotsorientierten Branche entwickeln.

5 Risiken von PPP für die Bauwirtschaft

Im Gegensatz zur herkömmlichen Angebotsbearbeitung (Kalkulation eines detaillierten Leistungsverzeichnisses) ist die Bearbeitung eines Angebots für ein PPP-Vorhaben wesentlich komplexer und erheblich arbeitsaufwändiger. Zu der Kalkulation der Bauleistungen treten bei einem umfassenden („echten“) PPP-Projekt Planungsaufgaben, Konzipierung und Kalkulation der Bauunterhalts-/ Betriebsphase sowie Fragen der Finanzierung hinzu. Das führt zu erheblich höheren Angebots- und Transaktionskosten, die bei Nichterhalt des Auftrags umsonst aufgewendet worden sind. Sofern der öffentliche Auftraggeber einen Kostenersatz für die erfolglosen Bieter in der Ausschreibung vorgesehen hat, deckt dieser regelmäßig nur einen kleinen Prozentsatz der tatsächlich angefallenen Angebotskosten ab.

Die langen Projektlaufzeiten von PPP-Maßnahmen bringen die Gefahr mit sich, dass sich Fehlkalkulationen (z.B. die Vernachlässigung oder fehlerhafte Einschätzung eines übernommenen Projektrisikos) über Jahre finanziell negativ auswirken.

Das (Bau-)Unternehmen, das sich an einem PPP-Vorhaben beteiligt, muss sich darüber bewusst sein, dass personelle und finanzielle Ressourcen des Unternehmens langfristig gebunden werden oder auch Investitionen für den Aufbau neuer Geschäftsbereiche getätigt werden müssen.

Ferner muss sich das (Bau-)Unternehmen der Risiken bewusst sein, die sich aus der Übernahme neuer Aufgabenfelder (z.B. Bauunterhalts-/ Betriebsleistungen) oder aus veränderten Beteiligungs- und Haftungsstrukturen (z.B. gesellschaftsrechtliche Beteiligung an der PPP-Projektgesellschaft) ergeben.

Schließlich kann die Beteiligung an einem PPP-Projekt für das (Bau-) Unternehmen auch späte Gewinnentnahmen bedeuten.

All diese Risiken müssen unternehmensseitig betrachtet und in den Entscheidungsprozess, sich zukünftig an PPP-Projekten zu beteiligen, mit einbezogen werden.

6 PPP-Projekte als wachsendes Betätigungsfeld für mittelständische Unternehmen

Nach einer aktuellen Untersuchung des Deutschen Instituts für Urbanistik (Difu) in Kooperation mit dem Institut für Site und Facility Management GmbH (ISFM) sind mittelständische Unternehmen überproportional stark als (Haupt-) Auftragnehmer an kleineren PPP-Projekten beteiligt. Bei größeren Projekten sind sie vor allem als Nachunternehmer „in der zweiten Reihe" einbezogen. Auf der zweiten und folgenden Ebene übernehmen sie durchschnittlich 70 bis 80 % der Arbeiten. Deutlich mehr als die Hälfte der durch diese Projekte erzielten Wertschöpfung bleibt in der jeweiligen Region.

Die Ergebnisse der Studie zeigen einerseits, dass die These der „Mittelstandsfeindlichkeit" von PPP nicht aufrechterhalten werden kann, dass aber andererseits durchaus Verbesserungspotenziale in der mittelstandsgerechten Ausgestaltung der PPP-Projekte bestehen.

Die immer wieder geäußerte Vermutung, dass es einen Zusammenhang zwischen Projektvolumen und Mittelstandsbeteiligung gebe, konnte trotz der vergleichsweise kleinen Zahl untersuchter Projekte (30) statistisch bestätigt werden. In großen Projekten finden sich praktisch keine mittelständischen Unternehmen als Hauptauftragnehmer, auch nicht als Partner in Konsortien. Dafür sind mittelständische Betriebe als (Haupt-)Auftragnehmer an kleineren PPP-Projekten überproportional stark beteiligt. Der (weiche) Schwellenwert, bis zu dem die Projekte mittelstandsgeeignet erscheinen, liegt nach der Studie jedoch nicht bei den vielfach in Fachliteratur und Praxis genannten zehn Millionen, sondern bei etwa 15 Millionen Euro. Die Hälfte aller untersuchten Projekte weist ein geringeres Investitionsvolumen als 15 Millionen Euro auf. Das entspricht etwa dem bundesweiten Durchschnitt. Gleichzeitig sind damit auch in 47 % der Projekte mittelständische Betriebe als Hauptauftragnehmer zum Zuge gekommen, entweder als Beteiligte an den Bieterkonsortien oder (in sechs Fällen) als alleinige PPP-Auftragnehmer.

Die Ergebnisse der Untersuchung weisen auch auf Optimierungspotenziale im Hinblick auf die mittelstandsgerechte Ausgestaltung von PPP-Projekten hin:

- die Bereitstellung von Informationen im Vorfeld einer Ausschreibung (z. B. Workshops, Informationsveranstaltungen, ausführliche Online-Informationen) und von Bietermemoranden als Ergänzung zur reinen Bekanntmachung,
- die detaillierte Darstellung der Ausgangssituation (inklusive der Zustandsbeschreibung bei Sanierungsprojekten),
- die angemessene Terminierung der Ausschreibungsfristen insbesondere bei Umbau- und Sanierungsobjekten über die vergaberechtlichen Mindestfristen hinaus,
- die vertragliche Festlegung einer angemessenen Beteiligung von mittelständischen Unternehmen als Nachunternehmer sowie ein besseres
- Controlling der Nachunternehmerbeteiligung nach der Auftragsvergabe.

7 Bayerisches Merkblatt „Kleine mittelstandsfreundliche PPP-Projekte"

Unabhängig von diesen Untersuchungsergebnissen wurden in Bayern diese Belange mittelständischer Unternehmen bei PPP-Projekten besonders aufgegriffen. In einer von der „Gesprächsrunde PPP" (Federführung Oberste Baubehörde im Bayerischen Staatsministerium des Innern) und dem von ihr eingesetzten Ad hoc-Arbeitskreis „Kleine mittelstandsfreundliche PPP-Projekte" (Geschäftsführung Bayerischer Bauindustrieverband) herausgegebenen Sonderveröffentlichung wird unter Berücksichtigung der speziellen Mittelstandsbelange hierzu wie folgt Stellung genommen:

Die Rahmenbedingungen richtig setzen – Hinweise für den Auftraggeber

- Projektvolumen, Finanzierungs- und Transaktionskosten
- Informationsmemorandum
- Bietergemeinschaften
- Bewertung der Bewerbungen und Angebote
- Fristen
- Angebotskosten
- Ausstiegsklausel
- Sonderzahlung
- Besicherung

Das Unternehmen richtig aufstellen – Hinweise für Bieter/Auftragnehmer

- Partnerschaften und Netzwerke bilden
- Unternehmensinterne Organisation an PPP ausrichten

- Kompetenzen aneignen
  - Planungsleistungen
  - Bauleistungen
  - Betriebsleistungen
  - Finanzierungsleistungen
- Lebenszykluskalkulation
- Finanzielle Voraussetzungen für PPP-Projekte schaffen
- Förderkredite einbinden
- Risikomanagement betreiben
- PPP-Erfahrungen sammeln

8 Fazit

Von Victor Hugo stammt das Zitat: „Nichts auf der Welt ist so mächtig wie eine Idee, deren Zeit gekommen ist".

Der Autor ist der festen Überzeugung, dass sich PPP in Deutschland wie auch in Bayern in naher Zukunft in den geeigneten Fällen als „ganz normale" alternative Beschaffungsvariante der öffentlichen Hand durchsetzen wird.

PPP im Staatlichen Hochbau Bayerns – Pilotprojekte und Beratung der Kommunen

Gabriele Engel

Inhaltsverzeichnis

Keywords

Architektenwettbewerb, Bauherrenfunktion, Bauunterhalt, Bayerischer PPP-Leitfaden, Bayerischer Weg, Betreibermodell, Effizienzvorteil, Genehmigungsplanung, Gestaltungskonzept, Justizvollzugsanstalten, Kommunales Forum, Lebenszyklus, Machbarkeitsstudie, PPP-AG Bayern, Probebetrieb, Projektabwicklung, Projekteignungstest, Qualitätssicherung, Referenzobjekt, Risikostruktur, Risikoverteilung, Sachverständiger, Transparenz, Verjährungsfrist für Mängelansprüche, Vertragsbedingungen, Vertragscontrolling, Wirtschaftlichkeit, Wirtschaftlichkeitsuntersuchung

1 Einführung

Wenn in Deutschland von Public Private Partnership – PPP – die Rede ist, bekommen manche leuchtende Augen, weil sie einen ihrer Meinung nach unterentwickelten Markt sehen, der großartige Chancen biete, während andere abwehrend die Hände heben, weil PPP nur für die Banken und vor allem die großen Unternehmen gut sei. Vertreter der Wirtschaft fordern, der Staat solle sich zurückziehen, während bereits einige Kommunen privatisierte Aufgaben zurückholen und wieder in öffentlicher Hand erledigen. Die einen sprechen vornehmlich von den Chancen und Vorteilen, die anderen vornehmlich von den Risiken und Nachteilen.

Wir – die Bayerische Staatsbauverwaltung – wollten es genauer wissen und haben daher im Jahr 2004 eine Struktur geschaffen, die wir den Bayerischen Weg nennen. Sie besteht aus dem Bayerischen Kooperationsmodell, in dem wir eine Reihe von Kooperationspartnern in einer Organisation zusammenfassen und welches selbst ein PPP-Modell ist. Vertreter staatlicher und kommunaler Behörden, der kommunalen Spitzenverbände und von Wirtschaftsverbänden haben sich zusammengefunden, um eine gemeinsame Haltung zu PPP zu erarbeiten und die Entwicklung von PPP in Bayern zu begleiten. Der ständige Diskussionsprozess gewährleistet, dass Chancen und Risiken gleichermaßen in den Blick genommen werden und damit die Haltung zu PPP ausgewogen bleibt.

Darüber hinaus ist es wichtig, eigene Erfahrungen zu sammeln. So führt die Bayerische Staatsbauverwaltung eine Reihe eigener Projekte im Hochbau und im Straßenbau durch. Aus dieser Erfahrung heraus sind wir in der Lage, die bayerischen Kommunen bei ihren Projekten zu unterstützen.

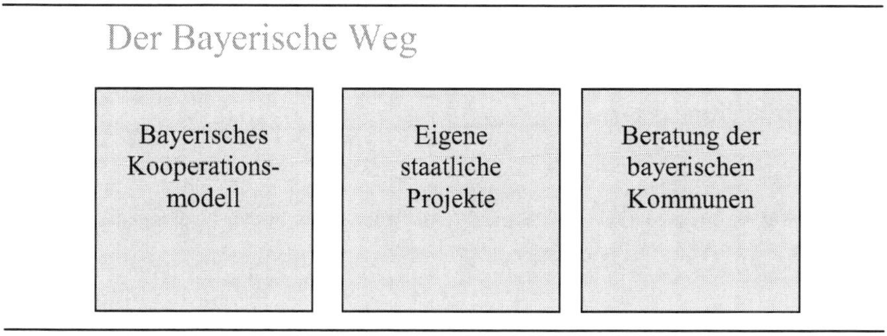

Abb. 1: Der Bayerische Weg
Quelle: eigene Darstellung.

2 Staatliche Projekte

Der Freistaat Bayern führt zur Zeit 11 PPP-Projekte durch. Davon sind 10 Pilotprojekte, also solche, deren Ablauf besonders dokumentiert und ausgewertet wird. Es handelt sich um 2 Hochbauprojekte (Justizvollzugsanstalten) und 8 Straßenbauprojekte, nämlich 7 Staatsstraßen und Brücken sowie die Autobahn A8 als Vorhaben des Bundes. Ein weiteres Projekt ist in Vorbereitung. Die beiden staatlichen Hochbauprojekte sollen hier dargestellt werden.

Mit den Pilotprojekten sollen Erfahrungen mit den Instrumenten und Funktionsweisen einer Public Private Partnership als Beschaffungsvariante hinsichtlich einer ganzheitlichen Projektbetrachtung – Lebenszyklus – gemacht und in Vergleich zu konventionell realisierten Maßnahmen gesetzt werden. Wichtig sind dabei u. a. Erkenntnisse über Vor- und Nachteile in Bezug auf den Personal- und Arbeitsaufwand, über die erforderlichen Organisationsstrukturen und Arbeitsschritte in den einzelnen Projektphasen sowie über die Zusammenarbeit zwischen Bauverwaltung, Nutzer und privatem Partner.

Mit den Neubauten für die Justizvollzugsanstalten München und Augsburg realisiert die Staatsbauverwaltung Pilotprojekte im Bereich des Hochbaus, bei denen erstmals private Partner Aufgabenfelder der öffentlichen Hand aus dem gesamten Lebenszyklus eines Gebäudes übernehmen, und zwar über einen Zeitraum von 20 Jahren.

2.1 Justizvollzugsanstalt München – Neubau eines Frauengefängnisses und einer Jugendarrestanstalt

Mit diesem Pilotprojekt des bayerischen Justizvollzugs erhält die Justizvollzugsanstalt München in unmittelbarer Nähe zur Stammanstalt Stadelheim für ihre Frauenabteilung 160 neue Haftplätze (davon 10 in einer Mutter-Kind-Abteilung) sowie 60 Plätze in einer neuen Jugendarrestanstalt. Ein privater Partner übernimmt die Planung, den Bau und die Finanzierung des Gebäudes sowie den Betrieb der technischen Anlagen einschließlich der Bereitstellung der Energie (Wärme, Strom) und die Abwasserentsorgung; weiterhin in öffentlicher Hand bleiben dagegen sämtliche vollzugliche und somit hoheitliche Aufgaben sowie der übrige Bauunterhalt.

Die Herausforderung für die Vergabestelle – das staatliche Bauamt – bestand darin, in einem frühen und im Verhältnis zur Vertragslaufzeit sehr kurzen Zeitraum alle erforderlichen und über viele Jahre wirksamen Eckdaten mit einem maximal möglichen Grad an Verbindlichkeit zu definieren und in einer Leistungsbeschreibung mit Leistungsprogramm ergebnisorientiert auszuschreiben. Diese Phase erfordert besondere Aufmerksamkeit und ein intensives Zusammenarbeiten innerhalb des Bauamtes und mit dem Nutzer, da hier die Weichen für den späteren Projektverlauf und schließlich für den Erfolg oder Misserfolg des Projekts gestellt werden: Was hier vergessen wird, kann der Auftraggeber später nicht – kostenneutral – fordern.

Nach der Durchführung eines öffentlichen EU-weiten Teilnahmewettbewerbs im August 2004, eines nichtoffenen Verfahrens und eines anschließenden Verhandlungsverfahrens wurde der Auftrag im März 2006 erteilt. Damit ging die Bauherrenfunktion vertragsgemäß auf den Auftragnehmer über, so dass nunmehr die Genehmigungsplanung auf Basis des vorab vom Bauamt erwirkten Vorbescheids zu erarbeiten war. Ende Januar 2007 konnte der Auftragnehmer mit der Vorbereitung des Geländes beginnen und im Mai 2007 die Grundsteinlegung für den Neubau durchführen. An die Baufertigstellung, die für Herbst 2008 vorgesehen ist, schließt sich ein zweimonatiger Probebetrieb an, ehe schließlich die Betriebsphase beginnt.

Insgesamt hat sich bei dem Projekt – bedingt durch ein Nachprüfungsverfahren im Teilnahmewettbewerb und die Aufhebung des nichtoffenen Verfahrens – eine relativ lange Vorlaufzeit von ca. 27 Monaten bis zur Auftragserteilung ergeben; im Gegenzug ist jedoch eine im Vergleich zu konventionellen Verfahren kürzere Bauzeit zu beobachten, u. a. weil der Auftragnehmer keine Vergaben nach VOB/A durchführen muss und darauf bedacht ist, die Zwischenfinanzierungskosten möglichst gering zu halten.

Bis auf die Erstellung des Wirtschaftlichkeitsvergleichs, der vor Auftragserteilung von einem externen Büro verfasst wurde, lag bzw. liegt die gesamte Projektabwicklung – also sämtliche Vorbereitungsarbeiten, die Erstellung der Vergabeunterlagen, die Wertung und schließlich die Projektsteuerung nach Auftragserteilung – vollständig in der Hand der staatlichen Bauverwaltung. Dies ermöglicht über den gesamten Projektverlauf eine genaue Beobachtung und Dokumentation der Vor- und Nachteile. Die ersten Erfahrungen zeigen, dass entgegen der oftmals geäußerten Erwartung, dass PPP-Projekte eine Reduzierung des Aufwandes auf Auftraggeberseite bedingen würden, gerade die Besonderheiten eines PPP-Verfahrens zu einem mit konventionellen Verfahren vergleichbaren Aufwand führen: Vor Auftragserteilung erfordert die Komplexität der Ausschreibung einschließlich der Wertung eine besonders hohe fachliche und personelle Konzentration, nach Auftragserteilung führt der Vertrag auf Grundlage des Angebotes zu einem zeitaufwändigen Vertragscontrolling, für das wiederum ein ganzes Projektteam zur Verfügung stehen muss – und zwar für die gesamte Laufzeit des Vertrages.

2.2 Justizvollzugsanstalt Augsburg

Mit dem Neubau für die Justizvollzugsanstalt Augsburg führt der Freistaat Bayern ein weiteres PPP-Projekt durch, bei dem nun auf die bei der Justizvollzugsanstalt München gewonnenen Erfahrungen zurückgegriffen werden kann. Wesentliche Unterschiede bestehen im Projektumfang – er ist deutlich größer – sowie in der Projektgeschichte: Die Neubaumaßnahme sollte zuerst als konventionelle staatliche Maßnahme durchgeführt werden.

Hierfür wurde im Jahr 2004 ein Architektenwettbewerb durchgeführt, den das Architekturbüro Schuster aus Düsseldorf für sich entscheiden konnte. Etwa eineinhalb Jahre später – inmitten der Planungsphase – fiel die Entscheidung, die staatliche Maßnahme in ein PPP-Projekt umzuwandeln. Die bis dahin weitgehend fertig gestellten Planungen wurden zu Ende geführt. Die Gebäudeplanung wurde als verbindliche Grundlage in der PPP-Ausschreibung vorgegeben. Damit werden im Gegensatz zur Justizvollzugsanstalt München die Planungsleistungen des Entwurfs nicht mehr Bestandteil der Ausschreibung; die übrigen Komponenten der Planung, die Finanzierungs- und Bauleistungen sowie der Betrieb der technischen Anlagen werden jedoch vom künftigen Auftragnehmer zu erbringen sein, so dass man auch bei diesem Projekt aufgrund des Lebenszyklusansatzes von einem ‚echten' PPP-Projekt sprechen kann. Die Angebote der Bieter wurden im Mai vorgelegt. Der weitere Projektverlauf wird sich nach dem Ergebnis des Vergabeverfahrens – es handelt sich um ein Verhandlungsverfahren – richten.

2.3 Absichten und Ziele – Vertragsbedingungen

Aus den Vertragsbedingungen, die unsere Absichten und Ziele widerspiegeln, sollen beispielhaft die Risikoverteilung und die Qualitätssicherung herausgegriffen und anhand der Justizvollzugsanstalt München erläutert werden.

2.3.1 Risikoverteilung

Identifikation, Definition und Zuweisung der wesentlichen Risiken eines langfristigen Projekts im Rahmen einer öffentlich-privaten Partnerschaft stellen einen entscheidenden Einflussfaktor für Projektverlauf, Projektkosten und Projekteffizienz dar. Nur eine beiden Vertragspartnern entsprechende und von diesen tragbare Risikostruktur kann zu einem ausgewogenen Projekt führen, was sich schließlich in der Wirtschaftlichkeit zeigen wird. Risiken, die der Auftragnehmer nicht oder nur schwer kalkulieren kann, sollten nicht übertragen werden, da dies nur zu hohen Kosten führt. Die „klassischen" Risiken, die mit der Erbringung der Planungs-, Bau- und Betreiberleistungen verbunden sind (wie Kosten und Termine), übernimmt der private Partner aufgrund der hohen Professionalisierung, die von ihm erwartet wird. Unabhängig davon ist die Risikostruktur eines jeden Projekts individuell zu konzipieren.

Für die Justizvollzugsanstalt München hat das Bauamt im Rahmen der Vorbereitung der Ausschreibung eine Machbarkeitsstudie erarbeitet und einen Vorbescheid als Grundlage der späteren Genehmigungsplanung erwirkt. Da es keinen qualifizierten Bebauungsplan gibt (wie z.B. für die Justizvollzuganstalt Augsburg), war dies die einzige Möglichkeit, das Genehmigungsrisiko für den Bieter kalkulierbar zu machen. Die Risiken aus dem Baugrund und aus Altlasten wurden dem Auftragnehmer so weit übertragen, wie sie aus den vom Bauamt zur Verfügung gestellten Gutachten erkennbar waren. Entstehen weitere Leistungen, bezahlt der Auftraggeber die anfallenden Kosten gesondert.

Während der Betriebsphase hat der Auftragnehmer für die Energieversorgung und für die einwandfreie Funktion der technischen Anlagen zu sorgen. Um zu vermeiden, dass Betriebsstörungen zu Sicherheitsproblemen in der Justizvollzugsanstalt führen, muss der Auftragnehmer solche Störungen innerhalb festgelegter Fristen beseitigen. Diese sogenannten Eingreifzeiten sind Vertragsbestandteil.

Das Auslastungsrisiko trägt dagegen der Auftraggeber. Nach der Erfahrung der vergangenen Jahre sind die bayerischen Justizvollzugsanstalten eher überbelegt als unterbelegt. Daher geht der Vertrag von einer vollständig belegten Anstalt einschließlich einer 10%igen Überbelegung aus. Steigt die Überbelegung darüber hinaus, ändert sich der Preis. Dieser war im Angebot anzugeben. Eine Unterbelegung von maximal 10% führt nicht zu einer Preisänderung. Eine weitere Unterbelegung ist nicht zu erwarten und bleibt daher unberücksichtigt. Das Risiko aus Gesetzesänderungen wurde ebenfalls nicht übertragen, da sich keine konkreten Prozesse abzeichneten, die den Bietern als ausreichende Kalkulationsgrundlage hätten dienen können.

2.3.2 Qualitätssicherung

Die Qualitätssicherung ist im Rahmen der Ausschreibung eines PPP-Projekts von besonderer Bedeutung, da die Einflussmöglichkeiten des Auftraggebers in die laufende Planung bzw. Bauausführung oder gar in die Art des Betriebs gering sind. Daher müssen Qualitätsansprüche für alle Leistungsbereiche – Planung, Bau, Betrieb – vorab definiert und die Instrumente zur Umsetzung in den Vergabeunterlagen festgelegt werden. Im vorliegenden Fall wurde versucht, mithilfe mehrerer Bausteine eine zuverlässige und ausreichende Regelung zu treffen. Ziel sollte sein, eine Art sich selbstregulierendes Qualitätssicherungssystem – Erzeugung und Erhaltung von Qualität im Interesse des Auftragnehmers – mit mehreren Komponenten herzustellen und damit den Personalaufwand auf Auftraggeberseite zu minimieren – gewünschter Effekt der Beschaffungsvariante PPP.

– Die Vergabe des Bauunterhaltes, hier zumindest für die technischen Anlagen, bietet einen guten Ansatz zur Selbstregulierung, da die gesamte Kostenverantwortung für die Dauer der Vertragslaufzeit von 20 Jahren, also sowohl für die Investition als auch für den Betrieb dieser Investition, gewissermaßen vollständig im Verantwortungsbereich des Auftragnehmers liegt.

- Für einige Gewerke (z.B. Dächer, erdberührte Bauteile, Fassaden) wurde die Verjährungsfrist für Mängclansprüche verlängert, da – wie oben erwähnt – eine Vergabe des gesamten Bauunterhalts nicht vorgesehen war.
- Weitere Bausteine der Qualitätssicherung sind die Durchführung von Bemusterungen sowie die Vorlage von Gestaltungskonzepten oder auch ein ständiges Betretungsrecht der Baustelle und damit die Möglichkeit der stichprobenartigen Baukontrollen durch den Auftraggeber.
- Ein vom Auftragnehmer beauftragter externer Sachverständiger hat zu überwachen und zu dokumentieren, dass die vereinbarten Leistungen vertragsgemäß erbracht werden. Auf diese Weise soll die Kontrollverantwortung des Auftraggebers durch die Nachweispflicht des Auftragnehmers ersetzt werden.
- Weiterhin wurden einzelne technische Details vorgegeben, z.B. im Bereich der Sicherheitstechnik, da hier unabdingbare Anforderungen bzw. Mindeststandards nicht zur Diskussion und damit nicht ins Ermessen des Auftragnehmers gestellt werden konnten.
- Zuletzt wurde für den Fall, dass sich trotz aller Vereinbarungen hinsichtlich der gewünschten Qualitäten während der Planungs- und Bauzeit Streitpunkte ergeben, ein Referenzobjekt festgelegt, dessen Qualitäts- und Ausstattungsstandard als Entscheidungsmaßstab für die Ausführung einzelner Bauteile dienen soll.

Weitere Informationen zum Projekt sind auf der Internetseite www.ppp.bayern.de bereitgestellt.

2.4 Wirtschaftlichkeitsuntersuchungen

Um zu prüfen, ob ein PPP-Projekt wirtschaftlich sein kann, ist eine Wirtschaftlichkeitsuntersuchung durchzuführen, für die ein von allen Bundesländern erarbeiteter Leitfaden (www.ppp-bund.de) als unverbindliche Arbeitshilfe mit Empfehlungscharakter vorliegt. Er kann von Kommunen ebenso genutzt werden wie von staatlichen Stellen. Für die Ermittlung des staatlichen Vergleichswerts können wir für die Justizvollzugsanstalten auf Datenbanken zurückgreifen, in denen die abgerechneten Investitionskosten ebenso gut dokumentiert sind wie die Betriebskosten. Abgerechnete Kosten bzw. tatsächlich angefallene Kosten beinhalten nach unserer Auffassung alle (normalen) projektbezogenen Risiken. Daher sind Risikokosten nur dann noch gesondert zu veranschlagen, wenn das Projekt solche besonderen Risiken aufweist.

Zum Einstieg in die Wirtschaftlichkeitsuntersuchung ist ein Projekteignungstest erforderlich. Dafür hat Bayern ein Werkzeug entwickelt, das im ersten Teil des bayerischen PPP-Leitfadens enthalten ist – den bayerischen Projekteignungstest. Danach ist zunächst anhand qualitativer Kriterien zu prüfen, ob das Projekt grundsätzlich geeignet ist. Erst danach findet der quantitative Test statt, der das Ergebnis des qualitativen Tests begleitet. Es kommt also nicht darauf an, zunächst einen (möglichst hohen) Effizienzvorteil auszuweisen. Nach dem bayerischen Haushaltsrecht sind seit 1994 Aufgaben und Einrichtungen „in geeigneten Fällen darauf zu untersuchen, ob und in welchem Umfang die Tätigkeit durch nichtstaatliche Stellen, insbesondere durch private Dritte oder unter Heranziehung Dritter, ebenso gut oder besser erledigt werden kann" (Art 7. Bayerische Haushaltsordnung – Entsprechendes gilt im kommunalen Haushaltsrecht).

Im Zusammenhang mit PPP werden Effizienzvorteile mitunter bis auf die zweite Kommastelle ausgewiesen. Dies erweckt den Anschein großer Genauigkeit, obwohl es sich bei den Wirtschaftlichkeitsuntersuchungen von PPP-Projekten immer nur um den Vergleich eines im Wettbewerb kalkulierten verbindlichen Angebotes – also eines Marktpreises – mit einer (theoretischen) Kostenschätzung bzw. -berechnung für die konventionelle Eigenrealisierung handeln kann. Zudem sind nicht alle Entwicklungen während der Vertragslaufzeit mit Sicherheit absehbar. Die zu Beginn des Projekts bzw. nach der Submission durchgeführte Wirtschaftlichkeitsuntersuchung ist also eine Momentaufnahme. Ob sich die Annahmen in dieser frühen Phase des Projekts als zutreffend erweisen, kann erst am Ende der Vertragslaufzeit festgestellt werden.

3 Beratung der Kommunen

Im kommunalen Bereich werden seit vielen Jahren kleinere und größere Projekte mit unterschiedlichen privatwirtschaftlichen Elementen durchgeführt. Die Kommunen haben dabei eine beachtliche Kreativität entwickelt. So sind die Betreibermodelle, die man als Vorläufer von PPP bezeichnen kann (vielleicht meinen sie auch das gleiche), eine häufig praktizierte Form der Realisierung öffentlicher Infrastrukturaufgaben. Seit 1991 gibt es dazu eine 7-seitige und seit 2001 eine 13-seitige Bekanntmachung der Bayerischen Staatsministerien zu privatwirtschaftlichen Realisierungsformen.

Die kommunalen PPP-Projekte sind vorwiegend Schulen, Bildungs-, Sport- und Freizeit- sowie Ver- und Entsorgungseinrichtungen. Es handelt sich also häufig um Projekte, bei denen zumindest ein Teil der Finanzierung durch die Nutzer jener Einrichtungen geleistet wird. Kommunale PPP-Projekte sind in erster Linie kleine Projekte. Nach einer Umfrage, die wir Ende 2006 durchgeführt haben, haben etwa 2/3 der kommunalen Projekte ein Gesamtvolumen von unter 10 Mio. €. Darin sind mindestens drei Lebenszyklusphasen enthalten, von denen eine der Betrieb ist.

3.1 Der Bayerische PPP-Leitfaden

Im März 2004 lud die Bayerische Staatsregierung unter der Leitung der Obersten Baubehörde Vertreter der öffentlichen Hand sowie der Bauwirtschaft und des Kreditgewerbes ein, um mit ihnen über Public Private Partnership bei der Realisierung von öffentlichen Baumaßnahmen in Bayern zu sprechen und eine gemeinsame Position zu erarbeiten. Daraus entstand der Bayerische Weg (vgl. Abb. 1 und 2). Diese OBB-Gesprächsrunde stellte Informationen zusammen, die in erster Linie den bayerischen Kommunen helfen sollen, sich in der komplexen Materie PPP zurechtzufinden. Wichtigstes Ergebnis dieser Zusammenarbeit ist der dreiteilige bayerische PPP-Leitfaden. Teil 1 des Leitfadens („Grundlagen") erläutert insbesondere Chancen und Risiken von PPP, dokumentiert bereits realisierte Projekte mit PPP-Elementen in Bayern, gibt Hinweise zur Projekteignung und enthält den bayerischen Projekteignungstest. Teil 2 des Leitfadens („Rechtliche Rahmenbedingungen und Finanzierung") stellt die aktuellen rechtlichen Rahmenbedingungen für PPP-Projekte in Bayern dar und erläutert das Thema Finanzierung. Seit Juni 2007 liegt der dritte Teil des bayerischen PPP-Leitfadens vor, der das Vergabeverfahren und die Vertragsgestaltung behandelt.

Der Leitfaden soll vor allem den Kommunen ermöglichen, in eigener Verantwortung und gut informiert den richtigen Weg für die Realisierung ihrer Vorhaben zu finden. Kein PPP-Projekt ist wie das andere. Deshalb enthält der Leitfaden auch keine Musterverträge und Musterabläufe. Der Bedarf bestimmt den Vertrag, nicht der Mustervertrag den Bedarf. Der einheitliche Rahmen aller PPP-Modelle besteht in den geltenden Rechtsvorschriften. Darauf aufbauend gibt es Charakteristika, die zum Wesen von PPP gehören und die Vergabe und die Vertragsgestaltung beeinflussen. Sie sind Gegenstand des Leitfadens. Darüberhinaus sind der Standardisierung im Sinne vorgefertigter Lösungen angesichts der Vielfalt der PPP-Modelle Grenzen gesetzt. Vor allem aus diesem Grund sind die Hinweise im Leitfaden als Hilfestellung ohne verbindlichen Charakter zu verstehen.

Im Dezember 2007 brachten wir darüber hinaus ein Faltblatt für „Kleine mittelstandsfreundliche PPP-Projekte“ heraus. Neben der Auftraggeberseite nimmt diese Ausarbeitung in gleicher Weise die Auftragnehmerseite in den Blick. Denn nicht nur der Auftraggeber – also die öffentliche Hand – muss sich auf den Mittelstand einstellen, sondern im Gegenzug auch der Mittelstand auf PPP, wenn er an Ausschreibungen teilnehmen und erfolgreich sein möchte.

Alle genannten Papiere sind im Internet bereitgestellt (www.ppp.bayern.de).

3.2 Die PPP-AG Bayern und das Kommunale Forum

Gemäß einem Auftrag des Bayerischen Landtags begleitet die Oberste Baubehörde im Bayerischen Staatsministerium des Innern Kommunen bei ihren PPP-Projekten, soweit sie dies wünschen. Allerdings handelt auch hier der Staat nicht allein, sondern in Zusammenarbeit mit den Kooperationspartnern. Dazu wurde eine Arbeitsgruppe, die PPP-AG Bayern, geschaffen (vgl. Abb. 2), deren Anlaufstelle die Oberste Baubehörde ist. Sie steht den Kommunen auf der Projektebene zur Verfügung und berät bzw. begleitet die kommunalen PPP-Projekte. In erster Linie handelt es sich dabei um die Beratung zu Beginn eines Projekts, also die sog. Frühphasenberatung. Einige Projekte werden während der Vorbereitungs- und Ausschreibungsphase begleitet. Mehr als 50 Kommunen haben dieses Angebot bisher genutzt.

Um die Kommunen besser miteinander zu vernetzen und den Wissenstransfer zu verbessern, hat die Oberste Baubehörde das Kommunale Forum ins Leben gerufen. Hier treffen sich Kommunen, die bereits Erfahrung mit PPP-Projekten gesammelt haben, mit solchen, die gerade erst ein Projekt beginnen oder sich für PPP interessieren. Das Forum trifft sich zweimal im Jahr.

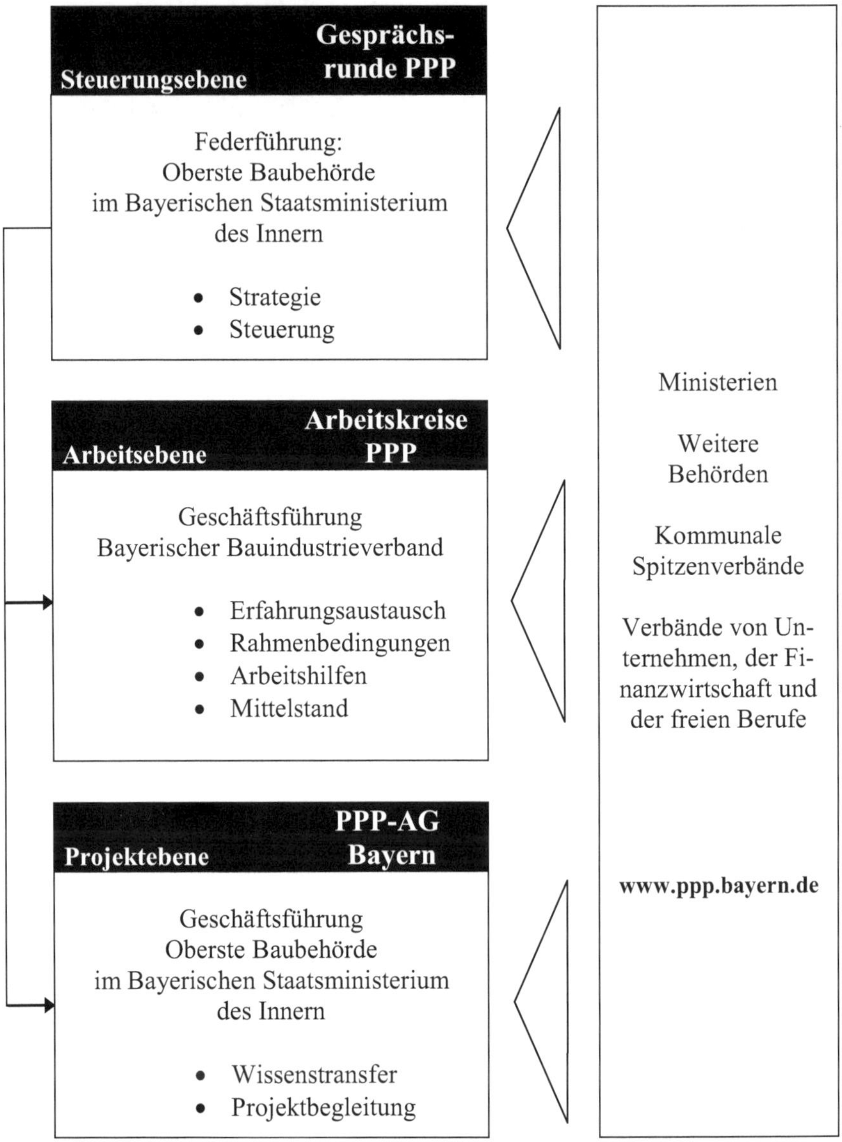

Abb. 2: Das Bayerische Kooperationsmodell
Quelle: eigene Darstellung.

4 Erfahrungen

Auch wenn sich die staatliche Bauverwaltung aufgrund von Synergieeffekten Vorteile erwartet, so darf nicht übersehen werden, dass PPP-Projekte sehr unterschiedlich und in jedem Einzelfall zu konzipieren sind. Die oftmals gewünschte bzw. erhoffte Standardisierung von PPP-Verfahren wird es somit nicht für den vollen Projektumfang geben können, so dass PPP-Projekte voraussichtlich auch in Zukunft aufwändige Beschaffungsverfahren bedingen werden. Unsere Erfahrungen lassen sich in folgenden Punkten zusammenfassen:

- PPP ist zwar ein weiteres Instrument, öffentliche Infrastrukturaufgaben in geeigneten Fällen zu privatisieren. Die Komplexität von PPP-Projekten erfordert aber von beiden Partnern ein hohes Maß an Kompetenz.
- PPP eignet sich insbesondere für Maßnahmen, deren Umfang über den üblichen Rahmen der Projekte eines Auftraggebers hinausgeht.
- PPP-Modelle binden die öffentliche Hand und private Unternehmen für lange Zeit und müssen daher wohlüberlegt sein.
- Das Interesse der privaten Partner an PPP-Projekten ist hoch.
- Öffentliche Auftraggeber können von PPP auch für die Realisierung ihrer sonstigen Bauaufgaben lernen. Insbesondere der bewusste Umgang mit Risiken, eine erhöhte Haushaltstransparenz durch die Erfassung von Lebenszykluskosten und eine verbesserte Projektdisziplin können auch auf die konventionelle Realisierungsvariante übertragen werden.
- Für diese Transparenz durch die Erfassung der Lebenszykluskosten gibt der öffentliche Auftraggeber die Steuerung der Kosten an den Auftragnehmer ab; dies erlangt immer dann besondere Bedeutung, wenn während der Vertragslaufzeit Veränderungen eintreten, die berücksichtigt werden müssen. Im Vertrag sollte also hierfür Vorsorge getroffen werden.

- PPP ist kein Selbstläufer: Die Angebotspreise bewegen sich bisher bei unseren Pilotprojekten in der Bandbreite konventioneller Verfahren.
- PPP darf kein Selbstzweck sein. Letztlich ist immer eine differenzierte Betrachtung – bezogen auf den Einzelfall – erforderlich, insbesondere hinsichtlich der Wirtschaftlichkeit. PPP-Modelle sind nur dann sinnvoll und erfolgreich, wenn sie tatsächlich Vorteile bieten.
- PPP ist kein Joker – für diese Form der Projektrealisierung muss sich der Auftraggeber bewusst entscheiden.
- PPP funktioniert nicht „über Nacht“ – auch der private Partner, der potentielle Auftragnehmer, muss sein Unternehmen auf PPP ausrichten.
- Eine Bewährung in der Betriebsphase steht vielfach noch aus.
- PPP kann fehlende Haushaltsmittel nicht ersetzen.

Entsprechend der „PPP-Philosophie“ kann eine öffentlich-private Partnerschaft nur dann wirklich funktionieren, wenn sich beide Partner auf gleicher Augenhöhe begegnen, sich gegenseitig und mit einer gewissen Fehlertoleranz respektieren und einander Entscheidungsfreiräume lassen. Dem stehen in der Praxis jedoch die ureigenen Interessen beider Seiten gegenüber, die mit der erforderlichen Toleranz nur schwer vereinbar zu sein scheinen. Die Lösung kann nur das beiderseitige Bestreben sein, der Sache zu dienen. Die Pilotprojekte werden zeigen, ob dieses Ziel eher durch die Gewährung von Freiraum oder durch feste Vorgaben erreichbar ist.

Effizienzsteigerung im öffentlichen Immobilienmanagement durch PPPs – Hintergründe und praktische Erfahrungen

Christian Glock & Julia Schultheis

Inhaltsverzeichnis

1 Einführung

In Deutschland besteht im Bereich der öffentlichen Infrastruktur ein sehr hoher Investitionsbedarf. Die derzeit schlechte Finanzlage der öffentlichen Haushalte führt jedoch dazu, dass Investitionen in den Aufbau, Ausbau oder Erhalt der öffentlichen Einrichtungen häufig aufgeschoben werden müssen oder vollständig unterbleiben. In den letzten Jahren wird in diesem Zusammenhang vermehrt über die Einbeziehung privaten Know-hows und Kapitals in die öffentliche Aufgabenerfüllung in Form von Public Private Partnerships, sog. PPPs, diskutiert.[1] Dabei geht es um die Kooperation zwischen öffentlichem Sektor und Privatwirtschaft, von der im Idealfall jede Seite profitiert. Privatwirtschaftliche Firmen realisieren mit ihrem Know-how und ihrer Marktübersicht öffentliche Bauvorhaben. Angefangen von der Planung und der Finanzierung eines Projekts, über Bau, Betrieb bis hin zur Nachfolgenutzung oder Verwertung fungieren privatwirtschaftliche Unternehmen als Baudienstleister und decken so die gesamte Wertschöpfungskette ab.

Besonders interessant für öffentliche Auftraggeber ist das Thema Effizienzsteigerung durch PPP, wodurch die öffentlichen Haushalte langfristig entlastet werden können. Da bei PPP-Projekten Investoren aus der Privatwirtschaft die komplette Umsetzung von Projekten übernehmen, kann das für die öffentliche Hand geringere Investitions- und Folgekosten, verkürzte Planungs- und Bauzeiten sowie einen verbesserten Betrieb und Unterhalt eines Projekts bedeuten. Umgekehrt können private Investoren mit Kommunen, Städten oder dem Land langjährige, vertrauensvolle Partner gewinnen. Im vorliegenden Beitrag werden die effizienzsteigernden Faktoren von PPP im Einzelnen analysiert und praktische Erfahrungen aus bereits realisierten PPP-Projekten aufgezeigt.

[1] Im vorliegenden Beitrag werden die Begriffe Public Private Partnership (PPP) und Öffentlich Private Partnerschaft (ÖPP) synonym verwendet.

2 Effizienzsteigernde Faktoren von PPPs

2.1 Grundlagen

Bei PPP handelt es sich um eine alternative Beschaffungsvariante der öffentlichen Hand für Leistungen im weitesten Sinne, bei der sich die öffentliche Hand mit privaten Partnern langfristig zur Erfüllung öffentlicher Aufgaben der Daseinsvorsorge zusammenschließt. PPP eignet sich dabei insbesondere zur Beschaffung und langfristigen Nutzung von Immobilien der öffentlichen Hand. Ziel der öffentlichen Hand ist es, durch die Investition, Risikoübernahme und Erbringung von Dienstleistungen des privaten Partners Effizienzgewinne zu erzielen und damit die öffentlichen Haushalte langfristig zu entlasten.[2] Die folgende Abbildung veranschaulicht den Grad der Aufgabenübertragung auf den privaten Partner im Rahmen von PPP-Modellen verglichen mit der konventionellen Beschaffung über die Einzelvergabe von Gewerken bis hin zur materiellen Privatisierung.

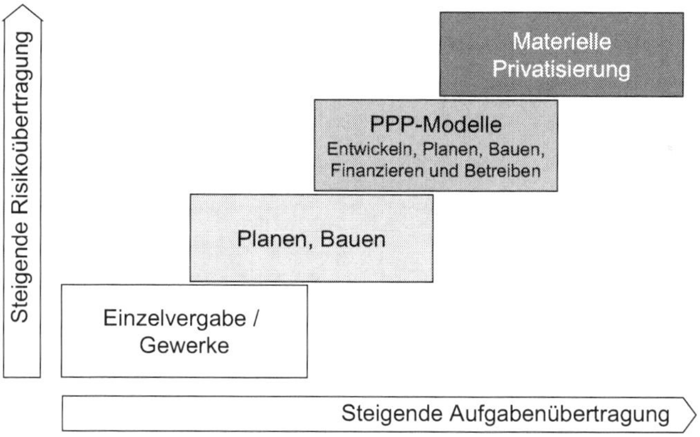

Abb. 1: Umfang der Aufgabenübertragung zwischen konventionellen und PPP-Modellen

Quelle: eigene Darstellung.

[2] Vgl. Schultheis, J. (2006).

Im Rahmen eines PPP-Projektes zur Realisierung einer öffentlichen Immobilie werden die Teilleistungen Planung, Bau, Finanzierung und Gebäudemanagement im Rahmen einer gesamtheitlichen Vergabe auf einen privaten Partner übertragen. Dieser wird dabei regelmäßig zur Realisierung des Vorhabens aus wirtschaftlichen und organisatorischen Überlegungen heraus eine Projektgesellschaft gründen, die alleiniger Vertragspartner der öffentlichen Hand wird. Die Projektgesellschaft schließt ihrerseits zur Erbringung der vertraglichen Leistung diverse Nachunternehmerverträge ab. Die folgende Abbildung zeigt die Grundstruktur einer PPP.

Abb. 2: Grundstruktur einer Public Private Partnership
Quelle: eigene Darstellung.

Das Konzept der PPP hat seinen Ursprung in den USA, wo ein Erfahrungshintergrund besteht, der bis in die 1940er Jahre zurückreicht. In Europa wurde das Konzept der öffentlich-privaten Partnerschaften erst in den 1980er Jahren aufgegriffen. Für den Bereich des öffentlichen Hochbaus nimmt Großbritannien mit seiner „Private Finance Initiative" (PFI) eine Vorbildfunktion für die deutsche PPP-Entwicklung ein. Die wachsende Bedeutung von PPP in Deutschland ist insbesondere Ausdruck einer Reaktion auf die desolate Finanzlage der öffentlichen Haushalte. In diesem Zusammenhang muss festgehalten werden, dass die öffentliche Hand zur Realisierung einer Immobilie auch in Form eines PPP-Modells ausreichende Mittel im Haushalt zur Verfügung stellen muss. In den meisten Fällen verpflichtet sie sich zur Zahlung eines regelmäßigen Leistungsentgelts an den Privaten über einen Zeitraum von 20 bis 30 Jahren. Diese zusätzliche langfristige Belastung des öffentlichen Haushalts durch das Eingehen einer PPP ist daher im Vorfeld intensiv zu prüfen.

Darüber hinaus sieht man vermehrt auch für die öffentliche Aufgabenwahrnehmung die Notwendigkeit, privatwirtschaftliches Managementwissen und Know-how für eine effizientere öffentliche Aufgabenerfüllung zu nutzen. Effizienz wird dabei häufig gleichbedeutend mit Wirtschaftlichkeit verwendet. Indikatoren sind Kosten, Qualität und Zeit, wobei die Kosten als Steuerungsgröße dominieren. Effizienzvorteile durch PPP entstehen immer dann, wenn eine öffentliche Immobilie über ihren Lebenszyklus mit einem geringeren Input als dem bisherigen der öffentlichen Hand realisiert werden kann. Als Vergleichsmaßstab dient der konventionelle Eigenbau und Eigenbetrieb der Immobilie durch die öffentliche Hand. Nach einer Studie des Deutschen Instituts für Urbanistik aus dem Jahre 2005 werden Effizienzvorteile als Hauptgrund für die Durchführung von PPP angegeben.[3]

Die Effizienzsteigerung bei PPP resultiert insbesondere aus der Lebenszyklusbetrachtung, der Risikoübertragung, der optimierten Finanzierungsstruktur und der Einbindung privatwirtschaftlichen Know-hows in Verbindung mit der Unabhängigkeit des Privaten von öffentlich-rechtlichen Bindungen.

---

[3] Vgl. Deutsches Institut für Urbanistik (Hrsg.) (2005).

2.2 Lebenszyklusbetrachtung

Immobilien unterliegen wie andere Vermögensgegenstände einem Lebenszyklus, der durch die Phasen Entwicklung, Planung, Bau, Betrieb sowie Revitalisierung gekennzeichnet ist und einen Kreislauf darstellt. Die Beurteilung der Wirtschaftlichkeit einer Immobilie macht es erforderlich, alle Kosten während ihres Lebenszyklus zu betrachten, denn fundierte Investitionsentscheidungen können nur auf Grundlage einer ganzheitlichen Betrachtungsweise getroffen werden. So entstehen bis zum Nutzungsbeginn der Immobilie Investitionskosten für Entwicklung, Planung und Neubau bzw. Sanierung. Nach Nutzungsbeginn sind die Kosten für die Finanzierung, das Facility-Management, die Instandhaltung und Instandsetzung sowie für den Energie- und Medienverbrauch zu berücksichtigen. Die Lebenszykluskosten entsprechen der Summe aller Kosten, die im Zusammenhang mit der Immobilie in allen Phasen des Lebenszyklus anfallen.

Durch eine ganzheitliche Betrachtungsweise der Immobilie eröffnet sich die Möglichkeit, die Lebenszykluskosten erheblich zu reduzieren. Dies beginnt mit einer lebenszyklusorientierten Entwicklung und Planung der Neubau- oder Sanierungsmaßnahme. Bei Büro- bzw. Verwaltungsgebäuden fallen beispielsweise nur etwa ein Viertel der Lebenszykluskosten in der Investitionsphase an, während die restlichen drei Viertel der Baunutzung zuzurechnen sind.[4] So können oftmals erhöhte Investitionskosten durch Einsparungen in der Betriebsphase bereits nach wenigen Jahren kompensiert werden. Die Weichenstellung für die Umsetzung einer entsprechend wirtschaftlichen Realisierungsalternative muss zu einem möglichst frühen Zeitpunkt in der Planungsphase vorgenommen werden, da hier die Betriebs- bzw. Folgekosten am stärksten beeinflusst werden können (vgl. Abb. 3).

---

[4] Vgl. Graubner, C.-A./Hüske, K. (2003); Herzog, K. (2005).

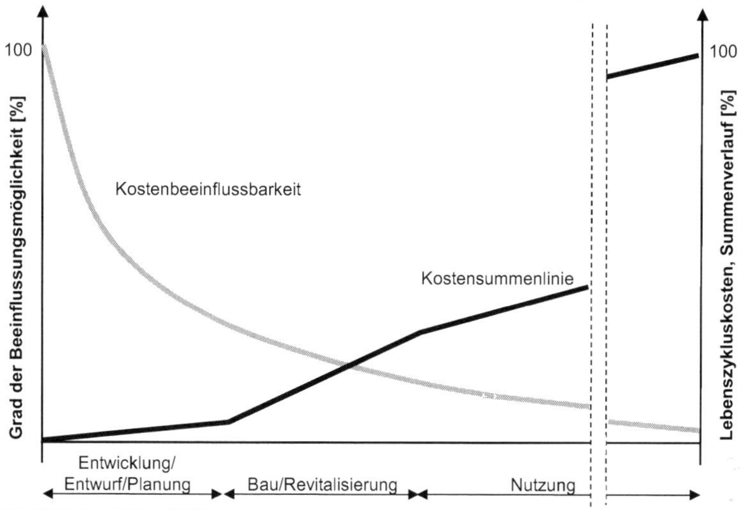

Abb. 3: Lebenszykluskosten und ihre Beeinflussbarkeit
Quelle: eigene Darstellung.

Die Lebenszyklusbetrachtung von Immobilien dient auch der Umsetzung der Ziele der Nachhaltigkeit und Energieeffizienz, die zunehmend Eingang in die Bau- und Immobilienwirtschaft finden. Es geht vermehrt darum, nicht nur kostengünstige, sondern auch energieeffiziente und ressourcenschonende Gebäude mit hoher technischer, funktionaler und gestalterischer Qualität zu planen und zu errichten, die über den Lebenszyklus wirtschaftlich betrieben werden können.[5]

Hinsichtlich der Investitionskosten des Bauwerkes liegt das Gesamtkostenoptimum über den Lebenszyklus betrachtet i.d.R. zwischen einer Spar- und einer Luxusvariante (vgl. Abb. 4). Eine geschickte Wahl der Bauwerksgeometrie, der Tragwerkskonstruktion und der zur Anwendung kommenden technischen Komponenten, Materialien und Qualitäten sowie eine sinnvolle Festlegung der Funktionsbeziehungen können die späteren Betriebskosten in starkem Maße

[5] Vgl. Herzog, K. (2008).

reduzieren. Übertriebene Sparmaßnahmen im Bereich der Investitionskosten verursachen dagegen unverhältnismäßig hohe Betriebskosten. Unangepasste Investitionen in teure Anlagen bzw. Materialien bis hin zur Luxusvariante amortisieren sich hingegen nicht über den Lebenszyklus und bieten ebenfalls nur suboptimale Gesamtlösungen.

Bei der Konzeption einer Immobilie ist daher eine geeignete Realisierungsvariante zu entwickeln, bei der die Summe aus Investitions- und Betriebskosten ein Optimum ergibt, und welche gleichzeitig die Nutzungsansprüche sowie eine ansprechende und funktionale Architektur berücksichtigt.

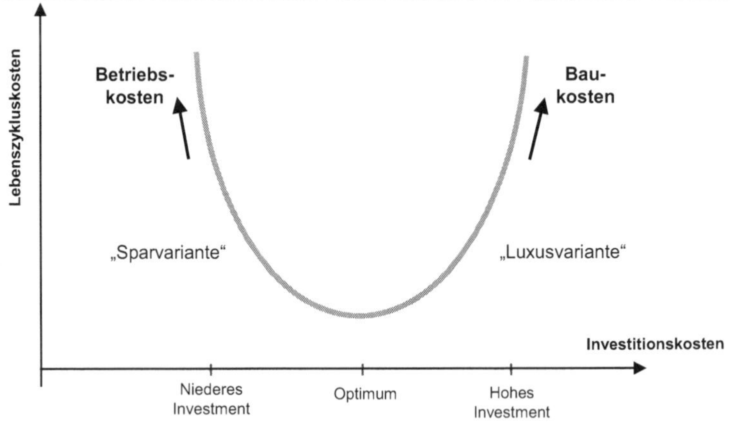

Abb. 4: Optimale Investition als Minimum der Lebenszykluskosten
Quelle: eigene Darstellung.

Beim konventionellen Eigenbau und -betrieb einer öffentlichen Immobilie koordiniert die öffentliche Hand in der Regel alle erforderlichen Teilleistungen in eigener Verantwortung. Die einzelnen Teilleistungen der Planung, des Baus und des Betriebes der Immobilie werden dabei regelmäßig getrennt voneinander betrachtet und vergeben. In den Prozess sind verschiedene Ämter der Verwaltung involviert, wobei die Verantwortlichkeiten nicht immer eindeutig zugeordnet sind. Während ein solches Vorgehen die wirtschaftliche Vergabe von

Einzelleistungen gewährleistet, wird auf diese Art und Weise jedoch die Sicherstellung einer wirtschaftlichen Gesamtlösung häufig nicht erreicht. Die einfache Addition der einzelnen Teilleistungen wie Projektsteuerung, Architektur, Fachplanungen, Roh- und Ausbau sowie Fassade und Technische Gebäudeausrüstung und das anschließende technische, kaufmännische und infrastrukturelle Gebäudemanagement stellt in den seltensten Fällen auch zugleich das wirtschaftliche Gesamtoptimum dar.

Einer PPP liegt hingegen eine ganzheitliche Betrachtung des Lebenszyklus einer Immobilie zugrunde. Durch die Gesamtvergabe der Planungs-, Bau-, Finanzierungs- und Betriebsleistungen wird die Verantwortung an einer Stelle gebündelt. Der Private wird über die geforderte Abgabe eines Gesamtangebots zur Optimierung der Lebenszykluskosten der Immobilie angeregt. Es stehen nicht – wie bei der Einzel- oder Generalunternehmervergabe – die günstigsten Bauinvestitionskosten im Vordergrund, sondern die simultane Optimierung von Planung, Bau, Finanzierung und Betrieb durch den Privaten.[6] So können höhere Erstinvestitionskosten, wenn sie zu einer Reduzierung der Kosten in der Betriebsphase führen, zu optimierten Lebenszykluskosten beitragen. Besonders wichtig für die Optimierung der Lebenszykluskosten ist die frühzeitige gegenseitige Einbindung von Planern und späteren Betreibern. Durch ein rechtzeitig entwickeltes Gebäudemanagement-Konzept können die Kosten für das Betreiben der Immobilie erheblich gesenkt werden.

2.3 Risikoallokation gemäß Risikomanagementkompetenz

Entscheidend für die Optimierung der Lebenszykluskosten und damit für die Effizienzsteigerung ist die gleichzeitige Übertragung von Verantwortung und damit von Risiken auf den privaten Partner. Die Risikoübertragung führt zu neuartigen Anreizstrukturen im Vergleich zur konventionellen Beschaffung der öffentlichen Hand, die den Privaten mit Blick auf seine Renditeziele zu einer

6 Vgl. Schultheis, J. (2006).

optimierten Umsetzung der Maßnahme im Sinne des gesamten Lebenszyklus anregen. Dabei geht es nicht darum, möglichst viele Risiken auf den Privaten zu übertragen, sondern unter Berücksichtigung der Risikozuschläge des Privaten und der Kalkulierbarkeit von Risiken die effizienteste Risikoallokation für das Projekt zu finden.

Um zu einer effizienten Verteilung der Risiken zu kommen, ist ein zielgerichteter Risikomanagementprozess erforderlich. Hierzu sind die Risiken zunächst zu identifizieren und anschließend zu bewerten. Im Rahmen der Risikosteuerung wird die Allokation der Risiken durch vertragliche Vereinbarungen festgelegt und Maßnahmen zur Minimierung der Risikokosten getroffen.[7]

Risikoidentifikation

Bei der Durchführung eines PPP-Projektes sind im Rahmen der Risikoidentifikation zunächst die projektspezifischen Risiken vollständig und systematisch zu erfassen und zu beschreiben. Hierbei sind insbesondere folgende Risikogruppen zu analysieren:[8]

- Planungs- und Genehmigungsrisiken (Planungsänderungen, Änderungen der technischen oder gesetzlichen Vorschriften),
- Grundstücks- und Gebäuderisiken (Bodenbeschaffenheit, Kontaminierungen, archäologische Funde, Altlasten von Gebäuden),
- Baurisiken (fehlerhafte Umsetzung der Bauplanung, mangelhafte Terminplanung, mangelhafte Qualität, Änderung der Materialkosten),
- Finanzierungsrisiken (Änderungen der Finanzierungskonditionen, Änderung des Finanzierungsvolumens),
- Betriebsrisiken (betrieblicher Stillstand, Betriebsstörungen und/oder Qualitätsprobleme, veränderte Leistungsanforderungen),

7 Vgl. Weber, M./Moß, O./Parzych, A. (2005).
8 Vgl. Arbeitskreis PPP im Management öffentlicher Immobilien im BPPP e.V. (2006).

- Marktrisiken (Änderung der Nachfrage/Auslastung, Änderung der Konkurrenzsituation, Änderung der Preise) sowie
- Verwertungsrisiko (Änderung des Restwerts der Immobilie bei vorzeitiger Beendigung des Vertrages oder am Ende der Vertragslaufzeit).

Um eine möglichst umfassende Risikoidentifikation sicherzustellen, sollten neben den direkt Projektverantwortlichen auch sachkundige Dritte in den Prozess der Risikoidentifikation einbezogen werden.

Risikobewertung

Grundsätzlich sind alle identifizierten Risiken in Form von Risikokosten zu bewerten. Eine Berechnung der monetären Auswirkungen des Eintritts von Risiken ist allerdings mit erheblichen Schwierigkeiten verbunden. In der Praxis wird derzeit überwiegend das Zuschlagsverfahren angewandt, bei dem für jede Risikoart ein risikobedingter Zuschlag ermittelt wird, der sich als Produkt aus möglicher Schadenshöhe und der entsprechenden Eintrittswahrscheinlichkeit ergibt.[9] Eine exaktere Bewertung der Risiken kann über eine simulative Risikoanalyse erzielt werden.[10]

Risikosteuerung

Im Rahmen der Risikosteuerung ist zu entscheiden, ob die Risiken bei der Umsetzung des PPP-Projektes bei der öffentlichen Hand verbleiben oder ob diese auf den privaten Partner übertragen werden können bzw. sollen. Entscheidungskriterium für die Verteilung der Risiken ist die Effizienz, die durch die gewählte Allokation für das Projekt erreicht werden kann.[11] Im Sinne einer effizienten Projektumsetzung kann es nicht darum gehen, alle mit Planung, Bau, Finanzierung und Betrieb einer Immobilie verbundenen Risiken auf den Privaten

---

[9] Vgl. Weber, M./Moß, O./Parzych, A. (2005).
[10] Vgl. Pfnür, A./Eberhardt, T. (2005).
[11] Vgl. Weber, M./Moß, O./Parzych, A. (2005).

zu übertragen. Die Risikoüberwälzung auf den Privaten schlägt sich in Wagniszuschlägen nieder, die die Wirtschaftlichkeit des Projektes verringern.

Die Verteilung der Risiken auf die Projektbeteiligten sollte prinzipiell nach dem Grundsatz der Risikomanagementkompetenz erfolgen. Danach hat jede Vertragspartei diejenigen Risiken zu übernehmen, die sie am besten beherrschen kann.[12] Die Beherrschungsfähigkeit ergibt sich wiederum im Wesentlichen aus der Fachkompetenz. Entsprechend hat der Private überwiegend die Risiken aus seinen übernommenen Aufgaben zu tragen. Risiken, die von keinem der Partner zu beherrschen sind, sollten bei der öffentlichen Hand verbleiben, denn in diesem Fall sind keine Effizienzgewinne aus der Risikoübertragung zu erwarten. Der Private wird, wenn er sich überhaupt zur Risikoübernahme bereit erklärt, einen hohen Risikozuschlag ansetzen. Die öffentliche Hand zahlt folglich einen hohen Preis für ein Risiko, das nicht kalkulierbar ist und entsprechend auch gering ausfallen kann.[13]

2.4 Optimierung der Finanzierungsstrukturen

Zur Effizienzsteigerung trägt bei PPP-Modellen weiterhin die Optimierung der Finanzierungsstrukturen bei. Beim konventionellen Eigenbau und -betrieb einer öffentlichen Immobilie stellt die öffentliche Hand als Bauherr die Finanzierung der Immobilie sicher. Die klassische Form der Finanzierung von Investitionsmaßnahmen auf kommunaler Ebene ist dabei der Kommunalkredit. Im Rahmen von PPP-Modellen wird nach Projektart, Projektgröße und Risikostruktur die für das Immobilienvorhaben optimale Finanzierungsstruktur entwickelt. Angesichts des teilweise hohen Anteils der Finanzierungskosten am Leistungsentgelt (je nach Projektstruktur zwischen 30 % und 60 %) und der dadurch bedingten hohen politischen Relevanz sind die Finanzierungslösungen stets von erheblicher Bedeutung.

---

[12] Vgl. Pfnür, A./Eberhardt, T. (2005).
[13] Vgl. Arbeitskreis PPP im Management öffentlicher Immobilien im BPPP e.V. (2006).

In der Praxis sind als Finanzierungsformen im Rahmen einer PPP-Beschaffung die Forfaitierung mit Verzicht der öffentlichen Hand auf sämtliche Einreden, Einwendungen und Aufrechnungen (Forfaitierung mit Einredeverzicht) sowie auch die Projektfinanzicrung vorherrschend.

Forfaitierung mit Einredeverzicht

In Deutschland wurde bislang die überwiegende Zahl der PPP-Hochbauprojekte über eine Forfaitierung mit Einredeverzicht finanziert.[14] Die Vorteile dieser Finanzierungsvariante liegen in den günstigen kommunalkreditähnlichen Finanzierungskonditionen kombiniert mit den Effizienzgewinnen durch PPP.[15] Unter einer Forfaitierung wird ein regressloser Verkauf bestehender oder künftiger Forderungen verstanden. Bei PPP-Projekten tritt als Forderungsverkäufer der private Auftragnehmer auf, der einen Teil der Ansprüche gegen die öffentliche Hand aus dem geschlossenen PPP-Vertrag an die finanzierende Bank verkauft. In der Regel handelt es sich dabei um den Teil des Leistungsentgelts, der den Werklohn aus dem Planungs- und Bauvertrag mit dem privaten Partner abdeckt. Die öffentliche Hand wird regelmäßig daran interessiert sein, die Werklohnforderung nicht in einem sofort zahlbaren Betrag zu entrichten, sondern den Betrag nebst Zinsen über die vereinbarte Vertragslaufzeit in gleich bleibenden Raten zu zahlen. Hierzu wird über eine Stundungsvereinbarung zwischen dem Privaten und der öffentlichen Hand ein weitreichender Zahlungsaufschub gewährt, aufgrund derer die öffentliche Hand periodische Zins- und Tilgungsleistungen zur Amortisation der Investition erbringt. Die Rückzahlung der Forderungen sollte über einen Zeitraum von 10 bis 30 Jahren erfolgen. Der Forderungskaufpreis errechnet sich als abgezinster Barwert der angekauften Entgelte und kann seitens des privaten Auftragnehmers für die im Projekt erforderlichen Investitionen verwendet werden. Die Bank zieht daraufhin die

---

[14] Vgl. Hauptverband der deutschen Bauindustrie (Hrsg.) (2007).

[15] Vgl. Grotowski, T. (2005).

Forderung von der öffentlichen Hand im eigenen Namen ein und erhält sämtliche Vertrags- und Nebenrechte.[16]

Kommunalkreditähnliche Konditionen werden bei einer Forfaitierung erreicht, wenn der öffentliche Vorhabensträger im Verhältnis zur Bank auf sämtliche Einreden, Einwendungen und Aufrechnungen verzichtet. Die öffentliche Hand muss folglich in jedem Fall die verkauften Forderungen an das Kreditinstitut auszahlen und kann berechtigte Minderungen bzw. Rückzahlungsansprüche nur gegenüber dem Privaten geltend machen.[17] Das ankaufende Kreditinstitut kann damit bezüglich seiner Konditionen – wie beim Kommunalkredit – auf die Bonität der öffentlichen Hand abstellen, da die Refinanzierung in diesem Fall über den öffentlichen Haushalt erfolgt. Folglich ist bei einer Forfaitierung mit Einredeverzicht (im Folgenden auch einredefreie Forfaitierung genannt) Eigenkapital nicht notwendigerweise erforderlich.

Der Werklohn wird regelmäßig erst mit Inbetriebnahme des Gebäudes durch die öffentliche Hand fällig. Entsprechend hat der Private die Planungs- und Bauleistungen vorzufinanzieren. Da der Einredeverzicht der öffentlichen Hand üblicherweise erst mit der Abnahme des gesamten Gebäudes gegeben wird, stellt die Zwischenfinanzierung während der Planungs- und Bauphase zumeist auf die Bonität des ausführenden Bauunternehmens ab. Dies führt zu einem entsprechend höheren Margenaufschlag der finanzierenden Bank. Zur Verbesserung der Konditionen der Zwischenfinanzierung auf Kommunalkreditniveau kann die öffentliche Hand die Bauleistungen abschnittsweise in Form sogenannter Bautestate anerkennen. Diese Bautestate können dann vom Bauunternehmer an die Bank verkauft werden. Der Bauunternehmer erhält damit auch die Abschlagszahlungen zu kommunalkreditähnlichen Konditionen. Diese Finanzierungsvariante ist auch unter dem Namen „Mogendorfer“-Modell bekannt.[18]

---

[16] Vgl. Weber, M./Moß, O./Schwichow, H. (2004).
[17] Vgl. Kumlehn, F. (2001).
[18] Vgl. Sester, P./Bunsen, Ch. (2005).

Die folgende Abbildung verdeutlicht die Grundstruktur einer einredefreien Forfaitierung.

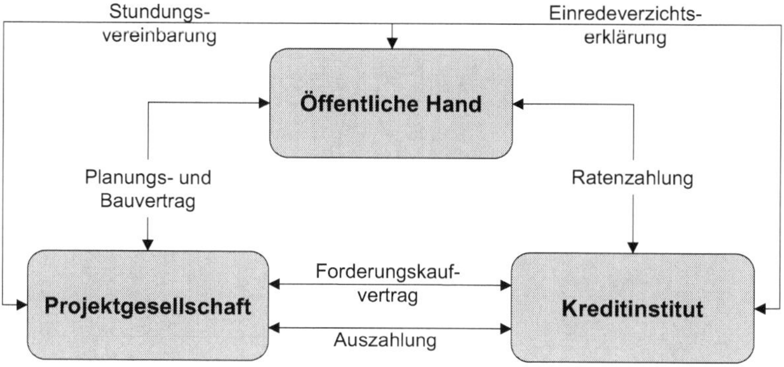

Abb. 5: Struktur einer Forfaitierung mit Einredeverzicht
Quelle: in Anlehnung an Eppinger, F./Käsewieter, H.-W./Miksch, J. (2005).

Vorteile der einredefreien Forfaitierung als Finanzierungsform für PPP-Projekte sind neben den günstigen Finanzierungskosten die kurze Transaktionszeit und die niedrigen Transaktionskosten. Aufgrund der geringen Risikoposition der Banken verzichten diese auf eine umfassende und kostenintensive Projektprüfung. Die Forfaitierung stellt darüber hinaus ein Standardprodukt für die Banken dar, das kostengünstig und schnell angeboten werden kann.[19] Damit eignet sich diese Finanzierungsform sowohl für große Projektvolumen als auch für PPP-Projekte mit kleinerem Investitionsvolumen.

Projektfinanzierung

Unter einer Projektfinanzierung versteht man die Finanzierung einer sich selbst tragenden Wirtschaftseinheit, bei der sich die Finanzierungsentscheidungen der Kreditgeber vornehmlich am prognostizierten Cashflow und den Aktiva des

[19] Vgl. Grotowski, T. (2005).

Projektes als Sicherheit für die Rückzahlung des bereitgestellten Kapitals orientieren.[20] Die Rückführung der Finanzierungsmittel wird demgemäß allein durch die generierten Zahlungsströme aus dem Projekt und den Vermögenswerten der wirtschaftlich abgrenzbaren Projektgesellschaft sichergestellt, die regelmäßig zur Durchführung des Projektes gegründet wird. Grundgedanke der Projektfinanzierung ist eine umfassende Risikoanalyse und anschließende Verteilung der mit dem Projekt verbundenen Risiken auf die Projektbeteiligten, einschließlich den Fremdkapitalgebern. Durch die Risikoteilung können Projekte realisiert werden, die aufgrund ihres hohen Gesamtrisikos für ein einzelnes Unternehmen nicht durchführbar wären.[21]

Zur Untersuchung der Risikostruktur sowie der wirtschaftlichen, technischen und rechtlichen Realisierbarkeit und Tragfähigkeit des Projektes führt das Kreditinstitut im Sinne einer Risikopräventions- und Risikooptimierungsstrategie eine sogenannte Due Diligence durch. Durch diese sorgfältige Projektprüfung wird zum einen die Gefahr unerwarteter oder eventuell unüberschaubarer Risiken minimiert und zum anderen ermöglicht, sich frühzeitig auf notwendige Maßnahmen einzustellen und Lösungskonzepte zu erarbeiten. Damit trägt die Qualität einer Due Diligence maßgeblich zum Erfolg oder Misserfolg einer Projektfinanzierung bei.

Die Fremdkapitalgeber übernehmen im Vergleich zur einredefreien Forfaitierung wesentlich höhere Risiken. Die Kreditinstitute fordern daher regelmäßig eine Eigenkapitalbeteiligung der privaten Investoren, um deren Projektverbundenheit zu erhöhen und somit Projektrisiken zu reduzieren. Als Alternative zum Eigenkapitaleinsatz können auch vom Privaten zu stellende Bank- oder Konzernbürgschaften als Sicherheit dienen. Zudem werden die Fremdkapitalgeber aufgrund der aufwendigen und kostenintensiven Prüfung eine Risikoprämie in Form einer höheren Marge verlangen. Der Margenaufschlag liegt je nach Risikogewichtung und Projektgröße 1 % bis 2 % über dem Kommunal-

---

[20] Vgl. Pfnür, A. (2004).

[21] Vgl. Weber, M./Moß, O./Bachhuber, F. (2005).

kredit.[22] Die Kosten einer Projektfinanzierung werden folglich deutlich über denen einer einredefreien Forfaitierung liegen. Zum einen führen die hohen Eigenkapitalrenditen zusammen mit der Risikoprämie der Banken zu deutlich höheren Finanzierungskosten. Zum anderen resultieren aus der umfassenderen Due Diligence der Fremdkapitalgeber höhere Transaktionskosten. Da die Transaktionskosten im Wesentlichen einen Fixkostencharakter aufweisen und damit vom Projektvolumen weitestgehend unabhängig sind, eignet sich die Projektfinanzierung grundsätzlich erst ab einer Projektgröße, bei der die realisierbaren Effizienzvorteile die hohen Transaktions- und Finanzierungskosten aufwiegen.[23]

Die Grundstruktur einer Projektfinanzierung stellt sich folgendermaßen dar:

Abb. 6: Struktur einer Projektfinanzierung
Quelle: in Anlehnung an Miksch, J. (2007).

[22] Vgl. Wegner, H.-J./Böing, B./Jürgenliemk, R. (2005).
[23] Vgl. Wegner, H.-J./Makowka, T./Hedrich, Ch. (2006).

2.5 Nutzung des Know-hows der Privatwirtschaft

Bei der Vergabe von PPP-Projekten findet unter den privaten Bietern neben dem Preiswettbewerb ein Innovationswettbewerb um die Schaffung von Produkt- und Verfahrensinnovationen statt. Die eingebrachte Kreativität und das unternehmerische Denken des privaten Sektors tragen ebenfalls zu effizienteren Formen der Leistungserbringung der öffentlichen Hand bei.[24] Private Unternehmen sind zudem wesentlich flexibler in der Anpassung von Personal- und Kapitalbedarfen, können ihre Ressourcen gezielter zum Einsatz bringen und Entscheidungen problemadäquater und schneller umsetzen. Der Amtsleiter eines Hochbauamtes ist an interne und externe Vorschriften, insbesondere bei Ausschreibung und Vergabe, gebunden und unterliegt den Weisungen der Verwaltungsleitung.

Wichtig zur Erzielung von Effizienzvorteilen ist, dass der Private sein Know-how bereits in einer frühen Planungsphase einbringen kann, denn hier ist der Einfluss auf die späteren Bau- und Betriebskosten am größten. Dabei muss das Projekt so strukturiert sein, dass sich das gewünschte Projektergebnis mit den Zielen der öffentlichen Hand deckt und dem Privaten die Möglichkeit gibt, seine Fähigkeiten und Fachkenntnisse effektiv einzusetzen. Hierzu trägt die outputorientierte Leistungsbeschreibung im Rahmen des Vergabeverfahrens von PPP-Projekten bei. Dabei wird die geforderte Leistung von der öffentlichen Hand im Gegensatz zum konventionellen Vergabeverfahren funktional beschrieben. So bleibt genügend Spielraum für innovative Lösungen der ausführenden Unternehmen und des Betreibers bei der Umsetzung der funktionalen Leistungsbeschreibung.[25]

---

[24] Vgl. Jacob, D./Kochendörfer, B. (2002).
[25] Vgl. Schultheis, J. (2006).

3 Beschaffung öffentlicher Immobilien inklusive Dienstleistungen als PPP

3.1 Grundlagen

Die öffentliche Hand hat ihre Entscheidung über das „Ob“ und „Wie“ einer Immobilienbeschaffung am Grundsatz der Wirtschaftlichkeit und Sparsamkeit auszurichten, der einen der zentralen Haushaltsgrundsätze darstellt. Aus ihm ergibt sich der in Abbildung 7 dargestellte Ablauf des PPP-Beschaffungsprozesses, der im Folgenden näher erläutert wird.

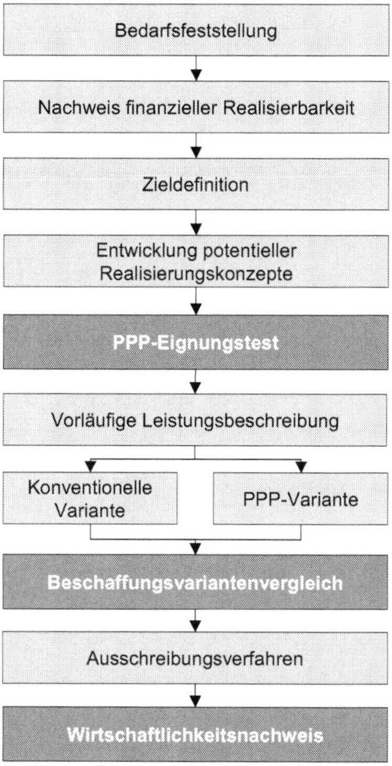

Abb. 7: Ablauf des PPP-Beschaffungsprozesses
Quelle: eigene Darstellung.

3.2 Ablauf des PPP-Beschaffungsprozesses

Nach dem Sparsamkeitsgrundsatz dürfen Projekte, die nicht unbedingt erforderlich sind, die finanzielle Leistungsfähigkeit der öffentlichen Hand nicht einschränken. Vor der Realisierung einer Immobilie hat die öffentliche Hand daher eine umfassende Bedarfsanalyse durchführen, um eine fundierte Entscheidung über das „Ob“ der Immobilie treffen zu können. Ergibt sich ein Bedarf für die Immobilie, ist die finanzielle Realisierbarkeit der Maßnahme durch die öffentliche Hand zu prüfen. Dies gilt unabhängig von der Beschaffungsvariante, d. h. für die konventionelle Eigenrealisierung und die PPP-Variante gleichermaßen.

Ist die Umsetzung der Maßnahme mit dem öffentlichen Haushalt vereinbar, kommt der Grundsatz der Wirtschaftlichkeit zum Tragen. Der Wirtschaftlichkeitsgrundsatz bezieht sich in erster Linie auf das „Wie“ der Aufgabenerfüllung, d. h. auf die Auswahl der verschiedenen Organisations- und Finanzierungsalternativen. Das Wirtschaftlichkeitsgebot fordert die öffentliche Hand dazu auf, das Effizienzpotential von partnerschaftlichen Lösungen im Rahmen einer Wirtschaftlichkeitsuntersuchung zu überprüfen. Jedoch ist nicht jedes Immobilienvorhaben für die Umsetzung in Form eines PPP-Projektes geeignet. Die Effizienzvorteile einer PPP können nur bei Vorliegen bestimmter Randbedingungen ausgeschöpft werden. Daher ist zunächst über einen sog. PPP-Eignungstest die grundsätzliche PPP-Eignung des Projektes festzustellen. Hierbei sind insbesondere nachfolgende Fragen zu beantworten:

- Leistungsumfang: Ist eine Integration von Planungs-, Bau- und Betreiberleistungen möglich?
- Risikoverteilung: Ist ein optimaler Risikotransfer auf den Privaten möglich?
- Leistungsbeschreibung: Ist eine outputorientierte Leistungsbeschreibung möglich?
- Wettbewerb: Ist das Projekt marktgängig? Ist ein Wettbewerb auf Bieterseite zu erwarten?

Der Leistungsumfang und die Risikoverteilung können als kritische Faktoren angesehen werden, da insbesondere über den Lebenszyklusgedanken und die Risikostruktur die Effizienzvorteile erzielt werden können.

Ist die PPP-Eignung des geplanten Projektes gegeben, sind potenzielle Realisierungskonzepte von der öffentlichen Hand zu identifizieren und zu entwickeln. Hierbei werden die übertragbaren Leistungen definiert – im Idealfall Planen, Bauen, Finanzieren und Betreiben – sowie die Vertragsgestaltung, die Finanzierungsform und der Umfang der Risikoübertragung festgelegt.

Der Beschaffungsvariantenvergleich dient der Ermittlung der günstigsten Realisierungsvariante für das geplante Immobilienprojekt. Hierbei ist der öffentliche Eigenbau und -betrieb mit der Beschaffung über das gewählte PPP-Modell zu vergleichen. Bei der Kalkulation des öffentlichen Eigenbaus und -betriebes der Immobilie sind insbesondere folgende Kostengruppen zu berücksichtigen:[26]

- Kosten der baulichen Infrastruktur (Kosten, die mit der Planung, dem Neubau, der Erweiterung, Sanierung oder Modernisierung der Immobilie verbunden sind),
- Baunutzungskosten (alle regelmäßig oder unregelmäßig wiederkehrenden Kosten der Nutzungsphase der Immobilie sowie der dazugehörigen Anlagen und Grundstücke),
- Sonstige Personal- und Sachkosten (nicht-gebäudebezogene Kosten des Betriebes, wie Kosten der allgemeinen Verwaltung und Kosten zusätzlicher Dienstleistungen, die über die Leistungen des Gebäudemanagements hinausgehen),
- Finanzierungskosten (Kosten der Bauzwischenfinanzierung und langfristige Finanzierungskosten),
- Risikokosten (Kosten sämtlicher relevanter und quantifizierbarer Projektrisiken, wobei zwischen Risiken, die auf den Privaten übertragen werden können, und zurückbehaltenen Risiken unterschieden werden muss),

[26] Vgl. Weber, M./Moß, O./Parzych, A. (2005).

– Steuern (Berücksichtigung der unterschiedlichen Besteuerung der konventionellen Variante und der PPP-Variante).

Bei der Kalkulation der PPP-Beschaffungsvariante hat die öffentliche Hand auf Grundlage der Daten und Informationen der konventionellen Beschaffungsvariante die potenziellen Kosten, Erlöse und Risiken abzuschätzen, die mit einer Realisierung des Immobilienprojektes als PPP verbunden sind. Für eine möglichst realistische Abschätzung ist gegebenenfalls ein Interessenbekundungsverfahren durchzuführen. Neben den Kosten und Erlösen aus dem Projekt sind der PPP-Beschaffungsvariante auch die Transaktionskosten zuzurechnen, die der öffentlichen Hand im Rahmen der Anbahnung, Vereinbarung und Kontrolle der PPP entstehen. Zudem sind Kosten für Risiken und Aufgaben zu berücksichtigen, die im Rahmen der PPP bei der öffentlichen Hand verbleiben. Weiterhin sind mittelbare Kosten anzusetzen, die der öffentlichen Hand beispielsweise durch einen von der PPP verursachten Personalüberhang entstehen. Im Anschluss an die Entwicklung der konventionellen und der PPP-Beschaffungsariante erfolgt der Beschaffungsvariantenvergleich auf Basis vollständiger Cashflow-Ströme im Rahmen der Kapitalwertmethode. Der Kapitalwert eines Projektes ergibt sich dabei aus der Summe aller relevanten, auf einen gemeinsamen Betrachtungszeitpunkt ab- bzw. aufgezinsten Ein- und Auszahlungen.[27]

Die folgende Abbildung zeigt die relevanten Kosten- und Erlösgruppen zur Durchführung des Beschaffungsvariantenvergleichs.

[27] Vgl. Weber, M./Moß, O./Parzych, A. (2005).

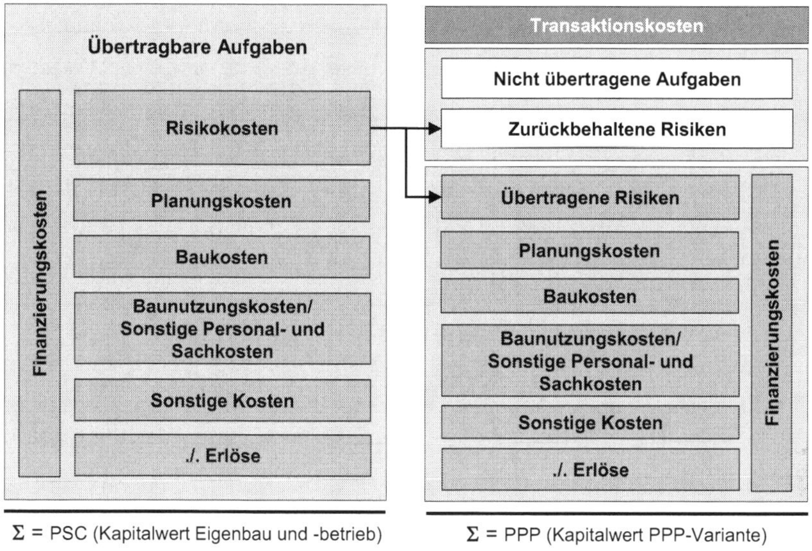

Abb. 8: Für den Beschaffungsvariantenvergleich relevante Kosten- und Erlösgruppen

Quelle: eigene Darstellung.

Ergibt der Beschaffungsvariantenvergleich, dass mit der PPP-Beschaffungsvariante ein insgesamt besseres Preis-Leistungs-Verhältnis im Vergleich zur konventionellen Beschaffungsvariante erzielt werden kann, erfolgt die Ausschreibung der PPP-Leistungen.

Als Vergabeverfahren kommt in Deutschland derzeit meist das strukturierte Verhandlungsverfahren zum Einsatz. Hier werden in einem vorgeschalteten Teilnahmewettbewerb – der sogenannten Präqualifikation – die bestgeeigneten Bieter ausgewählt und zur Angebotsabgabe aufgefordert. Nach Bewertung der von diesen Bietern eingereichten Angebote folgt die Verhandlung regelmäßig mit nur einem bevorzugten Bieter – dem „preferred bidder" – bis zur Zuschlagserteilung.

Der Wirtschaftlichkeitsnachweis wird kurz vor Zuschlagserteilung durchgeführt. Er dient dem abschließenden Nachweis der wirtschaftlichen Vorteilhaftigkeit des im Rahmen des Ausschreibungsverfahrens ermittelten bevorzugten PPP-Angebots. Als Vergleichsmaßstab dient die fortgeschriebene konventionelle Beschaffungsvariante. Fällt der Wirtschaftlichkeitsnachweis zugunsten der PPP-Variante aus, kann der Zuschlag auf das bevorzugte PPP-Angebot erteilt werden.

3.3 Angebotsprojektbearbeitung seitens der Privatwirtschaft

Die erfolgreiche Projektbearbeitung eines lebenszyklusbezogenen PPP-Projektes erfordert aufgrund der hohen Komplexität eine professionelle Projektvorbereitung und -organisation auf Seiten der Anbieter aus der Privatwirtschaft. Beginnend mit der EU-weiten Aufforderung zum Teilnahmewettbewerb müssen potentielle Bieter zunächst eine wettbewerbsfähige Bietergemeinschaft bestehend aus Architekten, Fachplanern, Baupartnern und Betreibern sowie Investoren, Banken und ggf. Beratern zusammenstellen.

Die Angebotsbearbeitung muss aufgrund der umfangreichen Projektbearbeitung und der kurzen Bearbeitungszeit von meist nur drei Monaten einem engen Terminplan folgen. Erste Entwurfsskizzen zur Umsetzung von vorgegebenen Raumprogrammen und der funktionalen Abhängigkeiten müssen in der Regel bereits nach einer Woche vorliegen, um auf dieser Basis in einen intensiven Dialog zwischen den Projektbeteiligten zu treten und ein Gesamtoptimum zu finden. Die gesamte Planung wird in der Regel innerhalb von nur wenigen Wochen ausgearbeitet, um dem Baupartner und dem Betreiber eine sichere Kalkulationsbasis zu ermöglichen. Die Optimierung der Lebenszykluskosten als erfolgsentscheidendes Kriterium erfolgt parallel zur Kalkulation der Bau- und Betriebskosten in der verbleibenden Angebotsfrist. Das Organisationsmodell und die Finanzierung werden zeitgleich zur Planung und Kalkulation auf Grundlage der mit den Ausschreibungsunterlagen vorgegebenen Rahmenbedingungen strukturiert und mit zunehmender Kalkulationssicherheit konkretisiert.[28]

3.4 Praktische Erfahrungen

Verglichen mit der Kalkulation für konventionelle Ausschreibungen erfordern PPP-Angebote auf Seiten der Privatwirtschaft grundsätzlich eine wesentlich detailliertere Planungstiefe, da der private Partner neben den Planungs- und Baukosten auch die Betriebskosten inklusive der Instandhaltung sowie des Medien- und Energieverbrauchs über meist 20-30 Jahre verbindlich anbietet. Komplexe PPP-Angebote erfordern daher auch bei den Privaten große personelle und finanzielle Ressourcen. Bei der Angebotsbearbeitung entstehen oftmals Kosten zwischen 200.000 EUR und 500.000 EUR je Bieter. Die gezahlte „Entschädigung" für nicht berücksichtigte Bieter deckt davon i.d.R. nur einen kleinen Teil der verursachten Angebotskosten. Um zu vermeiden, dass diese im Missverhältnis zur Chance auf eine Auftragserteilung stehen, muss die Anzahl der zum Angebot aufgeforderten Bieter gering gehalten und im Zuge des Verhandlungsverfahrens weiter reduziert werden.

In der Praxis sehen PPP-Vergabeverfahren der öffentlichen Hand jedoch häufig einen zu großen Bieterkreis von teilweise bis zu acht Bietern vor. In diesem Fall steht die Erfolgswahrscheinlichkeit in einem deutlichen Missverhältnis zum erhöhten Aufwand bei der Angebotsbearbeitung von PPP-Projekten. Dies kann dazu führen, dass private Anbieter von einer Angebotsbearbeitung absehen. In der Folge wird dadurch der Wettbewerb auf der Anbieterseite erheblich geschwächt. Eine starke Selektion der Bieter im strukturierten Verhandlungsverfahren ist somit auf Grund des hohen Aufwands für die Projektbearbeitung unabdingbar.[29]

---

[28] Vgl. Glock, Ch./Früh, T. (2007).
[29] Vgl. Schetter, H.-H. (2006).

4 Praktische Erfahrungen aus realisierten PPP-Projekten

4.1 Grundlagen

Die effizienzsteigernde Wirkung von PPPs im öffentlichen Immobilienmanagement verbunden mit der großen politischen Unterstützung dieser Beschaffungsvariante haben in den letzten Jahren dazu beigetragen, dass zahlreiche PPP-Projekte realisiert worden sind. Die überwiegende Zahl deutscher PPPs wird aktuell im Bereich öffentlicher Immobilien realisiert, dabei mehrheitlich von kommunalen Projektträgern, gefolgt von Projekten der Länder und des Bundes. Abbildung 9 zeigt die Anzahl der bereits vergebenen PPP-Projekte in Deutschland untergliedert in die einzelnen Bundesländer sowie die Projekte in Vorbereitung zum Stand Juli 2008 (Quelle: www.ppp-plattform.de). Aufbauend auf den zahlreichen realisierten und sich in Realisierung oder Verhandlung befindlichen PPP-Projekten werden nachfolgend die wichtigsten Projekterfahrungen zusammengefasst.

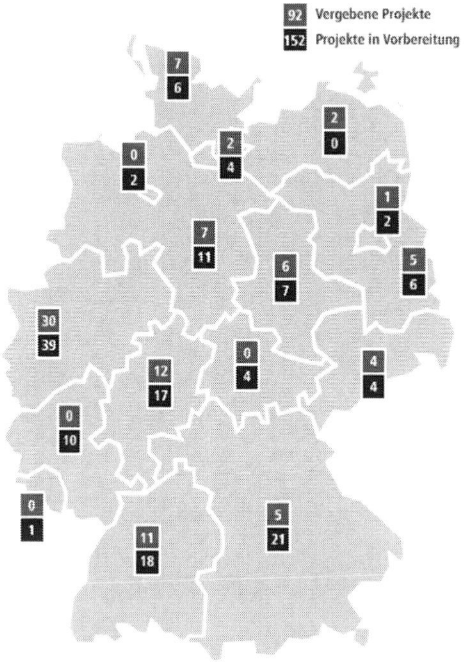

Abb. 9: Anzahl PPP-Projekte in Deutschland, Stand: Juli 2008
Quelle: *www.ppp-plattform.de*

PPP-Immobilienprojekte können nach verschiedenen Kriterien unterschieden werden:

- Immobilientyp (z.B. Verwaltungsbau, Schule, Klinik, Justizvollzugsanstalt, etc.)
- Leistungsumfang (Entwicklung, Planung, Neubau, Sanierung, Betrieb, Verwertung, etc.)
- Organisationsmodell (z.B. Inhabermodell, Mietmodell, etc.)
- Finanzierungsmodell (z.B. Forfaitierung mit Einredeverzicht oder Projektfinanzierung)
- Projektvolumen

- Projektträger (Kommune, Land oder Bund)
- Standort

Die Vielzahl der o.g. Unterscheidungskriterien verbunden mit der Schar an Untervarianten zeigt, dass vor der Realisierung eines PPP-Projektes jeweils individuell alle Randbedingungen geprüft werden müssen, um eine optimale Realisierungsvariante wählen zu können. Gleiches gilt auch für den Vergleich verschiedener deutscher PPP-Projekte und die Bewertung einzelner Projekterfahrungen. So kann z.B. eine suboptimale PPP-Projektrealisierung an einem zu geringen oder zu großen Umfang der Leistungsübertragung auf den Privaten, an einem unpassenden Organisationsmodell, an einseitigen Vertragsstrukturen oder anderen projektspezifischen Randbedingungen liegen.

Ein wichtiger Gradmesser für den Erfolg eines PPP-Projektes ist sein Effizienzvorteil, der in der Regel zwischen 5% und 20% liegt. Die PPP Task Force des Bundes im Bundesministerium für Verkehr, Bau und Stadtentwicklung hat eine umfassende PPP-Projektdatenbank aufgebaut, in der die o.g. Projektdaten einzeln abgefragt werden können (siehe dazu: www.ppp-projektdatenbank.de). Auf die Vorstellung einzelner Projekte wird daher im Folgenden verzichtet, die vorliegenden Erfahrungen werden zusammenfassend dargestellt.

Eine sehr gute Übersicht zu Erfahrungen aus PPP-Projekten gibt u.a. auch das Positionspapier „Die ersten PPP-Projekte im öffentlichen Hochbau – Lessons Learned“ des Hauptverbandes der Deutschen Bauindustrie mit folgenden Forderungen:[30]

- Echte PPPs mit angemessener Risikoverteilung
- Professionelle Vorbereitung und Steuerung der Projekte sowie Einführung eines standardisierten Leistungsbildes für Berater

[30] Vgl. Hauptverband der Deutschen Bauindustrie (Hrsg.) (2006).

- Standardisierung der Wirtschaftlichkeitsuntersuchung vor allem hinsichtlich der Berücksichtigung von Risiken im Public Sector Comparator (PSC)
- Festlegung der Rechtsform der Bietergemeinschaft erst nach Zuschlag
- Erstellung standardisierter Vergabeunterlagen vom Teilnahmewettbewerb mit angemessenen Wertungskriterien bis zu modulhaft anwendbaren Verträgen
- Angemessene Entschädigung der Bieter
- Berücksichtigung der outputspezifizierten Leistungsbeschreibung und des Lebenszyklusansatzes als wichtigsten Effizienztreiber für PPP-Projekte
- Klarheit über die Wirtschaftlichkeit der Finanzierungsformen

4.2 Lebenszyklusbetrachtung

Der Lebenszyklusbetrachtung von Immobilien kommt als zentraler Punkt des Generierens von Effizienzgewinnen bei PPP-Projekten eine besondere Bedeutung zu. Daher sollte die Beschreibung des Bedarfs der öffentlichen Auftraggeber bei PPP-Projekten derart erfolgen, dass die Privatwirtschaft effiziente Bedarfsdeckungsalternativen formulieren kann. Eine Ausschreibung muss daher funktional und outputorientiert sein, um ein Höchstmaß an Kreativität der Privatwirtschaft nutzen zu können. Im Zusammenhang mit der Planung bedeutet dies architektonische und fachplanerische Freiheiten anstelle von engen Vorgaben oder auch vorgeschalteten Architekturwettbewerben, wie sie immer wieder bei Projekten der Vergangenheit zu finden waren. Eine PPP-Ausschreibung sollte grundsätzlich eine möglichst genaue Beschreibung dessen liefern, „was" die öffentliche Hand benötigt, aber gleichzeitig offen lassen, „wie" dies zu erreichen ist.

Dies gilt auch für die Aspekte der Nachhaltigkeit und Energieeffizienz, die vermehrt Einzug in PPP-Ausschreibungen finden. Der Wunsch öffentlicher Auftraggeber nach Planung und Errichtung energieeffizienter und ressourcenschonender Gebäude muss sich zum einen in präzisen Vorgaben zum einzuhaltenden Standard widerspiegeln, zum anderen sollten die Kriterien Nachhaltigkeit und Energieeffizienz Eingang in die Bewertung der Angebote der Bieter finden, um eine nachhaltige Planung entsprechend zu belohnen.

Neben der funktionalen Ausschreibung ist auch von entscheidender Bedeutung, dass die wesentlichen Bausteine des Lebenszyklus einer Immobilie erfasst sind, um der Privatwirtschaft Motivation für dessen Optimierung zu geben. Dies sind insbesondere Planung, Bau und Betrieb über 20 bis 30 Jahre inklusive der Finanzierung des Projektes. In manchen Projekten werden entweder die Planungs- oder die Betriebsleistungen derart im Leistungsumfang reduziert, dass nicht mehr ausreichend Anreize für die Optimierung im Lebenszyklus vorhanden sind. Darüber hinaus müssen sich die vollständigen Leistungen auch ausreichend in den Bewertungskriterien seitens der öffentlichen Hand für die Angebote der Privatwirtschaft wiederfinden.

4.3 Risikoallokation gemäß Risikomanagementkompetenz

Die optimale Risikoallokation zwischen öffentlichem Auftraggeber und privatem Partner ist von entscheidender Bedeutung für eine erfolgreiche PPP. Wie in Abschnitt 2.3 erläutert, gilt grundsätzlich, dass ein Risiko am wirtschaftlichsten von demjenigen Partner übernommen werden kann, der es am besten steuern und bewerten kann. Dies bedeutet im Vergleich zur konventionellen Beschaffungsvariante, dass bei einer PPP Risiken auf die Privatwirtschaft übertragen werden, auf die sie mehr Einfluss hat als die öffentliche Hand. Die Übertragung von unkalkulierbaren Risiken auf die Privatwirtschaft ist grundsätzlich nicht möglich, da diese zu extremen Risikoaufschlägen führen würde. Trotz dieses Grundsatzes kommt es bei zahlreichen PPP-Projekten immer wieder zu Missverständnissen einer sachgerechten Risikoverteilung – teilweise mit dem Versuch, auch sehr schwer kalkulierbare Risiken auf den Markt zu übertragen. Da aus den Projekterfahrungen eindeutig hervorgeht, dass eine sachgerechte Risikoverteilung letztlich für eine erfolgreiche PPP zwingend erforderlich ist, sollte vor der vertraglichen Festlegung der Risikoverteilung die Privatwirtschaft befragt werden, z.B. im Rahmen eines Interessenbekundungsverfahrens.

Die öffentliche Hand hat jedoch in der Vergangenheit teilweise die schlechte wirtschaftliche Situation der Bauwirtschaft dazu genutzt, eine möglichst weitgehende Risikoübertragung zu erreichen. Diese Tendenz wird noch dadurch verstärkt, dass der PPP-Markt in Deutschland noch sehr jung ist. Es liegt daher im Interesse der Privatwirtschaft, Erfahrungen zu sammeln, um Referenzen nachweisen zu können. Die Risikobereitschaft der Privatwirtschaft wird entsprechend höher sein als in einem etablierten PPP-Markt (wie beispielsweise in Großbritannien). Aus Sicht der öffentlichen Hand ist zu bedenken, dass durch einen Risikotransfer auf den Privaten ohne angemessenen Risikozuschlag das Insolvenzrisiko bei der Umsetzung des Projektes steigt.

Aufgrund der großen Bedeutung der adäquaten Risikoverteilung befasst sich auch der Arbeitskreis „PPP im Management öffentlicher Immobilien" des Bundesverbandes PPP e.V. umfassend mit dem Thema und zeigt in seinem Arbeitspapier „Risiken immobilienwirtschaftlicher PPPs aus Sicht der beteiligten Akteure" eine vorteilhafte Risikoverteilung auf.[31] Im Thesenpapier „Optimierung von Wirtschaftlichkeitsuntersuchungen in immobilienwirtschaftlichen PPPs" des o.g. Arbeitskreises findet sich folgende Stellungnahme: „Aktuelle PPP-Projekte beinhalten häufig die Übertragung von Risiken, die weder von der öffentlichen Hand noch vom privaten Partner kalkuliert werden können. Da solche nicht kalkulierbaren Risiken keine fundierte Berücksichtigung im Wirtschaftlichkeitsvergleich finden können, muss eine Übertragung auf den privaten Partner ausgeschlossen werden. In Fachausschüssen sollten daher „nicht kalkulierbare" und

[31] Vgl. Arbeitskreis PPP im Management öffentlicher Immobilien im BPPP e.V. (2006).

damit auch vergaberechtlich nicht übertragbare Risiken definiert und in standardisierten Verträgen berücksichtigt werden."[32]

4.4 Optimierung der Finanzierungsstrukturen

Die Finanzierung eines PPP-Projektes ist wichtiger Baustein und Voraussetzung für eine erfolgreiche Leistungserbringung. Die Wahl eines geeigneten Finanzierungsmodells wurde und wird in der Fachöffentlichkeit nach wie vor kontrovers diskutiert. Grundsätzlich wird dabei, wie unter Abschnitt 2.4 beschrieben, zwischen Forfaitierung mit Einredeverzicht und Projektfinanzierung unterschieden. Gemäß dem Positionspapier „Die ersten PPP-Projekte im öffentlichen Hochbau – Lessons Learned" des Hauptverbandes der Deutschen Bauindustrie gibt die deutsche Bauindustrie keine grundsätzliche Empfehlung für eine Finanzierungsvariante ab und bemerkt, dass es bei der Diskussion um die richtige Finanzierungsform von PPPs „(…) vielfach an Transparenz über die Höhe der zu berücksichtigenden Finanzierungskosten und den Umfang der Risiko- und Aufgabenübertragung (…)" fehlt.[33]

Neben den o.g. Finanzierungsformen ist auch zwischen den einzelnen Projektphasen zu unterscheiden. Während der Planungs- und Bauphase eines Immobilienprojektes fallen in vergleichsweise kurzer Zeit sehr hohe Kosten an. Diese Kosten werden in einer PPP in der Regel bis zur Fertigstellung des Objektes von der Privatwirtschaft zwischenfinanziert und mit Abnahme des Objektes in eine Endfinanzierung mit meist 20- bis 30-jähriger Laufzeit überführt. Gegenüber den Investitionskosten fallen die Betriebskosten (Reinigung, Instandhaltung, Energie/Medien, etc.) der Immobilie überwiegend kontinuierlich über die Laufzeit an, so dass keine nennenswerte Finanzierung der Betriebskosten erforderlich ist. Ausnahme bilden hierbei die unregelmäßigen Instandsetzungs- und Instandhaltungsmaßnahmen, die teilweise finanziert werden müssen.

---

32 Arbeitskreis PPP im Management öffentlicher Immobilien im BPPP e.V. (2007).

33 Vgl. Hauptverband der Deutschen Bauindustrie (2006).

Tabelle 1 zeigt einen Vergleich der Finanzierungsformen aus Sicht praktischer Projekterfahrungen.

	Forfaitierung mit Einredeverzicht	**Projektfinanzierung**
Planungs- und Bauphase	Risiko beim privaten Partner, Zahlungsbeginn erst nach Fertigstellung und Abnahme	Risiko beim privaten Partner, Zahlungsbeginn erst nach Fertigstellung und Abnahme
Betrieb	Leistungsabhängige Vergütung über Service-Level-Agreements mit Malusregelungen	Leistungsabhängige Vergütung über Service-Level-Agreements mit Malusregelungen
Schlechtleistung	Kürzung bei Schlechtleistung durch Einbehalt des Betriebsentgelts	Kürzung bei Schlechtleistung durch Einbehalt des Betriebsentgelts
Schlechtleistung (gravierend)	Kürzung bei gravierender Schlechtleistung i. H. des Betriebsentgeltes möglich, darüber hinaus Rückgriff auf Bürgschaften und Versicherungen	Kürzung bei gravierender Schlechtleistung i. H. des Betriebsentgeltes sowie auch i. H. des Kapitaldienstes möglich
Sicherheiten	Sicherheitskonzept ist explizit zu regeln über Bürgschaften, Versicherungen, Instandhaltungsrücklagenkonto und Eintrittsrechten, etc.	Sicherheitskonzept ist implizit im Finanzierungskonzept enthalten
Kreditkonditionen	kommunalkreditähnlich	bezogen auf Projekt
Verträge	Standardisierte Finanzierungsverträge, geringer Prüfaufwand seitens Bank	projektbezogene Finanzierungsverträge, hoher Prüfaufwand seitens Bank (Due Diligence)
Fördermittel	Einbindung Fördermittel möglich	Einbindung Fördermittel möglich

Tab. 1: Vergleich der Finanzierungsformen

Quelle: eigene Darstellung.

4.5 Positiver Strukturwandel beim öffentlichen Immobilienmanagement

Die Effizienzgewinne einer PPP stehen in der öffentlichen Diskussion der Beschaffungsvarianten meist im Vordergrund, da diese wirtschaftlich messbare, monetäre Vorteile darstellen. Darüber hinaus bewirken PPPs auch einen positiven Strukturwandel beim öffentlichen Immobilienmanagement, der sich in verschiedenen Aspekten zeigt.

Modernisierung der Verwaltung

Das PPP-Konzept entfaltet auch Wirkungen auf das Immobilienmanagement der öffentlichen Hand. PPP zielt dabei insgesamt auf den Umbau des öffentlichen Aufgabenspektrums. Neben der reinen öffentlichen bzw. privaten Aufgabenwahrnehmung wird ein Mittelweg beschritten, um Effizienzsteigerungen und Leistungsverbesserungen zu erreichen, ohne den öffentlichen Einfluss aufgeben zu müssen. Für dieses neue Selbstverständnis der Aufgabenerledigung werden auch neue innere Strukturen benötigt, so dass verwaltungsinterne Organisationsstrukturen nicht unberührt bleiben werden. Durch die Einbeziehung privaten Kapitals und Know-hows werden im Rahmen von PPP-Projekten ökonomische Entscheidungskriterien bewusst in den Vordergrund gerückt. Dies führt dazu, dass die öffentliche Hand ihr Verwaltungshandeln verstärkt an Indikatoren wie Effizienz und Effektivität auszurichten versucht.

Die Verwaltungen können sich die Marktkenntnisse und die unternehmerische Kompetenz Privater zunutze machen und durch die Wahrnehmung von Aufgaben in Form von PPP die Verwaltung entlasten, unternehmerische Flexibilität gewinnen sowie die beteiligten Verwaltungseinheiten qualifizieren und flexibilisieren. Die öffentliche Hand kann sich auf ihre Kernaufgaben konzentrieren und bezüglich der betroffenen Aufgabe eine reine Gewährleistungsfunktion übernehmen. Dies fördert zum einen die angestrebte Verschlankung der Verwaltung, zum anderen verändert es das Aufgabenspektrum der beteiligten Einheiten. Mitarbeiter der Verwaltung werden sich im Rahmen der Durchführung eines PPP-Vorhabens insbesondere zusätzliches Wissen in den Bereichen Projektmanagement und Projektcontrolling aneignen.

Die PPP-Entwicklung dürfte die Kultur des öffentlichen Sektors daher insgesamt stärker ökonomisch prägen. Die mit der Übertragung von Aufgaben auf die Privatwirtschaft verbundene notwendige Verschlankung der Verwaltung ermöglicht es ihr, sich auf ihre Kernaufgaben zu konzentrieren, d. h. auf die Hoheitsverwaltung und auf die Rolle als Beschaffer und Steuerer wichtiger Leistungen, die Private oft besser erfüllen können.

Kostentransparenz

Durch eine PPP werden die gesamten Kosten für Planung, Bau, Finanzierung und Betrieb der Immobilie in Form des vereinbarten Leistungsentgelts transparent. Eine PPP trägt damit zu einer gewissen Planungssicherheit der öffentlichen Hand bei der Haushaltsaufstellung bei.

Das Ausmaß der Kostensicherheit hängt entscheidend von der Ausgestaltung des PPP-Vertrages und der Risikoverteilung zwischen der öffentlichen Hand und dem Privaten ab. In der Regel übernimmt der Private das Risiko für die Höhe des ermittelten Leistungsentgeltes, wobei die Zahlungen lediglich über die Vertragslaufzeit indexiert werden. Damit ergibt sich für die öffentliche Hand eine Kostensicherheit, die sie im Fall der konventionellen Eigenrealisierung der Immobilie nur selten erreichen wird.

Gesicherter Werterhalt

Der hohe Instandhaltungs- und Instandsetzungsrückstau bei öffentlichen Immobilien zeigt, dass die öffentliche Hand in der Vergangenheit zu wenig in ihren Immobilienbestand investiert hat.[34] Notwendige Ersatz- bzw. Erweiterungsinvestitionen in die öffentlichen Immobilien unterbleiben häufig aufgrund der

[34] Vgl. Reidenbach, M. et al. (2002).

Finanzlage der öffentlichen Haushalte. Der Instandhaltungsrückstau führt dazu, dass Immobilien teilweise nur noch eingeschränkt genutzt werden können oder gar abgerissen und an anderer Stelle neu aufgebaut werden müssen. Die dann erforderlichen Investitionskosten können im Verhältnis zu den Kosten einer regelmäßigen Unterhaltung und Instandsetzung erheblich höher sein, da sich die Schäden im Laufe der Zeit teilweise potenzieren.

Bei der Realisierung einer Immobilie als PPP-Modell wird hingegen die Werterhaltung der Immobilie von Anfang an vertraglich gesichert. Der private Partner hat im Allgemeinen eine regelmäßige Instandhaltung der Immobilie über die Vertragslaufzeit durchzuführen, sodass der vertraglich vereinbarte Zustand der Immobilie jederzeit sichergestellt ist und die öffentliche Hand am Ende der Vertragslaufzeit eine voll funktionsfähige Immobilie übergeben bekommt. Damit wird auch die Versorgung der Bürger mit öffentlichen Gütern und Dienstleistungen verbessert.

Beschleunigte Beschaffung

Über eine PPP-Beschaffung können öffentliche Bauvorhaben schneller realisiert werden, als dies bei einer konventionellen Beschaffung durch die öffentliche Hand der Fall wäre.[35] Die Beschleunigungseffekte resultieren zum einen aus der unternehmerischen Kompetenz des Privaten, da von ihm eine effizientere und marktnähere Arbeitsweise erwartet werden kann, und zum anderen aus der größeren Unabhängigkeit der Entscheidungen von den komplexen und zeitintensiven Abläufen der öffentlichen Verwaltung. Ein Privater ist in der Wahrnehmung von PPP-Aufgaben in der Regel unabhängiger von der politischen Einflussnahme als die Verwaltungsangehörigen. Zudem ist er nicht den vielfältigen rechtlichen Restriktionen des öffentlichen Rechts, insbesondere des öffentlichen Organisations-, Personal-, Haushalts- und Vergaberechts unterworfen. Dies beinhaltet die Chance, dass die Projekte von den Beteiligten fachorientierter

[35] Vgl. Deutsches Institut für Urbanistik (Hrsg.) (2005).

und professioneller durchgeführt werden können, was auch zu einer Steigerung der Qualität der zu erbringenden Leistung beitragen kann.

Steigerung der Nutzerzufriedenheit

Neben den wirtschaftlichen Vorteilen einer PPP in Form der Effizienzgewinne entfalten PPP-Projekte insbesondere auch erhebliche Vorteile im Bereich der Nutzerzufriedenheit. In diesem Zusammenhang haben Studien der TU Darmstadt zum PPP-Schulprojekt im Kreis Offenbach (Los West) gezeigt[36], dass die Motivation von Schülern und Lehrern sowie die Identifikation der Schüler mit ihrer Schule und die Arbeitszufriedenheit der Lehrer nach der Durchführung der im Rahmen einer PPP realisierten Sanierungsmaßnahmen signifikant gestiegen ist. Die Sanierung hat bewirkt, dass sich Schüler und Lehrer emotional stärker an ihre Schule gebunden fühlen. Dies wiederum geht mit einer höheren Motivation und höherem körperlichen Wohlbefinden einher. Grundsätzlich ist davon auszugehen, dass PPP-Maßnahmen allgemein zu einer erheblichen Steigerung der Arbeitsproduktivität führen, die zusätzlich zu den wirtschaftlichen Kriterien bei der Frage der PPP-Projektrealisierung bewertet werden sollte.

[36] Vgl. Pfnür, A./Hirt, K./Egres, P. (2007).

4.6 Zusammenfassung praktischer Erfahrungen zu PPP

Zusammenfassend sind in der folgenden Tabelle die praktischen Erfahrungen zu PPP, untergliedert in Vor- und Nachteile, aufgeführt.

Vorteil	Erläuterung
Optimierung der Lebenszykluskosten	Die Einbindung Privater in den gesamten Lebenszyklus der Immobilie stellt für sie aufgrund der damit verbundenen Risikoübertragung und der Langfristigkeit der Verträge einen großen Anreiz zur Lebenszykluskostenoptimierung dar.
Reduzierung von Schnittstellen	Durch die gesamtheitliche Vergabe aller Leistungen an einen privaten Partner („alles aus einer Hand") wird das Schnittstellenrisiko minimiert und Nachtragsforderungen aus Bau und Planung bzgl. der sonst üblichen Schnittstellenproblematiken aus Ausführungs- und Planungsgewerken werden eliminiert.
Optimierung der Risikoallokation	Im Rahmen einer PPP werden die Risiken zwischen Öffentlicher Hand und Privatem nach dem Grundsatz der Risikomanagementkompetenz optimal verteilt, wonach jeder diejenigen Risiken übernehmen sollte, die er am besten beherrschen kann.
Optimierung der Finanzierung	Im Rahmen eines PPP-Modells wird je nach Projektart, Projektgröße und Risikostruktur die für das Immobilienvorhaben optimale Finanzierungsstruktur entwickelt.
Nutzung des Know-hows der Privatwirtschaft	Bei der Vergabe eines PPP-Projektes findet unter den privaten Bietern neben dem Preis- auch ein Innovationswettbewerb statt, der zu effizienteren Formen der Leistungserbringung beiträgt.
Modernisierung der Verwaltungsstrukturen	Die Betonung ökonomischer Entscheidungskriterien im Rahmen einer PPP führt dazu, dass die Kommune ihr Verwaltungshandeln verstärkt an Indikatoren wie Effizienz und Effektivität auszurichten versucht. Die öffentliche Hand konzentriert sich auf ihre Kernaufgaben und übernimmt eine reine Gewährleistungsfunktion, was zur Verschlankung der Verwaltung beiträgt.
Kostentransparenz und Kostensicherheit	Die Lebenszykluskosten einer Immobilie werden in Form des an den Privaten zu zahlenden Leistungsentgelts in einer frühen Projektphase transparent.

Werterhaltung der Immobilie	Bei einem PPP-Projekt hat der private Partner die regelmäßige Instandhaltung der Immobilie über die Vertragslaufzeit durchzuführen, so dass die Werterhaltung der Immobilie vertraglich gesichert ist und die öffentliche Hand am Ende der Vertragslaufzeit einc voll funktionsfähige Immobilie übergeben bekommt.
Beschleunigte Beschaffung	Aus der unternehmerischen Kompetenz des Privaten und seiner größeren Unabhängigkeit von der öffentlichen Verwaltung, ihren Entscheidungsprozessen und rechtlichen Restriktionen resultieren Beschleunigungseffekte bei der Immobilienbeschaffung.
Steigerung der Nutzerzufriedenheit	Durch die beschleunigte und effektive Immobilienrealisierung im Rahmen einer PPP steigt die Zufriedenheit und Identifikation der Nutzer mit ihrer Immobilie, wodurch die Arbeitsproduktivität gesteigert werden kann.
Nachteil	**Erläuterung**
Hoher Planungs- und Abstimmungsaufwand in der Ausschreibungsphase auf Seiten der öffentlichen Hand	Oftmals wird der im Verhältnis hohe Planungs- und Abstimmungsaufwand in der Ausschreibungsphase und dessen Vorbereitung als Nachteil genannt. Dem im Vergleich zu einer konventionellen Beschaffungsvariante relativ hohen Aufwand der einmaligen PPP-Ausschreibung sind jedoch die ersparten Aufwendungen für die zahlreichen Einzelausschreibungen der Folgejahre gegenüberzustellen. Im Ergebnis zeigen die realisierten Projekte mit Effizienzgewinnen von bis zu 20%, dass in der Summe die Wirtschaftlichkeit gegeben ist.
Hoher Aufwand bei der Angebotsbearbeitung auf Seiten der privaten Bieter	PPP-Angebote erfordern in der Regel aufgrund des Umfangs der ausgeschriebenen Leistungen (Planung, Bau, Finanzierung und Betrieb) und der erforderlichen detaillierten Planungstiefe erhebliche personelle und finanzielle Ressourcen auf Seiten der privaten Bieter. Dieser erhöhte Aufwand sollte kompensiert werden durch eine angemessene Entschädgungszahlung an die unterlegenen Bieter sowie eine starke Selektion der Bieter im Vergabeverfahren zur Erhöhung der Zuschlagswahrscheinlichkeit.

Lange Dauer des PPP-Vergabeverfahrens	Als Nachteil wird häufig die lange Dauer des PPP-Vergabeverfahrens angesehen, die je nach Projektgröße und -umfang zwischen einem halben Jahr und 1 ½ Jahren liegt. Diesem Zeitraum ist jedoch die Dauer der ansonsten zahlreichen erforderlichen Einzelausschreibungen gegenüberzustellen, so dass der Zeitnachteil nicht ins Gewicht fallen sollte.
Hohe Komplexität der PPP-Projekte	Öffentliche Auftraggeber beklagen zum Teil die hohe Komplexität von PPP-Projekten aufgrund der umfassenden Leistungsübertragung und der langfristigen Verträge. Dies bietet jedoch auch die Chance, ein Projekt zu einem sehr frühen Zeitpunkt in seiner Gesamtheit zu betrachten und somit rechtzeitig Schwierigkeiten und Problemstellungen zu erkennen und zu beseitigen. Unterstützung erhalten öffentliche Auftraggeber zudem von zahlreichen PPP-Kompetenzzentren und sonstigen Beratern.

Tab. 2: Übersicht praktischer Erfahrungen zu PPP
Quelle: eigene Darstellung.

5 Ausblick

Die Realisierung öffentlicher Infrastrukturprojekte auf privatwirtschaftlicher Basis ist in Deutschland in den vergangenen Jahren ein wachsender Trend. Bei den bis Ende 2006 in Deutschland realisierten PPP-Projekten im öffentlichen Hochbau betrugen die Effizienzvorteile für die öffentliche Hand durchschnittlich 16 %. Das entspricht rund 220 Millionen Euro. Bis 2010 wird, so der Hauptverband der Deutschen Bauindustrie, mit PPP-Projekten mit einem Vertragsvolumen von zehn Milliarden Euro gerechnet.

Aufgrund dieser großen Optimierungspotentiale und des partnerschaftlichen Miteinanders ist zu erwarten, dass die vielfach angewandten und langjährig bewährten umfassenden Lebenszykluskonzepte der öffentlichen Hand künftig auch in privatwirtschaftlichen Projekten Anwendung finden werden. Von den hierdurch zu erzielenden Effizienzgewinnen kann die Privatwirtschaft im selben Maße profitieren wie die öffentliche Hand bei PPPs, sofern geeignete Vergabe-

und Realisierungsmodelle angewendet werden. Aufgrund der Unabhängigkeit der Privatwirtschaft von den Restriktionen des öffentlichen Rechts, insbesondere des öffentlichen Vergaberechts, ist zudem zu erwarten, dass bei rein privatwirtschaftlichen Modellen noch höhere Effizienzgewinne möglich sind. In der Bau- und Immobilienwirtschaft wurde dieser Trend längst erkannt und das Leistungsspektrum entsprechend der notwendigen Kernkompetenzen zunehmend vernetzt und systematisch erweitert.

So bietet Bilfinger Berger bereits seit mehreren Jahren die ganzheitliche Beratungs-, Bau- und Dienstleistungskompetenz unter dem Markennamen „i.volution" an. Das Unternehmen fungiert dabei als Partner für jede Phase im Lebenszyklus einer Immobilie (vgl. Abb. 10) und verweist auf die jahrelange Erfahrung mit ganzheitlichen, lebenszyklusphasenübergreifenden Projekten für öffentliche und private Kunden.

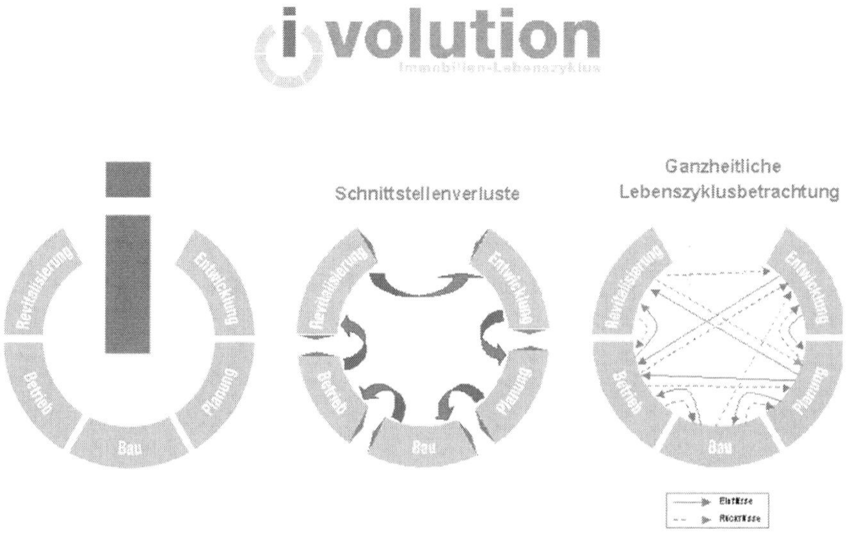

Abb. 10: Ganzheitliches Beratungs-, Bau- und Dienstleistungsangebot von Bilfinger Berger

Quelle: eigene Darstellung.

Literaturverzeichnis

Arbeitskreis PPP im Management öffentlicher Immobilien im BPPP e.V. (2006): Risiken immobilienwirtschaftlicher PPPs aus Sicht der beteiligten Akteure. In: Pfnür, A. (Hrsg.) (2006): Arbeitspapiere zur immobilienwirtschaftlichen Forschung und Praxis, Band Nr. 4. Darmstadt.

Arbeitskreis PPP im Management öffentlicher Immobilien im BPPP e.V. (2007): Optimierung von Wirtschaftlichkeitsuntersuchungen in immobilienwirtschaftlichen PPPs. Ein Thesenpapier. In: Pfnür, A. (Hrsg.) (2007): Arbeitspapiere zur immobilienwirtschaftlichen Forschung und Praxis Band Nr. 9. Darmstadt.

Deutsches Institut für Urbanistik (Hrsg.) (2005): Public Private Partnership Projekte: Eine aktuelle Bestandsaufnahme in Bund, Ländern und Kommunen: Endbericht. Berlin: Deutsches Institut für Urbanistik.

Eppinger, F./Käsewieter, H.-W./Miksch, J. (2005): Die Bedeutung der Finanzierung innerhalb eines PPP-Projektes. In: Meyer-Hofmann, B./Riemenschneider, F./Weihrauch, O. (Hrsg.) (2005): Public Private Partnership: Gestaltung von Leistungsbeschreibung, Finanzierung, Ausschreibung und Verträgen in der Praxis. Köln u.a.: Heymann, S. 290-333.

Glock, Ch./Früh, T. (2007): PPP-Pilotprojekt des Freistaates Sachsen: Justizzentrum Chemnitz. In: Knop, D. (Hrsg.) (2007): Public Private Partnership Jahrbuch. Frankfurt am Main: ConVent, S. 54-58.

Graubner, C.-A./Hüske, K. (2003): Nachhaltigkeit im Bauwesen. Berlin: Ernst & Sohn Verlag.

Grotowski, T. (2005): Projektfinanzierung versus kommunale Forfaitierung? In: Knop, D. (Hrsg.) (2005): Public Private Partnership Jahrbuch. Frankfurt am Main: ConVent, S. 56-58.

Hauptverband der Deutschen Bauindustrie (Hrsg.) (2006): Positionspapier: Die ersten PPP-Projekte im öffentlichen Hochbau – Lessons Learned. Berlin: Hauptverband der deutschen Bauindustrie.

Hauptverband der deutschen Bauindustrie (Hrsg.) (2007): Public Private Partnership im öffentlichen Hochbau: Eine Idee wird Realität – PPP-Projekte in Deutschland 2006/2007. Berlin: Hauptverband der deutschen Bauindustrie.

Herzog, K. (2005): Lebenszykluskosten von Baukonstruktionen: Entwicklung eines Modells und einer Softwarekomponente zur ökonomischen Analyse und Nachhaltigkeitsbeurteilung von Gebäuden. Darmstadt: Technische Universität Darmstadt, Institut für Massivbau.

Herzog, K. (2008): Wissensmanagement im Bereich Energieeffizienz zur Umsetzung nachhaltigen Bauens. Wuppertal: Bergische Universität Wuppertal.

Jacob, D./Kochendörfer, B. (2002): Effizienzgewinne bei privatwirtschaftlicher Realisierung von Infrastrukturvorhaben: Wie effizient ist die Einbeziehung Privater bei öffentlichen Hoch- und Straßenbaumaßnahmen? Köln: Bundesanzeiger-Verlag.

Kumlehn, F. (2001): Ausschreibungs- und Vergabemodell für private Vorfinanzierungs- und PPP-Projekte im Bausektor. Braunschweig: Institut für Bauwirtschaft und Baubetrieb.

Miksch, J. (2007): Sicherungsstrukturen bei PPP-Modellen aus Sicht der öffentlichen Hand, dargestellt am Beispiel des Schulbaus. Berlin: Technische Universität Berlin, Fakultät IV, Fachgebiet Bauwirtschaft und Baubetrieb.

Pfnür, A. (2004): Modernes Immobilienmanagement, Facility Management, Corporate Real Estate Management und Real Estate Investment Management. 2., akt. und erw. Aufl.. Berlin u. a.: Springer.

Pfnür, A./Hirt, K./Egres, P. (2007): Ergebnisbericht zur empirischen Untersuchung: Ganzheitliche Wirtschaftlichkeitsanalyse bei PPP Projekten dargestellt am Beispiel des Schulprojekts im Kreis Offenbach. In: Pfnür, A. (Hrsg.) (2007): Arbeitspapiere zur immobilienwirtschaftlichen Forschung und Praxis, Band Nr. 8. Darmstadt.

Pfnür, A./Eberhardt, T. (2005): Teilung von Risiken in PPPs am Beispiel der Immobilienwirtschaft. In: Keuper, F./Schaefer, Ch. (Hrsg.) (2005): Führung und Steuerung öffentlicher Unternehmungen: Probleme, Politiken und Perspektiven entlang des Privatisierungsprozesses. Berlin: Logos-Verlag, S. 195-221.

Reidenbach, M. et al. (2002): Der kommunale Investitionsbedarf in Deutschland: Eine Schätzung für die Jahre 2000 bis 2009. Berlin: Deutsches Institut für Urbanistik.

Schetter, H.-H. (2006): Public Private Partnership (PPP) – Eine interessante Beschaffungsvariante für öffentliche Hochbaumaßnahmen. In: Trend – Zeitschrift für soziale Marktwirtschaft, Heft 2. Berlin, S. 36-39.

Schultheis, J. (2006): Public Private Partnership bei Stadthallen: Rahmenbedingungen und Gestaltungsmöglichkeiten in Deutschland. Darmstadt: Technische Universität Darmstadt, Institut für Baubetrieb.

Sester, P./Bunsen, Ch. (2005): Vertragliche Grundlagen – Finanzierungsverträge. In: Weber, M./Schäfer, M./Hausmann, F.-L. (Hrsg.) (2005): Praxishandbuch Public Private Partnership: Rechtliche Rahmenbedingungen, Wirtschaftlichkeit, Finanzierung. München: Beck, S. 436-498.

Weber, M./Moß, O./Bachhuber, F. (2005): Anforderungen und Besonderheiten bei der Finanzierung von PPP-Projekten. In: Weber, M./Schäfer, M./Hausmann, F.-L. (Hrsg.) (2005): Praxishandbuch Public Private Partnership: Rechtliche Rahmenbedingungen, Wirtschaftlichkeit, Finanzierung. München: Beck, S. 599-640.

Weber, M./Moß, O./Parzych, A. (2005): Wirtschaftlichkeitsuntersuchungen als Erkenntnis- und Entscheidungsprozess. In: Weber, M./Schäfer, M./Hausmann,

F.-L. (Hrsg.) (2005): Praxishandbuch Public Private Partnership: Rechtliche Rahmenbedingungen, Wirtschaftlichkeit, Finanzierung. München: Beck, S. 499-597.

Weber, M./Moß, O./Schwichow, H. (2004): Finanzierungsleitfaden: Public Private Partnership im Hochbau. Düsseldorf: Finanzministerium des Landes Nordrhein-Westfalen.

Wegner, H.-J./Böing, B./Jürgenliemk, R. (2005): Projektfinanzierung auch bei leeren Kassen? In: Knop, D. (Hrsg.) (2005): Public Private Partnership Jahrbuch. Frankfurt am Main: ConVent, S. 52-55.

Wegner, H.-J./Makowka, T./Hedrich, Ch. (2006): Projektfinanzierung: Erfolgsfaktor für PPP-Projekte. In: Knop, D. (Hrsg.) (2006): Public Private Partnership Jahrbuch. Frankfurt am Main: ConVent, S. 89-92.

Erfolgsmodell für Seilbahnprojekte? PPP am Beispiel der Innsbrucker Nordkettenbahnen

Michael Seeber

Inhaltsverzeichnis

Abkürzungsverzeichnis

DLKV	Dienstleistungskonzessionsvertrag
HBB	Hungerburgbahn
IKB	Innsbrucker Kommunalbetriebe AG
INKB	Innsbrucker Nordkettenbahnen GmbH
IVB	Innsbrucker Verkehrsbetriebe AG
LTD	limited
m/s	Meter pro Sekunde
NK	Nordkette
Pers./h	Personen pro Stunde
TVI	Tourismusverband Innsbruck

1 Einleitung

Erklärtes Ziel dieses Beitrags ist ein kurzer Überblick über die Bedeutung und Struktur der Bergbahnen in Tirol im Allgemeinen. Weiters soll anhand des Beispiels der Innsbrucker Nordkettenbahnen im Besonderen dokumentiert werden, welche Möglichkeiten mit diesem PPP-Modell, verglichen mit dem vorherigen Betrieb durch die öffentliche Hand, ausgeschöpft werden konnten. Chancen und Risiken runden den Beitrag ab.

2 Situation der Bergbahnen in Tirol

Wenn in diesem Artikel von Tirol gesprochen wird, so beziehen sich die Angaben immer auf Nord- und Osttirol, also die österreichischen Landesteile Tirols. Mehr als 3/4 der Landesfläche besteht aus Gebirge. Etwa 1/3 der Landesfläche Tirols ist in Form von Schutzgebieten (Landschaftsschutz, Naturschutz, Ruhegebiete, etc.) ausgewiesen, 0,6% der Landesfläche sind Pisten-flächen, das entspricht 7300 Hektar. Bergbahnen als Transportsystem haben vor allem touristische Bedeutung, nur in wenigen Ausnahmefällen in entlegenen Gebieten stellen Seilbahnen für die dortigen Bergbewohner im Vergleich zu gefährlichen kurvenreichen Bergstraßen die schnellere Verbindung zwischen Bergsiedlung und Talboden dar, ohne dass diese Bahnen touristisch genutzt würden.

Tirol lebt zu einem großen Teil vom Fremdenverkehr, einen Schwerpunkt dabei bildet die touristische Nutzung der Berge. Die Seilbahnbranche beschäftigt in der Wintersaison bis zu 8.600 Personen und erzielt eine jährliche Wertschöpfung von 550 Mio. €, die Förderkapazität aller Bahnen beträgt mehr als 1,4 Mio. Personen in der Stunde und übertrifft dabei die Kapazitäten innerstädtischer Verkehrsmittel von Großstädten. Im Jahr 2007 verzeichnete man insgesamt 199,8 Mio. Personen-Beförderungsfälle.[1]

---

[1] Daten entnommen aus dem Wirtschaftsbericht der Wirtschaftskammer Tirol Bereich Seilbahnen.

Die unten stehende Aufstellung gibt einen Überblick über die zehn umsatzstärksten Seilbahnbetriebe.[2]

Unternehmen	**Ort**	**Umsatz (Mio. €)**
Silvretta Seilbahn AG	Ischgl	53,0
Arlberger Bergbahnen AG	St.Anton a.A.	32,0
Bergbahn AG Kitzbühel	Kitzbühel	31,0
Wintersport Tirol AG & Co Stubaier Bergbahnen KG	Neustift i. St.	27,5
Zillertaler Gletscherbahnen GmbH & Co KG	Hintertux	26,0
Ötztaler Gletscherbahnen GmbH & Co KG Sölden Tirol	Sölden	22,0
Schiliftgesellschaft Sölden Hochsölden GmbH	Sölden	22,0
Mayrhofner Bergbahnen AG	Mayrhofen	22,0
Seilbahn Komperdell GmbH	Serfaus	21,0
Fisser Bergbahnen GmbH	Fiss	16,5

Tab. 1: Übersicht über die umsatzstärksten Bergbahnen in Tirol
Quelle: ECONOVA.

Die Seilbahnbetriebe lassen sich nach ihrem wirtschaftlichen Erfolg in drei Gruppen einteilen:
Ungefähr ein Drittel der Bergbahnen verdient so viel, dass sie sämtliche Investitionen aus dem eigenen Cash flow finanzieren könnten. Ein weiteres Drittel kommt positiv über die Runden, der Rest sind „Bürgermeisterbahnen", also meistens kleinere Unternehmen, die nicht wirtschaftlich zu führen sind, aber mit regelmäßigen Zuschüssen aus der öffentlichen Hand überleben, bzw. Bergbahnen, die ganz oder teilweise im Eigentum von Gemeinden stehen. Gerechtfertigt werden diese Subventionen dadurch, dass erst durch die Infrastruktur einer Seilbahn viele andere Betriebe (Hotels, Gaststätten, Schischulen, Sportartikelhandel) eine wirtschaftliche Grundlage finden.

[2] Die größten unter den Bergbahnen liegen in weltbekannten Wintersportorten.

Die Innsbrucker Nordkettenbahnen, welche von der Nordpark Errichtungs- und Betriebs-GmbH geführt werden, gehören mit einem erwarteten Umsatz von unter 4 Mio. zu den kleineren Bergbahnen. Innerhalb der Bergbahnen hat die Nordpark Errichtungs- und Betriebs-GmbH eine Sonderstellung, weil sie nicht nur Bergbahn, sondern mit der Hungerburgbahn auch ein innerstädtisches Verkehrsmittel darstellt.

3 PPP am Beispiel der Innsbrucker Nordkettenbahnen

3.1 Geschichte der Bahnen

Die Hungerburg ist die Bezeichnung für eine Hochebene über Innsbruck, welche früher als ein Naherholungsgebiet galt und mittlerweile als Wohngebiet an Bedeutung gewinnt. Die alte Hungerburgbahn wurde am 12. September 1906 eröffnet. Diese Bahn wurde als Standseilbahn ausgeführt und stellte als zweite Seilbahn Tirols mit einer 156 m langen Schrägbrücke über den Inn und einem 160 m langen Viadukt bis zu 12 m über dem Boden im oberen Bereich damals eine technische Meisterleistung dar.[3] Eine weitere technische Sensation waren die beiden Pendelbahnen auf die Nordkette, die 1929 ihren Betrieb aufnahmen. Diese verbinden die Hungerburg (863 m Seehöhe) mit der Seegrube (1.905 m) und die Seegrube mit dem Hafelekar (2.256 m). Nicht nur die Seilbahn war damals zukunftsweisend, auch die Architektur des Tiroler Architekten Franz Baumann zählte zu den wichtigsten Beispielen alpinen Bauens in der Zwischenkriegszeit.

[3] Vgl. http://www.sagen.at/texte/sagen/oesterreich/tirol/innsbruck/hungerburgbahn.html vom 03.08.2008, Quelle: Franz-Heinz Hye, Vom "Grauenstein" zur Hungerburg, Geschichte des Stadtteiles Hoch-Innsbruck, Innsbruck 1982, S. 70 - 78.

3.2 Entscheidung für einen Neubau

Die Bahnen waren am Beginn des 21. Jahrhunderts am Ende ihrer technischen Leistungsfähigkeit. Die Stadt Innsbruck als Eigentümerin suchte nach einer Lösung für eine das Budget schonende Erneuerung der Bahnen, wobei mit dem neuen Projekt gleichzeitig ein Alleinstellungsmerkmal für Innsbruck gefunden werden sollte.

In einem 2003 von INKB (Innsbrucker Nordkettenbahnen GmbH) und Stadt Innsbruck veröffentlichten Bericht wurde festgestellt, dass die dringend notwendigen Investitionen für die Komplettsanierung und technische Neuinstandsetzung der Hungerburgbahn und der Sektionen I und II der Nordkettenbahn ca. 30,7 Mio. € erfordern würde. Zudem wäre ein wirtschaftlicher Betrieb durch die Innsbrucker Nordkettenbahnen GmbH, einer Gesellschaft im überwiegenden Eigentum der Stadt Innsbruck, trotz dieser Investitionen nicht möglich. Der seitens der Innsbrucker Nordkettenbahnen ausgearbeitete Businessplan für ein künftiges Gesamtunternehmen Hungerburg- und Nordkettenbahn hatte unter Zugrundelegung der bisherigen Situierung der Talstation und Trassenführung eine fundamentale Unwirtschaftlichkeit dieser Option aufgezeigt. Eine neue Trassenführung, mit der das Zentrum angebunden werden sollte, sollte die Erlöse laut einer Studie um ca. 50 % steigern können. Daher wurde eine Ausschreibung durchgeführt mit dem Ziel, im Rahmen eines Vergabeverfahrens jenen Anbieter auszuwählen, der die Hungerburgbahn zu den besten Konditionen neu errichtet und die Nordkettenbahnen als Generalunternehmer zu einem anzugebenden maximalen Pauschalpreis (Höchstbetrag) modernisiert.

Der Gemeinderat beschloss die Ausschreibung eines Dienstleistungskonzessionsvertrages und die Übernahme der Kosten in Höhe von 41,2 Mio. € in Form eines Gesellschafterzuschusses an die INKB.

Von sieben Teilnahmeanträgen an der Ausschreibung langten letztlich zwei Angebote von Bietern ein. Die Bestbieterermittlung führte zu einem Zuschlag an die Firma Strabag AG in Wien. Der Auftragnehmer musste sich verpflichten, spätestens bei Übernahme des Betriebs der Haupteinrichtungen einen Arbeitskräfteüberlassungsvertrag abzuschließen. Damit war von Anfang an geregelt, dass sowohl die bisherigen Dienstnehmer der IVB bei den Nordkettenbahnen, welche in einem pragmatisierten Arbeitsverhältnis stehen, als auch Vertragsbedienstete der INKB nach Übernahme durch einen privaten Betreiber weiterhin ihren Dienst bei den Bergbahnen auf der Nordkette versehen.

3.3 Projekt

Das Siegerprojekt konnte mit folgender Trassenführung, Ideen und Zielen reüssieren:

Eine Standseilbahn beginnt unterirdisch beim Congresshaus, stoppt bei der Station Löwenhaus, quert über einem auf zwei Pylonen hängenden s-förmigen Brückenbauwerk den Inn und wird durch einen Tunnel bis zur neuen Station Alpenzoo geführt. Von dort verläuft die Standseilbahn in einer leichten Linkskurve oberirdisch in die Trasse der alten Hungerburgbahn. Von der dortigen Bergstation ist die Talstation der Nordkettenbahn Sektion I fußläufig erreichbar.

Die alten Pendelbahnen der Nordkettenbahnen werden durch neue Pendelbahnsysteme ersetzt, wobei die vorhandenen denkmalgeschützten Gebäude in Abstimmung mit der Denkmalschutzbehörde restauriert, vergrößert und weiterverwendet werden. Die neuen Stationen der Standseilbahn sollen durch moderne Architektur beeindrucken, für die Planung konnte Zaha Hadid LTD in London gewonnen werden.

Abb. 1: Schematische Darstellung der Nordkettenbahnen
Quelle: Unternehmensdaten der Leitner GmbH.

Eigentümerin der neu zu errichtenden Anlagen bleibt die Innsbrucker Nordkettenbahnen GmbH. Diese ist nach wie vor Inhaberin der Seilbahnkonzessionen und schreibt die Bahnen steuerlich ab. Um die Verluste aus den Abschreibungen steuerlich zu nutzen, beteiligen sich die Innsbrucker Kommunalbetriebe an der INKB GmbH. Damit können für die Stadt Innsbruck als (Teil-)Eigentümerin der IKB für eine Dauer von 30 Jahren jährlich Ertragssteuerminderungen geltend gemacht werden. Dazu kommen für die Stadt monetäre Entlastungseffekte durch den Wegfall der doch beträchtlichen Betriebsabgänge. Somit hat sich für die Stadt Innsbruck der Wechsel zum PPP-Modell mit Sicherheit gelohnt.

3.4 Abwicklung des PPP-Projektes

Nachdem die Strabag den Auftrag erfolgreich erstanden hatte, gründete sie die Nordpark Errichtungs- und Betriebs-GmbH und holte sich in weiterer Folge die Leitner GmbH als Partner mit einer Beteiligung von 49 % mit ins Boot.

Im Dezember 2005 wurde mit dem Bau begonnen. Die Niedrigwasserperiode wurde genutzt, um die 241,5 m lange geschwungene Brücke, gespannt an zwei 34 m hohen Pylonen, über den ca. 70 m breiten Inn zu schlagen.

Bei den Vortriebsarbeiten für den Weiherburgtunnel gab es dabei immer wieder Rückschläge, zwei Mal brach eine Binge ein. Der Vortrieb musste teilweise von oben mit ca. 45° Steilheit nach unten erfolgen. Bei den von Zaha LTD geplanten Stationsgebäuden wurden die Gläser für die Umhüllung aus China geliefert. Abweichungen im Bereich mehrerer Millimeter bei den dreidimensional geschwungen geformten Bauteilen führten immer wieder zum Bruch beim Einbau einzelner Gläser auf der Baustelle. Die Lieferfristen der einzelnen nachzuliefernden Glasscheiben aus China betrug mehr als zwei Monate, was immer wieder Ursache für spitze Bemerkungen in den Medien war. Im Zuge der Untertunnelung des Rennwegs im Bereich des Congresshauses wurden zudem mehrere Bauvorhaben der Stadt mitrealisiert; so wurde z.B. der Inndüker modernisiert. Dies hatte zur Folge, dass der Rennweg monatelang für den Straßenverkehr gesperrt bzw. nur mit Behinderungen passierbar war. Auch wenn die Bahnbaustelle nur zu einem Teil die Ursache für die zusätzlichen Staus im innerstädtischen Straßenverkehr war, wurde mit den Staus einzig der Bahnbau in Verbindung gebracht.

Dies führte schon vor der Eröffnung der Bahn zu einem schlechten Image in den Medien. Bereits im Vorfeld war die Bahn immer wieder Zankapfel der Innsbrucker Gemeindepolitik. Es gab Bürgerinitiativen, welche die alte Bahn als Museumsbahn erhalten wollten, weiters Unterschriftenlisten gegen den Bau der neuen Bahn sowie Anrainerproteste von Hausbesitzern, die sich wegen möglicher Lärmbelästigung durch die neue Bahn auf die Hungerburg Sorgen machten. Leider ist es den Erbauern und Betreibern bis heute nicht gelungen, den Gegnern der Bahn den Wind restlos aus den Segeln zu nehmen. Bei jeder sich bietenden Gelegenheit steht die Bahn negativ in der Presse, sei es wegen Blitzschlag oder wegen Notbremsungen. Selbst strittige Personalentscheidungen werden von bestimmten Medien immer wieder breitgetreten.

Die Nordkettenbahn Sektion I wurde noch vor Weihnachten 2006 in Betrieb genommen, die zweite Sektion im Jänner 2007. Aufgrund der Verzögerungen beim Tunnelbau wurde die Hungerburgbahn erst im Dezember 2007 feierlich dem öffentlichen Verkehr übergeben. Bereits im ersten Monat zählte dic Bahn über 60.000 Eintritte.

4 Vertragswerk

4.1 Übersicht

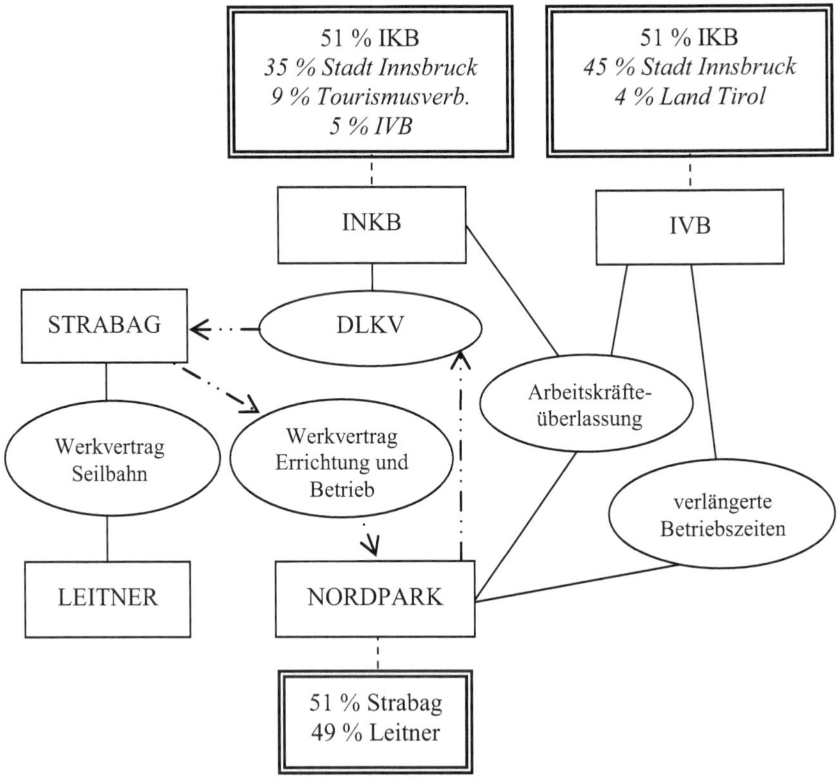

Abb. 2: Vertragsübersicht bei PPP – vereinfachte Darstellung
Quelle: eigene Darstellung.

4.2 Dienstleistungskonzessionsvertrag (DLKV)

Kernstück des Vertragswerks, welches eine Wiener Rechtsanwaltskanzlei federführend entworfen hat, ist der Dienstleistungskonzessionsvertrag.

Darin wird zwischen INKB als Eigentümerin der Bahn und der Strabag SE als Erbauer und Betreiber geregelt, welche Verpflichtungen zu erfüllen sind: Strabag baut die oberen Sektionen um sowie die Hungerburgbahn mit veränderter Trassenführung neu. Strabag bzw. eine Tochtergesellschaft betreibt die Bahn für 30 Jahre und muss ab dem 11. Jahr bei einer entsprechenden Erlössituation einen Teil der Gewinne mit den INKB teilen. Strabag hat das Recht, Partner mit ins Boot zu holen, muss aber stets die Mehrheit behalten. Die Konzessionszeit kann einvernehmlich über das 30. Jahr hinaus verlängert werden. Die INKB als Eigentümerin der Bahn muss sich an jenen Investitionen beteiligen, die fünf Jahre vor Vertragsablauf getätigt werden.

Der DLKV regelt Details über

- Planung
- Errichtung
- Betrieb
- Finanzierung und
- Übertragung der Seilbahninfrastruktur an den Eigentümer.

Durch den Vertrag sollen folgende Ziele erreicht werden:

- Effizienzsteigerung
- Know-how für Konzept, Planung, Realisierung und Betrieb
- Verkürzung der Realisierungszeit
- Übertragung des Betriebs- und Erlösrisikos im vereinbarten Rahmen
- Verhinderung des Verfalls öffentlicher Infrastruktur
- Schaffung einer neuen Attraktion für Einheimische und Touristen
- Begrenzung der Bereitstellung öffentlicher Mittel auf ein vereinbartes Maß

Zu den wesentlichen Elementen des DLKV zählen:

- DBOT-Projekt (Design-Build-Operate-Transfer)
- Konzessionsprojekt, d.h. Preis- und Frequenzrisiko liegen beim Betreiber

- Transfer nach dem 30. Betriebsjahr an die INKB mit Option auf Verlängerung
- Eigentümerin an den alten und neuen Anlagen bleibt die INKB
- der Konzessionär hat das Behördenverfahren im Namen der INKB zu führen
- der Konzessionär erhält einen maximalen Höchstbetrag für die Errichtung (Zuschlagskriterium)
- Entgelt für die Benutzung (Betrieb): fixes Entgelt für die ersten zehn Betriebsjahre, danach variables Entgelt (profit sharing)

4.3 Werkvertrag zwischen Nordpark Errichtung- und Betriebs-GmbH und Strabag AG

Die Nordpark Errichtungs- und Betriebs-GmbH wurde von der Strabag AG gegründet mit dem Zweck, die Bahnen zu bauen und für die nächsten 30 Jahre zu betreiben. Die Nordpark beauftragte die Strabag als Generalunternehmer, die Strabag ihrerseits beauftragte für den seilbahntechnischen Teil die Leitner GmbH.

4.4 Der Syndikatsvertrag

Im Syndikatsvertrag wurden jene Bedingungen festgelegt, zu denen Leitner und Strabag in diesem PPP zusammenarbeiten.

4.5 Arbeitnehmerüberlassungsvertrag

Bedingung bei der Auftragserteilung war, dass die bisherigen Beschäftigten von den neuen Betreibern mittels Arbeitskräfteüberlassung übernommen werden. Dies birgt im laufenden Betrieb ein hohes Konfliktpotential, weil die Arbeitnehmer arbeitsrechtlich völlig unterschiedlich behandelt werden, selbst wenn sie exakt die gleiche Tätigkeit ausführen.

Dabei gibt es drei Arten von Arbeitnehmern:

- Pragmatisierte Bedienstete, die in einem Dienstverhältnis zur IVB standen, als die alte Hungerburgbahn noch im Eigentum der IVB war,
- Vertragsbedienstete mit Dienstverhältnis zur INKB für jene Bedienstete, die bei den alten Nordkettenbahnen angestellt wurden, sowie
- Arbeitnehmer, die einen Dienstvertrag mit der Nordpark Errichtungs- und Betriebs-GmbH abgeschlossen haben

4.6 Verträge im laufenden Betrieb

Von Anfang an achtete die neue Betreibergesellschaft auf win-win-Situationen beim Abschluss von Verträgen für das laufende Geschäft: Egal ob für Restaurantbetrieb auf der Seegrube, Werbeverträge mit Banken oder Medien, Schischulbetreiber oder Gleitschirmfliegerverein, es wurde immer eine Basis für langfristige Zusammenarbeit gesucht.

Um die Hungerburgbahn auch als öffentliches Nahverkehrsmittel interessant zu gestalten, wurden die im DLKV vorgesehenen Betriebszeiten in Abstimmung mit den IVB verlängert. Ein Abrechnungsmodus wurde ausgehandelt, damit auch die Zeitkarten der IVB bei der HBB verwendet werden können. Angebotspakete wurden geschnürt, so bspw. dass beim Alpenzoo-Kombi-Ticket von der Tiefgarage über die Fahrt mit der Bahn bis zum Eintritt in einem niedrigen Package-Preis alles enthalten ist. Die Nordpark Errichtungs- und Betriebs-GmbH ist auch Partner der Innsbruck-Card, im Rahmen derer Wintersportler die Möglichkeit haben, mit einer Saisonkarte mehrere Schigebiete in der Umgebung Innsbrucks zu nutzen.

5 Vergleich der alten mit den neuen Bahnen

Hungerburgbahn:	Alt	Neu
Fassungsvermögen	92+1	130+1
Kapazität	690 Pers./ h	1200 Pers./h
Fahrgeschwindigkeit	2,5 m/s	10 m/s
Nordkettenbahn Sektion I	Alt	Neu
Fassungsvermögen	50+1	95+1
Kapazität	375 Pers./h	800 Pers./h
Fahrgeschwindigkeit	7,5 m/s	10 m/s
Nordkettenbahn Sektion II	Alt	Neu
Fassungsvermögen	50+1	69+1
Kapazität	500 Pers./h	620 Pers./h
Fahrgeschwindigkeit	7 m/s	7 m/s

Tab. 2: Vergleich der alten mit den neuen Bahnen
Quelle: eigene Darstellung, Unternehmensdaten der Leitner GmbH.

6 Chancen durch PPP

Durch die Entscheidung der Stadt Innsbruck, die Nordkettenbahnen über ein PPP-Modell zu erneuern, konnte die öffentliche Hand mit einem vertretbaren Aufwand ein Projekt verwirklichen, welches aufgrund der Superlativen in Bau und Architektur zu einem neuen Wahrzeichen von Innsbruck wurde. Das Interesse internationaler Reiseveranstalter, die neuen Bahnen in ihr Programm aufzunehmen, ist ungebrochen. Innsbruck erhielt mit den neuen Nordkettenbahnen Bauwerke, die für die Stadt ein Alleinstellungsmerkmal bedeuten. Der Anteil an der Finanzierung durch die Unternehmen Strabag und Leitner liegt dabei bei 27 %.

Bedenkt man, dass sich die neuen Betreiber unter anderem auch einen wirtschaftlichen Betrieb der Bahn zum Ziel gesetzt haben, so wurde der Beitrag der öffentlichen Hand an dem Neubau bzw. der Erneuerung gut investiert. Eine gut geführte Bergbahn soll auch umliegenden bzw. branchenverwandten Betrieben bessere Geschäftsmöglichkeiten eröffnen. Alteingesessene Gastronomiebetriebe auf der Hungerburg erleben eine Renaissance, neue Betriebe haben sich bereits dazugesellt. In diesem Zusammenhang wurden auf der Seegrube, am Hafelekar und auf der Hahnenburg neue Arbeitsplätze in der Gastronomie geschaffen; im Bahnbetrieb wurden weitere 14 Personen neu eingestellt. Zudem sind positive Auswirkungen auf die Innsbrucker Almen im Nordpark zu erkennen, der Alpenzoo konnte 2008 ein Besucherplus von 15 % verzeichnen.

Abbildung 3 fasst die Hauptmotive der Nutzer für ihre Fahrt mit den Innsbrucker Nordkettenbahnen zusammen.

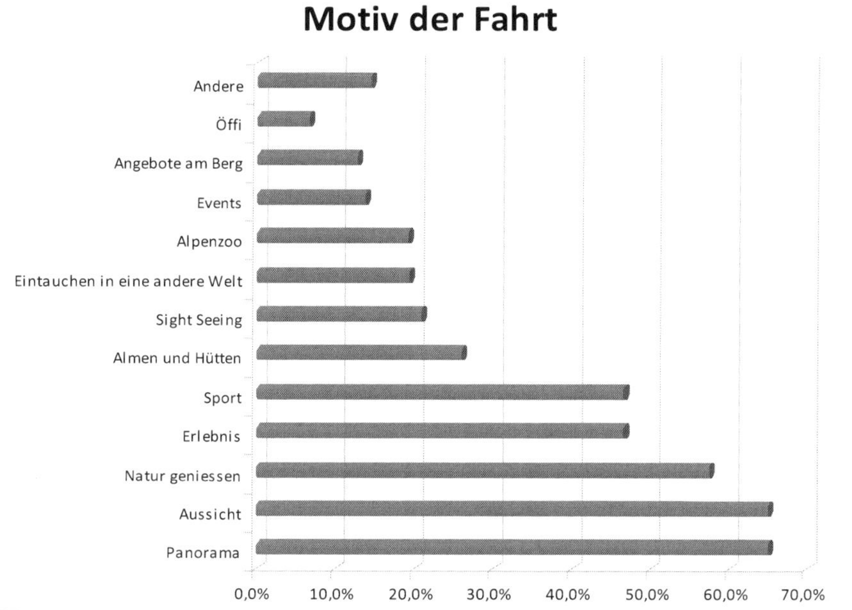

Abb. 3: Motive für eine Fahrt mit den Innsbrucker Nordkettenbahnen
Quelle: Bericht zum 1. Geschäftsjahr der Innsbrucker Nordkettenbahnen.

Schnellere Entscheidungen durch private Betreiber als durch Kollektiventscheidungen im Stadtsenat führen zu mehr Effizienz und letztlich mehr Effektivität im täglichen Betrieb der Bahnen.

Jene Mitarbeiter, die neu eingestellt werden, können nicht mit jenen Vorrechten spekulieren, welche den pragmatisierten Kollegen zu Teil werden. Letztere genießen Kündigungsschutz und dürfen mit fixen Biennalsprüngen rechnen. Die neuen Mitarbeiter steigen üblicherweise mit einer niedrigeren Einstufung in das Unternehmen ein und erhalten außerordentliche Lohnsteigerungen nur bei besonderen Leistungen. Zum Wohle des Unternehmens sinken damit die Durchschnittspersonalkosten. Eine leistungsorientierte Entlohnung führt zu einer sehr guten Einstellung zum neuen Produkt und zu einer hohen Motivation. Für besondere Leistungen werden Prämien ausgeschüttet (egal, zu welcher Kategorie von Mitarbeitern eine Person zählt).

Die Nordpark Errichtungs- und Betriebs-GmbH kann im Marketing mehr Möglichkeiten nutzen als bisher die INKB: Von der sehr aufwändigen Eröffnungsfeier der Hungerburgbahn wurde im ersten Halbjahr 2008 weltweit in 300 internationalen Medien berichtet. Die Veranstaltung stand unter dem Motto „Alpine Fusion: Architektur – Mensch – Natur“. In den Reden der Prominenten wurde – untermauert durch eine aufwändige Laser-Show – die Einzigartigkeit der Nordkettenbahnen betont. Innsbruck bietet die einmalige Chance, in weniger als einer halben Stunde vom Zentrum der Stadt ausgehend hochalpines Gelände zu erreichen. Das mediale Echo stellte eine ausgezeichnete Werbung für das Renommee der neuen Bahn dar.

Die ursprüngliche Betreiberin der Bahn – letztlich die Stadt Innsbruck – hätte die Kosten für eine derart aufwändige Inszenierung von urban zu hochalpin aus Steuermitteln mit Sicherheit nicht rechtfertigen können.

Was den Verkauf des Produktes „Hungerburgbahn neu“ anbelangt, lässt der neue Geschäftsführer der Nordpark Errichtungs- und Betriebs-GmbH, keine Gelegenheit aus, um entsprechend die Werbetrommel zu rühren. Ausstellungsstände auf Tourismusmessen in Zusammenarbeit mit Tirol Werbung und Tourismusverband werden ebenso betrieben wie eine intensive Zusammenarbeit mit Innsbrucker Hotels. Die Kooperation mit Alpenzoo und Tiefgarage führte zu kundenorientierten Paketleistungen, durch Verträge mit der IVB wurde die Hungerburgbahn für die Bewohner der Hungerburg zu einem idealen Nahverkehrsmittel. Dies schätzen nicht nur der Großteil der 6000 Bewohner auf der Hungerburg, sondern auch Tausende Anrainer in den engen Gassen der Stadtteile Hötting und St. Nikolaus, die vom Individualverkehr merklich entlastet wurden.

Das neue Management agiert um einiges flexibler und schneller als die Geschäftsleitung des Eigentümers INKB, welche die Nordkettenbahnen damals zusätzlich zum vergleichsweise viel größeren Betrieb der IVB mitführen musste.

7 Risiken bei den Nordkettenbahnen

Die neuen Strukturen bieten auch einige Risiken: die Financiers der neuen Bahn möchten alle entsprechend ihre eigenen Vorstellungen und Wünsche an der Bahn durchsetzen und verwirklicht sehen. Dabei prallen unterschiedliche Interessen aufeinander. Das Finden von Prioritäten bei den Vorlieben von Stadt und Tourismusverband als Vertreter der öffentlichen Hand, den Besonderheiten der Eigentümer Strabag und Leitner machten anfänglich der Geschäftsleitung das Leben nicht einfach. Nach einer gewissen Anlaufphase sind die Leitlinien jedoch heute relativ klar. Die Entscheidungen fallen innerhalb der Geschäftsführung in der Regel einstimmig.

Kopfzerbrechen bereiten immer wieder die negativen Presseberichte in einer sehr verbreiteten Lokalzeitung, die kleine Pannen der Bahn auf die Titelseite ihrer Lokalberichterstattung bringt. Das stärkt immer wieder die Gegner der Bahn, die sich in Leserbriefen mit meist fast identischer Wortwahl negativ zur Bahn äußern. Der Geschäftsführer Thomas Schroll ist als Olympiasieger im

Viererbob harte Schläge gewohnt und zuversichtlich, auch die Nordkettenbahnen optimal zu lenken.

Ein Risiko für Einnahmenausfälle stellen Schlechtwetter oder schlechte Sicht dar. Bei Nebel oder Wolken interessieren sich nur wenige Gäste für eine Fahrt mit der Bahn in den hochalpinen Bereich. Das führt zu enormen Auslastungsschwankungen, die kaum in den Griff zu bekommen sind.

Steigende oder hohe Zinsen sorgen für ein ausgeprägtes finanzielles Risiko. Der Darlehensvertrag wurde 2006 mit einem variablen Zinssatz abgeschlossen. Jeder Prozentpunkt an Veränderung des Euribor nach oben bringt im Moment Mehrkosten. Die Tilgung wird deshalb in der Anfangsphase auf ein Minimum reduziert.

8 Zusammenfassung

Die von Kohl & Partner im Jahre 2004 verfasste Studie für die Zukunftschancen der Nordkettenbahnen ging von folgendem Erlöspotential aus: realistisches Szenario 2,4 Mio. € jährlich, im optimistischen Fall ca. 2,6 Mio. €. Nachdem alle Bahnen noch kein vollständiges Jahr in Betrieb sind, kann diese Zahl nur mit der Vorschau für 2008 verglichen werden. Dieses Jahr ist wiederum kein Regeljahr, weil sich die Fußballeuropameisterschaft überproportional gut auf die Umsätze der Nordpark Errichtungs- und Betriebs-GmbH auswirkten. Es wird im Moment davon ausgegangen, dass die optimistische Variante übertroffen wird. Gegenüber der ursprünglichen Prognose stiegen allerdings auch die Kosten an. Aus heutiger Sicht wird der Betrieb der Bahnen in den ersten Jahren ein negatives Ergebnis erreichen, welches allerdings wesentlich geringer ausfallen dürfte als die genannten Verluste, als die Bahnen von der öffentlichen Hand betrieben wurden.

Laut der genannten Studie von Kohl & Partner hatten die Innsbrucker Nordkettenbahnen im Jahr 2002 insgesamt 230.000 Erstzutritte. Ohne Hungerburgbahn waren es 146.698 im Jahr 2002 und 130.666 im Jahr 1997. Erfreulicherweise erreichen die Eintritte im ersten Halbjahr 2008 bereits 222.000, somit wird im laufenden Jahr der Gesamtjahreswert von 2002 bereits im Juli überschritten. Mit im Gesamtjahr 2008 insgesamt 443.000 Ersteintritten wurde letztlich sogar die Prognose der Potentialanalyse bei Weitem übertroffen (plus 21 %). Aus dem Blickwinkel der Besucherzahlen ist das PPP-Modell schließlich sicher erfolgreicher als der Betrieb durch die öffentliche Hand.

Bei genauerer Betrachtung lässt sich erkennen, dass die Innsbrucker Nordkettenbahnen in ähnlichem Maße beiderseits von Einheimischen wie auch Gästen und dabei insbesondere von Ausflugsgästen (gut 85 %) sowie von Skifahrern (gut 14 %) genutzt werden. Jeweils etwa ein Viertel der Besucher waren Nächtigungs- und nicht-einheimische Tagesgäste, knapp die Hälfte der Nutzer waren Einheimische. Die positive Annahme der Bahnen belegt zudem die Tatsache, dass zum Zeitpunkt der Befragung bereits beinahe die Hälfte der Gäste die Bahnen bereits einmal oder mehrmals benutzt hatten. Dazu trugen als die wichtigsten Begeisterungsfaktoren vor allem die Seilbahntechnik, die Streckenführung, die Architektur der Stationen, die Fahrdauer sowie die Anbindung an die Stadt bei. Den bisherigen Erfolg untermauern zudem die beiderseits sehr hohe Kundenzufriedenheit und Absicht zur Wiederbenutzung. Schließlich ergab die Studie, dass 91,5 % der Besucher die Innsbrucker Nordkettenbahn weiterempfehlen würden.

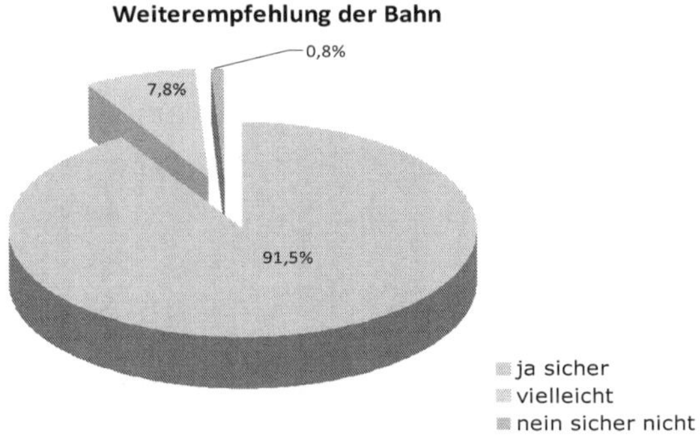

Abb. 4: Weiterempfehlungsrate für eine Fahrt mit den Innsbrucker Nordketten bahnen
Quelle: Bericht zum 1. Geschäftsjahr der Innsbrucker Nordkettenbahnen.

Für die Innsbrucker Nordkettenbahnen ist das PPP-Modell letztendlich erfolgreicher und unternehmerischer als der bisherige Betrieb, weil von allen Beteiligten – sogar von Mitarbeitern, die Nachteile gegenüber ihrer bisherigen Position befürchten – eine bilanziell positive Führung des Unternehmens erwartet wird. Auch wenn nicht alle mit derselben Kraft an einem Strang ziehen, ist seit Inbetriebnahme der Bahn jedem Mitarbeiter bewusst, dass verstärkt auf Leistung gesetzt wird.

Das Unternehmensziel, auch wirtschaftlich erfolgreich zu agieren, kann von privaten Betreibern besser kommuniziert werden. Politiker bzw. kommunale Kollektiventscheidungsorgane erweisen sich leider häufig nicht als Idealbesetzung für die Führung von Unternehmen. Als weiterer Grund für den wirtschaftlichen Erfolg des Unternehmens zählt auch, dass unpopuläre Entscheidungen von privaten Betreibern weniger schwierig durchzusetzen sind als von politisch gewählten Mandataren:
Es gab Beteiligte, die von bisherigen Entscheidungen der Stadtführung persönlich profitierten. Dazu zählen manche Anrainer, Mitglieder in bestimmten Kommissionen, der Stadtführung nahestehende Gruppen aber auch einige

Mitarbeiter. Auch wenn es am Verständnis dieser bisher Privilegierten mangelt, müssen diese wohl oder übel Maßnahmen akzeptieren, die für den positiven Betrieb der Bahnen für die nächsten 30 Jahre getroffen werden.

Das PPP-Modell der Innsbrucker Nordkettenbahnen steht eigentlich noch am Beginn seiner voraussichtlich 30-jährigen Laufzeit. Investitionen müssen am Anfang dieser Zeitspanne getroffen werden, um davon längstmöglich zu profitieren. Dadurch ergeben sich für die Anfangsphase neben einem hohen Finanzierungsbedarf auch Anlaufverluste. Die neuen Eigentümer bzw. deren Vertreter agieren dabei mit wirtschaftlichem Weitblick.

Wie sich das PPP-Modell bis zum Ende der Laufzeit der Konzession im Jahre 2038 entwickelt, wird unter anderem auch von der Qualität der Zusammenarbeit zwischen Eigentümerin (INKB als Konzessionär gegenüber der Behörde) und Betreibergesellschaft geprägt sein. Darüber kann heute – auch wenn in der bisherigen Zusammenarbeit immer gute Lösungen gefunden wurden – keine genaue Prognose erstellt werden.

Regional Governance und Public Private Partnership in der Wirtschaftsförderung

Voraussetzungen für das Engagement privater Unternehmen in der Wirtschaftsförderung unter besonderer Berücksichtigung von Regional Governance

Arno Brandt

Inhaltsverzeichnis

1 Einführung

Die Globalisierung und vor allem der Strukturwandel zur wissensbasierten Ökonomie haben den Blick auf die Standortbedingungen geweitet. Seit einigen Jahren rücken zunehmend „weiche“ Faktoren wie Kultur, Architektur und Naherholung in den Fokus der kommunalen Wirtschaftsförderung. Für die Zukunft ist eine größere Bedeutung insbesondere solcher Standortfaktoren zu erwarten, die auf die Entwicklung ausdifferenzierter Standort- und Innovationskulturen abstellen.[1] Diese Neuausrichtung ist nicht zuletzt Ausdruck einer veränderten Zielgruppenorientierung in der Standortpolitik: Nicht mehr nur Unternehmen, sondern insbesondere auch hochqualifizierte Arbeitskräfte werden umworben. Lebensqualität und urbanes Image treten im Marketing neben die harten Standortfaktoren wie beispielsweise Verkehrsanbindung und verfügbare Gewerbeflächen. Vor allem großen Städten wird eine herausragende Anziehungskraft auf die „creative class“ zugesprochen; bevorzugt konstituieren sich hier die kreativen Milieus und nur hier finden sich auch die urbanen Infrastrukturen, die von den Wissensarbeitern mit ihren besonderen Arbeitsverhältnissen nachgefragt werden. Entsprechend richten die wissensintensiven Dienstleistungen ihre Standortpräferenzen zunehmend nach dem Vorhandensein eines adäquaten, (hoch)qualifizierten Arbeitskräftepools aus.[2]

Diese Neuorientierung hat der Wirtschaftsförderung eine Vielzahl von neuen Aufgaben und Arbeitsbereichen zugewiesen, die im engen Korsett tradierten kommunalen Verwaltungshandelns kaum mehr zu bewältigen sind. Zudem hat sich mittlerweile die Erkenntnis durchgesetzt, dass der Ausweis urbaner Qualitäten allein keineswegs ein ausreichendes Marketinginstrument ist. Das liegt im Wesentlichen in vier Faktoren begründet: Erstens stellen Wissensarbeiter ein äußerst heterogenes Spektrum mit divergierenden Aufgaben, Arbeitsverhältnissen, Lebensläufen und kulturellen Milieuanbindungen dar;

[1] Vgl. Gärtner, S. (2008).
[2] Vgl. Brandt, A. (2008a).

zweitens ist vielfach die Hoffnung auf die Akquise neuer Unternehmen der nüchternen Einsicht gewichen, dass Bestandspflege und -sicherung zu den Hauptaufgaben der Wirtschaftsförderung zählt; drittens konzentrieren sich wissensintensive Tätigkeiten nicht nur auf Dienstleistungen, sondern in hohem Maße auch auf die Industrie und viertens kommen heute zusätzliche Standortfaktoren wie regionale Innovationskulturen bzw. innovative Milieus in den Blick. Insbesondere die Förderung und Weiterentwicklung dieser Innovationskulturen mit ihren regional sehr spezifischen Bedarfen, ihren Netzwerkstrukturen und ihren die administrativen Grenzen überschreitenden Raumbezügen stellen hohe Anforderungen an die Informations- und Steuerungskapazitäten der Wirtschaftsförderung.[3]

Vor diesem Hintergrund spielen Public Private Partnership- (PPP-) Modelle heute für die Wirtschaftsförderung eine immer größere Rolle. Neben verstärkter Kooperation mit anderen Ämtern und benachbarten Gebietskörperschaften gilt die Einbeziehung privater Akteure mittlerweile als unverzichtbare Säule einer professionalisierten Wirtschaftsförderungspraxis. Im Gegensatz zu Privatisierungen erfordern PPP-Projekte jedoch die dauerhafte Verzahnung marktwirtschaftlicher und hierarchischer Steuerungsmodi im Rahmen von Regional Governance.

2 Der institutionelle Rahmen: Regional Governance

Der im Zuge der Globalisierung proklamierte „death of the distance“ hat nicht stattgefunden, ein Bedeutungsverlust der ökonomischen Raumbezüge ist nicht erkennbar. Im Gegenteil: bei weiterhin tendenziell sinkenden Transport- und Kommunikationskosten (aber steigenden Kapazitäten) lassen sich signifikante Wettbewerbsvorteile zunehmend nur noch auf der regionalen Ebene mobilisieren. Vor allem moderne Clusterkonzepte und Implikationen der wissensbasierten Ökonomie, die für die unternehmensbezogenen Innovationsprozesse auf das

[3] Vgl. Gärtner, S. (2008).

personengebundene „tacit-knowledge“ angewiesen ist, weisen den Regionen heute eine entscheidende Bedeutung für wirtschaftliches Wachstum zu.[4]

Die bereits angesprochenen ökonomischen Raumbezüge in diesen Regionen sind jedoch außerordentlich komplex. In zunehmend netzwerkartigen Kooperationsverhältnissen finden sich oft lokale Akteure neben weltweit vernetzten Global Players. Diese Netzwerke lassen sich immer weniger von den tradierten administrativen Grenzen „einfangen“. Eine regionale Wirtschaftsförderung ist daher heute gefordert, nicht nur einen Überblick über die privatwirtschaftlichen Kooperationsbeziehungen zu erhalten, sondern auch den Schulterschluss mit allen beteiligten Kommunen zu suchen. Eine solche Konstellation aus mehreren öffentlichen und privaten Akteuren lässt sich nicht effektiv von nur einer „Partei“ koordinieren oder leiten, sondern erfordert ein eigenständiges institutionelles Arrangement.

Regional Governance bezeichnet zunächst allgemein Formen der regionalen Selbststeuerung und umfasst das Zusammenspiel politischer, privater und zivilgesellschaftlicher Akteure mit einem gemeinsamen räumlichen Bezug. Die konkrete Ausgestaltung von Regional Governance variiert in der Praxis stark und hängt weitgehend vom Zuschnitt der jeweiligen PPP-Projekte ab, welche sich wiederum an den spezifischen Bedarfen (oder Möglichkeiten) der einzelnen Regionen orientieren.

Der besondere Nutzen von PPP-Modellen in der Wirtschaftsförderung wird dabei nicht vorrangig in der Akquise privaten Kapitals, sondern eher in Effizienzvorteilen und einer größeren strategischen Flexibilität vermutet. Da das Vertrauen in die ökonomische Kompetenz und den strategischen Weitblick von Verwaltungen und Räten innerhalb den Unternehmen in der Regel nicht als besonders stark eingeschätzt wird, soll die Einbeziehung namhafter Firmen oder Persönlichkeiten aus der Wirtschaft die erforderliche Akzeptanz und Rückhalt für eine breitere Beteiligung und Unterstützung der Projekte liefern. Insbesonde-

---

4 Vgl. Brandt, A. (2008b); Brandt, A. (2008c).

re in der institutionellen Einbeziehung der Privatwirtschaft werden dabei entscheidende Informations- und Steuerungsvorteile erkannt.[5] Eine gezielte Förderung innovationsorientierter Netzwerkbeziehungen zwischen ansässiger Wirtschaft, Wissenschaft sowie Verbänden und Kammern, aber auch eine Unterstützung der für das innovative Milieu so wichtigen Soziokulturen lässt sich ohne aktive Teilnahme der involvierten Akteure nicht mehr durchführen.

Die aktuelle EU-Förderkulisse verschärft zudem die Konkurrenz der Regionen hinsichtlich der Zuteilung von Strukturmitteln aus dem europäischen Haushalt. Andererseits ergeben sich durch die neuen Vergaberichtlinien auch größere Chancen für innovative Projekte, die sich für die Wirtschaftsförderungen i.d.R. jedoch nur mithilfe externer Partner entwickeln lassen, welche über die notwendige konzeptionelle Intelligenz und Erfahrung verfügen.

Regional Governance schließt in diesem Zusammenhang auch in Richtung Privatwirtschaft an das Konzept der „Corporate Social Responsibility“ an. Urban Governance „(...) kann übersetzt werden als ein System lokaler Steuerung, in dem die öffentliche Verwaltung und die städtische Politik zwar weiterhin eine zentrale Rolle spielen, zu dem aber – und zwar mit wachsender Bedeutung – alle Organisationen und (Interessens-)Gruppen gehören, die bewusst einen Beitrag zur Stadt leisten.“[6]

Die Steuerung der Prozesse erfolgt über netzwerkartige Formen der Koordination. Hierzu ist ein partieller Rückzug des Staates aus der direkten Regelung, verbunden mit einer Verbesserung der Selbststeuerungsfähigkeit, erforderlich. Hierbei existiert letztendlich weiterhin der „Schatten der Hierarchie“ als Faustpfand für den öffentlichen Kooperationspartner, notfalls kann er hierarchisch intervenieren.

Diese komplexe Konstellationen beschränken sich nicht auf öffentliche oder private Handlungslogiken, sondern vermitteln zwischen den Sphären Public,

---

[5] Vgl. Ullrich, M. (2007).

[6] Häußermann, H. (2006), S. 124.

Private und Zivilgesellschaft.[7] Regional Governance beruht auf Freiwilligkeit. Kooperationen werden von den Teilnehmern nur aufgenommen, wenn sie einen komparativen Handlungsvorteil gegenüber anderen Formen kollektiven Handelns haben.[8] Wesentliches Steuerungsmuster von Regional Governance sind Verhandlungen zur Erzielung von gemeinsamen Lösungen. Dies bedeutet, dass ein Nebeneinander unterschiedlicher Governance-Formen existieren kann, die zu Projekten mit Regionsbezug arbeiten und unterschiedliche Mitglieder haben. Dabei entwickelt sich Regional Governance nur im Rahmen bestehender Institutionen, die Verlässlichkeit bieten. Sie benötigen einen „organisatorischen Kern" und klare Verfahrensregeln.[9]

Darüber hinaus ist es aber auch denkbar, dass Governance-Muster nur Übergangsphänomene darstellen, die in festere Government-Strukturen münden.[10] Institutionalisierungszwänge können sich zum Beispiel ergeben, wenn die Zahl der Teilnehmer steigt. Beispiele hierfür lassen sich in Kernstadt-Umland-Konstellationen finden, die neue Organisationen mit der formalen Struktur einer Gebietskörperschaft schaffen und eine Mischform aus Mehrheitsdemokratie, hierarchischer Steuerungsstruktur, funktional differenzierten Netzwerken und einem kooperativen Konfliktmanagement bilden. So ergeben sich in diesen Räumen durch Regional Governance mit einem organisatorischem Kern neue Gestaltungsressourcen.[11]

Regional Governance eröffnet verschiedene Optionen. Zum einen kann sie zur Gewinnung neuer Handlungsfähigkeit beitragen. Durch das Zusammenspiel öffentlicher, privater und zivilgesellschaftlicher Akteure ist es möglich, problemadäquatere Lösungen zu erreichen, da verschiedene Kompetenzen zusammenfließen und nach dem Verhandlungsprinzip im Vorhinein viele Probleme bearbeitet werden können: „Dort, wo sich Regional Governance bildet, entstehen

---

[7] Vgl. Einig, K. et al. (2005), S. II.
[8] Vgl. Fürst, D. (2004), S. 48 und 53.
[9] Vgl. Fürst, D. (2003), S. 445.
[10] Vgl. Fürst, D. (2004), S. 54 f.
[11] Vgl. Benz, A. (2003), S. 505 ff.

tendenziell auch Wettbewerbsvorteile für die Region."[12] Ein weiterer Nebeneffekt dieser Steuerungsform kann ein demokratischeres und effizienteres Verfahren sein, weil Beteiligte von Anfang an mit einbezogen werden. Leitbild ist hierbei die „Bürgergesellschaft", die dem Bürger die neue Rolle als „Mitgestalter" und „Ko-Produzent" gibt. Dabei darf die Einbeziehung der Bürger jedoch nur als Ergänzung, nicht als Ersatz angesehen werden.[13] Eine Beteiligung der Bürger ist insbesondere für die Legitimation von Regional Governance wichtig. Die Legitimationsfrage stellt sich dabei insbesondere dann, wenn demokratisch gewählte Gremien nicht mehr allein entscheiden, sondern zusammen mit anderen Gruppen. Vorentscheidungsmuster können zur Ausgrenzung anderer Akteure und Gruppen führen.[14]

3 Public Private Partnership in der Wirtschaftsförderung

In der Wirtschaftsförderung öffnet sich für PPP-Projekte ein weiter Gestaltungsspielraum. Dieser umfasst sowohl die Beteiligung ansässiger Unternehmen am Ausbau der wirtschaftsnahen Infrastruktur, als auch die Kooperation bei der Trägerschaft von Wirtschaftsförderungsgesellschaften. Dabei sind es längst nicht mehr nur Sparkassen oder andere regionale Kreditinstitute, die sich für derartige gemeinsame Trägerschaften ansprechbar zeigen. Öffentliche Institutionen und private Unternehmen kooperieren heute in vielfältiger Weise als Träger von Wirtschaftsfördereinrichtungen.

Ein modernes Instrument der Wirtschaftsförderung stellt die gezielte Initiierung und Koordination von Netzwerken und Plattformen wie Kompetenzzentren dar. Dabei handelt es sich in der Regel um informelle Kooperationsformen, bei denen sich Wirtschaft, Wissenschaft und Wirtschaftsförderung gemeinsam an Entwicklungsprozessen beteiligen, um Problemlösungen für Wirtschaft und

[12] Vgl. Fürst, D. (2003), S. 447.
[13] Vgl. Einig, K. et al (2005), S. III f.
[14] Vgl. Fürst, D. (2003), S. 446.

Beschäftigung vor Ort zu generieren. Aus derartigen Kooperationen gehen oft Innovationsprojekte oder Projekte im Bereich der wissensintensiven Wirtschaftsbereiche hervor. Grundsätzlich lassen sich drei Formen von PPP-Modellen differenzieren:

- **Informelle Kooperationen** sind insbesondere bei PPP-Konzepten in der Wirtschaftsförderung ein wichtiger Aspekt. So geht auch SCHUPPERT (2001) davon aus, dass unter dem Begriff Public Private Partnership informelle Kooperationsformen zu subsumieren sind, bei denen der Grad der formellen Institutionalisierung im Vergleich zu anderen Modellen relativ gering ist.
- Die **kontraktbestimmte PPP** ist auf die Erbringung von Leistungen (i.d.R. vom privaten Partner) ausgerichtet und erfordert ein professionelles Vertragsmanagement, da hier üblicherweise die Risiken und Kosten der Kooperation insbesondere für die öffentliche Hand nur unzureichend abschätzbar sind. Damit ergibt sich ein ständiger Gestaltungs- und Anpassungsbedarf[15], der kooperativ zu lösen ist.
- Im Fall der **Organisations-PPP** bringen die Partner Ressourcen in eine gemeinsame Gesellschaft ein, an deren Ertrag sie gemeinsam partizipieren. Die Organisations-PPP zeichnet sich durch einen hohen Grad der formellen Institutionalisierung aus.

Welche Motive treiben private Unternehmen dazu, sich an PPP in der Wirtschaftsförderung zu beteiligen? Im Bereich der Wirtschaftsförderung tritt das Motiv der direkten Gewinnerzielung in den Hintergrund, da es sich in weiten Bereichen der Wirtschaftsförderung um ein öffentliches Gut im klassischen Sinne handelt. Bei einem öffentlichen Gut können erstens keine potenziellen Interessenten zu vertretbaren Kosten von der Nutzung des Gutes ausgeschlossen werden (Nicht-Ausschluss). Zweitens existiert Nicht-Rivalität im Konsum, d.h. das Gut kann ohne Beeinträchtigung des Nutzens anderer Personen verwendet

---

15 Vgl. Budäus, D. (2005).

werden. Soweit diese beiden Bedingungen erfüllt sind, kann der in Märkten übliche Preismechanismus nicht funktionieren, d.h. das Gut wird vom Markt nicht bzw. nicht in hinreichender Menge zur Verfügung gestellt.[16]

Beide genannten Voraussetzungen sind bei vielen Maßnahmen der Wirtschaftsförderung gegeben. Von Aktivitäten des Standortmarketing oder von der Erzeugung von Wissensspillover im Rahmen regionaler Innovationspolitik sollen z.B. möglichst alle regionalen Unternehmen profitieren. Zugespitzt formuliert: ein Ausschluss von Unternehmen ist in diesem Fall auch gar nicht gewollt. Auch liegt die Rivalität im Konsum in derartigen Fällen, wo Wissen eine zentrale Rolle spielt, nicht vor – im Gegenteil: Wissen ist ein Gut, das durch seinen Gebrauch nicht gemindert wird, d.h. die Grenzkosten der Nutzung liegen bei Null.[17]

Anders gelagert ist die Sachlage, wenn es sich um Clubgüter handelt. Bei diesen Gütern gilt zwar auch Nicht-Rivalität, aber das Ausschluss-Prinzip ist grundsätzlich gegeben. Um derartige Clubgüter geht es bei einigen besonderen Ausprägungen von Unternehmensnetzwerken, die in den letzten Jahren auch für die kommunale Wirtschaftsförderung zunehmend an Bedeutung gewonnen haben. Dabei handelt es sich um zwischenbetriebliche Kooperationen, bei denen der verbundbedingte Mehrwert auf die formellen Netzwerkmitglieder begrenzt werden kann.[18] Da Netzwerke im Hinblick auf ihren Nutzen mit größerer Unsicherheit behaftet sind und sich zumindest in der Startphase nicht unerhebliche Vertrauensprobleme ergeben, kann es durchaus sinnvoll sein, dass die Wirtschaftsförderung bei der Initiierung derartiger Projekte in Vorleistung geht. Ist das Projekt erst einmal funktionsfähig, ist es unter günstigen Rahmenbedingungen zweckmäßig, dass sich die Wirtschaftsförderung so weit wie möglich zurückzieht.

[16] Vgl. Stiglitz, J. (1999), S. 176 f.
[17] Vgl. Stiglitz, J. (2006), S. 405.
[18] Vgl. Sperlich, M. (2007).

Ein wichtiger Beweggrund für die Beteiligung privater Unternehmen an den Aufgaben der Wirtschaftsförderung sind Nutzenerwartungen, die jenseits der direkten Gewinnerzielung zu verorten sind. Obwohl das Engagement direkt auf Belange des Gemeinwohls gerichtet ist, vermag es unter dem Aspekt der Umwegrentabilität durchaus die Entwicklung des regionalen Absatzmarktes, die Markterschließung und positive Imageeffekte zu befördern. Auch die Intention, durch politische Einflussnahme bestimmte Entscheidungen herbeizuführen (Gate-keeper-Strategie), darf in diesem Zusammenhang nicht außer Acht gelassen werden. Eine wichtige Rolle spielt zudem der Austausch von Know-how: Unternehmen beteiligen sich bevorzugt an innovations- und wissensorientierten Netzwerken, um von dem damit verbundenen Wissensaustausch zu profitieren und neues Wissen frühzeitig in eigene Strategien zu integrieren.

Unterscheidet man die Unternehmen hinsichtlich ihrer Bindung (regionale Bindung oder keine regionale Bindung) und ihres Absatzmarktes (regionaler Absatzmarkt oder überregionaler/globaler Absatzmarkt) so zeichnen sich insbesondere jene Unternehmen durch ein hohes Engagement im Bereich PPP aus, die über eine signifikante regionale Bindung verfügen. Dies sind zum einen mittelständische Betriebe mit Hauptsitz in der Region, die ihren Absatz regional generieren. In diesen Kontext fallen auch regionale Kreditinstitute, wie z.B. Sparkassen, die qua Auftrag auf ihr regionales Geschäftsgebiet begrenzt sind.[19] Zum anderen kann es sich auch um Industrieunternehmen mit Hauptsitz in der Region handeln, die überwiegend überregional und global absetzen, aber auf ein attraktives Umfeld an ihrem Standort angewiesen sind. Dies kann sowohl Einrichtungen der Infrastruktur wie zum Beispiel die Verkehrsanbindung betreffen, aber auch „weichere“ Faktoren, die den Standort für (hoch)qualifizierte Arbeitskräfte attraktiver gestalten und deren Rekrutierung bzw. Bindung erleichtern. Das Engagement von Unternehmen ohne regionale Bindung (Filialbetriebe, Zweigstellen, „verlängerte Werkbänke“) wird aus strukturellen Gründen weniger ausgeprägt sein.

---

[19] Vgl. Bredemeier, S. (2007).

4 Beispiele von PPP in der Wirtschaftsförderung

Die folgenden Beispiele von PPP in der Wirtschaftsförderung können im Rahmen dieses Artikels nur in Kurzform skizziert werden. Dennoch sollte diese Auswahl einen Eindruck von der Bandbreite der Möglichkeiten zur Umsetzung dieses Konzepts vermitteln. Allen Beispielen ist gemeinsam, dass es sich um „echte“ PPP handelt, die privaten Partner also auch als Träger der Projekte fungieren und nicht nur in beratender und unterstützender Form tätig sind.

HI-REG

Die HI-REG ist eine privatwirtschaftlich organisierte Gesellschaft, der die Wirtschaftsförderung für die regionale Ebene des Landkreises Hildesheim obliegt.[20] Zu den Trägern der GmbH zählen alle 19 Städte und Gemeinden des Kreises, die vier ansässigen Volksbanken und die Sparkasse Hildesheim. Letztere ist auch alleinige Gesellschafterin der GmbH, nimmt aber nur ihre „gesetzlichen Mindestrechte“ (HI-REG) wahr, den anderen Trägern sind gesellschafterähnliche Entscheidungsbefugnisse eingeräumt. Gefördert wird die HI-REG zudem von mehreren Wohnungsbaugesellschaften. Zu den Geschäftsbereichen der HI-REG zählen der Unternehmerservice (einschließlich Innovationsförderung), die Existenzgründungsberatung (Gründerlotse), das Standortmarketing für die Region und die Tourismusförderung. Der ansässige Mittelstand und die Existenzgründer sind erklärtermaßen die Hauptzielgruppen der Gesellschaft. Die HI-REG beschäftigt acht Mitarbeiter, wobei die Dienstleitungen „im Netzwerk von den Partnern erbracht“ werden. In einer neueren Studie der Initiative Neue Soziale Marktwirtschaft (INSM) und des Magazins Impulse wurde Hildesheim als gründerfreundlichste Region Deutschlands ausgezeichnet (HI-REG).

[20] Vgl. Ullrich, M. (2007).

Untere Ems

Das PPP-Projekt für ein Maritimes Kompetenzzentrum in Leer ist ein Vorhaben, das die Clusterformierungsprozesse in einem Wirtschaftssegment (Maritime Wirtschaft) unterstützen soll.[21] Der Aufbau dieser Einrichtung wird in besonderer Weise durch die regionale Wirtschaft und insbesondere die Reedergemeinschaft Leer gefördert, die in den vergangenen Jahren einen beachtlichen Aufschwung genommen und sich zu einem bedeutenden Standbein der regionalen Wirtschaft entwickelt hat. Diesem Prozess soll nun Rechnung getragen werden, indem bestehende Infrastrukturen in ihrem Bestand gesichert und weiterentwickelt werden. Das Maritime Kompetenzzentrum soll das maritime Cluster in seiner Gesamtheit fördern, indem Leistungen für die Reedereiwirtschaft wie auch für den Schiffbau und die Hafenwirtschaft entwickelt werden, und ist prinzipiell als regionale Schnittstelle der Maritimen Wirtschaft geplant. Nicht zuletzt sollen die Forschungs- und Entwicklungsaktivitäten der Region und insbesondere der Fachhochschule auf dem Gebiet der maritimen Technologien gefördert werden. Die Einrichtung der verschiedenen Module wird schrittweise stattfinden. Die inhaltliche Ausrichtung und die Struktur des Kompetenzzentrums orientieren sich dabei an den vordringlichen Problemfeldern der Maritimen Wirtschaft sowie an den spezifischen Bedarfen maritimer Unternehmen und insbesondere der Reedereiwirtschaft. Insgesamt umfasst das Maritime Kompetenzzentrum die Module Schiffführungssimulator, Weiterbildung und Qualifizierung, Netzwerkmanagement, Standortmarketing und Beratungsleistungen für Unternehmen.[22] Unternehmen aus dem Bereich der regionalen Reedereiwirtschaft beteiligen sich sowohl an den Kosten des Investments als auch am Betrieb einzelner Module des Kompetenzzentrums. So übernehmen zwei Reeder den Betrieb des Schiffsführungssimulators, der in der nautischen Aus- und Weiterbildung Einsatz finden soll.

---

[21] Vgl. NORD/LB (2007).

[22] Vgl. Brandt, A./Dickow, M. Ch. (2007).

Ein vergleichbares PPP-Konzept im Bereich der Maritimen Wirtschaft wird derzeit am Standort Elsfleth (Landkreis Wesermarsch) umgesetzt.

CFK-Valley

CFK-Valley-Stade mit dem Ziel, die regionalen Kompetenzen im Verbundwerkstoffbereich zu bündeln, verdankt sich einer Initiative des Landes Niedersachsen und der Stadt Stade. Der kohlefaserverstärkte Leichtbau ist vor allem auf die Bedarfe der ansässigen Luftfahrtindustrie ausgerichtet, aber auch in anderen Wirtschaftsbereichen, wie der Automobilindustrie oder dem Schiffbau einsetzbar. Das PPP-Projekt hat sich mittlerweile zu einer Integrationsplattform entwickelt, die weitgehend die gesamte vertikale Wertschöpfungskette abbildet, aber auch horizontal prozess- und branchenübergreifend aufgestellt ist. Im Kern stehen Forschung und Entwicklung von innovativen Verfahren für die Kohlenfaserverbundwerkstoff-Technologien. Am CFK-Valley sind sowohl Forschungsinstitute und klein- bis mittelständische Unternehmen, aber auch große Industriebetriebe integriert. Die Mitsprache- und Gestaltungsmöglichkeiten richten sich nach dem Engagement und sind nach einfacher Mitgliedschaft, der Vertretung mit einer Dependance sowie Produktion bzw. FuE-Dienstleistungen vor Ort gestaffelt („Levels"). Die strategische Entwicklungsplanung wird von einem „Steering Board" geleitet, das sich aus Mitgliedern des „Upper Level" und der regionalen Wirtschaftsförderung der Stadt Stade konstituiert. Die Projektumsetzung wird über Fachbeiräte organisiert und betreut. Eine hauptamtlich eingerichtete Geschäftsstelle bildet das koordinierende Zentrum, während eine Kommunikationsplattform für den regelmäßigen Informationsaustausch sorgt. In Kooperation mit der privaten Fachhochschule Göttingen und Unternehmen aus dem CFK-Bereich wurden zudem zwei Studiengänge entwickelt, die vom Land Niedersachsen und der Stadt Stade gefördert werden. Mittlerweile konnten durch die Aktivitäten des CFK-Valley 350 zusätzliche Arbeitsplätze am Standort geschaffen werden, bis 2010 sollen noch 150 weitere hinzukommen. CFK-

Valley ist bereits mehrfach als „Entwicklungsnetzwerk Nr.1“ ausgezeichnet worden.[23]

hannover innovation fonds

Der hannover innovation fonds(hif) stellt Beteiligungskapital für kleine und mittlere Hightech- und Life Science-Unternehmen bereit. In einer ersten Finanzierungsrunde wird durch den hif und seine Kooperationspartner Seed-capital zur Verfügung gestellt. Für eine Anschlussfinanzierung ist ein weiterer Fonds mit Beteiligungskapital in der Entstehung. Der Fonds wird mit 24 Mio. Euro dotiert. 50 Prozent der Mittel steuert die von Stadt und Region Hannover gemeinsam betriebene Wachstumsinitiative hannoverimpuls bei, die andere Hälfte soll aus EFRE-Mitteln bestritten werden. Bezogen auf die Gesamtfinanzierung der Unternehmen muss der Anteil privater Investoren mindestens 50 Prozent betragen.[24]

5 Erfolgsfaktoren für PPP in der Wirtschaftsförderung

Die im vorherigen Kapitel skizzierten Initiativen illustrieren die große Bandbreite an Möglichkeiten, die heute für PPP-Projekte in der Wirtschaftsförderung besteht. „Die Inspiration durch „Best-Practice-Beispiele“ kann durchaus förderlich sein, ersetzt aber nicht die eingehende Analyse der spezifischen regionalen Erfordernisse. Entscheidend ist die Orientierung der Wirtschaftsförderung an tatsächlich vorhandenem Wissen und regionalen Kompetenzen“.[25]

Die steigende Zahl von informellen und formellen Kooperationen ist auch ein Zeichen für ein verändertes Staatsverständnis und ein neues Verantwortungsbewusstsein vieler Unternehmen.[26] Dabei müssen sich die öffentlichen Einrich-

[23] Vgl. Sperlich, M. (2007).
[24] Vgl. Franz, U.-B./Meyer, M. (2007).
[25] Gärtner, S. (2008), S. 87.
[26] Vgl. Rehm, H. (2007).

tungen jedoch bewusst sein, dass sie bei PPP-Projekten gewissermaßen auf fremdem Terrain agieren. Die einzelnen Vorhaben müssen deshalb durch ein professionalisiertes Umfeld abgesichert werden.

Folgende Eckpunkte für PPP-Vorhaben lassen sich für die kommunale Seite aus pragmatischen Erwägungen hervorheben: Eine gewissenhafte Vorbereitung und eine Prüfung des Geschäftsmodells muss jeder PPP vorausgehen. Die Ergebnisse dieser Betrachtung müssen sich in einer sorgfältigen Vertragsgestaltung niederschlagen.[27] Für das Gelingen einer PPP ist zudem eine effiziente, an den Geschäftsprozessen ausgerichtete Gremienstruktur sowie ein konsequentes Controlling und Monitoring der Arbeit erforderlich. Nicht zuletzt muss „die Dienstleistung Wirtschaftsförderung in adäquater Weise in die Verwaltungsvorgänge eingebunden“[28] und für eine Einbeziehung der Politik[29] gesorgt werden, um ein möglichst hohes Maß an Akzeptanz und Unterstützung zu mobilisieren.

Dabei darf jedoch nicht aus dem Blickfeld geraten, dass Wirtschaftsförderung ein öffentliches Gut ist, das prinzipiell allen Akteuren zur Verfügung gestellt werden muss und für dessen Gestaltung die gewählten Gremien der Öffentlichkeit gegenüber rechenschaftspflichtig sind. In dem Maße jedoch, in dem betriebswirtschaftliche Logik Eingang in die Aktivitäten der öffentlichen Hand findet, wirkt sie auch auf das Beziehungsgeflecht von Rat und Verwaltung, von Staat und Zivilgesellschaft ein.[30]

Der britische Politikwissenschaftler Colin Crouch hat für diesen Prozess unlängst den Begriff „Postdemokratie“ geprägt. Seine Argumentation soll an dieser Stelle Anlass sein, nach den vorangegangenen Erörterungen über die Effizienz von PPP-Projekten das Augenmerk abschließend auf die Effektivität dieser Arrangements innerhalb eines demokratisch verfassten Gemeinwesens zu

[27] Vgl. Weil, S. (2007).
[28] Ullrich, M. (2007), S. 57.
[29] Vgl. Weil, S. (2007).
[30] Vgl. Sack, D. (2007); Weil, S. (2007).

richten. Auf zumindest zwei Fragen sollte bei der Planung von PPP-Vorhaben eine Antwort gefunden werden:

Die erste Frage stellt sich nach dem Erhalt von Qualität und Umfang öffentlicher Leistungen. Die Auslagerung profitabler Segmente an private Anbieter kann zu einer adversen Selektion führen, bei der die öffentliche Hand gewissermaßen auf den „Restposten" sitzen bleibt. Diese im öffentlichen Bereich verbleibenden Aufgaben sind anschließend einem deutlich höheren Kostendruck ausgesetzt – umso mehr, als die Nachfrager dieser „Restleistungen" in der Regel über keine oder kaum eine Lobby verfügen. Die Folge wäre eine Erosion dieser öffentlichen Leistungen einschließlich der zugehörigen Infrastruktur.[31]

Der zweite Einwand betrifft die Legitimation von PPP-Projekten. Konstitutiv für ein demokratisch verfasstes Gemeinwesen ist die Steuerung öffentlicher Aufgaben durch eine gewählte Legislative und die Kontrolle durch eine informierte Öffentlichkeit der Staatsbürger. Das Besondere an PPP-Projekten ist nun, dass sie sich außerhalb dieser Kontroll- und Steuerungsmöglichkeiten etablieren. Der Bürger hat keinen Adressaten mehr für seine Ansprüche: nicht mehr als Staatsbürger, weil die Kommune nicht mehr zuständig ist, aber auch nicht als Kunde, weil der private Dienstleister nur Vertragsbindungen mit der Gebietskörperschaft eingeht.[32] Die gewählten Ratsvertreter sitzen wiederum weit am Ende der Informationskette und haben keinen unmittelbaren Einfluss mehr auf die Gestaltung der einst öffentlichen Leistungen (Problem der asymmetrischen Information). Dagegen wird bei PPP-Projekten im Unterschied zu Privatisierungen die Beziehung zwischen kommerziellen Anbietern und Behörden auf Dauer gestellt.[33] Aus diesem Grund muss der Gewährleistung von Transparenz gegenüber den demokratisch legitimierten Gremien, aber auch gegenüber einer demokratischen Öffentlichkeit sowohl bei der Einrichtung als auch bei der Durchführung von PPP-Vorhaben ein hoher Stellenwert eingeräumt werden.

---

[31] Vgl. Crouch, C. (2008), S. 114 f.
[32] Vgl. Crouch, C. (2008), S. 131.
[33] Vgl. Crouch, C. (2008), S. 121.

Gerade Kommunen gehen mit der Einführung von PPP-Projekten vielfach das Risiko ein, dass der politische Handlungsspielraum erheblich eingeschränkt wird. Dieser ist jedoch für eine Demokratie unverzichtbar, „(...) damit eine Gesellschaft mit politischen Mitteln auf sich selber einwirken kann. [...] Je mehr Lebensbereiche der Regulierung des Marktes überlassen werden, umso weiter dankt [...] die Politik ab“[34]. Gerade deshalb kommt es entscheidend auf das institutionelle Arrangement an. Ohne eine demokratisch sensible Einbettung von PPP-Konzepten wäre eine Beschädigung der demokratischen Kultur unvermeidlich. Das wäre sicherlich ein zu hoher Preis für bloßen Effizienzgewinn.

6 Fazit

Eine Kooperation mit der Privatwirtschaft kann bei der Wahrnehmung öffentlicher Aufgaben also kein Selbstzweck sein. Das spricht jedoch nicht gegen die Nutzung von PPP für die Wirtschaftsförderung. Im Gegenteil müssen PPP-Projekte heute als wichtige und wirksame Instrumente der kommunalen Selbstverwaltung und gerade auch der Wirtschaftsförderung betrachtet werden. Sie verlangen jedoch nach einer professionellen Vorbereitung und Durchführung. Sinn und Zweck einer PPP-Konstruktion müssen zudem in jedem Einzelfall geprüft und auf die spezifischen regionalen Bedarfe ausgerichtet werden. Den tendenziellen Steuerungs- und Legitimationsproblemen kann mit dem Modell einer Regional Governance begegnet werden, das sich dem demokratischen Gemeinwesen verpflichtet sieht.

[34] Habermas, J. (1999), S. 39.

Literatur

Benz, A. (2003): Regional Governance mit organisatorischem Kern. Das Beispiel der Region Stuttgart. In: Bundesamt für Bauwesen und Raumordnung (Hrsg.) (2003): Aktionsraum Region – Regional Governance. Heft 8/9. Informationen zur Raumentwicklung. Bonn, S. 505-512.

Benz, A. (2004a): Governance – Modebegriff oder nützliches sozialwissenschaftliches Konzept? In: Benz, A. (Hrsg.) (2004): Governance – Regieren in komplexen Regelsystemen. Wiesbaden, S. 11-28.

Benz, A. (2004b): Multilevel Governance – Governance im Mehrebenensystem. In: Benz, A. (Hrsg.) (2004): Governance – Regieren in komplexen Regelsystemen. Wiesbaden, S. 125-146.

Behrens, M. (2004): Global Governance. In: Benz, A. (Hrsg.) (2004): Governance – Regieren in komplexen Regelsystemen. Wiesbaden, S. 103-124.

Bogumil, J. (2006): Ökonomisierung der Verwaltung. Auswirkungen einer zunehmenden Vermarktlichung der Verwaltung auf die kommunale Steuerungsfähigkeit. In: Neues Verwaltungsmanagement 06/2006, B12, S. 1-32.

Bogumil, J./Holtkamp, L. (2002): Liberalisierung und Privatisierung kommunaler Aufgaben – Auswirkungen auf das kommunale Entscheidungssystem. In: Libbe, J./Tomerius, S./Trapp, J.-H. (Hrsg.) (2002): Liberalisierung und Privatisierung öffentlicher Aufgabenerfüllung – Soziale und umweltpolitische Perspektiven im Zeichen des Wettbewerbs. Berlin, S. 71-91.

Brandt, A. (2007): Was heißt PPP in der Wirtschaftsförderung. In: Brandt, A. et al. (Hrsg.) (2007): Public Private Partnership in der Wirtschaftsförderung. Herausforderungen, Chancen und Grenzen. Stuttgart, S. 32-41.

Brandt, A. (2008a): Regionaler Strukturwandel in der Wissensökonomie. In: RegioPol 1/2008, Zeitschrift für Regionalwirtschaft, S. 11-19.

Brandt, A. (2008b): Regional Clusterprozesse zwischen Effizienzvorteilen und Marktversagen. In: Floeting, H. (Hrsg.) (2008): Cluster in der kommunalen und regionalen Wirtschaftspolitik (Edition DIFU). Berlin, S. 131-145.

Brandt, A. (2008c): Sind Cluster machbar? Zur ökonomischen Begründung von Clusterpolitik und der politischen Gestaltbarkeit von Clusterkonzepten. In: Kiese, M./Schätzl, L. (Hrsg.) (2008): Cluster und Regionalentwicklung: Theorie, Beratung und praktische Umsetzung. Dortmund, S. 119-135.

Brandt, A./Dickow, M. Ch. (2007): PPP am Reedereistandort Untere Ems – Maritime Partnerschaften. In: Brandt, A. et al. (Hrsg.) (2007): Public Private Partnership in der Wirtschaftsförderung. Herausforderungen, Chancen und Grenzen. Stuttgart, S. 112-121.

Bredemeier, S. (2007): Wirtschaftlichkeit und Wirtschaftsförderung – Zur Rolle der regionalen Kreditinstitute im Spannungsfeld zwischen Globalisierung und Standortwettbewerb. In: Brandt, A. et al. (Hrsg.) (2007): Public Private Partnership in der Wirtschaftsförderung. Herausforderungen, Chancen und Grenzen. Stuttgart, S. 58-68.

Budäus, D. (2005): Public Private Partnership (PPP/ÖPP). Expertise für die Vereinigte Dienstleistungsgewerkschaft (VerDi). Hamburg.

Crouch, C. (2008): Postdemokratie. Frankfurt/Main.

DIFU (2005): Public Private Partnership Projekte. Eine aktuelle Bestandsaufnahme in Bund, Ländern und Kommunen. Endbericht, Berlin.

Einig, K. et al. (2005): Urban Governance. In: Bundesamt für Bauwesen und Raumordnung (Hrsg.) (2005): Urban Governance. Heft 9/10. Informationen zur Raumentwicklung. Bonn, S. I-VIII.

Einig, K./Fürst, D./Knieling, J. (2003): Aktionsraum Region – Regional Governance. In: Bundesamt für Bauwesen und Raumordnung (Hrsg.) (2003): Aktionsraum Region – Regional Governance. Heft 8/9. Informationen zur Raumentwicklung. Bonn, S. I-VI.

Eppler, E. (2005): Auslaufmodell Staat? Frankfurt am Main.

Franz, U.-B./Meyer, R. (2007): Regionale Beteiligungsfonds – öffentliches Kapital für die regionale Strukturförderung. In: Brandt, A. et al. (Hrsg.) (2007): Public Private Partnership in der Wirtschaftsförderung. Herausforderungen, Chancen und Grenzen. Stuttgart, S. 91-95.

Frey, R. L. (2003): Regional Governance zur Selbststeuerung territorialer Subsysteme. In: Bundesamt für Bauwesen und Raumordnung (Hrsg.) (2003): Aktionsraum Region – Regional Governance. Heft 8/9. Informationen zur Raumentwicklung. Bonn, S. 451-462.

Fürst, D. (2003): Steuerung auf regionaler Ebene versus Regional Governance. In: Bundesamt für Bauwesen und Raumordnung (Hrsg.) (2003): Aktionsraum Region – Regional Governance. Heft 8/9. Informationen zur Raumentwicklung. Bonn, S. 441-450.

Fürst, D. (2004): Regional Governance. In: Benz, A. (Hrsg.) (2004): Governance – Regieren in komplexen Regelsystemen. Wiesbaden, S. 45-64.

Gärtner, S. (2008): Entgrenzung der kommunalen Wirtschaftsförderung. Regionale Wirtschaftsförderung in der wissensintensiven Ökonomie. In: Regiopol. Zeitschrift für Regionalwirtschaft. 1/2008. Hannover, S. 83-93.

Habermas, J. (1999): Auf dem Weg zu einer demokratischen Bürgergesellschaft. In: Theodor-Heuß-Stiftung: 50 Jahre Grundgesetz, 50 Jahre Theodor-Heuß-Stiftung. Stuttgart.

Häußermann, H. (2006): Die Stadt als politisches Subjekt. Zum Wandel in der Steuerung der Stadtentwicklung. In: HBS (Hrsg.) (2006): Das neue Gesicht der Stadt. Strategien für die urbane Zukunft im 21. Jahrhundert. Berlin, S. 121-136.

Jung, H.-U. (2007): Neue Herausforderungen der kommunalen Wirtschaftsförderung. In: Brandt, A. (Hrsg.) (2007): Public Private Partnership in der Wirtschaftsförderung. Herausforderungen, Chancen und Grenzen. Stuttgart, S. 15-31.

Leggewie, C. (2006): Nur noch Berater am Hof der Macht. In: Die Zeit, Nr. 39 vom 21.9.2006.

Leibfried, S./Zürn, M. (2006): Transformation des Staates? Frankfurt am Main.

Mayntz, R. (2004): Governance im modernen Staat. In: Benz, A. (Hrsg.) (2004): Governance – Regieren in komplexen Regelsystemen. Wiesbaden, S. 65-76.

NMW (2005) : Eckwertepapier des niedersächsischen Wirtschaftsministeriums zu regionalen Wachstumskonzepten.

Nord/LB (2006a): Wirtschaftsförderung unter veränderten Rahmenbedingungen Befragung der NORD/LB Regionalwirtschaft zur strategischen Ausrichtung der kommunalen Wirtschaftsförderung in Niedersachsen. Hannover.

NORD/LB (2006b): Tagung: „PPP in der Wirtschaftsförderung“. Online unter http://www.nordlb.de/index.jsp (07.12.2006).

NORD/LB (2007): Wind im Rücken – die maritime Wirtschaft in der Wachstumsregion Ems-Achse. Hannover.

Rehm, H. (2007): Regional Governance als institutioneller Rahmen für Public Private Partnership in der Wirtschaftsförderung. In: Brandt, A. et al. (Hrsg.) (2007): Public Private Partnership in der Wirtschaftsförderung. Herausforderungen, Chancen und Grenzen. Stuttgart, S. 43-48.

Schuppert, G. F. (2001): Grundzüge eines zu entwickelnden Verwaltungskooperationsrechts. Regelungsbedarf und Handlungsoptionen eines Rechtsrahmens für Public Private Partnership. Berlin.

Sack, D. (2007): Probleme der politischen Kontrolle von PPP-Konzepten in der Wirtschaftsförderung. In: Brandt, A. et al. (Hrsg.) (2007): Public Private

Partnership in der Wirtschaftsförderung. Herausforderungen, Chancen und Grenzen. Stuttgart, S. 198-205.

Sack, D. (2004): Public Private Partnership im "aktivierenden Staat". In: vhw Forum Wohneigentum. Zeitschrift für Wohneigentum in der Stadtentwicklung und Immobilienwirtschaft. Berlin, S. 285-288.

Schuppert, G. F. (2005): Governance-Forschung. Vergewisserung über den Stand und Entwicklungslinien. Baden-Baden.

Schuppert, G. F. (2006): Governance. In: Heun, W. et al. (Hrsg.) (2006): Evangelisches Staatslexikon. Stuttgart, S. 889-893.

Sperlich, M. (2007): CFK-Valley e.V. – ein erfolgreiches PPP-Modell. In: Brandt, A. et al. (Hrsg.) (2007): Public Private Partnership in der Wirtschaftsförderung. Herausforderungen, Chancen und Grenzen. Stuttgart, S. 122-130.

Stiglitz, J. (1999): Volkswirtschaftslehre. 2. Aufl., München/Wien.

Stiglitz, J. (2008): Die Chancen der Globalisierung. München.

Ullrich, M. (2007): Herausforderungen, Chancen, Grenzen – PPP als Trägerstruktur der Wirtschaftsförderung. In: Brandt, A. et al. (Hrsg.) (2007): Public Private Partnership in der Wirtschaftsförderung. Herausforderungen, Chancen und Grenzen. Stuttgart, S. 51-57.

Weil, S. (2007): PPP. Neue Herausforderungen für die Kommunale Wirtschaftsförderung. In: Brandt, A. et al. (Hrsg.) (2007): Public Private Partnership in der Wirtschaftsförderung. Herausforderungen, Chancen und Grenzen. Stuttgart, S. 227-234.

Woestoff, F. (2007): PPP-Ansätze regionaler Wachstumsinitiativen – Wolfsburg AG. In: Brandt, A. et al. (Hrsg.) (2007): Public Private Partnership in der Wirtschaftsförderung. Herausforderungen, Chancen und Grenzen. Stuttgart, S. 104-111.

Regionale Kooperation und Unternehmensentwicklung am Beispiel der AUDI AG

Werner Widuckel

Inhaltsverzeichnis

1 Globale Expansion und regionale Entwicklungsbasis

1.1 Wettbewerb, Unternehmensstrategie und Personalpolitik

Die Unternehmensentwicklung der AUDI AG ist insbesondere in den letzten zehn Jahren durch ein überdurchschnittliches Wachstum sowie eine massive internationale Expansion gekennzeichnet. So wuchsen Absatz und Produktion innerhalb dieses Zeitraums um jeweils 58 % bzw. 64 % (Abb. 1).

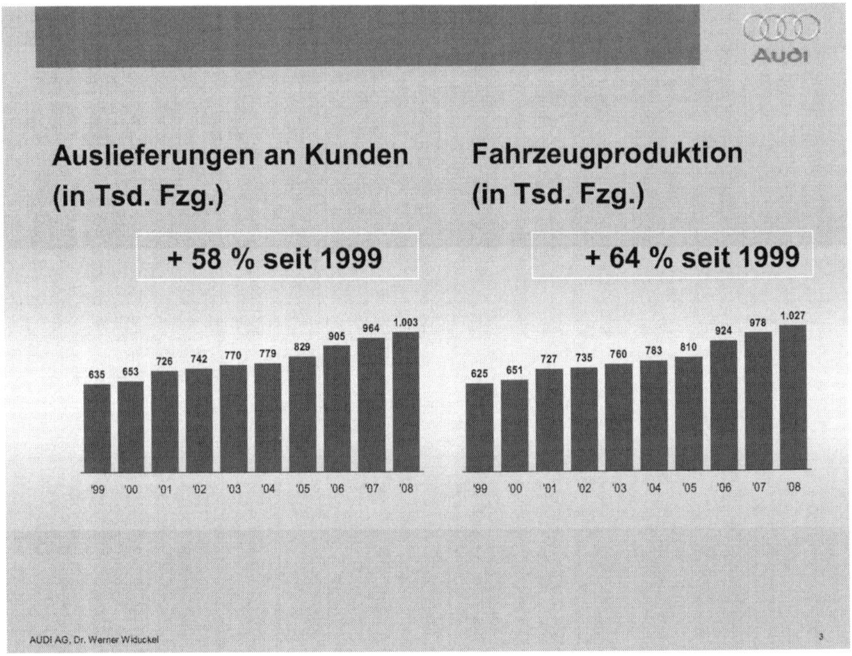

Abb. 1: Fahrzeugauslieferungen und -produktion der AUDI AG seit 1999

Quelle: AUDI AG.

Die Verteilung von Absatz und Umsatz verschob sich zugunsten Europas und Asiens, während sich das Gewicht des Absatzraums Deutschland trotz eines absoluten Wachstums verringerte (Abb. 2).

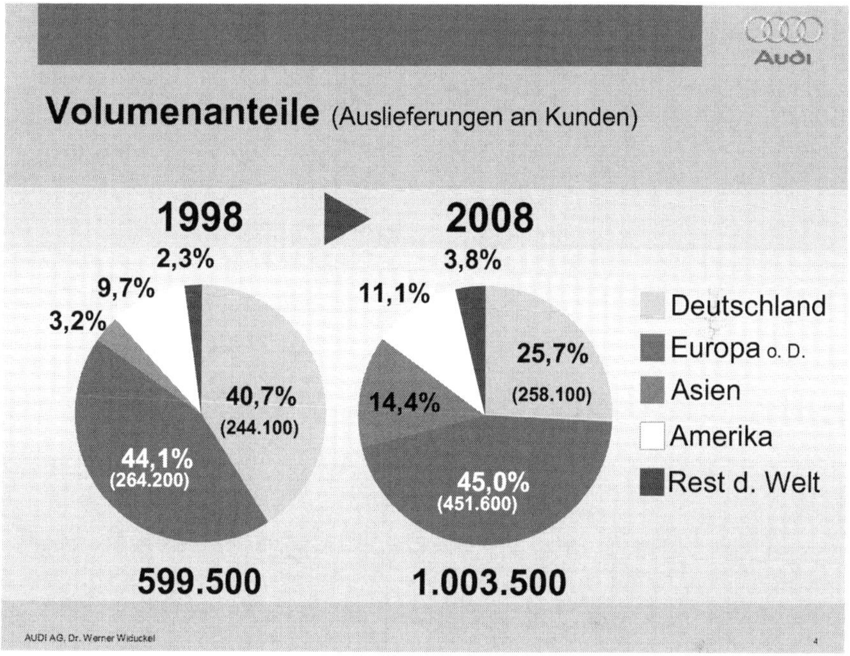

Abb. 2: Volumenanteile (Auslieferungen an Kunden)
Quelle: AUDI AG.

Diese Wachstumsentwicklung spiegelt den Markterfolg des Produktprogramms und der gezielten Aufwertungsstrategie der Marke Audi wider. Audi entwickelte sich bereits seit dem Ende der 1980er und dem Beginn der 1990er Jahre zu einer sportlichen Marke im Premiumsegment. Dieser Entwicklungsprozess wurde zwischen den Jahren 2002 und 2004 durch die Unternehmensstrategie 2015 weiter verdichtet und konsequent weiter entwickelt. In dieser Strategie werden vier Handlungsfelder und Zielgrößen definiert und konkretisiert (Abb. 3).

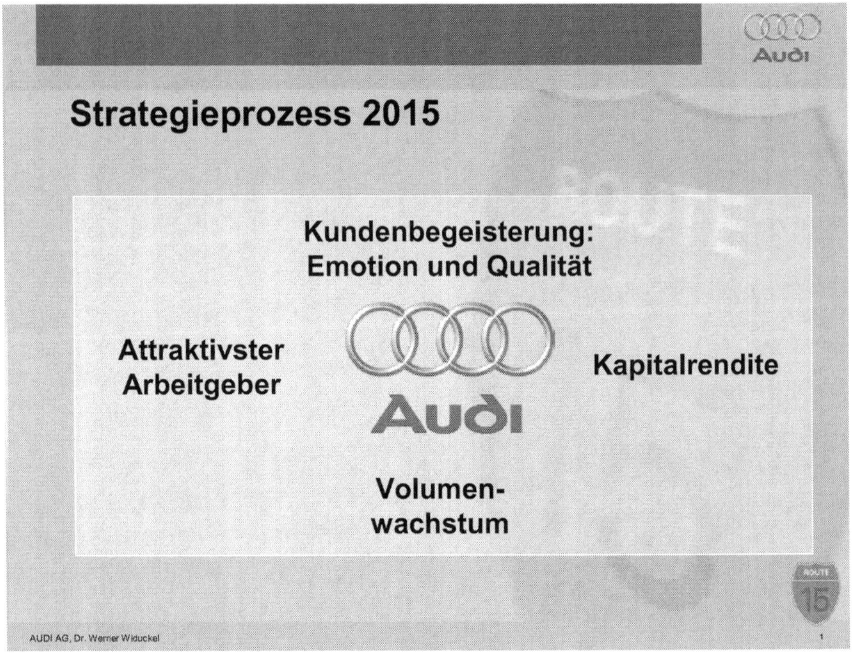

Abb. 3: Strategieprozess 2015
Quelle: AUDI AG.

Durch die weitere Aufwertung und Ausdifferenzierung des Produktprogramms soll sowohl die Voraussetzung für Wachstum als auch für die Steigerung der Ertragskraft gelegt werden. Darüber hinaus soll die Anziehung und emotionale Bindung der Kunden durch die besondere Wertigkeit und Qualität der Produkte sowie durch exzellenten Service deutlich gesteigert werden. Das Strategieziel „attraktivster Arbeitgeber" zielt auf die Gewinnung und Bindung motivierter und leistungsfähiger Mitarbeiter ab. Eine besondere Bedeutung hat für dieses

Strategieziel die Verbindung von Leistungsanforderungen mit einer aktiven Personalentwicklung und einer materiellen Beteiligung am Unternehmenserfolg sowie der Verknüpfung von Wettbewerbsfähigkeit und sicherer Beschäftigung. Die AUDI AG will nicht nur gegenüber ihren Kunden, sondern auch gegenüber ihren Mitarbeitern bindungsfähig sein, um somit die Identifikation mit und die Leistung für das Unternehmen nachhaltig zu einem Wettbewerbsvorteil werden zu lassen. Leistungsbereitschaft, Qualifikation und Kompetenzen der Mitarbeiterinnen und Mitarbeiter sind für Audi strategische Schlüsselgrößen, um wachsenden technologischen Innovationsanforderungen und einer steigenden Komplexität von Unternehmensprozessen Rechnung tragen zu können. In diesem Kompetenzwettbewerb können die Personalkosten nur ein Bewertungsfaktor sein. Leistungsbereitschaft, Leistungsfähigkeit und Kompetenzen der Mitarbeiter sind weitere Faktoren, die die Innovationsfähigkeit sowie Effizienz und Effektivität der Unternehmensprozesse wesentlich bestimmen. Hieraus ergeben sich besondere Faktoren der Standortbindung, die nicht vernachlässigt werden dürfen und auch nicht durch virtuelle Beziehungen ersetzt werden können. Hierbei ist im Blick zu behalten, dass die technologischen Innovationsprozesse in der Produkt- wie Verfahrensentwicklung nach wie vor extrem von den beiden deutschen Standorten Ingolstadt und Neckarsulm abhängen. Der „Vorsprung durch Technik" bei Audi ist nach wie vor durch die Qualifikationsbasis sowie die Forschungs- und Wissenschaftsinfrastruktur am Standort Deutschland geprägt. Dies reicht von der dualen Berufsausbildung bis zu Forschungskooperationen. Somit wird erkennbar: Globale Expansion, Wettbewerbsorientierung und Standortbindung schließen sich nicht aus, sondern können sich ergänzen. Für ein innovatives Automobilunternehmen ist dieser Zusammenhang von ganz besonderer Bedeutung. Denn Qualifikationen und Kompetenzen werden über mehrere Produktlebenszyklen für das Unternehmen gewonnen und weiter entwickelt. Diese sind nicht ausschließlich durch theoretisches Wissen, sondern auch durch Erfahrungswissen fundiert, das über längere Zeiträume gewonnen werden muss. Dies wird in einem Innovationswettbewerb an Bedeutung gewinnen, der die Ausschöpfung aller verfügbaren Potenziale zur

Reduzierung des Verbrauchs und der weiteren Verbesserung der Fahrzeugsicherheit erfordert, ohne hierbei die zahlungskräftige Nachfrage am Markt zu überfordern. Darüber hinaus verlangt ein komplexes Unternehmen wie Audi auch Organisationserfahrung von seinen Mitarbeitern, um die gestellten Kommunikations- und Kooperationsanforderungen bewältigen zu können. Auf die schnelle Auswechselbarkeit und Verfügbarkeit qualifizierter Mitarbeiter zu setzen, ist deshalb für Audi kein erfolgversprechender Weg der Unternehmensentwicklung.

Neben den genannten funktionalen Anforderungen muss sich Audi als großes Unternehmen auch normativen gesellschaftlichen Erwartungen und Ansprüchen stellen. Unternehmen sind neben ihrer Funktion im Wettbewerb auch in einen gesellschaftlichen Kontext eingebunden. Dieser Kontext „umschließt" die Wettbewerbsbeziehungen und die ökonomische Rationalität unternehmerischen Handelns. Hierin wird normativ an Unternehmen die Erwartung gerichtet, nicht nur einen betriebswirtschaftlichen Mehrwert für die Investoren zu erzielen, sondern gleichzeitig einen gesellschaftlichen Mehrwert darzustellen, der den Entwicklungsanforderungen der Umwelt, der Standortregion genauso gerecht wird wie den Bedürfnissen der Kunden und der Mitarbeiter. Hierbei handelt es sich nicht nur um eine mehr oder weniger vom Willen des Unternehmens abhängige Darstellung sozialer Verantwortung, die mit dem Kernbereich der Unternehmensentwicklung unverbunden wäre. Vielmehr ist das Unternehmen darauf aus zwei Gründen angewiesen, sich auf Arrangements mit den Wirtschaftsbeteiligten (stakeholdern) des Unternehmens einzulassen. Zum einen nutzen Unternehmen gesellschaftliche Ressourcen (z.B. Bildung, Forschung, Infrastruktur), zu deren Erhalt und Weiterentwicklung sie im Sinne einer nachhaltigen Entwicklung beitragen müssen. Darüber hinaus konstituieren insbesondere große Unternehmen durch ihren Einfluss auf gesellschaftliche Entwicklungen Machtpotenziale, die ihre Legitimation nicht allein aus dem betriebswirtschaftlichen Erfolg ableiten können. Vielmehr muss die von der Gesellschaft gewährte Handlungsfreiheit auch durch die Bereitschaft der

Bindung des Unternehmensinteresses an gesellschaftliche Interessen begründet werden können. Sind Unternehmen hierzu nicht bereit, entstehen Zielkonflikte, wie sie überdeutlich in der Finanzmarktkrise aufgebrochen sind, die im Jahr 2008 ihren Anfang nahm und deren Ende gegenwärtig nicht abschbar ist.

1.2 Regionale Umfeldbedingungen

Die regionalen Umfeldbedingungen sind ein Handlungsfeld, das vor allem für ein Unternehmen mit einer hohen „physischen Gebundenheit“ der Wertschöpfung von hoher Bedeutung ist. Physische Gebundenheit bedeutet, dass Kooperationsbeziehungen zwischen Akteuren innerhalb und außerhalb des Unternehmens nicht beliebig virtuell transferierbar sind. Von der Produktentwicklung über die Produktionsplanung bis zur Integration der Lieferanten steht am Ende des Wertschöpfungsprozesses ein physisches Produkt, das zusammengesetzt ist aus Komponenten, Baugruppen und Systemen. Dies verlangt einen hohen Grad an ortsgebundener Kooperation und Integration. Damit wird nicht ausgesagt, dass nationale oder internationale Kooperationsbeziehungen hierdurch ausgeschlossen wären. Im Gegenteil: Ein Automobilunternehmen, das seine Entwicklungspotenziale ausschließlich auf regionalen Beziehungen gründen wollte, wäre auf Dauer nicht wettbewerbsfähig. Dies gilt sowohl für Wissenschafts- und Forschungskooperationen als auch für Lieferantenbeziehungen sowie für die Erfordernisse einer globalen Marktpräsenz und hiermit verbunden eines globalen Produktionsnetzwerkes. Allerdings bedeutet der Verweis auf die Erfordernisse einer globalen Integration nicht, dass die Wettbewerbsfähigkeit von Unternehmen unabhängig von den regionalen Umfeldbedingungen wäre. Im Gegenteil: Gute regionale Umfeldbedingungen für Innovation bieten die Chance, sich durch die Vernetzung mit globalen Innovationspotenzialen zu verstärken. Wer glaubt, auf starke regionale Umfeldbedingungen verzichten zu können, lässt diese Chance ungenutzt. In dieser Erkenntnis liegt für große Unternehmen und Standortregionen eine gemeinsame Chance. Sie zu nutzen, erfordert einen gemeinsamen und gezielten Entwicklungszusammenhang zu organisieren, der beiden dient.

2 Die Initiative Regionalmanagement (IRMA) – eine Initiative der AUDI AG – ein Projekt der Region Ingolstadt

Zur Vorgeschichte

Die Beziehung zwischen der AUDI AG und der Region Ingolstadt hat sich seit der Ansiedlung des Unternehmens Ende der 1940er Jahre keineswegs reibungslos und spannungsfrei entwickelt. Auf der einen Seite stand eine Region mit einer vielfältigen Geschichte und sehr entwickelten historischen Wurzeln, auf der anderen Seite brach das Unternehmen in diese kulturell-historischen Wurzeln als „Fremdkörper" ein. Trotz vielfältiger und zahlreicher Bemühungen verschiedener Akteure waren die Beziehungen zwischen zentralen Entscheidungsträgern der Region und des Unternehmens von einer gewissen Fremdheit geprägt. Kooperationsbeziehungen und Kooperationsprojekte waren in diesem Entwicklungsstadium stark von Einzelpersonen und deren Engagement abhängig. Gleichwohl sind hierdurch wichtige Grundlagen gelegt worden, auf denen später aufgebaut werden konnte. Die Überlegung, einen systematisch organisierten kooperativen Entwicklungsprozess zwischen Unternehmen und Region zu initiieren, war Gegenstand einer Studie, die im Jahr 2004 durch eine Unternehmensberatung im Auftrag der Stadt Ingolstadt und der AUDI AG[1] durchgeführt wurde. In dieser Studie wurde eine erste Definition von Themenfeldern für die Standortentwicklung vorgenommen. Damit wurde ein entscheidender Schritt vollzogen, eine systematische Verbindung zwischen der Entwicklung des Unternehmens und der Standortregion vorzunehmen, die allerdings in diesem

[1] Vgl. The Boston Consulting Group (2004): Stadt Ingolstadt und AUDI AG. Öffentlich-Private Kooperation. Dokumentation.

Ansatz noch auf die Kooperationsmöglichkeiten zwischen der Stadt Ingolstadt und der AUDI AG beschränkt waren. Andere Gebietskörperschaften und Unternehmen waren hierin noch nicht einbezogen. Allerdings zeigt sich in dieser Studie eine erweiterte inhaltliche Perspektive öffentlich-privater Kooperation. Mit den priorisierten Themenfeldern „Fahrzeugsicherheit", „Kreislaufwirtschaft", „Tourismus" und „Freizeit" wird erkennbar, dass beide Akteure unternehmensrelevante Handlungsfelder und Standortfaktoren miteinander verkoppeln wollen, um sowohl die Innovationsstärke als auch die Standortattraktivität zu verbessern. In der Definition dieser Handlungsfelder werden regionale Aspekte genauso mit einbezogen wie die strategische Fokussierung von „Clustern" als Kompetenznetzwerke im Standortwettbewerb. Dies bezieht sich sowohl auf die Kooperation zwischen unterschiedlichen Unternehmen über die einzelnen Stufen der Wertschöpfung hinweg als auch auf die Entwicklung und Einbeziehung der regionalen Hochschulen und Universitäten.

Diese erweiterte Fokussierung spiegelt hierbei auch die Unternehmensentwicklung der AUDI AG wider. Das Wachstum des Unternehmens und sein sich erweiternder Innovationsfokus sowie das Erfordernis, beides abzusichern, stellte sowohl erweiterte Ansprüche an die regionalen Umfeldbedingungen und die Infrastruktur als auch an den Zuwachs qualifizierten Beschäftigungspotenzials durch „Zuwanderung". Damit rücken neben „harten" Standortanforderungen auch die Lebensbedingungen (soziale Infrastruktur, Schule, Gesundheitsversorgung, Lebensqualität) umfassend in das Blickfeld des Unternehmensinteresses.

Der Gründungsprozess und seine Motive

Dieser ausgeweitete Fokus führte in der AUDI AG zur Überlegung, den angedachten Entwicklungsprozess zu institutionalisieren, um damit eine stabile Grundlage für Vertrauen, Verbindlichkeit und Zielorientierung zu schaffen. Es wurde vorgeschlagen, im Sinne einer öffentlich-privaten Kooperation („Public

Private Partnership“) eine strukturierte Projektorganisation in Form eines Vereins zu gründen und hierin weitere wirtschaftlich prägende Unternehmen der Region schon im Gründungsprozess mit einzubeziehen. Dieser Kooperationsansatz verfolgte das Ziel der Gründung eines strukturierten Netzwerkes, das über die Grenzen zwischen Privatunternehmen und Gebietskörperschaften hinweg regionale Entwicklungsprojekte anstoßen kann. Der Vorteil dieser Kooperationsform ist neben ihrer Flexibilität, dass sie die Möglichkeit bietet, für die jeweiligen Entwicklungsthemen die jeweils inhaltlich und formal besten bzw. erforderlichen Kompetenzen zu bündeln und zu koordinieren. Somit können gemeinsame Interessen sichtbar gemacht und aufeinander bezogen verfolgt und in Projekten umgesetzt werden. Hierbei ist besser als in anderen Organisationsformen erreichbar, dass die jeweiligen Interessen der unterschiedlichen Unternehmen und Gebietskörperschaften geklärt und die jeweils unterschiedlichen Perspektiven zusammengeführt werden können. Dies bietet die Chance, Ressourcen zu schonen, jene Konkurrenzsituationen zu vermeiden, welche die Region zersplittern würden, aber auch im Abgleich zu ermitteln, worauf sich die Region konzentrieren sollte, um ein klares Profil zu entwickeln. In dieser Absicht haben die vier genannten Gebietskörperschaften, die AUDI AG, die EADS, die Media-Saturn AG, die Bauer AG sowie EDEKA Süd bei der Gründung der INITIATIVE REGIONALMANAGEMENT Region Ingolstadt e.V. (IRMA) Pate gestanden. Damit wird von Beginn an die Absicht deutlich, IRMA nicht auf eine Kooperation der AUDI AG zu reduzieren, was den regionalen Entwicklungspotenzialen und der Wirtschaftsstruktur nicht gerecht geworden wäre.

3 Das Handlungskonzept als gemeinsame Handlungsbasis

Eine der schwierigsten Herausforderungen regionaler wie öffentlich-privater Kooperation besteht in der Herausarbeitung einer gemeinsamen Interessen- und Handlungsperspektive. Dies schließt sowohl die räumliche Definition der jeweiligen Region mit ein wie auch die Handlungsfelder, die gemeinsam gestaltet werden sollen. Eine weitere Herausforderung besteht in der Einbringung von Ressourcen und die Verteilung der hieraus resultierenden Lasten zwischen den Akteuren. Um hierfür eine gemeinsam getragene Ausgangsbasis zu schaffen, wurde von den vier Gebietskörperschaften und der AUDI AG das Zentrum für Entrepreneursh!p an der Katholischen Universität Eichstätt mit der Ausarbeitung eines Handlungskonzepts beauftragt, das neben einer Analyse der Stärken und der Schwächen der Region auch eine inhaltliche Strukturierung von Handlungsfeldern vornehmen sollte. Dieses Handlungskonzept bildet die Basis für die Arbeit der Initiative; folglich wurde dessen Erstellung der Gründung des Vereins vorangestellt. Die räumliche Definition der Region ergab sich aus den Grenzen der beteiligten Gebietskörperschaften. In einer Analyse, die durch Experteninterviews und einem Workshop untermauert wurde, konnten vier Handlungsfelder herausgearbeitet werden, die in den Augen der beteiligten Akteure die relevanten Entwicklungsfelder der Region und der öffentlich-privaten Kooperation darstellen. Diese lauten „Wirtschaft", „Bildung und Wissenschaft", „Lebensqualität/Wohn- und Erlebnisraum" sowie „Wahrnehmung der Region". Im Rahmen dieser Handlungsfelder wurden die in der nachstehenden Tabelle dargestellten Themenschwerpunkte festgelegt.

Wirtschaft	**Bildung und Wissenschaft**	**Lebensqualität/ Wohn- und Erlebnisraum**	**Wahrnehmung der Region**
– Beschäftigungsmanagement – Handel & Versorgung – Regionale Clusterentwicklung	– Bildungs- und Wissenschaftsstandort	– Gesundheit, Fitness, Sport, Soziales – Touristik, Kongresse; Freizeit, Kultur – Mobilitäts- und Verkehrsmanagement – Urbanität & Shopping	– Regionalmarketing – Räumliche Lage der Region

Tab. 1: Die Themenschwerpunkte innerhalb der Handlungsfelder
Quelle: eigene Darstellung.

Das Handlungskonzept verfolgt damit drei gedankliche Entwicklungslinien: Die erste Linie beantwortet die Frage, wo die spezifischen Stärken und Entwicklungspotenziale der Region liegen. Die zweite Linie klärt die Frage nach Schwächen der Region, die in der Zukunft zu einem Problem werden könnten, weil sie einen Modernisierungsrückstand oder Entwicklungshindernisse auslösen würden. Und die dritte Linie nimmt die Fragestellung auf, welche Handlungsfelder am ehesten durch eine übergreifende Kooperation besser gestaltet werden können oder sogar müssen als durch das einzelne Handeln der beteiligten Unternehmen und Gebietskörperschaften. Das heißt: Neben der notwendigen inhaltlichen und strategischen Orientierung wird mit dem Handlungskonzept auch Klarheit über die jeweiligen Rollen und Aufgaben im regionalen Entwicklungsprozess geschaffen. Dies ist vor allem deshalb erforderlich, weil das Regionalmanagement hoheitliche Aufgabenstellungen und kommunalpolitische Willensbildungsprozesse genauso wenig ersetzen kann wie unternehmenspolitische Entscheidungen. IRMA kann nur dann Impulse setzen, wenn die Rückkoppelung zu den Akteuren fließend und durchgängig gewährleistet ist, um deren eigenständige Interessenpositionen und Sichtweisen auch aufnehmen zu können. Das ist die Grundvoraussetzung dafür, dass in dieser Kooperation für die Gebietskörperschaften und Unternehmen auch ein „Mehrwert" entsteht, der als solcher wahrgenommen wird. Deshalb hat IRMA die Form einer flexiblen Projektorganisation angenommen, in der in unterschiedlicher Zusammensetzung die jeweils relevanten Themen von den Akteuren bearbeitet werden, die hieran das jeweils größte Interesse haben und die höchste Kompetenz aufweisen. Der hauptamtliche „Stab" von IRMA wird schlank gehalten und nimmt die Aufgaben der Projektorganisation und -koordination, der Kommunikation und der operativen Steuerung der Ressourcen wahr. So soll einerseits ein professioneller Handlungsrahmen gewährleistet werden, der allerdings sehr bewusst die Anbindung an die Interessen und die Expertise seiner „Basis" gewährleistet.

4 Die ersten Projekte

In diesem Handlungsrahmen sind nach der formalen Gründung des Vereins erste Projekte initiiert worden. Übergeordnet wird die **Entwicklung eines Leitbildes** für die Region vorangetrieben, das in einem ersten Schritt die unterschiedlichen Sichtweisen von Bevölkerungsgruppen aus unterschiedlichen Teilräumen konsistent miteinander verknüpfen soll. Das Leitbild soll aussagen, wie sich die Region selber sieht und von anderen gesehen werden soll. Es stellt somit das begriffliche und kommunikative Dach bereit, wobei ausdrücklich nicht die Entwicklung eines „Logos" vorangestellt wurde. Hiermit verbunden wird die Entwicklung eines **Regionalportals** vorgenommen, das die Region sowohl als Wirtschafts- wie auch als Lebensraum profilieren und wahrnehmbar machen wird. Hieran anschließen wird sich ein Tourismusportal, das die touristische Attraktivität der Region Ingolstadt aufzeigen und hierbei regional „Verbundangebote" für Freizeit und Kultur in den Mittelpunkt stellen wird.

Im Bereich Bildung und Wissenschaft wird zum einen in einer **Grundlagenstudie** die **Bildungs- und Wissenschaftsinfrastruktur** der Region dargestellt, um Verknüpfungsmöglichkeiten für Bildung und Qualifizierung wie auch Wissenschaft und Forschung aufzuzeigen. Es wird von besonderer Bedeutung sein, diese Synergien zwischen den öffentlichen Einrichtungen und den Unternehmen mit Hilfe dieses Atlasses herzustellen und zukunftsweisende Kooperationspotenziale aufzuzeigen. In einem zweiten Schritt werden in einer weiteren Studie **Zukunftserfordernisse für Bildung und Wissenschaft** in der Region einfließen, um hieraus Hinweise für die Weiterentwicklung dieser Infrastruktur ableiten zu können. Dies umfasst ausdrücklich auch den Bereich der beruflichen Bildung. Als konkretes Umsetzungsprojekt wird darüber hinaus die **Gründung einer internationalen Schule** in Ingolstadt forciert, die von mehreren international tätigen Unternehmen der Region ausdrücklich begrüßt wird.

Mit diesen Projekten bekommt das Regionalmanagement durch IRMA konkrete Gestalt und liefert als kooperatives Netzwerk eine Handlungs- und Kompetenzbasis für Regionalentwicklung, die keiner der beteiligten Akteure allein darstellen könnte. Dies zeigt auch: Öffentlich-Private Kooperation im Rahmen von Regionalentwicklung ist ein Lernprozess. Dieser Lernprozess bezieht sich aber nicht nur auf die konkreten Projekte, sondern auch auf die Notwendigkeit, das Handlungskonzept und die hiermit verbundenen Entwicklungsziele immer wieder zu überprüfen. Dies schließt die dauerhafte wissenschaftliche Begleitung und methodengeleitete Reflexion über den Stand des Erreichten und die verfolgten Ziele mit ein.

5 Perspektiven

Unter den Bedingungen der derzeitigen Krise der Finanzmärkte und ihre Rückwirkungen erhält die Zukunftsperspektive für IRMA eine besondere Brisanz. Denn wirtschaftliche Krisen lösen in Unternehmen und Gebietskörperschaften gleichermaßen finanzielle Restriktionen aus, die auch das Engagement im Rahmen der Regionalentwicklung auf den Prüfstand stellen. Es ist bemerkenswert, dass die Mitgliederzahlen bei IRMA gegenwärtig steigen und das Engagement der in den Projekten arbeitenden Beteiligten genauso wenig zurückgenommen wird wie der Finanzierungsbeitrag durch die Mitglieder. Hinzu kommt, dass auch der Freistaat Bayern in die finanzielle Förderung des Vereins eingetreten ist, um den hier dargestellten Ansatz der öffentlich-privaten Kooperation zu unterstützen. Es scheint bei den Akteuren eher das Bewusstsein vorzuherrschen, dass wirtschaftlich schwierigere Entwicklungen eher mehr als weniger Kooperation zur Entwicklung von Standortpotenzialen erfordern, die letztlich auch der Schonung von Ressourcen dienen. Am Ende müssen aber die auf den Weg gebrachten Projekte zeigen, dass sie diese Potenziale auch tatsächlich in der Realität entwickeln. Dies erfordert, möglichst zügig aus dem Stadium der Grundlagenarbeit (z.B. Leitbild, Grundlagenstudie Bildung und Wissenschaft) hinauszuwachsen, ohne die hierfür erforderliche Gründlichkeit und Professionalität zu vernachlässigen. Ohne Frage wird dieses Spannungsfeld durch die gegenwärtige wirtschaftliche Entwicklung verschärft. Ganz entscheidend ist darüber hinaus, dass die zentralen Entscheidungsträger der Region ihre Identifikation und ihr gegenseitiges Vertrauen mit diesem Entwicklungsprozess öffentlich erkennbar dokumentieren. Hierfür ist in der Region Ingolstadt eine gute Basis gegeben.

Als vorläufiges Fazit lässt sich deshalb ziehen, dass der Erfolg von IRMA letztlich messbar sein muss. Die erfolgreichste Region in Deutschland zu werden, ist das Ziel unseres regionalen Entwicklungsprozesses. Dies gilt für Beschäftigung, Wachstum, Innovation und Attraktivität von Leben und Arbeiten. Voraussetzung für diesen Erfolg wird sein, dass nicht nur Unternehmen und Gebietskörperschaften sich mit dieser Aufgabe identifizieren, sondern die Menschen, die in der Region Ingolstadt leben und arbeiten. Regionalentwicklung ist kein technokratischer Prozess der Gestaltung von Strukturen, sondern muss Anschluss haben und halten an die Lebenswelt der Bevölkerung und ihre Zukunftserwartungen. Hierfür weitere Schritte zu unternehmen, wird eine der nächsten wesentlichen Aufgaben von IRMA sein, die mit dem Projekt „Leitbild" begonnen wurde. Ein guter Anfang ist gemacht.

PPP und Stadtwerke – Public Private oder Public Public?

Horizontale Kooperationen als Strategieoption für Stadtwerke im liberalisierten Energiemarkt

Michael Wübbels

Inhaltsverzeichnis

1 Stadtwerke im Kontext von Daseinsvorsorge und Kooperationen

Die Kommunalwirtschaft hat als zuverlässiger Anbieter von hochwertigen Infrastrukturdienstleistungen eine große Bedeutung in Deutschland. Die Bandbreite kommunalwirtschaftlicher Dienstleistungen umfasst die Versorgung mit Strom, Gas, Fernwärme und Wasser, die Entsorgung von Abwasser und Abfällen sowie deren umweltgerechte Behandlung und die Straßenreinigung. Stadtwerke bieten diese umfangreichen lokalen Infrastrukturgüter sicher, umweltverträglich und preisgünstig an. Ein häufig anzutreffendes Merkmal ist die Zusammenfassung mehrerer Sparten im Querverbund, wodurch die Erschließung von Synergievorteilen – auch zur Kostenentlastung der Kunden – möglich ist.

Für die Kommunen als Eigentümerinnen ist die Daseinsvorsorge durch ihre Unternehmen aus zwei Gründen von großer Bedeutung. Erstens orientieren sich die Unternehmen in ihrem Wirtschaften am Gemeinwohl, dem Public Value. Über alle Sparten hinweg erwirtschafteten kommunale Unternehmen beispielsweise im Jahre 2007 rund 71 Mrd. Euro Umsatzerlöse. Rund 80 % der Investitionen, die sich für 2007 auf 6,7 Mio. Euro belaufen, wurden als Aufträge an regionale Unternehmen vergeben, vor allem an lokale Handwerks- und Gewerbebetriebe. Zusätzlich ist die Kommunalwirtschaft mit ca. 233.000 Beschäftigten und einer überproportionalen Ausbildungsquote ein wichtiger Arbeitgeber. Zweitens verfügen Städte und Gemeinden mit der Eigentümerschaft über die Stadtwerke über eine wichtige Einnahmequelle für den kommunalen Haushalt. In erster Linie trifft das für die Energiesparte zu, deren Gewinne den größten Anteil der Einnahmen aus kommunalen Unternehmen ausmachen. Diese Einnahmen können wiederum in lokale Bürger- und Infrastrukturdienstleistungen investiert werden. Insgesamt tragen kommunalwirtschaftliche Unternehmen damit mittel- und unmittelbar zur Steigerung der regionalen Wertschöpfung bei und leisten einen wichtigen Beitrag zur Verbesserung der kommunalen Standortqualität.

Diese Funktionen konnten Stadtwerke bis zum Ende der 1990er Jahre ohne größere Friktionen wahrnehmen. Seit der Liberalisierung der europäischen Strom- und Gasmärkte und der nachfolgenden Regulierung der jeweiligen Netze sind Stadtwerke mit einer Vielzahl von Herausforderungen konfrontiert, die es zu meistern gilt. Fakt ist, dass viele Stadtwerke, insbesondere aber die kleinen und mittleren Unternehmen, den sich hieraus ergebenden Anforderungen nur begegnen können, wenn sie mit anderen Unternehmen kooperieren.

Unter Kooperationen im streng betriebswirtschaftlichen Sinn wird die Zusammenarbeit zwischen meist wenigen, rechtlich und wirtschaftlich selbständigen Unternehmen verstanden, die zur Steigerung der Wettbewerbsfähigkeit in einzelnen Geschäftsbereichen gemeinsam tätig werden. Kooperationen sind in vielfältiger Form denkbar und praktiziert; sie unterscheiden sich zum einen in der horizontalen oder vertikalen Ausrichtung innerhalb der Wertschöpfungskette, zum anderen im Grad ihrer vertraglichen Festlegung. Kooperationen auf der gleichen Ebene, also kommunales Unternehmen mit kommunalem Unternehmen, werden als horizontale Kooperationen bezeichnet, während vertikale Kooperationen mit über- oder nachgelagerten Wertschöpfungsstufen eingegangen werden. Sie können als formlose Zusammenarbeit oder als vertraglich feste Struktur etabliert werden. Unter den letztgenannten stellen Joint Ventures eine spezifische Kooperationsform mit Kapitalbeteiligung dar, bei der rechtlich selbständige gemeinsame Unternehmungen zweier oder mehrerer Partner gegründet werden.

Beteiligungen sind keine Kooperationen im engeren Sinn. Jedoch sind die hiermit verbundenen gewünschten Ergebnisse – so z. B. Kosteneinsparungen, Synergieeffekte, Zugang zu bislang verschlossenen Märkten – vergleichbar, so dass sie im Folgenden als eine Unterform von Kooperationen behandelt werden. Beteiligungen können auch zu Kooperationen im engeren Sinn ausgebaut werden (vertikale Kooperation). Fusionen stellen einen Unternehmenszusammenschluss dar und können daher nicht zu Kooperationen gezählt werden; sie werden im Rahmen dieses Beitrags daher nicht behandelt.

Offen ist bei diesen (und weiteren denkbaren) Formen der Kooperation zunächst, ob die Kooperation zwischen zwei oder mehreren öffentlichen Unternehmen oder aber zwischen privaten Betrieben stattfindet, oder aber in einer gemischten Form. Letztgenannte Variante, bei der sich private und öffentliche Partner formell oder informell zusammenschließen, entstand in den 1940er Jahren in den USA, um die Entwicklung und Erneuerung in städtischen Problemzonen voranzutreiben.

Im Folgenden wird diskutiert, inwieweit die zugrunde liegende Idee für den Bereich der Stadtwerke sinnvoll erscheint. Dargestellt werden die zwei Alternativen für kommunale Unternehmen, die ermöglichen, sich den aktuellen ordnungs- und strukturpolitischen Herausforderungen zu stellen und dabei ggf. noch weitere Kosten- und Synergiepotenziale zu erschließen. Der Beitrag geht von der These aus, dass Kooperationen in der gemischten Form (also Public Private Partnership) nicht zwingend die optimale Lösung sind. Für kommunale Unternehmen bieten sich aus verschiedenen Gründen vor allem auch rein kommunale Kooperationen, also Public Public Partnerships, an.

2 Public Private Partnership oder Public Public Partnership?

Kommunalwirtschaftliche Unternehmen sind heute überwiegend in privater Rechtsform organisiert, vorzugsweise als GmbH. Einer Erhebung des VKU zufolge sind nur noch knapp 14 % der Mitgliedsunternehmen mit den Sparten Strom oder/und Gas so genannte Eigenbetriebe[1]. Die überwältigende Mehrheit von über 73 % ist als GmbH organisiert, weitere gut 7 % als AG.

[1] Ein Eigenbetrieb ist ein aus der Verwaltung ausgegliedertes Sondervermögen der Gemeinde/Landkreise ohne eigene Rechtspersönlichkeit und damit unselbständiger, aber organisatorisch abgegrenzter Teil des Gemeindevermögens. Die Haftung der Gemeinde erfolgt unmittelbar und unbeschränkt. Eigenbetriebe unterliegen den Eigenbetriebsgesetzen, die von den Ländern erlassen werden.

Von der Organisationsform sind die Eigentumsverhältnisse zu unterscheiden. Einer Erhebung des VKU aus dem Jahre 2007 folgend befinden sich knapp die Hälfte (48 %) der befragten rund 1.000 kommunalen Unternehmen im Eigentum einer einzelnen Kommune. Weitere knapp 13 % Unternehmen sind in der Hand von mehreren Kommunen. Privatwirtschaftliche Beteiligungen bestehen bei gut 39 % der kommunalen Unternehmen. Nur etwa 3 % dieser befragten Unternehmen weisen private Beteiligungen von mehr als 50 % auf, für die Mehrzahl ergibt sich eine Beteiligungsquote zwischen 25 und 50 % (Abb. 1).

Aus der Sicht der einzelnen Kommune ist zusätzlich wichtig, inwieweit die auf dem Gemeindegebiet aktiven kommunalen Unternehmen von ihr „gelenkt“ werden können. Hält die Kommune die Anteile zu 100 %, so spricht man von direkter oder unmittelbarer Beteiligung, und die Entscheidungsfindung findet unter direkter Steuerung der Kommune statt. Ähnlich steht es bei indirekten Beteiligungen, bei denen die Kommune zwar unmittelbar keine Anteile besitzt, aber indirekt durch eines ihrer Tochterunternehmen. Solange die Kommune eine Mehrheitsbeteiligung hat, also direkt oder indirekt mindestens 50 % der Anteile hält, können keine Entscheidungen gegen die Interessen der Kommune getroffen werden. Anders sieht es bei Minderheitsbeteiligungen aus. Hält die Kommune weniger als 50 % der Anteile direkt oder indirekt, sind unternehmerische Entscheidungen auch gegen die Interessen der Kommune möglich.

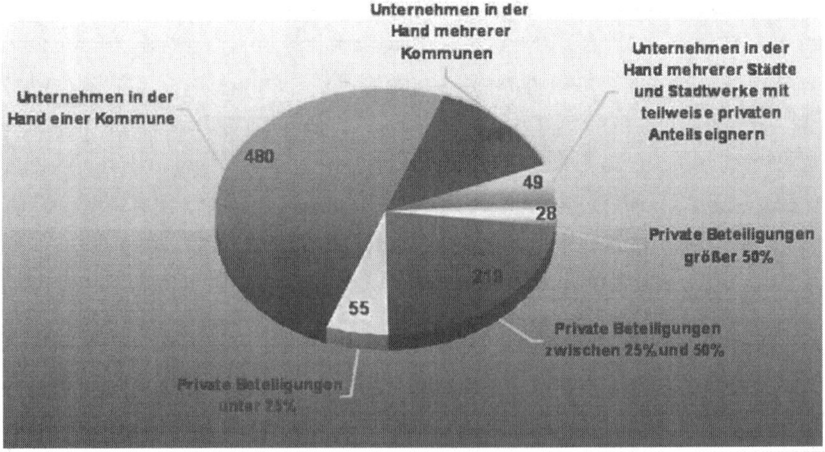

Abb. 1: Beteiligungsverhältnisse kommunaler Unternehmen

Quelle: *VKU 2007.*
(Die Grafik basiert auf Erhebungen des VKU bei rund 1.000 kommunalen Energie-, Trink- und Abwasserversorgern, davon 732 Stadtwerke in der Rechtsform AG/GmbH.)

2.1 Public Private Partnership

Die Beteiligung der Privatwirtschaft an kommunalen Unternehmen unter grundsätzlicher Beibehaltung der öffentlichen Trägerschaft ist eine Unterform des Public Private Partnership (PPP). Erwarteter Effekt einer PPP ist, dass öffentliche Dienstleistungen schneller und günstiger erbracht werden. Bei in der Regel defizitären kommunalen Sparten wie dem öffentlichen Personennahverkehr (ÖPNV) besteht beispielsweise die Erwartung, dass durch effizientere Betriebsführung die Zuschüsse seitens der Kommune sukzessive zurückgefahren werden können. Zudem wird durch einen Anteilsverkauf ein einmaliger Betrag für die oft finanziell notleidenden Haushalte der Städte und Gemeinde eingenommen.

Die Ausgestaltungsmöglichkeiten von Public Private Partnerships beispielsweise im Energiebereich sind vielfältig. Eine Möglichkeit für private Unternehmen besteht darin, sich finanziell durch die Übernahme von Unternehmensanteilen an kommunalwirtschaftlichen Unternehmen zu beteiligen. Eine andere Möglichkeit stellt der Verbleib der Infrastruktur im Eigentum der öffentlichen Hand dar, während der Privatsektor die Betriebsführung (z. B. eines Strom- oder Gasversorgungsnetzes) übernimmt.

In Deutschland wurden als Folge der Unsicherheit kommunaler Eigner über die künftige Entwicklung ihrer Unternehmen nach der Liberalisierung der europäischen Strom- und Gasmärkte im April 1998 sowie der angespannten Haushaltslage vieler Städte und Gemeinden Anteile an Stadtwerken an die Energiekonzerne respektive deren Regionaltöchter verkauft.

In den meisten dieser Fälle lag der Umfang des veräußerten Anteils zwischen 25,1 % und 49,9 %. Die untere Grenze ergibt sich daraus, dass die Sperrminorität bei GmbHs bei 25 % des gezeichneten Kapitels liegt; bei Aktiengesellschaften sind dies 25 % des Grundkapitals. Mit einer solchen Sperrminorität können Beschlüsse, die konträr zur eigenen Unternehmensposition liegen, verhindert werden[2]. Auf Grundlage der Minoritätsrechte im Aktienrecht können allerdings auch bei Beteiligungen von weniger als 25 % des Grundkapitals bestimmte Rechte durchgesetzt werden, wie z. B. die Einberufung einer außerordentlichen Hauptversammlung.

Das Bundeskartellamt hat zwischenzeitlich in mehreren Entscheidungen festgestellt, dass Beteiligungen von Verbund- und Regionalunternehmen an Stadtwerken bereits in der Höhe von 20 % ein Hindernis für effektiven Wettbewerb im Energiemarkt darstellen. Im November 2008 untersagte der Bundesgerichtshof die Übernahme von 33 % der Stadtwerke Eschwege GmbH durch E.ON, weil hierdurch der Wettbewerb in der deutschen Energiewirtschaft noch weiter eingeschränkt würde; Dritte hätten demnach nicht die Möglichkeit, eine ähnliche Marktposition aufzubauen.

---

2 Dies gilt, sofern der Anteil am Stammkapital mit den Stimmrechten übereinstimmt. Abweichungen von diesem Grundsatz sind allerdings eine äußerst seltene Konstellation.

Interessant ist in diesem Zusammenhang auch eine Analyse der Determinanten der Strategien von Stadtwerken im Klimaschutz[3], in der festgestellt wurde, dass Stadtwerke mit steigendem privatem (Teil-)Eigentum ihr Engagement im Bereich der erneuerbaren Energien zunehmend einschränken. Diese negative Korrelation, so die Vermutung der Studie, könnte mit der Risikoaversion privater Anteilseigner erklärt werden.

Es lässt sich somit vorläufig festhalten, dass Eigentumsstrukturen einen Einfluss auf den Wettbewerb und die Technologiewahl haben sowie in der Strategiewahl nicht unbedingt kohärent mit den Zielen der kommunalen (Teil-) Eigentümer sind.

2.2 Public Public Partnership

Eine – wachsende Bedeutung erlangende – Alternative zu privatwirtschaftlichen Beteiligungen an kommunalen Unternehmen sind Kooperationen zwischen kommunalen Unternehmen sowie Beteiligungen anderer Kommunen an einem solchen Unternehmen. Das Akronym „PPP" könnte dann auch für Public *Public* Partnerships stehen. Ein denkbarer Grund für eine solche Beteiligungsstrategie ist der begrenzte Erfolg von Beteiligungen der Privatwirtschaft. De facto haben in den vergangenen drei Jahren einige Kommunen nach einer ersten Privatisierungswelle ausgegliederte Unternehmen rekommunalisiert. Hauptgrund dafür war häufig, dass kommunale Unternehmen ihre Dienstleistungen genauso preiswert oder preiswerter als private Unternehmen anbieten können, oft jedoch mit einer höheren Qualität.

Aktuell werden im Hinblick auf Ursachen und Auswirkungen der weltweiten Finanz- und Wirtschaftskrise seit dem Herbst 2008 die Vorteile kommunaler Unternehmen zunehmend deutlicher. Die krisenhaften Entwicklungen zeigen die existenzielle Bedeutung auf, welche volkswirtschaftsrelevante

3 Vgl. Ostertag, K. et al. (2007).

Infrastrukturdienstleistungen wie die Energieversorgung haben. Solche Infrastrukturen müssen unabhängig von Marktzyklen und privatwirtschaftlichem Shareholder Value oder Unternehmensinsolvenzen gewährleistet sein. Das gilt auch und gerade für die lokalen und regionalen Infrastrukturdienstleistungen.

Die Bereitstellung solcher Infrastrukturen erfordert – unabhängig von der Eigentümerschaft über das erbringende Unternehmen – eine politische Steuerung, die durch eine stringente und aufwändige Regulierung privatwirtschaftlicher Unternehmen geschehen kann. Vorteilhaft ist zugleich die Beauftragung staatlicher Strukturen, also beispielsweise der Kommunen, die als Ausdruck des gesellschaftlichen Konsenses eines demokratisch verfassten Gemeinwesens dem Gemeinwohl verpflichtet sind. Die Kommunen können diese Aufgabe durch die entsprechende Steuerung kommunaler Unternehmen erfüllen oder durch Beauftragung privatwirtschaftlicher Unternehmen, die sie wiederum entsprechend extern regulieren müssten. Das Letztere ist, wie die Erfahrung und die Rechtslage zeigt, eine weitaus komplexere Herausforderung als das erstgenannte Modell, da die Interessenslagen der Unternehmen und der Kommune nicht zwingend kohärent sind.

Die Akzeptanz und das Vertrauen in die Privatwirtschaft sind zugleich auch in der Bevölkerung eher rückläufig. War die Privatisierungswelle am Anfang auf relativ wenig Widerstand in der Gesellschaft gestoßen, so hat sich das Bild – 2006 beginnend – deutlich gewandelt. Die kommunalen Energie- und Wasserversorgungsunternehmen erfahren hohe Zustimmungswerte. Eine im Auftrag des VKU Anfang 2008 durchgeführte Umfrage bestätigt die starke Unterstützung der Bürgerinnen und Bürger für die Kommunalwirtschaft. Demnach lehnen 69 % der Befragten eine Privatisierung kommunaler Unternehmen ab. Die Umfrage hat auch gezeigt, dass in einer direkten Gegenüberstellung etwa 58 % der befragten Haushaltskunden von den Stadtwerken mit Strom versorgt werden wollen und nur 11 % von Privaten. Diese Tendenz spiegelt sich auch in der steigenden Zahl an Privatisierungsablehnungen in Bürgervoten wider. Ein prominentes Beispiel ist der Teilverkauf der Stadtwerke Leipzig an Gaz de France, der in einem Bürgerentscheid Ende Januar 2008 mit deutlicher Mehrheit abgelehnt wurde.

Der Trend zugunsten einer möglichen „Renaissance der Kommunalwirtschaft“ wird dadurch verstärkt, dass bis Mitte des nächsten Jahrzehnts viele Konzessionsverträge für kommunale Strom- und Gasversorgungsnetze auslaufen. Daraus resultierend setzen sich immer mehr Kommunen mit der Frage einer Rekommunalisierung bis hin zur Neugründung von Stadtwerken auseinander. Schon jetzt befinden sich verschiedene Kommunen in der Planungsphase für neue Stadtwerke, so beispielsweise Mühlheim, Staufen und Schmalkalden. Zudem gib es in einer Reihe von Städten und Gemeinden Diskussionen um Neu- oder Wiedergründungen, wie z. B. in Warendorf, Herford oder in Hamburg. Dem Privatisierungstrend der ersten Phase der Energiemarktliberalisierung wird daher nicht nur durch Kartellgerichte und -behörden mit hohen Hürden begegnet, vielmehr reflektieren auch Städte und Gemeinden zunehmend die strategische kommunalpolitische Bedeutung von Partnerschaften zwischen kommunalen Unternehmen.

3 Kooperationen von kommunalwirtschaftlichen Stadtwerken als strategische Handlungsoption

3.1 Aktuelle energiewirtschaftliche Herausforderungen für Stadtwerke

Im Folgenden wird ausgeführt, welche Bedeutung Kooperationen für kommunale Energieversorgungsunternehmen bei der Bewältigung der aktuellen europäischen sowie deutschen ordnungs- und strukturpolitischen Herausforderungen haben. Die Auswirkungen des Liberalisierungs- und des Regulierungsprozesses sind vielfältig. Daher werden einige besonders prägnante Aspekte, die bei der Entscheidung zugunsten der Strategieoption Kooperation Berücksichtigung finden, exemplarisch vorgestellt.

3.1.1 Klimaschutzpolitische Herausforderungen

Die Bundesregierung hat mit dem Integrierten Energie- und Klimapaket (IEKP) aus dem Jahre 2007 das Ziel gesetzt, bis zum Jahre 2020 den Anteil regenerativer Energien im Strombereich auf mindestens 30 % zu erhöhen, im Wärmebereich auf 14 %. Die Energieeffizienz soll verdoppelt werden (was eine jährliche Steigerung um 3 % bedeutet) und die Kraft-Wärme-Kopplung soll deutlich ausgebaut werden. Zur Umsetzung dieser Ziele sind 2008 eine Reihe von Gesetzesvorhaben umgesetzt worden, darunter Revisionen des Kraft-Wärme-Kopplungs-Gesetzes sowie des Erneuerbare-Energien-Gesetzes, ein neues Erneuerbare-Wärme-Gesetz sowie die Liberalisierung des Mess- und Zählwesens.

Im Erzeugungsbereich setzt die Bundesregierung auf den zielstrebigen Ausbau der Kraft-Wärme-Kopplung (KWK), denn die KWK ist ein Technologiepfad, der wirkungsvoll und wirtschaftlich den Ausstoß von Kohlendioxid vermindert und zugleich den Wettbewerb auf dem Energiemarkt fördert. Die Stadtwerke sind Protagonisten dieser Effizienztechnologie. Aber auch erneuerbare Energien und Biomasse sind – abgesehen von großen Windparks – eine dezentrale Technologie, die auf lokaler Ebene umgesetzt werden. Darüber hinaus kann Energieeffizienz durch die Entwicklung von Energiedienstleistungsangeboten vor Ort optimal realisiert werden.

3.1.2 Eigenerzeugung

In der Praxis allerdings hat sich die Eigenerzeugung der Stadtwerke – und damit auch die Nutzung der KWK – in der Vergangenheit eher rückläufig entwickelt. Mit der Liberalisierung 1998 änderten sich auch die Rahmenbedingungen für die Betreiber kommunaler Energieerzeugung. Die überregionalen und regionalen Energieversorger fusionierten zu vier auch den Erzeugungsmarkt dominierenden Konzernen. Zahlreiche Stadtwerke wurden teilweise oder – in wenigen Fällen – vollständig privatisiert. Parallel ging die Eigenerzeugung kommunaler Energieversorger deutlich zurück und liegt heute bei etwa 15 % der deutschen Stromerzeugung. Die Eigenerzeugung von Stadtwerken wird in 9.900 MW an installierter Leistung generiert, wobei nahezu jedes zweite Stadtwerk Erneuerbare-Energien-Anlagen betreibt bzw. daran beteiligt ist. Der Anteil des erzeugten Stroms aus KWK-Anlagen beträgt 80 %. Die Stadtwerke sind seit wenigen Jahren jedoch wieder verstärkt engagiert, den Anteil ihrer Erzeugung durch die Errichtung von konventionellen Kraftwerken, die Modernisierung bestehender und den Neubau von KWK-Anlagen sowie die Ausweitung der Stromproduktion aus Erneuerbaren Energien insgesamt zu steigern.

3.1.3 Wettbewerb um Kunden

Seit der Liberalisierung des deutschen Elektrizitätsmarkts im April 1998 können Kunden ihren Energieversorger frei wählen. Dies hat erwartungsgemäß zu einer deutlichen Verschärfung des Wettbewerbs geführt, der vor allem in den letzten Jahren stark zugenommen hat. Zahlreiche neue Anbieter werben heute mit zum Teil neuen Produkten und Preismodellen um Kunden. Zunehmend ist der Wettbewerb auch bei den Verbrauchern angekommen. Nach einer anfänglich eher verhaltenen Bereitschaft ist in den vergangenen Jahren ein deutlich zunehmender Trend zum Wechsel des Stromversorgers zu beobachten. Kunden sind heute im Vergleich zu früher viel eher bereit, ihren Energieversorger zu wechseln, und zwar gerade im für Stadtwerke wichtigen Segment der Industrie- und Gewerbekunden. Der Differenzierung und Verbesserung des Produktangebotes und der Energiedienstleistungen kommt daher zunehmend strategische Bedeutung zu. Kommunale Energieversorger sind gefordert, noch aktiver als bisher im Wettbewerb mit attraktiven sowie zielgruppenorientierten Produkten um Kunden zu werben.

3.1.4 Regulierung der Netzentgelte

Seit Inkrafttreten des neuen Energiewirtschaftsgesetzes im Jahr 2005 müssen Netzbetreiber ihre Kosten für Betrieb und Erhalt der Netzinfrastruktur nach einer aus den Netzentgeltverordnungen Strom und Gas abgeleiteten Methode ermitteln und von der Regulierungsbehörde genehmigen lassen. Man spricht hierbei vom System der Kostenregulierung. In den beiden Genehmigungsrunden 2006 und 2008 wurden die zulässigen Kosten um jeweils durchschnittlich 15 % gekürzt. Dieses System der Kostenregulierung wird seit Januar 2009 von der so genannten Anreizregulierung abgelöst. Durch das zukünftige System sollen Netzbetreiber Anreize für einen noch effizienteren Betrieb ihrer Gas- und Stromnetze gesetzt werden. Die von den Regulierungsbehörden im Rahmen eines Effizienzvergleiches ermittelten Ineffizienzen müssen innerhalb von zwei Regulierungsperioden abgebaut werden.

Insgesamt unterliegt der Netzbetrieb mittelfristig deutlich veränderten Rahmenbedingungen, die sich in betriebswirtschaftlicher Hinsicht bemerkbar machen werden. Es ist davon auszugehen, dass durch die Implementierung der Anreizregulierung erhebliche – und für einige Stadtwerke sehr nachteilige wirtschaftliche – Auswirkungen auf die Unternehmen zukommen. Des Weiteren verursacht die Regulierung einen exorbitanten zusätzlichen administrativen Aufwand (siehe unten).

3.1.5 Administrativer Aufwand und IT-Kosten durch Umsetzung der Entflechtungsvorgaben

Mit der Novelle des Energiewirtschaftsgesetzes wurde auch die informatorische, organisatorische, rechtliche und buchhalterische Entflechtung der Erzeugung und des Vertriebs vom Netzbetrieb innerhalb von Energieversorgungsunternehmen vorgeschrieben. Vormalige organisatorische und prozessoptimale sowie betriebswirtschaftlich rationale Synergien wurden „aufgehoben“. Die Bundesnetzagentur, der die Formulierung der Anforderungen (auch) für die Umsetzung der informatorischen Entflechtungsvorgaben obliegt, erließ zwischenzeitlich für dieses Segment die gemeinsamen Auslegungsgrundsätze der Regulierungsbehörden des Bundes und der Länder. Diese umfangreichen Auslegungs- und die zusätzlichen Konkretisierungsvorschriften bedeuten für die Unternehmen, dass diese erhebliche Investitionen in die Organisation und Steuerung sowie in „entflechtungskonforme" IT-Systeme tätigen müssen, die nicht nur den betrieblichen Aufwand erheblich ausweiten, sondern auch kostenwirksam in die Energiepreise für die Verbraucher einfließen.

3.1.6 Administrationsaufwand und Bürokratiekosten durch diskriminierungsfreie Prozesse und verschärfte Dokumentationspflichten

Die diskriminierungsfreie Umsetzung der Vorgaben zur Neugestaltung des Lieferantenwechsels sowie der Öffnung des Zähl- und Messwesens für den Wettbewerb führen durch die notwendigen Anpassungen der jeweiligen Prozesse zu zusätzlichem monetären und organisatorischen Aufwand.

Zudem ist der administrative Aufwand für die Stadtwerke aufgrund zahlreicher Dokumentations- und Berichtspflichten nach der Novellierung des Energiewirtschaftsgesetzes und durch vielfache Anforderungen der Regulierungs- und Kartellbehörden stark gewachsen. Mussten vor 1998 einige wenige Formulare für den Preisgenehmigungsantrag ausgefüllt werden, so sind heutzutage Regalmeter an Antrags- oder Nachweisdokumenten einzureichen. Dieser immens gestiegene Bürokratieaufwand generiert beim einzelnen Unternehmen einen hohen Zeit- und Personalaufwand mit entsprechend höheren Kosten. Weiterhin entstehen durch die Erfüllung dieser behördlichen Auflagen erhebliche Opportunitätskosten, weil die für die Abarbeitung der Dokumentations- und Berichtspflichten erforderlichen unternehmensinternen Ressourcen nicht für andere, ggf. den Umsatz steigernde Tätigkeiten (wie z. B. Key-Account-Management) eingesetzt werden können. Aufgrund ihrer begrenzten Personalbestände sind gerade kleinere und mittlere Stadtwerke von diesen Anforderungen – kosten-, personal- und zeitökonomisch – überproportional belastet.

3.2 Handlungsoptionen im Rahmen von Kooperationen

Die genannten Herausforderungen können als Risiko angesehen oder als Chance genutzt werden. Wichtig ist, dass kommunalwirtschaftliche Unternehmen vorhandene und abschätzbare Handlungsoptionen identifizieren und aktiv werden. Wettbewerbs- und Kostendruck muss vorausschauend begegnet und zukunftsrobuste, unternehmensindividuelle und wachstumsorientierte Strategien in den einzelnen Wertschöpfungsstufen müssen entwickelt werden. Jedes Unternehmen muss für sich prüfen, welche Instrumente und Management-Tools es zur zukünftigen Unternehmenspositionierung nutzen möchte. Eine mögliche Option im Umgang mit den Herausforderungen stellen, wie nachfolgend erläutert wird, Kooperationen dar.

Unter Kooperationen ist eine verbindliche Verpflichtung der Partner auf ein oder mehrere abgestimmte Ziele sowie ein verlässliches gemeinsames Handeln zu verstehen. *Horizontale* Kooperationen finden sich in allen Bereichen der kommunalen Wirtschaft. In der Wasserver- und Abwasserentsorgung sowie der Abfallwirtschaft sind sie im Rahmen von interkommunalen Kooperationen seit Jahrzehnten ein bewährtes Instrument für eine effiziente Aufgabenerledigung auf horizontaler Ebene. In aller Regel erfolgen sie auf freiwilliger Basis – ein deutlicher Unterschied zu den oft erzwungenen Kooperationen mit privaten Unternehmen. Zudem agieren die Partner auf Augenhöhe.

Public Private Partnerships können durch Beteiligungen von Verbund- oder Regionalunternehmen oder anderen privaten Unternehmen über reine Liefer- und Leistungsbeziehungen hinaus zu *vertikalen* Kooperationen ausgebaut werden. Diese sind derzeit überwiegend im Netzbereich oder im IT-Bereich angesiedelt und beruhen zumeist nicht auf dem Prinzip „gemeinsames Agieren auf Augenhöhe“, sondern werden eher über eine Machtbeziehung ergänzt.

Kooperationen sind für viele Stadtwerke bereits heute eine strategische Option. Nach Umfragen des VKU steht das Thema „Kooperationen“ ganz oben auf der Strategieagenda. Knapp über 60 % der Stadtwerke befinden sich bereits in einer Kooperation. Mehr als 50 % der Stadtwerke wollen ihre bereits bestehenden Kooperationen noch stärker ausbauen, 43 % planen einen Beitritt oder wollen mit anderen Stadtwerken eine neue Kooperation gründen. Es zeichnet sich ab, dass immer mehr Stadtwerke *multikooperativ* tätig sind, das heißt, sich mehreren, unterschiedliche Geschäftsfelder abdeckenden Kooperationen anzuschließen. So sind schon knapp 15 % der Unternehmen auf diese Weise engagiert. Es ist davon auszugehen, dass multikooperative Kooperationen von Stadtwerken weiter zunehmen werden. Nur 9 % verfolgen derzeit keine konkreten Planungen hinsichtlich einer institutionalisierten Zusammenarbeit. Stand während der ersten Jahre kommunaler Kooperationen im Energiebereich die Zusammenarbeit ohne gesellschaftsrechtliche Verflechtungen im Vordergrund, so weisen heute über 80 % der Kooperationen eigene gesellschaftsrechtliche Konstruktionen auf. Dabei dominiert das so genannte Joint-Venture-Modell.

Die Vorteile von Kooperationen sind dabei so vielfältig wie ihre Ausgestaltungsmöglichkeiten. Übergeordnet lassen sich vor allem folgende Vorteile von Kooperationen auflisten:

- Durch Kooperationen lassen sich Synergie- und Kostensenkungspotenziale realisieren, so z. B. durch die Bildung von Netzgesellschaften oder gemeinsame IT-Organisationseinheiten.

- Durch die Zusammenarbeit mehrerer Unternehmen können neue Geschäftsfelder, z. B. im Bereich der Energiedienstleistungen, auf- oder ausgebaut werden. Gerade bei einem Einstieg in bisher erst teilweise oder noch nicht erschlossene Geschäftsfelder können durch Kooperationen im eigenen Unternehmen notwendige Kompetenzen aufgebaut oder von Dritten abgerufen werden. Auch können Kooperationen in diesem Zusammenhang zur Strategieimplementierung genutzt werden.

- Kooperationen bieten Stadtwerken auch die Möglichkeit, strategische Allianzen (z. B. mit einem großen oder einem oder mehreren gleichberechtigten Partnern) zu schmieden, die über eine bloße Synergiegenerierung oder Kostensenkung hinausgehen.

- Vor allem kleinere und mittlere Unternehmen können durch Kooperationen teilweise ihre Begrenzungen von Kapital und Ressourcen überwinden, ihre Leistungsfähigkeit steigern und damit leichter wachsen als aus einer „stand-alone-Position".
- Durch Kooperationen können zudem fehlende Größeneffekte und die Kapitalkraft der konkurrierenden Regional- und Verbundunternehmen – zumindest teilweise – kompensiert werden.
- Kooperationen sind für kleinere und mittlere Stadtwerke oft die einzige Möglichkeit, um an der Strombörse zu handeln.
- Kooperationen können vielfach auch eine Lösung sein, Synergieeffekte zu nutzen, ohne aber die Eigenständigkeit, den – aus Sicht der Eigentümerkommunen relevanten – politischen Einfluss oder die Orts- und Kundennähe aufzugeben.

3.3 Kooperationen entlang der Wertschöpfungskette

3.3.1 Einkaufskooperationen

Bei der Analyse des bestehenden Kooperationsgrades entlang der Wertschöpfungsstufen wird deutlich, dass der Bereich der Energiebeschaffung ein besonders relevantes Kooperationsfeld ist. Die überwiegenden Beispiele dafür sind Stromeinkaufsgemeinschaften, die häufig bereits mit Beginn der Marktliberalisierung im Jahre 1998 gegründet wurden.

Auch im Bereich der Gasbeschaffung sind verstärkte Kooperationstendenzen zu beobachten. Aufgrund der Lieferstrukturen im Gasbereich ist die kritische Masse für Erfolg versprechende Gasbeschaffungskooperationen jedoch deutlich größer als im Strombereich. Gleiches gilt für alle Bestrebungen zur Verlängerung der Wertschöpfungskette Gas in Richtung Upstream, wie z. B. für die Errichtung und den Betrieb von Gasspeichern, die Beteiligung an Erdgasfeldern oder den Bezug von verflüssigtem Erdgas (LNG). Daher ist es nicht verwunderlich, dass die Mehrzahl der kommunalen Energieversorgungsunternehmen ebenso wie in der Strombeschaffung auf Kooperationsmodelle zur Generierung von Kosteneinsparungen setzt. Eine VKU-Umfrage ergab, dass die überwiegende Anzahl der kommunalen Energieversorgungsunternehmen eine horizontale Kooperation in der Gasbeschaffung als strategisch relevant ansieht. Bei Stadtwerken mit weniger als 100.000 Kunden sind dies sogar knapp 80 %.

3.3.2 Erzeugungskooperationen

Der Erzeugungsmarkt wird durch vier Energiekonzerne dominiert. Für viele Stadtwerke war und ist es ein notwendiger Schritt, selbst im Bereich der Eigenerzeugung zu investieren. Durch den Ausbau ihrer Erzeugungskapazitäten verfolgen die an Kraftwerken beteiligten Stadtwerke das Ziel, sich eine von Vorlieferanten unabhängigere Position in der Energieversorgung aufzubauen und damit eine wettbewerbs- und zugleich preisfähige Energieversorgung für die Kunden zu sichern. Zwar erzeugen viele Stadtwerke einen Teil ihres Strombedarfs selbst, überwiegend aber in mittelgroßen oder kleineren KWK-Anlagen. Wegen der hohen Investitionssummen und den damit verbundenen wirtschaftlichen Risiken sind auch in diesem Segment horizontale Kooperationen die vorteilhafteste Handlungsoption zur Sicherung von Größenvorteilen im Erzeugungsbereich, so z. B. beim Bau von Kondensationskraftwerken.

Auch für kleinere und mittlere kommunale Energieversorgungsunternehmen wird eine Beteiligung an Gemeinschaftskraftwerken immer wichtiger. So können sie – gerade vor dem Hintergrund der stark steigenden Energiebezugspreise am Rohstoffmarkt – Einfluss auf ihre individuelle Bezugspreisentwicklung nehmen und damit auch ihre wirtschaftliche Eigenständigkeit sichern. Ein Beispiel für eine erfolgreiche Stadtwerkekooperation im Erzeugungsbereich ist die 1999 gegründete Trianel-Gruppe, an der sich aktuell fast 30 Unternehmen beteiligen. Ein anderes Beispiel ist die Südweststrom (Südwestdeutsche Stromhandels GmbH), die Dienstleistungen für Stadtwerke auf dem Strom- und Gasmarkt sowie Beteiligungsmöglichkeiten an modernen Kraftwerksprojekten (wie z. B. an einem Steinkohlekraftwerk am Standort Brunsbüttel) anbietet. Insgesamt betragen die geplanten Erzeugungskapazitäten Ende des Jahres 2008 rund 6.300 MW, davon etwa 40 % (2.300 MW) in Form von Kraft-Wärme-Kopplung und ca. 10 % (610 MW) in Erneuerbare-Energien-Anlagen.

3.3.3 Shared Services

In der Regel verfügen das Kerngeschäft unterstützende Verwaltungs- und Querschnittsfunktionen über ein hohes Maß an Optimierungs- und Einsparpotenzialen. Dies gilt insbesondere für standardisierte bzw. standardisierbare Prozesse wie Einkauf, Materialwirtschaft, Personalwesen, IT/Rechenzentrum oder auch Zählerwesen und Abrechnung.

Wurden in der Vergangenheit diese Aufgaben von den Unternehmen meist in Eigenregie erbracht, werden seit einiger Zeit, bedingt durch die Entflechtungsvorgaben und den regulierungsbedingten Kostendruck, Kooperationen angestrebt. Überwiegend wird dabei ein Kooperationsmodell bevorzugt, bei dem Stadtwerke einzelne oder mehrere ausgewählte Querschnittsfunktionen in ein Joint-Venture-Unternehmen auslagern. Dieses erbringt dann Leistungen als so genanntes Shared Service Center vorrangig für die Kooperationspartner, aber ggf. auch für externe Kunden.

Gegenüber einem stand-alone-Ansatz bringt diese Kooperationsvariante beachtliche Vorteile: Skaleneffekte durch die Volumenvergrößerung, Sicherstellung eingelöster Entflechtungsvorgaben sowie ggf. zusätzliche Deckungsbeiträge bei einer Geschäftsausweitung auf dem Drittmarkt. Dabei droht im

Unterschied zum „reinen“ Outsourcing an Dritte kein nachhaltiger Know-how-Verlust, da die Kooperation in ihrer Struktur als Beteiligung ein Organisationsteil der kooperierenden Stadtwerke bleibt. Auch die in der Vergangenheit durch fehlendes energiewirtschaftliches Know-how ggf. aufgetretenen Prozess- und Qualitätsmängel werden durch die horizontale Kooperation in Form eines Joint Ventures vermieden.

Eine Umfrage des VKU ergab, dass der überwiegende Teil der Mitgliedsunternehmen die strategische Relevanz alternativer Organisationsmodelle für den IT-Bereich sehr hoch einschätzt. Die befragten Unternehmen ordneten beim Vergleich der Handlungsoptionen „Abgabe an strategische Partner“ und „Outsourcing an spezialisierte Dienstleister“ der „horizontalen Kooperation“ eine zwei- bis fünfmal höhere Relevanz zu.

3.3.4 Energiedienstleistungen

Aufgrund des zunehmenden Wettbewerbs um industrielle, gewerbliche und private Kunden setzen immer mehr kommunale Energieversorgungsunternehmen auf den Auf- oder Ausbau des Geschäftsfeldes Energiedienstleistungen und damit auf eine Verlängerung der Wertschöpfungskette.

Die Bedeutung der energienahen Dienstleistungen wird noch verstärkt durch das Integrierte Energie- und Klimaprogramm der Bundesregierung, das zahlreiche Perspektiven für den Ausbau oder die Erschließung von Geschäftsfeldern im Bereich der Energiedienstleistungen bietet. Bereits in der Vergangenheit hatten viele Stadtwerke Energiedienstleistungen in ihrem Produktportfolio, meist jedoch ohne eigenen Wertbeitrag. Nach den dem VKU vorliegenden Einschätzungen liegt der zukünftige Schwerpunkt im zweifellos interessanten Markt für Industrie- und Geschäftskunden.

Dem Auf- oder Ausbau neuer Geschäftsfelder geht ein langer Weg der Markt- und Wettbewerberanalyse voraus. Ziel ist hierbei zunächst, zu identifizieren, welche Dienstleistungen erfolgreich bei welchen Kundengruppen platziert werden können. Bei der anschließenden Implementierung der entwickelten – neuen/auszubauenden – Geschäftsfelder bieten gezielte Kooperationen mit anderen Stadtwerken oder aber auch laterale Kooperationen mit Fachfirmen (wie Herstellerfirmen oder bei kleineren oder mittleren Energieversorgungsunternehmen auch Ingenieurbüros) nicht außer Acht zu lassende Vorteile zur Schließung etwaiger Kompetenzlücken.

3.3.5 Smart Metering

Durch das im Juni 2008 verabschiedete Gesetz zur Liberalisierung des Zähl- und Messwesens wurde der Startschuss für eine zusätzliche Intensivierung des Wettbewerbs um Strom- und Gaskunden eingeläutet. Intelligente Zähler sollen Kunden unterstützen, zukünftig Einsparpotenziale durch eine aktive Steuerung des eigenen Energieverbrauchs zu nutzen.

Es ist davon auszugehen, dass sich auch dieses Geschäftsfeld für Kooperationen anbietet, z. B. durch eine Zusammenarbeit mit Herstellerfirmen von Smart Metern oder zusätzlich durch ein Joint Venture von mehreren Stadtwerken. Kooperationsvorteile liegen in der Bündelung von Fachwissen sowie in der Generierung von Größeneffekten beim Einkauf, z. B. von Zählern.

Der VKU hat daher die Bildung einer internetgestützten Serviceplattform zum Zähl- und Messwesen mit dem Ziel initiiert, eine Informations- und Angebotsplattform für Mitgliedsunternehmen zu schaffen, die dadurch auch die Möglichkeit erhalten, geeignete Kooperationspartner zu finden.

4 Diskussion und Fazit

Stadtwerke sind durch den Liberalisierungs- und den Regulierungsprozess sowie die Klimapolitik mit einer Vielzahl von Herausforderungen konfrontiert, die überwiegend durch einen extrem gestiegenen administrativen Aufwand, durch erhebliche Reduzierung der Netzentgelte sowie einen verstärkten Wettbewerb im Energieerzeugungs- und Vertriebsbereich gekennzeichnet sind.

Stadtwerke leisten bei der Umsetzung der energie- und klimapolitischen Ziele, die international, europäisch und national definiert werden, einen wichtigen Beitrag. De facto können Stadtwerke in ihrer Wirtschaftstätigkeit Energie- und Klimaschutzpolitik verknüpfen und auf diese Weise die Erwartung attraktiver Energiepreise, nachhaltigkeitsgerechten Klimaschutzes und sicherer Energieversorgung miteinander verbinden – Ziele, die auch dem IEKP zugrunde liegen. Gleichzeitig sind Stadtwerke in der Lage, sowohl angebotsseitig zu agieren als auch die Nachfrageseite durch eine Vielzahl von Energiedienstleistungen und Beratungsangebote zu stimulieren. Kommunalwirtschaftliche Unternehmen haben bereits zahlreiche Angebote für alle Kundengruppen entwickelt, um bei der Identifikation und Umsetzung von Maßnahmen zur nachhaltigen Energieeinsparung zu unterstützen.

In den Anfangsjahren der Liberalisierung wurden viele Stadtwerksanteile an privatwirtschaftlich agierende Unternehmen verkauft, und Public *Private* Partnerships hatten eine stärkere Bedeutung. In den letzten Jahren hat jedoch ein Gegentrend eingesetzt: Zunehmend lautet die strategische Antwort der Kommunen und ihrer Stadtwerke, horizontale Kooperationen mit anderen Stadtwerken einzugehen – also Public *Public* Partnerships. Ein wesentliches Element dieser horizontalen Kooperationen von Stadtwerken ist es, auf gleicher Ebene zu agieren. Das Eingehen weiterer Public Private Partnerships, u. a. durch Beteiligungen von Verbund- oder Regionalunternehmen, werden aus Sicht der Stadtwerke als in der Regel nicht zielführend eingestuft. Die mit dem Thema (Re-) Kommunalisierung verbundenen Fragestellungen haben entsprechend stark an Bedeutung gewonnen. Umfragen sowie auch die zunehmende Anzahl von Bürgerbegehren gegen Anteilsverkäufe von Stadtwerken belegen diese Entwicklung. Stadtwerke sind im Gegensatz zu privatwirtschaftlichen Anbietern dem Public Value, also dem gemeinwohlorientierten Handeln für Bürger und lokale

Wirtschaft, verpflichtet und nicht den vorherrschenden Renditeinteressen privatwirtschaftlicher Eigentümer. Horizontale Kooperationen bieten sich hierbei entlang der gesamten Wertschöpfungskette an. Lag der Fokus der Kooperationen zu Beginn der Liberalisierung und Regulierung im Beschaffungsbereich, nimmt die Bedeutung kooperativer Aktivitäten in den anderen Geschäftsbereichen deutlich zu. Durch Kooperationen können Kosten- und Synergiepotenziale gehoben, neue Strategien implementiert sowie Know-how aus- oder aufgebaut werden.

Damit sich *kommunalwirtschaftliche Kooperationen* als Bestandteil strategischen Verhaltens auf dem liberalisierten Energiemarkt weiter entwickeln können, müssen für alle Akteure auf dem Energiemarkt vergleichbare und faire Rahmenbedingungen gelten. Für Stadtwerke, die im direkten Wettbewerb zu privatwirtschaftlichen Unternehmen stehen, bedarf es einer bundesweit anzustrebenden, marktkonformen und europarechtsangepassten Reform des Gemeindewirtschaftsrechts der Bundesländer. Bisher bestehen in den Bundesländern sehr unterschiedliche ordnungspolitische Bedingungen, die sich in den jeweiligen Gemeindeordnungen wiederfinden.

Mit den europäischen Binnenmarktrichtlinien für Elektrizität und Gas sowie dem darauf aufbauenden deutschen Energiewirtschaftsrecht wurden alle Energieversorgungsunternehmen in den Wettbewerb überführt, unabhängig von öffentlicher oder privater Eigentümerschaft. Nach den europäischen Vorgaben sind die Mitgliedstaaten zur Gleichbehandlung aller im Energiemarkt tätigen Unternehmen verpflichtet und müssen die Liberalisierung daher „eigentumsneutral" ausgestalten, ohne eine wie auch immer geartete Vorrangstellung für bestimmte Unternehmen. Mit dem deutschen Energiewirtschaftsgesetz (EnWG) sind diese europäischen Vorgaben vom Bundesgesetzgeber umgesetzt worden. Während das EnWG von einer gleichberechtigten Teilnahme kommunaler Unternehmen im Markt ausgeht, setzen die Gemeindeordnungen der Länder den kommunalen Unternehmen allerdings im Wettbewerb hohe Hürden (wie das Subsidiaritäts- und das Örtlichkeitsprinzip). Es entstehen ausgeprägte Wettbewerbsnachteile der kommunalen Unternehmen gegenüber ihren privaten Mitwettbewerbern aufgrund der beschränkten Möglichkeiten, zur Stützung des Kerngeschäfts oder zur Diversifizierung das Angebot an Produkten und Dienstleistungen zu erweitern und sich in gleicher Weise wie private Unternehmen auch jenseits der Gemeindegrenzen auf den Energiemärkten zu betätigen. Nach dem Subsidiaritätsprinzip dürfen kommunale Unternehmen überhaupt nur tätig werden, wenn sie den sehr schwer zu führenden Nachweis erbringen, besser zu sein als ein privater Mitkonkurrent.

Von ebenso zentraler Bedeutung ist eine sachgerechte Ausgestaltung der Anreizregulierung, die es erlaubt, die Investitionsfähigkeit und damit Versorgungssicherung durch die Stadtwerke zu erhalten. Gerade kleine Unternehmen sind durch die zunehmende Bürokratisierung in überproportionaler Weise benachteiligt. Der gesetzlich bedingte administrative Aufwand muss daher auf ein vernünftiges Maß zurückgefahren werden.

Es ist und bleibt die Aufgabe von Stadtwerken und Kommunen, auch zukünftig Daseinsvorsorge im Interesse der Gesellschaft auszugestalten und als wesentlichen Baustein der kommunalen Selbstverwaltung zu verfestigen. Mit einem fairen Ordnungsrahmen können Stadtwerke weiterhin die wettbewerblichen und regulatorischen Herausforderungen annehmen. Horizontale Kooperationen im Sinne von Public Public Partnerships sind hierfür eine wichtige strategische Handlungsoption.

Literaturverzeichnis

Bleicher, A./Gleiche, C. (2008): Kooperationsmöglichkeiten von Stadtwerken. Studie im Auftrag des Verbandes kommunaler Unternehmen. Unveröffentlichter Zwischenbericht. Leipzig, im November 2008.

Cronauge, U./Westermann, G. (2006): Kommunale Unternehmen, Eigenbetriebe, Kapitalgesellschaften, Zweckverbände. 5., überarbeitete Auflage 2006. Erich Schmidt Verlag, Berlin.

Ostertag, K. et al. (2007): Local utilities, liberalisation and the EU Emission Trading Scheme: Emerging strategies and their determinants. Paper für die 6th Conference on Applied Infrastructure Research, 5.-6. Oktober 2007, TU Berlin, Berlin.

Trapp, J.H./Bolay, S. (2003): Privatisierung in Kommunen – eine Auswertung kommunaler Beteiligungsberichte. Deutsches Institut für Urbanistik.

Verband kommunaler Unternehmen e. V./YourSales Unternehmensberatung (2007): Stadtwerk der Zukunft II – Perspektiven im Geschäftsfeld Energiedienstleistungen. Handbuch.

Von Weizsäcker, E. U. (2007): Grenzen der Privatisierung – Wann ist des Guten zu viel? Bericht an den Club of Rome. 2., korrigierte Auflage. S. Hirzel Verlag, Stuttgart.

PPPs im Strafvollzug: Ökonomisch effizient, gesellschafts- und sozialpolitisch gefährlich

Christian Jäkel

Inhaltsverzeichnis

Abkürzungsverzeichnis

BHO	Bundeshaushaltsordnung
GG	Grundgesetz
JVA	Justizvollzugsanstalt
PPP	Public Private Partnership
StVollzG	Strafvollzugsgesetz

1 Einleitung

Wer die Nachrichten aufmerksam verfolgt, wird feststellen, dass kaum noch ein Tag vergeht, an dem nicht eine neue Nachricht über den Bildschirm flimmert, in der von Haushaltslöchern und leeren staatlichen Kassen die Rede ist. Bund, Länder und Kommunen fahren seit geraumer Zeit ihre Investitionen zurück, da das hierfür notwendige Geld nicht vorhanden ist.[1] In der Konsequenz hat sich der Investitionsbedarf in den vergangenen Jahren immens aufgestaut.[2]

Das Deutsche Institut für Urbanistik hat errechnet, dass sich dieser Bedarf allein für den Zeitraum von 2006 bis 2020 bei den Kommunen auf 704 Mrd. Euro belaufen wird.[3] Daraus ergibt sich für sie ein jährlicher Investitionsbedarf von rund 47 Mrd. Euro basierend auf den Preisen des Jahres 2000.

Aber auch Bund und Länder sind von dieser Misere betroffen. Laut einer Studie von McKinsey muss der Bund bis 2020 in den Bereichen Energie, Verkehr und Telekommunikation mit Investitionen von rund 220 Mrd. Euro rechnen. Lediglich 160 Mrd. Euro sind aber bis jetzt erst eingeplant.[4] Um diesem beachtlichen Volumen nachkommen zu können, muss die öffentliche Hand nach neuen Wegen der Umsetzbarkeit notwendiger Projekte suchen. Knappe finanzielle Ressourcen müssen effizient genutzt werden. Dies kann u. a. dadurch geschehen, dass sich der Staat nur noch auf die Erledigung seiner Kernaufgaben beschränkt oder sich von privater Seite Kapital und Know-how beschafft.[5]

Ein wichtiger Bereich auf Landesebene, der zunehmend in der öffentlichen Diskussion um Sanierungs- und Ausbaumaßnahmen zu finden ist, ist der Strafvollzug. Überbelegungen der Hafträume, defekte und veraltete Sicherungs-

1 Vgl. Friemel, K. (2005), S. 39.
2 Vgl. o. V. (2004), S. 5.
3 Vgl. o. V. (2008a), S. 12.
4 Vgl. o. V. (2008b), S. 17.
5 Vgl. o. V. (2004), S. 5.

anlagen, Geiselnahmen und Ausbruchskandale sind Schlagworte, die sich vermehrt in den Medien wiederfinden.[6]

Die marode Haushaltssituation macht auch vor diesem Bereich nicht Halt. In diesem Zusammenhang wird insbesondere von politischer Seite immer wieder der Ruf nach einer Privatisierung von Justizvollzugsanstalten (JVAs) laut. Während es sich hierbei über viele Jahre hinweg um ein Tabuthema in der deutschen Politik handelte, da diese Verantwortung des Staates gegenüber der Gesellschaft als oberstes Primat erachtet wurde, kam es hierüber in den USA bereits in den 1980er Jahren zu ersten Diskussionen. Die Umsetzung der Projekte ließ dort schließlich nicht lange auf sich warten. Erst nachdem sich der Europarat mit der Thematik in den 1990er Jahren auseinandersetzte, stieß die Privatisierung von deutschen JVAs nach und nach auch auf das Interesse der hiesigen Politik.[7] Der Betrachtungswinkel änderte sich dahingehend, dass die Strafanstalten wie Unternehmen erachtet werden, die unter strategischen, betriebswirtschaftlichen und finanzwirtschaftlichen Aspekten geführt werden müssen.[8]

Dabei wird das Augenmerk immer wieder auf die USA gerichtet, die mittlerweile eine Vorreiterrolle im Bereich des privaten Strafvollzugs eingenommen haben. Mit 2,3 Mio. Gefangenen im Jahr 2007 boomt das Geschäft mit Kriminellen dort förmlich.

Ähnlich wie der deutsche Staat leidet auch die amerikanische Regierung unter immensen Haushaltslöchern im Budget.[9] Eine Maßnahme, dieser Tatsache entgegenzuwirken, war u. a. die Privatisierung zahlreicher JVAs. Hierdurch ist es dem Staat möglich, Kosteneinsparungen in Höhe von ca. 30 % in diesem Sektor zu erzielen. Marktführer im Bereich der Betreibung privater Gefängnisse ist die Corrections Corporations of America. Im Jahr 2007 unterhielt sie 64 JVAs

6 Vgl. Friemel, K. (2005), S. 32.
7 Vgl. Jung, H. (1988), S. 377.
8 Vgl. Kloff, J. (1997).
9 Für das Hauhaltsjahr 2009 wird eine Etatlücke von 482 Mrd. Dollar prognostiziert. Vgl. o. V. (2008c).

mit insgesamt 70.000 Gefangenen. Und das Geschäft lohnt sich. So schaffte es das Unternehmen, bei einer konstanten Bettenbelegung von fast 95 % binnen einen Jahres seinen Nettogewinn in 2006 auf damals umgerechnet 783 Mio. Euro zu verdoppeln. Der Aktienkurs nahm um 95 % zu und fand bei den Anlegern große Beliebtheit.[10]

Vor diesem Hintergrund ist es verständlich, dass solche Modelle auch in Deutschland zunehmend Beachtung finden. Im Folgenden wird daher diskutiert, wie sinnvoll derartige Projekte für Staat und Gesellschaft sind.

2 Public Private Partnerships

Wie im vorangegangenen Kapitel bereits dargestellt wurde, bringen die leeren Staatskassen Überlegungen zur Haushaltskonsolidierung und Verkleinerung des Staatsapparates mit sich. In diesem Zusammenhang fällt immer wieder der Begriff der Public Private Partnerships (PPPs).

Die Idee, die sich hinter dieser Bezeichnung versteckt, beruht auf dem Gedanken einer Partnerschaft zwischen der öffentlichen Hand und der Privatwirtschaft. Staat und private Unternehmen gehen dabei Kooperationen ein, um öffentliche Leistungen bereitstellen zu können.[11] Die Zusammenarbeit geschieht vor dem Hintergrund, eine Entlastung der angespannten Haushaltssituation herbeizuführen, indem der Staat die Bereitstellung bestimmter Güter und Leistungen an Dritte ausgliedert.[12] Die Staatsverschuldung soll auf diese Art und Weise zurückgeführt und Effizienzgewinne durch eine Ausweitung der Marktwirtschaft erzielt werden.[13] Die Europäische Investitionsbank hat errechnet, dass

[10] Vgl. o. V. (2007a).
[11] Vgl. o. V. (2004), S. 8.
[12] Vgl. Kulas, A. (2001), S. 2.
[13] Vgl. Giefers-Wieland, N. (2002), S. 3-4.

der Staat so über einen Zeitraum von 20 bis 30 Jahren mit Einsparungen in Höhe von 10 % bis 20 % rechnen kann.[14]

Für den Bereich der JVAs kann im Rahmen einer PPP von einer Dreierbeziehung gesprochen werden, die sich wie folgt darstellt: Der Staat tritt als Kunde gegenüber einem Sicherheitsunternehmen auf, das sich dazu verpflichtet, ein Gefängnis zu bauen und zu betreiben. Die bereits angesprochenen Leistungsempfänger wären in diesem Fall die Gefangenen.[15]

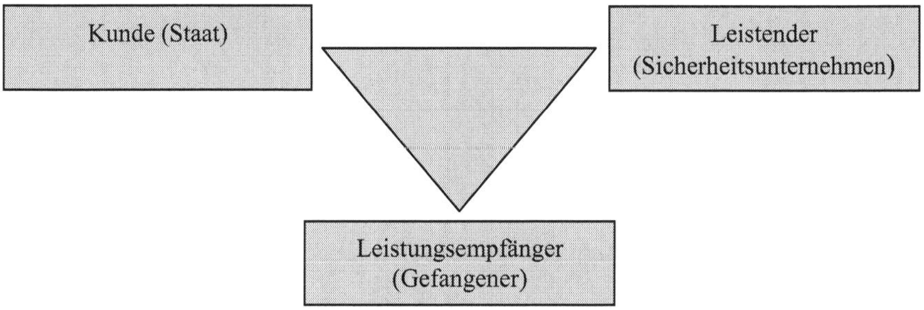

Abb. 1: PPP-Beziehung bei JVAs
Quelle: Salewski, B. (2001), S. 83.

3 Rechtliche Grenzen eines Einsatzes von Privaten

Bevor nachfolgend über die ökonomischen sowie gesellschafts- und sozialpolitischen Konsequenzen eines Einsatzes privater Unternehmen nachgedacht wird, muss in diesem Kapitel zunächst herausgearbeitet werden, inwieweit es überhaupt möglich ist, eine Privatisierung deutscher JVAs vorzunehmen. Kann ohne weiteres das amerikanische Modell, bei dem der Betrieb eines Gefängnisses gänzlich an die Privatwirtschaft übergeben wird, auch in Deutschland über-

14 Vgl. Friemel, K. (2005), S. 39; o. V. (2003a).
15 Vgl. Salewski (2001), S. 83.

nommen werden oder gelten hierzulande Gesetze, die diesen Schritt nicht ermöglichen?

Eine mögliche Schranke könnte in den Artikeln 83ff des Grundgesetzes (GG) liegen. Sie enthalten eine Auflistung von staatlichen Bereichen, bei denen es zu keiner vollkommenen Privatisierung kommen darf. Der Strafvollzug findet sich hierin nicht wieder. In der Konsequenz stellen die Artikel kein Hindernis für Privatisierungsmaßnahmen dar.[16]

In Artikel 33 Abs. 4 GG wird vom sog. „Funktionsvorbehalt für Beamte" gesprochen: *„Die Ausübung hoheitsrechtlicher Befugnisse ist als ständige Aufgabe in der Regel Angehörigen des öffentlichen Dienstes zu übertragen, die in einem öffentlich-rechtlichen Dienst- und Treueverhältnis stehen."* Hierdurch soll eine Sicherstellung der Kontinuität hoheitlicher Funktionen des Staates gewährleistet werden. Kraft Gesellschaftsvertrag wird vom Staat die Gewährleistung einer gerechten Ordnung und Sicherheit mittels des Strafvollzugs erwartet. Der Strafvollzug wird als Kernaufgabe des Staates definiert und ist somit in seiner Gänze nicht privatisierungsfähig.[17] Mit der Formulierung „in der Regel" werden aber gleichzeitig Tore für Ausnahmen geöffnet. Hierunter fallen Aufgaben, die nicht dem hoheitlichen Tätigkeitsbereich des Staates unterliegen und somit nicht „in die Grundrechte und sonstigen Rechte der Gefangenen eingreifen und diese u. U. sogar einschränken".[18] Damit ist es möglich, Privaten einzelne Bereiche innerhalb des Strafvollzugs zu überlassen, in denen sie tätig werden können. Allerdings ist es hierbei notwendig, dass diese Bereiche zum einen nicht das Gewaltmonopol des Staates betreffen und zum anderen auch nicht mit der Ausübung physischer Gewalt einhergehen.[19]

Eine weitere Schranke könnte im §155 Strafvollzugsgesetz (StVollzG) bestehen. Nach § 155 Abs. 1 S. 1 StVollzG *(„Die Aufgaben der Justizvollzugs-*

[16] Vgl. Giefers-Wieland, N. (2002), S. 142; Kulas, A. (2001), S. 91.
[17] Vgl. Giefers-Wieland, N. (2002), S. 147-149.
[18] Giefers-Wieland, N. (2002), S. 150.
[19] Vgl. o. V. (2003b), S. 18.

anstalten werden von Vollzugsbeamten wahrgenommen.") ist die Vollziehung physischer Gewalt sowie die Durchführung von Behandlungsmaßnahmen ausschließlich Vollzugsbeamten vorbehalten. Dementsprechend können aber andere Aufgaben von privaten Unternehmen übernommen werden.[20] Hierauf wird in § 155 Abs. 1 S. 2 StVollzG eingegangen: „*Aus besonderen Gründen können sie auch anderen Bediensteten der Justizvollzugsanstalten sowie nebenamtlichen oder vertraglich verpflichteten Personen übertragen werden.*" Unter „besonderen Gründen" sind all solche Aspekte zu verstehen, die dazu beitragen, dass das Vollzugsziel der JVAs erreicht wird und dem Wohle des einzelnen Gefangenen dienlich sind. Der Mangel an eigenem Personal kann unter diesem Gesichtspunkt durch einen Rückgriff auf qualifiziertes Fachpersonal privater Unternehmen kompensiert werden.[21] Als besonderer Grund gilt auch die Verbesserung der Wirtschaftlichkeit der JVAs bzw. die Reduzierung des staatlichen Aufwands. Mit § 7 Abs. 1 Bundeshaushaltsordnung (BHO) wird der Staat sogar zur Wirtschaftlichkeit und Sparsamkeit verpflichtet.[22]

Zusammenfassend kann aus § 155 Abs. 1 S. 1 und 2 StVollzG resümiert werden, dass der Einsatz privater Unternehmen im Strafvollzug grundsätzlich möglich ist, wenn die auferlegten Gründe zutreffen. In diesem Kontext werden die Privatpersonen als Beliehene bezeichnet. Sie nehmen als natürliche oder juristische Person eigenständig eine öffentliche Aufgabe des Staates wahr und handeln dabei im eigenen Namen.[23]

Im Gegensatz hierzu stehen die sog. Verwaltungshelfer. Sie treten nicht in eigenem Namen auf und arbeiten nach Auftrag und Weisung der jeweiligen Behörde. In der Regel werden sie für Verwaltungsaufgaben herangezogen. Für ihren Einsatz bedarf es keiner besonderen Gründe, solange es sich um bloße Dienstleistungen handelt und es zu keinem direkten Kontakt mit den Gefangenen

---

20 Vgl. o. V. (2003b), S. 20.
21 Vgl. o. V. (2003b), S. 20; Calliess, R.-P./Müller-Dietz, H. (2005), § 155 Rn 2.
22 Vgl. Bonk, J. (2000), S. 441.
23 Vgl. Burgi, M. (2001), S. 44; Gusy, Ch. (2001), S. 8.

kommt. Andernfalls muss immer ein Beamter zugegen sein.[24] Nicht-hoheitliche Aufgaben können in diesem Kontext somit ohne Weiteres von privaten Unternehmen vollzogen werden. Hoheitliche Aufgaben werden jedoch im Normalfall und auf Dauer verboten.[25]

Somit ergeben sich für private Unternehmen folgende Einsatzmöglichkeiten in einer JVA: [26]

- Sofern Sonderkenntnisse im Bereich der Objektüberwachung vorliegen, können sie als Verwaltungshelfer bei der Kontrolle der technischen und baulichen Sicherheit, der sachbezogenen Raumkontrolle sowie der Überwachung der Gefangenen außerhalb ihrer Zellen eingesetzt werden. Ein bewaffneter Wachdienst ist allerdings auf Grund der Hoheitlichkeit der Aufgabe an sich nicht erlaubt.
- Die Essenszubereitung kann ebenfalls Privaten übertragen werden. Allerdings dürfen sie sich dann nicht alleine mit Gefangenen in einem Raum befinden.
- Die Reinigung der Anstaltswäsche kann an Private vergeben werden.
- Teile des Fahrdienstes können selbstständig übernommen werden, sofern der Kontakt mit Gefangenen ausgeschlossen werden kann.
- Die Materialbeschaffung und -verwaltung kann ebenfalls übertragen werden.
- Gebäudearbeiten (Reparaturen, Reinigung) können ausgegliedert werden.
- Die Buchführung einer JVA kann an Private vergeben werden.

---

[24] Vgl. Pitschas, R. (2000), S. 47, 64; Gusy, Ch. (2001), S. 9; o. V. (2003b), S. 21.
[25] Vgl. Gusy, Ch. (2001), S. 16.
[26] Vgl. o. V. (2003b), S. 22-24.

4 Aspekte der Privatisierung

Nachdem im vorangegangenen Kapitel aufgezeigt wurde, inwiefern es nach deutschem Recht möglich ist, den Strafvollzug zu privatisieren, wird im Folgenden die finanzwirtschaftliche Motivation des Staates für eine solche Maßnahme erörtert. Hieran anknüpfend werden die Konsequenzen einer Privatisierung aus dem gesellschafts- und sozialpolitischen Blickwinkel dargestellt.

4.1 Ökonomische Aspekte aus staatlicher Sicht

Wie im Vorfeld bereits ausführlich erörtert wurde, ist die Ursache für die zunehmenden Überlegungen zur Privatisierung staatlicher Einrichtungen in den leeren Haushaltskassen des Staates zu sehen. Es müssen neuen Wege gefunden werden, sich der Kostenlast dieser Einrichtungen zu entledigen und neue Investitionen zu vermeiden. Outsourcing-Maßnahmen scheinen in diesem Zusammenhang eine geeignete Lösung für das Problem zu sein.[27] Der Ruf nach einem Umdenken unter Wirtschaftlichkeits- und Effizienzgesichtspunkten staatlicher Aktivitäten wird seitens der Politik immer lauter.[28]

Vor dem Hintergrund einer steigenden Anzahl von Strafgefangenen in deutschen Gefängnissen sowie der steigenden Haftkosten pro Gefangenem stellt der Strafvollzug eine zunehmende finanzielle Belastung für den Staat dar.[29] Der Ruf nach neuen Haftplätzen und zusätzlichem Personal wird laut.[30] In diesem Zusammenhang scheint die Hinzuziehung privater Sicherheitsdienste in den Strafvollzug eine kostengünstige Lösung zu sein. Wenngleich dieses Gewerbe in der Vergangenheit noch nicht mit großen Werbekampagnen in der Öffentlichkeit erschienen ist, zeichnet es sich aber ab, dass es sich hierbei um einen deutlichen Wachstumsmarkt handelt, der zunehmend um die Übernahme staatlicher Aktivi-

[27] Vgl. Fuest, W./Kroker, R. (1981), S. 16.
[28] Vgl. Giefers-Wieland, N. (2002), S. 138-139.
[29] Vgl. o. V. (2006a); o. V. (2007b); o. V. (2006b).
[30] Vgl. Sucher, J. (2005).

täten wirbt. Die Anzahl der Wach- und Sicherheitsunternehmen hat sich in den letzten Jahren stetig erhöht. Allein im Jahr 2007 erwirtschafteten sie einen Umsatz von geschätzten 4,5 Mrd. Euro.[31]

Die Vorteile, die sich der Staat durch eine Hinzuziehung Privater erhofft, liegen in einer Reduzierung der bisherigen Kosten, da davon ausgegangen wird, dass sie auf Grund vertraglicher Vorgaben Kontrollmaßnahmen sowie sonstige Aktivitäten innerhalb einer JVA effektiver ausführen.[32] Dem Staat könnte es durch die eingesparten Kosten in der Folge gelingen, weniger Kredite für den aktuellen Haushalt aufzunehmen oder gar eine Ablösung bestehender Kredite zu tätigen.[33]

Vor allem bei den JVAs wird davon ausgegangen, dass es zu erheblichen Einsparungen bei den Bau- und Unterhaltungskosten sowie in bestimmtem Ausmaß auch im Personalbereich kommt.[34] Da sich ein privates Unternehmen beim Bau eines Gefängnisses bei weitem nicht so zahlreichen Ausschreibungs-regularien zu unterziehen hat, wie es der Staat bei der Erstellung eines solchen Gebäudes vorzunehmen hat, liegt die Planungs- und Bauzeit bei einem privaten Bauherren nur bei ca. drei Jahren. Der Staat hingegen bräuchte hierfür ungefähr sechs bis acht Jahre.[35] Allein durch diesen verkürzten Zeitraum hätte der Staat Einsparungen immensen Ausmaßes erzielt. Darüber hinaus könnte der Staat durch kostensparende Fortschritte im Bereich der Sicherheitstechnik, zu deren Umsetzung und Erneuerung ein privates Unternehmen vertraglich verpflichtet werden könnte, den bestehenden Sicherheitsstandard bei geringeren Ausgaben gewährleisten.[36]

Ein weiterer Kostentreiber innerhalb einer JVA ist das Personal. Der Staat versucht auch hierbei, seine Ausgaben zu reduzieren. Dies kann, wie bereits

---

31 Vgl. o. V. (2008d).
32 Vgl. Aumüller, Th. (2001), S. 62.
33 Vgl. Fluhrer, H. (1984), S. 69-70; Stern, V. (1992), S. 39.
34 Vgl. Kulas, A. (2001), S. 9.
35 Vgl. Aumüller, Th. (2001), S. 63.
36 Vgl. Kulas, A. (2001), S. 11.

erwähnt, bspw. durch den Einsatz von mehr Sicherheitstechnik geschehen. Eine weitere Option ist die Hinzuziehung privater Sicherheitsdienste, soweit dies nach deutschem Recht möglich ist. Durch günstigere Tarifstrukturen ist es diesem Sektor möglich, sein Personal wesentlich billiger anzubieten, als es dem Staat durch die Beschäftigung von eigenen Angestellten oder Beamten gelingt. So liegen die Einkaufspreise für einen privaten Sicherheitswächter bei 50% bis 60% der Stundenkosten, die der Staat einem Beamten des mittleren Dienstes zahlt.[37] Des Weiteren bieten die Privaten eine wesentlich höhere Wochenarbeitszeit an, so dass ihrerseits der Betrieb einer JVA im Zwei-Schicht-Betrieb vorgenommen werden könnte. Momentan wird in den Gefängnissen in einem Drei-Schicht-Betrieb gearbeitet, was einen erheblich höheren Koordinationsaufwand erfordert.[38]

Darüber hinaus besitzt dieses Modell für den Staat einen weiteren großen Vorteil. Weil dieser vom Privaten lediglich die Arbeitsstunden einkauft und nicht einzelne, bestimmte Arbeitskräfte, verpflichtet sich das private Unternehmen, für erkrankte oder beurlaubte Personen einen sofortigen Ersatz zur Verfügung zu stellen. In der Konsequenz liegt die Abwesenheitsquote bei den Mitarbeitern des privaten Sicherheitsgewerbes bei Null.[39] Die im Gesetz vorgeschriebene Kontrolle privater Sicherheitsdienste in einem Gefängnis könnte von der dortigen Verwaltung vorgenommen werden, die ohnehin zugegen ist. Wesentliche Mehrkosten würden hierdurch nicht entstehen.[40]

Zusammenfassend bleibt festzuhalten, dass der Staat durch die Hinzuziehung privater Unternehmen im Bereich des Strafvollzugs erhebliche Kosten einsparen könnte. Aufgrund der erwähnten Wettbewerbssituation im Markt der Sicherheitsgewerbe sind die dort tätigen Unternehmen gezwungen, unter gänzlich anderen Kostenstrukturen zu arbeiten, als dies beim Staat der Fall ist. In ihren Strukturen sind sie so organisiert, dass sie einer plötzlich veränderten

[37] Vgl. Aumüller (2001), S. 63.
[38] Ebd.
[39] Ebd.
[40] Vgl. Kulas, A. (2001), S. 9.

Nachfrage flexibel begegnen können. Das Anstreben einer kostengünstigen Leistungserstellung zwingt sie dazu, Leerlaufkosten einzusparen.[41]
Diesen Aspekt macht sich der Staat zu Nutzen, indem er mit Privaten zusammenarbeitet. Gleichzeitig trägt er somit dem ihm auferlegten Wirtschaftlichkeits- und Effizienzgedanken Rechnung.

4.2 Gesellschafts- und sozialpolitische Aspekte

Wie die vorangegangene Darstellung gezeigt hat, stellt die Teil-Privatisierung einer JVA für den Staat offensichtlich eine gute Möglichkeit dar, Kosteneinsparungen vorzunehmen. Unter finanzwirtschaftlichen Aspekten handelt es sich hierbei somit um eine erfolgversprechende Lösung des Problems leerer Haushaltskassen. Doch wie gestaltet sich eine Betrachtung der Privatisierung unter gesellschafts- und sozialpolitischen Gesichtspunkten?

Kostenvorteile entstehen unter anderem dadurch, dass mit weniger Personal und mehr Technik gearbeitet wird. Die Überwachung der Gefangenen geschieht aufgrund des möglichen Einsparpotentials weniger durch Mitarbeiter eines privaten Unternehmens als durch die Nutzung von Sicherheitselektronik. Die Unternehmen folgen in diesem Fall einem natürlichen Gewinnmaximierungsstreben. In der Konsequenz kommt es dann aber zu geringeren persönlichen Kontakten zwischen Inhaftierten und Bewachungspersonal. Gute zwischenmenschliche Beziehungen stellen jedoch eine wichtige Grundlage zur erfolgreichen Resozialisierung eines Gefangenen dar, der während seiner Haftzeit keine größeren Kontakte zur Außenwelt hat.[42]

Darüber hinaus gibt es einen weiteren gravierenden Unterschied zwischen fest angestellten Justizvollzugsbeamten und privaten Sicherheitskräften. Während Erstgenannte dauerhaft in einer JVA tätig sind und hierdurch eine persönli-

---

[41] Vgl. Steiner, U. (1975), S. 290-291; Mayer, B. (1990), S. 165; Fuest, W./Kroker, R. (1981), S. 20.

[42] Vgl. Suhrbier, W. (2001), S. 76; Friemel, K. (2005), S. 35.

che Beziehung zu den Häftlingen aufbauen können, kommt es bei den Privaten zu häufigeren Personalfluktuationen, weil deren Mitarbeiter flexibel und nach Bedarf bei den verschiedenen Kunden des Sicherheitsunternehmens eingesetzt werden. Im vorangegangenen Kapitel wurde bereits dargestellt, dass der Staat nur Arbeitsstunden bei den Privaten einkauft und somit keinen Anspruch auf bestimmte Arbeitskräfte hat. Der flexible Personaleinsatz hat auch zur Folge, dass sich die Privaten weniger mit ihrer Arbeit in einer JVA identifizieren können. Zusammen mit dem Aspekt der niedrigen Löhne, die sie erhalten, und ihrem indirekten Umgang mit Gefangenen wird vermutet, dass sie für Einflussnahmen innerhalb und außerhalb von Gefängnissen wesentlich anfälliger sind als dies bei den Beamten der Fall ist.[43]

Es ist wichtig, zu betonen, dass eine erfolgreiche Behandlung der Häftlinge nur dann geschehen kann, wenn die notwendige Sicherheit der JVA-Mitarbeiter gewährleistet werden kann. Im Gegenzug kann diese Sicherheit aber nicht nur mittels der Sicherheitstechnik erreicht werden, sondern muss auch durch erfolgreiche Behandlungsmaßnahmen geschehen.[44] Genau vor diesem Aspekt fürchten sich jedoch die Justizvollzugsbeamten, wenn sie mit Privaten zusammenarbeiten müssen. Während sie in einer zweijährigen Ausbildung auf den Kontakt und den Umgang mit Straffälligen vorbereitet werden, unterliegen die Mitarbeiter keiner besonderen Schulung hierzu.[45] Dies kann sich ihr Arbeitgeber auch nicht erlauben, da ihre dauerhafte Beschäftigung in einem Gefängnis nicht sichergestellt ist und somit jede Schulungsmaßnahme im Falle eines anderweitigen Einsatzes des Mitarbeiters unnötige Kosten verursacht hätte. Aufgrund dieses Ausbildungsdefizits fürchten die Strafvollzugsbediensteten um die Sicherheit innerhalb der Gefängnisse.[46]

Ein weiteres Problem ist im Tätigkeitsbereich der Privaten zu sehen. Im dritten Kapitel wurde bereits herausgearbeitet, in welchen Bereichen private

[43] Vgl. Friemel, K. (2005), S. 36.
[44] Vgl. Suhrbier, W. (2001), S. 77.
[45] Vgl. Friemel, K. (2005), S. 37.
[46] Vgl. Sucher, J. (2005).

Sicherheitskräfte eingesetzt werden dürfen. Hierzu gehören unter anderem die Anstaltsküche, die Wäscherei oder die Gestaltung der Außenanlage. Während zuvor Beamte abgestellt werden mussten, die die Gefangenen in diesen Bereichen bewachten, können die Staatsdiener hierbei nun eingespart werden, da die anfallenden Tätigkeiten von günstigeren Privaten erbracht werden. Dies führt aber dazu, dass die Inhaftierten ihre dortigen Arbeitsplätze verlieren und ohne Aufgabe sind. Schlimmstenfalls endet hierdurch der Strafvollzug in einem bloßen Verwahrvollzug.[47] Es ist unumstritten, dass sich solche Maßnahmen letztendlich auch im Verhalten der Gefangenen widerspiegeln. Je mehr Zeit die Inhaftierten miteinander unbeschäftigt verbringen, umso mehr steigt deren Gewaltpotential und umso geringer ist deren erfolgreiche Wiedereingliederung in die Gesellschaft.[48] Ein Blick in die Länder, in denen Gefängnisse privat oder teil-privat betrieben werden, zeigt, dass sich dort die Anzahl von Selbstmorden der Häftlinge stark erhöht hat.[49] Dieser Tatbestand ist nicht zuletzt auf die vorangegangenen Aspekte zurückzuführen.

Darüber hinaus muss auch hinterfragt werden, ob der Staat nicht seine gesellschafts- und sozialpolitische Verantwortung gegenüber seinen Angestellten und Beamten im Justizvollzug verletzt, wenn er diese durch private Sicherheitskräfte ersetzt. Unabhängig davon, dass Staatsbedienstete nach und nach durch „Billig-Arbeitskräfte“, die einen Stundenlohn zwischen sechs und acht Euro erhalten, ausgetauscht werden, führt ein solches Verhalten auch dazu, dass der Staat Arbeitgeber fördert, die sozial schlechter abgesicherte Arbeitsverhältnisse anbieten.[50] Ein weiterer Punkt, der dem Staat vorgeworfen wird, ist, dass durch das Outsourcing bestimmter Bereiche des öffentlichen Dienstes auch die Gewerkschaften in ihrer Position geschwächt werden. Auf diese Art gelingt es dem Staat, die Vertretung von Arbeitnehmerinteressen zu reduzieren.[51]

47 Vgl. Sucher, J. (2005).
48 Vgl. Friemel, K. (2005), S. 38; Suhrbier, W. (2001), S. 76.
49 Vgl. o. V. (2007a).
50 Vgl. Sucher, J. (2005); Kulas, A. (2001), S. 12.
51 Vgl. Kulas, A. (2001), S. 13.

5 Schlussbetrachtung

Ausgangspunkt für die aufgestellte These ist die schlechte Haushaltssituation des Staates mit seinen leeren Kassen und den damit verbundenen Überlegungen zu verschiedenen Konsolidierungsmaßnahmen. Ein scheinbar gangbarer Weg zur Verbesserung der Kostensituation ist das Outsourcing staatlicher Einrichtungen und Dienstleistungen an private Unternehmen im Rahmen von sog. Public Private Partnerships. Die Privaten erhalten dabei den Auftrag, Leistungen des Staates zu übernehmen bzw. zusammen mit ihm durchzuführen. Dabei werden sie in den unterschiedlichsten Bereichen wie bspw. bei der Betreibung von Schwimmbädern, der Abfallbeseitigung oder der Unterhaltung von Schulen tätig.

Seit einiger Zeit wird, auch mit Blick auf das Ausland, eine Privatisierung von JVAs heftig diskutiert. Steigende Gefangenenzahlen sowie eine Zunahme der Haftkosten zwingen den Staat entweder mehr Geld in diesen Bereich zu investieren oder ebenfalls auf eine Zusammenarbeit mit Privaten zu setzen.

Der Justizvollzug fällt unter die sog. hoheitlichen Aufgaben des Staates. Nach § 2 StVollzG verpflichtet sich der Staat zu Resozialisierungsmaßnahmen bei straffällig gewordenen Menschen. Eine rechtliche Überprüfung des Privatisierungsgedankens von Gefängnissen ergibt, dass es nach deutschem Recht aufgrund der Hoheitlichkeit der Aufgabe nicht möglich ist, den Betrieb ganzer Haftanstalten an private Unternehmen auszugliedern. Lediglich einzelne Teilbereiche können von Privaten übernommen werden. Somit kann es in diesem Zusammenhang nur zu einer Zusammenarbeit zwischen Staat und privaten Unternehmen kommen. Die Motivation der Politiker liegt bei einer solchen Kooperation in der Erzielung von Kostenvorteilen und somit in der Entlastung staatlicher Kassen. Bei einem von der Deloitte Business Consulting GmbH erstellten Gutachten findet die Politik Bestätigung.[52] Demnach kann sich der Staat wesentliche Einsparungen beim Bau, dessen Unterhaltung sowie dem Facility Management erhoffen. Ausstattung und Gebäudebetriebskosten lassen

[52] Vgl. o. V. (2003b).

hingegen keine wesentlichen Kostenvorteile erkennen, da die privaten Betreiber Risikoaufschläge berechnen, welche die vermuteten Einsparungen bei der Anschaffung und Bewirtschaftung verschwinden lassen. Grundsätzlich lassen sich für den Staat wesentliche Effizienzvorteile erzielen. Allerdings werden diese durch die zu erwartenden Gewinnzuschläge der Privaten sowie der anfallenden Mehrwertsteuerbelastung auf das Serviceentgelt in erheblichem Ausmaß aufgezehrt. Die Wirtschaftlichkeitsrechnung lässt somit auf ein Einsparpotential von ungefähr 8 % gegenüber einer ausschließlich staatlichen Betreibung schließen. Das Ziel des Staates, Kosten zu dämmen, wäre somit erreicht.

Demgegenüber stehen aber zahlreiche gesellschafts- und sozialpolitische Ansichten, die eine PPP in diesem Bereich stark in Frage stellen. Hierbei geht es vor allem um den Aspekt der Sicherheit innerhalb und außerhalb der Gefängnisse. Durch die bedingte Einsatzfähigkeit privater Sicherheitskräfte sowie die zunehmende Einführung elektronischer Überwachungssysteme wird von Seiten der Justizvollzugsbeamten mit einer steigenden Gewaltbereitschaft bei den Inhaftierten gerechnet. Die persönliche Betreuung der Gefangenen wird hierdurch sowie durch die geringere Anzahl von Gefängnisbeamten erschwert. Resozialisierung kann in der Konsequenz nur noch unter erschwerten Bedingungen stattfinden. Folglich ist das Anfälligkeitspotential der Häftlinge zu erneuten Straftaten nach ihrer Entlassung aus dem Gefängnis sehr hoch. Die innere Sicherheit des Landes würde zu Gunsten erhoffter Kostenvorteile verschlechtert. Der Staat kann seiner Verantwortung gegenüber der Gesellschaft nicht mehr nachkommen. Vor diesem Hintergrund ist es als äußerst bedenklich anzusehen, PPPs in diesem Bereich allein aufgrund erwarteter Effizienzvorteile einzugehen.

Literaturverzeichnis

Aumüller, Th. (2001): Motive und Argumente für eine Privatisierung im Strafvollzug aus der Sicht der Politik. In: Stober, R. (Hrsg.) (2001): Privatisierung im Strafvollzug?. Carl Heymanns Verlag, Köln et al., S. 59-70.

Bonk, J. (2000): Rechtliche Rahmenbedingungen einer Privatisierung im Strafvollzug. In: JuristenZeitung, 55. Jahrgang, Heft 9, 2000, S. 435-442.

Burgi, M. (2001): Statement „Beleihung im Strafvollzug". In: Stober, R. (Hrsg.) (2001): Privatisierung im Strafvollzug?. Carl Heymanns Verlag, Köln et al., 2001, S. 43-54.

Calliess, R.-P./Müller-Dietz, H. (2005): Strafvollzugsgesetz. 10. Auflage. Verlag C. H. Beck, München.

Fluhrer, H. (1984): Weniger Staat – Mehr Privat. Christine Hasenzahl Verlag, München. Zugl. Diss. Ludwig-Maximilians-Universität München.

Friemel, K. (2005): Gefängnis mit beschränkter Haftung? In: McK Wissen, Nummer 13, 2005, S. 32-39.

Fuest, W./Kroker, R. (1981): Privatisierung öffentlicher Aufgaben. Deutscher Instituts-Verlag, Köln.

Giefers-Wieland, N. (2002): Private Strafvollzugsanstalten in den USA. Centaurus, Herbolzheim. Zugl. Diss. Universität zu Köln.

Gusy, Ch. (2001): Zulässigkeit und Grenzen des Einsatzes privater Sicherheitsdienste im Strafvollzug. In: Stober, R. (Hrsg.) (2001): Privatisierung im Strafvollzug? Carl Heymanns Verlag, Köln et al., 2001, S. 5-33.

Jung, H. (1988): Paradigmawechsel im Strafvollzug? In: Kaiser, G./Kury, H./Albrecht, H.-J. (1988): Kriminologische Forschung in den 80er Jahren. Eigenverlag Max-Planck-Institut für ausländisches und internationales Strafrecht, Freiburg, S. 377-388.

Kaiser, G./Kury, H./Albrecht, H.-J. (1988): Kriminologische Forschung in den 80er Jahren. Eigenverlag Max-Planck-Institut für ausländisches und internationales Strafrecht, Freiburg.

Kloff, J. (1997): Management-Methoden im Justizvollzug? In: Neue Kriminalpolitik, 9. Jahrgang, Heft 3, 1997, S. 12-15.

Kulas, A. (2001): Privatisierung hoheitlicher Verwaltung. Carl Heymanns Verlag, Köln et al. Zugl. Diss. Philipps-Universität zu Marburg.

Mayer, B. (1990): Die Bundespost: Wirtschaftsunternehmen oder Leistungsbehörde. Duncker & Humblot, Berlin. Zugl. Diss. Albert-Ludwigs-Universität in Freiburg.

o. V. (2003a): Public Private Partnerships für öffentliche Infrastrukturvorhaben? – Ziele und Erfahrungen in Deutschland und Europa. URL: http://www.eib.europa.eu/about/press/2003/2003-037-public-private-partnerships-objectives-and-experiences-in-germany-and-europe.htm?lang=-de vom 8. September 2008.

o. V. (2003b): Pilotprojekt „Neubau und Betrieb einer Justizvollzugsanstalt“ im Rahmen der Public Private Partnership Initiative des Landes Nordrhein-Westfalen. Deloitte Business Consulting GmbH.

o. V. (2004): Public Private Partnership – Chance für die Modernisierung von Infrastruktur und Verwaltung. Bundesverband deutscher Banken, Berlin.

o. V. (2006a): Mehr als 64000 Strafgefangene in deutschen Gefängnissen. URL:http://www.destatis.de/jetspeed/portal/cms/Sites/destatis/Internet/DE/Presse/pm/2006/12/PD06_517_024.psml vom 4. Juni 2008.

o. V. (2006b): Die durchschnittlichen Haftkosten je Gefangenen im Jahre 2004 mit Baukosten. URL: http://www.manfred-schraepel.de/2.html vom 3. Juni 2008.

o. V. (2007a): Geschäfte hinter Gittern. URL: http://derstandard.at/?id=2931020 vom 3. Juni 2008.

o. V. (2007b): Justizvollzug – Zahl der Anstalten, Belegungsfähigkeit und Belegung am 31.03.2007. URL: http://www.destatis.de/jetspeed/portal/cms/Sites/destatis/Internet/DE/Content/Statistiken/Rechtspflege/Justizvollzug/Tabellen/Content75/Belegungskapazitaet.psml vom 4. Juni 2008.

o. V. (2008a): Der kommunale Investitionsbedarf 2006 bis 2020. Deutsches Institut für Urbanistik, Berlin.

o. V. (2008b): Deutschland 2020 – Zukunftsperspektiven für die deutsche Wirtschaft. McKinsey & Company, Inc., Frankfurt am Main.

o. V. (2008c): Bush präsentiert Rekorddefizit. URL: http://www.n24.de/news/newsitem_1189890.html vom 29. Juli 2008.

o. V. (2008d): Bundesverband Deutscher Wach- und Sicherheitsunternehmen e.V. URL: http://www.bdws.de/cms/index.php?option=com_content&task=view&id=510&Itemd=32 vom 3. Juni 2008.

Pitschas, R (2000): Polizei und Sicherheitsgewerbe. Bundeskriminalamt, Wiesbaden.

Salewski, B. (2001): Erfahrungen im Ausland. In: Stober, R. (Hrsg.) (2001): Privatisierung im Strafvollzug?. Carl Heymanns Verlag, Köln et al., S. 81-85.

Steiner, U. (1975): Öffentliche Verwaltung durch Private. Hansischer Gildenverlag, Joachim Heitmann & Co, Hamburg. Zugl. Habil. Universität Erlangen-Nürnberg.

Stern, V. (1992): Vorrang für Private in der öffentlichen Energieversorgung. Karl-Bräuer-Institut des Bundes der Steuerzahler e.V., Wiesbaden.

Stober, R. (Hrsg.) (2001): Privatisierung im Strafvollzug? Carl Heymanns Verlag, Köln et al.

Sucher, J. (2005): Lebenslänglich in der Knast AG. In: Spiegel Online, URL: http://www.spiegel.de/wirtschaft/0,1518,336343,00.html vom 3. Juni 2008.

Suhrbier, W. (2001): Privatisierung im Strafvollzug. In: Stober, R. (Hrsg.) (2001): Privatisierung im Strafvollzug?. Carl Heymanns Verlag, Köln et al., S. 71-79.

PPP und Mittelstand – Risikoanalyse und Risikobegrenzung mit neuen Instrumenten

Daniel Kloss & Gerhard Steyer

Inhaltsverzeichnis

1 Einführung

Public Private Partnership (PPP) ist eine Beschaffungsalternative der öffentlichen Hand mit dem Ziel, die Fähigkeiten und Erfahrungen des privaten Sektors bei der Bereitstellung einer normalerweise öffentlichen Infrastruktureinrichtung zu nutzen. Die Vertragsmodelle unterscheiden sich insbesondere mit Blick auf das Eigentum an der erstellten Anlage, der Art der Refinanzierung (Leistungsentgelte durch öffentlichen Auftraggeber oder Nutzerentgelte) sowie die notwendigen Endschaftsregelungen am Ende der Vertragslaufzeit. Das Grundprinzip ist die Effizienzsteigerung durch Risikoallokation und Leistungsorientierung. Das heißt:

- Optimale Risikoallokation: Wer ein Risiko am besten beurteilen und beeinflussen kann, sollte es tragen und bepreisen (insbesondere Kontrahenten- und Leistungserstellungsrisiken).
- Funktionale Leistungsbeschreibung anstelle von inputorientierten Bauvorgaben in einem Leistungsverzeichnis.
- Planungs- und Innovationspotenzial sowie fachliches Know-how und Kreativität der privaten Anbieter werden zum Erfolgsfaktor.
- Lebenszyklusansatz: Planung, Bau, Finanzierung, Betrieb und Verwertung.
- Durch ein langfristiges Anlagenmanagement werden Effizienzsteigerungen erzielt und Betreiberrisiken auf die private Partei übertragen.
- Über genaue Spezifikation der zu erbringenden Leistungen im Vertragswerk können die Zahlungen an die Nutzbarkeit und Verfügbarkeit der Anlage anknüpfen. Damit werden Performancerisiken auf die private Partei übertragen.

2 Finanzierung von PPP-Maßnahmen

Die Finanzierung eines PPP-Projektes erstreckt sich über die Bau- und die Betriebsphase. In der Bauphase bis zur Fertigstellung und Abnahme durch den Auftraggeber ist eine Fremdfinanzierung des Projektes durch eine Bank grundsätzlich auf die Bonität des Bieters abzustellen. Ist dies eine Projektgesellschaft, so muss die notwendige Bonität über Garantien der Gesellschafter (Bieterkonsortium) hergestellt werden. Gesellschafter sind in der Regel Unternehmen aus der Bauwirtschaft, dem Facility Management und auch Finanzinvestoren.

Hinsichtlich der Finanzierung des Gesamtprojektes kann PPP als Projektfinanzierung oder als Forfaitierung mit Einredeverzicht des öffentlichen Auftraggebers (z.B. einer Kommune) ausgeschrieben und realisiert werden. Daraus ergeben sich unterschiedliche Risikopositionen mit direkten Konsequenzen für den Prüfungsaufwand (Due Diligence) der Bank und die Konditionen.

Nach der Fertigstellung wird der Werklohn in beiden Fällen über die Betriebsphase gestundet. Im **Forfaitierungsmodell** kauft die Bank dem Auftragnehmer (AN) die Werklohnforderung ab. Die Kommune erklärt gegenüber der Bank den Einredeverzicht, so dass die Bank auf die Bonität der Kommune abstellt und daher kommunaldarlehensähnliche Konditionen möglich werden. Regressansprüche gegenüber dem AN bleiben bestehen. Zu beachten ist, dass es im Insolvenzrisiko des AN in der Gewährleistungsphase für die Kommune zu unerwarteten Mehrkosten und finanzieller Doppelbelastung kommen kann.

Bei der Realisierung als **Projektfinanzierung** bleibt der Aufragnehmer (z.B. ein Bieterkonsortium) Kreditnehmer auch in der Betriebsphase. Die Bank unterzieht daher das PPP-Projekt und den Auftragnehmer einer eingehenden Prüfung, einer so genannten Due Diligence. Bei der Projektfinanzierung wird von den Kapitalgebern ein dem Projektrisiko entsprechender Eigenkapitaleinsatz des Auftragnehmers erwartet, meist bis zu 10% des Finanzierungsvolumens. Die Bank quotiert risikoadäquate Kreditmargen, die regelmäßig höher als bei der

Forfaitierung sind. Die Due Diligence der Bank bei PPP-Modellen erstreckt sich dabei über 3 Phasen:

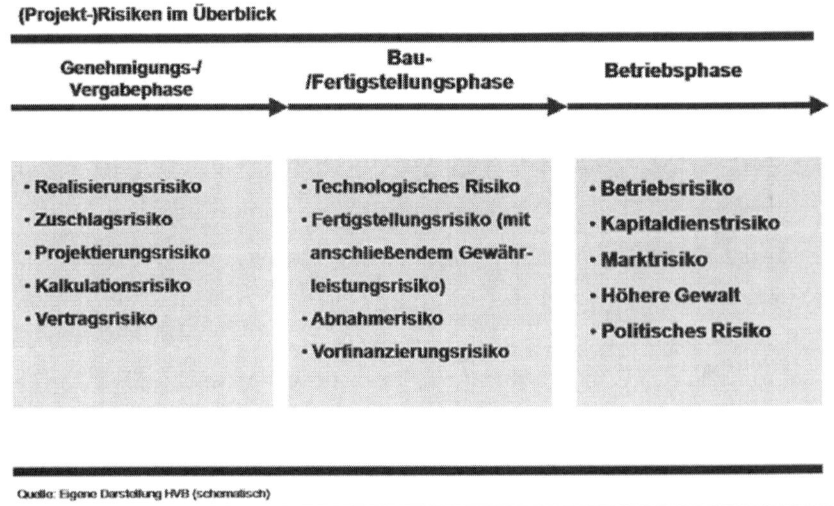

Abb. 1: (Projekt-)Risiken im Überblick
Quelle: eigene Darstellung.

Es ist grundsätzlich zu prüfen, ob Sonderkreditinstitute oder öffentliche Förderbanken über ihre diversen Förderprogramme zinsgünstige Refinanzierungsmittel zur Verfügung stellen können und damit die Finanzierung und somit das Gesamtprojekt wirtschaftlich attraktiver für den Auftraggeber machen.

3 Verbesserung des Finanzierungsrahmens und der Risikoverteilung

Neben der klassischen Risikotragung von Bau- und Unterhaltensrisiken stellt die weitere Verbesserung des Finanzierungsrahmens und der Risikoverteilung für PPP-Maßnahmen eine besondere Herausforderung dar. Es ist unbestritten, dass PPP-Projekte wichtige Impulse in den deutschen Baumarkt geben können. Einerseits setzt das kommunale Haushaltsrecht für die Kreditaufnahme wie auch für kreditähnliche Rechtsgeschäfte die dauerhafte Leistungsfähigkeit der Kommune voraus – d. h., durch eine PPP-Maßnahme darf deren Leistungsfähigkeit nicht beeinträchtigt werden. Andererseits führt das daraus resultierende Sicherheitsbedürfnis des öffentlichen Auftraggebers zu einer zu beobachtenden Präferierung besonders finanziell leistungsstarker bauindustrieller privater Projektpartner, so dass sich der Mittelstand des Baugewerbes und der Bauindustrie aufgrund der vorgegebenen Rahmenbedingungen nicht wieder finden. Hier gilt es, Voraussetzungen zu schaffen, die diesen Mittelstand der Bauwirtschaft in die Lage versetzen, ein ebenbürtiger Partner bei PPP-Maßnahmen zu sein.

Im Hinblick darauf stehen die Finanzierung sowie die Sicherheiten für die öffentliche Hand für den Fall der Schlechterfüllung oder Insolvenz des privaten Auftragnehmers im besonderen Fokus bei der Einbringung von Lösungsansätzen durch einen Versicherer.

Dabei spielt es eine entscheidende Rolle, auf welches Public Private Partnership-Modell zurückgegriffen wird. Wichtig ist, dass für beide Projektpartner und auch für die finanzierende Bank die Rahmenbedingungen der Risikoallokation so geschaffen werden, dass die Risikotragungen durch den Versicherer eine günstigere Finanzierung zulassen.

Bei allen Finanzierungsformen haftet die Baufirma bei den derzeitigen Ausgestaltungen mit einer **revolvierenden Vertragserfüllungsbürgschaft** über 5 – 10 % der Auftragssumme pro Jahr gegenüber der Kommune zur Absicherung im Wesentlichen für die Kosten einer notwendig werdenden Vergabe an eine neue Baufirma.

Die folgende Grafik veranschaulicht den Komplexitätsgrad hinsichtlich der Koordination der Projektbeteiligten und der notwendigen Vertragsgestaltungen. Dies gilt insbesondere für Projektfinanzierungen, bei denen die Risikoverteilung eine zentrale Rolle spielt.

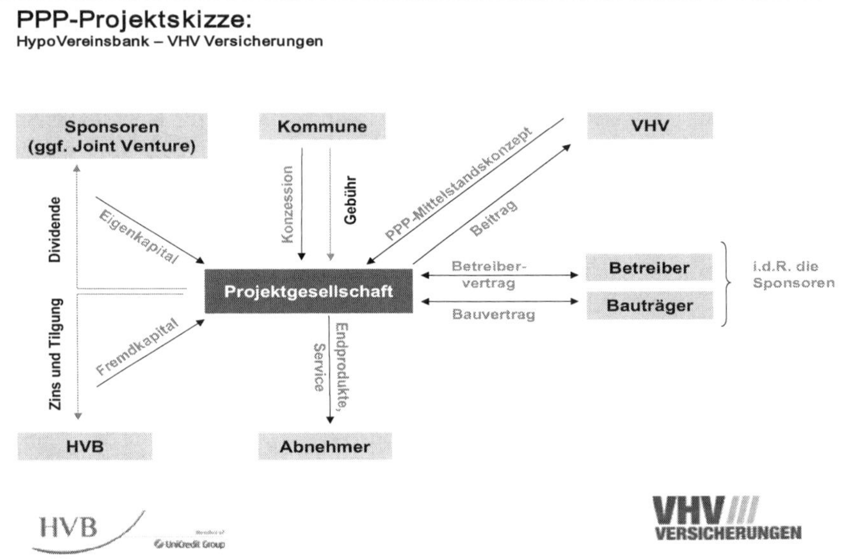

Abb. 2: PPP-Projektskizze
Quelle: eigene Darstellung.

4 Alternative Sicherheiten

Als alternative Sicherung empfiehlt sich die Baufertigstellungs-Versicherung, die nur gemeinsam mit der Baugewährleistungs-Versicherung abgeschlossen werden kann. Beide Versicherungsformen setzen im Hinblick auf die Eigenschadenproblematik voraus, dass sie nur für die PPP-Finanzierungsmodelle zur Anwendung kommen können, bei denen der öffentlich-rechtliche Projektpartner Grundstückseigentümer ist bzw. bei Vertragsende verbleibt.

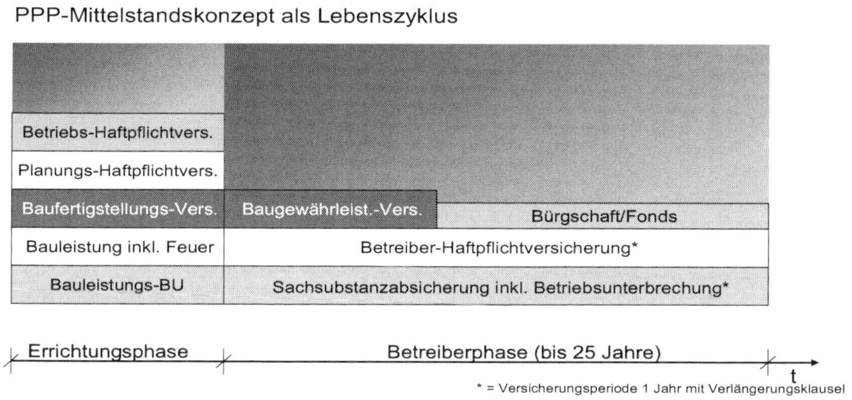

Abb. 3: PPP-Mittelstandskonzept als Lebenszyklus
Quelle: eigene Darstellung.

Diese Problematik ist für die mittelständische Bauwirtschaft insoweit unbeachtlich, da überwiegend das Inhabermodell in der Praxis zur Umsetzung kommt und das Einbringen von eigenen Grundstücken in PPP-Maßnahmen aufgrund der Gesamtkostenbetrachtung in der Regel die wirtschaftlichen Möglichkeiten des Mittelstandes übersteigt.
Im Gegensatz zur Bürgschaftslösung bietet die **Baufertigstellungs-Versicherung** eine 20%-ige Sicherheit, die für den öffentlich-rechtlichen Partner eine deutliche Verbesserung im Insolvenzfall bedeutet.

Hinzu kommt eine Liquiditätsentlastung für die Bauunternehmung, da diese nicht – anders als eine Bankbürgschaft – die Kreditlinie belastet und zum anderen keine Sicherheitenstellung erfordert. Beiden Projektpartnern kommt zusätzlich zugute, dass die technische Baubegleitung bei Durchführung des Bauvorhabens, die bei der Baufertigstellungs- und Baugewährleistungs-Versicherung obligatorisch ist, letztlich zu einer verbesserten Bauqualität führt, die sich insbesondere auch im Rahmen der Nutzungsphase bei notwendig werdenden Instandhaltungsarbeiten kostenmindernd auswirkt.

Die damit verbundene Gesamtprozessoptimierung von Bau und Betrieb im Lebenszyklus beim PPP-Modell bringt grundsätzlich eine höhere Bauqualität und als Folge eine Senkung der Bewirtschaftungskosten.

Auch im Segment der Betriebsphase lässt sich bei Einbindung von präqualifizierten Nachunternehmern innerhalb der Mittelstands-Arge eine Risikominimierung im Hinblick auf eine Insolvenz erreichen.

Die nach Abnahme auftretenden Baumängel, die in der Nutzungsphase auftreten, können für einen Zeitraum von 5 Jahren über die so genannte **Baugewährleistungs-Versicherung** dem Grunde nach zu 100 %, jedoch höchstens in Höhe der zu vereinbarenden Deckungssumme abgesichert werden.

Die Absicherung über eine Bankbürgschaft ist zu einem hohen Maß mit Eigenkapitalbindung verbunden und schränkt den Liquiditätsspielraum und die Kreditlinie der Unternehmen ein. Voraussetzung für die Stellung solcher Bürgschaften ist eine Bonitätsprüfung durch Auswertung von geeigneten Bonitätsunterlagen (wie z. B. Jahresabschlüsse, Wirtschaftsauskünfte u. ä.). Gegebenenfalls wird der Nachweis von Sicherheiten wie z. B. Bankrückbürgschaften, Abtretungen und Verpfändungen von Guthaben bzw. Wertpapieren u. ä. bonitätsabhängig erforderlich.

Die damit einhergehende Kapitalbindung gerade im Zusammenhang mit den gängigen Nachunternehmerketten – auch hier muss jeder Nachunternehmer eine entsprechende Bürgschaftsstellung nachweisen – stellt sich in der Gesamtbetrachtung als potentielle Zusatzbelastung zum Eintritt in eine PPP-Maßnahme dar.

Der dadurch geschmälerte Finanzierungsrahmen fehlt für das operative Geschäft, für das durch die Vorfinanzierung der Baumaßnahme bereits enorme Geldmittel gebunden sind.

5 Verbesserte Risikolage als Konsequenz

Mit diesem Lösungsansatz über die **Baufertigstellungs- und Baugewährleistungs-Versicherung** wird auch die Finanzierung der Investitionen über die Vertragslaufzeit von 25 – 30 Jahren in Form einer Forfaitierung (Forderungsverkauf) mit Einredeverzicht seitens des Auftraggebers deshalb problemloser möglich, weil die öffentliche Hand nunmehr aufgrund der verbesserten Risikolage in den ersten fünf Jahren der Nutzungsphase sich auch bei einem mittelständischen Unternehmen auf einen Einredeverzicht einlassen kann und damit die finanzierende Bank eine erhöhte Sicherheit zur Verfügung hat, die ihr den Spielraum gibt, bis zu kommunalkreditähnlichen Konditionen bieten zu können.

Mithin erfährt der mittelständische Bauunternehmer in einem PPP-Ausschreibungsverfahren eine Gleichwertigkeit bei der Abwägung der Sicherheitenstellung zu großen bauindustriellen Mitbewerbern.

Hinzu kommt, dass zu den unten beschriebenen Leistungsmerkmalen der Baugewährleistungs-Versicherung der öffentlich-rechtliche Projektpartner trotz Einredeverzicht im Insolvenzfall des privaten Projektpartners die Sicherheit hat, dass auftretende Bauschäden (Nachbesserungsansprüche) – im Gegensatz zu den bisherigen Sicherungskonzepten – zumindest in der Nutzungsphase in einem Zeitraum von 5 Jahren durch einen Direktanspruch gegen den Versicherer zur Regulierung kommen und zu keiner Haushaltsbelastung führen.

Die vertragliche Ausgestaltung einer PPP-Maßnahme verändert nach der Abnahme die werkvertraglichen Verpflichtungen der Bauausführenden in die durch den Nutzungsvertrag festgelegten Verbindlichkeiten. Soweit die Leistungsstörungen auf Baumängeln resultieren, greift der Leistungsumfang aus der Baugewährleistungs-Versicherung. Die Baugewährleistungs-Versicherung nimmt vom Grundsatz den zu Werksvertragsleistungen verpflichteten Bauausführenden dieses Risiko ab. Das heißt, es besteht ein Anspruch auf

- Erstattung der Nachbesserungskosten für Mängel an der Bauleistung, die erstmals nach der Abnahme auftreten,
- Erstattung des angemessenen Minderungsbeitrages, soweit die Mängelbeseitigung unmöglich bzw. unverhältnismäßig ist, und
- vertraglich vereinbarte Gewährleistungszeiten bis zu maximal 5 Jahren.

Im Gegensatz zur Gewährleistungsbürgschaft kennt die Baugewährleistungs-Versicherung keine Regressierung.
Dieser Leistungsumfang wird die Bauleistung betreffend für die ersten 5 Jahre nach Abnahme bei PPP-Maßnahmen in der Nutzungsphase gewährt.

Rückstellungen sind weitestgehend entbehrlich. Auch hierdurch verbessert sich die Liquidität des Bauunternehmens. Hinzu kommt, dass Rückstellungen für Nachbesserungsansprüche in aller Regel nur bedingt steuerlich anerkannt sind. Die Prämie für die Baugewährleistungs-Versicherung hingegen ist uneingeschränkt und in voller Höhe als Betriebsausgabe absetzbar.

Bei einer Aufteilung in Zinsen und Tilgung für die Bauabnahme einerseits und Entgelt für den Betrieb andererseits erfolgt im Gegensatz zur Bauleistung eine Bezahlung der Bewirtschaftung erst, nachdem die Leistung erbracht wird. Bei Festschreibung der Qualitäts- und Leistungsstandards über ein Bonus/Malus-System kann eine Schlechterfüllung durch Einbehalt kompensiert werden. Für die darüber hinausgehenden Leistungsverpflichtungen in der Lebenszyklusphase bietet sich die traditionelle Vertragserfüllungsbürgschaft über 5 – 10 % der Auftragssumme pro Jahr gegenüber dem öffentlich-rechtlichen Projektpartner an, die als Versicherungslösung den Vorteil gegenüber einer Bankbürgschaft hat, die Kreditlinie nicht zu belasten. Hinzu kommt, dass eine solche Absicherung um die der potenziellen Baumängel für die ersten 5 Jahre nach Abnahme durch die Baugewährleistungs-Versicherung entbehrlich ist.

Mit den innovativen Versicherungslösungen der Baufertigstellungs- und Baugewährleistungs-Versicherung in Ergänzung zum konventionellen Versicherungskonzept bei PPP-Maßnahmen werden die Rahmenbedingungen insbesondere im Hinblick auf den Aspekt der Risikoallokation zwischen dem öffentlich-rechtlichen und privaten Projektpartner und der finanzierenden Bank signifikant verbessert, da wesentliche Teile der Risikotragung insbesondere in der Bau- und den ersten Jahren der Nutzungsphase durch den Versicherer vorgenommen werden, was bei bisherigen Projekten nicht der Fall war. Als Konsequenz daraus hat die Bank die Möglichkeit, mittelständische Bauunternehmen ebenfalls als geeignete Projektpartner zu identifizieren und die finanziellen Rahmenbedingungen bei der Durchführung von PPP-Maßnahmen im Gegensatz zur bisherigen Praxis günstiger zu gestalten.

6 Die Vorteile des PPP-Mittelstandsmodells Bau aus Sicht der Bank

Die Kombination aus Finanzierungs- und Versicherungspaket bietet aus Sicht der Bank für alle Teilnehmer verschiedene Vorteile:

- Hohe Vorfinanzierungsvolumina blockieren im Mittelstand schnell limitierte Kreditrahmen. Risikomindernde Strukturen schaffen Freiräume, für die unter Umständen ansonsten kein Platz mehr in den Linien wäre.
- Da die Versicherung auch Gewährleistungsrisiken abdeckt, kann der kommunale Auftraggeber evtl. Mängelansprüche auf die Bonität der Versicherungsgesellschaft abstellen. Für das Bauunternehmen bedeutet dies eine Risikoverlagerung infolge des ersparten Gewährleistungsaufwands und eine Verbesserung der Bilanzqualität (Versicherung vs.

klassische Gewährleistungsrückstellung). Bei signifikantem Volumen kann sich das auch positiv auf sein Rating auswirken.

- Den Kosten für die Versicherung steht durch verringerte Avalbeanspruchung eine Einsparung von Avalprovision bei gleichzeitiger Schonung der vorhandenen Linien gegenüber.

- Auch die Konditionen während der Bauzwischenfinanzierung, das heißt während der Fertigstellungsphase, können gegenüber einer klassischen Unternehmensfinanzierung positiv beeinflusst werden. Die Baufertigstellungs-Versicherung bietet eine auf 20 % erhöhte Sicherheit im Insolvenzfall. In der solventen Phase wird die Mängelbeseitigung im Rahmen der Nachbesserung dem über die Baugewährleistungsversicherung abgesicherten Bauausführenden bis zu 100% ersetzt.

- Ein weiterer Baustein ist gegeben, wenn dadurch verbindliche Teilabnahmen bereits während der Fertigstellungsphase eine Kostensenkung bei den forfaitierungsfähigen Abschnitten auf kommunaldarlehensähnliche Konditionen ermöglicht wird.

- Der Einredeverzicht gegenüber der finanzierenden Bank spielt dabei und auch für die Endfinanzierung eine entscheidende Rolle. Hier lassen sich hohe Kosteneinsparungen generieren. Relevant ist der Einredeverzicht bzgl. der Zahlung an die finanzierende Bank; eventuelle Regressansprüche der Kommune gegenüber dem Facility-Manager bleiben davon unbeschadet.

- PPP als ganzheitliches Modell der Planung, des Baus, der Finanzierung, des Betriebs und der Verwertung öffentlicher Hochbau- und Infrastruktureinrichtungen durch Private wurde in den vergangenen fünf Jahren nur zögerlich entwickelt. Der deutsche Mittelstand hat in puncto Erfahrung und Expertise auf diesem Sektor Aufholbedarf.

- Mittelständische Unternehmen sehen sich wegen des systemimmanenten Risikotransfers und der Langfristigkeit der Projekte insbesondere auf der Finanzierungsseite besonderen Herausforderungen gegenüber.
- Die Kombination von Finanzierungs- und Versicherungskomponenten kann gerade den mittelständischen Unternehmen in PPP-Projekten helfen und einen Mehrwert bieten.
- Das Zusammenwirken mehrerer risikotragender Partner erhöht die Erfolgschancen mittelständischer Bieter/-gemeinschaften aufgrund kompetitiver Gesamtfinanzierungskosten und einer Risikoverlagerung auf bonitätsmäßig einwandfreie Partner.

Die Herausgeber und Autoren

Prof. Dr. Harald Pechlaner

Nach Jahren in der Praxis und zahlreichen internationalen Forschungsaufenthalten und Gastprofessuren setzte Prof. Dr. Harald Pechlaner seine wissenschaftliche Karriere nach seiner Habilitation fort, indem er den Ruf an die Katholische Universität Eichstätt-Ingolstadt im Jahr 2003 annahm. Er baute die Stiftungsprofessur Tourismus sukzessive zum Lehrstuhl für Tourismus an zwei Fakultäten (MGF, WWF) auf. Prof. Dr. Harald Pechlaner ist Vorsitzender und Mitglied in zahlreichen (inter-) nationalen, wissenschaftlichen Institutionen und Organisationen (z. B. DGT Deutsche Gesellschaft für Tourismuswissenschaft, AIEST Association Internationale d'Experts Scientifiques du Tourisme, ICRET International Center for Research and Education in Tourism) und verfügt somit über ein großes Beziehungsnetzwerk, welches ihm erlaubt, seine Lehre und Forschung sehr praxisorientiert und aktuell zu gestalten. Er ist Autor und Herausgeber zahlreicher wissenschaftlicher Publikationen, Beiträge und Journalartikel und zudem Leiter des Instituts für Regionalentwicklung und Standortmanagement der Europäischen Akademie Bozen.

Mag. Wolf von Holzschuher

Nach seiner Tätigkeit in den Bereichen Structured Finance und Investment-Banking ist Herr Mag. Wolf von Holzschuher seit dem Wintersemester 2004/05 Teil des Stiftungslehrstuhlteams. Er promoviert bei Prof. Dr. Harald Pechlaner und ist als freier Mitarbeiter insbesondere am weiteren Aufbau des Zentrums für Entrepreneursh!p beteiligt. Wolf von Holzschuher wirkt aktiv am Aufbau eines nationalen und internationalen Beziehungsnetzwerkes, an der Organisation von Konferenzen und Symposien sowie an der Akquisition von Drittmitteln für das Zentrum mit.

Diplom-Kulturwirtin Monika Bachinger

Nach ihrem Studium der Kulturwirtschaft an der Universität Passau arbeitete Monika Bachinger zunächst mit dem Schwerpunkt „Standardisierung von Corporate Social Responsibility“ bei der Siemens AG, bevor sie 2004 die Stabsstelle „Wirtschaftsförderung und Regionalentwicklung“ am Landratsamt Mühldorf a. Inn übernahm. Dort leitete sie Projekte in den Bereichen Infrastrukturausbau, Bildung, Wirtschaft und Tourismus. Seit November 2007 ist sie wissenschaftliche Mitarbeiterin am Zentrum für Entrepreneursh!p und betreut dort vor allem die INITIATIVE REGIONALMANAGEMENT Region Ingolstadt e.V., deren Ziel es ist, in einer öffentlich-privaten Partnerschaft zwischen Arbeitgebern und kommunalen Gebietskörperschaften die Attraktivität und Wettbewerbsfähigkeit der Region nachhaltig zu sichern. Frau Bachinger promoviert bei Prof. Dr. Harald Pechlaner.

Josef Johann Bernhart

Abgeschlossenes Diplomstudium der Betriebswirtschaftslehre sowie Doktorat der Sozial- und Wirtschaftswissenschaften an der Leopold-Franzens-Universität Innsbruck, Österreich. Stellvertretender Leiter des Institutes für Public Management der Europäischen Akademie Bozen (EURAC research), Italien. Vortrags- und Lehrtätigkeit u.a. an der Universität Innsbruck, der Fachhochschule Kärnten und der Universität der Italienischen Schweiz in Lugano.Forschungs- und Beratungsschwerpunkte liegen in den Bereichen Qualitätsmanagement, Sozialmanagement, Gemeindeentwicklung und Internationale Public Management Reformen.

Dr. Arno Brandt

Geb. 1955, Studium der Wirtschaftswissenschaften an der Universität Hannover, Abschluss: Diplom-Ökonom. Von 1985 bis 1990 wissenschaftlicher Mitarbeiter am Institut für Markt und Konsum der Universität Hannover, Promotion 1994, seit 1990 Mitarbeiter der Norddeutschen Landesbank, dort Bankdirektor und

Leiter der NORD/LB Regionalwirtschaft. Arbeitsschwerpunkte: Standortmanagement und -marketing, Clusterpolitik, Wirtschaftsförderung, Kulturtourismus und regionalwirtschaftliche Effekte von Großprojekten, Mitglied des Beirates der Zeitschrift „Neues Archiv für Niedersachsen", Chefredakteur der regionalwirtschaftlichen Zeitschrift „RegioPol", Mitglied des Konvents der Evangelischen Akademie Loccum, Lehrbeauftragter am Institut für Politische Wissenschaft der Gottfried Wilhelm Leibniz Universität Hannover.

Prof. Dr. Gralf-Peter Calliess

Gralf-Peter Calliess ist Inhaber des Lehrstuhls für Bürgerliches Recht, Internationales Wirtschaftsrecht und Rechtstheorie am Fachbereich Rechtswissenschaft der Universität Bremen. Er ist Autor der Bücher „Grenzüberschreitende Verbraucherverträge" (Tübingen Mohr 2006) sowie „Rough Consensus & Running Code. A Theory of Transnational Law" (zusammen mit Peer Zumbansen, Oxford Hart Publ. im Erscheinen). Prof. Dr. Calliess leitet zusammen mit Prof. Dr. Freiling das Forschungsprojekt Rechtssicherheit und Gerechtigkeit in globalen Austauschprozessen am Bremer Sonderforschungsbereich 597 „Staatlichkeit im Wandel". Nähere Informationen unter www.staat.uni-bremen.de.

Germana Di Domenico

Germana Di Domenico is currently National Expert in the DG Employment and Social Affairs of the European Commission, in the Unit in charge of Employment Services and Mobility. Before joining the Commission, she has been working for 7 years as research fellow in the Italian Institute for the Development of Workers' Vocational Training (ISFOL) based in Rome; more specifically she has dealt with: Quali-quantitative analysis of labour market dynamics and trends; Monitoring and Socio-economic impact assessment of reform processes and new regulatory frameworks concerning employment policies; Cross-countries studies with focus on Labour Market Institutions and Performance in a benchmarking key. Within the DG Employment of the European Commission, she is currently in charge of coordinating the Expert Working Group for Monitoring Vacancies of Public Employment Services, aiming at developing effective ways of processing data on vacancies to face labour market mismatches and recruitment difficulties in the Member States.

Ministerialrätin Dipl.-Ing. Architektin Gabriele Engel

Frau Ministerialrätin Gabriele Engel ist Architektin. Ihr Studium der Architektur an der TU München schloss sie mit einer Diplomarbeit im Städtebau ab. Danach arbeitete sie in einem Architekturbüro in München und ist seit dem Eintritt in den Staatsdienst in verschiedenen Bereichen der Staatlichen Bauverwaltung tätig. Seit mehreren Jahren leitet sie ein Sachgebiet in der Hochbauabteilung der Obersten Baubehörde im Bayerischen Staatsministerium des Innern. Sie ist zuständig für die Steuerung staatlicher Hochbaumaßnahmen im Geschäftsbereich einiger Ministerien. Seit 2004 ist Frau Engel auch für PPP zuständig; dies umfasst u.a. die Durchführung staatlicher Pilotprojekte und die Leitung der PPP-AG Bayern, der bayerischen Arbeitsgruppe für PPP, die Kommunen und kommunalen Zweckverbänden als Ansprechpartner für PPP-Projekte zur Verfügung steht. Die wesentliche Aufgabe der PPP-AG Bayern besteht darin, Informationen und Erfahrungen über die konkreten Projekte zu sammeln und auszuwerten sowie Wissen weiterzugeben. Die PPP-AG Bayern und weitere Informationen zu PPP, z.B. die bayerischen PPP-Leitfäden, findet man im Internet unter www.ppp.bayern.de.

Prof. Dr. Jörg Freiling

Jörg Freiling ist Inhaber des Lehrstuhls für Mittelstand, Existenzgründung und Entrepreneurship am Fachbereich Wirtschaftswissenschaft der Universität Bremen. Er ist Herausgeber mehrerer akademischer Schriftenreihen und Zeitschriften sowie Autor zahlreicher Publikationen (Einzelheiten unter www.lemex.uni-bremen.de). Seine Forschungsgebiete sind Wissens- und Kompetenzmanagement, Internationalisierung von Mittelstandsbetrieben,

Gründungsmanagement, Kooperationsstrategien in dynamischen Märkten, Unternehmertum, Dienstleistungs-Management, Change Management und Governance im internationalen Kontext. Prof. Dr. Freiling leitet zusammen mit Prof. Dr. Calliess das Forschungsprojekt Rechtssicherheit und Gerechtigkeit in globalen Austauschprozessen am Bremer Sonderforschungsbereich 597 „Staatlichkeit im Wandel“. Nähere Informationen unter www.staat.uni-bremen.de.

Tobiolo Gianella

Abgeschlossenes Studium der Wirtschaftswissenschaften mit betriebswirtschaftlicher Ausrichtung. Doktorand in Management an der Universität der Italienischen Schweiz (USI) in Lugano sowie Assistent von Prof. Marco Meneguzzo am Institut für Mikroökonomie und Öffentliche Wirtschaft (MecoP) der USI. Seine Forschungsschwerpunkte liegen im Public Management, im Besonderen Public Private Partnership (PPP) auf Gemeindeebene in der Schweiz.

Dr. Christian Glock

Christian Glock ist promovierter Bauingenieur mit einem ganzheitlichen Blick auf den Lebenszyklus von Immobilien und fundierter technisch-wissenschaftlichen Berufsausbildung. Dr. Glock ist Mitglied der Geschäftsleitung der Niederlassung Project Development der Bilfinger Berger Hochbau GmbH. Seit 1999 hat er in verschiedenen Funktionen innerhalb der Bilfinger Berger Gruppe zahlreiche Immobilienprojekte der öffentlichen Hand und der Privatwirtschaft begleitet. Während der letzten Jahre realisierte Dr. Glock insbesondere Public Private Partnership Projekte des öffentlichen Hochbaus mit den Leistungen Entwicklung, Planung, Bau, Finanzierung und Betrieb. Innerhalb des Bundesverbandes PPP e.V. leitet er seit 2006 gemeinsam mit Professor Dr. Andreas Pfnür den Arbeitskreis „Management öffentlicher Immobilien“. Dr. Glock ist Autor zahlreicher Veröffentlichungen im Zusammenhang mit der wirtschaftlichen und technischen Optimierung von Immobilienprojekten.

Prof. Dr. Dieter Jacob

Dieter Jacob ist der Inhaber des 1997 gegründeten Lehrstuhls für Baubetriebslehre an der TU Bergakademie Freiberg. Nach seinem Studium der Betriebswirtschaftslehre an der Universität Mannheim begann er seinen Berufsweg bei der BASF AG. Dort war er zuletzt als Handlungsbevollmächtigter für Finanzplanung, Finanzkontrolle und Sonderfinanzierungen (insb. Immobilien- und Projektfinanzierungen) zuständig. Gleichzeitig promovierte er nebenberuflich bei Prof. Drees in Stuttgart zum Dr.-Ing. Nach einer kurzen Zeit bei der Linotype AG, wo er mit dem Aufbau und der Leitung des Bereichs Steuern und Finanzen tätig wurde, baute Prof. Jacob seine Ingenieurskenntnisse aus. Er diplomierte in Berlin zum Bauingenieur und absolvierte in Edinburgh ein Studium zum Master of Science. Anschließend ging er zur Ph. Holzmann AG. Dort war er als Bauingenieur in der technischen Federführung und Projektleitung involviert, bevor er den Ruf auf die Professur in Freiberg annahm. Prof. Jacob vereint praktische kaufmännische Managementerfahrung in verschiedenen Branchen mit dem Know-how eines Bauingenieurs, und kann so den Brückenschlag zwischen Technik und kaufmännischem Denken und Handeln ausgezeichnet vermitteln.

Dr. Christian Jäkel

Christian Jäkel, geb. 1978, studierte Betriebswirtschaftslehre mit dem Schwerpunkt International Business Administration an der Wirtschaftswissenschaftlichen Fakultät (WFI) der Katholischen Universität Eichstätt-Ingolstadt. Nach Beendigung seines Studiums arbeitete Christian Jäkel zunächst für zwei Jahre als Geschäftsführer des Weiterbildungsbereichs der Fakultät. Im Herbst 2005 begann er seine Promotion zum Thema „Der Einsatz mono- und multikultureller Teams in Abhängigkeit von der zu bearbeitenden Aufgabe“ am Lehrstuhl für Internationales Management der WFI. Seine Lehr- und Forschungsschwerpunkte lagen im interkulturellen Management und dem organisatorischen Aufbau von multinationalen Unternehmungen. Seit Januar 2009 ist Christian Jäkel bei der Bauer AG, Schrobenhausen, als Referent im Bereich Unternehmensentwicklung beschäftigt.

Dr. Daniel Kloss

Daniel Kloss absolvierte eine Banklehre bei der Deutschen Bank und anschließend ein Betriebswirtschaftsstudium an der Westfälischen Wilhelms Universität Münster und der Universität zu Köln. Nach der Promotion setzte er seine berufliche Laufbahn im Corporate Finance der Bayerischen Vereinsbank in München fort. Er war dort bis Mitte 2007 in mehreren Funktionen in der internationalen Projektfinanzierung tätig und zuletzt überwiegend in Osteruropa mit Schwerpunkt Russland mit der Arrangierung von Konsortialfinanzierung für Großprojekte beschäftigt. Seit Mitte 2007 ist er bei der HypoVereinsbank (Unicredit Group) in leitender Funktion im Bereich strukturierte Finanzierung zuständig für die Strukturierung und Arrangierung von komplexen Finanzierungen für mittelständische Firmenkunden und PPP-Projekte in Deutschland. Im PPP Segment konnten einige Finanzierungen erfolgreich arrangiert werden, unter anderem die Projektfinanzierung der Autobahn A1 (Hamburg - Bremen).

Dr. Frank Littwin

Frank Littwin ist seit 2002 Leiter der Public Private Partnership-Task Force der Landesregierung Nordrhein Westfalen und Referatsleiter für den Bereich „Neue Förder- und Finanzierungsmodelle“ im Finanzministerium des Landes NRW in Düsseldorf. Die Task Force initiiert und begleitet im Auftrag der Landesregierung sektorenübergreifend PPP-Pilotprojekte, insbesondere im Bereich des staatlichen und kommunalen Hochbaus, im Verkehrsbereich sowie der IT-Infrastruktur. Er ist Mitglied im Lenkungskreis PPP der Bundesregierung, Sprecher des PartnerRegio-Netzwerkes der Förderbanken und PPP-Beauftragter der Finanzministerkonferenz der Bundesländer sowie Herausgeber und Autor von zwei PPP-Handbüchern. Dr. Frank Littwin studierte Rechtswissenschaft an den Universitäten Bochum und Münster (Promotion an der Rechtswissenschaftlichen Fakultät in Münster) und ist nach seiner Anwaltstätigkeit und Sachgebietsleitertätigkeit im Finanzamt seit 18 Jahren in verschiedenen Bereichen der Landesregierung, u. a. im Ministerium für Europa- und Bundesangelegenheiten sowie der Staatskanzlei tätig.

Dr. Detlef Lupp

Lupp ist Geschäftsführer und Leiter der Abteilung Recht und Steuern im Bayerischen Bauindustrieverband e.V., München. Den Schwerpunkt seiner juristischen Tätigkeit bildet das Bauvergaberecht mit seinen EU-rechtlichen Bezügen sowie das Bauvertragsrecht mit seinen angrenzenden Rechtsgebieten. Ferner betreut Dr. Lupp u.a. die verbandlichen Querschnittsthemen "Verkehrsinfrastruktur" und "Privatwirtschaftliche Realisierung öffentlicher Investitionsmaßnahmen" (PPP). In diesem Zusammenhang leitet er seit März 2004 den von der Obersten Baubehörde im Bayerischen Staatsministerium eingesetzten Institutionen übergreifenden bayerischen PPP-Arbeitskreis. Darüber hinaus ist Dr. Lupp Geschäftsführer des Trägervereins EMB-Wertemanagement Bau e.V., München.

Prof. Dr. Sulev Mäeltsemees

Sulev Mäeltsemees (born 7 August 1947 in Estonia) received his degrees from the University of Tartu and worked, among other employment, as Director of the Department of Social Infrastructure and Regional Economics of the Estonian Academy of Sciences' Institute of Economics in1986-1992. He is currently Professor of the Local Self-Government and Regional Policy and Dean of the Faculty of Social Sciences at the Tallinn University of Technology. In 1992-1993, during the times of "heavy transition", he was Chairman of the Tallinn City Council, and from 1993-1997 the Director of the Estonian Institute of Public Management, the state's central in-service training agency for civil servants. Since 1997 Prof Mäeltsemees is a member of the Group of Independent Experts of the European Charter of Local Authorities at the Congress of Local and Regional Authorities (CLRAE) of the Council of Europe. Since 2002 Prof. Mäeltsemees is the Estonian expert of internationally recognized local Self-Government Finance-Economical Research Center DEXIA in Paris. He has published internationally dozens of articles.

Prof. Dr. Marco Meneguzzo

Ordentlicher Professor für Public und Nonprofit Management an der Universität der Italienischen Schweiz (USI) in Lugano. Lehrtätigkeit für Public und Nonprofit Management sowie Cultural Management an den Fakultäten für Wirtschafts- und Kommunikationswissenschaften. Wissenschaftlicher Koordinator am Institut für Mikroökonomie und Öffentliche Wirtschaft (MecoP) für den Bereich Management des Master of Advanced Studies Net-MEGS und des Executive Master in Öffentlicher Verwaltung (EMAP) in Zusammenarbeit von USI, Fachhochschule der Italienischen Schweiz (SUPSI) und Tessiner Kantonalregierung. Ordentlicher Professor an der Wirtschaftsfakultät der Universität Rom Tor Vergata und wissenschaftlicher Koordinator zahlreicher nationaler und internationaler Beratungsprojekte.

Prof. Dr. Andreas Pfnür

Andreas Pfnür ist seit 2004 Professor für Immobilienwirtschaft und Baubetriebswirtschaftslehre am Fachbereich Rechts- und Wirtschaftswissenschaften der TU Darmstadt. Zuvor war er nach der Habilitation an der Universität Hamburg mehrere Jahre in leitender Funktion bei einer auf Immobilienthemen spezialisierten Managementberatung in Hamburg tätig. Seine Tätigkeitsschwerpunkte sind Public Private Partnership, Immobilieninvestmentmanagement und die betriebliche Immobilienwirtschaft (CREM/PREM). Er ist Präsident des Instituts der Deutschen Immobilienwirtschaft e.V. (iddiw) sowie Mitglied im Vorstand des Bundesverbands PPP e.V.

Prof. Dr. Kurt Promberger

Kurt Promberger, Jahrgang 1959, A. Univ.-Prof. für Betriebswirtschaftslehre, Leiter des Lehr- und Forschungsbereiches für Verwaltungsmanagement, E-Government & Public Governance am Institut für Strategisches Management, Marketing und Tourismus der Universität Innsbruck und wissenschaftlicher

Leiter des Instituts für Public Management der Europäischen Akademie Bozen (EURAC Research) Italien.
Weitere Informationen: http://www.verwaltungsmanagement.at

Dr. Stefan Rufera

Stefan Rufera begann seine berufliche Karriere 1999 als Universitätsassistent am Institut für Betriebswirtschaftslehre des Außenhandels an der Wirtschaftsuniversität Wien. Nach einem halbjährigen Forschungsaufenthalt an der Università LUISS Roma im Jahr 2002 kehrte er für weitere zwei Jahre an die Wirtschaftsuniversität Wien zurück. Seit 2004 ist Dr. Rufera im Bereich Corporate Finance der KPMG Wien beschäftigt. Einer seiner Schwerpunkte liegt dabei in der Beratung bei der Konzeption und Umsetzung von PPP-Projekten, insbesondere im Infrastrukturbereich. Er war bereits bei mehreren nationalen und internationalen PPP-Projekten beratend tätig, wie etwa im Rahmen des Autobahnprojekts „PPP-Ostegion" in Österreich oder im Zuge der Analyse möglicher PPP-Lösungen zur Umsetzung des Brenner Basistunnels zwischen Italien und Österreich.

Prof. Dr. Edwin Rühli

Edwin Rühli ist emeritierter Professor für Betriebswirtschaft an der Universität Zürich. 1970 gründete er das Institut für Betriebswirtschaftliche Forschung und leitete es bis ins Jahr 2000. Von 1984 – 1990 war er Prorektor der Universität Zürich. Im Frühlingssemester 1994 war er Gastprofessor am Chazen Institute for International Management an der Columbia Business School in New York. Er war und ist Verwaltungsratsmitglied bei verschiedenen Schweizer Firmen.

Prof. Dr. Sybille Sachs

Sybille Sachs ist seit 2003 Titularprofessorin an der Universität Zürich und steht dem Center for Strategic Management: Stakeholder View an der HWZ (Hochschule für Wirtschaft Zürich) vor. Zurzeit leitet sie die Forschungsprojekte „Good Practices of Stakeholder View“ und „ICT-gestütztes Stakeholdermanagement als unternehmerischer Erfolgsfaktor“ und wird dabei von zahlreichen namhaften nationalen und internationalen Institutionen in Wissenschaft und Forschung unterstützt. Neben vielfältigen nationalen und internationalen Mitgliedschaften und dem Einsitz in Komitees und Boards von wissenschaftlichen Institutionen, Expertenkommissionen, Think Tanks und Verbänden ist Sybille Sachs Mitbegründerin des Forums Stakeholder View, welches zum Ziel hat, den nachhaltigen Erfolg einer Unternehmung durch die professionelle Ausgestaltung der Beziehungen zu relevanten Stakeholdern zu stärken.

Nadine Schröter

Nadine Schröter studierte Bauingenieurwesen und Wirtschaftsingenieurwesen an der TU Berlin und schloss dort ihr Studium als Diplom-Bauingenieurin ab. Im Rahmen der Tätigkeit als Wissenschaftliche Mitarbeiterin am Lehrstuhl von Prof. Dr.-Ing. Bernd Kochendörfer an der TU Berlin betreute sie verschiedene Studien zum Thema PPP im Fernstraßenbau. Im Dezember 2006 übernahm sie als Projektleiterin verschiedene Projekte des Verkehrsinfrastrukturbereichs in der Private Sector Participation Consult GmbH (PSPC). Dazu zählten u.a. die Durchführung der Machbarkeitsstudien zum nordrheinwestfälischen Landesstraßenbauprojekt sowie zur Einbindung der Privatwirtschaft in Brücken- und Betriebsdienstprojekten. Derzeit zeichnet Frau Schröter als Prokuristin und Bereichsleiterin Infrastruktur der PSPC GmbH für alle Verkehrsinfrastrukturprojekte für Länder und Kommunen verantwortlich.

Dr. Julia Schultheis

Dr. Julia Schultheis absolvierte als promovierte Wirtschaftsingenieurin mit technischer Fachrichtung Bauingenieurwesen eine interdisziplinäre wirtschafts-, rechts- und ingenieurwissenschaftliche Berufsausbildung, die sich mit den technischen und ökonomischen Aspekten einer Immobilie ganzheitlich befasst. Ihre

Promotion über Public Private Partnership bei Stadthallen entstand in einer Forschungskooperation zwischen der Technischen Universität Darmstadt und Bilfinger Berger. Seit 2004 gehört Frau Dr. Schultheis dem Unternehmen Bilfinger Berger an und hat in verschiedenen Funktionen Erfahrungen mit lebenszyklusorientierten Immobilienprojekten gesammelt. Als Projektleiterin der Niederlassung Project Development der Bilfinger Berger Hochbau GmbH bearbeitet Frau Dr. Schultheis seit 2007 Public Private Partnership Projekte in den Bereichen Verwaltung, Bildung, Sicherheit und Gesundheit.

Michael Seeber

Michael Seeber, geboren 1948 in Sterzing (Italien), war nach dem Studium der Rechtswissenschaften an der Universität Wien als Unternehmensberater tätig. Heute ist er Präsident von zwei international agierenden Unternehmen mit Hauptsitz in Südtirol: von der Seeste Bau AG, die er 1973 gründete, und von Leitner Technologies, bei der er im Jahre 1992 einstieg. Die Seeste Bau AG zählt zu den bedeutendsten Südtiroler Baufirmen und ist außerhalb von Italien in Österreich, Deutschland und China tätig. Die Leitner Gruppe arbeitet in den Bereichen Seilförderanlagen, Pistenfahrzeuge, urbaner Personentransport und Windkraft.

Gerhard Steyer

Rechtsanwalt Gerhard Steyer war in den Jahren 1976 bis 1978 Bereichsleiter für das Industrie- und Gewerbegeschäft bei einem internationalen Industrieversicherer. 1984 kam er zu den VHV Versicherungen als Leiter der Regionaldirektion Mitte in Frankfurt und ist seit Juli 2005 bundesweit verantwortlich als Leiter des Verbands- und Kooperationsmanagements Bau der VHV.
Im Rahmen seiner Beiratstätigkeit der Rationalisierungsgemeinschaft Bau setzte er sich für die Schaffung eines mittelstandsfreundlichen PPP-Modells ein, das er auch bei verschiedenen Taskforces der Bundesländer präsentierte. Als Beirat des Bauforums Rheinland-Pfalz konnte er gemeinsam mit den Vertretern der Bauverbände erreichen, dass in Rheinland-Pfalz die Baugewährleistungs-

versicherung als „Mängelansprücheversicherung" per Erlass verbindlich für öffentliche Bauvorhaben als mögliche alternative Sicherheit eingeführt wurde.

Michael Wübbels

Stellvertretender Hauptgeschäftsführer, Verband kommunaler Unternehmen e.V. (VKU). Der VKU vertritt seit 60 Jahren die wirtschaftspolitischen Interessen von rund 1.360 kommunalen Unternehmen der Energieversorgung, der Wasser- und Abwasserwirtschaft sowie der Abfallwirtschaft und Stadtreinigung. Nach seinem Studium war Michael Wübbels als Vorstandsassistent bei den Klöckner Stahlwerken tätig. Nach mehreren Jahren bei der Gewerkschaft ÖTV, u. a. als Leiter des Verbindungsbüros in Berlin, ist Michael Wübbels seit 2002 beim VKU. Dort ist er u. a. verantwortlich für energie- und klimaschutzpolitische sowie Unternehmensstrategien in der Energiewirtschaft und das gesamte Spektrum der stadtwerkebezogenen Regulierungs- und Wettbewerbsthemen. Zudem beschäftigt er sich mit der kommunalen Infrastrukturwirtschaft im Verhältnis zu Kommunalpolitik und Privatwirtschaft. Er vertritt die energiepolitischen und -wirtschaftlichen Interessen der Stadtwerke durch Kontakte zu den europäischen und nationalen Gesetzgebungsinstitutionen, der EU-Kommission und der Bundesregierung, zu Parteien und Verbänden. Der Autor dankt Sebastian Bolay, Christian Herrmann, Simone Käske, Dr. Barbara Praetorius und Rainer Stock (alle VKU) für wertvolle Hinweise und Beiträge.

Dr. Werner Widuckel

Dr. Werner Widuckel, geb. 1958 in Salzgitter, arbeitete nach seinem Abitur in Wolfsburg als Produktionsarbeiter bei Volkswagen. Im Anschluss an den Zivildienst im Klinikum Wolfsburg begann er sein Studium der Sozialwissenschaften an der Universität Göttingen, welches er 1984 als Diplom Sozialwirt abschloss. Daraufhin war er als wissenschaftlicher Mitarbeiter am soziologischen Seminar der Universität Göttingen tätig. Nach mehreren Jahren als Referent beim Gesamt- und Konzernbetriebsrat der Volkswagen AG setzte er seinen beruflichen Werdegang als Leiter der Koordination des Europäischen Konzernbetriebsrats, des Weltkonzernbetriebsrats sowie des Gesamt- und Konzernbetriebsrats fort, bevor er im Jahre 2003 an der Technischen Universität Carolo-Wilhelmina zu Braunschweig zum Doktor der Sozialwissenschaften promovierte. Nachdem er seit 2005 den Bereich Personalpolitik und Grundsatzfragen der AUDI AG leitete, ist Herr Dr. Werner Widuckel seit Dezember desselben Jahres Mitglied des Vorstands der AUDI AG und hier für den Geschäftsbereich Personal- und Sozialwesen zuständig.